In the Ring
With
James J. Jeffries

Adam J. Pollack

Win By KO Publications
Iowa City

In the Ring With James J. Jeffries

Adam J. Pollack

(ISBN-13): 978-0-9799822-1-7

(hardcover: 55# Acid-free alkaline paper)

Library of Congress Control Number: 2009932948

Includes footnotes and index.

Cover design by Van-garde Imagery, Inc., www.van-garde.com ©

Manufactured in the United States of America.

Win By KO Publications

Iowa City, Iowa

winbykopublications.com

Contents

Preface:
The Undeniable Talent

This is the story of one of the greatest heavyweight champions who ever lived. Listed at about 6'1½", James J. Jeffries was a well-built 205-220 pounds. He was known for his excellent stamina, strong chin, ability to absorb punishment, and solid punching power, especially with the left, which could knock out opponents at any time. His defense was good enough to ensure that no one was able to land debilitating blows upon him. It was quite difficult to hit him with clean punches to vital areas. Jeff was able to absorb any blows that did land solidly. Although very strong, Jeffries was a calm, economical, often patient fighter with his offense. As he developed as a champion, he became even more aggressive. His skills were designed to capitalize upon his strengths and to minimize his opponent's long-term effectiveness in a lengthy bout. James J. Jeffries' strengths were perfect for an era where title bouts were 20-25 rounds. By the end of his reign, he was not only considered invincible, but the greatest heavyweight champion who ever lived.

As with the previous three books in this series (*John L. Sullivan: The Career of the First Gloved Heavyweight Champion, In the Ring With James J. Corbett,* and *In the Ring With Bob Fitzsimmons*), this book closely follows Jeffries' career using next-day local primary source newspapers, but also some later sources, in particular Jeff's two autobiographies.

Early on, many writers and experts recognized Jeff's talent. However, that talent had to be developed and his skills honed over time. It is interesting to note how the print media observed the development of his skills, and how the analysis of his abilities changed over time. Opinions of Jeffries often depended upon whether a reporter wanted to highlight his strengths or weaknesses, or how he had recently performed against a given opponent. Over time, Jeffries consistently improved and the media gradually grew to appreciate him. There is no doubt that by the end of his reign as champion, he had a lofty status the likes of which had not been seen since John L. Sullivan. In a fight to the finish, the true test of a champion's mettle, Jeffries was indeed that good. Even to this day, when historians analyze head-to-head matchups of all the champions who ever lived, Jeffries ranks amongst the best.

CHAPTER 1

Foundation of Strength:
Establishing a Local Reputation

James Jackson Jeffries claimed that the "original stock of the Jeffries family was Scandinavian or Norse Viking." His ancestors were traced back to Normandy in around A.D. 900. Jeff was of Scotch descent on his father's side, and Holland Dutch descent on his mother's side. Some Jeffries lived in Wiltshire, England. In 1681, Robert Jeffries moved from Great Britain to Pennsylvania, in America. Subsequent family lived in Virginia, and eventually Ohio.

Back row (l to r): Jack, Thomas, Calvin, Alexis, James, and John.
Front row (l to r): Almeda, Rebecca, Lillian, and Lydia/Lizzie.

Jeff's father, Alexis Cehon Jeffries, was a large and powerful man, like all of the Jeffries family. He married Rebecca Boyer, whose descendants dated back to the earliest Holland Dutch settlers of America. "Mother there is just Pennsylvania Dutch." Supposedly, Rebecca's father was a big fellow and a natural fighter. Because Jeff had a dark look about him, some thought that he was part Spanish, but he was not.[1]

Alexis Jeffries was both a farmer and an evangelical preacher who believed that churches were a useless expense and that the money spent on them should be used for the poor. His family lived on a 160-acre farm which had a two-story log cabin on it, three miles northeast of Carroll, Ohio.[2] It was there that James J. Jeffries was born, on April 15, 1875.

In 1881, when James was six years old, his family moved to a northeast suburb of Los Angeles, California, in the Arroyo Seco Canyon, which today is Cypress Park. They lived in a pretty fourteen-room house on a large ranch which had 97 acres of fruit trees. The ranch was near the Arroyo Seco Bridge. Today, the location is just northeast of Dodger Stadium, where the 5 Freeway meets the 110 Freeway. Their home was on Cypress Avenue, on the block north of Huron Street and south of Jeffries Avenue, the latter street name homage to its past residents.[3]

James had three sisters and four brothers who lived in their large home. Charlie Jeffries, better known as Jack Jeffries, was two years younger than James. He too eventually took to boxing, and primarily boxed as James J.'s sparring partner.[4]

The Jeffries home in Los Angeles.

A young James J. Jeffries enjoyed the open air, and particularly liked hunting with his rifle, learning to shoot at age 11. When Jeff was older, between bouts, the avid outdoorsman loved to hunt and hike about, taking long trips in the mountains. It was his true passion. Jeff was what they called a "natural man." His long hikes helped with his conditioning.[5]

As of 1890, Los Angeles only had a little over 50,000 residents, but it would double in size over the next ten years. At that time, San Francisco was the much larger city, with a population of around 300,000. It is hard to imagine Los Angeles as a small town, given that today the population is

---

1 "Jeffries is so dark that many people incline to the belief that he has Spanish blood in his veins. As a matter of fact, Jeffries' parents are both Americans." *San Francisco Chronicle*, July 4, 1896.
2 Robert Edgren and James J. Jeffries, *My Life and Battles* (N.Y.: Ringside Publishing Co., 1910), 9-10; *New York World*, June 11, 1899; William Brady, *Life and Battles of James J. Jeffries* (1900), 11-13.
3 The family ranch and home no longer exist, as Florence Nightingale Middle School currently occupies the block.
4 Jack Jeffries' home is currently located at 571 Cypress Avenue, the last existing remnant of the Jeffries family homes. Special thanks to Edith Weil and Philip Halprin.
5 *My Life and Battles* at 11; *New York World*, June 11, 1899; *Los Angeles Times*, March 14, 1902.

around 4 million, with the surrounding metropolitan area home to nearly 13 million residents.

During the early 1880s, John L. Sullivan rose to stardom. Well aware of Sullivan's popularity, when he was about 14 years old, James J. told his father that he wanted to wear the prize-ring championship belt. His father replied, "You young rascal; I'll spank you if you talk like that. ... You can't be a pugilist as long as you're under my roof." He considered boxing "devilment." According to Mr. Jeffries, James "always worshipped strength, and some who think they're his friends have egged him on. ... I don't just know how he first took to fighting, but he was always crazy to own a pair of boxing gloves."[6]

Every fighter has stories of childhood scuffles; Jeffries included. "All through my school days I had little scraps, like other boys, but none of them serious." One fight that Jeff recalled at the Arroyo Seco School was with a much bigger and older boy named Fred Hamilton. Jeff might have been smaller, but even then, he was stocky, broad and strong. Following a verbal argument, Hamilton hit Jeff, who then told him that if he did it again, that he would get mad. Hamilton hit him a second time and Jeffries proceeded to rush in, catch him with a hip lock, and throw Fred onto the ground. Jeff then jumped on top of him and hammered away with both hands, giving Hamilton a fierce beating. Upon seeing all the damage that the smaller boy had done, the teacher merely laughed in disbelief. "Hamilton and I had many a good laugh over it years afterward when I had grown up to a man's size, and he didn't mind the idea of having been beaten by me."[7]

Regarding his early frays, Jeff's father said,

> What kind of a lad was Jim? Why he was always quiet and never quarrelsome. I remember he did get into a couple of scraps while at school – one with a boy and the other with his master. ... Jim was never looking for trouble, but he could cope with it when he had to. I remember his telling us of some boyish trouble at school when the other fellow hit him. Jim didn't hit back at first, but lisped (he's got over that now), 'Just hit me once more and I'll get mad.' The boy was rash enough to hit our Jim again. The result, so Jim said: 'The boy just rolled his eyes back like a sick calf as I brushed his back hair against the barn.'

> His row with his teacher? Oh! That wasn't much. Teacher thought he would be funny, and was showing the boys how to play ball. He took a special interest in Jim, and I guess wanted to see how much he would stand. So he hurled the ball at Jim's head. Jim picked it up and hurled it back right into teacher's face. Only, much harder than

6 *New York World*, June 11, 1899.
7 *My Life and Battles* at 13.

teacher had thrown it. The teacher said he had enough and left Jim to teach the other boys ball. [8]

In 1904, Jeff admitted to engaging in more early fisticuffs than he claimed in other accounts. "Oh, yes, I did do considerable 'scrapping' when I was going to school, and I remember I licked most of the boys in our neighborhood on one occasion or another."[9] His mother said that a young Jeff had tremendous strength, and was always stronger than his fellows were. She said that he was 190 pounds even at age 16.[10]

Future manager William Brady told a story in 1900, explaining how Jeff realized his great fighting ability. One evening, Jeff's sister Margaret and a party of girl friends, along with younger brother Jack, were returning home, and came upon a drunken crowd of six black men. One of them was Bob Luckett, a large fighter with a reputation. After the girls were grossly insulted, they called for Jeff. Their burly brother came out and told Luckett and his crowd to clear out unless they wanted trouble. Luckett drew closer and threw a punch, but Jeff blocked it and dropped him with a body blow. When the others came after Jeff, he beat them up too. Naturally, this gave Jeffries a reputation for being able to hold his own in a scrap.[11]

Jeffries went to school until he was 14 or 16, depending on the source. Like Corbett, Jeff was expelled from school. He had passed a note to a girl, and she refused to give it to the teacher when requested to do so. The teacher grabbed her and whacked her hand with a ruler. Jeff saw red and pummeled him.[12]

LACY MANUFACTURING COMPANY, LECOUVREUR STREET.

After leaving school, Jeff went to the Los Angeles Business College for a year, but preferred physical labor. He became an apprentice for the Lacy Manufacturing Company to learn the ironwork trade. William Lacy owned both the Lacy Manufacturing Company, which made pipes and boilers, as well as the Puente Oil Company. Lacy Manufacturing was located in the modern day Lincoln Heights section of Los Angeles on Lecouvreur Street/Avenue 23, walking distance from Jeff's home. Today,

8 *New York World*, June 11, 1899.
9 *San Francisco Bulletin*, August 21, 1904.
10 *New York World*, June 11, 1899.
11 William Brady, *Life and Battles of James J. Jeffries* (1900), 12-13.
12 Hugh Fullerton and James J. Jeffries, *Two Fisted Jeff* (Chicago: Consolidated Book Publishers, Inc., 1929). Written in first person as an autobiography, and the copyright was taken out in Jeff's name.

there is a nearby street named Lacy Street, within a mile of where the Jeffries home had been located.[13]

Owing to his early profession, Jeff was later known as "The Boilermaker." Working as a boilermaker for a number of years further developed Jeff's great strength. According to Jeffries, at age 17, he stood over six-feet tall and weighed over 220 pounds. Jeff was so large and strong from a young age that most thought he was older than he was. He would become famous for his feats of strength.

One day, while working at the Punta oil wells, Jeff and his fellow workers were putting up a big tank, which required them to lift and set massive 800-900-pound plates. A big derrick made up of a mast sixty-feet long and twelve by twelve inches square, supporting a boom of the same size, was used to lift the plates into position. Unfortunately, one of the iron pegs holding the ropes came out of the ground, and the mast and boom fell on one of Jeff's co-workers, pinning and almost killing him. Jeff quickly sprung into action, lifted the heavy timbers off of his co-worker and threw them to the side, saving his life.

To their surprise, afterward, it required eight men, including Jeffries, to move the timbers one at a time. But in the moment, when it required unexplainable strength, Jeff was able to move them off of the man in peril. Everyone was amazed at what James had done. His boss, Mr. Smalley, stared at him in awe. Jeff recalled, "I felt embarrassed, for even as a boy I never did like to be stared at as a freak – a thing I've never gotten over." Mr. Smalley said, "I've known some strong men in my time, but none that could do what you did. Some of them were as big as you, so it isn't just the muscle. ... It's superhuman. ... I don't understand it." Later on, Jeff would often hear Mr. Smalley tell the story to people visiting the camp, pointing out the massive mast and boom, and bringing them to look at Jeffries.[14]

According to Jeffries, at age 17, "I could hold my own in any little scrap or wrestling bout, and do more than my share of heavy work." During his career, in most discussions about his early informal fighting experience, Jeff either mentioned few details or claimed that he knew almost nothing about boxing. However, in his later autobiography, he indicated that he did have at least some informal boxing experience.

> At the shops, no one could stand against me, and I was getting a reputation as a wrestler, foot racer and boxer. We did a lot of boxing around the shops in the evenings and about forty of us rented a hall in East Los Angeles where we had a gymnasium. We called ourselves the East Side Athletic Club, and had boxing every night.[15]

Jeff was always stronger than his peers, and was just having fun.

---

13 *San Francisco Examiner*, May 28, 1899; *Life and Battles* at 13; *Two Fisted Jeff* at 17-18.
14 *My Life and Battles* at 14-15.
15 *My Life and Battles* at 14; *Two Fisted Jeff* at 26.

The thought of following pugilism as a profession, however, never dawned on me until after I began work in the boiler factory. One day I concluded that I could make more money in the ring. Others that I knew I could whip were in the business and so I just jumped in and tried my luck.[16]

At that time, Jim Corbett was the world's heavyweight champion, having won the championship from Sullivan in late 1892. Corbett was a product of the San Francisco athletic clubs up in Northern California, whereas Jeff was a Southern California boy, down in Los Angeles.

---

16 *San Francisco Bulletin*, August 21, 1904.

CHAPTER 2

Hank Griffin
and the Professional Hiatus

James J. Jeffries' first professional fight was against a black boxer named Hank Griffin. Young Jeff did not realize how significant this fight would be to his legend, at least for boxing historians. Griffin would become known as one of the best black fighters in the country. He was a solid fighter who had fought a number of times in the Los Angeles area prior to meeting Jeffries, including, according to secondary sources, 1891 KO11 Happy Jack, 1892 KO4 Harris Martin (a.k.a. "the Black Pearl"), and April 1893 D20 Frank Childs, the "colored cyclone." The 175-pound Childs would later become the "colored heavyweight champion." According to later sources, Hank Griffin stood 6'2", weighed in the 180-pound range, and had a very long reach of 81 ½ inches, amongst the longest in the business.[17]

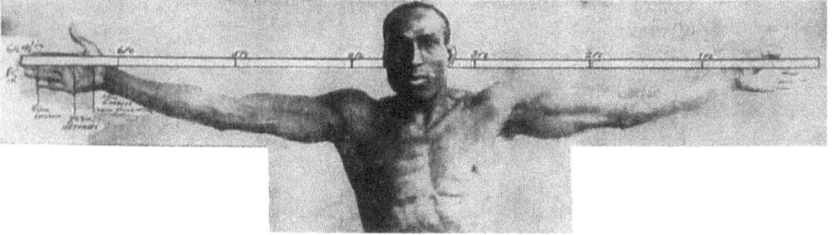

Hank Griffin

Unfortunately, no one has ever located a primary source news account of the Jeffries-Griffin bout, so its date and exact result remain uncertain and unconfirmed. The bout likely took place somewhere from 1893 to 1895. In his first autobiography (*My Life and Battles*, written in 1910), Jeff said that he was 17 years old at the time, which would have been about 1892-1893. In the much later *Two Fisted Jeff* (written in 1929), Jeffries said that he was about 19 years old, which would have been 1894-1895. He has also said that he did not fight professionally again until a couple years later, in 1896, when he was 21.[18]

An 1898 *San Francisco Chronicle* reproduction of Jeffries' record lists an 1893 bout against Hank Griffin in Los Angeles as a 15-round knockout victory for Jeffries. That was the earliest listing of the fight.

---

17 Boxrec.com cites the April 4, 1900 *Oakland Tribune* as reporting at least five bouts for Griffin up to 1893. Some of these are unconfirmed. *San Francisco Evening Post*, July 21, 1902.
18 *San Francisco Chronicle*, May 6, 1898; *My Life and Battles* at 16; *Two Fisted Jeff* at 27.

In May 1899, Jeffries told the earliest known printed account of the Griffin bout. His various retellings of the fight and its circumstances remained fairly consistent over the years, with only some minor variations. As we all know, typically the accounts closest in time to the actual event tend to be the most accurate, although not necessarily complete. What follows is the story that Jeff told in 1899.

At the time, Jeff was working in the boiler shop, and he claimed to have never worn a boxing glove in his life. This claim may be questionable. Based on subsequent statements, it is more likely that he had done some boxing at a local club, or at least had some informal boxing experience. In 1929, Jeff said that he looked no worse after the Griffin bout than he did after boxing four or five fellows at the club.

A big black fighter named Hank Griffin, who stood about 6'3", made a living traveling to small towns and challenging the best local man to fight. He was pretty clever, and "in a big city would be considered a tough proposition in the ring."

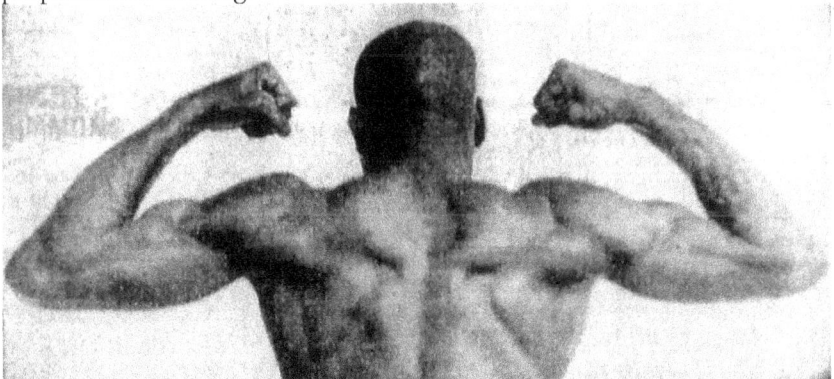

Having heard that Jeffries was in the habit of taking care of bullies, Griffin insisted that he could whip Jeff or any man in town. Jeff's chums told him about Griffin's claims and brought him to the saloon where Griffin was making his boasts. Jeff asked Hank if he really thought he could whip him. "He looked me over and said he had never seen anything that he couldn't whip." Jeff told him "to peal his duds for I was going to thrash him." Jeff was ready for a fist fight right then and there. "He looked at me, laughed and explained that he meant with gloves." Jeff moved towards Griffin, who again insisted that he only wanted a boxing match.

Griffin required some time to train, so Jeff consented to a delay. They fought a couple weeks later. "My preparation had been work in the boiler shop and twice I had on gloves with a man who knew about as much as I and that was nothing." Basically, Jeff claimed to be a street fighter (or at best an informal gloved scrapper) with little to no knowledge about the skill of boxing.

The fight took place in a nearby club [likely the Los Angeles Athletic Club or its nearby theater] in a regulation boxing ring, before a crowded house. In the 1st round, Jeffries attacked, but missed his punches by a mile. Griffin was never within reach. When Jeff finally settled down and tried to box (as best as he could at that point), Griffin "feinted me all into a snarl. I was covering up and dodging and ripping away without being touched or ever landing a blow." Eventually, Griffin landed an awful straight left to Jeff's nose. "Of course, I went after him to kill, but I never could get him fair. The blows were always blocked or he would duck or get away. That first round was the biggest surprise party of my life."

Thereafter, round after round, Jeff got jolted and jabbed, "and although I was not being weakened particularly, I was bleeding and being generally made to look foolish." Jeff tried all the tricks that he knew from his rough and tumble affairs, but nothing worked.

However, Jeffries then tried to figure Griffin out, and mimicked some of Hank's own tricks and used them on him. Early on, Jeff credited himself with the ability to learn and adapt during a fight. He also had a great ability to take a punch, and a natural endurance and strength that lasted over time.

> I guess it was about the tenth or eleventh round that I discovered how he managed to get away from my straight punches. In fact, he didn't get away but slipped past them into me. I decided I would try this also. Of course I had touched him a few times as every awkward man will touch a clever man, but my work did not amount to much. He had simply had one pleasant evening, and jabbed me fair to the face pretty often. His right hand peppered me also, but his left was the one that worried most.

> Finally, in the fourteenth round, as he led for my face with the left, I ducked a little and shot my left into his body. I knew it hurt him, and I crowded in till he tried the left again, then I slipped past it and let the left go fair into his face. He dropped like a log. My left hand was always good as my right, and I assure you I let the punch go. He got up after about five seconds, and I jolted him on the jaw with the left. His knees bent a bit and he stumbled toward me. I knew it was my chance, and let the right hand go at the jaw. I got him on the spot, and he stayed down till they carried him to his corner.

I was badly bruised up, but I had won, so it was all right. I guess I learned more about boxing in that first ten rounds than I ever have in any ten rounds since."[19]

It was an amazing feat to go 14 rounds so early in his career, with little to no formal training, against a more knowledgeable and experienced boxer, and to win by knockout. It was a sign of his natural durability, condition, adaptability, and power. Jeffries had undeniable raw talent.

This victory is historically significant because years later, in 1901, Hank Griffin would a defeat a then 22-year-old Jack Johnson, a future champion, via a 20-round decision. They fought several rematch draws, but Jack Johnson never defeated Hank Griffin, let alone stop him.

It should be no surprise that the punches from Jeff's left were of particular importance in his fights. Jeffries was actually a natural southpaw (left-handed), but typically fought from the conventional right-handed stance. Thus, his left hooks, jabs and left uppercuts were his most powerful blows. That said, he had a strong right, and particularly liked using it to the body or as a finishing blow. One 1899 article noted that Jeff was naturally "left handed, but he has, owing to the requirements of boxing, been obliged to learn to use his right hand so that he can now use either one with equal facility and hit as hard with the right as with the left."[20]

In 1901, recalling Jeff's first fight, Eugene Van Court (who was likely present at the fight) told his version of matters.

> Griffin was matched with somebody at Los Angeles, and he backed out. Jeff was working at his trade, but used to box some, and the club insisted that he should box Griffin. In the first twelve rounds Griffin hammered him all over the ring, and it was such a bloody affair that the police were in the act of stopping it three times, and after the twelfth did interfere. Jeff begged them to give him one more round. At first the police were obstinate, but finally let the fight go on, and the result was Jeff knocked Hank stiff in the thirteenth.[21]

This account suggests that Jeffries had been doing some boxing before taking on Griffin. It also backed Jeff's story that although he was getting outboxed and cut up, he eventually managed to land the knockout blow.

Naturally, the accounts changed slightly over the years, with the exact manner of the knockout sometimes changing a bit, or in much later accounts, the knockout coming later in the fight, but the basic story remained the same.

---

19 *New York Journal*, May 29, 1899. Shortly after printing this version of Jeff's story, another newspaper said that Jeff's first glove fight was "the result of the boasts of a certain burly colored man who came to Jeffries' town looking for a fight. He was a fighter, he said, and could whip any man in town." Jeffries took him on. "He took a jabbing, for the man was clever, but he kept his word, finally putting his opponent to sleep." *New York Herald*, June 10, 1899.
20 *National Police Gazette*, May 27, 1899.
21 *San Francisco Bulletin*, November 13, 1901.

In 1903, Jeff told the *Los Angeles Times* that despite the beating that he took, Griffin could not knock him out, and he noticed that Hank was getting tired, perhaps having punched himself out, while he was just as strong as when he started. In about the 14th round, "I punched him a good one in the stomach. He curled up on the floor and couldn't get up, so that was all there was to it."[22]

In 1905, Jeff told the *Police Gazette* that he liked to box even at an early age, and would spar with his brother Jack. He had agreed to quit because his father did not like the sport.

However, when Jeff was 17 (or 19), he attended a big picnic. During the afternoon dances, "I saw a big coon in a mix-up with a bunch of fellows, and right away I wanted to get in and fight him." However, the cops put a stop to the fight. Hank Griffin had the reputation of being a strong and clever boxer, and somewhat of a bully.

Despite Griffin's reputation and experience, Jeffries was not afraid. Griffin was told that Jeff was looking for his head. A bout between them was scheduled to take place in two weeks in a local hall. "Nine days before that fight I had never worn a boxing glove, but I started then and trained until the night of the fight." "We fought with small gloves and I won in less than fifteen rounds. It was a slashing bout, and I made a hit with my chums by bringing the negro to his level."[23]

According to Jeff's 1910 autobiography, a welterweight fighter named Billy Gallagher told Jeffries that he had the making of a great heavyweight, and urged him to fight Griffin, despite the fact that Jeff had never worn gloves before. The fight took place at a local hall in a regulation boxing ring on an elevated platform.

Griffin hit him at will and made Jeff miss most everything he threw. Eventually, Jeff stopped rushing at him. This made Griffin confident and he attacked Jeffries. However, Hank wore himself out trying to knock Jeff out. After about 10 rounds, Jeff noticed that the blows no longer had the same sting, and he began walking into Hank slowly, with a slight crouch. In the 14th round, cut and bruised, but still strong, Jeff landed a left to the body that knocked Griffin out. "The referee counted his ten – he could have counted a hundred. All the boys were slapping me on the back and telling me I was a wonder."[24]

---

22 *Los Angeles Times*, November 29, 1903. But see a *Los Angeles Times* September 11, 1899 claim that it was a draw. Most semi-primary accounts and later secondary accounts listed Jeffries-Griffin as a KO14 win for Jeff. *Los Angeles Times, New York Times*, July 3, 1910. Jeff likely stopped Griffin somewhere between the 13th and 15th rounds.
23 *Police Gazette*, June 10, 17, 1905. During the fight, Jeffries went at him like a wild bull, battering him on the body and ribs "until I thought that I had smashed him in two." Griffin fought back savagely for a while, but discovered that his blows had no effect upon Jeff. Hank then began backing up. When Griffin broke ground, Jeff grew confident, and he punched him around the ring until Hank could no longer stand up. "It was a great win for me."
24 *My Life and Battles* at 15-16.

Jeffries said that he made between $400 and $500 for the Griffin fight. This gave him a taste for the very good money that professional boxing could bring, much better than the $20 a week he was likely making as a boilermaker.

However, after his mother learned about the bout, she insisted, "Young man, you are not of age and you're still under my care. Please remember one thing, you're not going to fight until you are twenty-one." Jeff obeyed and did not have another pro bout until 1896, when he was 21, which at that time was the age of adulthood, not 18 like today. Jim Corbett had experienced the same type of opposition from his family. Both of Jeff's parents were religious, and at that time, religious folk were amongst the staunchest anti-boxing lobby. Although Jeff's father was against boxing, he still felt that overall Jeff was a good boy.

Billy Gallagher, who was in Jeff's corner as a second for the Griffin fight, was very impressed with Jeffries. He encouraged Jeff to go on the road and fight everybody. He felt that they could make a lot of money together. However, Jeff did not feel like leaving home. Furthermore, as a minor, he respected his family's wishes. It was not until two years later that Gallagher's urgings began to sink in. Jeff was glad that he did not listen to Billy right away, because he gained two years of experience and maturity that gave him a level head.

Although a number of promoters offered him matches, Jeffries turned them down. Still, that did not mean he couldn't learn a few things. At the Los Angeles Athletic Club (LAAC), Jeff boxed in occasional exhibition bouts, and sparred and trained with Gallagher and other pupils. "Billy Gallagher, coach of the Los Angeles Athletic Club, invited me to the club to box two or three evenings a week and I worked under him and learned much about boxing. When he resigned as coach...De Witt Van Court replaced him."[25]

Billy Gallagher

Founded in 1880, the LAAC was the city's first private club, and its officers contained the city's elite. It had a $5 initiation fee and $1 monthly dues. Its motto was "Health, Recreation, Grace and Vigor."

The LAAC's first president was Colonel James B. Lankershim, whose family owned a good portion of the San Fernando Valley. Remember that if you drive on Lankershim Boulevard in the San Fernando Valley. By 1895, another member was O.N. Van Nuys – now a street and city name in the San Fernando Valley.

The club quickly emerged as the center for physical culture in Southern California. It was to Los Angeles what the Olympic Club was to San

25 *Two Fisted Jeff* at 29-33, 36; *My Life and Battles* at 16; *New York World*, June 11, 1899.

Francisco. Members trained and competed in a myriad of athletic endeavors, such as gymnastics, acrobatics, bicycling, track and field, baseball, and boxing.

From 1889 to 1896, the LAAC was located at 226 South Spring Street, only about 3.5 miles from Jeff's home. That is where Jeffries primarily trained. From 1896 to 1901, the LAAC was located on the Wilson Block at 534 ½ South Spring Street, which was still very close to Jeff's home and place of work, about 4 miles away.[26]

According to *Our First Century: The Los Angeles Athletic Club 1880-1980*, Billy Gallagher became the club's boxing instructor in 1894. He was a graduate of Oakland's Acme Athletic Club. In the San Francisco area, his pro record included 1892 LKOby42 George Dawson, and 1893 LKOby19 Tom Tracey and KO5 Bill Mahan.

As the LAAC instructor, Gallagher organized Friday night smokers, likely held at the Los Angeles Theatre across the street, which had a myriad of pro and amateur boxing bouts, sometimes with himself as one of the combatants. In a November 1894 bout sponsored by the LAAC, Gallagher fought Joe Cotton to a 35-round draw. The Jeffries-Griffin bout likely took place at one of these smokers.[27]

Jeff said that after the Griffin fight, "I boxed at every opportunity in the gymnasium and at every club smoker with the best men, understanding the bouts to be mere exhibitions." He was itching to pursue a professional career, but remembered the promise he had made to his mother.[28]

The referee for the Griffin bout was a fellow by the name of John Brink. Brink was a boxing promoter who also worked as a referee in amateur and professional bouts. Brink had once been the LAAC's heavyweight champion for several years. He became the club's president in 1895. When he took office, he sought to stress boxing.

Brink hired De Witt Van Court, a San Franciscan recognized as a great boxing trainer. Van Court had joined Corbett as an Olympic Club professor in San Francisco in 1889 and succeeded to the top post when Corbett left. From 1895/1896 on, Van Court was the LAAC's chief boxing coach. Jeffries received coaching from both Gallagher and Van Court.

Jeff said that as a 19-year-old at the Los Angeles Athletic Club, he once had what was supposed to be a friendly bout with Brink. John Brink was fast and clever, much older and more experienced, and a master at infighting. Jeff discussed how he learned from Brink about the efficacy of a left hook to the body, which became one of his most effective blows. Brink hit him with a left hook to the liver and it paralyzed him for a moment.

---

26 Preparations for the move to the gym at 534 ½ South Spring Street began in April 1896. The gym there was large enough to contain a suitable boxing arena.

27 Betty Lou Young, *Our First Century: The Los Angeles Athletic Club 1880-1980* (Los Angeles: LAAC Press, 1979).

28 *Two Fisted Jeff* at 33.

Funny thing about that punch. Let me tell you about it. When I was putting on the gloves up at the old Los Angeles Athletic Club – raw young Indian I was then, but strong as a bull – I got up against John Brink. He sparred with me one day and caught me a frightful wallop in the stomach, and it hurt me. It hurt me bad – and then some. I never got a poke like that before, and I says to myself, 'That's the punch for me!'[29]

Jeff doubled over to protect his body, but kept fighting from that position. From the crouched position, Jeff struck Brink a number of times, and actually found that he hit harder from that position. Brink said that Jeff was getting mad. He pulled off the gloves and refused to continue, thinking that Jeff was hitting too hard. Brink did not realize that he had hurt Jeff.

After that, Jeffries always tried to crouch over a bit to protect his body. It also helped protect his jaw, and allowed him to use his reach. He used the crouch in all his fights, but not constantly, and in some bouts more than others. He could shift back and forth between being erect and crouching, which puzzled opponents and made it difficult to figure out his defense.[30]

Jeff also informally semi-fought/wrestled a big and powerful fellow boilermaker named Jim Barber. They were at the Santa Monica beach in their bathing suits, and, while on the sand, "we started scuffling, grabbed hold of each other, and from play we went at it to see which was the better man. We fought and wrestled all over that beach." After they stopped, Barber said, "By gosh, Jim, it's lucky they didn't get us to fight. You're a better man than I am." Jeff had thought of Barber as the strongest man in California, and to beat him "at rough and tumble wrestling" convinced Jeff to become a fighter. "If I was strong enough to beat Jim Barber, I need fear no one." At that time, his 21st birthday was approaching.[31]

The first known next-day newspaper account of a Jeffries bout is a late October 1895 bout against Hank Lorraine. The previous month, on September 4 at the LAAC, Lorraine, who hailed from Cripple Creek, Colorado, boxed 4 lively rounds against Hank Griffin. Griffin was a head taller and had two inches greater reach. In that bout, Lorraine proved to be a lively ringster who was light as a feather on his feet and "smilingly dodged the big colored man's stomach blows." They boxed 4 scientific rounds and were as fresh at the end as when they began. The local press called Lorraine a "clever fighter" and a "very good man," who "can handle himself in splendid style."[32]

29 *San Francisco Bulletin*, August 24, 1903.
30 *Two Fisted Jeff* at 138-140. Jeff used the crouch less in Sharkey I but more in Sharkey II. He said that Tommy Ryan did not teach him the crouch, but later helped him make it more effective. He used the crouch less after Ryan was no longer his trainer, after the first Corbett fight. This made him faster on his feet and more aggressive.
31 *Two Fisted Jeff* at 34.
32 *Los Angeles Express*, September 5, 1895; *Los Angeles Herald*, September 9, 1895.

In early September 1895, Lorraine said that he wanted to meet Jeffries in the ring, so even then, Jeff was well known. In early 1898, Jeffries claimed to have been boxing for three years, which would put the start of his career sometime in early 1895. The fact that Lorraine called Jeffries out in late 1895 gives the impression that Jeff had been sparring and taking lessons before that, and had gained some sort of local reputation.[33]

After Lorraine made his challenge, Jeffries responded in the next-day newspaper, saying that he was willing to fight Lorraine for a purse from $500 to $5,000. Of course, a pro fight would have been a violation of his parents' edict.[34]

A 20-year-old Jeffries boxed Hank Lorraine on October 29, 1895 in the Los Angeles Athletic Club's gymnasium. 300 well-known men of the city were in attendance. After a preliminary wrestling bout, "Jim Jeffries, a local heavyweight, came in to box Hank Lorraine of Colorado four rounds." As it was only scheduled for 4 rounds, it appears that this bout was considered a mere exhibition, not a pro fight, which might explain why Jeffries failed to mention it in his autobiographies.

According to the *Los Angeles Herald*, Lorraine weighed 175 pounds to Jeffries' 220 pounds. The weight difference told heavily. "In the first round Jeffries swung savagely and rushed his opponent around the ring. In the second a tremendous blow on the jaw knocked Lorraine higher than a kite, and he was carried to his corner in a very dazed condition."

Another local newspaper said that Jeffries had at least a fifteen-pound weight advantage, and "had no trouble in doing what he pleased with Lorraine, although the latter is known to be a game boxer. Time was called in the second round after Lorraine had been punished quite severely by his big antagonist."[35]

In January 1896, the local newspaper again mentioned Jeffries' name, but in a comical way. At an LAAC smoker on January 10, 1896, the 223-pound Jeffries boxed 3 rounds with little 80-pound Isidore Magnin.

> Such a comical sight as this pair made, drew tears of laughter from the assembled audience. When Magnin wished to hit the big man he would climb up his legs and slap him gaily with his glove. Big Jeffries swung gigantically at the smoky air, his huge fists acting as a sort of Indian punkah to clear the atmosphere.

So, this was just Jeff having some playful fun with a young boy.[36]

---

33 *San Francisco Examiner*, March 22, 1898.
34 *Los Angeles Herald*, September 10, 1895.
35 *Los Angeles Herald, Los Angeles Express, Los Angeles Daily Times*, October 30, 1895. Several other bouts followed, including one with Billy Gallagher
36 *Los Angeles Herald*, January 11, 1896.

CHAPTER 3

It Wasn't Long

According to Jeffries, the two years of hard work (boxing training and boilermaking) following the Griffin bout had helped him. He had grown tired of boxing for fun (exhibition/gym sparring bouts) and decided to see if he could make money with it. He stood 6'1 ½" and weighed 228 pounds, with a 33-inch waist.

Billy Gallagher was preparing to fight Danny Needham, and wanted Jeff to go to San Francisco to train with him, which he did. This makes sense, because Jeffries turned 21 and became a legal adult on April 15, 1896.

In May 1896, Jeff was in the San Francisco area training with the welterweight-sized Gallagher. Jeff claimed to have sparred with him for five weeks, preparing Billy for his early June bout with Needham. "He would swing on me as hard as he could and never budge me and he seemed surprised and would say: 'Big Fellow, you take an awful wallop.' I was learning."[37]

During May, the local *San Francisco Chronicle* listed Jeffries as 6'1" and 195 pounds, but he was likely much bigger. During most of his career, Jeff's weight tended to be underestimated. Because there was no official weigh-in for heavyweight bouts, reported weights were rarely objectively confirmed.

The Chronicle discussed Jeff's ability and career to that point. "Jeffries has fought not a few men, and has won every battle he has had." It described him as splendidly proportioned, having a frame like a "youthful Hercules, and quick-footed as a cat."

> Such force of propulsion, such speed, such controlled violence of force is fascinating. Jeffries has bested his opponents in short order. Two rounds, three rounds, five rounds is the history of his fights. He put George Griffin out in eleven seconds. Frank Childs, the "colored cyclone" of Los Angeles went out in two rounds, and Childs had bested La Blanche and "Billy" Smith. It took the young giant the same length of time to put out Joe Cotton. Jeffries is a clever and scientific boxer. His training in this line began early in life…. When he was about 14 years old Jeffries was put under instruction in the Los Angeles Athletic Club…. Jeffries' first professional engagements

---

37 *Two Fisted* Jeff at 36.

21

were under Gallagher's management. He made a tour of Southern California, Arizona and New Mexico, meeting all comers.[38]

This report's accuracy is questionable. No subsequent printing of Jeffries' record ever mentions any of these bouts. This same newspaper, reporting Jeff's record as of 1898, lists an 1893 KO15 against Hank Griffin in Los Angeles, but lists no other fight until Jeff's 1895 bout with Hank Lorraine.[39]

Jeffries did not mention any of these bouts in his autobiographies. In fact, his autobiographies contradict the claims, at least in regard to the out-of-state bouts. Jeff said that he refused to go on the road with Gallagher for two years, and did not have any professional fights until mid-1896, first fighting Dan Long. The wily Gallagher might have been generating false press releases in order to build up interest in Jeffries.

It is possible that Jeff did box Childs, who often fought in the Los Angeles area, as well as Cotton, who was later listed as a Los Angeles heavyweight.[40] It is unclear as to how often or whom Jeffries boxed from 1893 to late 1895. Jeff appears to have been doing some training and boxing in the L.A. area, and could have fought these men in exhibition bouts, as he did with Hank Lorraine. This has never been confirmed. Certainly, a victory over Childs would be significant, given his prior and later successes. Childs later won the world colored heavyweight championship. However, given its significance, it would be curious for Jeffries never to mention such a bout.

The day after the *Chronicle* report hyping Jeffries, the *San Francisco Examiner* reported that it was said that Jeffries was an "embryo world's champion who combines the strength of Sandow and the punching ability of Bob Fitzsimmons, with the agility of Jim Corbett." Again, it was probably relying on Gallagher as its source.[41]

On June 3, 1896, Billy Gallagher fought Dan Needham to a 10-round draw. According to Jeff, for whatever reason, Gallagher ditched him after that, leaving him penniless. However, perhaps as a result of the press hype, Jeffries was quickly matched to take on Dan Long of Denver, the bout scheduled to take place one month later in San Francisco.

In preparation for Long, Jeffries sparred with the very experienced veteran, Australian Billy Smith, who was preparing for a late June bout. Smith had been boxing since the mid-1880s and had fought and exhibited at Australia's Foley's Hall, where Bob Fitzsimmons had boxed. In America in 1889, Smith had lost two 6-round decision bouts to Jim Corbett. In 1895,

---

38 *San Francisco Chronicle*, May 22, 1896. Cotton was another black fighter, one who was listed by the L.A. *Times* as a member of a "distinguished colored trio" that included the Black Pearl and Henry Peppers, who seconded Childs in his bout with Soldier Walker.
39 *San Francisco Chronicle*, May 6, 1898.
40 *San Francisco Call*, December 3, 1897.
41 *San Francisco Examiner*, May 23, 1896.

Tom Sharkey stopped Smith in 7 rounds. The 172-pound Smith had fought on the same June 3rd card as Gallagher, stopping Patsy Corrigan in the 6th round.

Jeffries also sparred again with Gallagher, when Billy returned to the San Francisco area to train for a match with welterweight Mysterious Billy Smith, which would be the main event of the card in which Jeffries-Long would take place.[42]

On June 24, 1896 in San Francisco, after watching his sparring partner Australian Billy Smith defeat Jack Davis via KO2 in the preliminary, Jeffries watched world heavyweight champion James J. Corbett box 4 rounds to a draw against Tom Sharkey. Although Corbett was not in the best condition, and struggled with the strong and aggressive Sharkey, Jeff saw how clever Jim was.[43]

The day before the Long fight, the *San Francisco Bulletin* said, "Considerable curiosity has been aroused over Jeffries. He has the reputation of fanning Childs to sleep in two rounds in Los Angeles. Childs is remembered here as a very shifty bruiser. Now, if a novice like Jeffries has really accomplished this feat there certainly must be some cleverness in him. Tomorrow night will tell." Gallagher's promotion of Jeffries had helped secure him a fight with Long for what Jeff later claimed was for a $1,000 purse, to be split $750 winner, $250 loser, which was very good money.[44]

The Jeffries-Long fight took place on July 2, 1896 at San Francisco's Pavilion in a show sponsored by the Occidental Athletic Club. Dan Long reportedly had a number of bouts in Colorado and the Northwest. Jeff was called the "Los Angeles cyclone" and the "Los Angeles Hercules."

Both combatants were described as giants. Reports of their weights varied from 178-185 pounds for Long, and about 190-195 pounds for Jeffries. Another said that Jeff had perhaps a 20-pound weight advantage. Because they were heavyweights, and could weigh whatever they wanted, there was no official weigh-in. The day after the fight, Jeff said that he weighed over 200 pounds for the fight.[45]

Joe Choynski, who would later fight Jeffries, refereed the bout.[46]

---

42 *Two Fisted Jeff* at 39; Boxrec.com.

43 *Two Fisted Jeff* at 52.

44 *San Francisco Bulletin*, July 1, 1896; *My Life and Battles* at 17; *Los Angeles Times*, July 3, 1910; *Two Fisted Jeff* at 36-38.

45 *San Francisco Chronicle*, July 2, 4, 1896; *San Francisco Evening Post*, July 1, 1896; *San Francisco Bulletin*, July 3, 1896; *San Francisco Call*, July 3, 1896. There rarely was an official weigh-in for any heavyweight fight at that time. Therefore, the weights were just estimates or self-reported.

46 The following is an amalgamation of the local accounts. *San Francisco Chronicle*, *San Francisco Call*, July 3, 1896.

1st round

At the start, Long was smiling and confident, doing some pretty dancing. Jeffries, "on the other hand, was serious in aspect, but cool and collected." Jeff feinted several times as Long moved about. There were some exchanges and clinches. Jeffries landed a blow over the heart that weakened Long.

Jeffries followed Long around, until there was a rally, and Long received a sledge-hammer right or right uppercut to the point of the chin that floored him. Long rose, but "had hardly regained his feet when Jeffries again countered on the point of his jaw with a right-hand blow that knocked him off his feet again." The bell saved him.

2nd round

Long began with a rush, but in missing a blow, fell to the ground. After Long rose, Jeffries banged him with his right and left. Hot infighting followed, with Jeff hitting Long every which way. Dan was on the defensive.

Jeffries finally landed a terrific left uppercut on the point of the jaw, and Long sank to the floor. After rising, another left uppercut knocked him out for the ten-count. With little apparent effort, Jeffries picked up the defeated man.

The local reporters were very impressed, quickly noticing Jeff's undeniable potential. They were taken with his magnificent physique and hard-hitting ability. Having outclassed Long from the beginning, decking him twice in the 1st round, and twice more in the 2nd round, Jeffries was unanimously described as a new star.

One local newspaper said that before the fight, "many doubted his capability of coping with the sturdy knight of the squared circle. But it did not take Jeffries a week to convince the audience that he can hit a lick."

> The mere fact that he whipped Long does not count for much, but the way he went at it was what impressed the onlookers. Though only a novice at the game, he handled himself like a man of many battles. He was not stage-frightened, nor did he lose his head at any stage. He was as cool as the proverbial cucumber all the way through. Moreover, he had good command of his driving apparatus. Every blow arrived at his destination and Long was perfectly aware of the time and place. Jeffries has a fierce left upper-cut which he used effectively, in fact, he whipped Long with it.[47]

Another observer said that Jeffries "showed himself to be a hard hitter and is not wedded to any particular blow, using both the right and left when

47 *San Francisco Bulletin*, July 3, 1896.

opportunity presented itself. If Jeffries is handled with judgment he may prove a thorn in the side of the best men in the business in a year or two."[48]

Yet another local newspaper said that Jeff was "in the field as a prominent candidate for the pugilistic championship." For a novice, Jeffries had shown himself to be "extremely clever, and what is more, he has a punch such as has not been seen since the days of Sullivan; and it is doubtful if that great knocker out had in his prime so effective an uppercut and short arm blow as that displayed by the Southern youth." Although Long was a big man, he was "like a child" in Jeff's hands, who floored him every time that he struck him.[49]

The favorably impressed audience voted that Jeffries would have an excellent chance with Tom Sharkey, who was coming off his impressive late-June 4-round draw with James J. Corbett.

> He is large and strong and could fight Tom the way Tom fights. In other words, meet him on a level. It is a question if Jeffries, notwithstanding his magnificent powers and developments could withstand Sharkey's cyclonic rushes. The sailor would certainly make him prance about, at any rate compel him to move twenty miles an hour faster than he did last night.[50]

Another local paper's analysis of the two emerging contenders said,

> A comparison of Sharkey and Jeffries results in favor of the latter. He is in the first place the taller, stronger and younger of the two. While not so quick on his feet he is fully as swift in the delivery of his blows, and, what is more, he is ten times as precise and effective with his hands, which he uses equally well.
>
> Jeffries has more blows than the sailor. His uppercuts and hooks are superb and to top off other natural advantages, he is built on the lines which lead to the conclusion that he has recuperative powers of high order, combined with the power to take punishment. ... So good a judge of boxers as Jimmy Carroll, after witnessing Jeffries' performance last night declared the boxer to be the most likely man he has seen in many days. "He has a punch and knows how to land it," was the concise way in which the great lightweight sized up the latest "phenom."[51]

---

48 *San Francisco Chronicle*, July 4, 1896.
49 *San Francisco Evening Post*, July 3, 1896. Later during the evening that Jeff fought Long, Jeffries helped corner Billy Gallagher for Bill's fight against "Mysterious" Billy Smith, which Police Captain Wittman stopped in the 1st round, declaring that he would not tolerate slogging. The referee initially declared it a draw, but later changed it to a no contest. As a result of the premature termination, it was the Jeffries bout that everyone wanted to discuss.
50 *San Francisco Bulletin*, July 3, 1896.
51 *San Francisco Evening Post*, July 3, 1896.

Perturbed by the analysis, Tom Sharkey claimed that he could knock Jeff out in the 1st round. He did say though that Jeffries was "a good, strong fellow and a hard worker and will make a fighter."

About a week later, it was said that amongst good judges of boxers, the opinion widely prevailed that Jeffries was the strongest candidate in the field for the championship. They wanted him to be placed in good hands, so that he could be properly developed.[52]

Jeffries had earned another taste of the big money that boxing could bring him. The $750 that he had won "would make a man's wages for six or eight months in the boiler shop, and at good pay, too." Jeff could make in one night as a boxer that which he could make in half a year as a boilermaker.

Eager to earn more money following the Long fight, Jeffries was next matched to fight Theodore Van Buskirk. However, unfortunately, James J. came down with a severe case of pneumonia. He lost a lot of weight, and the doctors feared that he might die. Fortunately, he eventually fought it off, but the doctors told Jeff that he would never be able to fight again. However, Jeffries returned to Los Angeles to recover fully, which he eventually did.[53]

The Van Buskirk fight was re-scheduled, but the real reason that it did not take place in late 1896 was financial. Both boxers wanted more than the $1,500 purse that the Occidental Club offered. Instead of complying with the boxers' "unreasonable demand," in mid-November, the club's manager "wisely called the match off."[54]

On December 2, 1896 in San Francisco, although Bob Fitzsimmons knocked out Tom Sharkey in the 8th round, referee Wyatt Earp disqualified him, claiming that Bob had struck a low blow. Most thought that Earp had been fixed to rule in Sharkey's favor. Fitz next scheduled a heavyweight championship match with Corbett.

A sign of what a strong prospect the press considered him, Jeffries was being discussed even when he was not fighting. During December, the *San Francisco Evening Post* said,

> In local sporting circles there is a decided feeling that Jeffries, the Los Angeles heavy-weight, can beat Sharkey, and an attempt will be made to bring them together. While Sharkey has had more ring experience than the Southern lad, the latter is by far the more powerful puncher of the pair. He is also very clever with hands and feet, and in the opinion of many is the most promising man in the ring to-day."[55]

---

52 *San Francisco Evening Post*, July 7, 1896. In late July, Dan Long boxed in a 4-rounder with Hank Griffin at the Los Angeles Athletic Club. *Los Angeles Times*, July 25, 1896.
53 *My Life and Battles* at 17-18.
54 *San Francisco Evening Post*, November 17, 1896.
55 *San Francisco Evening Post*, December 18, 1896.

CHAPTER 4

Sparring with the Champion

While in San Francisco, James Jeffries had met and befriended Harry Corbett, Jim Corbett's brother. Harry asked Jeff if he would like to become a sparring partner for Jim, who was preparing for a heavyweight championship title fight with Bob Fitzsimmons, set to take place on St. Patrick's Day, March 17, 1897. Jeff accepted. He figured that he would gain invaluable experience. He could also see how a champion trained.

James J. Corbett had been boxing seriously since 1885, and had an advantage of ten years experience on Jeffries. He had fought and sparred with the likes of 220-pound William Miller, 220-pound Joe McAuliffe, the knockout artist Joe Choynski, 205-pound Jake Kilrain, 197-pound Peter Jackson, and 212-pound John L. Sullivan. Jim Corbett was comfortable in the ring with big and strong men.

Bill Delaney, Corbett's trainer, trying to put a scare into Jeff to see if he was the type of man who was worth bringing to camp, warned Jeffries that Corbett worked hard. Jeff responded that no one ever set too fast a pace for him. Delaney told him that he would be lucky if Jim didn't scar him up. Jeff responded, "He'll be lucky if I don't put my mark on him." That was good enough for Delaney.[56]

In February 1897, boxing aficionados were excited about the prospect of Jeffries sparring with Corbett.

> The engagement of Jeffries, the Los Angeles wonder, to act as Corbett's sparring partner during his residence here [in Carson City, Nevada], is creating a good deal of interest among the sporting men now gathered in Carson. They look on Jeffries as one of the coming men in the pugilistic world, and believe that his connection with Corbett will not only test his merits but will give him a great deal of valuable experience.[57]

A couple days later, when speaking about top boxer Peter Maher, it was said, "Jeffries is the man who is being figured on to lower the Irishman's colors." Clearly, his performance in the Long fight had put Jeff's name on the sports writers' pens. They were not shy about giving him free advertising, even for fights not yet made.

Jeffries had been scheduled to meet Jack Stelzner on February 22 at San Francisco's Woodward's Pavilion, under the promotion of the newly

---

56 *My Life and Battles* at 18.
57 *San Francisco Chronicle*, February 14, 1897, from a Carson City, Nevada, dispatch.

revived California Athletic Club. Stelzner was a Bob Fitzsimmons sparring partner who had fought Theodore Van Buskirk to a 10-round draw.

However, Stelzner pulled out of the fight, claiming a bad back from his last bout with Van Buskirk. Jeff believed that it was not a sore back but "cold feet" that troubled Stelzner. The real reason was either fear or Stelzner's obligation to Fitzsimmons. Stelzner joined Bob's training camp as a sparring partner on February 24, and sparred and trained with Fitz all the way up to the Corbett fight. His back was fine. Jeffries and Stelzner would be sparring at competing camps.

An alternate 4-round exhibition with Alex Greggains was proposed, but Jeff refused, saying that he was a fighter, not an exhibition pugilist. Besides, Jeff was scheduled to go to Carson in a few days anyway.[58]

Prior to leaving, Jeffries learned the meaning of the word 'fickle,' suffering his first criticism in the press. *The San Francisco Evening Post* called him a "dub" as a result of a recent sparring session with Soldier Walker.

> Jeffries, the Los Angeles heavyweight, about whom so much has been written and so little seen, has been tried out and found wanting. A few days ago, while he was preparing for the go with Stelzner, Jeffries put on the gloves with the prince of dubs, Soldier Walker. The latter smashed the Los Angeles Hercules on the nose, and the latter turned tail and could not be induced to face his man.

> Jeffries has gone to Nevada to spar with Corbett. If he is as represented, the champion will keep him less than two days.[59]

The criticism seems overly harsh. Given that they were just sparring in preparation for a fight, it is understandable that Jeff might want to protect his nose from injury just prior to a fight with money on the line. Remember, they did not wear headgear back then and they usually sparred with 8-ounce gloves. They fought with 5-ounce gloves.

However, seeing Jeff retire from the sparring like that raised some concern amongst those who were trying to get a line on him. In boxing, the greater the media hypes and praises a fighter, the greater the criticism that follows. Often, such is the narrative arc of a boxer's career – up, down, up again.

On the morning of February 24, 1897, Bill Delaney arrived with Jeffries at Corbett's training camp at Shaw's Hot Springs, just outside Carson City, Nevada. Corbett had already been training there, at the higher altitude, since February 16. Jeff was to be a member of the sparring staff, which included Jim McVey, Billy Woods, and Jim Corbett's brother, Joe Corbett.

> Joe Corbett is as quick as the proverbial cat and Billy Woods strikes a blow like a mule kicks. These two represent the extremes in a way and

58 *San Francisco Chronicle*, February 16, 18, 1897.
59 *San Francisco Evening Post*, February 24, 1897.

of course gives the champion plenty of exercise, but in Jeffries, the California boy, Corbett hopes to find all these virtues combined in one man and he will have plenty of variety in his sparring. Jeffries is said to be a wonder and a coming man in ring circles.[60]

The following day, on February 25, 1897, the 30-year-old Corbett began sparring with the 21-year-old Jeffries. A *New York Journal* writer who was on the scene described the sparring between the well-muscled 210-pound Jeffries and the 180-pound Corbett. Jeff wore a light-colored sleeveless undershirt with snug-fitting knee breeches of maroon tint. Corbett wore his orthodox ring costume so that he would be able to move about rapidly. They looked to be about the same height.

> Jeffries has more freedom of action than most heavily muscled men. His go with Corbett also made this manifest. He wasn't the least bit timorous at the outset, but went at Jim vigorously. His favorite punches were a left swing at the head and a right body punch, and during the first minute of sparring he landed them on Jim several times. It soon became apparent, though, that Corbett was simply playing himself on good terms with the new man and gaining his confidence. After a few visitations from Jeffries's ponderous paws Jim infused more ginger into his defence and began to attack the man before him.
>
> He knocked Jeffries's left swings and brought his own left around on the ear. When Jeffries lashed out at the ribs with his right Jim steadied him with straight lefts on the face. When Jeffries stood away and sparred for an opening, Jim feinted in such a manner as to bewilder the big novice. In all they boxed for about twenty minutes, several slight rests being indulged in while Jeffries recovered his breath. ...
>
> Throughout the work was of the fastest description, the men taking in every corner of the spacious court. When Corbett went at Jeffries hand over hand the novice threw up his gloves in such a way as to protect his face from the swinging blows. The straight punches he did not avoid so well, and it was also noticed that his defence of his body was not of the best. He was thoroughly aggressive, though, and on most occasions used his best endeavors to give blow for blow.
>
> There was not much clinching during the bout, as Jim wished to acquaint himself thoroughly with Jeffries's idea of long range fighting. Once, when they did clinch, and Jeffries exerted his strength in pushing Corbett away, I noticed that the novice made no provision

---

60 *The News* (Carson), February 24, 1897. That same day, Jack Stelzner arrived at Fitzsimmons' training camp. Fitz manager Martin Julian said, "Stelzner is a great man and I really think he could whip Jeffries."

for warding off a blow in the breakaway. It is very evident that he is not up to date in his notions of ringmanship. …

The set-to was brought to a sudden termination during a rally, by Jeffries slipping and straining one of the sinews of his right leg. He had on new shoes, and having shuffled over to a spot on the floor which was not sprinkled with rosin, he received a rather awkward fall. The injury, however, is not serious, and he will be able to tackle Corbett tomorrow. Taking all in all, Jeffries' initial showing was a highly creditable one. He used his arms with a nice, free movement, and proved that he was a good judge of distance and direction. His footwork was remarkably fast for such a heavy man, and there was nothing ungainly about his carriage. When facing an opponent possessed of less speed than Corbett his weak points would not be nearly so palpable.[61]

The local Carson report of their sparring merely said,

Yesterday was Corbett's first day with Jeffries, the Los Angeles heavyweight, and the bout was held in private, only trainer Delaney and Examiner-Journal representatives being present. The new man proved all that has been claimed for him and will be a substantial addition to the Corbett staff of trainers.[62]

Another description of this sparring session, relying on a dispatch, said that Jeff was a bit cautious at first, but cut loose after Corbett urged him to do so. However, his blows failed to land, and Corbett's feinting and fiddling confused him.

Time and again Jim would throw his head within striking distance, and when the big blacksmith would see Corbett's head so close he could not resist the temptation of letting his left or right hand fly at it. Corbett, however, timed him so well that he would move his head just out of distance, thus forcing Jeffries to fan the air. He did this so often that the Los Angeles man was dumfounded.[63]

Afterwards, Corbett said that he found Jeffries to be a big, husky fellow, strong as a giant, a terrific puncher, and very game and aggressive, displaying unexpected activity and quickness of foot. He also said that Jeff handled his 210 pounds of brawn and muscle with considerable skill and cleverness. Further, Jeff was not simply a quarter horse (which excelled at sprinting short distances), but a man who appeared able to keep up the pace. "I can't see his finish yet."

---

61 *New York Journal*, February 26, 1897.
62 *The News*, February 26, 1897.
63 *Rocky Mountain News*, February 28, 1897. It should be kept in mind that the reporters from the *New York Journal* and *San Francisco Examiner* actually witnessed the sparring, and were not merely relying on dispatches.

However, Corbett was still able to give Jeffries troubles. He noted that Jeff was not accustomed to his feints, which were all puzzling to him, or Jim's tricks in drawing him out. "I encouraged him to go and lead, but he seemed perplexed when he hit nothing." Jeff hardly knew what to make of Jim's moves at first, which made him appear to disadvantage. Still, Corbett said, "I didn't have to coax him to keep coming after he got started, and I like that. He kept me on the move every minute, and took his medicine without flinching." Jim felt that Jeff would figure out his moves in a day or two and then be of even more usefulness.

When asked what he thought of Jeff's prospects, Corbett said, "In my opinion, he is a corker." He also said that he could tell better after he was with him for about a week. "He has all the ear marks of a good one, and it would not surprise me a bit to see him on top shortly. He is only 21 years of age, a kid in fact, and has a good pugilistic career before him. I intend to teach him all I can, and if he does not learn it will be his own fault."[64]

Corbett's trainer, Bill Delaney, said,

> Jeffries is a good, strong, active fellow and quite clever. He made a very creditable showing. I told him as soon as he put on the gloves to go at Jim and do his level best to land as hard and as often as possible. He carried out my instructions to the letter, and the result was a right good exhibition. Corbett's feints bothered Jeffries considerably, but nevertheless he behaved splendidly. Jim hit him pretty hard but Jeffries took the hard knocks in good part, showing that he is a game fellow and just the man to give Corbett plenty of

64 *New York Journal, Salt Lake Herald*, February 26, 1897. *Rocky Mountain News*, February 28, 1897.

hard work. In point of reach and height Jeffries and the champion are very evenly matched, and they shaped up well. As I told you yesterday, I thought Jim was a dead one after his fight with Sharkey, but his bout with Jeffries today completely changed my mind. Corbett never sparred with better judgment in his life. He also showed all his old-time speed. I was very agreeably surprised by his work, I can assure you, and I now feel that Jim can't lose.

That day, Jeffries discussed their first sparring session.

Corbett is a wonder. I thought I could land on him effectively in view of his poor fight with Sharkey, but I must confess that I was very much mistaken. I never laid a glove on him and I tell you frankly I tried very hard to do so. He is the quickest boxer with his hands I ever sparred with, and it is my candid opinion that Fitz will hit the air instead of Corbett when they meet on March 17th.[65]

The next day, on February 26, Corbett sparred 4 rounds with Jeffries, and then another 4 rounds with Billy Woods. Jim said that Jeff was as good a sparring partner as he wished to find.

Corbett is greatly pleased with Jeffries, the Los Angeles boxer who has been secured as a punching bag for the champion. While the big fellow has not great science, he is exceedingly fast on his feet and will give Corbett just the kind of work he needs. He made a better showing today than he did yesterday and the prospects are that he will keep on improving from day to day.[66]

In speaking of his sparring that day, Corbett said,

I sparred with both Woods and Jeffries today, and each of them hit me a lively clip. My work with Jeffries was more on the slugging order than it was on the first day. We had it hot and heavy for a stretch of fifteen minutes. This is the kind of thing I need, for no matter how scientific a man may be he requires to do some hard hitting before the fight, so as to accustom himself to the shock of countering resistance. Jeffries swings like a pile driver, and as Fitz is said to be a good deal of a swinger himself, it is to be presumed that the practice I will get in avoiding Jeffries's smashes will prove useful to me on St. Patrick's Day.[67]

One paper said that Jeff's muscular development was remarkable, and he had the potential to develop into something. "He is by occupation a boilermaker and if he can acquire a little more speed, Corbett thinks he will

---

65 *San Francisco Chronicle*, February 26, 1897.
66 *San Francisco Evening Post*, February 26, 1897.
67 *New York Journal*, February 27, 1897.

eventually become a great fighter. Jeffries never took a boxing lesson in his life and his practice with Corbett cannot but be of great benefit to him."[68]

Still, Corbett was looking good against Jeffries. Corbett manager Bill Brady said, "Jim is stronger than I ever knew him to be. That man Jeffries is a young giant, and Jim threw him about like a cork when they clinched."[69]

What happened in their February 27, 1897 sparring session has been the subject of some later discussion and debate. On that date, as they had done on the previous two days, Jim and Jeff boxed with no headgear and 8-ounce gloves.

The San Francisco Examiner's W.W. Naughton witnessed the sparring. His article, which the *New York Journal* mirrored, was entitled, "PUNCHED TWO MEN ALMOST OUT... Dazes and Floors Jeffries with a Right Up Swing."

According to these *Examiner-Journal* accounts (both papers owned by William Randolph Hearst), that day, instead of doing a lot of exercises before sparring as he usually did, this time a fresh Corbett did his sparring first, and both sparring partners were informed that he intended to go at them hard.

> Jeffries was warned that the bout was to be in the nature of a try-out, and braced himself for heavy weather. ... Jeffries, who has the true fighting spirit in him, cut out the pace. He knew that it was Corbett's intention to lay on hard and fast, and he sensibly concluded that he might as well do a bit of thumping while being thumped.

> Corbett kept drawing back so as to allow Jeffries' big fists to skim past his nose, but never failed to return with counters that covered the novice's face with inflamed patches and caused his nose and lips to trickle with blood.

> In the clinches, and there were several of them, Jeffries was all at sea, the champion gripping his opponent's shoulders and neck and forcing his head back until Jeffries was compelled to loosen his hold and

68 *Rocky Mountain News*, February 27, 1897. See also *Leadville Herald Democrat*, February 28, 1897.
69 *Salt Lake Herald*, February 27, 1897.

totter away. The hard blows and the pressure on his neck had no deterring effect on him. Just as soon as he could pull himself together he went after Corbett again, and such a seasoned fight followed that Delaney and White were loud in their praises of the new man's grit.

On one occasion Corbett backed into a corner and Jeffries made heroic efforts to swat him before he escaped. It was like a move on a checkerboard, Corbett see-sawing and the swarthy giant from the orange belt stepping from side to side, intent on preventing the champion's escape…. He drove Jeffries back with a straight left-hander and went past him into the open space. Jeffries was bewildered…. He pressed Corbett hard and Jim fell back. Suddenly Corbett made a stand and waited for one of Jeffries' left swings. Jim bent his head so as to avoid contact and sent his right in with a jerky up swing. He reached Jeffries' jaw and the big fellow flopped on his knees, his face resting against Corbett's stomach. Corbett placed the palms of his hand to the side of Jeffries' head and steadied him for a few seconds. When the fog cleared from Jeffries' brain Corbett assisted him to his feet and the bout was over.

Billy Woods then took over, clad in his face and body protectors, called pneumatic armor. Corbett was the aggressor and in half a minute had him staggering. A swift left to the body dropped him. A half-minute later, a right to the jaw dropped Woods again. Jim said that he had enough.

Praising Corbett, trainer Charley White said, "His ways of attacking a man and defending himself are an interesting study. Take this man Jeffries, who is far above the average in speed of delivery, and he cannot place a glove on Corbett unless Jim allows him to do so in order to be able to put in a more damaging return." He also said, "He dropped Jeffries this morning with the shortest of short-arm punches, and he doubled Woods up and floored him with the left body blow."

Trainer Bill Delaney said, "The blow that he dropped Jeffreys with was a right jolt, and as usual it was delivered from short range. That punch that sent Woods down was a left-hander fair in the pit of the stomach and was a knockout blow."

Jim Corbett described the blow. "The punch I caught Jeffries with was a right hook at close quarters."

At the time, Jeffries allegedly admitted the knockdown.

Jeffreys himself entertained mixed feelings. It was thought that he would sulk after his unpleasant experiences, but such was not the case…. "An awful hitter, isn't he?" said Jeffreys in a confidential whisper. "Now, I knew about his cleverness before I came up here, but they told me that he hadn't a punch that would hurt. I know differently now. I was never slugged like that before in my life. I know that I can take a hard smash, and I had an idea that it was next to impossible to put me out. Well, I was not completely out, but I was so close to it that there was no fun in it. He hit me from such short range, too. I was right on top of him when he let go, and the jar was the funniest thing I ever felt. My knees struck the floor and I had pins and needles all over me. I suppose I am in for some thumpings before this thing is through, but I hope to learn from Corbett and that will compensate me for the hammerings I get."[70]

Many newspapers around the nation reported the alleged events that day, based on the dispatches that were sent out. However, the only reporters who actually saw the sparring were the Hearst-owned *Journal-Examiner* reporters, who had an exclusive.

The local Carson newspaper said that both Jeffries and Woods were floored. "The bout was short because of the limited number of men available that cared to be knocked out, but it satisfied White that Jim is in as good condition as he ever was and he is of the opinion that the man doesn't live who can best him in the ring."[71]

The Rocky Mountain News reported that Jim scored when and where he pleased, while Jeff found it very difficult to land his slugging blows.

Jim allowed the big fellow to corner him and then, seeing a good opening after one of Jeffries' wild swings, he threw himself forward and shot out his right arm from a half bent position, catching Jeffries squarely on the point of the jaw. The big fellow went flat on the floor and was assisted to his dressing room by Delaney and White. Jim was rather surprised himself and quickly came to his partner's assistance. Jeffries took it good naturedly, saying he certainly "got a good one that time."[72]

Even the *San Francisco Chronicle* reported that Corbett had knocked out Jeffries. Prior to their sparring, Corbett told him to do his best to take him out, because he was going to do the same to him.

They went at each other in terrific fashion, Jeffries on the aggressive. The Los Angeles fighter was very active, and tried in every possible way to land effectively on Jim's anatomy, but all to no purpose. Corbett either met him with a straight left or a left swing on the jaw or body, getting away each time without a counter. Finally Jeffries let his right go at full speed. Jim threw his head back out of range and immediately came back, landing a swinging left and right on Jeffries' jaw. The blow knocked the Los Angeles man groggy, but Corbett gave him time to recover.

---

70 *San Francisco Examiner, New York Journal*, February 28, 1897. Some sources called him "Jeffreys" or "Jefferies," but the usually accepted spelling was "Jeffries."
71 *The News*, March 1, 1897.
72 *Rocky Mountain News*, February 28, 1897.

When Jeffries was himself again and they had been sparring briskly for about two minutes Corbett suddenly stepped in close, a la Fitzsimmons, and landing a stiff right-hand jolt on the jaw knocked Jeffries down and out. The time was about seven minutes. As soon as Jeffries collapsed White and Delaney rushed to his assistance and applied restoratives. Five minutes later the Los Angeles heavyweight was again in shape.[73]

A couple weeks later, Naughton again wrote of Corbett's improved power. "I saw him send big Van Buskirk down with a half-speed right at the Olympic Club a few months ago, and I saw him drop Jeffreys with a right jolt not many days since."[74]

Joseph Pulitzer's *New York World* similarly said,

> [Corbett] has worked up a short arm jolt which seems to be driven with little effort, but in which and behind which is all the terrible strength of those mighty arms and shoulders, combined with the full momentum of his 178 pounds of bone and muscle. It is this blow that unexpectedly knocked out Jeffries, the 210-pound youth, who acts as an animated gymnasium for Corbett.[75]

However, years later, Jeffries said that the reports of his being knocked down were fabrications. He said that he had never been dropped in his life. The suggestion was that Naughton had made up the stories in order to increase the circulation of the Hearst papers, to boost his friend Corbett, and/or to intimidate Fitzsimmons. The dispatches sent out propagated the falsehoods, and then newspapers around the country relied upon them.

In 1900, Corbett claimed to have knocked out Jeffries in sparring. Corbett said, "As I planted my right he was coming toward me and when he went 'out' lurched forward. He would have fallen flat on his face if I had not caught him in my arms. He was 'out' clean as a whistle and it took several minutes to bring him around."[76] The question was whether Corbett spoke the truth, or just used the claim as a way to upset Jeff, as Jim liked to do with his opponents.

In response to Corbett's claims, at that time, Bill Delaney said that Corbett had never knocked Jeffries out. He said that Jeff made creditable exhibitions with Corbett. "Jeffries is a big, strong fellow, and it will take a mighty powerful blow to put him into the land of dreams and shadows."[77] Of course, at the time he said this, Jeff was champion, and Delaney was his trainer, so he might not have wanted to upset his man. Delaney was quoted

---

73 *San Francisco Chronicle*, February 28, 1897.
74 *San Francisco Examiner*, March 15, 1897.
75 *New York World*, March 16, 1897.
76 *New York Journal*, May 8, 1900.
77 *New York Herald*, May 9, 1900.

in 1897 as describing the knockdown. The question was whether that was actually him speaking, or the imagination of a good writer.

Jeffries denied it, saying, "I want to tell Mr. Corbett that he lies when he says he ever knocked me out at Carson… The truth is, he never would box with me on the level in Carson, and he much preferred to do his exercise punching upon Billy Woods with his jaw and stomach protector."[78]

In William Brady's 1900 book, *Life and Battles of James J. Jeffries*, written while he was still managing Jeffries, Brady wrote,

> The writer is in a position to say that after the first day that Corbett and Jeffries sparred at Carson, Corbett never afterward would spar with the big fellow on their merits. … In order to give the papers something to write about and to scare Fitzsimmons, Jeffries was persuaded to allow a fake story to be sent broadcast through the country that Corbett had knocked him out in a practice bout. This was a lie, and should not be given credence. *Jeffries, in his ring career, has never been knocked down, nor has he ever shown the slightest sign of grogginess in a sparring encounter.*[79]

In Brady's 1916 book, *The Fighting Man*, he again said, "Yarns were published in the newspapers about Corbett knocking out Jeffries in practice, but no such thing ever occurred."[80]

The question is whether Delaney and Brady told the truth when they said that Jeffries was not dropped. Often, trainers and managers change their stories over time based on their allegiances. When Brady and Delaney were with Corbett, they talked about how great Corbett looked in sparring with Jeffries. When they were with Jeff, they built up Jeffries and put down Corbett's stories. It seemed that they also liked Jeff more on a personal level than Corbett. However, these two would be in a position to know the truth.

In his 1910 autobiography, Jeffries continued to cast doubt on the story, claiming that a news reporter (likely Bill Naughton) fabricated it. Jeff said of the reporter, who generated the fake story,

> He must have had a friendly feeling for Jim, or, perhaps, it was just the natural inclination to boost a champion. At any rate, I believe he sent a story to his paper to the effect that Jim had beaten me all over the place, and had finally knocked me out. That was just a joke, of course, for nothing of the sort happened. Corbett didn't knock me out, or knock me down. I've never been knocked down in my life.[81]

---

78 *San Francisco Examiner*, May 9, 1900.
79 William Brady, *Life and Battles of James J. Jeffries* (1900), 15.
80 William Brady, *The Fighting Man* (Indianapolis: Bobbs-Merrill Co., 1916), 144.
81 *Life and Battles* at 19.

In his later autobiography, Jeffries again said that there was never a knockdown in their sparring. He also claimed to have told Corbett, "If that's as hard as you can hit, you're not going to do much to Fitz."[82]

Of course, a cynic might say that Jeff was so concussed that he did not remember it. Corbett insisted that it did happen. In 1897, Jeff was quoted as saying that Corbett indeed hit hard and had decked him, but there are lingering questions as to whether those really were Jeff's words.

Many years later, in his autobiography, Corbett described the incident in question. "Without intending to hurt him I hit him a short uppercut with my right, but with little force behind it, as I thought, and he fell helpless in my arms." Corbett said of the 1897 version of Jeffries that he was big and strong, with a "hefty left," and was able to keep up with him during roadwork. That said, although Jeffries was "very willing," he "didn't know the simplest fundamental of the game." Corbett claimed to have handled him quite easily in sparring, and tried to teach him something. The news reports generally backed him up, although they also said that Jeff gave him the toughest time of all of his sparring partners.[83]

It is not entirely improbable that the knockdown story was a fabrication. Naughton and the Hearst-owned *Examiner* and *Journal* newspapers were not always known for their complete honesty. They were associated with a form of reporting in this era called "yellow journalism," which used exaggerations, eye-catching headlines, scandal-mongering, sensationalism, heavy reliance on unnamed sources, and unprofessional practices in order to boost sales. Truth was of secondary importance. The Hearst and Pulitzer papers (*New York World*) did battle with each other, competing for circulation in this manner. Their methods often came under attack from other newspapers. In fact, the competition was so fierce that Hearst paid Fitzsimmons to allow his reporters exclusive access to his training camp. Hearst's various reporting methods worked, rapidly growing the circulation of his newspapers, proving that the public preferred sensational falsehoods to simple truths. Of course, some of these sensational stories were true. However, because of the era's yellow journalism, a number of sensational boxing stories have to be taken with a grain of salt, or at least further scrutinized.

So, was the story of Jeffries being dropped a fabrication? If it was, it was a very good one, given all the detail in the descriptions and the quotes from everyone involved. These writers had to be very good at what they did. This should actually give one pause for concern when writing history.

However, even if the story was true, there is no shame in getting dropped in sparring by an experienced world champion with a perfectly timed speedy punch when you are green and rushing forward into the

---

82 *Two Fisted Jeff* at 56.
83 James J. Corbett, *The Roar of the Crowd* (New York: G.P. Putnam's Sons, 1925), 250-251.

punch. How many fighters today with only three or so bouts could step into the ring with *the* world champion and spar daily with no headgear, no mouthpiece, and 8-ounce gloves, and not get dropped once? No one dropped Jeffries before or for over a decade thereafter, and he was known for having a granite chin. Of course, the fact of his proven iron jaw over the years also boosts Jeff's claims that he was not dropped.

Even Bob Fitzsimmons indirectly supported Jeff's claims that he was under a pull and not allowed to let himself out fully during the sparring sessions. At the very least, the suggestion was that Corbett was more interested in making sure that his partners did not hit him, more than he was in hitting them. Fitz liked to take cuts at Corbett and his training. Unlike Jim, Bob said that it was "not his style to restrain his sparring partners and make monkeys out of them that the public might think nobody could hit him." Bob felt that Jim was trying to look good for reporters and to boost his confidence. Fitzsimmons was not intimidated by the stories about how good Jim was looking.

> A man must learn to take blows as well as to give them. ... Corbett won't allow any of his men to lay a glove on him, for fear people might think he was not the marvel he believes himself. I'll show him that he can be hit just like the rest of us when we get together.[84]

Regardless, at the time, Jeffries was quoted as being thoroughly impressed with Corbett's speed and power. "I never dreamed that any human being could hit so hard. ... Actually, you cannot see his fists coming. I can tell which hand he used by recollecting which side of the head I was punched on, and that is all." Although Jeffries had sparred Australian Billy Smith in preparation for the Long fight, his blows did not compare to Corbett's punches.

> I remember once when I thought I put myself to quite a test, so far as being punched is concerned. I was training Australian Billy Smith for a fight near San Francisco, and one day when we were boxing I asked Smith to cut loose. I wanted to know how it felt to be slugged. Now, Smith has the name of being a terrible puncher, and if you don't think he let out for keeps, you had better ask some one who was there. Really, though, Smith's blows were only gentle taps as compared to the smashes I got from Corbett.[85]

Jeffries and Corbett continued running and sparring almost daily up to the world championship bout. Jeffries was happy to be working with Corbett. "I'm learning a great deal...but it's rather discouraging to reach out all the time and find nothing. If I could only get in just one punch every

84 *New York Journal,* February 28, 1897.
85 *San Francisco Examiner,* March 1, 1897.

day, it would satisfy me, but even that is denied me." Corbett most certainly was a defensive specialist. No one ever disputed that.[86]

Despite the alleged knockdown, Corbett and his trainers were impressed with Jeffries, and they all saw potential in him. "Corbett's admiration for his new sparring partner, Jeffreys, increases hourly. For that matter, every one around the camp is attached to the lad from the orange belt. He is such a genial giant when off duty, and such a brave fellow when under the fire of Jim's blows, that they all like him." Jim said, "I have nothing but good words for Jeffreys. He is a willing fellow, and when I am skipping around trying to dodge those great big fists of his I am attending strictly to business all the time. He gives me splendid exercise and I appreciate it thoroughly." He also said, "I have every confidence in him turning out well, and I think, with a fair amount of coaching, he will be able to hold his own against all comers." It was further said, "White and Delaney think with Corbett that Jeffries has the making of a top-notch fighter. They believe that his experiences with Jim will be of no end of benefit to him, and that before many years he will be in line for the championship." Perhaps all of these positive statements about Jeffries were generated in order to make up for the fib about his being knocked down.

On March 1, 1897, Corbett sparred 15 rounds total, which consisted of 3 rounds each with Jeffries, Jim McVey, Billy Woods, Joe Corbett and Robert Edgren. Although the report did not specifically say, usually for his lengthy sparring sessions, Corbett rotated each boxer in and out for 1 round each, until each sparring partner had gone 3 total rounds. "Jeffreys sent in a lot of left and right smashes with fairly good speed. Corbett evaded and so timed himself that Jeffreys came within a sixteenth of an inch at him every time." Corbett said,

> The two 'Billies' [Delaney and Brady] have been putting a flea into Jeffrey's ear, for this morning when his number was reached on the programme he came at me like a cyclone, swinging blows that would have knocked my head off if any one of them had happened to land. Jeffreys has the arm and physique of a giant and the quickness of a cat, but the quick eye and the capacity to judge distance which the critics award me saved me from disaster.[87]

Another non-local report of their sparring on that date said,

> Jefferies, who is the strongest man on the force, does rushing work. Much has been sent out from Carson about Corbett's sparring with Jefferies, some writers claiming that Jefferies gave the latter all he could do to avoid the rushes. As a matter of fact, Jefferies' instructions are to rush and corner Jim if possible, giving the

---

86 *Salt Lake Herald*, February 28, 1897. "It leaked out today that Jim put Jeffries out twice in one bout yesterday. The Los Angeles lad wears no protection." *Salt Lake Herald*, March 1, 1897.
87 *San Francisco Examiner*, *New York Journal*, March 2, 1897. *The New York Journal* called him "Jeffries."

champion practice at extricating himself from tight places. He allows the big fellow to corner him, but usually gets away without having the gloves put on him. He reaches Jefferies when and where he pleases. In his bout this morning with the new aspirant for championship honors, Corbett landed a particularly vicious upper-cut, which caused Jefferies' jaws to come together with a snap. Unfortunately his tongue was caught between them and for several seconds the big fellow held his jaws with both hands and howled with pain.

Corbett took his sparring sessions seriously, never allowing himself to be outpointed.

[Corbett] never allows one of the men with whom he boxes to score off him. The instant they make a point that causes the onlookers to whisper, the champion sends in a swift return. He is so jealous of his reputation that he won't for an instant allow the idea to get out that he is not invincible.[88]

March 2 was a day off.

On the morning of March 3, Corbett and Jeffries covered 12 miles of walking, jogging, hill-climbing, and sprinting. One source said that Jim "left Jeffries on the road far, far away, tired out."[89] In his autobiography, Jeff disputed that Corbett ever outran him.

Other than his run, Corbett mostly rested on the 3rd and 4th because he was visiting with his wife.

Jeffries and Woods were said to have swelled hands and lumpy wrists from coming into contact with Corbett's arms. On the other hand, Corbett knew how to protect himself from the shock of his sparring partners' blows. Corbett said,

If my arms were not as flinty as they are this fellow (Jeffries) would cripple me in a half hour's boxing…. His arms are as big and as heavy as legs, and he keeps swinging them for all he is worth. Now while I ward off his blows I see that my arms do not get the full shock of the contact. It is a good deal like catching a base ball. If you throw your hands out against the ball you are liable to get your finger smashed by the concussion, but if you stretch your hands and bring them back gradually when you are sure of making connection with the ball you lessen the chances of injury. It is all in judging distance. I take Jeffries' swings on my forearm, wrist, or hand, and relax sufficiently to kill the force of the blow, and at the same time protect my guard arm.[90]

Of Jeff's participation in the training camp to that point, Harry Corbett said, "Jeffries is making a mighty handy man for Jim. … He is big, strong

88 *Rocky Mountain News*, March 2, 4, 1897. Also using a dispatch from the *New York Journal*.
89 *San Francisco Examiner, New York Journal*, March 4, 1897.
90 *New York Journal*, March 4, 1897; *Rocky Mountain News*, March 6, 1897.

and a bit clever. He keeps coming for his medicine all the while and seems to like it."[91]

On the morning of March 5, Jim and Jeff went on a walk and run lasting one hour and twenty minutes. Later, Jeffries, along with Robert Edgren, Jim McVey, and Billy Woods, sparred Corbett 3 or 4 rounds each, depending on the source.

On the 6th, Jeff, Woods, and Corbett's brother Joe all sparred 4 rapid rounds with Jim. Corbett boxed them all at long range, altering his usual style of working on the inside against them.

On the 7th, Corbett played handball, punched the bag, and then sparred alternating rounds with Jeffries, Edgren, McVey (wrestling), and Woods, repeating the round robin circuit four times (16 total rounds). "He first went at Jeffries, and waded into him in a manner that made that gentleman a trifle nervous."[92]

On the 8th, in addition to his usual preliminary work, Corbett boxed Jeffries, wrestled with McVey, and sparred with Edgren and Woods in the typical round robin fashion. "As usual, Jeffries was first, and Jim went at him like a whirlwind, hitting him all over the body and driving him all over the place." After working with McVey, Edgren, and Woods for 1 round each, Jeff was up again.

> Then everything began all over again and was gone through in much the same manner as before, save that Corbett, instead of going after Jeffries, kept that gentleman coming after him. Again and again Jeffries rushed and made desperate efforts to land, but not once could he reach the champion. ... Corbett is the grand master of the art of getting away from a punch...the next best thing to punching the other fellow. It may not be a winner of fights, but it is a tolerably sure preventative from losing them.

One source claimed that in the late afternoon, Corbett repeated the routine circuit again in the same fashion, working the pulleys before boxing and wrestling 16 rounds.[93]

On March 9, Corbett again did his road work with Jeffries, plodding through the slushy snow for about two and a half hours, running at least 10 miles. Later, as usual, Jim played handball, punched the bag, and sparred and wrestled with Jeffries, McVey, Edgren, and Woods. Instead of working on his short-arm blows, on this day Corbett again fought at longer range, practicing stops and evasions, left hand leads and cross counters.[94]

91 *San Francisco Bulletin*, March 3, 1897.
92 *San Francisco Examiner, New York Journal, Rocky Mountain News*, March 6-8, 1897.
93 *Rocky Mountain News*, March 9, 1897.
94 *Rocky Mountain News, Salt Lake Herald*, March 10, 1897.

The New York World, which had a correspondent on the scene, reported that on the 9th, Corbett dropped both Jeffries and Woods. The title of the article was, "Big Jeffries Knocked Out."

> It was not given out for publication even to contract holders at Corbett's quarters, but it is fact nevertheless that last night Jim knocked out both Jeffries and Woods. While sparring with the former he hooked in a slow right that reached the kidneys. Jeffries lost control of every joint and sinew in his mighty frame and collapsed into limpness at the blow, which didn't appear to be a very hard one. … A little later Corbett fetched a hard left swing across on Billy Woods' mushroom face armor. … Billy was slammed against the wall of the handball court and fell to the floor.[95]

Other newspapers repeated this report. Again, it is unclear whether such unconfirmed dispatches were fabrications designed to boost Corbett, affect the odds, generate interest in the fight, and/or to stimulate newspaper sales. Perhaps the *World* was simply mirroring the *Journal's* tactics, seeing that readers eagerly lapped up and enjoyed such stories.[96]

Jeffries supposedly told the *Examiner*, "I was quite convinced before I came here that Corbett was a kingpin boxer so far as cleverness went, and I have discovered since I arrived that he is a terrific puncher. I cannot figure out how Fitz can hope to discount Corbett's cleverness and punching power combined."[97] Of course, years later Jeff denied giving such quotes, saying that Corbett could not punch very hard, although he admitted that Jim hit him a lot.

On the morning of the 10th, in a same-day special from a staff correspondent who was there, the *New York World* reported,

> Corbett took a jaunt of about nine miles all told, deviating from his former route and turning off near Fitz's quarters.… The Evening World's correspondent followed Corbett on horseback during his long jaunt. At no time did the champion breathe hard, although Jeffries was done up before they were within a mile of Shaw's Springs on the return trip.[98]

That was the morning when they allegedly came upon Bob Fitzsimmons while both parties were doing their roadwork. Jeff confirmed that Corbett refused to shake Bob's hand.

That afternoon, Corbett hit the bag, worked the wrist machine, and then sparred 4 rounds each with Jeffries and Woods, followed by two games of handball.[99]

---

95 *New York World*, March 10, 1897.
96 *Rocky Mountain News*, March 11, 1897, reporting a March 10 dispatch discussing the 9th.
97 *San Francisco Examiner*, March 10, 1897.
98 *New York World*, March 10, 1897.
99 *Salt Lake Herald*, March 11, 1897.

On March 11, Corbett (and likely Jeffries) jogged 8 miles, sprinting the final quarter of a mile. He then engaged in his usual exercises of handball (four games), bag punching, and sparring. Jeffries, Woods, and Joe Corbett "gave the big fellow three hot rounds each, while McVey did his share of the wrestling."[100] Discussing Corbett's sparring, the *New York World* said,

> In his bouts he used some new maneuvers in fighting. Trainer White had coached each man who faced the champion upon a lot of Fitzsimmons's tricks of hitting in clinches and breakaways. Jeffries and Billy Woods suffered accordingly. One of the prettiest and most effective bits of work with the former was shown in the clinches. Another trick of Corbett was to stand apparently off guard with both hands down and meet Jeffries's rushes with straight jabs that steadied him up with a jerk, then clinching and working his right free to beat a tattoo on the place where Jeffries feels hungry between meals.[101]

On the 12th, Corbett (and likely Jeff) ran 10 miles in the morning. In the afternoon, after working the wrist machine, punching the bag, and playing five games of handball with brother Joe, Corbett sparred. First, he wrestled 1 round with McVey. After that, "Without a moment's intermission, Trainer White sent 'Big' Jeffries into the arena and the California giant had a decidedly unpleasant three minutes' experience with the swift gloves of the champion." Woods immediately followed, and then brother Joe. The four boxers were given 3 rounds each in round-robin circuit fashion, for a total of 12 rounds for Corbett. "Although they all made vigorous efforts to land on the champion, Jefferies was the only one to mix anything like honors with his punishment, he having succeeded in landing a blow on Corbett's cheek, the latter failing to get his head entirely out of the way of the splendidly aimed right."

On the 13th, in the morning, Corbett ran 10 miles with Jeffries. Later, after his usual preliminary work, Corbett did his usual round-robin sparring. He wrestled McVey for 1 round, then immediately took on Jeffries for "three minutes of hot sparring," then Joe Corbett for a round, and then Woods. Each sparring partner went 4 rounds total in the round-robin circuit, while Corbett went round after round without any rest in between the 16 rounds. Jim would taper in subsequent days. "The change will be a relief to the big fighter and none the less so to McVey, Jeffries and Woods, who have been punched and hammered to the limit of endurance in the vigorous work."[102]

100 *Salt Lake Herald*, *Rocky Mountain News*, March 12, 1897.
101 *New York World*, March 12, 1897.
102 *Rocky Mountain News, San Francisco Bulletin, San Francisco Evening Post*, March 13-14, 1897.

Another source said of the sparring that day that Corbett puffed up Jeffries' lip with a straight left, and did the same with Woods, who was wearing the armor. Joe Corbett was more cautious and kept at a distance.[103]

On the 14th, Corbett did his usual pre-sparring work before taking on his sparring partners one after another. Without any intermission between rounds, Corbett wrestled McVey for five minutes, and then boxed a round each with Joe Corbett, James Jeffries, and Billy Woods. The circuit was repeated once more, each of the four men going 2 rounds with Jim. William Muldoon said of Corbett, "I saw for myself that he is practically tireless. His wind is superb, and more than two hours constant work did not distress him in the least."

On March 15, Corbett did his last sparring, working only 3 total rounds in a slow and easy fashion, 1 round each with McVey, Jeffries, and Woods. Jim was tapering, for the fight was only two days away.[104]

On March 17, 1897, Jeffries watched Bob Fitzsimmons knock out Jim Corbett with left hook to the body in the 14th round to win the world heavyweight championship. Jeff was in Jim's corner that day. On the films, the huge Jeffries can be seen entering the ring after the knockout.

James J. Jeffries had been sparring with world heavyweight champion James J. Corbett for nearly three weeks, almost every day. Jeff had been in the ring with Jim on fifteen separate days. The experience with Corbett was invaluable to Jeffries, who was essentially an inexperienced novice when he entered that camp. When it is considered that he only had a few known bouts up to that point, and was boxing against an undefeated champion with well over ten years of experience, it is a testament to Jeffries' talent to be able to keep up that type of daily training and sparring regimen. How many boxers today, with only three total fights, could step into the ring with the reigning world heavyweight champion and box him every day with no headgear, no mouthpiece, and wearing only 8-ounce gloves? These were the conditions in which a green Jeffries was working with Corbett. Most heavyweights today could not even handle their roadwork regimen.

Jeffries learned a great deal from sparring with Corbett. In his autobiography, he wrote, "I'd be patient and let Corbett hammer me as much as he chose, but every day I'd tuck some new information away in the back of my mind." For a number of days, the trainers asked Jeff to fight like Fitzsimmons, whom he tried to imitate, but it was not easy, and it handicapped him.

> Every man has his own instinctive style of fighting. Fitzsimmons had his, and it wasn't like mine at all. It was a style designed to fit his own build. Fitzsimmons had light, thin legs and narrow hips. ... Everything about his build helped him to pivot at the hips and knees

103 *Salt Lake Herald*, March 14, 1897.
104 *San Francisco Examiner, Rocky Mountain News, San Francisco Bulletin*, March 15, 1897.

and swing his whole body into the blow. My style was different. I didn't need to pivot like Fitzsimmons. All I did was to stick my left arm out like a piece of scantling and let them try to run into me. I could hold them off with the left and could hit a hard blow with my arm nearly straight, swinging it a few inches like a club. I could whip that arm down to the body in a good stiff punch and plunge in with it. And the right I used for a good dig into the body whenever I came to close quarters. I crouched a little and my chin was partly protected by my left shoulder. When I began using more of my own style I did better, and especially after I had begun to try to equal Corbett's fast footwork.[105]

Years later, an expert who had observed Jeffries at Corbett's camp said that Jeff could take endless punishment, and seemed to enjoy the hardest kind of punching without distress. Jeff was ambidextrous, and could hit equally hard with either hand. When he sparred with Corbett, sometimes Jeff stood with his right hand forward, from the southpaw stance. This was perhaps a result of Jeffries being naturally left-handed, something few realized.

When, to all intents and purposes, Jeffries should have been sparring with his left hand forward and his right covering his heart, it was not unusual to find him shifting with great rapidity and entirely reversing his position for some advantage that presented itself. He was frequently rebuked by his friends and associates for this gross violation of accepted rules, but Jeffries, nevertheless, continued to plant his terrible left fist, and then to follow up with his right, punching and jabbing and hammering with it before his opponent knew what was going on…. Through Jeffries' ambidextrous method of attack he is enabled to assume the reversed position, and to throw his terrible left in a vicious swing with as much facility and force as he does his right. Coming as it does from an unexpected quarter, the movement disconcerts his antagonist and Jeffries scores a distinct advantage.

One must see Jeffries in action to fully appreciate the importance of his methods. While he does not disregard the importance of protecting his body and face with his right he also strives to utilize the left for that purpose, at the same time throwing in a quick, hard blow with the right. Another peculiarity of Jeffries is his system of quick hammering with his right. He very often strikes four and five blows with the right short arm, all in quick succession, while other prizefighters save that arm for a final and single smash…. But with

---

Jeffries, by the time he has put in a few right handers his gifted left is far enough back to come in with frightful velocity and power.[106]

However, in his autobiography, Jeffries claimed that Corbett's trainers had him shift his feet around to an unorthodox stance, and to draw back his left, so as to imitate some of Fitz's positions and moves. Fitzsimmons was famous for shifting his feet, stepping forward with his right foot to set up a left hand punch.

Still, Jeffries admitted that he was left handed, which explains why his most noted and powerful punches were often those thrown with his left, even though he usually stood in the orthodox stance. "I'm naturally left handed. I fight and write and shoot left handed. I fight with my left foot and my left arm advanced, but I have a big advantage in holding the left out because it's my best arm. At that the right is nearly as good, and just as good for body punching."

In that training camp, Jeffries learned a lot about boxing, and also a lot about Corbett.

> Corbett was a master of footwork, and I picked up many a neat trick through watching him. … When we first boxed he was as hard to reach as a shadow. I soon grew tired of wasting my blows on the air and determined to force my way to close quarters before letting go a single punch. … At last, in closing, I struck my toes against his, and, lunging at the same moment, managed to get home a good whack on his ribs. As soon as I started forward again I tried the same trick, feeling around for him with the toes of my left foot and then shooting out one hand or the other. … Corbett knew what I was doing, as I could see plainly, for when we boxed again he took care to keep shifting about rapidly to confuse me.
>
> Another thing was the feinting. Corbett was the best man I've ever seen at that. He was like a fencing master, feinting to draw you into a position that would leave an opening somewhere else and then taking advantage of it. I had an advantage that few men have at this game, however. An ordinary blow doesn't affect me at all, and even a heavy smash doesn't shake me. So all that I needed to do when Corbett feinted was to pay no attention to it, but step right in toward him and lash out with either hand, according to his position. This I've always found to be very disconcerting to a boxer. It makes half of his cleverness of no use at all.
>
> The part of the training that I liked the best was the work on the road. … Corbett and I…went out every day for a ten or twelve mile spin. Sometimes we walked and ran alternately, sometimes we ran the whole way at an easy trot, finishing with a two or three hundred yard

106 *National Police Gazette*, June 3, 1899; May 19, 1900; July 26, 1902.

spurt. … I was a natural runner. … Billy Delaney thought that Corbett was doing too much road work, especially when he went out for a long, slow jog on the day before he was to meet Fitzsimmons. "He's leaving his fight on the road," Delaney complained.[107]

Jeffries felt that Corbett was nervous; trying to make up for years of easy living that had followed the Sullivan victory. So, Jim over-trained. Jeff watched Corbett beat on Fitzsimmons, but fail to finish him. Fitz recovered well after the 6th round knockdown, no trace of grogginess to be found. After that, Jeff saw a change in Corbett. The laughter left and Jim's face turned gray. Corbett had fatigued himself. Subsequently, Fitz gradually wore him down, and even knocked Jim's teeth out. Following the 14th round knockout, even after Corbett was brought back to the dressing room, Jim "was in agony from that last blow at the joining of the ribs, and looking at him I determined that it was a good blow to finish a man with in any fight. Since that time I have used it often myself, and it's a winner."

Corbett co-trainer Charlie White told Jeff that he had just seen the two greatest men that ever met in a ring. "I stopped to think that over, but I didn't feel convinced." Jeff told White, "Then I'm going to be champion of the world. … I can beat either of them, and I know it." He would have the opportunity to prove it against Fitzsimmons two years later, and against Corbett the year after that.

Following Corbett's loss, Bill Delaney, Corbett's chief trainer, became Jeffries' trainer and manager. Obviously, Delaney had liked what he had seen of Jeff against Corbett in that camp, enough to take him on. Jeffries was starting to feel like somebody.[108]

107 *My Life and Battles* at 19-20, 39.
108 *My Life and Battles* at 22-23; *Two Fisted Jeff* at 62-63.

CHAPTER 5

Driving the Van Downtown

A week before Jim Corbett took on Bob Fitzsimmons, it was announced that San Francisco's National Club had matched James Jeffries and Theodore Van Buskirk for a go in April 1897. This match had been in the making since the previous year.

Van Buskirk had some good experience. Like Corbett, he had learned to box at San Francisco's Olympic Athletic Club, and had been the club's heavyweight champion.

On paper, Van Buskirk was no walkover, for his pro experience included: 1895 KO2 Joe Kennedy and 1896 KO2 James "Soldier" Walker, KO2 Patsy Corrigan, KO2 Jack "Bubbles" Davis, D10 Jack Stelzner, and KO4 Bill Johnson.[109] Corbett had sparred Van Buskirk in late 1896. In January 1897, Van Buskirk fought Jack Stelzner to another 10-round draw. Certainly, Van had more pro experience than Jeff did. Furthermore, Van Buskirk was about as big as Jeffries was. "So far as the size of the performers go, that mill will be the biggest ever decided here, as the boxers will scale about 200 pounds each."[110]

There was some discussion of having the winner of Jeffries Van Buskirk go against the winner of the Pruett-Bob Armstrong fight, which was between two black boxers. However, this was the first time that Jeffries (or his new manager Delaney, speaking on his behalf) drew the color line.

Theodore Van Buskirk

---

109 William "Bill" Johnson was described as a trainer at a local athletic club and remarkably clever. Van Buskirk was described as much heavier, a far harder hitter, and almost as clever with his hands. *San Francisco Chronicle*, December 12, 1896. Going 10 rounds with Jack Stelzner was impressive, given that Jack was able to go round after round of sparring with the hard-punching Fitzsimmons. Joe Kennedy would go on to have some good results as well.
110 *San Francisco Evening Post*, March 10, 1897; *San Francisco Evening Post*, April 3, 1897; Boxrec.com; Cyberboxingzone.com; *San Francisco Examiner*, March 15, 1897; *New York Journal*, March 19, 1897.

Should Jeffries carry off the honors the plan will have to be abandoned, as the Los Angeles youth draws the color line. He does not take the position as a matter of sentiment, but simply because there is something so strong about the aroma of the average colored slogger that it nauseates the boxer from the South. Under the circumstances he cannot be blamed, for it is one thing to be knocked out by a fist and another to be defeated by a bad smell.[111]

Leading up to the fight, both men were training hard. Jeffries was a 10 to 7 betting favorite, and at those figures, much money was invested. "As both of the men are in fine fettle a splendid battle is looked for."[112]

On April 8, 1897 in Oakland, California, the day before the fight, Jeffries gave an (advertised for 4 rounds) exhibition with Billy Woods, his fellow Corbett training camp member. Woods was a 200-pounder who in the past had sparred with both Corbett and Fitzsimmons, and had likely been sparring with Jeff to help prepare him for the upcoming fight. During his career he had suffered losses to Joe Choynski (1891 LKOby34) and Steve O'Donnell (1895 LKOby15). Woods wore his pneumatic armor, which consisted of a body protector that bulged out, and also a thick padded leather headgear that made him look like an Eskimo dressed for winter. The exhibition closed with an imitation of the Corbett knockout, showing the appreciative audience how Fitz had won the title.

The day of the big fight, a reporter predicted, "The men are such big strong punchers and aggressive fighters that it seems impossible that a knockout will not result." Jeff said that he was never in better shape in his life, and expected to win inside of 10 rounds. Delaney remarked that Jeff would enter the ring at over 200 pounds. Van Buskirk was reported to be weighing at least 195 pounds.[113]

> In his first fight, and only one here, Jeffries set the wiseacres to thinking. They fancied they saw an embryo wonder. He knocked his man out in such workmanlike fashion that it caught the house.
>
> Corbett then took him and boxed with him. He pronounced him a hard, conscientious worker, and had some cleverness. Certainly he is game; he showed that at Carson. Van Buskirk is a rushing fighter, and will give an interesting exhibition. He was the heavyweight champion at the Olympic Club for some time, and since then has bested a number of men.[114]

Just over three weeks after the Corbett-Fitzsimmons fight, on April 9, 1897 at the People's Palace, under the auspices of San Francisco's National

111 *San Francisco Evening Post*, April 3, 1897.
112 *San Francisco Evening Post*, April 6, 8, 1897.
113 *Oakland Tribune, San Francisco Evening Post*, April 9, 1897.
114 *San Francisco Bulletin*, April 9, 1897.

Athletic Club, James Jeffries took on Theodore Van Buskirk. The battle was scheduled for 15 rounds. An immense crowd of 5,000 packed the building "from pit to dome." Several hundred had to be turned away because there simply was no more room left. Already, Jeffries was a gate draw.

Jeff's seconds were Billy Delaney, Billy Woods, and Danny Needham.[115]

The 20-year-old Van Buskirk was listed at 203 pounds, while Jeff (just six days short of his 22nd birthday) "was all of that weight, if not heavier." Van looked as big as an elephant, but did not appear as Herculean as "the Los Angeles wonder" when Jeffries removed his sweater. Jeff had to strain to insert his huge hands into the small 5-ounce gloves.

Referee Hiram Cook introduced the boxers. Both received generous applause, although Van Buskirk's friends, mostly local Olympic Club members, were in the majority.

Before the fight began, Henry Baker, the Chicago heavyweight "who has fought many of the best big men of the world and has won many victories," entered the ring and challenged the winner to a fight. "After it was over he probably felt like changing his mind."[116]

1st round

At the start, there was the "usual inaugural fiddling and cautious sparring for an opening." Both danced and skipped about. However, Van Buskirk soon took the aggressive, rushing as Jeff retreated. Van swung his left, but Jeff cleverly ducked under the blow, and as they collided, he countered with a "thunderbolt" to the lower stomach that doubled Van over and "sent the German reeling to his corner in agony."

Another account of this sequence said that they "clinched and swung round violently, Jeffries' left catching his opponent below the belt as they struggled together." "Van made up all sorts of grimaces and put his hands in the region of his groin."

Van Buskirk was on the verge of going down, but his seconds entered the ring and held him up, claiming a foul. They brought the chair into the ring and sat Van down. However, Referee Hiram Cook shook his head, said, "No foul," and ordered them out of the ring.

The local papers all rendered their opinions as to whether or not the blow was foul or fair. Three reports said it was a legal punch. *The Evening Post* said it was in the body. *The Bulletin* said it was in the stomach. *The Call* said it was a left shot into the lower ribs under the heart. Jeff's very first blow was a "veritable Fitzsimmons heart punch, and had the effect of temporarily paralyzing Van Buskirk's entire working system." However, the *Examiner* said the blow might have strayed low. *The Chronicle* insisted that it

---

115 Dan Needham was a middleweight who had trained and sparred with Tom Sharkey to help Tom prepare for his December 1896 fight with Fitzsimmons. Jeff had possibly also been sparring with him. Typically, a fighter's cornermen included the men who had been his sparring partners and trainers.

116 The fight discussion and analysis is taken from the *San Francisco Examiner, San Francisco Evening Post, San Francisco Bulletin, San Francisco Call, San Francisco Chronicle*, April 10, 1897.

was below the belt. "There is no doubt that Jeffries delivered a foul blow, though the punch was unintentional." Clearly though, referee Hiram Cook felt that the blow was legal.

Jeff might have thought it was low, because he stepped back to his corner instead of going in to finish Van Buskirk. Both went to their corners and essentially took a time-out during the round. However, the fact that the seconds had entered the ring and Van was holding his hands by his groin might have puzzled Jeff, so he stepped back in sportsmanlike fashion. Perhaps the fact that his very first blow had done so much damage surprised him. "And all this time Jeffries stood looking on with an expression of astonishment on his countenance and had apparently forgotten that he was one of the principals in the contest." Jeff's seconds rushed him back to business.

Van Buskirk had recovered sufficiently to continue, but he was still suffering a bit, and some of the dash and ginger had been taken from him. Still, he managed to fight fiercely and desperately, showing a lot of pluck. However, the fighting was all in Jeff's favor, and he gave Van an "unmerciful drubbing." The first blow of the fight was the beginning of the end.

During the remainder of the 1st round, Jeffries sent crushing left-handers into the German's wind, now and then varying with a "poorly aimed right for the head." After landing a hard body punch, Jeff landed two terrific left-handers in the face, staggering Van badly. Van Buskirk ducked and attempted to defend, but Jeff hit him with several more hard blows. A Jeffries left to the face and a left to the ribs sent Van back to a corner.

Another left rattled Van Buskirk, but then he fought back hard, attacking Jeffries. Jeff eventually backed around the ring and scored with straight lefts. Even when backing up, he was the better fighter. Jeffries finished the round with a hard left to the stomach.

> It was Jeffries' round throughout. He had no style to speak of and his footwork was rather slovenly, but he judged distance well and it was rarely that he aimed for either the face or the body with his left and failed to make connections. He was quick at ducking too, managing to get under some well meant lefts from the other man.

2nd round

Van Buskirk had recovered, and attempted to hurry matters by attacking, fighting evenly at the start of the round. However, he "made little progress as his opponent showed considerable speed and cleverly avoided and at the same time dealt out hot blows." Jeff retreated and ducked, allowing Van to force the fight, but continued landing his hard left to the body. Van kept pressing, until Jeff held, each time landing his right to the body or head on the break. This was legal under straight Queensberry rules, which required the men to protect themselves at all times. The breakaway right was a move that he had learned from Corbett.

After Delaney called on Jeffries to go in and punch, Jeff complied, jolting Van whenever and wherever he wanted to, "throwing his whole force into every blow." "He tattooed his face and body with uppercuts and terrific punches."

After a minute of slugging in which Jeff landed punishing lefts to the stomach, Jeffries caught him with one especially effective left hook to the body which caused Van to bend over, doubled up. Jeff followed with a right over the left eye, drawing first blood. Another version said that a clinch followed after Van bent over, and in the breakaway, "Jeffries delivered a right on Van's left optic that left it puffed up like a tomato."

Jeffries followed Van Buskirk around the ring, swinging vicious lefts and rights, missing more than he landed, but he eventually drove Van to the ropes with a left jab in the throat. While Van was on the ropes, there was a terrific exchange of head blows. Van Buskirk "landed but one blow of consequence on his opponent's anatomy. That was a right cross on Jeffries' jaw, a fairly stiff one at that, but even then it was one of those desperate swings which a fighter resorts to when he is pinned against the ropes."

After this exchange, Jeff again worked Van Buskirk into a corner, and, crowding his man, ripped a left into the body. As Van doubled up and his head came forward, Jeff quickly crossed with a crushing right on the jaw and Van went down, his limp and quivering form colliding with the resined floor. Another version of the knockdown said that Jeff landed three straight rights to the stomach, and then followed with a left uppercut to the jaw which stretched Van onto the boards, insensible.

The "pride of the Olympic Club" was counted out. "It was a complete knockout." Still out cold, Van Buskirk was carried to his corner. "It was fully four minutes before the defeated fighter was brought to." The fight had ended at 2 minutes into the 2nd round.

The match had been "short and decisive." Van Buskirk had as much chance to win "as a grasshopper would have in the midst of a prairie fire." He was an easy mark, and "had no right to get into the same ring with his opponent, who had the fight won from the moment they got together." Jeffries "was hit four times by the ex-champion of the Olympic Club and in return got in over thirty punches, every one of which helped a little to bring about the final result."

Once again, the local papers lauded Jeffries' abilities. *The Call* said, "This man Jeffries can hit." *The Examiner* said, "Jeffries' clean and powerful hitting and his quickness to see an opening and take advantage of it were the subject of glowing comment." *The Chronicle* echoed, "Jeffries proved himself quite as hard a hitter as has been claimed for him and with a little more science he will make a dangerous opponent for any fighter at present before the public." *The Bulletin* gave its analysis of Jeffries:

While Jeff has yet lots to learn, few will question his ability to punch hard. A clip that can set big Van Buskirk down on the floor must have some power behind it. Furthermore, Jeff is mighty quick for a big man. He is so gross that he looks to be slow, but he isn't. He is plenty fast enough to whip any man. What he has to learn most is to guard his body. He seems to lay himself open. A clever man last night would have landed him frequently on the body.

The Evening Post commented,

The fight demonstrated beyond a doubt that Jeffries is in line for championship honors and it goes without saying that he has advantages over all other fighters, as he is undoubtedly the biggest, strongest and youngest of the heavyweights of the day. In addition, he is remarkably quick for a big man. He has a cool head, gauges his blows nicely, wastes no effort, and, what is of the greatest importance of all, he hits like a pile driver.

The locals agreed that Jeff was of championship material, a "rising star in the championship horizon." The caption to a drawing of Jeffries said, "Experts Pronounce Him The Coming Heavyweight Champion."

Before the fight, when Jim Corbett said that Jeffries had considerable talent and would make a favorable showing in front of most any man, many laughed. However, "None who saw the fight last night will do so any more." *The Chronicle* said, "It is the general opinion…that if he meets Sharkey, the Irishman will be badly worsted." *The Evening Post* agreed. "That Jeffries can whip Tom Sharkey is almost certain."

Jeffries was paid the 80% winner's share of a $1,500 purse ($1,200 winner/$300 loser).

After the fight, Dr. Lustig examined Van Buskirk, who was complaining of severe pain in his right side. The physician declared that Van had sustained a hernia. He could not say whether a blow or a strain caused it. Van Buskirk claimed that a low blow at the start of the fight was the culprit. Dr. Somers, an ex-police surgeon, said that a blow undoubtedly brought on the hernia.

The next day, Van said, "I do not believe that Jeffries struck me where he did intentionally, but he has a bad habit of stooping very low in a clinch and doesn't seem to know just where he is striking." Van claimed that he received the blow several inches lower than where the spectators believed he did. Regardless of whether the blow was fair or foul, it did not change the high opinion that the fans, writers and experts had of Jeffries.[117]

117 *San Francisco Call*, April 11, 1897.

CHAPTER 6

How the Baker
Got His Goose Cooked

After defeating Theodore Van Buskirk in 2 rounds in San Francisco in early April 1897, Jeffries returned to Los Angeles. On April 27, 1897 in Los Angeles, Jeff and sparring partner Billy Woods boxed 6 rounds in an imitation of the Fitzsimmons-Corbett bout. Jeff played Fitz, while Woods, wearing his pneumatic armor, played Corbett.[118]

A 20-round bout between Chicago heavyweight Henry Baker and Jeffries was scheduled to be held in San Francisco in May. Baker was the boxer who had entered the ring prior to the Jeff-Van Buskirk fight and challenged the winner.

Henry Baker was a "thick-set fellow with a fair amount of speed and unlimited pluck and punching power." Having been a professional since 1889, Baker had boxed in some 3-round exhibitions with Bob Fitzsimmons in 1892 and 1893. His record included: 1889 LKOby3 Tommy Ryan; 1892 D4 Con Riordan, LKOby7 and KO15 Dick Moore; 1893 W6 Frank Kellar and KO6 William Mayo; 1894 W8 Kellar, W8 Billy Woods, and EX4 Jim Hall (Hall contracted to knock him out and failed); 1895 D6 Dan Creedon; and 1896 D6 Frank Slavin and L20 Dan Creedon, in addition to many other bouts. Baker was called the champion of the Chicago slaughter-houses and the Northwest.[119]

Jeff trained and sparred with his brother Jack Jeffries and Billy Woods at Oakland's Reliance Club, which would be his training quarters for many of his San Francisco bouts. De Witt Van Court helped with his conditioning work.[120]

Less than a week before the fight, when Jeff was observed training in Oakland, sparring, punching the bag, and working on the gymnasium machines, he appeared to have "lots of speed and his wind was perfect."[121]

---

118 *Los Angeles Daily Times*, April 28, 1897. "Jeffries is the better fighter of the two, so in order to allow him to get in realistic blows without killing off Mr. Woods before the end of the six rounds, it was necessary to pad the latter effectually before beginning the contest." The final round was an imitation of the 14th round of the Fitz-Corbett bout, with Woods going down to his hands and knees from a body blow, then clutching the ropes and attempting to rise. Jeff was listed at 198 pounds to Billy's 185 pounds.
119 Cyberboxignzone.com; Boxrec.com; *San Francisco Examiner*, April 20, 1897; *San Francisco Bulletin*, May 18, 1897.
120 *Two Fisted Jeff* at 71-72.
121 *San Francisco Bulletin*, May 13, 1897.

Although on the day of the fight, the "dusky bruiser" Jeffries was a 1 to 2 favorite in the poolrooms, the local *San Francisco Bulletin* did not think that was fair. Baker had the reputation for "striking a murderous blow," and was definitely far more experienced than Jeffries was.

> It is hard to see what he has done to install him at such prohibitive odds. Van Buskirk is the only man of note he has subdued, and he is not a wonder. Baker is accredited with being fairly clever, can hit like a mule and is remarkably game. He is strong and his powers of endurance are above par.

> It seems absurd to lay such prices against Baker. At these odds he should be played. Billy Kennedy saw both Jeff and Baker yesterday, and pronounces them in tip-top shape. He says the Chicago-man will be a genuine surprise.

Steve O'Donnell, who had seen Baker go 20 rounds with Dan Creedon, dropping Dan in the 1st round, felt that Baker would surprise everyone and defeat Jeffries. O'Donnell said, "Jeffries has got to be a first-class man to win."[122]

James Jeffries and Henry Baker fought their scheduled 20-round bout on May 18, 1897. Sponsored by the Olympic Club, the fight took place in San Francisco's spacious Woodward's Garden Pavilion on Fourteenth Street. It was "literally packed from floor to rafter" with 6,000 fans, of which about 3,500 were in the gallery. "The ticket office closed with men clamoring for admission."

After some preliminary bouts, one of which included Joe Gans defeating Mike Leonard, Jeffries came on, looking like a giant next to Baker (who Jeff said weighed 185 pounds). *The Call* called Baker a "fat boy," with rolls of fat hanging over his belt. On the other hand, Jeffries was a "magnificent specimen." It said that Baker weighed 175 pounds to Jeff's 201 pounds, "which is nine pounds lower than he has ever fought." Delaney and Woods seconded Jeffries.

---

122 *San Francisco Bulletin*, May 18, 1897.

Woodward's Pavilion

Before the battle, manager Billy Madden announced that he would match Gus Ruhlin against the winner. "Ruhlin is the man who made a monkey out of Steve O'Donnell."

Most of the local sources did not give a complete round by round account. However, the *Call* gave an abbreviated version.

1st round

From the start, Baker showed that he was clever and nimble on his feet, creating a favorable impression. He knew how to move fast and hit hard, landing a number of good blows. However, Baker could not land nearly often enough, for Jeffries "ducked with remarkable cleverness for a big man." Defensively, "Baker relied principally upon his clever foot work in getting away from Jeffries' heavy swings." He also relied on clinching when close. "Considerable clinching was indulged in and as the round closed Baker landed a left and right on Jeffries' mouth."

2nd round

"Jeffries caught a hard right-hand punch in the left eye which left its imprint. Jeffries ducked cleverly from several swings and in the clinches which followed he was hissed by the gallery because he struck at Baker when both men had one hand free, which was perfectly proper and according to rule."

3rd round

Jeff played for the stomach, in hot pursuit as Baker backed away and danced around.

4th round

"Jeffries sent Baker under the ropes with a body blow, but near the end of the round Baker landed a hard right on Jeffries' mouth." Obviously, Jeff's body attack was starting to work, but Baker was game.

Rounds 5-7

In subsequent rounds, Jeffries "scored a strong lead."

The Examiner summarized that for 6 rounds, Baker used some pretty footwork which baffled his opponent, and occasionally landed a left and right. When held, Jeffries got rough in the clinches, causing the crowd to turn against him.

As the fight progressed, Baker mostly missed, while Jeff landed his left to the body and head quite often. Jeffries "ducked marvelously well for a big man, getting well under Baker's left swings and picking the Chicagoan clear off his feet as he straightened up."

8th round

Jeffries twice knocked Baker down with left-hand swings on the jaw. Although Baker was on Queer Street and got hammered all over the ring, Jeffries could not finish him in this round.

9th round

Another left on the chin dropped Baker again. After he rose, Jeffries repeated the left hand blow and sent Baker between and partly through the ropes. Baker hung over the lower rope, his head nearly touching the floor. His second, "Spider" Kelly, threw up the sponge to retire him, entered the ring, picked Baker up, and brought him to his corner. "Though Baker was not entirely knocked out he was so very near it that his seconds were satisfied to allow the Los Angeles giant to receive the decision."

The Bulletin praised Jeffries for defeating a tough opponent.

> Baker gave a better account of himself than the majority expected. He is fairly clever, hits hard and seems game. Jeffries deserves a lot of credit for his victory. The only match now to make is to put Sharkey against Jeffries. The club that can bring this off can retire from the business after it is over.

The Chronicle called it an exhibition of hard hitting, with both demonstrating an ability to take punishment. However, nitpicking, it criticized Jeffries for not knowing enough to follow up and take Baker out in the 8th round. In contrast to the *Bulletin*, it was not all that high on Jeff.

To put it mildly, Jeffries' showing last night did not prove that he had become surfeited with cleverness. His hitting powers showed up in great shape, and some of the punches he got in on Baker were terribly heavy. But from the first round to the ninth, when he ended the fight with a swing like the blow of a sledgehammer on his opponent's jaw, he showed no science whatever.[123]

Apparently, the fight showed both Jeffries' strengths and weaknesses at that point. He was a developing young fighter. Still, he was pretty good for a boxer with only about five known bouts under his belt. He had dropped the far more experienced, in shape and motivated Baker once in the 4th, twice in the 8th, and twice more in the 9th round.

Jeff later said of Baker that he was a game, tough fellow who hit hard. He said that Henry had been so confident of winning that he had bet heavily on himself; so much that he came away with nothing, and actually owed money.[124]

123 *San Francisco Examiner, San Francisco Chronicle, San Francisco Bulletin, San Francisco Evening Post, San Francisco Call*, May 19, 1897. *The Call* gave a contrary view from its local counterparts, saying that there were only 1,500 spectators.
124 *My Life and Battles* at 23.

CHAPTER 7

The Closer

Following his victory over Henry Baker in May, James Jeffries continued his busy 1897, being matched to fight Ohio's Gus Ruhlin for a July fight. The 25-year-old Ruhlin was called a "high class performer" as a result of his recent May 1897 splendid 10-round decision victory against the experienced and respected Steve O'Donnell. This win put Ruhlin's name on the map.[125]

A primary source listed Ruhlin's record as: defeated Jim Woods, 8 rounds (1893), Con Tobin, 5 rounds (1893), Doc Payne, 4 rounds (1894), drew with Peter Maher, 4 rounds (1895), beat Tony Gelder, 2 rounds (1896), Dominick Kano, 4 rounds (1896) and Steve O'Donnell, 10 rounds (1897).[126] Going 4 rounds with Peter Maher was significant, given that Maher had the reputation for being one of the hardest one-punch knockout artists in the game.

Jeffries trained at Oakland's Reliance Club under Delaney's guidance. Approaching the fight, as a result of his hard training, Jeff was in excellent condition, which showed in "his improved form and appearance." Ruhlin was also in "fine fettle" and

---

125 *San Francisco Evening Post*, July 5, 1897. O'Donnell had been a Jim Corbett sparring partner and was highly regarded by Corbett. O'Donnell's record included 1895 KO21 Jake Kilrain and LKOby1 Peter Maher. The retiring Corbett then declared Maher the world heavyweight champion. O'Donnell also held an 1896 KO5 over Frank Slavin, although Steve was once again been knocked out in the 1st round by Maher in a rematch, and also lost an 1897 6-round decision to Maher. Boxrec.com.
126 *San Francisco Bulletin*, July 16, 1897. Secondary sources indicate that in 1895, Yank Kenny knocked out Ruhlin in the 16th round, but this has not been confirmed.

"prime condition." *The San Francisco Evening Post* opined, "They will put up a great fight, and the winner will be justified in going at any of the big fellows for the championship belt." Jeff was the 10 to 6 odds favorite.[127]

Alex Greggains had seen Ruhlin, and felt that he would be a surprise.

> I don't know as I have ever seen a better-built man of his size. He is nicely proportioned. Ruhlin handles himself cleverly, is quick on his feet, and seems to be moderately clever. I think he will make an excellent showing against Jeff, and I wouldn't be surprised to see him beat him. Jeffries is not a marvel. He can be whipped.

Noted was the fact that Ruhlin was taller than Jeffries was (6'2 ½" vs. 6'1 ½") and also had a decided reach advantage of a few inches. Jeff only had a slight weight advantage of about twelve pounds. "Ruhlin's record stamps him as a good performer, with a prospect of moving ahead into the front rank. The winner of this contest will undoubtedly be heard from as an aspirant for championship honors."[128]

On July 16, 1897 at San Francisco's Mechanics' Pavilion, under the sponsorship of the Columbian Athletic Club, a 22-year-old Jeffries took on fellow young contender, 25-year-old Gus Ruhlin, in a scheduled 20-round bout. Jeff was listed at 212 pounds, while Ruhlin was listed at 198 or 199 pounds. By fight time, Jeff was a 2-1 betting favorite. Ruhlin's well-respected manager Billy Madden predicted a surprise for the over-confident Californians.[129]

The men entered the ring at about the same time, at 10:20 p.m., with a house full of over 5,000 spectators. Bill Delaney, Billy Woods, and Billy Gallagher seconded Jeffries. Ruhlin's squires were Billy Madden, Steve O'Donnell (then Ruhlin's trainer and sparring partner), and Jimmy Anthony.

127 *San Francisco Evening Post*, July 12-14, 1897.
128 *San Francisco Bulletin*, July 15, 16, 1897.
129 *San Francisco Chronicle, San Francisco Evening Post, San Francisco Call*, July 16, 1897.

Both boxers had difficulty getting on the mittens, as they were too small. One said that Jeff's problems were in part owing to the fact that he "wore such an innumerable number of bandages on his paws." After some tight shoving, with assistance from his seconds, Jeff finally got his hands into the gloves. The fact that he was wearing such a large amount of bandages was perhaps the first hint that he had been having hand troubles. Wearing small 5-ounce gloves was not going to help matters.

Delaney and Madden had some dispute over the rules regarding the breakaway, although it is unclear what their positions were. Apparently, the men agreed not to hit in clinches, and to break away cleanly.[130]

THE NEW ARENA IN MECHANICS' PAVILION.

1st round

Jeffries immediately cut out a fast pace. Ruhlin was not afraid and engaged Jeffries, who in return "played a hot tune on his body." Jeff missed a swing and clinched, and as they separated Ruhlin landed a hot left to the mouth and right to the body. Quick exchanges to the head followed. After a hot rally, the cool-headed Ruhlin smashed Jeff twice in the mouth, but Jeff ducked a wicked swing at his jaw. Ruhlin rushed and attacked as Jeff cleverly ducked, dodged and clinched. Gus hit the ribs with a right but Jeff shook him up with a left jolt. Gus rushed at intervals and clinches were

---

130 The following account, analysis, and discussion are an amalgamation of the *San Francisco Chronicle, San Francisco Examiner, San Francisco Evening Post, San Francisco Call, San Francisco Bulletin,* July 17, 1897.

frequent. Jeff slowed the pace when he saw that he had a tough customer in front of him.

2nd round

This too was a warmly contested round. Jeffries "sailed in to knock Ruhlin's head off his shoulders, but he received hot pepper in the nose and mouth, and withdrew in astonishment." The calm Ruhlin watched him closely, "and sent home good medicine whenever Jeffries run his face within shooting distance." Gus became the aggressor again and Jeff countered and clinched. Ruhlin made a good showing, following him up every second, although neither landed any really powerful blows.

3rd round

This was a red-hot round. After Gus scored a few times with the left, Jeff went in and landed a heavy left on Gus's ear, which started Ruhlin's blood boiling, and he mixed it up with his powerful opponent. It was give and take. "Jeffries relied altogether on a left-arm swing and hook, and while his glove was making a wild swat through the air Ruhlin was planting straight-arm shots on the local man's proboscis." Ruhlin landed some vicious straight lefts to the eye and followed with heavy rights that sent Jeff backwards momentarily.

When they drew close again, there was a savage short-range rally in which Jeffries landed the more telling blows, which were "sufficiently heavy to down a Jersey bull." Jeff landed two rights to the body and two lefts to the jaw and Ruhlin grabbed to avoid punishment. Jeff worked his heavy left upon the jaw and body repeatedly. The thunderbolts took a lot of steam out of Gus. Just before the round concluded, Jeffries landed a heavy smash on the neck that staggered Ruhlin to the ropes. Gus was glad when the round ended.

4th round

They sailed into each other like bulldogs and fought hammer and tongs. A Ruhlin left to the nose brought blood. Jeff retaliated fiercely to the body with his own famous left, rushing like a madman.

Ruhlin stopped a left swing, but caught a right in the stomach near the belt and dropped to the floor. Ruhlin claimed it was a foul, but the referee did not recognize his claim. It was a legal blow. Gus was down for nine seconds.

Upon rising, Jeff was on top of him, but Gus ducked away and then dashed in. They landed simultaneous swinging lefts. Hot fighting followed, and Jeff actually got the worst of the majority of exchanges. They mixed it up at the bell, with Gus landing several hard rights that made Jeff seem a bit unsteady on his legs, momentarily staggered. Still, Jeff had edged the round with his swift and powerful rushes, one of which had led to the knockdown.

5th round

This was another hot and rough round, as they engaged in several fierce rallies. Jeff hit in the clinches, which had been barred by agreement, so the referee warned him. Delaney cautioned Jeff to be careful of Ruhlin's right. Jeffries swung both arms wildly, while Ruhlin executed some great work with his left and right. The round was mostly Ruhlin's, drawing blood from Jeff's nose, partially closing and cutting Jeff's left eye, and bloodying his mouth.

However, Jeffries again knocked Ruhlin down in this round, each local source giving its version of how it happened. *The Call* said Ruhlin went down from a body shot. Ruhlin again claimed the blow was foul, but the referee did not allow his claim. *The Chronicle* said that a Jeffries left swing sent Ruhlin stumbling to his knees. *The Examiner* said that a Jeffries right dropped Ruhlin. Gus was down for seven or nine seconds, depending on the source. Ruhlin rose and boxed well for the remainder of the round, despite the fact that Jeffries continually pressed him.

6th round

Ruhlin had the best of this round. He punched Jeff's face a number of times with his right. They fought briskly, with Jeff ducking the onslaught. Ruhlin hit Jeffries with a flush right on the mouth "that caused the receiver to see all kinds of stars." Another Ruhlin right cut Jeffries. Jeff's left eye began to swell, which bothered him and caused him to take the defensive, backing away and becoming more cautious. Ruhlin chased him about but only landed an occasional punch, one of which landed on the jaw and "jarred the stage." However, the pace slackened in this round.

The San Francisco Chronicle described the bout as initially fast, the two mauling each other through the first 5 rounds, but after that, the bout dragged on, with only occasional short but hard rallies. It said that they did very little from the 6th to the 19th rounds.

7th round

Jeff was wary of the Ruhlin right. Gus was the aggressor. In an attempt to get away from one right, Jeff slipped and fell near his own corner. Towards the close of the round, there was a warm exchange of blows.

The Call said that after this round the fighters took things easy, for the pace was too severe for big men to hold out. *The Chronicle* said the 7th through 12th rounds were tame. *The Bulletin* said there was no heavy fighting until the 14th round.

8th round

Jeffries landed several strong lefts, but there was not much action.

9th round

Ruhlin was more cautious as Jeff forced the pace. They did little damage though, for each was waiting for an opening which never came.

10th round

Gus cut loose again. While avoiding a Ruhlin rush, Jeff slipped down to his knees in the center of the ring. However, overall, very little fighting was done in this round.

11th round

This was a faster round, with both landing fierce blows. Jeff got the worst of the exchanges. At the close of the round, there was a mix-up, each giving and taking several hard blows.

12th round

The Examiner said that this round was in Ruhlin's favor, and he held the lead until the 15th round.

13th round

Jeff landed a left that marked Gus's face for the first time.
The Chronicle said that from the 13th to the 19th rounds, the fight was a succession of sparring and clinching, the fighters rarely landing hard.

14th round

Following Delaney's advice, Jeff revived in this round and forced matters, doing the most effective work. However, he "found that his opponent had ammunition up his sleeve and after a few short rallies he took matters easy." Still, Jeff was the aggressor in the next 4 rounds.
The Call said that from this point on until the 18th round, there was no fighting worthy of note.

15th round

The Examiner said that Jeff caught his second wind and sent in multiple left swings, causing Gus's right cheek to swell. Jeff also landed blows to the heart, and Ruhlin's ribs became reddened.

16th and 17th rounds

There was not much to report, for the men continued sparring and clinching, doing little effective work.

18th round

Jeff again assumed the aggressive. He had seldom used his right up to this point, but discovered that he could plant the right with telling effect to Ruhlin's body, under Gus' left arm. Jeffries administered some severe punishment to Ruhlin's body and ribs.

19th round

At this point, the fight was even. However, Jeff's body blows had weakened Ruhlin. Jeff landed lefts to Gus' swollen jaw. Gus scored straight lefts. Jeff hit the ribs. "Jeffries forced the pace and pitched Ruhlin over his shoulder to the floor. It finished in a give-and-take, and Jeffries scored a success."

20th round

In this round, Jeffries showed what would become one of his trademark attributes - his endurance and ability to finish strong. In doing so, he demonstrated that he would be an effective fighter in a fight to the finish. Jeffries almost knocked Ruhlin out.

Both made a strong and desperate finish, picking up the pace and engaging in some wicked exchanges. Jeff did the rushing. Coming at Gus, he received some hard smashes in the mouth.

The Chronicle felt that up to this point, Ruhlin had the best of the bout, having landed more blows. He hit Jeff's head a dozen times in the final round. However, undaunted, Jeff kept right after him and eventually got the better of it.

Once again, Jeffries knocked Ruhlin down. According to the *Call*, Jeff caught Ruhlin with a left hook under the chin which staggered him. Jeff swung with both right and left until a right landed to the jaw and Ruhlin went down on his back. *The Examiner* agreed that a right to the jaw had dropped Ruhlin. However, the *Chronicle* said of the knockdown sequence that Jeff got Ruhlin on the ropes and "sent him to the floor hard, dazing him badly with a left swing on the ear."

The Call said that Gus staggered to his feet after eight and a half seconds, while the *Chronicle* said he rose after seven seconds. Gus rushed, but got the worst of the exchange, getting banged on the jaw with a left that sent him to the ropes. Ruhlin was rattled, and it looked as if he would not last the round. However, just as Jeff was about to finish him off, Ruhlin clinched and the gong sounded, saving him from defeat.

Referee Phil Wand declared the bout a draw. Both of Jeff's eyes were black and his lips were swollen. Ruhlin had sore sides and a lump over his right cheekbone "as large as a full-grown tomato." As Jeff later said in his autobiography, they both had been "well pounded up at the end of it."

The Chronicle called the referee's draw decision "undoubtedly fair and just." *The Bulletin* said that the decision "satisfied the majority."

However, the *Evening Post* said that the decision "created general surprise." Generally, how a fighter finished the fight weighed heavily in a referee's ultimate decision, as did overall effective damage and who was in better condition to continue at the end. At the close of the mill, Jeffries had Ruhlin on the ropes in a dazed, defeated condition. "Had the encounter been allowed to go on another round Jeffries would almost certainly have put his man out." It felt that Jeffries deserved the victory.

The local papers had mixed praise and criticism of Jeffries and Ruhlin. *The Call* said it was a hot fight, but "Fitzsimmons can easily whip both men in the same ring." *The Examiner* said the contest "was interesting in spots only." While not providing a round by round account, the *Evening Post* gave a nice overview and analysis.

> During the early rounds of the battle fighting was fast and furious, but after the boxers had dealt each other a few sharp blows they showed marked consideration for one another and were content to do business at long range and at rather a slow pace.
>
> So far as natural advantages go, Jeffries was a few pounds heavier…but he did not appear any stronger. He was inferior in reach and a trifle slower in his delivery.
>
> Ruhlin was, if anything, the cleverer of the pair and used straight lefts…with speed and precision. During last night's mill he stood terrible punishment, but was about finished when the last gong sounded, as he had reached the end of his limit and was succumbing to the fierce body blows dealt out by Jeffries, who was apparently as strong as when he entered the arena.
>
> So far as championship form is concerned neither of the opponents in last night's battle displayed it. Jeffries used his left hand almost exclusively, and time and time again could have driven in his right had he half tried. It may be said, however, that his second, Billy Delaney, instructed him to make a left-handed fight. Probably that precaution resulted in spreading the mill out to the twenty-round limit.
>
> As he gains experience as a fighter Jeffries seems to lose form. In his first mill in this city the Los Angeles slogger was prolific of upper cuts. He used both hands equally well and gave promise of developing into a hurricane boxer. Since then, however, he has lost the use of his right and has discarded the upper cuts and other serviceable blows. If such is the result of tuition in the art of boxing a man had better let the professors alone.

The Chronicle similarly said that Jeff had not displayed an improvement in science. It called him a one-blow puncher, using his right infrequently, depending almost entirely on his left. That left "does not come straight from the shoulder, but is a half swing, missing as often as it lands. The only redeeming feature of Jeffries' performance last night was his body work in the clinches."

The Call agreed, criticizing, "If Jeffries could strike straight from the shoulder he would prove to be a dangerous man. His only blow is a left-hand hook, which he telegraphs every time he leads."

The Bulletin also said,

> Jeffries showed little improvement. He relied upon his left swings; his right was pressed into service only a few times in the whole twenty rounds. Jeff's aim was to get his left in on Ruhlin's jaw. He whipped it around scores of times, but the best he could do was to bruise Ruhlin's neck. At the end it bore the resemblance of rare sirloin.

The Examiner said that Jeffries was "not quite as good as was claimed for him. His best efforts in the punch line are a left swing at the head and a right-hander at the body. In delivering the former he frequently holds his left arm rigid, working it in the manner of a pump-handle." However, by the end of the bout, those lefts had made the right side of Ruhlin's face swollen out of proportion. Jeff's rights left Ruhlin's ribs well marked.

Ruhlin made a favorable impression. His graceful form was pleasing to the eye. He was a quick, straight hitter, cool, scientific, and clever, but not as strong as Jeffries was. His punch form, reach and footwork enabled him to land to the face and keep out of range. His straight lefts brought blood from Jeff's nose and mouth. Well-timed right counters had partially closed Jeff's left eye. *The Bulletin* said, "His blows were clean cut and right from the shoulder. There were no swings or roundabout efforts made. He sent his fists straight out and was clever enough in landing a majority. Ruhlin was light on his feet, in view of his colossal size. He was not a bit clumsy." It further said that at several stages Ruhlin had Jeffries on Queer Avenue, and came within an ace of taking his scalp. However, Ruhlin was "deficient in headwork to complete his job."

However, the more critical *Call* said that Ruhlin "showed some white feather last evening." Ruhlin was the prettier boxer, but Jeffries was the stronger, more effective, and more rugged of the two.

Ruhlin manager Billy Madden was glad that the experts thought more highly of Ruhlin after the fight than they did before it. Madden was also high on Jeffries, impressed by his performance.

> I believe Jeffries can whip Sharkey. No one need to laugh at Jeffries; he is a better man than the majority will give him credit to be. He can punch and take a punch. If he hadn't been game he couldn't have stood some of them blows Gus landed him. Only a game man can stand up against such thunderbolts. I will bet that Jeff can whip Sharkey.[131]

The critics were probably a bit too hard on Jeffries, underestimating just how tough and good his opponent was. In subsequent years, Ruhlin would become a top world contender. Sometimes tough opponents have a way of exposing some weak points. The fight showed both Jeff's strengths and weaknesses to that point. He needed to work on his punch form, defense,

---

131 *San Francisco Bulletin*, July 20, 1897.

and versatility. However, he also showed power - dropping Ruhlin in the 4th, 5th, and 20th rounds, a good chin, having taken several hard blows from a similarly-sized man, and wonderful endurance, carrying his strength late into the fight, which would become a Jeffries signature. Jeff was a closer. He almost had Gus out at the end, demonstrating his ability to land effective blows and break his opponents down over time. Going 20 rounds against a solid fighter after what was really only 22-year-old Jeff's first full year of pro boxing has to be recognized as impressive, particularly by today's standards. How many fighters today could go 20 rounds after only one full year of pro boxing?

In Jeff's autobiography, he claimed that he went into the fight with swollen hands, explaining why he had so much bandaging on them, and why he had such great difficulties getting them into the gloves.

A report three days after the fight backed Jeff's claims about his hands. "Jeffries' friends say that his disappointing showing was due to crippled hands. When he came into the ring he wore a couple yards of bandage around each hand." With hurt hands, he probably could not punch quite as hard as usual. Towards the end of the fight, "it was noticeable that Jeff's right was idle."

Why did they allow Jeff to box if his hands were not right? *The Bulletin* opined that his backers probably realized that his hands were not in proper condition, but felt that he could beat Ruhlin anyway, erroneously looking upon him as a dub.[132]

Still, in his autobiography, Jeff did not really use his hands as an excuse for his performance. He admitted that Ruhlin was very tough and knew a few things about the game that he did not. Jeff was relatively green and inexperienced at this point, and realized that he had a lot to learn. Regardless, he had Ruhlin nearly out at the end and had landed plenty of damaging blows.[133] The two would meet again four years later.

---

132 *San Francisco Bulletin*, July 19, 1897.
133 *My Life and Battles* at 24. Jeff made between $2,000 and $3,000 for this fight. *Two Fisted Jeff* at 77.

CHAPTER 8

The Master Veteran

In October 1897, there was some talk of Jeffries potentially being matched to fight Joe Choynski. This was seen as a very dangerous test for Jeff. When Delaney initially failed to make the fight, one newspaper opined, "Perhaps it is just as good…as [Choynski] is feeling in great fighting shape, and will probably render a very good account of himself. … Jeffries is young yet, and, though being coached by a great ring teacher and tactician, he has plenty to learn that will do him good."[134] Some thought that such a fight would be premature for a still developing Jeffries. However, by early November, the Jeffries and Choynski representatives had finalized an agreement to fight late in the month.

What most historians fail to realize is that Choynski was the favorite to win. This was considered a very tough matchup for Jeffries. Despite the fact that Choynski was smaller, because he was such a seasoned veteran, famous for his hard punch, and had been able to defeat much larger men, most thought that he would defeat Jeffries. Choynski had fought the best in boxing for over a decade. Many saw young Jeff as just another notch in Joe's belt, not the other way around. In fact, Choynski's supporters not only thought Joe would defeat Jeff, but that he would knock him out. Still, many of those who had seen Jeff in his four recent San Francisco fights recognized his talent, and felt that he had a chance to win.

> Eddie Graney [Choynski's manager] visits the Olympic Club daily to see Choynski work. He thinks Joe is looking better than he ever did before. Graney has the greatest confidence in his ability to beat Jeffries in a few rounds. … There are people who look at the matter totally in another light. It is predicted that Choynski has a harder scrap on his hands than he imagines.[135]

A San Francisco native, the 29-year-old Jewish Joe Choynski was vastly more experienced than the 22-year-old Jeffries. Joe Choynski is one of the few fighters in history who can legitimately say that he fought every top fighter in his division, and did it over several generations. To say that Joe Choynski was an experienced and active fighter would be a gross understatement. Choynski had been in the ring with every heavyweight champion. He barred no one, and did not draw the color line.

---

134 *San Francisco Bulletin*, October 2, 1897.
135 *San Francisco Bulletin*, November 10, 1897.

Although only weighing about 165-175 pounds, Choynski's fights were usually highly entertaining, exciting wars because of his aggressive and vicious hard-punching style. Because he punched so hard and was so aggressive, at times he either got tired or ran into his opponents' punches, leading to his losses. But even in defeat, his foes usually hit the deck or were badly hurt at some point in the fight, and they always came away with increased respect for him. Joe was a drawing card by himself. "He always makes a fight which satisfies the audience."

Back in 1889, Choynski had given Jim Corbett a great battle before being stopped in the 27th round. In 1891, in two all out wars in which both were down multiple times, Joe Goddard twice stopped Choynski in 4 rounds. That same year, Choynski scored a KO34 over Billy Woods, and boxed a friendly 3-round exhibition with John L. Sullivan. In 1892, Joe scored a KO15 over black veteran George Godfrey. During 1894, Choynski was a Peter Jackson sparring partner. In June 1894, Choynski dropped Bob Fitzsimmons in the 3rd round and had him badly hurt. However, over the next two rounds, Fitz beat up Choynski until the police stopped the fight in the 5th round with Joe on the verge of being knocked out, technically causing the fight to be declared a draw.

In 1896, Choynski scored a KO13 over the skillful and dangerous Jim Hall, and essentially whipped Tom Sharkey in a good tussle over 8 rounds, but lost the decision due to the fact that he had agreed that if he failed to knock Sharkey out that he would lose. Joe then scored a KO4 over the hard-hitting 220-pound Joe McAuliffe, who, like Jeffries, had at one time been a hot prospect.

However, at the end of 1896, the very hard-punching 174-pound Peter Maher knocked out the 165-pound Choynski in the 6th round. At that time, Maher was one of the best heavyweights in the world. In May 1897, Choynski won on a 4th round disqualification over the experienced veteran Denver Ed Smith. Joe had boxed in scores of other bouts and exhibitions. Certainly, he had a huge edge in experience over a fighter with only five pro bouts.

Analysts today, looking back, place too much emphasis on weight. Because Choynski was much smaller than Jeffries was, some want to denigrate the significance of the matchup. That is not how the experts of the time viewed the bout. They saw weight as but one factor. Size had its advantages. However, smaller fighters, less than 200 pounds, were typically seen as ideal and superior to larger ones. They were often quicker, more agile, had better conditioning, kept a better pace, and, if they knew how to punch hard, as Choynski did, could score knockouts over bigger men, particularly when wearing 5-ounce gloves.

Size could be a detriment in a lengthy fight because a bigger fighter had to carry more flesh, as opposed to a smaller more efficient boxer. The big fighter would have to pace himself more, because if he did not score a knockout early, he could be left spent and finding it quite difficult to last 20 rounds. How many big fighters today could last 20 rounds? Also, with more rounds to work with, smaller fighters could afford to be active on their feet, cautious and elusive against bigger fighters, biding their time until the larger man grew tired.

Leading up to the fight, Choynski was the betting favorite, opening at odds of 10 to 6 and 10 to 7. Most thought that he would win in short order. Some disagreed, particularly as the fight drew closer.

Jack Stelzner, who had been one of Fitzsimmons' chief sparring partners, was sparring with Jeffries almost daily in preparation for the fight. In 1897, Stelzner had fought Theodore Van Buskirk to a 10-round draw, Alex Greggains to a 20-round draw, and had won a 15-round decision over 220-pound Joe McAuliffe.

Stelzner said that he was digging up his money to bet on Jeff, and felt that Choynski would get the biggest surprise of his life. Stelzner said that Jeff was tough, and credited him with hitting harder than Fitzsimmons did. Many agreed that Jeff was being underrated.

> It is predicted that the odds will go up, for there are hundreds who fancy Jeffries. When the match was first made it was "Choynski in a walk," but opinion lately has changed materially. Sports who were clamoring that it was a walkover for Choynski now allow that he has a fight on his hands.[136]

In addition to Coach Bill Delaney, Olympic Club brothers De Witt and Eugene Van Court were also training Jeffries. One report said that Jeff was weighing 216 pounds to Choynski's 165 pounds. "That the mill will be a hot one goes without saying…. Each is training faithfully, Jeffries having been at work about two months, as the match has been postponed twice."

Choynski said that he felt first rate and was confident. He had seen Jeffries box before, having refereed Jeff's 1896 KO2 win over Dan Long, and had seen him in action in his subsequent local San Francisco fights. He knew what Jeff had, and was still willing to fight him. Joe was not concerned by Jeff's size, and felt that he had defeated men equally as formidable as Jeffries. He intended to enter the ring weighing 165 pounds.

> I saw Jeffries fight in this city. He is a large, stalwart, husky fellow. Bob Armstrong is also a large, stalwart, husky fellow. He stands six feet four inches, and at one time was a baby in my hands; I could do anything that I wished in an athletic way with him. [They had boxed some exhibitions in 1895 and 1897.] In [Jeff's] fight with Baker he demonstrated the fact that he was a great pugilist. I do not consider, while not wishing to speak in the least disparagingly of my coming opponent, that Jeffries, physically, is the equal of Armstrong.

---

136 *San Francisco Bulletin*, November 27, 1897.

As the fight approached, Choynski said that he was never in better condition. In his sparring, he was looking as quick and active as ever.

Both trainer Delaney and Jeffries said that he was in tip-top shape and would have no excuses to offer if he was defeated. Bill said that Jeff's hands were sore for the Ruhlin fight, but were fine now. He was confident that Jeff would give an excellent account of himself and surprise the fistic world. Delaney was said to be a very good judge of a man. When he had first seen Jeffries, he had declared that he was a comer.

Actually, Jeffries might have been overconfident. He said that he was weighing 220 pounds, and considered Choynski an easy mark. Both combatants were trying to appear as confident as possible.[137]

Although the betting was in Choynski's favor, as the fight approached, more and more experts were saying that Jeff had a good chance of winning. He was 50 pounds bigger, had a longer reach, a stiff punch, and was "moderately clever." "Choynski may defeat the giant, but it will be no picnic." One said, "The way I see that Choynski can beat this fellow, is to stand away and punch him. If he goes to mix it up with Jeffries I think he will get the worst of it. This man Jeffries is no slouch." That was sound advice, which Choynski may well have considered.

By the night before the fight, Jeffries money had been pouring in, moving the odds to almost even, but then Choynski money followed, and the odds once again shifted in his favor at 10 to 8 ½. It was said that should Jeff defeat Joe, he would stand in the way of Champion Fitzsimmons.

The general opinion of Choynski's friends was that he would go right at Jeff and finish him as quickly as possible, which was his typical fighting style.

> In Jeffries he will find a big husky opponent who will take considerable punishment, as was demonstrated by him when he fought Ruhlin. He will also go the distance unless he be shipped to dreamland by one of Choynski's favorite left-hand jolts to the jaw. ...
>
> Choynski will have a great advantage from the knowledge he has gained by years of hard experience in the ring and he should find little difficulty in landing on Jeffries, who is really too heavy a man to be shifty.
>
> Jeffries will handicap Choynski in weight and age and if he proves to be as clever as his trainer states he may possibly give the old warhorse a surprise, but to do this trick he must have improved considerably in hitting and footwork since his fight with Ruhlin.[138]

137 *San Francisco Call*, November 28, 1897; *San Francisco Examiner*, November 29, 1897; *San Francisco Evening Post*, November 27, 29, 1897; *San Francisco Bulletin*, November 29, 1897.
138 *San Francisco Call, San Francisco Evening Post, San Francisco Bulletin*, November 30, 1897.

Over four months after the Ruhlin bout, in his fourth and final 1897 fight, on November 30, 1897, Jeffries took on veteran Joe Choynski at San Francisco's Woodward's Pavilion, under the auspices of the National Athletic Club.

At 9:50 p.m., wearing blue trunks, Joe Choynski entered the ring, accompanied by Eddie Graney, George Green (a.k.a. Young Corbett) and Tom Murphy. The house, which was fully packed from floor to roof with 5,000 people, loudly cheered for Choynski, the native San Franciscan.

Fifteen minutes later, at 10:05 p.m., wearing black trunks, Jeff entered the ring, along with De Witt Van Court, Billy Delaney, and Jack Stelzner. He too received lots of applause, although the house was "decidedly for Choynski," the local man. Joe walked across the ring and shook hands cordially with Jeffries.

According to the *Chronicle*, Jeff weighed 220 pounds to Choynski's 171 pounds, a difference of about 50 pounds. *The Call* said Jeff weighed 30 pounds more than Joe did. *The Stockton Evening Mail* gave Choynski's weight as 167 pounds, while Jeffries "balanced the scales this afternoon at 230." *The Chronicle* said it appeared like a giant and a dwarf. Still, before the fight began, Choynski was a 10 to 6 ½ betting favorite. Joe had to be some fighter to deal so well with men of that size and strength.

Announcer Billy Jordan brought the standard 5-ounce gloves, which Police Captain Wittman inspected and approved.

The referee and sole judge of the fight was the famous baseball umpire Jim McDonald, whom both parties had agreed upon as an honest and fair-minded man. Referee McDonald announced that the men had agreed to hit in the clinches, with one arm free. However, there was some later indication that Captain Wittman demanded that agreement be changed, requiring only clean breaks without hitting in the clinches. This favored the smaller Choynski because it hindered Jeff's inside game.[139]

1st round

The round featured cautious sparring, fiddling and feinting by both men. Jeff led, but missed. "Not a blow was struck in the entire round." "Jeffries appears very nervous, and Choynski is cautious."

As the fight would further reveal, it seems clear that Choynski had decided to fight Jeffries as a cautious outside boxer-counterpuncher rather than attacking puncher. He had seen Jeff fight and knew that he was very big and strong, and had never been really hurt. He seemed cognizant of the fact that the best way for him to fight was to show Jeffries respect and not leave himself open too often. Also, by fighting at long range, Jeff could not use his weight in the clinches. Choynski held his right in reserve and mostly used his left jab.

2nd round

Jeff frequently lead, but Joe ducked and dodged. Choynski quickly darted in and out "like a shadow" and landed his left jab to the mouth and nose; knocking Jeff's head back a little. However, neither landed any hard or damaging blows in the round.

Although more of the aggressor, Jeff was fairly cautious himself, obviously not wanting to fall into one of Joe's traps and run into one of Joe's famous knockout wallops. Choynski was known for timing his opponents very well and maximizing his power.

3rd round

Jeff kept attacking, but Joe used clever footwork to evade. Both landed light lefts to the face. Joe could not get through Jeff's guard. Jeff landed a right to the body and missed a left lead for the head. Jeffries rushed and twice landed his right on the body. Choynski landed a hard left hook on the neck.

At the end of the round, Jeffries landed a hard left swing that glanced off the shoulder and went into Joe's neck, and Choynski went down to the floor. He remained down for seven seconds, but rose spryly. "The blow does not do much harm." Joe seemed fine, so Jeff approached cautiously, and the gong sounded to end the round. Choynski had the reputation for landing murderous punches when hurt, so it was perhaps wise for Jeff to use some caution.

---

139 As usual, the following account and analysis is an amalgamation of local sources: *San Francisco Examiner, San Francisco Chronicle, San Francisco Call, San Francisco Evening Post, San Francisco Bulletin, Stockton Evening Mail*, December 1, 1897.

Some later questioned Jeffries for not attacking and following up more often. However, Jeff had a wholesome respect for Choynski's vaunted punching power. Delaney had coached him to watch out for Joe's traps. Choynski liked to get his opponents to expose themselves so that he could time them and run them into his own powerful blows. However, this caution might have allowed Choynski to set a pace that was more comfortable for him. Still, as the fight wore on, Jeff was almost exclusively the aggressor and rushed plenty. But he did not want to swing blindly or expose himself more than was necessary. Furthermore, when he did attack, he often missed. Chasing after a quick and elusive target could be both tiring and discouraging.

4th round

Both landed hard lefts on the body. Choynski jumped away from several straight left leads, fighting cautiously. They exchanged hard left swings, landing simultaneously, and Joe reeled a bit from the effect. Still, Joe landed a hard straight left to the forehead, and got away from a Jeffries rush. The round was generally tame though, with Choynski fighting at long range, using his jabs.

5th round

They really commenced working in this round. Choynski moved about, but had the better of it, landing lefts to the nose and blocking Jeff's lefts. Joe showed his generalship by avoiding Jeff's rushes, slipping out of reach, getting out of corners, and ducking blows.

Jeffries landed a left to the temple and rushed in, lashing out with both hands. However, Joe returned the assault with a clean left between the eyes that jarred Jeff. Joe then sent Jeff's head back three times in succession with straight lefts. Jeff rushed in with left swings several times, but only landed lightly once. Finally, a Jeffries straight left sent Choynski's head back. The first clinch in the fight took place as the round ended.

6th round

This round was more intense. Jeff opened the round with a hard straight left on the face. After a clinch and break, Jeff twice landed his left hard on the face. He rushed in and landed a hard right on the body. Joe responded with a terrific right to the face and they clinched, with Jeff hitting hard twice with his right on the back before the referee broke them. Jeff chased him and landed a left to the body. Joe landed straight lefts to the nose and mouth, but a Jeffries counter left to the jaw was the hardest blow of the round. Jeff twice countered to Joe's nose. *The Call* said, "Jeffries seems to have the best of the fight so far."

7th round

To open the round, Choynski landed a terrific right swing to the head. Jeff's rushes were ineffectual, as Joe always managed to get away. Jeff tried again but received a hard straight left to the face. Joe lightly landed a left swing, but received a hard right on the body in return. Some Jeffries lefts reddened Choynski's forehead. Jeff was fighting well. However, Joe kept cool and jarred Jeff with some lefts in return. Joe landed a hard left to the face as the round closed.

According to the *Chronicle*, the 7th through 10th rounds were similar. Jeffries would rush while Choynski ducked and dodged, coming back with his left jab to Jeff's face.

8th round

Jeffries continued as the aggressor. He landed several hard blows in the round, including a glancing right swing on the head and two straight lefts on the face. Choynski hit him a bit as well with his jab, but was on the defensive. There were several clinches, but neither attempted to fight in close, despite the fact that the articles of agreement allowed them to do so. Jeff ended the round with several straight lefts to Joe's face.

Jeffries was later criticized for not hitting in the clinches when one arm was free. On the inside, his strength advantages could have told more. However, after the fight, Jeff said that the Chief of Police had told him that if he hit in the clinch that he would stop the fight. "That is why I did not hit Choynski during the dozen or more clinches when I had a free arm and could have knocked him out easily."

Many folks do not realize this, but a referee or a rules interpretation can dramatically affect the manner in which a fight is fought, and can often alter outcomes. Such a requirement forced Jeffries to fight mostly from the outside.

9th round

This was another lively round with some good exchanges. Joe landed some hard body blows, but only landed to the face once, with a hard left to the nose. Although Joe blocked several jabs, a hard Jeffries left swing on the jaw made Choynski dizzy.

10th round

Jeff rushed continually, while Joe retreated and dodged. In one rush, Jeff landed a hard left swing to the face. However, Choynski blocked several blows with his gloves, which brought calls of approval from the crowd. Jeff landed a hard right swing to the head.

11th round

Choynski kept away for a while, but then altered his style of fighting, standing close, anticipating leads, and beating them with his own straight lefts to the nose and mouth. Using this tactic, Joe landed two very hard lefts to the face. Jeff got mad and rushed, but Joe got away. Following a clinch and breakaway, as Jeffries advanced; Joe landed a huge left square on Jeff's nose, which began bleeding. Jeff rushed with right and left swings, but without success. Jeff's lips puffed and blood trickled from his nose. It was clearly Joe's round.

Years later, Jeffries said that the left that Choynski landed in this round was the hardest blow that he ever felt. "Nobody ever hit me before or since as hard as Joe Choynski did. … He was very fast and could time his punches perfectly." Jeff said that Joe whipped over a straight punch that caught him on the mouth. "My teeth are very even and grow close together, but that was such a terrific blow that it drove my upper lip through between the two in front, wedging them apart." Such was the case when fighting in the days of five-ounce gloves and no mouthpieces. Jeff tried to pull his lip away with the glove and force it out with his tongue, to no avail.

The lip that was wedged between his teeth bothered him so much that a round or two later, he had his seconds take a knife and cut away a piece of lip to release it. "I had to keep spitting the blood out as I went on fighting, for nothing makes a man so sick as swallowing warm blood. Besides that, Joe kept on popping his left over to my mouth and nose from that time on and had me smeared up more or less."[140]

12th round

Jeff kept pressing, but Joe ducked and dodged, peppering him with lefts. Jeff landed a hard left jab to the face. Choynski landed two left jabs on the nose. The round ended in a hot mix up with Joe getting the better of it,

---

140 *My Life and Battles* at 24-25.

landing his right hard on the jaw. Jeff was bleeding from the right cheek and nose.

13th round

The round was a footrace, with Choynski avoiding Jeffries until he eventually clinched when Jeff drew near. Joe always managed to roll away as Jeff lunged, so he did not receive the full force of blows. A Choynski straight left to the nose sent Jeff's head back. Jeff rushed in with lefts and rights, but without success. Joe landed on the nose again. Choynski's jabs at the end of the round puffed Jeff's face.

According to the *Chronicle*, the 13th through 15th rounds had less heavy work. Jeff kept pressing, but Joe gave him little chance to use his superior weight.

In his autobiography, Jeff said,

> I went after him as hard as I could and whenever a punch caught him it counted. But he was so clever at ducking that the crowd cheered even when he was getting away from me. I couldn't help admiring Choynski myself that night. Every now and then I'd stop and take a good look at him. He had a lot of nerve to give away so much weight and put up such a fight.[141]

14th round

Jeff charged ferociously and landed some, but also received some blows too. In one of Jeff's rushes, Joe slipped to his knees. Jeff rushed him to the ropes and landed a hard left on the face and a right on the top of the head. Joe sent Jeff's head back with his left, and then they exchanged left jabs. Joe ducked Jeff's vicious left swings.

15th round

Jeff rushed, and after landing a light left swing, landed another hard as Joe tried to duck away. Jeff rushed Choynski to the other side of the ring and landed again. Jeffries missed more often than he landed, but when he landed, he landed hard.

Jeffries rushed again and dropped Choynski to his knees with a left to the jaw. For the remainder of the round, Jeff kept forcing matters as Joe moved about and was defensive.

16th round

This round had some of the fiercest fighting, as Joe stood his ground more. Both landed hard and often. However, Jeff's face looked worse. Joe's jab had bloodied his face. They exchanged hard left jabs. Jeffries worked him into a corner and planted half a dozen straight lefts on the face. However, when Jeff was setting to throw a right, Joe landed a right swing to

---

141 *My Life and Battles* at 25.

the head that drove Jeff back a few steps to the center of the ring. The punch puffed Jeff's cheek. A stiff left to the face almost closed Jeff's left eye. Joe followed with a few lefts to the mouth and nose.

According to the *Chronicle*, Choynski clearly won the 16th and 17th rounds.

Sam Austin later said that Choynski's ducking was superb and he brought down the house in the 16th round. "Choynski caught the big fellow four smashing lefts in the jaw, ducked a terrific swing, which threw the Los Angeles boy against the ropes, and then flew in with his right on the side of the head – the only time he used it effectively in the whole fight."

17th round

Joe again landed lefts, but a hard Jeffries left made Choynski move about. Jeff landed his left to the face with terrific force. They exchanged many jabs. Near the close of the round, Choynski landed two terrific left swings on the jaw.

18th round

Joe ducked all of Jeff's attempts to land a jab, and again used his jab with success, landing several jabs which sent Jeff's head back.

Jeffries became more successful at rushing Joe about the ring, landing lefts to the body and head. Jeff caught him on the jaw and sent him to the ropes. However, Joe escaped danger and landed two lefts that sent Jeff's head back to end the round.

The Chronicle said, "Both were blocking each other's blows well for the past few rounds, but Choynski was the neater and cleverer."

The Call said that in the 18th and 19th rounds, "Neither scored much of a lead."

19th round

Choynski did well with his left, jabbing and keeping Jeff bleeding. Jeff tried for the body, rushing like a maddened bull, but Joe would jump away.

20th round

They shook hands to start the final round. The round was lively. Jeff missed several left swings and jabs. Joe was cautious, landing his jab. Jeff countered with his left and Joe moved back. Jeff rushed him around the ring and tried to mix it up. Joe ran away, but turned and blocked several leads. Jeff was careful to leave no opening for anything significant. Jeff pursued, and Joe landed jabs, but Jeff's heavy returns forced him to his heels again. Joe momentarily fought back, but a Jeffries right to the body made him move again, tripping and falling down in his haste. After Joe rose, Jeff rushed him to the ropes and landed a hard blow on the top of the head. Choynski responded with a terrific straight left to the face. They exchanged some blows until the round ended.

Referee Jim McDonald declared the fight a draw, the second such decision in a row for Jeffries. According to the *San Francisco Call*, the decision "was received with satisfaction by the entire audience." The public, which had read the live bulletins, also cheered the decision. Three of the local papers felt that the decision was fair and just. However, not everyone agreed. A couple local papers, the *Call* and *Chronicle*, either questioned the decision, or noted that many questioned it, feeling that Choynski should have won.

Despite the audience's satisfaction, the *Call*'s writer felt that Choynski deserved the decision.

> From a scientific point of view Choynski should certainly have been acknowledged the winner. He ducked cleverly away from Jeffries' push leads and time and again he planted his left on the big fellow's nose and eyes. Choynski most assuredly scored the most points, but Referee McDonald, to please the majority of betting spectators, decided the contest a draw. Possibly in a fight to a finish Jeffries would have outlasted his opponent, but from a scientific point of view Choynski certainly had the better of last evening's contest, having scored the cleanest hits and in defensive work he more than proved his superiority over the big Los Angeles heavyweight.

The Call said that neither man did what was expected of them. Joe's supporters had thought that he would knock Jeff out within 10 rounds. Likewise, "Jeffries did not warm up to the expectations of his most ardent admirers." It gave each man both credit and criticism.

On one hand, the *Call* described the fight as "twenty furious rounds," but it also said that the fight moved along at an even tenor all the way through.

> The fight was interesting in a way. Choynski, having many years of experience, discovered at an early stage of the game that he was up against a big, husky fellow whose blows were at least punishing if not dangerous.
>
> He had been informed that Jeffries was slow in movement, and all that was necessary for him to do was to draw the big fellow out and then put his "big bunch of fives" on the point. But Joseph was misinformed. He tried all kinds of devices, and repeatedly feinted in the hope of getting Jeffries to lead. The big fellow would not be led into a trap, and notwithstanding the fact that Choynski left several openings in the hope that Jeffries would swing either left or right he failed to draw out his game.
>
> Seeing that Jeffries intended to remain on the defensive Choynski fiddled around the big fellow like a cooper around a barrel, and whenever the opportunity offered Joseph would plant his left glove

on Jeffries' nose. Choynski pursued this order of attack from start to finish. He was not taking the least chance of receiving a knock-out blow, and his ducking and generalship were admirable.

Time and again Jeffries had Choynski at his mercy near the ropes, but the artful Joseph, by clever ducking and quick footwork, would invariably slide out of harm's way and come up like a Jack-in-the-box, ready to resume the attack at long range. It was amusing to note the look of surprise on Jeffries' face whenever he missed a wild left swing. ...

Choynski having sized up his game early in the fight, figured upon a cautious style of battle. He seldom let go his right, fearing a return. He relied upon his trusty left hand to do execution, and the frequent application of that "duke" on Jeffries' nose and eyes satisfied him that straight left-hand punching would eventually land him a winner.

Of Jeffries it must be said that he has shown marked improvement in his footwork since his fight with Gus Ruhlin. He also manifested improvement in hitting and stopping blows aimed at his face. His generalship, however, was very poor. Frequently he had Choynski in a very tight box near the ropes, but instead of following up an advantage a la Walcott he invariably moved away and allowed his opponent an opportunity to dodge under his arm and resume the attack at long range. Jeffries, with all the advantages he possessed in weight and size, should have held Choynski against the ropes when the latter was cornered and smashed him hard. But instead of doing so he backed away, thus giving his opponent an opportunity to resume a favorite position in the center of the ring.

The San Francisco Chronicle called it an exciting battle, with Jeff showing improvement and Choynski showing cleverness. It reported,

The decision was questioned by a great many people, as Choynski clearly outpointed his opponent in cleverness, hitting prowess and ring generalship generally. On the other hand, Jeffries was strong and aggressive all through and put up an excellent battle, showing such improved form and giving such evidence of gameness that in many ways the encounter was a triumph for him.

It believed the fact that Choynski was not the aggressor might have counted against him with the referee. However, he made his style work. Choynski covered himself with glory, for he was as quick and clever as ever. He was not reckless for a minute, contrary to his general tactics. Joe exhibited ring intelligence by boxing and staying away, ducking Jeff's rushes, and boxing superbly despite a 50-pound weight disadvantage.

On the other hand, Jeff had changed his style. Instead of making a series of wild swings, he guarded his head and body closely and threw out leads with considerable speed and judgment. *The Chronicle* believed that Jeff's weakness was his legs, having slow footwork. Still, he was game, being punished and cut up as he came forward.

In contrast, the *San Francisco Evening Post* wholeheartedly agreed with the decision.

> It was almost the unanimous opinion of the spectators that the men had put up a good fight and that the decision of Referee McDonald was all that could be given under the circumstances … [I]f the referee had given a decision in favor of either man after the showing they made he would have been mobbed.
>
> Jeffries did the forcing from start to finish. Choynski fiddled in very close to him to draw him out, but for two or three rounds the big fellow was very wary. He had heard of Choynski's countering. After that, he gained confidence and kept jabbing away with his left, landing frequently on Choynski's face and body. Joe countered very heavily with his left, but at no time did his punches "faze" the big fellow. Choynski escaped Jeffries' rushes by ducking away, but several times he met a hard left upper-cut that straightened him up.
>
> Several times Jeffries weakened Choynski, and it looked as if he could have finished him if he had gone in and mixed things, but he fought warily and gave Joe time to recover.
>
> Neither of the men was badly punished. Jeffries had a cut lip that bled freely and Choynski was very red around the body where the big fellow had landed some of his rib-roasting lefts.
>
> Jeffries has improved wonderfully, and did some very clever stopping, leading and countering, and there is little doubt that he can beat Choynski. Joe succeeded in making a draw by his cleverness and ring generalship, and Jeffries lost a decision in his favor by lack of experience and excessive caution. He is yet a novice, but he has the making of a first-class fighter in him.

The San Francisco Bulletin said that the draw decision was "quite fair, although the opinions of the crowd were, as usual, with the man upon whom they had their money." Although it did not give a round by round account, it too provided a nice overview of the fight.

> For the first few rounds it was a case of sizing up each other and looking for an opening. Throughout the entire contest there were few damaging blows struck and there were but four or five of what could be termed "rattling" rounds. Each man seemed to have a wholesome respect for the other.
>
> The privilege of hitting with one arm free was not used by either of the contestants to any extent. On the part of Choynski he had no

desire to get into a clinch with his massive opponent. In the first clinch Jeffries used his free arm with good effect, but the crowd hissed his action and it was not repeated but a few times thereafter, although he was perfectly at liberty to do so, according to the agreement.

There is no doubt that Jeffries has improved wonderfully since his bout with Gus Ruhlin, and last night showed him quicker on his feet and in the use of his hands. He also guards his body better. In previous fights he made the mistake of swinging his left arm free, leaving a large opening toward the heart. Some opinions are to the effect that in a finish fight Jeffries would win.

As for Choynski he has not gone back.... He is just as clever and as shifty as ever, and he certainly showed up much better last night than he did before Sharkey. ... It was feared that...his legs would go back on him, as has been the case in a few previous battles. His lower extremities did not weaken, however. His ring experience stood him in good stead, and his ducking and retreating from the long reach of his opponent saved him a deal of punishment.

Had a couple of Jeffries' lefts caught Joe it would have been "all off" with the San Franciscan.

Joe tried several times to lead Jim to follow up, but Jim was evidently not rushing into any of Joe's traps, and followed up but few of his leads. Neither man seemed much punished at the end of the contest, although the several plants on the heart that Joe received and the numerous jabs in the face that Jim got will probably be felt for a few days.

The San Francisco Examiner said that the referee's draw decision was a just one. Jeff had the advantage in the early rounds. He was a master at covering ground and could make "merciless lunges with that powerful left arm of his." However, Joe was tricky enough to escape. Jeff nailed him once or twice with lefts near the ropes, and even sent Joe to his knees, but Choynski was good at rolling with the punch and never felt its full force. Joe was also able to roll away from body shots to diminish their power. It was mostly a battle of lefts. Jeff was the aggressor, but Joe was effective with his straight left, landing many times.

Jeffries has the stamina of a young draft colt, however, and although he bled freely, his speed was not diminished. Ringsters not as thick-ribbed and shortnecked as he would have weakened under the constant stabbing, but Joe's lefts only seemed to enrage him.... He fought more wildly, perhaps, on occasions, but he was as strong as an ox at all stages of the game.

Some wondered why Choynski remained cautious after landing so many lefts, but possibly, "the glancing blows Jeffries dealt him occasionally might furnish the explanation."

Like the *Evening Post*, the *Examiner* was quite high on Jeffries. "After last night few will dispute Jeff's claims to be considered as a possibility for the world's championship. He is a clever boxer, and while little more than a novice, he fairly puzzled a man who, while young in years, is a veteran at fisticuffs."

The Stockton Evening Mail said that Jeffries "displayed much improvement in the art of defense and attack," but needed more experience. Joe tried to land his famous left hook, but Jeff cleverly blocked almost every attempt. "It can be said of Jeffries that under Delaney's coaching he has wonderfully improved. His defense was especially good, while he was quick both with his hands and on his feet for so large a man. It was the opinion of many experts who saw him tonight that he is a coming man."

Both Choynski and Jeffries believed that they had earned a victory. Choynski told the *Examiner*,

> I feel that the bout should have been decided in my favor. I realize that it was a hard matter to judge such a closely contested battle…. [M]y blows were cleaner and more damaging than Jeffries'…. Many of my punches made him groggy, but he has wonderful recuperative powers…. I landed on him several times hard enough to knock an ordinary man out of the ring.

The Chronicle quoted Choynski as saying, "I did the cleanest and by all odds the most frequent hitting…. I came out of the encounter with scarcely a scratch."

Jeffries told the *Examiner*,

> I think I was given the worst of the decision by the referee…. I had him going several times, and at no point of the fight was I groggy. I was very cautious all through, as I had heard so much about Choynski being a terrible fighter…. The police warned me that if I hit in the breakaway they would stop the fight…and that partly spoiled my chances.

Jeff told the *Chronicle*, "I was on the aggressive all the time. Choynski never forced the fighting once. I landed oftener than he did. I knocked him down twice. I had him running around the ring a good deal of the time." He had made Choynski fight a style which he had never utilized before.

Choynski's cornerman said that after Joe had been knocked down, he told him to be more cautious, not to use the right and leave himself open by being too aggressive. That was how he had suffered his previous losses. He said that Joe had put up one of the cleverest fights ever seen and had the better of it in every way.

Tom Sharkey said it was a fair, even fight with a just decision. "If he had decided in favor of either man he would have done one of them an injustice." Of Jeffries, Tom said that he is a "big, strong fellow and his peculiar method of fighting makes it rather difficult for a man like Choynski to land on him. ... It was a case of give and take all through the contest." However, he also said, "Jeffries will never make a champion. He is too heavy."

A few days later, Choynski would not express an opinion as to whether Sharkey or Jeffries was the better fighter. "But judging from the way he spoke of Jeffries he has a wholesome regard for the big fellow and would doubtless tip him to whip Sharkey."[142]

The day after the fight, Peter Jackson observed, "Jeffries is a splendidly built young fellow and put up a very good fight last night. He was boxing with a skilled man who knows all the tricks of the game. He matched his strength against the other's science." However, Peter still felt, "It is evident that the man who fought Choynski...has a long road to travel."

Joe Goddard said that the decision was just.

> The referee could not under any circumstances have given a decision in favor of either man in last night's battle. Choynski landed the hardest blows, but Jeffries seemed to balance matters by being aggressive.... I hardly think that Jeffries will ever be a champion, though with careful coaching he may turn out to be a fairly good man. At present he makes a poor fight. He seems to be slow at seeing and taking advantage of openings. He is as yet somewhat of a novice.

All three – Goddard, Jackson, and Sharkey – would fight Jeffries the following year, in 1898, and learn first hand about his ability.

In his autobiography, Jeffries said of Choynski,

> He was the first really clever man I ever met in the ring. He was a great man in those days and I was still practically a beginner and learning slowly. Joe was one of the hardest hitters in the ring. ... Fitz has told me that nobody ever hit him such a wallop before, and I can easily believe it. ... Choynski was a very light man to be fighting me.... I often wonder how men like Fitzsimmons and Choynski can hit so hard.

Joe Choynski had it all. He was fast, could punch hard, move and duck well, and had superior generalship and knowledge that comes from experience. He was the odds favorite, whom many thought would knock Jeff out quickly. Still, Jeffries had held his own, dropping him in the 3rd and 15th rounds, and was fresh and fighting hard at the end.

---

142 *San Francisco Call*, December 2, 1897.

Of the decision, Jeffries said, "I did the forcing, and landed the only knockdowns, but Choynski deserved a lot of credit for his cleverness. I was satisfied."[143]

One fighter who a few years later would learn about Choynski's power was Jack Johnson. In February 1901, Joe Choynski would knock out future heavyweight champion Jack Johnson in the 3rd round. Like Jeffries, Johnson was 22 years old at the time that he fought Choynski.

In 1901, Jeff said that the only man who ever hurt him was Choynski, who landed a blow on his nose that made him see stars. "It was a corker, but it did not have any disabling effect and I went after him all the harder." A couple years after that, in 1903, Jeff said, "Joe Choynski struck me the hardest blow I ever received. I was chasing him along the ropes in our fight at Woodward's Pavilion, when he suddenly turned on me. He let go his right and I thought my head left my body. The blow dazed me, but I recovered quickly. That was the closest call I ever had in the ring."[144]

The day after the fight, National Club manager J.J. Groom said that the gate was $7,000 (which seems low given the attendance), of which the fighters divided 70%, or $2,450 each. It was estimated that over $100,000 had been bet on the fight.

Continuing their discussion of the fight in subsequent days, the newspapers called it a "terrific battle, which reflected credit on both the participants." Neither man showed signs of severe punishment. Both of Joe's eyes were a bit discolored underneath. Jeff's left eye was black and swollen, but otherwise he was unhurt.

Both the Choynski and Jeffries camps thought they won, but did not complain too much about the decision. The general public was content. "Everybody would have liked a decision in favor of one or the other of the pugilists, but nobody is raising a howl over the matter."

The "agile and skillful" Choynski was "discreet in conversation and philosophical in temperament." He said that he was all right, and did not get hurt a bit in the fight. "He knocked me down once or twice, but that didn't amount to anything. I was up and at him again right away. I was never distressed at any time and could have fought right on." Choynski denied having anything wrong with his right arm. Many thought it was hurt because he rarely used it, but Choynski held it back for tactical reasons. With disdain, the veteran said, "Oh, everybody knows your business better than you know it yourself." Joe observed,

> I see by the papers that the referee says that he didn't give the decision to me because the other man came after me all the time. Well, why shouldn't he? He weighed about sixty pounds more than I did. He is a great big quick young fellow, very strong, and why

143 *My Life and Battles* at 24-25.
144 *San Francisco Evening Post*, December 2, 1901; *San Francisco Call*, August 16, 1903.

shouldn't he make the fighting? But I was there all the time, wasn't I? I have no complaint to make.

As usual, Jeffries did not say much. He was not much of a talker. "Jim Jeffries is a better fighter than a conversationalist. Billy Delaney, his manager, is also his thinker and talker." Delaney said that Jeff's solid performance against a crafty and well respected veteran who was supposed to defeat him moved his man up a notch or two on the scale of pugilistic fame. He too thought that Choynski fought the fight of his life.

> If he had fought like he did last night nine years ago, when we had them out here on a barge, he would have licked Corbett that day. He is one of the very best men in the world. I think the referee did the best thing in the circumstances. We ought to have had the decision, as our man did most of the leading, but it's all right I suppose. It would have meant a whole lot to either man to have decided against him, and it's just as well, I guess. …

> Jeffries never tires in a fight. He was as strong last night at the close as he was at the beginning. He is a wonderful young man.

Ultimately, Referee Jim McDonald was thought of as a fair arbiter. In fact, as a result of making such an "excellent impression" in the Jeffries-Choynski fight, he was chosen to referee the upcoming Needham-Gallagher bout.[145]

Although only receiving a draw, the *Evening Post* said that Jeffries' "stock has been greatly inflated since his recent good showing before Joe Choynski." *The Bulletin* echoed this sentiment.

> Jeffries stock has gone up about the city. Before he met Choynski he was pronounced a dub of the first water who would fall on his knees when he caught a punch. When Choynski poked him in the face nobody saw him manifest quitting signs. On the contrary, he came after more of the same stuff, and this is what won the house for him. Above all things ring-goers like to see a man keep coming. Not to back up when he receives a jolt, but to advance like a brave soldier in battle. The oftener Choynski would jab the harder Jeffries would press him. It demonstrated completely that the big fellow was game to the back bone, and it will take a pugilist with a terrific punch to lay him hors de combat.[146]

Thus, at the time, earning a draw against a dangerous, highly touted, favored veteran like Joe Choynski was viewed in a positive light and gained Jeff high marks.

---

145 *San Francisco Bulletin*, December 2, 1897.
146 *San Francisco Evening Post*, December 3, 1897; *San Francisco Bulletin*, December 2, 1897.

When writing of the fight a month later, Sam Austin opined that if any mistake was made in Choynski's corner, it was in not allowing Joe to go at his big opponent more at the start, because Jeffries seemed a bit rattled and lacking confidence for the first few rounds. However, after Jeff loosened up, "it was only by exercising all his knowledge of ring tactics that Choynski was able to hold his own with the giant." Of course, what Austin failed to realize is that early on, neither fighter wanted to run into something big – hence their cautiousness. Choynski was complimented as being "as clever and as quick as ever, and he fought the first calculating battle he has ever been mixed up in."

As would be seen, James Jeffries had a way of sometimes causing otherwise aggressive punchers to box and move when going against him. However, Austin believed that the fact that Joe was not the aggressor, a factor in the referee's decision, should not have counted against him, for the reason that with the big weight disparity, "it was the best kind of generalship to keep away from the rushes and to duck." Regardless, "the big fellow was in front of him all the time, and due credit must be given him for putting up the fight he did against such an accomplished exponent of boxing as Choynski."

Ultimately, Austin and the public were very high on Jeffries. "From all that can be gleaned from the spectators…Jeffries…has a better right to be regarded in the light of an aspirant for heavy-weight fame than any of the youngsters now battling toward the championship goal."[147]

---

147 *San Francisco Bulletin*, December 30, 1897.

CHAPTER 9

No Show

In the days following the Jeffries-Choynski match, there were discussions of Jeffries possibly fighting either Peter Jackson or Tom Sharkey. After years of inactivity, Jackson was making a comeback. However, there was great interest in seeing Jeffries and Sharkey in the ring, for such a match between two young, hungry, strong warriors would be a great drawing card. "Thousands upon thousands would go miles to see these men meet."

On December 4, 1897, Jeffries and Sharkey signed to fight before the National Club for a $10,000 purse on January 7, a month away. It was said to be the biggest fistic deal since Fitzsimmons-Sharkey. "Jeffries, by his showing against Choynski, demonstrated that he has class, and will give the sailor a battle royal."

On December 8, Jeffries returned from a hunting and rowing trip near Petaluma. He was set to begin training for the Sharkey fight the following week. On the 9th, the Occidental Club matched Peter Jackson to fight Peter Maher. Jackson would go right into training.

However, on the 10th, the local San Francisco Board of Supervisors refused to grant three boxing permits, a sign that they were looking to place a damper on the pugilistic industry. As time passed, it became evident that the local authorities were refusing to grant all boxing licenses, possibly as a result of the November 18 Sharkey-Goddard fight. Sharkey scored a KO6 over Goddard, but some suspected it was fixed.

In late December, the National Club announced that it had to postpone the Jeffries-Sharkey fight because it was unable to obtain its permit. Sharkey said that because no forfeit money was posted as a guarantee, and he was losing money in training expenses, he was going to make other matches, because it was uncertain whether the match could be brought off. Thus, the fight was off and Jeffries-Sharkey would have to wait for another day. Jeffries returned home to Los Angeles to visit.[148]

Because San Francisco boxing was in a state of limbo, Delaney scheduled Jeffries to box in Los Angeles in late February 1898 against Joe Goddard. However, while Jeff was in training, San Francisco began issuing boxing licenses again. In early February, Delaney negotiated a Jeffries-Peter

---

[148] *San Francisco Bulletin*, December 2, 6, 9-11, 28, 1897; *San Francisco Examiner*, April 1, 1898; *San Francisco Chronicle*, April 8, 1898.

Jackson bout, set to be held in San Francisco in late March. Jeffries would fight Goddard and then Jackson.

While training at Oakland's Reliance Club, Jeffries sparred with world welterweight and middleweight champion Tommy Ryan, who was preparing for a fight in San Francisco with George Green (a.k.a. Young Corbett). Tommy Ryan was a tough, very experienced, highly skilled fighter who would be middleweight champion for years to come.[149] It was later said, "While Tommy Ryan was training at the Reliance Club for his bout with George Green, Jeffries boxed daily with the phenomenally clever middleweight, and it is hinted improved his knowledge of swings, jabs and uppercuts considerably." In his autobiography, Jeffries called Ryan "the greatest boxer, the finest ring general and the best and fastest man of his size that ever lived." Jeff credited Ryan with "teaching me more of the finished touches of boxing than any man with whom I ever associated."[150]

Both Jeffries and Peter Jackson attended the February 25, 1898 Ryan-Green middleweight title fight in San Francisco, won by Ryan via an 18th round knockout. Jeff and Peter met and shook hands for the first time. "The two big boxers gazed interestingly at each other for several moments and then parted. The two heavy-weights are rapidly getting into trim for their contest and last night showed plainly the results of faithful work."[151]

In the meantime, Jeffries took on another match that had its own significance, at least on paper, against Joe Goddard. The Australian Goddard was another experienced and well-respected veteran, who during the early 1890s was one of the most feared fighters in the world. He had been a professional for almost ten years. Some said that he had about sixty fights.

"The Barrier Champion" Goddard had fought the great Peter Jackson to an 1890 8-round draw. At that point, the 186-pound Goddard had a ferocious, all-out, non-stop, hard-hitting, attacking style. He had "boundless energy, pluck, dash, and devil," putting faith in his "grit and staying powers." Most said that he would have defeated Jackson if it had been a fight to the finish. In 1891, in all-out wars with multiple knockdowns on both sides, Goddard twice knocked out Joe Choynski in the 4th round. In 1892, he scored a KO15 over big 220-pound Joe McAuliffe and a KO3 over hard-hitting Peter Maher. At that point, he was the top contender to Jim Corbett's heavyweight championship, outside of Peter Jackson. However, in an 1893 war, "Denver" Ed Smith stopped Goddard in the 18th round. Goddard later avenged the loss in 1896 with a KO4 over Smith. He

149 Having begun his career in 1887, champion Tommy Ryan's career to that point included: 1891 KO76 Dan Needham; 1894 W20 Mysterious Billy Smith; 1895 KO3 Jack Dempsey; 1896 LKOby15 Charles "Kid" McCoy (his only loss), KO6 Joe Dunfee, W20 Dick Moore, and KO7 Billy McCarthy; 1897 KO9 Tom Tracey, KO18 Patsy Raedy, KO3 Paddy Gorman, KO6 Raedy, KO5 Jimmy Ryan, and KO6 Billy Stift, amongst many others.
150 *San Francisco Examiner*, March 15, 1898; *Two Fisted Jeff* at 86; Boxrec.com.
151 *San Francisco Evening Post*, February 26, 1898.

had suffered some other losses in the intervening years, but picked up some good wins as well. But Goddard was getting on in years for a boxer, particularly for one with a relentless style who was willing to take punishment. As is often the case for such aging fighters, he had mixed results.

On November 18, 1897 in San Francisco, Tom Sharkey knocked out Goddard in the 6th round. There was some controversy surrounding the knockout as most thought it was a fast count. Others said the whole fight had been a fix and that Goddard's horrible performance demonstrated that he was in on it. Sharkey easily outboxed and outslugged him, dropping Joe in the 1st, 5th, and 6th rounds.

> [It was an] unpleasant exhibition between a young man who hasn't the remotest idea of the manner in which a straight, clean blow should be delivered [Sharkey] and an old warhorse [Goddard], so stiff as to be unable to get out of the way and so slow that an ice wagon could distance him in a test of speed. The mill certainly had an air of pre-arrangement about it.

Controversy was never far from a Tom Sharkey bout. The reality was that Goddard had seen his better days, and had gone up against a young lion whose style was reminiscent of his own back in his prime.[152]

In early January 1898, Goddard lost an 8-round decision to Theodore Van Buskirk because Joe had agreed to stop him in 8 rounds and failed. At his best, Goddard was known as a hard-punching, very aggressive, well-conditioned rusher who came to fight, who was willing to take punches in order to give them. However, at age 36, Goddard was clearly past his prime and could no longer fight as he used to.[153]

Against Goddard, Jeffries was a slight odds favorite, having "vastly improved in boxing ability during his training under Delaney, when he sparred with Ryan, a past master of the art." However, the fact that he was only a slight favorite showed that Goddard still commanded respect. Joe had been "training faithfully for four weeks" at the Los Angeles Athletic Club, the fight's sponsor. "He is said to be in excellent condition." Both

152 *San Francisco Examiner, San Francisco Chronicle, San Francisco Evening Post,* November 19, 1897.
153 Boxrec.com; Cyberboxingzone.com.

men were "so well known all along this coast as to require no special mention." If Jeffries won, "he will be in a position to, in a measure, dictate terms to other heavyweights."[154]

The Jeffries-Goddard fight took place at Hazard's Pavilion in Los Angeles on February 28, 1898, before 1,500 spectators. Goddard entered the ring first. Jeffries followed several minutes later, accompanied by Billy Delaney, Charles Jeffries (a.k.a. Jack Jeffries), and J.D. Burkhart. As he entered the ring, the crowd cheered and applauded Jeff, who bowed in appreciation.

Oddly enough, although Goddard wanted hitting in the clinches and breakaways, which would seem to suit Jeffries, it was finally agreed that there must be clean breakaways.

Referee John Brink announced Goddard's weight as 194 pounds, and Jeffries' weight as 201 pounds. The reporters all felt that Jeff looked much bigger than his listed weight, estimating that he really weighed about 215 pounds, which was probably closer to the truth.

The fight was scheduled for 15 rounds. It began at 9:58 p.m.[155]

1st round

The fight began cautiously. Goddard landed lightly with a left and right. Jeff missed a right but immediately followed with a left that landed over Joe's heart. A clinch followed. After breaking, the men exchanged what appeared to be light blows, but after Jeff landed a seemingly light left, Goddard fell to his knee. Some thought he slipped. He rose but again fell down. "The audience supposed something was the matter with his shoes, for he seemed to trip each time." It is possible that they underestimated the power in Jeff's punches. Jeffries landed a left to the stomach rapidly followed by a right to the heart. Goddard began sprinting around the ring. The round ended in a clinch. Joe obviously did not want to mix it up with Jeff, and had quickly gone into survival mode.

2nd round

During most of the round, Goddard tried to keep away as Jeff vainly tried to hit him. Goddard twice slipped or intentionally fell to the floor without being hit, perhaps in order to avoid punishment. Joe seemed weak and frightened, uncharacteristic of his previous aggressive and powerful fighting style. "He was on the defensive throughout and seemed to be afraid of Jeffries, making only a few efforts to lead, none of which resulted in a blow." Perhaps Jeffries really hit that hard.

---

154 *Los Angeles Daily Times, Los Angeles Herald,* February 28, 1898.
155 As usual, the following is an amalgamation of the local primary sources: *Los Angeles Evening Express, Los Angeles Daily Times, Los Angeles Herald,* March 1, 1898.

Jeff chased Goddard about the ring. A right and left to the jaw sent Joe to the ropes, and while there, Jeff hit him twice more. Joe tripped over a post and went down again.

After they resumed, Jeff ducked a right and countered with a right that dropped Goddard. He rose and continued his survival tactics.

The press criticized Goddard for making little to no offensive attempts, and for falling to the ground often without any excuse.

> In the second round, Goddard sprawled all over the stage, clinched, grabbed Jeffries by the legs and misbehaved generally in such a foolish fashion that the crowd hissed, and even Jeffries lost patience and cuffed his ears as he fell. Apparently Jeffries concluded that if Goddard would not fight he should be soundly drubbed for making such an obvious fizzle, for he quit handling him gently and put in a few uppercuts that must have caused discomfort.

3rd round

Goddard was even worse in this round, ducking, falling down, and grabbing Jeff's legs in order to avoid Jeff's rushes. Jeffries did all the fighting, while Goddard relied on survival tactics.

As Joe ducked, Jeffries landed a heavy left uppercut and Goddard went down. Another left dropped him again. Joe later slipped to his knees without being hit, and then rose and clinched.

After the round was over, Goddard pulled off the gloves and quit. His seconds threw up the sponge to retire their fighter. Joe said that there was no use in fighting, for he was unfit to cope with his opponent.

Jeffries technically won at this point, and referee John Brink awarded him the decision. However, oddly enough, the referee also insisted that Goddard continue or no pay would be forthcoming. Apparently, the referee felt either that Goddard had not put up much of an effort or was not sufficiently hurt to quit. Perhaps he did not feel that the fans had received their money's worth. "The mention of money caused Goddard to quickly put on his gloves again, and after two minutes' intermission he again faced his opponent."

4th round

Goddard "made no effort to fight, and was evidently looking for an opportunity to lie down." Jeff mostly dropped him with uppercuts. Whenever he was not on the floor, Goddard kept taking punches. "But the exhibition became too contemptible, and Brink, in disgust, stopped it and ordered the men out of the ring." Another local source said that the referee soon stopped it when he saw that Jeffries was making a helpless chopping block of Goddard. Only half of the round had elapsed.

Referee Brink renewed his decision for Jeffries, which he had previously awarded to him. "The two men left the ring without shaking hands. The crowd was disgusted and showed it by hissing."

Afterwards, Goddard said, "I didn't want to be knocked out, and that man outclassed me so much that I had no show. There was nothing for me to do but quit." Joe could not understand his poor condition, for he just had no energy. He was also surprised by how strong and clever Jeffries was. It quickly became evident to Goddard that he would lose, "and he thought the easiest way was to throw up the sponge before he should be pummeled severely by the active and powerful young man who was making of his battered old carcass a ring in the ladder of pugilistic fame."

Some alleged that Goddard had been drinking before the fight. Goddard vehemently denied it, saying that he was just weak and Jeffries too strong. "He is a good heavy puncher – the best I ever met. I have been in the ring with Sharkey and many others, but that man Jeffries is a wonder, and I do not want to meet him again." Sometimes, dazed fighters' movements made them appear drunk.

Regardless, Goddard was labeled as a quitter and an easy mark. "He declared that he was not drunk, but his actions called to mind his recent fiasco with Sharkey, in which the latter bested him in a put-up job" that was so bad that no boxing permits were issued for two months thereafter.

A San Francisco report said, "Goddard is a back number, and has been for several years. ... There was, consequently, much surprise when he was matched to fight Jeffries, for no one doubted the outcome."[156]

Almost a week after the fight, it was said,

> Sports down in Los Angeles are denouncing the recent Jeffries-Goddard fight as a fake and there seems to be good reason for their suspicions. It has been discovered that just prior to entering the ring the two pugilists agreed to cut the purse, and while the fight was progressing the referee says Goddard several times remonstrated with Jeffries for the manner in which he was hitting. The referee, however, fails to explain why he did not declare the fight no contest.[157]

At that time, splitting the purse evenly or agreeing upon a fixed percentage split, regardless of winner, was perceived as a disincentive for fighters to do their best, or would make it more likely that they would retire, not having to fear obtaining only the much smaller loser's share. These agreements probably took place more often than the public realized, but efforts were usually made to keep them secret. This is because such divisions were taken as a sign that a fight was fixed for one man to lose in return for a better share of the proceeds. This was not usually the case, but

---

156 *San Francisco Examiner, San Francisco Evening Post*, March 1, 1898.
157 *San Francisco Evening Post*, March 5, 1898.

that is how such deals were perceived. Such agreements were often necessary to incentivize a fighter to take the risk of a loss against a renowned fighter. However, the public and press wanted divisions based on winner and loser, which would cause fighters to give it their best in order to earn the larger share. What many considered evidence of a fix back then is actually how the purse is divided for most fights today.

If Goddard did ask Jeff to lighten up, it could have been proof that there was some sort of silent agreement between them. Or, it could have been Goddard realizing that he was overmatched, and trying to convince Jeff, who was doing his best to knock him out quickly, to ease up and give the public a show for their money. However, none of the immediate local post-fight reports mentioned anything about Goddard speaking to Jeffries in such a way.

Giving Goddard the benefit of the doubt, he had been in a lot of wars. Sometimes such fighters burn out faster. Perhaps all of the desire and willingness to absorb punishment had left him.

The heavy-handed Jeffries had decked all of his opponents, so perhaps his powerful blows would have stopped even a young Goddard. Clearly, Jeffries was a puncher. Although Joe said that it was his last battle, two months later, Goddard scored a KO1 over hard-hitting Peter Maher, although Maher subsequently avenged the loss a couple months later with a KO8. However, it did show that Joe had something left. During the rest of 1898, Goddard went the full 6-round distance with men such as big Bob Armstrong, Joe Choynski, and Gus Ruhlin. Jeffries was the only man to stop him that quickly and easily, so he has to be given some credit.

In his autobiographies, Jeff defended Joe. He said that he went at Goddard as hard as he could and hammered him so badly that he made Joe want to quit for the first time in his life. When the referee announced that it would be a no-contest if he quit, and the men not paid, Goddard vainly attempted another round, but the referee stopped it when he saw that Joe had no chance. "Goddard was accused of lack of gameness, but he was as game a man as I ever faced. He was badly hurt." Jeff said that after meeting the clever Choynski, it was fun to meet a slugger, because that was his own game.[158]

Speaking of Joe Choynski, coming off the 20-round draw with Jeffries, on March 11, 1898 in San Francisco, before a crowd of 6,000, he fought a rematch with Tom Sharkey. As usual, Sharkey fought in a foul fashion, much to the chagrin of the crowd, which hooted and howled at his tactics. Sharkey continually hit in the clinches and on the breakaways, at least twenty times, despite the fact that the agreed-upon rules prohibited it. Throughout the fight, he wrestled and pushed Choynski, bulled him about, pushed his head back, landed low blows, often held and hit, struck rabbit

---

158 *My Life and Battles* at 25; *Two Fisted Jeff* at 84.

punches (to the back of the head), choked him, and thrust him to the floor. The crowd often called for the referee to disqualify Sharkey, but Choynski did not complain.

Sharkey dropped Choynski three times in the 5th round, using punches to the body and head with both hands. However, the spectators continued their cries of foul because Tom utilized several foul tactics to set up the knockdowns, including choking Joe with one arm and hitting with the other.

In the 6th round, the audience went wild as Sharkey again used foul tactics in conjunction with his punches until a right to the jaw dropped Joe. However, Choynski rose and started landing more often, as Tom was fatiguing and grabbing to get a rest. Sharkey eventually pushed Joe's head back and threw him to the floor.

They were both tired early in the 7th, but eventually, Tom held Joe on the ropes and beat him. Joe jabbed him often until Sharkey again rushed him to the ropes and dropped Choynski with a left to the jaw.

Sharkey was fresher in the 8th, and used head butts. The crowd continued howling for the referee to award the fight to Choynski on fouls. The two engaged in a number of fierce exchanges. Sharkey eventually hammered Choynski towards the ground, but before he went down, while Joe's head was lowered, Sharkey rushed into him and pushed him head first through the ropes upon the heads of the front row spectators. Another local source said that Sharkey rushed him, and "Choynski lowered his shoulder to meet the rush, but his force sent him through the ropes and to the floor below." This enraged the spectators to a "boiling point," and the police began entering the ring. At that point, referee George Green announced that he had declared the fight a draw. One local paper wrote that Sharkey "has absolutely no control over himself."

Many criticized the decision.

> Green's decision is as mysterious as it is unfair. As far as punishment and condition at the finish were concerned, ignoring, as the referee did, the claims of foul, Sharkey should have had any decision that was coming. But, on the other hand, the sailor's brutal and consistent ignoring of the rules would, with a fair referee, have lost him the battle twenty times over. Such a decision as "draw" is preposterous.... He had friends on both sides of the house, and in his desire to cater to all of them fell down hard and got himself roundly hooted for his trouble.

The reporters called the referee timid and Sharkey dirty and shameful. It was par for the course with Sharkey. It appeared that the referee had split the baby by calling it a draw, rather than giving Sharkey a decision on the merits which he did not entirely deserve because of his fouling, or awarding Choynski a disqualification victory when no foul had actually been claimed by him or his seconds during the contest.

Justifying his decision, Referee Green said,

> In the last round Sharkey rushed Choynski to the ropes and both men clinched. Sharkey kept pushing, and when one of his hands became free – I don't know which hand it was – he shoved it up under Choynski's chin and pushed him through the ropes. That was a foul, but I was not sure whether the foul was intentional on Sharkey's part or not. There was a mint of money on both men, and I did not wish to burn up either end of it. If I had been positive that Sharkey committed the foul intentionally, I would have decided the battle in Choynski's favor ... When a man falls three or four feet and strikes on his head he is not, in my opinion, fit to fight any longer. .... My attention was called to several fouls which Sharkey committed earlier in the fight, but as they were trivial breaches of the rules I allowed them to pass, especially as Choynski lodged no objections. I will admit that Sharkey employed tactics that were not in strict keeping with the rules. I had to warn him several times. I thought it best not to interfere, as a knockout on either side would have been more satisfactory to the people who bet money on the men than a decision rendered on a foul.

True to form, Sharkey claimed that he was robbed.

Choynski said that he should have had the decision on repeated fouls, that it was the roughest fight of his career. He said that he was never hurt when Tom fought fairly, that Sharkey's punches did not hurt, but the wrestling and football tactics were what damaged him.

> Even though he injured me repeatedly by fouls I had him groggy in the sixth round and but for more fouling on his part would have put him out.... In his last rush he landed on me only lightly and then butted me through the ropes. It wasn't a clinch. He threw me off the stage and I struck on the back of my head.

Afterwards, Jeffries, who had attended the fight, said,

> If Choynski had fought me in the way he did Sharkey I would have licked him in two rounds. In our fight he kept away, but in to-night's go he went right at Sharkey. ... Sharkey fought foul all the way through. Had Choynski kept away he would have done better. At one time he had Sharkey at a standstill. There is no one that I would rather go against than Sharkey, and as soon as my fight with Jackson is over I am willing to go against him, and I think I can lick him.[159]

Within the next two months, Sharkey and Jeffries would meet.

---

159 *San Francisco Chronicle, San Francisco Evening Post, San Francisco Call, San Francisco Examiner,* March 12, 1898.

CHAPTER 10

The Legend

Peter Jackson was a huge name in boxing, one worth having on the resume. Since early December 1897, he had been training for prospective comeback matches against either Peter Maher or James Jeffries.

However, Peter Jackson had not had an official fight since his late May 1892 KO10 over Frank Slavin. Therefore, there was some serious doubt about how much he could possibly have left, particularly since there had been strong rumors in the intervening years that Jackson had not taken the best care of himself and had been drinking a fair amount of alcohol. Even if the rumors were untrue, the question was how good he could be physically after such a long layoff, regardless of his immense talent and vast experience.

> Some of his friends contend that he has been on the retrograde since he whipped Slavin, and that his physical condition has been run down to such an extent that any husky young fighter like Jeffries will stop the once great fistic general in short order. But Peter holds a very different view. … He contends that he is physically sound. …
>
> If the champion heavy-weight of Los Angeles should whip Jackson the feat will prove a great feather in his cap, as he will then be crowned fighting king of Australia and England, with the chances for meeting Bob Fitzsimmons for the world's championship most favorable.[160]

Thus, it seemed that the newspapers were simultaneously hyping the value of the bout, while at the same time questioning its significance given Jackson's years of inactivity and questionable physical state. This would continue.

Experts throughout the land were speaking kindly of Jeffries, and "go so far as to proclaim him the next champion." In late December 1897, it was said that Peter Jackson nearly got himself into a bad match when he had agreed to fight Jeffries.

> Jackson was up against a great beating…and his friends made the discovery just in time to pull him out of danger. My! But what Billy Delaney missed when the coon escaped. Jeffries would have become famous in that fight, and Delaney would have had another champion,

---

160 *San Francisco Call*, December 3, 1897.

as he is likely to get later, at any rate, in the same person, for Jeffries looks like a comer. Jackson…has been doing the booze business to such an extent that it would be difficult to condition him for a fight with any of the big guns of the present time.[161]

However, in early 1898, the match was on again. Jackson had already been training consistently for at least a couple months. In early February, one report said, "The colored champion is, as a result of recent work, in excellent shape and will need little severe exercise to put him in good fighting trim." When Jeff and Peter met on February 25, reporters were encouraged by the fact that Jackson was looking fit. Their fight was still a month away. [162]

Peter Jackson was at one time one of the best, if not the best fighter in the world. Jackson's career began in the early 1880s in Australia, and his results included: 1884 LKOby3 Bill Farnan (his only loss); 1886 KO30 Tom Lees; 1888 KO19 George Godfrey and KO24 Joe McAuliffe; 1889 KO10 Patsy Cardiff, WDQ2 Jem Smith, and KO2 Peter Maher; 1890 W5 "Denver" Ed Smith and D8 Joe Goddard; 1891 NC/D61 Jim Corbett; and 1892 KO10 Frank Slavin. Over the next couple of years, he had remained in shape and gave a number of exhibitions, hoping to obtain a championship bout with Jim Corbett, but it never materialized.

Because of the color line, a social norm against mixed race bouts, many boxers, including John L. Sullivan, openly refused to fight Jackson. Because most everyone avoided him, he essentially retired in 1895. He only boxed in occasional 3- or 4-round exhibitions, and he eventually opened a boxing

161 *San Francisco Bulletin*, December 20, 1897.
162 *San Francisco Evening Post*, February 9, 1898.

school in England in early 1897. By 1898, he was well past his prime at age 36, and had been inactive from serious bouts for nearly six years, so whatever he once had was pretty much gone.

Yet, Jackson chose to make a comeback fight against Jeffries, and claimed to be in good shape and perfect health. Because of Jackson's legendary status, the bout garnered much media attention. His reputation stood the test of time.

One report in early March 1898 said,

> There are many who think that the colored pugilist is no longer even a shadow of his former self. … If so, the month of training through which he has just passed has done wonders for him. He weighs 195 pounds at present, the same weight as when he entered the ring with Corbett in 1891. … How far the vitality of the man has been sapped can only be judged when he is viewed in the heat of actual battle.[163]

Another report a week later said that Jackson was looking good in training.

> It was thought that the clever colored boxer might have some difficulty in getting into condition, but the manner in which Peter has rounded to has surprised all his old friends. So far as personal appearance is concerned he does not seem to have altered a bit. His work in the gymnasium seems to indicate that he is as sprightly in his movements as ever.[164]

Jeffries was favored by 10 to 6 odds. Although it was conceded that Jackson was "the more scientific fighter and better ring general, it is feared that he will never be able to stand any length of time against the younger and hardier Jeffries." Parson Davies, who for many years had been Jackson's manager, "expressed himself as rather dubious as to Jackson's ability to get into good shape for the fight, notwithstanding reports to the contrary." Jeff himself "contends that every fighter has his day, and that Jackson has long passed the zenith of his prime; still he expects to see Peter give a great account of himself for ten or twelve rounds."[165]

As usual, Jeffries trained at Oakland's Reliance Club under Delaney. He sparred with brother Jack Jeffries and DeWitt Van Court. While sparring with his brother on March 15, just one week before the bout, James caught a head butt to the left eye, which left it slightly gashed and blackened. He was not concerned though, and did not request a postponement of the fight.

The next day, on March 16, Jeffries was listed as 6'1" and 213 pounds to Jackson's 6'½" and 197 pounds. Jeff said, "I am lighter than I have been for

163 *San Francisco Call*, March 7, 1898.
164 *San Francisco Examiner*, March 13, 1898.
165 *San Francisco Evening Post*, March 15, 17, 1898; *San Francisco Call*, March 16, 1898.

months." In the morning, he punched the bag, used dumbbells, worked the wrist machine, skipped rope, and ran several laps on the club's indoor track. He then boxed with brother Jack and Professor DeWitt Van Court. After working for a couple hours in the morning, in the afternoon, Jeff put in one hour doing roadwork. "I walk out a couple miles and run all the way back."

As of mid-March, Peter Jackson had been in hard training for about eight weeks at Croll's Garden in Alameda. In the mornings, he usually ran about 12 miles. In the afternoon, Jackson tossed the medicine ball, punched the bag, and sparred with three different sparring partners, putting in about two hours of work.[166]

Those who visited Jackson's training quarters were satisfied with how he looked.

> The thing most of them would like to know is: Can Jackson keep up a pace in the actual heat of battle similar to the one he sets in his gymnasium? On this point comparisons with John L. Sullivan, George Dixon, Young Griffo and other once brilliant fighters are in order. It is pointed out that the fact that these fellows had retrograded was not made manifest until they stepped into the ring. Their training told nothing, and as one local wiseacre has remarked, "All fighters look well in training."[167]

Both men claimed to be in the best of condition. Jeff said, "I can say honestly I never felt better than I do right now. In some of my former matches, the one with Ruhlin, for instance, my hands were in bad shape, but they are all right now."

Although many doubted Jackson's ability to be what he once was physically, "Nevertheless, numbers of them have taken his end of the betting, figuring that if he cannot win he will at least be able to make it a draw." After all, he had the superior experience, ring generalship, and skill. "It is generally conceded that Jackson knows about all that can be learned in the game." Because he had been looking good in training, some felt that Jackson would last the distance "unless Jeffries puts up a much faster and more spirited fight than he has heretofore in contests with Ruhlin and Choynski."

> Choynski did not hurt Jeffries in the least, still the big white man remained on the defensive all through the mill, expecting at any moment that Choynski's once famous left hook would crash on his jaw. ... Jackson can, to-day, deliver a much harder blow than Choynski, who, judging from his last fight, has gone completely to pieces. If Jeffries hopes to be declared the winner of Tuesday night's fight, he must, so to speak, get a move on, otherwise Jackson will win

---

166 *San Francisco Evening Post, San Francisco Examiner,* March 15, 1898; *San Francisco Call, San Francisco Examiner,* March 16, 1898.
167 *San Francisco Examiner,* March 17, 1898.

the battle on points, if he does not happen to end it before the limit is reached.[168]

Former heavyweight champion James J. Corbett gave his pre-fight analysis. Jim had heard that Jackson had been drinking himself to death during the past few years, although he also heard that Peter had been looking good recently in training. Corbett said that he had sparred with Jeffries once, sometimes twice a day for a month prior to his fight with Fitzsimmons. He described Jeffries as a "big, strong, healthy young man. He is not as clever as Jackson, nor as quick. He has not had the ring experience that Jackson has, and is not as great a ring general. He has a great deal of strength, and can hit hard." He recommended that Jeff press the pace and not allow Peter to "jolly him by feinting and ring generalship. … For instance, it is one of Jackson's plays, when he is tired and does not want to fight, to rush up as soon as the gong sounds and begin fast fighting. His opponent thinks that he is strong and keeps away, giving Jackson the rest he wants."

The night before the fight, the odds fluctuated back and forth, but settled on Jeff as the 10 to 7 favorite. The day-of-the-fight analysis said that the Jackson of old surpassed "all men of the Jeffries caliber." Jackson was much cleverer, and had the advantage of having seen Jeffries fight, while Jeff had never before seen Jackson in a ring. However, years of reckless living and inactivity had to take its toll. Discussing the odds favorite, the *San Francisco Evening Post* said,

> In the few engagements that Jeffries has participated in here he has created the impression that he is a hard man to beat. Not particularly clever with his hands nor possessing more than the ordinary ring generalship, he is a persistent fellow who can stand a pretty hard punching. Furthermore, Jeffries believes with the majority that Jackson is not as strong as he was in years gone by.

The San Francisco Call called Jackson a great master of the manly art and a polished artist, while Jeffries was young, powerful, and fairly scientific, but who still had "much to glean in the art of self-defense." Still, it felt that every dog has its day, and Jackson's years of inactivity and easy living were likely to "land him a member of the John L. Sullivan army; viz., men who have seen better days." "Jeffries should certainly defeat Jackson, all things considered, if he can be induced to sail in and fight to win."

The San Francisco Bulletin was doubtful about Jackson and very high on Jeffries, feeling that Jeff's skill and talent was underrated.

> Jackson in his prime was a prodigy. By the cleverest critics he was pronounced the best man of his day. But time and alcohol will work infinite destruction in a human system. It cannot be denied but what

---

168 *San Francisco Evening Post*, March 21, 1898; *San Francisco Call*, March 19, 1898.

the colored heavy-weight has tasted of the cheering spirits often and freely since he gave way to other aspirants. He has failed to travel the narrow path of virtue and temperance and sobriety. His friends tell us that he has been working consistently and he seems as strong and vigorous and clever as he ever was...but the writer entertains grave doubts. ... Jeffries, young, vigorous...is armed to go the route without faltering. He has protected himself by an ideal constitution, and having a deadly punch ought to be able to lay Jackson hors de combat as soon as he begins to weaken. Jeffries is no slouch of a boxer, and Jackson's friends will find that he will be bothered in planting his blows. After Jeffries has beaten a couple more good men the public will have a keener appreciation of his talents.[169]

Peter Jackson and James J. Jeffries fought on March 22, 1898 in San Francisco's Woodward's Pavilion, under the sponsorship of the Olympic Club. The arena was filled to overflowing, and many hundreds were unable to gain admittance. In his first autobiography, Jeff said that there were 8,000 in attendance. Big names tend to be big draws, regardless of age.

The men had agreed on referee Jim McDonald, who had refereed Jeff's fight with Choynski. They also agreed to no hitting in the clinches, but that if after the referee ordered a break, one persisted in holding, the other would be free to strike.[170]

The 22-year-old Jeffries entered the ring at 9 p.m., accompanied by Billy Delaney, lightweight "Spider" Kelly, and De Witt Van Court. Jeff wore blue trunks with a red and white belt. "Jeffries looked his weight – said to be about 210 pounds – when he threw his dressing robe." However, after the fight, Delaney said, "Jeffries went into the ring weighing 216 pounds, much lighter than he has ever fought before." The night before the fight, Jeff said that he would weigh about 215 pounds.

Five minutes later, the 36-year-old Jackson entered the ring, and the crowd "yelled itself hoarse" for "Peter the Great," who bowed and grinned before taking his seat across from Jeffries. He was the sentimental favorite. "His weight was stated to be 195 pounds, and when stripped he appeared well trained." Jackson wore long white trunks and a black belt, with kidney plasters on the small of his back, mostly hidden by his trunks and belt.

At 9:11 p.m., the gong sounded to begin the scheduled 20-round bout.[171]

169 *San Francisco Examiner, Evening Post, Call, Bulletin*, March 22, 1898.
170 *San Francisco Examiner*, March 22, 1898; *San Francisco Call*, March 23, 1898; *San Francisco Evening Post*, March 18, 1898.
171 As has been the case throughout the book, and will continue throughout, the following is an amalgamation of the local primary sources. *San Francisco Examiner, San Francisco Chronicle, San Francisco Call, San Francisco Evening Post, San Francisco Bulletin*, March 23, 1898.

1st round

At the start, Jackson feinted, while Jeff circled around him. After a half-minute of fiddling, Jeff lead with a straight left that fell short because Jackson jumped away. Peter blocked and ducked some lefts. "There was a noticeable difference in Jeffries' style from the time when he fought Choynski. Then he kept his guard well up and fought at the start almost entirely on the defensive. Last night he kept his guard low and his left arm well extended, playing for an opening."

Jackson jabbed, and landed a right to the body. Jeffries mostly focused on the body. They exchanged light counters on the body, ending in a clinch and clean break. Jeff rushed him to the ropes and they clinched. Peter ducked a hard left to the head and then countered with a stiff left on the stomach. Pete again eluded a Jeff left and countered with a right under the heart. After clinch and break, Jeff swung his left on the ear and Peter landed his right to the body.

During the fight, Jackson's favorite counterblow for Jeff's left to the head was his right to the heart. Jeff in turn often countered Pete's right with his left for the head.

Jackson landed a right on the body, left on the nose and right on the body again. Jackson jabbed between the eyes and on the nose. Jeffries grinned and kept away for a moment, before landing a hard left in the stomach. Jeff rushed a few times but Peter met him with solid rights under the heart. Jeff missed a left around the neck and they clinched.

Jackson looked good, showing much of his old form during the 1st round. He landed jabs to the head and some clean body punches, particularly with his straight right. Pete ducked most of Jeff's lefts. Another writer noted that although Peter was cool, quick, and skillful, his punches "did not carry sufficient force to hurt a fly." Jackson had never been known as a big puncher. He usually methodically broke his opponents down. Summarizing, "Jackson's body blows were the cleanest ones landed, but, taken all in all, honors were even during the round." Pete's showing in this round caused many to believe that it would be a long fight.

2nd round

Between rounds, Delaney told Jeff to hurry up and try to finish Jackson as quickly as possible. As requested, Jeff picked up the pace and rushed in, forcing matters from the start of the round. "Jeffries kept his left in his usual menacing half-swing attitude, but seemed to reach out more with his other hand whenever they came close together." Jeff fired in several rights to the head and body. He jumped in and landed a left to the wind and a right to the ear.

They mixed it up, with Jeff landing the left on the side of the face and Peter landing hot rights to the heart. Jackson jabbed, but Jeffries kept pressing in. Jackson focused his right on the heart and ducked Jeff's left swings. There were several clinches. Jeff landed a hard right to the face. Peter cleverly ducked a left. Jeff missed a right but landed a heavy left swing to the ear. They exchanged and landed simultaneous left jabs to the nose. Jeff rushed and Peter cleverly ducked and jumped away.

Jackson came back and landed some blows, but they lacked steam. "Fighting at close quarters, Jackson put in twice the number of blows, but they did not seem to have much effect." On the other hand, Jeff's blows affected Jackson. "The blow that turned the battle decidedly in favor of Jeffries was a short arm left swing on the jaw, which Jeffries landed several times with telling effect."

Jackson stepped in and threw a right to the heart, but Jeff countered with a sudden left to the jaw that dropped Peter backwards onto the floor, his hands outstretched to brace his fall before he landed on his back. Another version of this first knockdown said that Jeff laughed at Jackson's punches and rushed him back to the ropes and landed a left swing to the jaw that dropped him. He was down for either seven or nine seconds, depending on the source.

Upon rising, Jackson was dizzy and hurt. Jeff immediately landed another left hook smash 'to the chin that dropped Pete to his back again. "He rolled to the ropes, and was pulling himself to his feet when the gong sounded." The bell had saved him. One of Jackson's seconds rushed over, helped him up, and brought him to the corner. Jeff's friends cheered wildly, while Jackson was very dazed and groggy.

3rd round

Jeffries rushed in and forced the fight, anxious to finish Jackson off. He realized that Peter had not fully recovered. Full of confidence, Jeff did not try to guard the heart blows, but ignored them and fired off left hooks, nailing Jackson often. Pete kept at the body with his right, but Jeff kept landing several hard lefts to the face. Jackson was unable to resist Jeff's terrific rushes. Jeffries landed several left hooks to the body and head, as well as some rights, all of which eventually sent Jackson staggering. Although Peter fought back, he was stumbling around. Jeff had little difficulty landing, and with disastrous effect.

Jeffries kept rushing and hammering away, including two hard left hooks to the body, until Peter tottered back to the ropes. Jeff threw left and right swings to the head, until, "An extra hard left-hander from Jeffries placed Jackson in a sitting posture on the lower rope. His head was drooping. He was powerless and helpless." That left hook to the head had basically knocked Jackson out. Sitting on the lower rope, he was partially leaning against a ring post, both his hands at his sides, at Jeff's complete mercy. Instead of attacking again, Jeff held back.

At that point, the referee wisely stopped the fight, although it was not entirely clear as to whether the referee, the police, or both simultaneously ended the fight. One said that Referee Jim McDonald, seeing that Jackson was helpless on the ropes, quickly moved from the center of the ring in between the fighters, motioned Jeff to his corner and awarded the fight to him, while Peter remained oblivious to his surroundings. Another said that the police timely interfered and ensured that there was no useless brutality. Disagreeing, another said that the referee had stepped in and stopped it, but that the police captain was preparing to stop it when the referee did so. Yet, another writer quoted Referee McDonald as announcing, "The police have stopped the fight, and I proclaim Jeffries the victor."

Describing the end, the *Call* said,

> Here was where Jeffries showed the instincts of a gentleman, for instead of rushing up in brute fashion…he humanely stepped away and let him gradually sink against the post and ropes for support. The referee, seeing that Jackson was done for, raised his hand to stop the fight, and awarded it to Jeffries, who walked to his corner and out of the ring, cheered as victors always are. Jackson was able to stagger to his own corner with some help.

The San Francisco Bulletin said that as predicted, Jackson met his demise when he met "the most formidable candidate for heavy-weight honors in the ring today. The battle was short, decisive and pathetic." It was over after only 8 minutes of actual fighting (two minutes into the 3rd round).

> In the initial round Jackson showed a spark of his best form. For just a minute the king was himself…but it soon relaxed, and died away. The spirit was strong but the flesh weak. Peter repeatedly tried to make a rally, but his powers were gone and for a round his shattered hulk drifted helplessly about, completely at the mercy of the young Hercules. Referee McDonald interfered at the opportune moment and rewarded the worthy. Thus ends the career of a great man. Poor Peter.

The San Francisco Chronicle complimented Jeffries' improvement. "He has taught himself how to feint, how to use his feet and how to block his man with his gloves and shoulders." Jeffries did not use the cautious style seen in the Choynski fight, but attacked ferociously. Therefore, his critics would have to rethink their suspicion that he had a "yellow streak" and "stage fright."

The San Francisco Evening Post also lauded Jeff's progress.

> Although the contest last night was a one-sided affair, Jeffries nevertheless showed some improvement, particularly in the use of both hands. When he made his first appearance here with Long he used right and left, but in his recent bout with Ruhlin he relied entirely on his left. Last night he appeared again as a two-handed fighter, coming back frequently with his right after a lead with the left.

For a big man he is exceedingly agile. He has a great advantage in strength, and apparently is a cool-headed fellow.

A Los Angeles paper said that Jeff "showed considerable improvement in cleverness, using his hands with both judgment and precision."[172]

It was a virtual walkover. Jeff had little difficulty hitting Peter when and where he pleased, while Jackson was unable to resist the attack or administer punishment. *The Call* felt that age and dissipation had finally caught up with Jackson. *The Evening Post* agreed that Peter had gone the route of John L. Sullivan and other boxers. "Last night he paid the penalty of riotous living – a fault common to most all successful boxers." Peter's cleverness only served him meagerly. Still, the match had some significance. "Now Jeffries is the champion of England and Australia, and must whip Fitzsimmons to become champion of the world."

Afterwards, Jeffries said,

> In the first round I fiddled with him a little bit, just to find out how clever he was and if he had a good punch in him. It was not long in finding that I was just as clever and knew as much about the game as he did. Then I sailed right in and turned the trick. If people think that Peter Jackson cannot punch, they are badly mistaken. He landed several stiff punches under my heart. ...

> I had Jackson practically beaten in the second round, but the gong saved him. When we came together for the third round the first blow I gave him practically ended the fight. After I had sent him against the ropes with two or three left swings I saw he was completely gone and I stepped back.

Jeffries only had a slight cut over the eye, which injury he had sustained in training, and was reopened during the bout.

Jackson said that Jeffries was "wonderfully strong and active." Of the fight, he said,

> It was in the middle of the second round that I knew I was going. He hit me a punch under the ear that dazed me and that was why I was such an easy mark at the end of that round. When I got up for the third I hardly knew where I was, and when he got me on the ropes after that everything was a blank to me.

Bill Delaney said,

> In the first round he sparred with his dusky antagonist to get a line on him, but when he saw that he was just as clever he determined to make it a short fight. At the end of the first round I saw that Jackson could not hurt him, and instructed Jeffries to go at him. Many of

172 *Los Angeles Evening Express*, March 23, 1898.

Jackson's blows whizzed around Jeffries' head, which showed that he still had hitting power. Although he was defeated by Jeffries it does not prove that other men can defeat him. In my opinion Jackson has still a few fights in him. Jeffries has been improving right along, and, coupled with tremendous hitting powers, he has a cool head and fights fairly.

Tom Sharkey called Jackson a "has been" and said that allowing him to fight after so many years of dissipation was a sin.

I must say that I admired Jackson's style. It was Jeffries' fight from the start, though, for Peter's blows did not bother him much. They lacked steam. After a little exertion, Jackson became slow, and of course was an easy mark for any kind of a blow. I pitied the poor fellow. I could have had a fight with him shortly after his arrival here, but as I had promised my friends that I would never fight a negro I declined to make a match with him.

Both Sharkey and Jeffries said that they would like to meet each other. Delaney said that Jeffries "does not underrate Sharkey's ability and knows he will have a fight on hand when he meets him, but feels confident that he can do the trick."

Some have debated the significance of Jeffries' victory over Jackson. Given Jackson's years of inactivity, it was not much of a shock that Jeff won. However, what was impressive was the rapidity in which he did it. Peter Jackson was a vastly experienced, skilled and knowledgeable veteran whose last and only defeat had been fourteen years ago. He had trained faithfully. Even those who thought that Jackson would lose still felt that he would last many rounds before being worn down. The speed at which Jeffries took him out was surprising. Fighters with that type of experience, skill, and durability usually did not get taken out so quickly. But that is all the credit, if any, which can be awarded to Jeffries for a victory over a man who was likely not much more than a shell of himself.

In his later autobiography, Jeffries said, "I have been given credit for being one of the few boxers who dared meet the great negro, who, many thought, was one of the greatest of all fighters." Jeff had heard arguments that he was the best because he beat Jackson. However, Jeffries recognized the fact that Jackson was a diminished fighter. "A few years before, perhaps, Peter was a great fighter, but against me he was only a shell."[173]

Following the Jackson fight, Jeffries signed a contract to give nightly sparring exhibitions at a local San Francisco theater on Market Street.[174]

---

173 *Two Fisted Jeff* at 85-86. Over a year later, in August 1899, a very large Jim Jeffords would knock out Jackson in 4 rounds. Jackson would eventually die in July 1901 of tuberculosis, just shy of his 40th birthday.
174 *San Francisco Examiner*, March 22, 23, 1898; *San Francisco Chronicle, San Francisco Call*, March 23, 1898.

In the subsequent days, new and revised assessments of Jeffries were printed. "Some claim that on account of his youth and strength, coupled with a fair amount of science and backed by his vitality and ability to stand punishment, he can defeat any man whom he can hit…. It is a sure thing that if he lands one good blow that the fight will be his." However, there were some mixed reviews, one saying,

> [E]ven in his fight with Jackson the other evening he went back to his old clumsy foot movement, and…he pumped his left arm up and down out to one side when preparing to let go one of his swings. This is true…but it is also true that he delivered his blows much more quickly, landed true and dodged and blocked better. In other words, he was more on the aggressive and was not held by any restraint.[175]

Another paper wrote, "Several Eastern sporting scribes seem to think that Jim Jeffries did not show any marked improvement in his fight with Peter Jackson. … Local opinion differs with that entertained in the East. Jeffries is improving rapidly." The locals felt that neither Gus Ruhlin nor Peter Maher would last 8 rounds with the Jeffries that fought Jackson.[176]

---

175 *San Francisco Chronicle*, March 24, 1898.
176 *San Francisco Evening Post*, March 31, 1898.

CHAPTER 11

Mexican Pete

During late March and early April 1898, the Sharkey and Jeffries camps continued their ongoing negotiations for a fight between them. For the past couple of years, writers had been building, discussing, and analyzing this prospective fight. It was the big fight that local fans most wanted to see.

In the meantime, while those negotiations were ongoing, in early April, the Olympic Club tried to match Jeffries with someone else. Peter Maher out-priced himself, demanding a $10,000 purse. The Olympic instead matched Jeffries with "Mexican" Pete Everett for a 20-round bout, to be held in its own gymnasium, originally set for April 26. Everett insisted on hitting in the clinches, which was fine with Jeffries. They agreed to split 60% of the gate receipts, 75% to the winner and 25% to the loser.

Pete Everett had been fighting for about four years. He had never been stopped. Pete claimed to have won 38 fights. It was said that he had defeated respected fighters such as Jim Williams in 5 rounds (some say 7), Mike Queenan in 7 or 9 rounds, and in February 1898, Billy Woods of Denver in 6 or 7 rounds. Woods had lasted 34 rounds with Choynski and 15 with Steve O'Donnell before being taken out, and had been a sparring partner for Corbett, Fitzsimmons, and Jeffries.

Everett was called a big fellow, standing 6' ¼" or 6' ½". He had a long reach and weighed 190-192 pounds. He was 23 or 24 years old. Everett's father was an Irishman and his mother was half Mexican. However, he was living in an era where a drop of blood from a race other than white deemed you a member of that race. So, he was called "Mexican Pete."[177]

At that time, uncertain as to whether he would finalize a match with Jeffries, Tom Sharkey also challenged Jim Corbett. Corbett said that he was retired and would only return to fight Fitzsimmons. Jim said,

> Everyone knows what Sharkey is. The public is tired of seeing him try to fight and of listening to his talk. … Why don't he fight Jeffries? He can make a match with him before the Olympic Club if he is anxious to fight him. Sharkey always wants a shade, and he knows he cannot get it from the Olympic Club.

---

177 *San Francisco Evening Post, San Francisco Examiner,* April 2, 1898.

In response, Sharkey said,

> Corbett, I assert, is a 'dub' and is making capital on his gall. He is afraid of me, and is well aware that in a twenty-round contest he will have no show whatever with me. Corbett is apparently looking for notoriety in the theatrical line, and when it comes to pugilism he is well aware that he is a back number. ... Jeffries is afraid of me, and in consequence he made a contest with Mexican Pete. This is a subterfuge on his part.[178]

The promoters and some members of the press touted Pete Everett as a tough customer and an exceedingly dangerous fellow.

> Jeffries' opponent is not wanting in confidence, but he is nevertheless training faithfully and already shows the effects of his work. He is described as a hard hitting man who delivers straight from the shoulder and if such is his style of fighting he ought to experience little difficulty in landing frequently on Jeffries' broad countenance.

That said, the local paper wondered whether such promotion was simply being done to affect the betting odds or to stimulate ticket sales.[179]

While training for Everett, Jeffries allegedly took a short tour of Northeastern California. On April 6, he arrived at Angels Camp, about 134 miles northeast of San Francisco.[180] Although the San Francisco newspapers provided no details of Jeff's trip, there were non-local reports printed over a year later which claimed that on April 6, 1898 at Angels Camp, Jeffries boxed a 4-round exhibition with Jim Jeffords.

> On the evening of April 6, 1898, Jeffries and Jeffords met in a four-round boxing exhibition at Dolling's Hall at Angels Camp, and though the decision was a draw, it is asserted that Jeffords had the best of the mill and that he had the now champion of the world all but out in the fourth round.

Jeffords said, "Then I was in the best of condition; being in complete training, while Jeffries was not in the best condition, as he was simply traveling through our country giving sparring exhibitions with Billy Delaney. The fact that I was able to make a good showing is owing to the good condition I was in." A few months later, it was again claimed that the 6'4" 195-pound Jeffords had once bested Jeffries in a 4-rounder.[181]

Naturally, the question is whether this was just advertising puffery circulated by Jeffords' backers in order to secure some free publicity for him. They might have gone 4 rounds in an exhibition, but it is unlikely that Jeffords did as well as he alleged. His subsequent career results (1899 KO4

178 *San Francisco Examiner*, April 4, 1898.
179 *San Francisco Evening Post*, April 6, 1898.
180 *San Francisco Examiner*, April 7, 1898.
181 *Los Angeles Express*, July 10, 1899; *New York Evening Journal*, October 23, 1899.

Peter Jackson – Pete's final fight, LKOby5 Gus Ruhlin, LKOby3 Bob Armstrong, 1900 LKOby2 Tom Sharkey) do not give one the impression that Jeffords could do very well with Jeffries unless Jeff handled him lightly owing to the fact that it was just an exhibition. After Armstrong and Ruhlin stopped Jeffords, one writer said that he had "a manufactured reputation of having bested champion Jim Jeffries – a pleasing bit of fiction which originated in the fanciful mind of a zealous, but perhaps not too truthful promoter of publicity, as press agents are sometimes designated." If he had really bested Jeff, such an event would likely have been discussed at the time, instead of a year later.[182]

Jim Jeffords

Jeffries and Delaney returned from their "trip to the interior" on the evening of April 7. Jeffries had allegedly been on a brief barnstorming trip. However, "There is a strong suspicion existing among the local sports that Jeffries has not as many matches made in the East as his manager would have the public believe. … The belief is that Delaney circulated these stories…but for what particular reason no one but himself seems to know."[183]

On April 11, the Sharkey and Jeffries camps agreed to a match between them, to be held on May 6. Because of this more important and financially lucrative upcoming bout, the Jeffries-Everett fight date was advanced from April 26 to April 22.

Jeffries trained at Oakland's Reliance Club, sparring with Jack Jeffries, who weighed almost 200 pounds, as well as Jack Stelzner. Stelzner had previously sparred with Jeffries before the Choynski fight, and had also sparred Sharkey when Tom was preparing for his March 1898 Choynski rematch.

At that time, as a fighter grew more popular, there were an ever-increasing number of daily training regimen reports. The fight-worshipping

182 *National Police Gazette*, December 16, 1899.
183 *San Francisco Evening Post*, April 8, 1898.

public enjoyed them. Gamblers found such reports to be valuable. World heavyweight championship fights would often have daily reports from the training camps for weeks ahead of the fight.

On the hot day of April 13, Jeff took a 6-mile run, accompanied by trainers Bill Delaney and De Witt Van Court, who were on bicycles. In the afternoon, Jeff worked the wrist machine for half an hour. Next, wearing heavy gloves, Jeff sparred 4 rounds with brother Jack, "who is by no means a green hand at the game. After the first round, the 'big fellow' let himself out, and his brother received more than one solid cuff on the body and head." Jeff frequently used his left hook. Van Court said, "That's his favorite punch. Jeffries has that blow down so 'pat' that I don't know anybody who can get away from it." After the sparring, Jeff put on smaller gloves and hit the punching bag with "wonderful dexterity" for another half hour. Van Court said that he had known Jeff for a long time, had worked with him in the gym in Los Angeles, "and I can truthfully say that I never saw him box so cleverly as he does now. He is much faster than he used to be."[184]

Jeffries said, "Friday night I will go against "Mexican Pete" at the Olympic Club. I don't know much about him, except that he is a big man, and of course there is always a chance of a surprise when you have that kind of a man for an opponent."

On the morning of April 17, Jeff walked 7 miles into the hills, and then ran 3 miles "at a pace that astonished" Delaney and the Van Court brothers, Eugene and De Witt, who accompanied him on bicycles. At the Reliance Club gym, Jeff worked the punching bag and had a brisk 4-round set-to with his brother Jack. James J. "made some of the spectators wonder at his agility."

Jeffries was a tireless worker, both on the road and in the gymnasium. On the 18th, he practiced footwork while holding weights, working for 10 minutes without showing any fatigue. Jack Stelzner and Jack Jeffries then alternated sparring single rounds with Jeff for a total of 7 rounds, roughing it, hitting hard, and clinching repeatedly, preparing him for Sharkey's style. Jeff was engaging in hard sparring so that he would be prepared for a tough fight. "I like to take a stiff punch occasionally. It is well to feel the sting of the glove, as then you know what to expect when you go in the ring."[185]

On April 19, an *Examiner* reporter said of Pete Everett,

> I watched him box half a dozen rounds with big Joe Kennedy yesterday afternoon and was rather favorably impressed with his workmanship. He certainly knows how to box, and he has some tricks of attack and defense which appear to be original. … He is not a one-punch man by any means. He utilizes his wonderful reach by hitting

---

184 *San Francisco Evening Post*, April 13, 1898; *San Francisco Examiner*, April 14, 1898, March 9, 1898.
185 *San Francisco Examiner*, April 16, 18, 19, 1898.

straight from the shoulder and uses good judgment in snapping his head back out of the way of returns. He varies his system of avoidance by ducking.... Pete in action is all arms. His opponent never seems to get far enough away to be out of range. ... His length of arm enables him to indulge in certain "fancy shots." ... He proved that he can cover ground at a rapid gait and that his pipes are attuned to fast work. ... In reality, he stands six feet one and one-quarter, or a quarter inch taller than Jeffries.

Everett was confident. "They thought I was in for a drubbing when I went against Queenan, the stockyard giant. He weighed 230 pounds trained, but I took his measure in nine rounds." Pete again claimed to have won 38 knockouts, including his victory over 200-pound Billy Woods.

Pete was clever, but Jeff had a granite jaw and the punching ability. Everett was listed as weighing 190 pounds to Jeffries' 213 pounds.

As the fight approached, there were further attempts to promote and hype Everett. One said that Pete had more varied experience than Jeff did, "as his record shows he has engaged in over thirty battles and has on all occasions been returned a winner."

"MEXICAN PETE," THE COLORADO BOXER, WHO WILL DON THE GLOVES TWENTY ROUNDS WITH JEFFRIES TO-MORROW NIGHT.

However, the publicity was not all true. Better judges of pugilists did some investigating into Everett's record and found that "it has not been published as fully as would be desired." They learned that although "Everett did whip Williams some years ago it is claimed that the two men met a second time when Williams easily disposed of his opponent. It is also said that Everett has several other defeats which he has failed to account for in his record."

Ultimately, on the day of the fight, the *Examiner* felt that the Jeffries-Everett match was an unequal one. Although Pete had trained faithfully and had an abundance of confidence, he was not a hard hitter, and "lacks the other qualities of a fighter which are so prominent in his opponent." Jeffries had advantages in weight, strength, and punching ability. He also had an "iron jaw" and a midsection covered with an amalgam of muscle and hard flesh. At that point, Jeff's weight was given as 216 pounds to Pete's 190. Jeff was the 10 to 4 betting favorite, and some were giving 10 to 3, with not many takers. It was said that if Jeff failed to knock him out, it would be a great surprise.[186]

Jeffries was a hot item. *The Bulletin* said, "Jeffries, the Los Angeles giant, looms up as the most likely to succeed to the title. ... He is unquestionably the most important factor in the heavy-weight situation today." It also said,

> The fistic world is just commencing to recognize that Jeffries has more than a passing show of attaining the top of the ladder. Little by little the wise ones are dropping into line, and it will not be long before the I-told-you-sos will be sounding his praises. ... The truth of the matter is, Jim made an excellent showing while in the Corbett camp at Carson City, and conservative sportsmen predicted a new Richmond in the field when he had a bit more experience. Thus far he has more than exceeded their most sanguine expectations.[187]

Another hot topic in the newspapers at that time was the beginning of the Spanish-American War, a war in part spurred on by the journalism of William Randolph Hearst's newspapers, including his *San Francisco Examiner*. On February 15, 1898, the USS Maine sunk on an official visit to Havana, Cuba. It is unclear whether it was an internal accident or an enemy had sunk it. Hearst's newspapers did everything they could to promote a war with Spain, including accusing the Spanish of blowing up the Maine.

In March 1898, the U.S. under President William McKinley issued an ultimatum to Spain to end its presence in Cuba. Spain refused, and on April 20, Congress declared war.[188]

Referencing the just-declared Spanish-American War, the April 22, 1898 *San Francisco Examiner* headline exclaimed, "WAR IS FAIRLY ON!" That was the day that James Jeffries fought "Mexican" Pete Everett, the "Colorado Cyclone," in the Olympic Club's gymnasium, exactly one month after the Peter Jackson fight.

The men entered the ring at 9:30 p.m. Jeff was seconded by Delaney, Stelzner, De Witt Van Court, and "Spider" Kelly. Referee Phil Wand announced that they had agreed to hit in the clinches.[189]

---

186 *San Francisco Evening Post*, April 16, 19, 22, 1898; *San Francisco Examiner*, April 19, 22, 1898; *San Francisco Bulletin*, April 22, 1898.

187 *San Francisco Bulletin*, April 21, 22, 1898.

188 Eventually, Lt. Col. Theodore Roosevelt's Rough Riders were victorious in Cuba. Spain was also defeated in the Philippines. A peace protocol ended hostilities on August 12, 1898. Under the subsequent peace treaty signed at Paris on December 10, 1898, Spain relinquished title to Cuba, which became independent, and ceded Puerto Rico, Guam, and the Philippines to the United States. The U.S. also took Hawaii.

189 The following is from the *San Francisco Chronicle*, *San Francisco Examiner*, *San Francisco Call*, *San Francisco Evening Post*, *San Francisco Bulletin*, April 23, 1898.

1st round

Everett backed away as Jeffries feinted. Jeff tried to get him to lead, but Pete would not take the offensive. Jeff rushed and swung his left, with Pete ducking and clinching. Jeff backed him into a corner and twice landed his left to the jaw. Everett mostly moved, ducked and clinched. Pete made a couple short leads for the body, one right only landing on the elbow. Pete ducked a right and covered up his forehead with his left arm. Jeff suddenly rushed and landed his famous left hook. Pete bent over and "enveloped his head and neck in his long arms." Jeff laughed.

When Jeffries would swing his left, Pete would duck and receive blows on the top of his head. Pete missed a right to the body and then backed around the ring as Jeff leisurely followed. When Pete ducked a left and went in for a clumsy clinch around Jeff's body, Jeff landed a heavy right to the ribs. Everett backed away with his arms held high up to shield his ears. The crowd began to laugh. One yelled, "Don't hurt him, Pete." Overall, little damage was done in the round.

2nd round

Jeff kept trying to draw Pete on, but Everett would not lead. Pete jumped around, far away. His right for Jeff's body from the outside was half-hearted. Jeff got close enough to land several light lefts to the head, and in the clinches, he landed some stiff kidney blows with the right. Jeff mostly hit the body with the right on the inside. It was similar to the previous round, though Jeff grew a bit rougher. When Pete tried some feeble rights to the body in the clinches, both Jeff and the crowd laughed.

Jeffries grew determined to force matters, and landed a volley of short left jolts. Pete crouched low and covered his jaw and ears by crossing his arms in front of his face. The spectators jeered, so Pete tried a right to the body. Jeff chased him and swung his left but Pete grabbed his arm. Jeff followed with his hard right to the body before pulling away.

Jeff landed a left swing to the neck, which sent Pete to the ropes. One source said that Jeff almost pushed Pete through the ropes. "It looked as if Jeffries was only practicing some roughing tactics as a sort of preparation for Sharkey. He shoved the crouching Everett about as he pleased."

Another source said that when Everett was punched to the ropes, he fell and was down for five seconds. When he rose, Jeffries was after him again, swinging his left. Pete again stooped down and covered his face with his arms. Jeff tried a left uppercut for the nose, but Pete smothered it and clinched. Jeff followed with a right to the ribs. Pete then backed away until the gong rescued him.

3rd round

Under instructions from Delaney, Jeffries pressed Everett, determined to punch through Pete's guard. A couple of stiff punches on Pete's arms soon lowered them. Jeff measured him with a light left to the jaw and landed a right. He landed a left, right, and left that staggered Pete, who clinched. On the outside again, as Pete was in the process of attempting a right to the body, Jeff "nabbed him with one of those lefts of his which come from no great distance, but are remarkably damaging in their effects." Pete staggered back, reeling about as Jeff nailed him with lefts. Everett tried to clinch, but a long left hook clean on the jaw dropped him.

After seven seconds, Everett rose in an awkward way, looking a little wobbly. Pete covered up again, and Jeff landed a right to the body. Everett turned away and made for his corner. Jeff landed a right to the jaw, and Pete clinched.

Jeff followed up, knocking the wobbly Everett about the ring. One said, "All the fight was knocked out of him, and when he appeared to be on the point of shoving his head out through the ropes, Wand held up his hand to Jeffries to cease firing." Another said, "Pete was half down at the time, with his hands on the floor." A third local source said, "Everett exhibited a strong inclination to quit, and the referee, fully appreciating the ridiculous situation, promptly awarded the 'fight' to Jeffries."

Everett mildly protested the stoppage. Jeffries just laughed and said, "What was the matter with you? Why didn't you fight? I was only playing with you." *The Evening Post* noted, "Even the victor felt as if he were obtaining money and glory under false pretenses." It was thought that Everett was lucky, because Jeff had not put full force into his blows, wanting to protect his hands for the upcoming Sharkey fight. Another called Referee Wand humane, because when he stepped between them, Jeff had settled himself to deliver a knockout blow.

Those who had paid $3 to witness the alleged "coming man" Everett give Jeff a "hard argument" felt fooled, and withdrew from watching the "treat" in disgust. The local reports all called Everett a rank "dub" of the worst kind who could not fight at all. *The Evening Post* said that Everett had nerve to style himself as the Colorado champion when he "not only lacks the ordinary knowledge of boxing, but is further hampered by cowardice, which showed itself before he had been in the ring a minute last night." *The Examiner* called Pete slow and timid, having made a sorry showing. He was there only trying to survive, ducking and clinching as Jeff rushed and swung his lefts.

The Call criticized the Olympic for matching Everett with "a powerful man who has already proven his ability as a prize-fighter." It called the fight a hippodrome and an even bigger matchmaking blunder than the Jackson fight. "An account of the fight cannot be given for the very good reason that there was no fight to report. Pete sheltered his dark-skinned face with his gloves each time Jeffries made an attempt to land, and although spun about like a top from cuffs and pushes, the Mexican kept his face and neck always guarded."

The Chronicle agreed, "[Everett's] method was to fold his arms about his body and duck his head at the least move by Jeffries and to rush into a clinch. Jeffries did not seem to know what to make of his opponent's style, and let two rounds go by without doing much." Jeff merely played with him until he decided to end it. Pete never landed a real blow in the 3 rounds, despite Jeffries leaving openings.

The Bulletin said,

> [Everett] smiled and bowed and acted like a winner, but it was all assumed, for down deep in his bosom a coward's heart throbbed and beat until it nearly choked his wind. It took less time for him to show the yellow feather than it did for the Spanish lumber scow to surrender to the Nashville. The first punch Jeff presented his Mexican friend made him double up like a school boy hit in the stomach with an apple, and he never took his arms away from his face and chest after that. Jeff gave him a couple stiff jolts in the back, and even these didn't straighten him. He was tied up in a knot that could not be unraveled, and as soon as Jeff had shown him as a genuine fraud Referee Wand stepped in and gave the decision to the right man.

After the fight, Bill Delaney said that he cautioned Jeff not to hit with all his might, fearing a hand injury. "I didn't want him to take any chances, so I told him to go slow and take care of himself." The fight only lasted two and a half rounds, no blood was spilled, and neither man was marked.

Years later, Jeff wrote, "Poor old Pete, I do not know whether he was scared to death or just clowning, but he was the only man in my career who ever faced me that did not show gameness and courage."[190]

Perhaps history should revise its assessment of Everett and give Jeffries more credit for his quick and easy 3-round victory over him. Interestingly enough, Everett would prove to be at least competitive against other top fighters, including Bob Armstrong (1898 LKOby14), Joe Choynski (1899 LDQby7), Tom Sharkey (1901 WDQ2), and Frank Childs (1899 L6, 1900 L10). In 1902, Pete Everett would lose a 20-round decision to future champion Jack Johnson. However, Jeffries made him seem like nothing. Everett's other results make Jeff's performance against him all the more impressive.

---

190 *Two Fisted Jeff* at 87.

CHAPTER 12

The Shark

The Jeffries-Sharkey fight was what the fans and experts most wanted to see. It was a great matchup, because Tom Sharkey was not a pretty boxer, but a rough and tough bareknuckle style fighter. He had the reputation of being a foul fighter, fouling in almost every one of his bouts, leading to some controversy in most of them. He hit low, grabbed, pushed and wrestled, head butted, and hit after the bell. He had a vicious, hard-hitting, rushing style. He could keep a fast pace, take punishment and keep coming back for more.

Sharkey was another fighter who had met the who's who of boxing, and had been in the ring with all the champions. He had begun his career in 1893 while in the Navy, and had knocked out about fourteen military opponents. He held an 1895 KO7 victory over Australian Billy Smith.

In April 1896, Joe Choynski contracted to stop Sharkey in 8 rounds, but failed to do so. In that fight, Sharkey showed his foul habits, striking Joe with a vicious low blow, as well as using his clinching and wrestling tactics. However, he also showed his durability and spirit, fighting hard throughout, taking and giving punishment, getting dropped three or four times, but showing his recuperative powers. He was then described as "a perfect glutton for punishment and does not know when he is defeated. He is a fighter of the Goddard type." Tom was "famous for stamina, recuperative powers and courage," as well as "remarkable physical development as to make him proof against the assaults of all ordinary men."[191]

In June 1896 in San Francisco, the 180-pound Sharkey fought world champion Jim Corbett to a 4-round draw that was filled with clinching and wrestling. He took punishment in the first 2 rounds, but came back strong in the last 2 rounds. He had Corbett dead tired at the end, and most felt that he would have won had it been fought to a finish. After the fight, taking a dig at Corbett, Sharkey said, "Choynski is the greatest fighter that I ever yet met." Many called Tom a quick and powerful pugilistic wonder with irresistible rushes.

In August 1896, Sharkey sparred 3 tame exhibition rounds with John L. Sullivan.

In December 1896 in San Francisco, Bob Fitzsimmons dropped Sharkey in the 1st and 5th rounds and knocked him out in the 8th round. Referee

191 *San Francisco Chronicle*, April 18, 1896; *San Francisco Examiner*, April 17, 1896; *San Francisco Evening Post, San Francisco Bulletin*, June 24, 1896; *New York Sun*, June 25, 1896.

Wyatt Earp controversially called the final punch a foul low blow and disqualified Fitzsimmons, but most believed that the referee had been paid to fix the fight for Sharkey.[192]

In June 1897 in New York, Sharkey fought the hard-punching Peter Maher. Since his 1896 1st round knockout loss to Fitzsimmons, Maher's victories included 1896 KO4 Frank Slavin, KO6 Joe Choynski, and KO1 Steve O'Donnell. Sharkey dropped Maher in the 6th round, but was himself dropped in the 7th. He then resorted to foul tactics, rushing in like a wild bull, clinching and wrestling, and hitting after the bell, causing a brawl in the ring until the police stopped the bout. The referee declared it a 7-round draw.

After scoring several knockouts over lesser-knowns, in November 1897, Sharkey stopped Joe Goddard in 6 rounds. Tom's last fight was the March 1898 foul-laden 8-round rematch draw with Choynski in San Francisco.

During late March 1898, while negotiations were ongoing, Sharkey said that he did not want to fight Jeffries in San Francisco because the city was against him. However, San Francisco was where the fight was likely to

---

192 Sharkey began calling himself the champion, although almost no one recognized him, particularly after Fitzsimmons defeated Corbett in March 1897. Sharkey's best argument was that Corbett had briefly retired and given the title to Peter Maher, who then lost to Fitzsimmons. Thus, when Fitz "lost" to Tom, Sharkey became the champion, at least in his own mind. However, Maher had not accepted the title and Corbett repudiated his gift and retirement before Maher fought Fitzsimmons. Furthermore, most felt that Fitz forfeited his title claim when he had refused Corbett's challenges during 1896. Finally, everyone knew that Fitzsimmons had bested Sharkey, so when Bob subsequently knocked out Corbett, Fitz was universally recognized as the champion. Of course, for those who want to recognize Sharkey as champion, then James Jeffries stood to become world champion with a victory over Sharkey.

generate the most revenue. "There is no doubt that Sharkey has, by his actions, made many persons prejudiced against him, but he could win back all his former admirers if he would fight fairly."[193]

Bill Delaney did not want the fight to take place at the National Club, because it had been associated with the Sharkey-Fitzsimmons fix. Delaney preferred the Olympic or another reputable club. He said,

> We do not propose to take chances by signing for a go with any organization of mushroom growth. [National Club managers] Messrs. Gibbs and Groom are all right, but there are men identified with the National Club which, according to my information, took prominent part in the Sharkey-Fitzsimmons fiasco. That being the case it would be unwise for a man who had any thought of the future to consent to a meeting there.

However, Sharkey wanted the National. "The National Club has managed all my fights and has given me a square deal every time." He noted that he and Jeff had previously been matched to fight at the National [in late 1897], but the match fell through because the authorities refused to grant permits at that time. "Surely if the National Club was all right then it is all right now." Sharkey proposed that they draw lots to settle the matter.

National Club Manager J.H. Gibbs said, "Delaney has never once complained about us before, and I cannot understand his action. He matched Jeffries with Sharkey before us some months ago, and there certainly has been no change of conditions since."[194]

On April 11, Delaney agreed to flip a coin to determine the club. The National Club won. It secured the match for May 6 at the Mechanics' Pavilion. The winner/loser split would be 75%/25% of a 65% share of the gate receipts. "Sharkey and Jeffries should draw one of the biggest crowds that has ever assembled about a local ring. Their past performances may be accepted as a guarantee of a good fight. They are both aggressive and hard hitting fighters."[195]

Sharkey and Jeffries agreed to strict adherence to Queensberry rules, which meant that hitting in the clinches and on breakaways was legal. "It was also agreed that the two pugilists should wear bandages on their hands if they so desired." They agreed to Alex Greggains as the referee. Greggains had fought Sharkey to an early 1896 8-round draw.

---

193 *San Francisco Chronicle*, March 24, 1898.
194 *San Francisco Examiner*, April 1, 1898; *San Francisco Chronicle*, April 8, 1898.
195 *San Francisco Evening Post, San Francisco Examiner*, April 12, 1898. Interestingly enough, when the *Examiner* printed Jeff's record, it listed a couple bouts that it had never listed before or since: "He defeated Henry Baker in nine rounds; Henry Griffin, fifteen; Charles Allen, two; J. Morrissey, one; Dan Long, two; T. Van Buskirk, two; Goddard, three; and Jackson, three. The draws were each twenty-round bouts, his opponents being Gus Ruhlin and Joe Choynski." It inaccurately listed Jeff's year of birth and location as 1877 in Los Angeles. Jim Morrissey was a Los Angeles fighter, so it is possible that Jeff faced him at some point, perhaps at an LAAC smoker.

Sharkey trained with former Jeffries opponent Henry Baker in Vallejo. On April 13, Sharkey sparred 8 rounds with Baker.

Some saw the bout as being for the championship, owing to the fact that Fitzsimmons and Corbett had not done any fighting since early 1897. *The Evening Post* later said that the boxers were practically meeting for the world's championship. Fitzsimmons claimed to be retired (sort of) and Corbett would not fight anyone but Fitz, so Jeffries and Sharkey appeared to be the best out there. Thus, the *Post* felt that they were fighting for the vacant championship should Fitzsimmons or Corbett not fight again any time soon.

> Corbett and Fitzsimmons, if they do not get a move on, will soon be lost sight of as pugilists. The new faces that have come into the arena to take their places are live, progressive fellows, and just now the eyes of the pugilistic world is on them. In a very few days Jeffries and Sharkey will meet and Ruhlin and McCoy will come together. Later the winners of these two bouts will probably be matched, and it is safe to say the victor in this final bout will be hailed champion of the world, and Corbett and Fitzsimmons will be lost sight of for good.[196]

Jeffries expected to defeat Sharkey, but granted that Tom was a tough proposition. Even if victorious, he did not want any vacant title.

> Sharkey is a strong, shifty, game fighter and is entitled to all the credit which such a man should have. As to his methods and style of fighting, Delaney and myself agree that the only trouble with Sharkey has been his disposition to "rough it" in the ring. But I am satisfied this match will be as clean a fight as was ever held in San Francisco. Why? Because I have thirty pounds advantage of Sharkey in weight, and it will be rather difficult for him to toss me about the ring.

> If I win I shall not make any claims to the championship. I don't want the championship by claims, but by fight. … Anybody who whips Sharkey will know after he is through that he has been in a fight. …

> As to the referee, I am perfectly satisfied. In fact, we consider ourselves very fortunate that such a man as Alex Greggains could be secured to referee so important a fight as this. He hasn't got much money, but there is not wealth enough in San Francisco to get him to do anything wrong. A fairer man could not have been selected.[197]

Jeffries noted that most of Sharkey's opponents said afterwards that they wore themselves out trying to punch him out. He felt that although Tom could hit, Sharkey could not hit hard enough to damage him. "If he

---

196 *San Francisco Evening Post*, May 3, 1898.
197 *San Francisco Examiner*, April 16, 1898.

wants to mix things he will find me right there. I am not afraid of that proposition."[198]

One issue being discussed as a potential hindrance to Jeff's career was the fact that he had hand problems. "In the fight with Ruhlin…Jeffries broke his right early in the encounter. The weapon is still weak. … The left hand has also been broken by being struck over the back of the member with a club. … Jeffries is in the position of a great race horse with bad legs." Sharkey's manager said that Jeff's hands were weak, and that a punch on Tom's skull would not hurt Tom, but hurt Jeff's hands. "Consequently the inference is that an effort will be made by the sailor to win by crippling his big opponent." Jeff would have the option of wearing hand bandages. However, striking hard blows inside of 5-ounce gloves over the course of 20 rounds could have a debilitating effect upon the hands.

Analyzing Jeffries, the famous referee George Siler said,

> I saw the husky Californian repeatedly while Corbett was training at Carson, but I really could not get a correct line on him, simply because he appeared slow when boxing with Jim, as almost anybody would. He struck me at times as being a swinger with both hands, and one a clever man could easily avoid, but probably not as easily as did Corbett. He is a wonderfully strong fellow, and it appears to me as though he ought to be able to trim anybody in a slash-away mix-up battle. Maher, McCoy, and Choynski are more scientific, and to win over any of the above named he would, to my way of thinking, have to do it by mixing.[199]

On April 25, Sharkey punched the bag for nearly an hour, and boxed a few rounds with each of his sparring partners, Jim Casey and Henry Baker. Tom also added Tim McGrath and big Joe Kennedy to his sparring staff for the last ten days of his training.

Jeffries resumed training at the Reliance Club on the 25th, after having taken a two-day rest following the Everett bout, which had been held on the 22nd. Jeff continued sparring with Jack Jeffries and Jack Stelzner, engaging in plenty of rough work.[200]

As the fight approached, the poolroom betting odds were tight, for most thought it would be a close contest. The official betting opened with Jeff a slight 10 to 8 favorite. Harry Corbett thought that large sums of money would be bet, including from the East, where the sports thought that Jeffries would win. Apparently, Eastern experts looked upon Jeffries as "the greatest heavy-weight pugilist of the present day."[201]

On May 2, Bill Delaney reacted to the odds still being in Jeff's favor.

198 *San Francisco Examiner*, April 18, 1898.
199 *San Francisco Examiner*, April 17, 1898.
200 *San Francisco Call*, April 23, 1898; *San Francisco Examiner*, April 26, 1898.
201 *San Francisco Evening Post*, April 30, 1898; *San Francisco Bulletin*, May 2, 1898; *San Francisco Call*, May 4, 1898.

I am surprised to see that Jeff is such a strong favorite in the betting. They tell me that he is 10 to 7 favorite. To me this seems not a fair odds. Sharkey is a big, stout fellow and has fought the best men of the day. While I expect that Jeffries will whip him, I don't look for any easy victory. Anyone who has seen this sailor fight knows perfectly well that he is a tough game. If anybody should be favorite in the betting it should be Sharkey.[202]

Reacting to Jeffries being the odds favorite, Sharkey said that betting odds did not win a fight. He thought that Jeff did not like punishment, and a few good punches would discourage him. He intended to go right at Jeff and try to finish him quickly. Delaney responded that Jeffries would be able to take all that Sharkey had to offer and be able to ask for more.

Both men were confident. Sharkey had rapidly improved as a boxer during the past two years. However, Jeff was bigger and stronger, having "superhuman strength and vigor," and would be the first man that Sharkey would be unable to hustle about.[203]

Jeffries was training hard. "It is astonishing the amount of exercise the big fellow can stand, but he says he is used to it, owing to the long hours he put in when working at his trade. He is strong as an ox now." Jeff said that he was ready for a fight of any distance. "Of course I shall fight entirely under instructions from my manager, Billy Delaney. ... I am in excellent condition, in fact, never felt better in my life."

Both fighters realized that "in order to be returned victors, they will have to put up one of the greatest battles ever fought in the roped arena." Tickets were selling like hot cakes.

Sharkey responded to those who said that he was a foul fighter.

Why, all those other fellows ran away from me, and because I followed them up and punched them hard when I got near to them a howl went up from those who are anxious to see me licked that I was a foul fighter and should not be given a match. What do these squealers want me to do? Stand in the middle of a ring like a dummy and wait until the other fellow comes after me? Why, if I had done that there would have been no fighting at all, and then the sports would cry 'Fake! Faker!'

It's a wonder that those fellows who have always crucified me for what they call foul fighting don't cry foul now because Commodore Dewey of the American squadron did not wait for the Spanish to make the attack, but instead he went right after the game himself and hammered the Spaniards out of the ring. I suppose those kid-gloved sports who take fits at the sight of a drop of blood will say

202 *San Francisco Bulletin*, May 3, 1898.
203 *San Francisco Evening Post*, May 2, 1898.

Commodore Dewey should not be allowed to command a fleet because he fights from the drop of the hat and stands no nonsense. Well, I am going to fight just like Dewey. I will not wait for the enemy, but I will go right at him, hammer and tongs…. Jeffries is a big, powerful gunboat, but I will throw a broadside into him just as the gong sounds that will cause something to drop. You wait and see.[204]

Regarding the Spanish-American War, ex-navy-sailor Sharkey said that he would be willing to fight. Jeffries also said, "If my services are needed I, too, am ready to enlist."

Referee Alex Greggains was "well aware of the fact that Sharkey so far forgets himself when he once enters into the heat of battle, that blows aimlessly directed may land on any part of his opponent's anatomy." Greggains informed both men that he would not tolerate foul fighting, and that the man who resorted to rough and unfair work would lose.

On May 4, two nights before the fight, before a large audience at the Reliance Club, Jeff gave a 3-round sparring exhibition with his brother Jack. At that point, the *Call* listed Jeffries as weighing 230 pounds.

Although the gamblers were divided in their opinions, the consensus amongst those playing Jeffries was that he had the best of the argument from a physical standpoint, although they were about equal scientifically. Sharkey followers said that if the contest lasted more than 10 rounds that Jeff would be compelled to show the white feather. Odds were 10 to 8 at that point, with Jeff the favorite.[205]

The Call said the men would be put to a severe test, and the one with the stoutest heart and clearest head would win. "If the mill settles down to a slogging affair at close quarters Jeffries should triumph, as he punches straight and with much greater force than Sharkey." Still, Tom had speedy feet and was clever at avoiding counters.

Jeffries was "held by many expert judges of pugilism as being the superior of all the fighters, excepting the invincible Fitzsimmons." However, "the sports who are supposed to know a 'thing or two' about pugilistic contests are about equally divided in their opinions." Although Sharkey was the slight underdog, the night before the fight, wagers on him were heavy enough that the odds shifted to about even money. Both men were in splendid condition.

Sharkey looked 15 pounds heavier than he was for the Choynski fight, and he was happy to be bigger. He likely weighed in the mid-180-pound range. Tom said, "I feel more confident of beating this fellow than I did of beating Choynski. … I am glad he is so big, because I can't miss him. I can get at a big fellow like that, while a smaller man might get away from me. I

204 *San Francisco Call*, May 2-4, 1898.
205 *San Francisco Call*, May 4, 1898; *San Francisco Bulletin*, May 6, 1898.

don't care how big they are if they will only come to me." Sharkey was brimming with confidence. However, he might have been underestimating his opponent. One writer opined, "Jim Jeffries has improved at least 50 percent since his battle with Choynski."[206]

The Evening Post said that both men had trained faithfully and thoroughly, in part because a promising future awaited the winner. Its day-of-the-fight analysis said,

> Jeffries has not had so wide an experience as the sailor, but in the battles he has fought he has shown that he is made of the right stuff. In size he exceeds all fighters of the past and present. In strength he is supreme and as a judge of time and distance he is the equal of any man. Certainly he has not the agility of a Corbett...but on the other hand while he wastes no action he has the eye to see openings and the speed to deliver with certainty. ... If he wins, he will be the most prominent figure in the pugilistic world and will be hailed as its champion.[207]

The Bulletin in even-handed fashion said,

> It is not an easy matter to settle your mind upon the probable winner of tonight's contest, which is attracting world-wide attention. ...There is no gainsaying the fact that it is a tough fight to come to a sound, solid opinion upon. Each man has his strong points, which put upon the scale produce nearly a balance. There is the aggressive, ever-fighting Sharkey, who has measured his powers with the very pink of the talent.... Jeffries possesses a greater bulk of avoirdupois.... The strongest point in Jeffries' favor the writer believes to be his knack of hitting hard. Not only can he strike a fatal blow, but it does seem to arrive at its destination with greater precision. ... Sharkey may be quicker, more agile with his arms, livelier on his feet, but his driving propensities are not as dangerous. Jeffries is a two-handed fighter in every sense of the word. He can write with either hand, and he can strike as well. This is an advantage in his favor. Should Sharkey be inclined to rough it it will be interesting to see what opposition Jeffries will offer. ...
>
> The betting evened up last night. Sharkey money came in at Corbett's in large amounts and brought the odds up to 10 to 9 in Jeff's favor.[208]

Sharkey said that Jeffries had more weight, more reach, and more height, but Tom had five years more experience and was five times as

---

206 *San Francisco Call, San Francisco Bulletin*, May 6, 1898.
207 *San Francisco Evening Post*, May 5, 6, 1898.
208 *San Francisco Bulletin*, May 6, 1898.

quick. "I am going to beat Jeffries…and then claim the championship of the world."[209]

Just two weeks after the Everett fight, on Friday, May 6, 1898 at San Francisco's Mechanics' Pavilion, the 23-year-old Jeffries took on yet another more experienced fighter in the tough "Sailor" Tom Sharkey. Some said that Sharkey was 26 years old, while others said he was only 24. He stood about 5'8", but was stocky, strong, quick, and well-conditioned.

Because interest in the fight was so great, in order to support more spectators and to give them a better view, the National Club via its managers Gibbs and Groom hired a construction company to build a number of extra grandstands of gradually raised rows of seats. Carpenters took two weeks to erect the stands.

Before the preliminary fight between Henry Baker (Sharkey's sparring partner) and Jack Stelzner (Jeff's sparring partner), a big section of improperly constructed temporary seats on the main floor containing 500-600 spectators crashed down. "The master of ceremonies had stepped into the ring to announce the first contest, when there came a sound of cracking timbers followed almost instantly by a roar as of thunder." The helpless spectators were hurled headlong to the floor on top of each other, amid an avalanche of chairs and broken lumber. Joe Corbett said,, "That no one was killed outright is the greatest of miracles." Injured men cried and cursed in anger. A cloud of dust obscured one end of the building. The ensuing chaos caused a stampede in the hall as many rushed out of the building, seeking safety.

Things settled down a bit, and Stelzner and Baker were called to the ring. However, the creaking of timbers gave warning of yet another catastrophe. Another section of the platform on which the seats were placed gave way and came down with a crash, sounding a terrible roar. Nearly 2,000 spectators scrambled towards the door amidst the cloud of dust and the dense sea of broken timbers and chairs.

Most of the injuries were painful, but not deadly. 23 people were seriously injured and taken to the hospital. Only one man was hurt internally. A broken nose was the next worst injury.[210]

Despite the incident, the show went on. An immense crowd had paid $10, $5, $3, and $2 each to witness the battle. Eventually, the crowd from the fallen seats fought its way into the reserved sections.

Following the preliminary, Jeff and Tom had to force their way through the jam to reach their corners.[211]

---

209 *San Francisco Chronicle*, May 6, 1898.
210 Blaming the district fire engineer, the contractor said he should have discovered the fact that the stands were not strong enough. Engineer Shaughnessy had ordered the insertion of a few extra uprights and braces, which was done, and he then approved the structure. Clearly, this was insufficient to render it sound. The club managers claimed that the contractor was not stinted in the cost of his work. However, the contractor replied by saying that he only had a short time to do the work and the limit of the expenses that the club would stand for was $1,125.

Before the main event started, the closing odds were 10 to 7 in Jeff's favor. Harry Corbett said his gambling hall alone took in about $70,000.

Jeffries was first to enter the ring. He bowed as the crowd loudly cheered him. When Sharkey entered, the crowd gave him an ovation. Referee Alex Greggains handed the men their gloves. The rules for this one allowed the men to hit in the clinches and on the break.[212]

1st round

The men began cautiously, feeling each other out. Jeffries took the aggressive and began to set the pace, but the quick-footed Sharkey nimbly pranced around him. They fiddled and feinted, rarely striking a blow. Each took turns making some offensive attempts. Tom landed a right to the jaw, but Jeff only smiled. Jeff landed a solid right to the ribs. Near the end of the round, Jeff went in and planted his left on Tom's neck. "Jeffries seemed to show that he was the stronger." Referee Greggains scored this round even.

2nd round

Jeff was more aggressive and forced Tom about the ring. Jeff landed some lefts to the head and body and a right to the heart. Tom mostly moved around, but would intermittently rush in with blows, which were mostly glancing.

After Jeff hit Tom with a straight left on the nose, Sharkey attempted to introduce his favorite game of pushing with his shoulder and dashing in with left and right swings to the head. However, "Just as soon as Sharkey bore in Jeffries put his gloves on the Sailor's shoulders and held him against the ropes. Sharkey quickly came to the conclusion that at rough work he had an opponent who was his superior in weight, and afterward he did not resort to rushing and shoulder butting." Jeff was strong enough to meet Tom's rush and to simply hold him up against the ropes and rough him as a warning. Sharkey "looked very surprised at the manner Jeffries held him and shook him." That was not something Sharkey was used to, for he was usually the physically stronger fighter.

Tom's respect for the bigger and stronger man explains why he did not rush and rough in this fight as much as he usually did, and used more footwork and ducking than was typical for him.

Later in the round, Sharkey struck Jeff in a clinch, which drew hoots from the crowd, but it was perfectly legal. Jeff tried multiple short-arm blows and hooks, but the sailor was too quick, avoiding them by clever

---

211 *The Call* said that Baker won the fight on a controversial disqualification in the 6th round. Most thought the fouls were relatively minor, and that Stelzner would have won but for being disqualified. *The Evening Post* said that Stelzner was in better condition, but that Baker hit harder. Stelzner hit in the clinches, which led to his disqualification.

212 The following fight analysis and discussion is from *San Francisco Examiner, San Francisco Chronicle, San Francisco Call, San Francisco Evening Post*, May 7, 8, 1898; *Two Fisted Jeff* at 89.

ducking. However, it was Jeff's round, according to the newsmen. Referee Greggains scored it for Jeffries as well.

3rd round

Jeff was the aggressor as Tom moved about. They exchanged some rushes and clinches, with both landing lefts to the jaw. Referee Greggains scored this round for Jeffries.

4th round

The heavy punching began in this round. Jeff hit Sharkey with left jabs, which drew Tom in. Sharkey rushed in and landed a left to the stomach. Jeff hit the jaw with his left, and as Tom turned to make a remark to the crowd, he received another left.

Jeffries took some of the fire out of Sharkey's attack by landing short-arm blows to the ribs, which troubled Tom to no little extent. Jeff kept landing his good right under the heart, and it looked like that blow would eventually break him. "One hard smash caused the sailor to grunt, and he then wildly rushed Jeffries, only to receive a left stop in the nose." Sharkey ducked some blows, and after a rally, Tom said to his seconds, "Why, he's easy." However, Jeff landed a left to the neck, and the sailor quickly retreated. Greggains scored it for Jeffries.

5th round

Jeff forced Sharkey around the ring. Tom eventually clinched and hit on the inside. However, in the clinches, Sharkey met his match at wrestling. Whenever Sharkey would duck a left swing, Tom would smile and make some remark. Tom was often found ducking below Jeff's waist, fearful of his punches.

During this round, Jeffries "proved that his blows were dangerous." "Jeffries lands a stiff left swing on Sharkey's neck which proved a staggerer to the sailor." A right swing to Sharkey's arm sent him staggering against a post. Jeffries, "whether it was because he did not desire to take the least chance of being hit in the face or was obeying instructions, failed time and again to follow up his game and especially was this noticeable when he had Sharkey in a corner under his wing, so to speak." Perhaps he was concerned that he would punch himself out, fearing Tom's well-known recuperative powers, or he did not think that Sharkey was all that badly hurt. After the fight, Jeff revealed that he had badly swollen hands. He said that he could not punch hard on a consistent basis, owing to the pain in his hands.

Referee Greggains scored this round "even Jeffries a little," meaning that Jeffries had a shade the best of the round.

6th round

Jeff landed some hard left hooks and some rights to the body which caused Tom to clinch. Sharkey taunted Jeff by mimicking his swings.

Nevertheless, Jeff did the landing, striking left hooks and rights to the jaw. Sharkey ducked under some blows, rushed in and clinched. On the inside, Tom landed a left to the body. Greggains scored the round for Jeff.

7th round

There was some hot fighting at close range. Sharkey made a wild rush with left and right swings. Jeff backed away, but Tom was quickly on top of him. Tom swung his gloves continuously and in a fierce rush shoved Jeff half through the ropes, his head going under the upper rope. He came close to falling out, onto the floor. There were some heavy, spirited exchanges and clinches, but it was Sharkey's round. Greggains scored it for Tom.

8th round

They exchanged blows. Tom's arms whirled around wildly. When Sharkey raised his glove to acknowledge someone in the crowd calling to him, Jeff hit him with a clean left to the jaw. Although Tom was being hit, he was still lively and quite active. Referee Greggains scored this round for Sharkey.

9th round

Sharkey swung his left for the body and Jeffries nearly floored him with a stiff left. Jeff followed with another left and the crowd cheered as Sharkey ducked wildly. "Sharkey, although the recipient of many stiff punches, was jaunty in the eighth and ninth rounds." *The Examiner* felt that to this point, the fight was even. Greggains gave Jeffries this round.

10th round

Sharkey rushed in with wild swings and tried to push Jeff, but initially did not succeed. He landed a left, but received one in return. Undaunted, Tom kept up his rushing.

Sharkey "rushed Jeffries to the ropes time and again, smashing him around the shoulders and neck with lefts and rights. Jeffries tried in vain to beat him back with those terrible body blows, but Sharkey was not to be denied." There were many clinches and Tom had the better of it during the last exchange. Referee Greggains scored this round even.

11th round

Jeffries scored a knockdown, the first of the fight. "After some feinting Jeffries lands a heavy right on the jaw which sends Sharkey to his knees." Another version said Jeff led short with his left and followed with a right that hit Tom on the temple and knocked him under the ropes. Sharkey rose and Jeff landed rights to the body before Sharkey clinched. "This was clearly Jeffries' round." Greggains agreed.

12th round

Jeff rushed in with a straight, stiff left to the jaw. Tom seemed afraid of Jeff's lefts. However, Sharkey fought like a wildcat, and drew first blood with a left on the nose. Still, Greggains gave the round to Jeff.

13th and 14th rounds

During the 13th and 14th rounds, "Jeffries tried to mow the stalwart sailor down with sweeping lefts and rights." There was some fierce fighting as Jeff was trying for a knockout, landing some hard blows. Sharkey won the last half of the 14th, but it was still Jeff's round.

Greggains said that Jeff had a trifling advantage overall in the rounds prior to the 13th round. He scored the 13th even or "even Jeffries," meaning that he had a little the best of it, but said that Jeff won the 14th round.

The Chronicle said that from the 14th round on, Jeff had the advantage.

15th round

During this round, Sharkey "took a terrible drubbing." Jeff had landed a strong right to the ribs in every round, although Tom took it well. However, Jeff was starting to hurt him more in this round. A Jeffries right to the ear brought blood. Sharkey was game, but Jeff landed more. One account said that Sharkey was decidedly groggy at the end of this round. However, the pace was telling on both. Greggains said that Jeff did the most work in the round, and gave it to him.

16th round

Jeff stopped Sharkey's rushes with lefts to the face or rights to the body. He also landed a jolting left uppercut, but Sharkey kept coming. Jeff grew wilder with his punches. Greggains scored this round for Jeffries.

17th round

Jeff landed a hard right to the body, but when Sharkey swung a left, he caught Jeff in the face with his wrist, the blow making a cracking sound like a whip. Greggains scored this round even.

18th round

Jeffries did most of the scoring in the round, the right to the ribs doing the most effective work, but Sharkey continued rushing in. Greggains said Jeff did the most work, and he scored it for him.

19th round

Jeff landed heavy rights to the ribs, landing the harder blows in the round. Still, Sharkey held his own during the last two rounds, showing his gameness. Greggains gave this round to Jeffries as well.

20ᵗʰ round

Sharkey forced the pace, but Jeff responded with the cleaner blows. Still, he could not put Tom off balance. Tom landed one right between the eyes. They exchanged blow for blow, interspersed with clinching. Greggains gave this round and the fight to Jeffries.

The Chronicle said that the 14ᵗʰ to the 20ᵗʰ rounds "were marked by Jeffries' heavy swings. … In fact, from the fourteenth on Jeffries had it pretty much all his own way until the conclusion of the twentieth round, when Referee Greggains gave the decision to Jeffries."

Save for one even round, Greggains had essentially scored the 14ᵗʰ to the 20ᵗʰ rounds for Jeffries. Quite frankly, he scored most of the rounds for Jeffries, or even. He said that Jeff's marked superiority appeared from the 14ᵗʰ round and thereafter, although he had a slight advantage prior to that.

Neither Sharkey nor Jeffries showed many signs of having fought a long, hard battle. Sharkey only had a slight abrasion on the ear. Jeff had a slight black eye and swollen hands.

Explaining and justifying his decision, Referee Greggains said,

> Jeffries was the aggressor throughout and practically had the advantage all through…. The fact of the matter is that Jeffries was too heavy for him. In my opinion, Sharkey was very tired toward the end. Besides inflicting the most punishment, Jeffries scored the most points, and if he had followed up some of the advantages he gained after the eleventh round he would have won on a knockout blow.

The day after the fight, Greggains further said,

> I gave a decision in favor of Jeffries because I thought him justly entitled to it. The fact that there was many thousands bet in the poolrooms on Sharkey did not affect me in the least. Henry Quigg, my brother-in-law, and my sister had money on Sharkey, as also did my best friends, but this did not deter me. I kept tab during the progress of the fight, and when, at the end of the twentieth round, I summed up, I could not decide otherwise. …

> With the score before me and from my knowledge of the game, I thought there was only one man in the fight and his name was Jeffries. In my opinion Jeffries could have put Sharkey out had his hands been in good condition. He had him groggy two or three times and should have followed him up.[213]

After the fight, Jeff's thumbs were in poor condition, badly swollen and discolored. Jeffries said that during the fight, his hands caused him a great deal of pain, and as a result, he was unable to hit with much force, for every

---

213 *San Francisco Call*, May 8, 1898.

blow caused a twinge of pain to shoot through his arm, causing him to flinch. That was his explanation for why he did not punch even harder or try to finish Tom off. "I would have put Sharkey out if it were not that my hands were in such poor condition. During the fight I hurt them by hitting Sharkey on the head."

Jeff said that his hands were not well even going into the bout. "If my thumbs had not been injured I would have whipped him in nine or ten rounds. My thumbs have been in bad condition ever since I boxed with Van Buskirk." Jeffries had fought several times in the past year and had not had sufficient time to heal his hands. "I am going to rest until my hands get in shape again, as I can't hit with them." One writer confirmed that Jeff's hands were a bit swollen before the fight started.

Regardless of his hand problems, Jeff still felt that it was a relatively easy victory. He had punched Tom plenty of times and with the harder blows, even dropping him in the 11th round. "I did not find Sharkey as formidable an opponent as I was led to believe he would be. I think my fight with Choynski was much harder.... After the first two rounds I was certain that I was his master."

> At no stage of the game could he lick me. His blows did not faze me, and I told him at different times during the fight that he would lose if he did not do more fighting and less running away. This would anger him, and he said he would knock my roof out into the audience, and when he hit me he would say: 'How do you like that?' I joshed him throughout the fight, and it got him crazy. The only injury I received was when he butted me in the nose and eye. He blackened it, and it hurt me no more than his blows. I was not tired at the end of the fight, but was as fresh as a daisy.

Jeff was also quoted as saying, "Well, Sharkey's a foxy customer and a tough one. He is a game fighter and is a credit to his trainers. He couldn't hit me, though."

As usual, Sharkey and his friends thought that he had won. Sharkey called the decision a robbery and a conspiracy to cheat him, feeling that he had outpointed Jeff. He felt that the worst the referee should have done was call it a draw. "When Greggains gave Jeffries the decision I nearly dropped dead with surprise." He said that there was not a mark on him from Jeff's blows. "Sharkey, after the fight, abused the referee. In speaking about the mill the defeated man foolishly commented on the victor in a sneering way." He called Jeffries a dub. "I don't know of any heavyweight in the ring that he can lick." Sharkey further said,

> That - - Greggains did me nicely. His decision was the most barefaced rob I ever saw in my life. I fought a clean, straight fight, and punched the head off that big Jeffries, and he weighed thirty-five pounds more than me. Look at him and then look at me and see who go the worst

of it. ... I outpointed him all the way and should have had the decision. A draw would have been better than what I got, but I was entitled to the fight.

Jeffries can't hit, and he does not know how to guard at all. I was afraid the crowd would yell foul at me, so I changed my plan of going right at the man and finishing him up quick. I decided to go at him easy and punch him out slowly. I had him going in the last round. He couldn't hit me in that round. He landed his right, but didn't hurt at all. I had the whole face punched off him, and ought to have had the decision.

Justifying his more cautious, defensive, moving around style, attacking only in rushing spurts, Tom said, "I suppose if I had gone in and mixed things, the decision would have gone against me on a foul. I was surprised at the decision, as after the showing I made the worst I looked for was a draw."

Of course, Sharkey was one to claim that he was robbed in every fight that he had lost or drawn, and was given to great exaggeration. That said, some writers backed him, agreeing that the fight should have been a draw. It was odd that he would have approved of Alex Greggains as referee, given that Tom had previously fought Greggains to an 1896 8-round draw. Sharkey said that he would not fight again in San Francisco, and that he knew that he could not get a return match, for Jeff would be afraid to enter the ring with him again.

The broader discussions of the fight were actually more descriptive and useful towards obtaining an overall feel for the bout than were the round by round descriptions.

The Call said it was not a great battle from a scientific point of view, but it was exciting enough for the thousands who attended. It also said that the fight was not as interesting as most had expected, owing to the fact that Jeffries "put a quietus on the sailor lad whenever the latter attempted rushing and pushing tactics, for which style of fighting Sharkey has been noted." Jeff was able to neutralize Tom's usual roughhouse tactics and force him to fight in a different manner.

Early in the fight, the sailor was much quicker on his feet than Jeffries was, and managed to avoid punishment by ducking and clinching. However, late in the fight, Jeff stopped the ducking by sending in straight rights to the ribs.

Jeffries fought a very slow and careful fight, but he left his face unguarded and Sharkey found little difficulty in reaching it with straight blows, but the sailor wanted to land a swing, which blow Jeffries looked out for.

Jeffries invariably telegraphed his blows. Before hitting he would pull his arm back and Sharkey made ready to duck. The only hard blows that were landed were delivered at close range, and the sailor must have a sore left side this morning. Still, Jeffries received his share of punishment in the face. One or two blows that Sharkey landed on Jeffries' mouth and nose must have bothered its receiver.

The fight was not very interesting from the fact that both men resorted to round-arm blows and swings in the hope of scoring a knockout. There were very few straight blows landed. Jeffries should have whipped Sharkey in one or two rounds during the contest when the sailor was groggy from blows he received in the head.

Fitzsimmons can whip Jeffries easily, and will certainly do so if they ever meet.

Although Greggains gave the decision at the end of the twentieth round in favor of Jeffries, there were many of the spectators who said that a draw would have been proper.

Joe Corbett said that although the fight was a big disappointment to those who expected a knockout, it was as good a fight as had been witnessed in California for quite some time.

Both men fought very carefully during the early stages of the fight, apparently afraid to try the prowess of each other, Jeffries, however, landing body punches at intervals which hurt and finally won for him the decision. He forced the fighting from start to finish, following Sharkey from one side of the ring to the other, but was unable to land a knockout punch, owing to Sharkey's quickness and cleverness. He, however, kept trying, mixing it up whenever Sharkey was so disposed, his body punches having a terrible effect, especially in the last few rounds, when he devoted most of his time to that part of Sharkey's anatomy.

Jeffries' judgment of distance was very poor, as was Sharkey's, punch after punch cutting the air, but as Jeffries forced the fighting, landed oftener and did more damage, he deserved the decision, which was a just one.

Sharkey fought a good, clean fight. However, the *Call* said,

He was almost continually on the defensive, his rapid footwork and clever ducking saving him from many a hard punch. He tried hard and often to land a damaging punch, but Jeffries was too big and long. He made a game fight, however, yet should not complain as Jeffries outpunched him, having him on queer street three or four different times. Both men have much to learn in the way of science before they will be able to cope with such men as Corbett and Fitzsimmons.

The Evening Post said that Jeffries "now occupies the most prominent position in the pugilistic world." Although it applauded the decision, it called the bout one of the least interesting mills ever seen.

> There was no change in style of fighting from start to finish. The mill was not enlivened by any sensational rushes or hard hitting. Clean blows were scarce, decisive ones few and far between.

> So far as Sharkey is concerned the fight demonstrated that he is not to be dreaded by a man larger and stronger than himself, as is Jeffries. In the bout last night he started in the early part of the mill to hustle his opponent. With a smile Jeffries placed his hands on the sailor's shoulders, and, forcing him against the ropes, held him there. Sharkey was surprised at his helplessness, and did not attempt during the balance of the mill to resume his rough tactics.

> So far as effective work is concerned, the decision of the referee is to be commended. Jeffries landed continually while rounds went by in which the sailor failed to connect. Certainly during the mill he landed a few swings, but they were not put in on dangerous localities and were not hard enough to do material damage, even if they had struck on the chin or jaw.

Of the fight, the *Chronicle* said,

> Save for the title that was at stake and the bigness of the men the contest was not an interesting one. It lacked the dash and vim that the huge crowd wanted… It was a cautious, watchful fight, lacking signal displays of cleverness to compensate for its deficiency in whirlwind rush and savage encounter. … [I]n the main it was an unsatisfactory affair. There was a lack of heavy punching, Jeffries taking his honors by outpointing his opponent.

It had expected an all-out war terminating with a knockout. Instead, it was a stand-away fight, with little effective work done at close range. Of the decision, it said, "Jeffries' margin to the good in the aggregate of punches was not a wide one, and not a few of the crowd were prepared to see the despised Sharkey given a draw."

Apparently, both men were so strong that their common respect made it a somewhat cautious boxing affair. Plus, Jeff's hands were hurt. Owing to Jeff's size and strength, Sharkey did not use his usual boring-in tactics, but used leads, ducks and counters, as well as some outside defensive footwork. The few times that he used his old tactics, Jeff stopped and held him. Jim Jeffries had a way of making previously aggressive fighters take the defensive. Sharkey was given credit for putting up a clean fight for once.

Jeffries was credited with showing "marked improvement over his past performances." Furthermore, "Jeffries' victory was well earned, especially since he fought with a pair of sore hands. Before he entered the ring he displayed his swollen thumbs… He was ever on the alert to repel the attacks of the redoubtable sailor."

Still, there was criticism. "Jeffries towered over his opponent, and had advantage in every element that goes to make the fighter, yet he has much to learn of defense and footwork." *The Chronicle* further said that Jeff "still leaves himself open to attack, lacks accuracy in punching and does not seize opportunity."

Of the decision, the *San Francisco Examiner* said,

> It wasn't an overwhelming victory by any means. … [L]ast night's affair might have been called a draw without working injury to any one. It is true that if blow for blow were tallied, Jeffries had a credit balance in his favor. But when it was all over there was scarcely a mark to show for his blows. It was with the right hand at the body that he scored mainly. His dread left hook did not reach the mark once in every, possible ten times, and what baffled it was as marvelous an exhibition of avoidance on the sailor's part as was ever witnessed within the ropes. …

> Considering the gay and gallant contest the sailor put up, his clever footwork, his capacity for punishment and the unflinching manner in which he stood up against a man taller, heavier and apparently stronger than himself, the writer, had he been the referee, would have certainly called the contest a draw.

The day after the fight, the decision was further discussed. *The Call* said, "There are many who believe that the fight should have been declared a draw, but others agree with Referee Greggains, and say that Jeffries can whip Sharkey any mark of the road. … It is thought by the majority of sporting people that Greggains acted in the way he thought best, but many criticize his judgment."

The Bulletin reported that the general opinion was that Greggains should have declared the fight a draw. It too felt that a draw would have been more appropriate, but did not strongly criticize the decision.

> Although Tom Sharkey lost the battle last night he lost nothing of his reputation. ….. [T]he congress of sporting men…declare that a draw decision would have been more equitable. There is a respectable minority which agrees with Greggains, and admits a general prejudice against draw decisions, but the wise judgments pick weak spots in the referee's reasons as printed in the morning papers. It is true that Jeffries fought more aggressively than his opponent. … Jeffries weighed thirty-five pounds more than Sharkey and should be expected to do most of the attacking. It was good strategy for the lighter man to take the defensive. Therefore, it should not be counted against him that he did not adopt a line of action which would have been obviously injudicious. …

The merits of the fight consist of the conduct of the men in the ring and their condition at the conclusion of the battle. A referee's decision should be given solely on the merits. The man who takes on himself to say that Sharkey was more nearly played out than Jeffries at the end of round twenty, assumes to posses more than ordinary discernment. Greggains is quoted also as saying that Jeffries outpointed the smaller man. The reasoning is hardly sound, because the pugilists were not trying to make points.

In a fight such as that of last night, it is the worst judgment in the world to waste energy on harmless taps. Sharkey tried as he always does, to land blows which could do damage. ... Greggains made a mistake when he based his decision on his arithmetic, with courage.
...

It is not right, however, to censure Greggains. He decided according to his honest opinion, and gave reasons for his judgment. Had he done otherwise he would be dishonest. ...

Both men last night fought fairly and with courage. Sharkey showed considerable improvement in skill ... Through the twenty rounds he employed his head as a thinking machine and less as a battering ram, than has been his wont.

Jeffries fought well, but not so skillfully as Sharkey. He has not acquired sureness. His defense is awkward. His fists don't land where he tries to place them. But in each successive fight he shows such marked improvement that his chances of being some day champion of the world are not remote.[214]

On the other hand, the *Evening Post* was quite strong in its subsequent support of the referee's decision. It saw the fight the way the referee and Jeffries did.

The fact of the matter is that Jeffries would have been robbed had any other decision been given. He clearly outpointed and outfought Sharkey at every turn, and, judging by the battle as far as it went, there appears no doubt that the Los Angeles man would have won had the event been prolonged to a finish.

In boxing the first requisite in a champion is the power to administer punishment of a decisive, clear kind. That essential Sharkey lacks. He has a few swinging blows at his command, but he does not possess the knack of landing a clean, hard and effective straight lead. For that reason his friends must conclude after Friday night's battle that he is not a championship possibility. ...

---

214 *San Francisco Bulletin*, May 8, 1898.

So far as cleverness is concerned, the sailor is qualified to go against anybody, but in his battles he has demonstrated that he has nothing like the dash and confidence when meeting a big, strong fellow like Jeffries, as when he has a man like Choynski for an opponent. One man he can hustle, but the other on account of superior strength he respects and seeks to win by dodging and prancing what he would avoid from the weaker man by rushing and rough tactics.

Sharkey claims that he failed to pick Jeffries up and throw him through the ropes on the ground that he wanted to show the spectators that he is a fair fighter. Such a proposition is humorous. He did not resort to his usual rough and tumble style of battle for the very reason that he and not the other fellow would have been apt to have taken a flying trip to the spectators. He tried Jeffries and found that the latter could toss him about with ease. The experiment satisfied Sharkey that he would have to make a clever battle at long range in order to win, but even at that style he was outfought and easily defeated.[215]

The next day, the *Evening Post* said that Sharkey's attempt to break into the Corbett-Fitzsimmons argument caused a smile to pass over the faces of those who saw Fitz knock him out, and who "witnessed the decisive fashion in which Jeffries made a punching bag of him."

On the East coast, the reports were more favorable for Jeffries and the fight. *The National Police Gazette* wrote, "The fight was a lively one from beginning to end, and during the entire twenty rounds the action was incessant." Of Jeffries, it said,

He is a natural fighter, unusually quick and shifty on his feet for a man of such ponderous proportions. He is a two-handed fighter, using right or left with equal facility, and possesses what few pugilists can boast of, good temper and cool, calm and collected judgment…. In the fight with Sharkey, every time the latter came at him with one of his wild rushes he either waited with deliberate coolness, prepared to block, cross or counter, or stepped nimbly out of the way to avoid the impact…. The result of the fight was a foregone conclusion after the third round, when it became apparent that Sharkey's rough, rushing style of fighting had no effect upon the human stone wall which controlled him.[216]

There were some conflicting reports regarding how much money was generated from ticket sales. Some reported $15,000, but the *Post* did not believe it, as $10,000 had already been taken in the night before the fight. On the night before Sharkey-Fitzsimmons, $9,000 in tickets had been sold,

---

215 *San Francisco Evening Post*, May 9, 1898.
216 *National Police Gazette*, April 1, 1899.

but after it was over, it was learned that $30,000 had been collected in admission fees. Therefore, it believed that the Jeff-Shark fight had grossed much more than what had been represented. "Surely on Friday night last as large a crowd was in attendance as has ever gathered at a fight in this city. The question naturally arises as to what became of the gate money." The fighters were to receive their share of a percentage of the gate. Thus, representing the gate as smaller than it was would enable the club to retain more money. Remember, the National Club was associated with the Fitz-Sharkey fix, so its integrity was questionable.[217]

The Bulletin reported that the split of 75%/25% of the fighters' share of the proceeds yielded a payment of $7,300 to Jeffries and $2,400 to Sharkey. If $9,700 was the fighters' share, which was 65% of the ticket sales, then the total ticket sales which the club was claiming were a little over $14,900, which was questionable.[218]

Jeffries returned to his home in Los Angeles. "The new champion injured his hands in the battle with the sailor and declares that he will now rest until the weapons return to their natural form. As he has gathered in a number of good purses of late, it is hardly likely that he will suffer from a shortage of cash during his outing."[219]

The victory over Sharkey made Jeffries a top contender for the real title. In his autobiography, Jeff said, "It was hard to realize that, in two brief years, I had battled my way from an obscure sparring partner without experience to challenger of the champion. There was never a doubt in my mind, but that I could beat Fitzsimmons, if I could get him to fight me."[220]

Tom Sharkey would continue to prove his merit as a top contender. On June 29, 1898 in Brooklyn, New York, a 177-pound Sharkey (who looked 10 pounds bigger) scored a 1st round knockout over 190-pound Gus Ruhlin, the man who had fought Jeff to a 20-round draw. Ruhlin had previously lost a 20-round decision to Kid McCoy, in late May. Of course, Sharkey's subsequent success only made Jeff's victory over him more noteworthy.[221]

217 *San Francisco Evening Post*, May 10, 1898.
218 *San Francisco Bulletin*, May 9, 1898.
219 *San Francisco Evening Post*, May 11, 1898.
220 *Two Fisted Jeff* at 93-94.
221 In the Sharkey fight, Ruhlin mixed it up with Tom. After Gus ducked a swinging left, Sharkey knocked him out cold with a terrific right at 2 minutes and 17 seconds of the 1st round. *Brooklyn Daily Eagle*, June 30, 1898.

CHAPTER 13

The Cost of High Expectations

James Jeffries wanted his name in the mix as someone whom Bob Fitzsimmons should fight. However, few Easterners had ever seen him in action. Therefore, Bill Delaney thought that he could stir up further interest in Jeff by matching him to fight both Bob Armstrong and Steve O'Donnell 10 rounds each *on the same night* on August 5, 1898 at New York's Lenox Athletic Club. Jeff was not only expected to defeat both, but to knock them out. Only problem was that both of these guys could really fight, and were experienced at the game. Delaney's wild offer was great for generating publicity, but would be difficult in actual execution.[222]

Jeffries trained for his upcoming bouts at Boehm's Beach, near New Dorp, Staten Island, New York.

Ex-champion James J. Corbett was in training at Asbury Park, New Jersey for his upcoming fight with the very skilled Kid McCoy, who had recently won a 20-round decision over Gus Ruhlin. Perhaps seeing all of the attention that Jeffries was receiving, particularly after defeating Tom Sharkey, Corbett said that he wanted to fight Jeff after the McCoy fight. Corbett manager George Considine said that Jeffries was entitled to greater consideration than Sharkey, and that "Fitzsimmons has acted like a man fighting for show and time instead of for money."[223]

Bob Fitzsimmons had been catching heat, taking what he called "silly abuse and petty snarlings" by those who felt that he should defend the title. Fitz noted that the "would be sports" were alleging that five men were more entitled to the championship than he was – Jeffries, McCoy, Sharkey, Corbett, and Maher. "The very fact that I have met and defeated the three last named proves that their unscrupulous mouthings are as false as they are ridiculous." Upset by "the abuse that these soreheads continually heap upon me," on August 1, 1898, Fitzsimmons issued a statement saying that these five men should fight each other to determine the best man, and that he would fight the winner.

However, Fitz also said that since he had already defeated Corbett, Sharkey, and Maher, and because Corbett was already matched to face McCoy, if Jeffries wanted, he would fight him. Bob posted $2,500 for a fight before October 1. "Jeffries is the only man that I have not defeated who is at liberty, and for his benefit I will say once more that, providing he

---

222 *Two Fisted Jeff* at 93-94. The 1896 Horton Law had legalized boxing in New York State.
223 *New York World*, July 28, 1898.

is agreeable and that the details can be arranged so that the fight will take place before Oct. 1, I will accommodate him." Bob's manager Martin Julian noted that Jeff was a "reputed world-beater," and had defeated Sharkey, so Fitz wanted to fight him. Of course, Jeff was already scheduled to fight within a week.

Jim Corbett said that after defeating McCoy, if Fitz did not accept his challenge, he would take on and defeat Jeffries, after which Fitzsimmons would not be able to decline meeting him. Criticizing Bob, Corbett said,

> With strange and suggestive insincerity he points to Jeffries as the only man that can fill the bill, choosing to forget that I used to whip Jeffries every morning before breakfast at Carson City. If this red-headed fakir really wants to meet the best man in the world why doesn't he fight me? He knows I can whip Jeffries, and this challenge business is merely another big bluff to deceive the people and make them believe he is not really a coward. ... If Fitzsimmons really wants to fight the best man in the world let me fight Jeffries, and then Fitz may fight the winner.

Both Corbett and Sharkey were talking badly about Jeffries, which perhaps showed that he had arrived as a legitimate contender who stood in their way to obtaining a championship match. Bill Delaney sarcastically said, "Sharkey claims he was robbed...in his contest with Jeffries; Corbett states...that he used to whip Jeffries every morning... I would like to give the New York public a chance to see how Sharkey was robbed, and also how easy it will be for Corbett to whip Jeffries." Delaney said that he had deposited $1,000 as a guarantee of good faith for a match with either man. "I think Fitz's challenge to Jeff was made in good faith, but for the present he will give him the go by for either or both of those great pugilists (?) Sharkey and Corbett." This kind of back and forth bravado was commonplace in generating publicity for fighters.[224]

By the day of the Armstrong/O'Donnell bouts, Delaney had signed articles of agreement for Jeff to fight Corbett next. Tom O'Rourke of the Lenox Athletic Club said, "There is some doubt as to whether Jeffries is really a better man than Corbett, owing to the fact that the latter has repeatedly said that he used to whip Jeffries most every day."[225]

But first, Jeffries had a tall order to fill. *The New York Journal* said that Jeffries was going to attempt something new to pugilism – defeat two men in the same night, with a half hour's rest in between bouts. Sure, others had done it, but what distinguished Jeff's scheduled feat was that the bouts were each scheduled for 10 rounds, not 4 rounds, and his opponents were of high quality, not local dubs who knew nothing and were out of shape.

---

224 *New York World*, August 2-4, 1898.
225 *New York Sun*, August 5, 1898.

Jeffries has the heart of a lion and the head of a general. ... He believes he will some day be the heavy weight champion of the whole wide world, and he is doing everything he can to demonstrate that he has a right to fight for that title right now. He has come from practically nowhere in the pugilistic world in less than two years. Never has he been defeated or had a decision rendered against him, and he has gone up against some pretty hard propositions. ... This is his first appearance in the East and he starts in by doing something which will show his metal, to say the least. ... [A] few real, wise people who have seen all three men perform at different times and places declare that Jeffries has undertaken an awful task and one which he has no right to undertake. ... This Jeffries is a fighting fighter, and a whole lot better one than most people think.

Steve O'Donnell was very experienced, had fought a number of good fighters, and was a former Corbett sparring partner.

Chicago's Bob Armstrong "is a strong, burly negro, who for a time was thought good enough to fight with anybody. His fault, if he has one particular one, beyond lacking cleverness, is that he hits too hard. ... One thing is certain – he can hit an awful punch with either hand." Armstrong was a big man, taller than Jeffries and with a longer reach, strong as they grow, "and those colored boys grow pretty strong sometimes," and quite willing.

He is a rusher, a swinger, a taker of long, long chances with a perfect disregard for the crowd, the man's reputation before him and what happens. He is going in the ring to land that left a few times and that awful right just once. ... He is not bothered with knowing any too much about the technique of boxing. He knows more about walloping and rushing and chopping. He has knocked a few people cold and senseless with that system, and he believes in it.[226]

In fact, most historians do not realize what a serious test and threat Armstrong was to Jeffries. The big, strong and experienced Armstrong had sparred and exhibited with both Joe Choynski and Tom Sharkey. In November 1895, Armstrong scored a KO10 over the hard-punching Frank Slavin, who at one time had been one of the top three contenders in the world. In a November 1896 rematch, the then 185-pound Armstrong scored a KO4 over the 178-pound Slavin. Against Slavin, Armstrong was described as young and vigorous, standing 6'3" tall, "put together like a giant" and "quick, shifty and clever, and the hard punching he took in the first two rounds bore eloquent testimony of his ability to stand the gaff." Others said Armstrong stood 6'4", and from various photographs, this appears to be accurate.

226 *New York Evening Journal*, August 4, 1898.

In December 1896 in New York, Armstrong scored a KO19 over Charlie Strong, a fellow colored fighter. The well-conditioned Armstrong showed that he could land often and gradually break down an opponent.

In 1897, Armstrong scored a KO6 over Joe Butler, but lost a 6-round decision to Frank Childs, both of whom were fellow black fighters. An 1897 *San Francisco Examiner* article discussing who would succeed Fitzsimmons mentioned Armstrong as a possible contender. "Then there is the big negro, Bob Armstrong of Chicago. He is making his way to the front by slow stages, and the only reason advanced for his failure to pit himself against good men is that the good men won't meet him."

In January 1898, Frank Childs knocked out Armstrong in 2 rounds. However, Armstrong claimed to have thrown the fight. Subsequent significant 1898 bouts included: KO5 Yank Kenny, W/D10 Ed Dunkhorst, KO3 Joe Butler, and W6 Tom "Stockings" Conroy.[227]

Although Armstrong was likely to "give him a roughing game of a rare and startling order," Jeffries was still expected to take care of both him and O'Donnell.

> [Jeffries] is not only strong and big, but fast. His feet are as nimble as a light weight's, and he has learned to use them to advantage. He is clear headed, cool and fearless. His temper, one of the things which often causes a new man to make mistakes, is as sweet as a nun's. He takes an unexpected jab without growing hasty or getting rattled. If he has the worst of a round it does nothing but steady him. He has the temperament to make a champion.
>
> So far as hitting goes, the pipe can produce no more beautiful dreams than Jeffries. He is a strong man whose one effort since he began to box has been to learn to hit accurately and hard. He has strength to burn, and he has learned how to exert it. The left hand, which wins more fights than the other, ten to one, has been educated. ...
>
> Of course he has not the brilliancy of Corbett, but he hits accurately and handily. His right was good from the start, in a rough, uncertain way, but Jeffries has worked at it in spite of that. ... In clinches and infighting, it is perhaps enough to state that Sharkey broke away from Jeffries time and time again. The boilermaker is a hard man to hurt, and that is, after all, quite a part of a man's ability to mix.[228]

However, another local paper noted the difficult task that Jeff had undertaken.

> Many men well qualified to judge such matters think that Jeffries has undertaken a work that he will find it difficult to finish. ... Armstrong is a big Chicago negro, standing over six feet tall, as strong as a horse, and he deals in right and left swings that have terrific force. He pays little attention to the science of the game and is willing to take any kind of punishment in order to land his right. ... "Parson" Davies, who manages Armstrong, offers to bet $200 to $500 that his man will stay the entire ten rounds.[229]

---

227 *New York Herald*, June 28, 1895; *National Police Gazette*, December 5, 1896; *San Francisco Call*, November 24, 1896. *Rocky Mountain News*, December 22, 1896; *New York Clipper*, December 26, 1896; *San Francisco Examiner*, June 20, 1897; *San Francisco Evening Post*, February 5, 1898; Boxrec.com. There are unconfirmed claims that Pete Everett scored a KO5 over Armstrong in July 1898. In December 1898, Armstrong would score a KO14 victory over Everett. There is also an unconfirmed claim that Frank Childs scored an 1898 KO10 over Armstrong. Cyberboxingzone.com; Boxrec.com.
228 *New York Journal*, August 5, 1898.
229 *New York World*, August 5, 1898.

Just three months after his bout with Sharkey, on August 5, 1898 at New York's Lenox Athletic Club, the bold Jeffries undertook to knock out two men in one night, with a half-hour rest between each bout. Jeffries was first going to take on Bob Armstrong, and was then to fight Steve O'Donnell.

At 8:30 p.m., even for the preliminary, the towering bleachers were jammed with about 4,000 enthusiasts who had paid $1 or more to see the fun.[230]

Once again, that evening, a number of critics opined that Armstrong would prove to be a pretty tough customer, and if he was in any kind of good trim, Jeffries would have a tough time stopping him. "Armstrong has always been looked upon as a muscular marvel, a hard hitter, but slow and almost elephantine in his movements." Still, his manager assured everyone that he was in great shape and would last the distance.

Armstrong entered the ring at 9:45 p.m. to faint applause. He looked to be in first-class condition, as "black and muscular-looking as ever." Bob allegedly weighed 187 pounds, but looked bigger. He was 24 years old, one month shy of his 25th birthday. He stood "almost two inches taller" than Jeffries and had a longer reach.

When Jeff came into view, there was a cheer of great magnitude. "He weighed 212 pounds, it was said, and his appearance excited favorable comment on all sides. Massively built in limbs and body, with a broad, hairy chest, dark skin, and heavy muscles, he looked bigger and more powerful than did John L. Sullivan in his palmiest days." Another said that Jeff was built like a Hercules. "He is big everywhere... His weight was announced as 212 pounds, and he looked every ounce of it." Although the 23-year-old Jeffries was listed as weighing 212 or 213 pounds, much later reports claimed that Jeff was closer to 230 pounds. He was "truly a mountain of flesh, swarthy and muscled and so big and broad that with 6 feet 1 inch he looked stocky. A sight of him was enough to terrify an ordinary individual." Bill Delaney, Marty McCue, G. Martin and Dick Toner all handled Jeff.

The boxers agreed to spar until ordered to break.[231]

1st round

Jeff feinted wickedly with an odd left hook, and side-stepped handily. Armstrong gave him plenty of room, moving around, being cautious. "Jeffries carries his hands well and hits very fast with them. The right is well back and the left is always way off to the left, feinting a hook." Jeff tried to get him to lead, but Bob kept away. Jeff smiled and followed.

---

230 Jack Root of Chicago, a promising young middleweight, scored a 2nd round knockout over Jim Watts, a colored fighter from Louisville. Root would years later fight for the heavyweight crown.
231 The fight description and analysis is taken from the *New York Herald, New York Sun, New York World, New York Journal, Brooklyn Daily Eagle, New York Times*, August 6, 1898.

Jeffries occasionally charged in on the dancing Armstrong with some rights and left hooks to the head and body. When close, Jeff landed some solid left uppercuts.

Although defensive-minded, Armstrong fought back, landing some jabs and counter rights of his own. Jeff laughed at him and kept swinging. Bob used his legs well in order to get away from most of his powerful opponent's blows. *The New York Journal* criticized, "The round was slow and far from promising. Jeffries, though fairly shifty, seemed to be badly mixed on distance, and feinted without any definite idea of what came next."

After the fight, it was revealed that Jeffries had broken his left thumb during the 1st round. "After this his left blows appeared to be more smacks than punches and he waited always for a chance to use his right." Nevertheless, Jeffries kept throwing with his left, despite the fact that it hurt. But he could not punch as hard or as often with it as he otherwise would have done.

2nd round

When Jeff came up to begin the round, his right eye was red. Armstrong was on the defensive from the start, but was the first to land, getting in a quick jab to the eye and a light right to the cheek. He made a good showing with his left jab, landing several without return during the round. Jeff would feint and slide into range, but receive a jab to the jaw before Bob would move away. When hit, Jeff would smile and start his approach again. *The Journal* again criticized, "Jeffries worked about as if trying to figure something. This is one of his oddities. He appears to be undecided at times just what he should do. ... He begins over often. Oh, but he has a bookful to learn!"

Although Jeff appeared to have strength and hitting power, throwing his blows quick as a flash, his footwork lacked speed. Bob kept out of reach with good movement, which received applause. Jeffries made some vicious and occasionally wild swings and lunges to the head and body, but did no substantial harm. Despite his movement, Bob was not entirely averse to occasionally mixing it up. "The negro handled himself very well indeed."

3rd round

Jeffries was very aggressive, quickly starting operations. He landed an awful left hook to the face. "It was a tough one and its effect lasted the full three minutes." He missed a couple follow-up lefts, but a third left brought blood from Armstrong's nose. Jeff landed a left jab to the mouth and followed it with a left to the stomach.

An angered Armstrong retaliated, landing lightly with a left on the jaw. "Both men worked like demons and neither had an advantage for at least a minute." Jeff could not land very much to the head, but successfully hit the body. Armstrong retaliated with both hands to the face. He appeared to want to mix things, but when Jeff ducked low, Bob did not try to land.

In a mix-up, Armstrong claimed that Jeff had hit him low, but the referee did not acknowledge the claim. Bob continued fighting, landing lefts to counter Jeff's powerful rushes of terribly hard punches. Bob landed three lefts to the face and escaped a return. Jeff rushed furiously, but Bob stopped him with a jab and showed confidence in his ability to cope. Jeff sailed in, but Bob blocked and broke away, moving about. Jeff kept after him and landed the left as Bob ducked.

Armstrong led with a left, but Jeff countered with a right cross to the jaw that sent him flying across the ring. "Armstrong was staggered, but hugged and then kept away till the bell." Bob admirably stood the gaff.

4th round

They mixed it up and clinched. Armstrong used some roughing tactics. However, Jeff's bulk served him well, and Bob soon tired. Jeff landed a hard left on the body and a right over the heart that distressed Armstrong. Jeffries was doing the most damage, particularly with his right to the body, using it steadily with effect.

Armstrong did not use his right very often, for fear of the return. Instead, he jabbed and sprinted about. Bob landed hard left jabs to the nose that rocked Jeff's head. The crowd cheered, and Jeff responded with a bull-like rush, hitting the body a couple times. Armstrong was growing more confident, and attempted a rush of his own. However, by attacking, Bob "laid himself open to some tremendous swings, which, when they were reduced to half arm punches in a partial clinch, were surely hurtful."

Jeff forced matters a little, but landed no telling blows on the defensive Armstrong. At the bell, Bob went to his corner still in good trim. Some felt that Jeff seemed a bit worried, perhaps concerned that he had a tough customer whom he was not going to be able to stop within 10 rounds.

5th round

They started cautiously, but after thirty seconds of sparring, Jeff landed a good left on the ribs, then another above the right eye, and followed it up with a right on the ribs. Jeff kept rushing and landed his right to the heart. Bob landed a left on the eye and blocked a couple sledge-hammer swings. "The negro was not tired nor injured in the least up to this time, and was just as active as Jeffries. The double-header business looked rather blue."

Jeff was getting desperate to knock him out, and grunted audibly when punching. However, Bob was clever enough to counter savagely each time, and once drove Jeff to the ropes. Still, Jeffries frequently laughed after Armstrong's blows landed, and he continued trying to knock Bob out. A left brought blood from Armstrong's nose. A swift chopping left cut Armstrong's right eye open. Jeff went at him like a tiger, but Bob never faltered, doing some good ducking, which brought cheers from the crowd.

One report said that Jeff eventually landed a left uppercut that dazed Armstrong. He again rocked Bob with left and right swings and had him going rapidly as the bell rang. Another writer opined that Jeff was slowly wearing him down.

6th round

Jeffries waited for Armstrong to come in. Bob picked up the pace, but Jeff hit him twice with lefts to the jaw. Jeff followed with a rush that sent Bob bounding off the ropes. Jeff smashed the face and body. One said, "Jeffries rushed again and this time Bob slipped down." Another said, "Armstrong slipped under the ropes in trying to get away from a left aimed at the jaw." Although Bob was not groggy, he was puzzled, "probably because he found that Jeffries was stronger every minute."

Jeff followed up and tried for a knockout with a storm of swings to the head, but in doing so, got staggered by several desperate punches that Bob landed, in particular a very hard left in the stomach and a counter right. This deterred Jeff's aggression for a while. They were sparring vigorously at the bell.

7th round

Both were cautious at the start. When Jeff went in, Bob clinched. Jeff landed a left in the stomach that made Armstrong grunt. Bob retreated with his good footwork. Jeff was not quick in following, which allowed Armstrong to recover.

Bob jabbed and backed away until Jeff rushed in and landed heavy body blows with both hands. Jeff followed up with a left above the right eye which re-opened the cut and drew blood. Using his left, Jeffries stopped an Armstrong rush. It was clearly Jeff's round. He landed the greater number of blows as well as the most effective blows.

8th round

In this round, Armstrong tried to keep away, running and moving about, jabbing and trying to fight Jeff off. Jeffries followed him around the ring, and made several vicious attempts to put him to sleep. Jeff was trying to knock him out, while Armstrong was trying to last the limit. Jeff smiled faintly at Bob when he used his legs to get away. A smash to the eye drew blood from Armstrong again. Jeffries also landed his right to the ribs.

The last minute of the round was slow. Jeff was possibly getting tired, although he later claimed that he was pacing himself for the second fight. One reporter called him "slower than molasses in the winter time." There was some hissing as they took their seats. Still, reporters agreed that Jeff outpointed him easily.

9th round

Jeffries started off as if he was tired, for he was slow to attack, although he was possibly trying to get Armstrong to come to him so that he could counter. Jeff eluded a hard left but missed a counter. Bob was wary, so Jeff eventually had to rush him. Jeffries tried to end the fight with rights to the head and body. He landed some powerful body blows and a couple punches to the face, but Bob was only temporarily jarred. Jeff was very slow in the last half of the round, missing many chances to seize openings, as he was visibly puffing for wind. The round was overall fairly mild, with honors in Jeff's favor.

10th round

Jeffries began dancing around "clumsily," and Armstrong landed his left to the nose, rushed Jeff to the ropes, and swung a right to the jaw. In a mix-up, Armstrong landed a left on the ribs and followed it up with a left on the jaw. An angered Jeffries rushed viciously and swung blindly. He threw hard rights to the body and head.

Each local New York source gave a different version of what happened next. Some gave the impression that Jeff dropped Armstrong. Others said that Bob fell in ducking a blow. Still others felt that Jeff pushed him over. *The Herald* said Jeff threw a right, and then, in avoiding that blow, "Armstrong collided with Jim's left and fell. He arose quickly and then used the greater part of his time in sprinting out of range." *The Journal* said Jeff knocked him down with a short left hook, but it was too high to do harm. *The World* said Armstrong "fell in getting away from a left swing by Jeffries." *The Sun* said that in a half clinch Jeff pushed Bob down. Armstrong rose and laughed, and the crowd cheered him. *The Brooklyn Daily Eagle* said, "Armstrong rushed and tripped and Jeffries pushed him over, the negro taking the limit to rise from his knees."

Jeffries acted as if he had hurt Armstrong, because when Bob rose, Jeff attacked furiously, and smashed him with a right and left on the jaw. Jeff followed up with numerous punches and rushed Bob to his corner. The shock of the blows almost sent Armstrong out of the ring. "Jeffries got to close quarters and almost did the trick with a right on the jaw. It was such a painful blow that Armstrong deliberately ran away from two rushes that followed." Jeff chased him and landed three "piledrivers" to the head. Armstrong retreated. When Jeff got close again, Bob ducked way down, and Jeff was landing on his back when the bell rang.

Referee Charlie White awarded Jeffries the decision. *The Journal* said, "The decision in Jeffries's favor was the only thing possible." *The Sun* said, "The referee decided that Jeffries had won on work and points, and when this was announced there were cheers and some hisses." For lasting the 10 rounds, Armstrong left the ring to an ovation. He went over to Corbett and whispered something in his ear.

Jeffries went to his dressing room for the half-hour break between bouts. However, despite his desire and intention to do so, Jeff did not meet O'Donnell, because his left thumb had been broken. "The club's doctor ordered Jeffries not to go on, although the latter insisted upon having cocaine injected in the injured hand with the idea that he might be able to continue." 4,000 fans waited impatiently, and were not in good humor when eventually told that there would not be any more fighting.

> There was a delay and then Jeffries got into the ring with Delaney and a doctor, Charles F. Fivey. It was announced that the Californian had injured his left hand in the bout with Armstrong and, though anxious to meet O'Donnell, who was present and ready to fight, his physician would not permit it. The doctor explained to the newspaper men that Jeffries' thumb had been shattered, and the big fellow showed his hand as evidence. It was swollen. The announcement was received unfavorably, and the crowd yelled for fight. O'Donnell was cheered until he disappeared. The spectators, still retaining their seats, howled in derision. The managers explained the matter over again, and that was the end of it. The crowd got up and slowly poured out into the streets, hooting and catcalling.

Jeffries said that he was sorry and disappointed that he was not able to go on with the second bout.

> In the first round of the bout with Armstrong I shattered a bone in my hand. I felt it give way and was unable to use my left to advantage after that. I could have put Armstrong out, but kept in mind the fact that there was another man to face, so I did not exert myself. I fully expected to go on with O'Donnell, but the orders of the club physician, R. E. Fivey, were positive. I was not in the least apprehensive about myself during the bout. The probability is that it will be impossible to fight for some time, but just as soon as I recover sufficiently I will be in the ring again willing to meet anybody.

In another interview, Jeff said that the break resulted from the very first blow that he landed on Bob's head, and after that, he was unable to close his fist. He was nevertheless still willing to meet O'Donnell, but Delaney and the doctor prevented him from doing so.

Bob Armstrong said,

> Jim Jeffries can hit as hard as any man I ever stood before, and I think a little harder. His left-hand blow isn't delivered with the fist. As a rule he lands with his forearm and lands hard. He hits a hard body blow with his right, but I found it easy to ward off. He hurt my left arm early in the fight, and after that I could not use it with good effect. A right-hand uppercut landed rather low in the second round and distressed me considerably. But I know Jeffries didn't mean it.

Armstrong advised Jeffries not to fight the top men (Corbett and Sharkey) for a while, feeling that they would make him regret it.

Although the press agreed that Jeffries had defeated Armstrong, and there were some positives for Jeff, the majority of the post-fight reports were critical of him. They had expected much more from Jeffries. In fact, the local New York press was pretty hard on him, perhaps unfairly.

The Herald said that Armstrong "fought surprisingly well, and although Jeffries got the decision the colored man made a good showing. Jeffries was clumsy and painfully slow, and the general opinion expressed by the old fighters present…was that he would prove an easy mark for Fitzsimmons, McCoy and Corbett."

The Sun said, "Jeffries was slow, awkward and apparently too heavy to do quick execution. He fought with an injured hand, it is true, but as Armstrong was never a first-rater, the big fellow's showing was a bitter disappointment."

> The sporting men…were united in declaring that Jeffries was anything but the wonder he had been heralded. That he is a wonderfully strong man physically cannot be denied, but it is also a fact that there are many things about the game which he does not know. In the first place he is slow on his feet and to see and take advantage of openings, and he does not possess a scientific left hand. He can swing either hand with terrific power, and to a man who does not possess ability to get out of the way he will undoubtedly administer a terrible beating. But Armstrong, who has always been slow on his feet and a second rater in other respects, made a creditable showing and at no time in the ten rounds did Jeffries have him in serious trouble.

> It is conceded that in a finish contest Jeffries would be dangerous for most of the big fighters to tackle because of his wonderful physique and ability to hit with terrific force at almost any stage. Against Fitzsimmons or Corbett it is the general belief that Jeffries would have a hard time to put up a winning fight, chiefly for the reason that he would be outclassed by Fitzsimmons in both science and hitting and by Corbett in science and generalship. As several sports put it: "Fitz or Corbett would cut him into ribbons and would escape without marks. Jeffries could not reach them, because of his awkwardness and clumsy attack." … "If Jeffries is the most scientific heavyweight on the coast," the sports said last night, "then science must be at a low ebb. He is a big giant, who can beat a lot of men with brute force, but against a clever, shifty boxer, who knows how to inflict punishment and at the same time keep out of harm's way, he would be outclassed."

The Brooklyn Daily Eagle was much harsher in its critique of Jeffries. It literally called him a "failure" in its headline and said that he was not a championship possibility. It said that Jeff was far from clever and could not hit with the power that his body size promised. "Jeffries had only a few shades the better of it."

That said, it agreed that Jeff's hand was badly swollen and discolored, that after the 1st round his left-handed blows had lost their power, were thrown in smacking fashion, were used less often, and that Jeff mostly tried to set up for and use his right, which most often landed to the body.

The Eagle complimented Armstrong for putting up a good battle. Bob's agility, quickness, and footwork were first class, as was his two-handed blocking. What blows to the body and head Jeff did land; Armstrong took them well. He successfully blocked and countered Jeff's vicious rushes and swings, and often took the aggressive himself, doing most of the leading even when he was backing away. Jeff "had a wholesome regard for the negro's fists at all times." Armstrong's one bad habit was ducking too low.

The Times said that because of his injury, Jeff was unable to fulfill his self-imposed task of knocking out two men. Armstrong surprised everyone by giving a performance that was "sufficiently interesting to keep Jeffries guessing."

> The Californian, in short, proved a disappointment to his friends, and, while he landed several good body and face blows on Armstrong, he was slow and clumsy, and received not a little punishment in return. At the end of the stated tenth round, Armstrong was far from being knocked out. … Some of the spectators say that if Armstrong had been properly handled he would have defeated Jeffries.

The World had more positives mixed in with its criticisms. Jeff claimed to have shattered his thumb in the 1st round, "and two physicians declared that he told the truth." Despite being crippled, Jeff punished Armstrong in an entertaining affair. Jeffries had proven that he could win even when handicapped and in pain, something not every fighter could do.

Still, after his showing against Armstrong, many believed that O'Donnell would have bested him, because Jeff was tired.

> At the outset it was apparent that Jeffries had the better of Armstrong, but the superiority was by no means as great as the champions of the big fellow had claimed it would be. The negro was lively and alert, though always on the defensive. Jeffries was aggressive enough, but was as slow as a cart horse. He landed frequently; but never did he have his man anywhere near out.

> Once the negro got in a punch in the stomach that looked like a finisher, but Jeffries kept away from him for a few seconds, and the gong saved him. As a matter of fact, Armstrong was a harder proposition than Jeffries ever dreamed he would be, and even though Jim won; he was in no condition for O'Donnell within a half hour after the finish. That is the way it looked to the crowd. The broken thumb was a good thing for Jeffries.

The Journal said that the build-up and reputation that Jeffries had to live up to was "nothing short of colossal." Despite his swinging, jolting, jabbing, chasing and cornering, and trying all he knew, he was not able to take Armstrong out, which was a disappointment. Everyone had expected a knockout.

However, Jeff had a very bad hand, crippling his chances. It complimented Jeff for completing the 10 rounds with such an injury. The hand swelled and he was unable to close it. If he had gone on with O'Donnell, "he would have been showing bad judgment."

Its assessment of Jeffries said,

> It is hard to class Jeffries. He was up against a man who knew two or three things about staying in the ring. Armstrong's punches seemed to have no effect at all. Jeffries just wallowed along and took everything going, for a chance to get back. He puffed considerable, but at no time did he appear distressed. It would be hard to say what he would do to a man who would come and fight him. He can hit with both hands, and it is likely any one who faces his right will find something. He is not fast, nor never will be, nor does he show the least shadow of generalship. Twice, at least, he should have put Armstrong out. He waits, and one gets nothing by waiting when a man is going. He is a man with whom second-raters can fight draws, but who, because of his ability to stand punishment, it will take a first-class man to beat.

This writer believed that Jeff would not defeat Fitz, Corbett, or McCoy, but granted that he was still young yet and could improve.

The later, more positive *New York Clipper* report said, "Armstrong managed to stay the limit, but he was floored in the final round, and had so much the worst of the bout that the award of the referee was in Jeffries' favor." *The New York Daily Tribune* echoed that Armstrong "took a great deal of punishment." That said, the *Clipper* also noted that Armstrong gave Jeff "pretty nearly as much work as he wanted to do."[232]

Jim Corbett, who saw the bout, said that Jeff did not make a favorable impression. "What the audience expected to see was a man with wonderful science, and because Jeffries did not show any cleverness, thought he was a stiff." Jim said that Jeff had science, but because he was so big, he appeared awkward.

> He is an aggressive fighter, and a hard man to beat. His style of fighting is a peculiar one, and while he cannot always knock his man out, he can generally get a draw. I do not think Jeffries showed his real form last night. He knew he was to meet another man, and was cautious not to leave any opening for his opponent. I think Jeffries is capable of putting up a much better battle than he did and will prove

---

232 *New York Clipper*, August 13, 1898; *New York Daily Tribune*, August 6, 1898.

it in the near future. Jeffries has improved a little since I sparred with him at Carson, but I still think I am his master.

The day after the fight, Corbett told reporters that Jeffries made a bad showing and would have to do some fighting before he could win back the reputation that he lost. Tom O'Rourke said that the potential fight between Corbett and Jeff was off. Jeff's hand and reputation needed to heal.[233]

Tom Sharkey again reiterated his claim that he was robbed against Jeff, and said that Jeffries did not know the least thing about fighting. "He is a good, strong fellow and willing to mix things up, but that lets him out. As a pugilist, I think Jeffries's career is ended. He has no chance with a good man, and had better go back to riveting boilers in 'Frisco." Tom admitted that Jeff put up a better fight against him than he did with Armstrong. "Armstrong put up a great fight and should have received a draw. If the colored man had a little more confidence and started out to do fast work in the early stages, he might have received the decision."

John L. Sullivan defended Jeff. "Jeffries did not show his true form. He was fully ten or twelve pounds overweight. With that much off he would be quicker on his feet. … The verdict was a proper one." He also said,

> I do not believe that people should be hasty in criticizing Jeffries's showing against Armstrong last night. True, he did not knock the colored man out, therefore disappointing many people, but the fact that he fought nine rounds with a broken hand must not be overlooked. I know how it hurts to fight with smashed bones, and I can appreciate the suffering which the Californian endured. Jeffries fought under a great disadvantage, and did well at that.

> I mean to defend Jeffries. For he is not champion. He will have to gain considerable experience and employ superior training methods in order to reach the top of the heavyweight class. To my mind, Jeffries was not properly trained. He looked fat and heavy, and to these facts was due his slowness in getting around. I think he should take off at least fifteen pounds in order to be at his best.

> He is unquestionably a very plucky and willing fellow, and I think with a little more experience will win many fights. He punches hard, and if his hand had not failed him early in the fight he would have put Armstrong to sleep.

Sullivan could relate with Jeffries. He too had been a big-sized puncher who endured some criticism during his career. He had at times fought in an overweight condition, and had also fought Patsy Cardiff with a broken arm.

Bill Delaney revealed that the left hand was more seriously injured than was at first supposed. "The metacarpal of the thumb was fractured, and

233 *New York World, New York Sun*, August 7, 1898.

inflammation had full sway for several hours, causing the injured member to swell to an enormous size." It was so bad that Jeff had to wait until the following day to have the bone set. He was unable to obtain much sleep, and spent most of the night with his left hand in a basin of hot water. Of course, today it is known that ice is what should be applied to a swelling, not heat. Delaney said that he would refrain from talking business until he learned with some definiteness when Jeffries would be able to box again.

Two days after the fight, the *New York World* said that the general opinion was that Jeff was nowhere near the champion class. "Armstrong resembled a greyhound and Jeffries a St. Bernard. The former moved around in a very sprightly manner, would occasionally land on his husky opponent and rebound like a rubber man to the ropes." Despite his size and muscles, Jeff was "a great disappointment," "slow as a horse car and is nowhere near the scientific boxer that Corbett or McCoy is."

Still, the *World* understood how Jeff was just the man to go against and best Sharkey, as he had already done. "They are a pair of giants, have similar movements, can stand each other's jolts and wallops, and Jeffries is just a shade the cleverer with his fists. But neither man is a boxer in the most approved sense. They are physically unable to get out of their own or their opponent's way."

Regardless of the criticism, the sports were eager to see Jeff in with a top fighter such as Corbett, Fitzsimmons, or McCoy, so that they could judge his merits against a star.

> Many are willing to bet that any one of them will put him to sleep in less than ten rounds. However, these enthusiasts may be fooled. The big fellow undoubtedly shattered his left thumb early in the fight with Armstrong, so he had to proceed with care. And, strange to say, he invariably led with his left fist, and landed nearly all of his blows with it.[234]

Jeff was set to return to San Francisco on Tuesday, August 9, to nurse his injured hand and reputation for a while. Bill Delaney said,

> I think we have been unjustly condemned, and that the public has jumped too quickly to conclusions. In my opinion Jeffries did well under the circumstances. He fought gamely, and would have surely put Armstrong and O'Donnell to sleep were he not badly handicapped. Jeffries, as soon as his hand gets well, will fight any of 'em.[235]

In his autobiography, Jeff said that his hand was put in a plaster cast for several weeks. He was likely protecting it even after that, wanting it to

---

234 *New York World*, August 7, 1898.
235 *New York Sun*, August 7, 1898.

strengthen before risking further injury. He was out of the boxing scene for several months, and was not heard from again until the following year.

Clearly, the post-fight analysis demonstrated a great backlash against the big Jeffries build-up. Ordinarily, earning a decision victory over a tough and durable fighter was a good thing, but the hype surrounding Jeffries had led to high expectations for a dominant knockout victory. Despite the general agreement that he had defeated Armstrong, he had not been as impressive as hoped for or represented. The fans were doubly harsh on him when he did not complete the self-imposed two-bout task. In sports, when the bar gets set so high, anything less can be portrayed as a disappointment. Without the hype and self-imposed tasks, this would have been a good win.

The critics failed to give Jeffries the credit that he deserved, and failed to adequately take into account the hurdles that he faced. With a broken left hand, his dominant lead hand and most powerful wing, Jeffries simply could not meet expectations. It was very impressive for a left-handed man to win despite boxing for ten rounds with only a good right hand. Despite the pain, he still threw his left. Jeffries had shown heart and willpower by fighting the best he could under the circumstances, in a winning effort against a solid fighter.

Jeffries not only had to deal with the handicap of a broken hand, but the fact that he was expected to fight twice in one night also affected how he boxed against Armstrong. Fighters generally pace themselves with an understanding of how many rounds they will be expected to box. Jeff paced himself in anticipation of another bout. He did not want to rush matters too much, lest he would wear himself out for the second fight. This impacted the manner in which he fought Armstrong.

Another factor to consider is the fact that Armstrong was able to pace himself for 10 rounds, whereas Jeff had to pace himself for the possibility of having to go 20 rounds. Thus, Bob could give it his all, knowing that his task would be over after 10 rounds, whereas Jeff had to hold back somewhat, concerned about having the energy for the next fight. Jeff felt that he appeared slow because he was protecting his hand to a certain degree, and was pacing himself for the second bout. This caused him not to look as impressive as had been expected.

Also, Armstrong was simply an in-shape, motivated fighter with good experience. He was big, tall, strong, and had a long reach. Many reporters beforehand had predicted that he would put up a good fight and give Jeff a much tougher time of it than anticipated. So, it seems surprising that the press was so incredulous at the fact that Jeff had not stopped him.

These factors all handicapped Jeffries' chances for a knockout or an impressive performance. Yet, the press seemed to discount or minimize all of these points.

Clearly though, at this point in his career, the reviews on Jeffries were mixed. On one hand, New York writers lauded Jeff for his strength and durability, but they also criticized his skill, speed, and footwork. During his career, sometimes the press would compliment his improvement in these areas, but at others, it would be less than impressed. The book was still out on him.

One man in the audience for the Armstrong fight who did not agree with the general criticism of Jeffries was a boxing manager with an eye for talent: William A. Brady. Bill Brady had taken Corbett to the championship, and had seen Jeffries spar with Corbett in Carson. Brady had then felt that it was only a matter of time before Jeff would become champion. During the period of time that Jeff disappeared from public view and was allowing his hand to strengthen, Brady convinced Delaney that it would be wise to place Jeff under his co-management. They struck a deal in early January 1899. Brady was instrumental in securing a title shot for Jeffries.[236]

236 Brady, *Life and Battles of James J. Jeffries*, 16-17.

CHAPTER 14

A Strange Ending

On August 16, 1898, just eleven days after the Jeffries-Armstrong fight, Jim Corbett's father went temporarily insane, shot and killed his wife (Jim's mother), and then shot and killed himself. "He had been ill and acting strangely for several weeks."[237]

Having suddenly lost both of his parents, a despondent James J. Corbett called off his upcoming September 10 fight with Kid McCoy.[238]

Eventually, Corbett concluded his mourning, and he again resumed his long-time clamoring and lobbying for a rematch with Fitzsimmons. However, Fitz kept telling Jim that he needed to prove himself. Jeffries was recovering from his hurt hand. Kid McCoy had scheduled a December bout with Peter Maher (which was later canceled). Therefore, the big fight that New Yorkers wanted to see was Corbett-Sharkey II. If Corbett could win, he would be able to force Fitzsimmons into a rematch.

On October 11, 1898, Jim Corbett and Tom Sharkey signed articles of agreement for a late November rematch between them. Back in 1896, Jim had struggled with Tom in a 4-round draw. This time, the five-ounce gloved fight was scheduled for 20 rounds at the Lenox Athletic Club for a $20,000 purse, to be divided 75% winner/25% loser. In preparation, Sharkey sparred and trained with Bob Armstrong and the black Canadian world featherweight champion George Dixon. Corbett trained with Jim "Con" McVey and Charlie White.[239]

The articles of agreement provided for clean breakaways and prohibited any hitting in the clinches. Failure to comply with the articles could be grounds for disqualification. These terms were favorable to Corbett, because Sharkey liked to rough it on the inside and use his strength. Because of the prohibition against hitting in the clinches, Jim would be able

---

237 Corbett attributed the possible cause of his dad's insanity to an accident some years ago in which his father was thrown out of a wagon and had hit his head. Some speculated that his father had lost a great deal of money betting on Jim in the Fitzsimmons fight and that the banks were about to foreclose on his home. It was later revealed that Jim's sister Margaret had been an inmate of the Napa Insane Asylum for six years. "As in the case of her brother, her insanity is periodic." Hence, it might have been a hereditary issue.

Patrick Corbett was 64 years old, had come from Ireland in 1854 to settle in New Orleans, married in 1858 and moved to San Francisco, where he and his wife Katherine had eleven children, ten still living – Joseph, Harry, Thomas, Frank, John, Esther, Theresa, Kate, Mary, and James J. Notwithstanding his bitter denunciations of boxing, he took a keen interest in his son's fights and often wagered on them.

238 *New York Journal*, August 16, 17, 1898; *New York Clipper*, August 27, 1898. McCoy did not claim Corbett's forfeit money.

239 *New York Sun, New York World*, November 22, 1898.

to primarily box on the outside. This was the reason why Kid McCoy picked Jim to win. He felt that Corbett could only win a decision because Tom would be able to stand all the punishment that Jim could inflict. "If the fight was to be continued to a finish my choice would be Sharkey. I don't think Corbett can knock him out, and sooner or later 'Pompey Jim' would get tired, and when he gets tired it's all up with him."[240]

The matchup was exciting because the two were polar opposites. Tom Sharkey liked to fight and never grew tired, despite his constant rushing. Punishment had little effect on him, and he could marvelously recover from hard punches. One expert said, "The man never stops. He is like the great Sullivan when Sullivan was but twenty-one. He looks like him, acts like him, is always boring in, always keeping the enemy on the defensive. The idea that the enemy may hit back never seems to occur to him." On the other hand,

> There is no argument as to what Corbett possesses. He is, beyond a question, the cleverest fighter of all time. He can reach any man with either hand. He figures his man out, leads him into traps and confuses him beyond belief. He knows more about the art of smothering than all the heavyweights of the day combined. His eye is the best, his blocking the most perfect, and his shiftiness the most illusive.[241]

Another expert analyzed Corbett by saying,

> When Corbett shakes hands with you in the ring his fierce hazel eyes look deep into yours, as if he wanted to burn holes right through your head. The glare says: 'I am the boss of this ring. You get out.' Yet the first move Corbett made was a half step backward. He wanted to draw his adversary on, coax him into a lead, crack him on the eye or chin with a counter blow and then slip away. There is the whole story of Corbett's ring tactics. … His plan of battle is always evasiveness, with a constant attack as the enemy comes rushing in. He knows that the average man is most exposed to danger when forcing the pace … [H]e compels the other fellow to lead, and then cuts him up as he chooses. He refuses to leave any opening for the enemy.[242]

Although the odds favored Corbett, the experts were about evenly divided. One writer asked, "Is it not possible that Sharkey's strength and vitality may win for him in the end? This question should be seriously considered by those who think that cleverness is the whole thing in fighting." It was staying power versus strategy.

Some said that as hard as Corbett was training, with only a month and a half of work after such a long period of inactivity, he could not last longer

---

240 *New York World*, November 17, 1898.
241 *New York Journal*, November 18, 1898; *New York World*, November 21, 1898.
242 *New York World*, November 21, 1898.

than 10 rounds with a man like Sharkey. It was Corbett's first fight since he lost the title back in March 1897, one year and eight months earlier. During that same time span, Sharkey had eleven bouts and several exhibitions.

George Dixon said that Tom would win. "I base my prediction on the fact that Sharkey had the better of their four-round bout two years ago, and as he has advanced very rapidly in science, foot and head work, I have no doubt as to his ability to do so again."[243]

Ticket prices were $3, $5, $7, $10, $15, and $20. By the night before the fight, over $25,000 in tickets had already been sold. The arena was completely sold out, and so some extra seats were placed in each box, which were sold for $30 each. "It is one of the greatest fights held in New York in years. The interest in it is intense, and hundreds of sporting men have come to see it, even as far West as California."[244]

The Corbett-Sharkey rematch took place on November 22, 1898 at New York's Lenox Athletic Club on 100th Street and Lexington Avenue. Estimates of crowd size varied between 7,000, 8,000, and 10,000. Estimates of the total receipts were reported to be $45,000, $47,000, $50,000, and even $60,000.

With the tattoo of a ship on his chest, Sharkey entered the ring, along with manager Tom O'Rourke and trainers George Dixon, Jack Dougherty, and Bob Armstrong. Attending Corbett were manager George Considine, trainer Charles White, and sparring partner Jim "Con" McVey.

Corbett wore a white breech cloth with an American flag for a belt. Sharkey wore a breech cloth with a green sash around his waist. Both men wore soft bandages on their hands, as allowed by the articles of agreement.

Corbett had claimed that he would weigh 183 pounds, but on fight night, he said that he did not know what he weighed. Sharkey gave his weight as 178 pounds, and he looked every ounce of it. Many thought he weighed as much as Corbett did. No official weigh-in was required. Corbett was 32 years of age to Sharkey's 24 or 26 (depending on the source).

Before the fight, Referee "Honest" John Kelly told the men that the rules called for clean breaks and no hitting in clinches or on breakaways.[245]

The big fight began at about 10:50 p.m.[246]

1st round

Corbett was as light as a feather on his feet, feinting and dancing circles around Sharkey. Jim blocked or slipped Tom's aggressive rushes of wild swings, displaying his cleverness. Tom worked diligently to land, while Corbett laughed at him. A Sharkey right over the heart left a little red mark.

---

243 *New York Journal*, November 18, 1898; *New York World*, November 19, 1898.
244 *New York Sun*, *New York World*, November 22, 1898; *New York Times*, November 23, 1898.
245 Kelly was a former baseball player, manager and umpire who became a boxing referee. He had refereed Corbett's 1894 title defense against Charley Mitchell.
246 The following account and discussion is taken from the *New York Herald, New York Journal, New York Sun, New York World, New York Times, Brooklyn Daily Eagle*, November 23, 1898.

Tom showed improvement in speed. He played for the body with his right as Jim danced around with his devilish smile. Corbett was mostly on the defensive throughout the round and allowed Tom to do the work. What punches Jim did land to the head and body were quick and sharp, but did not worry or deter Tom at all. At the round's conclusion, Jim was laughing heartily.

2ⁿᵈ round

Most of Sharkey's swings were short. Jim hooked a left to the head that made Tom stop for a moment. Another tremendous hook rocked Tom's head. However, Sharkey was right back on the attack again. "Corbett was quick as lightning on his feet. His defence was superb. His left hand worked beautifully on Sharkey's mouth, but the Sailor paid no attention to it and kept on swinging and rushing until he finally got a right across on the neck." Corbett landed a light tap, and when Sharkey missed, Jim smiled derisively and landed a short left counter to the ribs.

Sharkey then got to close quarters and struck a lead left that landed low in the groin area. There were loud cries of foul, but the fight continued. Jim shook his head and landed his left to the body. During a furious clinch, both of Sharkey's hands punched away. Corbett hit the body and head, moved and clinched. When Jim feinted, Tom raised his hands and ducked.

Late in the round, Sharkey scored a knockdown, each local New York source giving its own version of events. Some said a right to the jaw decked Corbett, while others said it was a left.

Herald: Sharkey rushed Corbett to the ropes, and delivered two blows with fearful force to the body before sending Jim to the floor with a vicious blow to the head (it fails to say whether right or left).
Sun: Sharkey "rushed to close quarters again and with a tremendous right on the jaw sent Corbett down."
World: Sharkey came in with a left swing to the chin. Another rush followed and Tom missed a left and landed a right on the jaw, dropping Corbett to a sitting position, grinning.
Journal: From a running start, Sharkey landed a right to the body and left to the head and Corbett went to the floor.
Professor Mike Donovan: Jim got away and Sharkey landed a light left on the face. "Then followed a left hand blow in the jaw by Sharkey which felled Corbett."
Times: Sharkey landed a hard left on the jaw which sent Corbett down.

Corbett jumped up quickly, smiling. Some opined that he was not hurt. Others felt that Jim was hurt, but was doing his best to bluff and play it off. Mike Donovan said, "Jim got up quickly, but looked like a licked man if ever I saw one." He immediately clinched to save himself. Tom bore in with terrific blows, one or two punishing punches landing on the head and jaw. However, Jim kept cool and clinched, ducked, moved, and even threw some counters. At the end of the round, Jim laughed and smiled, showing his gameness. However, the *Sun* said, "It looked rather bad for Corbett, though, for Sharkey's hitting powers were tremendous."

3rd round

Corbett was busy keeping Sharkey off, and was more careful. Jim jabbed the eye and Tom landed a hard right jolt to the body that shook Jim and made a red contusion. Corbett looked a bit nervous. Sharkey continuously kept up his attack, fighting fast, chasing Jim around and leading often, but Corbett was quick on his legs, landing as he backed away, and ducking well when Sharkey got close. Still, Tom utterly disregarded any blows that Jim landed to the body or head, and kept Corbett defending his hard blows. Sharkey had twice the steam in his punches. When Tom landed on the arms and shoulders, the blows made loud thuds, which drew cheers.

Corbett showed his cleverness at footwork by evading several vicious swings. Jim's best work was in side-stepping and throwing a hard left to the head. He tried to annoy Tom with his smiles and laughs. Sharkey was serious and emotionless. *The Sun* said that neither had much advantage in this round. However, Mike Donovan said that Jim had decidedly the best of the round.

4th round

Corbett moved about and sparred well, stepping in and out, continually peppering Tom with punches to the head and body, clinching in between. Tom landed a hard left to the body and Jim clinched. The referee ordered them to step back. Sharkey asked, "Why doesn't he step back?" Sharkey kept swinging as Corbett blocked or moved. Tom landed left swing a bit low, and Corbett called attention to it.

Jim was being careful, showing even more clever footwork than in the previous round. He landed on Tom's face whenever he wanted to. Sharkey countered and led often, but Jim's science was too much.

There were two ways of looking at this round. On one hand, most of the locals agreed that Corbett clearly won the round and was outpointing Sharkey. On the other hand, the blows did not affect Tom, and he was willing to take some in order to land a big one. Also, the pace of the fight was very fast, which was to Sharkey's liking.

The Times opined, "The conqueror of Sullivan was displaying more of his old-time form now, and landed at will. Sharkey was willing to take the blows, apparently waiting for a heavy blow to put his opponent out." *The Sun* observed, "Corbett had done very little leading in the fight so far, but he had landed more blows perhaps than Sharkey. But his punches did not have the steam on them that his friends expected, and when Tom threw in a tremendous left on the ear there were cries of distress from the crowd." Sharkey took all of Corbett's blows without concern. "He was simply trying to put in a knockout, and Jim knew it. Corbett was not laughing now."

Donovan noted that although Jim easily won the round, "The pace was something terrific and told on Corbett."

5th round

This was a fast-paced and competitive round. When Tom started by boxing on the outside, Corbett jabbed and jolted him savagely. Tom's corner told him to quit sparring, and he then cut loose and attacked, but Jim got away. In the next rush, Tom landed to the body and followed up with the left to the face. A couple tremendous swings on the jaw made Corbett clinch. "There was no advantage for either man so far, and it looked like a great fight."

Jim outboxed him thereafter, and laughed at Tom, but his blows were not hard enough to make Sharkey wince. By taking so many chances, Tom left openings, and Corbett took advantage of them by pegging away with counters. Jim landed a hard left hook that momentarily shook Tom, but he broke no ground and went at Corbett with renewed vigor. Corbett feinted, laughed when Tom missed, landed counter hooks, and danced and skipped about. Sharkey rushed in and clinched several times. Jim was cleverer, but Tom was stronger.

The local sources agreed that Corbett outpointed him easily, but that Sharkey was not in trouble and was still as strong as a lion. They also agreed that it was as fast a heavyweight fight as ever seen.

6th round

In some ways, this was a repetition of the previous round. "Sharkey began by trying to box and do something from long range, but Corbett's left hand work at the head, together with a right or two at the body which sounded like the boom of siege guns, made him resort to the general result rushes." Tom rushed Jim around the ring like a mad bull. Corbett generally blocked, slipped or got away from the tremendous blows.

However, eventually Sharkey hit Corbett with some body shots. A Sharkey left to the jaw rocked Jim's head and took the smile off the ex-champion's face. Corbett jabbed away in return and eventually landed a hard left hook to Tom's eye. Both landed good body shots. Corbett landed a right over the heart that made Tom wince for a moment. Tom took the medicine and kept forcing, throwing punch after punch, which kept Jim busy avoiding.

While clinched, Sharkey landed two hard body blows, which drew cries of foul from Jim's seconds. Hitting in clinches had been barred, but the referee overlooked it, probably because Jim was doing the holding. "Corbett was growing excited now and made some remarks to Sharkey, who was fighting with vigor." Sharkey landed a hard right to the body, rushed Jim to the ropes, and landed several more body shots while Corbett clinched. Both appeared a bit tired at the end. It was a Sharkey round.

7th round

Sharkey made continual charges of showering chops, which kept Corbett busy dodging. Tom wanted to rush in and fight in give and take fashion. Jim landed hard counter lefts to the body and clinched. Sharkey rushed fiercely, landing some good shots to the head and body. He rocked Corbett's head with a good hook to the mouth, perhaps the best he had landed to that point.

Corbett came back and scored the larger number of blows. Clinches were frequent. Jim landed his left often. He jabbed, ducked and side-stepped, but the sailor was after him all the time, forcing Jim to clinch. Jim landed a heavy left and right on the jaw. "Sharkey's blows were still more powerful than Jim's and a blow on the stomach made Corbett clinch." However, Corbett landed some strong body punches that seemed to make Tom show some fatigue for the first time. Jim smiled and jabbed. Both were tired, but Sharkey was stronger. However, it was Corbett's round on points.

8th round

Sharkey rushed and induced Corbett to mix matters with him. Tom landed a left to the face and several strong body jolts. Jim landed some left and right rips to the body of his own which made Tom grunt. Tom rushed in and landed a swing on the jaw that sent Corbett toward the ropes. Jim came back like a tiger and landed a right on the mouth. The clinches continued. The referee warned them both repeatedly. Corbett's seconds protested Sharkey's wrestling tactics.

Sharkey was after him with no rest. Corbett cleverly dodged his swings. The sources all agreed that Corbett landed a hard, perfectly timed right to the jaw that staggered Tom. It was his best blow in the fight to that point. Sharkey was momentarily wobbled, but quickly recovered and hit out wildly. His well-known recuperative powers were in evidence. Corbett kept hitting him in the head and body, laughing and eluding, but Sharkey kept rushing in, forcing Corbett to clinch.

Sharkey landed a right to the ribs that hurt and nearly knocked Jim off his feet. Tom was in-fighting and landed a few hard punches. Jim landed an uppercut before the gong. Both were tired. The round was even. The crowd was cheering the fight.

9th round

Mike Donovan said, "Corbett was very shaky on his legs, and it looked as if he would not be able to go more than four or five more rounds at the furthest." Although the *Sun* said that Corbett was improving in his work and outpointing Sharkey, it also noted that Tom had the strength and was constantly trying to get in a finishing blow.

Sharkey came up "willing, feverishly anxious and as good as new. He refused to be kept at a distance and, coming in fast, got both hands to the body with speed." Corbett mixed it up with Tom. The referee broke up four successive clinches. Corbett landed a low blow and Sharkey protested. Jim responded, "Oh! Go on and fight." The referee did not allow the claim. As Corbett ducked, Tom clinched, and Corbett angrily said, "Oh, you go away." There were several more clinches. "Both men seemed to be clinching share and share alike." Neither man showed a disposition to break. Therefore, the referee had to give them a talk. The men continued fighting hard on the inside, clinching often.

What happened next became the subject of much controversy and debate. Various sources gave different versions. "[T]he one hand free clause was certainly forgotten. Both were offending and showing other tricks about breaking holes in the body when a cry of 'Foul!' went up from Corbett's corner and McVey went half through the ropes." Corbett's cornerman and sparring partner, Jim "Con" McVey, began climbing through the ropes into the ring to claim a foul. Apparently, he felt that Sharkey was holding and hitting with one hand free, in violation of the rules. *The Sun* version said that when McVey began entering the ring, he claimed that time was up, but there was no reason for it. There was plenty of time left in the round, as only about 1 minute and 48 seconds had elapsed. One thought that Sharkey hit in a clinch rather low and that McVey was protesting that.

Depending on the version, either a police sergeant, Police Chief Devery, or George Considine, Corbett's manager, grabbed McVey by the collar before he got more than his left foot and three-quarters of his body into the ring, and yanked him back out through the ropes. At this point, Referee John Kelly allowed the transgression to slide. During this time, the boxers kept fighting.

However, a determined and very excited McVey yelled again and this time came full into the ring, asking something to the effect of "John, why don't you get them apart and make them break?" "While McVey was in the ring protesting, Corbett and Sharkey were clinched and fighting under almost any old rules except those which governed the contest."

The referee threw up his hands, put one hand between the boxers, and as they broke, motioned Corbett to go to his corner. Corbett asked, "What is the matter?" The referee responded, "You have lost the fight. Your second has broken the rule; he has gotten into the ring." Corbett had been disqualified.

Upon learning that he had lost, "Corbett stood a second speechless, then ran after the referee, telling him things. Getting no satisfaction, he ran at McVey, but was prevented from striking him." Another version said that in a rage, Corbett rushed at McVey, and either swung or attempted to swing at him, calling him names, but either he held himself back or the police held him back. McVey attempted to retaliate, but Police Chief Devery threw him out of the ring.

There was confusion for a minute, as more police entered the ring. The referee consulted with ring announcer Charley Harvey, who then announced that the referee declared that because one of Corbett's seconds jumped into the ring, that he gave the decision to Sharkey on a disqualification. There was a wild uproar. The crowd yelled, "Fake! Robbery! Job! Skin!"

Perhaps in response to the crowd's displeasure, a subsequent announcement declared that the referee had decided that all bets were off. One said that the referee "made a great hit with the crowd by declaring all bets off." However, that was just with those who had bet on Corbett. Another observed of the announcement, "This was received with wild yells, catcalls, howls, shrieks, and hisses." Those who had bet on Sharkey felt cheated out of their winnings and questioned Kelly's power to call off the bets.

The massive post-fight debate and discussion addressed several issues. The biggest issue focused on what the true reason and motivation was for McVey's ring entry. Newspapers, experts, and participants had three distinct viewpoints and theories. One belief was that the fight was a fake - that McVey was in on a scheme with gamblers to fix the fight for Corbett to lose in a certain round or before a certain round was reached. Another position was that McVey was trying to save Corbett from a knockout loss, but at the same time preserve Corbett's reputation. A third view was that McVey simply lost his head, upset at the referee's failure to ensure that the agreed upon rules were followed, the failure of which was hurting Corbett.

Another big issue was whether the referee had the right to call off the bets but at the same time award the decision to Sharkey. Most analysts based their opinion of Kelly's decision upon whether they thought that Corbett was winning or losing at the time, and whether they thought the fight was fixed or McVey simply entered for more benign reasons. Those who believed either that Corbett was winning at the time of the stoppage or was at least even, were typically the ones who believed that the fight was fixed and therefore Kelly correct in calling off bets. Those who felt that Corbett was tiring and would eventually lose felt that McVey realized this and wanted to save Corbett from an ignominious defeat on the merits, and on the spur of the moment got him disqualified. Therefore, they felt that the bets on Sharkey should have still been recognized.

Referee Kelly believed that McVey had no reason to enter the ring, and that the ring entry was intentional and part of a preconceived plan with gamblers who had bought McVey. That is why he declared all bets off. He did not want to allow the public to be robbed of its money, feeling that it would be a rank injustice if he allowed the bets to be decided based on a prearranged act. McVey had been handling fighters long enough to know the rules, "and if he was on the level and had jumped in the first time while excited, he would not have gone in again after being warned." He perceived McVey's determination to enter, even after being pulled back the first time, as evidence of a plan that he should enter the ring and get Corbett disqualified. Kelly said,

> I called all bets off, because I believe the action of McVey was paid for by somebody who had bet on Sharkey, and I did not propose to decide public money on a palpable fake. ... No one can tell me McVey lost his head. He has been behind fighters for years, and there was some fraudulent deal behind his movement. So far as I can see, the fighters were on about even terms when I stopped the bout. ...

> While I know of no precedent for declaring all bets off, it was compulsory on my part, as it looked preconceived, and my decision concerning bets went as it did because I could see no reason why the many should suffer for the seeming intentional offence of one of the seconds.

Referee Kelly further said that he had heard of some crooked work several days ago, and made up his mind that nothing of the kind would be pulled off if he could help it. "When I saw McVey climbing into the ring I thought, By George, here it is now! And as soon as he got fairly in I stopped the fight and declared all bets off." However, he did not believe that Corbett or Sharkey were connected with the crooked work.

Some applauded Referee Kelly, while others severely criticized him for making a decision without precedence. Typically, the bets went according to who won, and if the referee wanted to call bets off, he had to declare the fight a no-contest. If he believed Corbett had a chance to win and was not in on the scheme, then awarding the fight to Sharkey penalized Corbett. If Sharkey had legitimately won the decision, then calling off bets penalized those who had won their bets on Tom. His two decisions seemed inconsistent. Corbett trainer Charlie White said Kelly had no right to declare the bets off, that if he suspected crooked work; he should have called it a no-contest.

Kelly felt that Corbett had to be penalized for the act of his cornerman. However, because he also felt that Corbett had a good chance to win and the end was fixed, he did not want to give Sharkey gamblers something they did not rightfully earn, nor cost Corbett betters when they might have won.

One noted that Kelly did not call off the bets until ten minutes after he had already awarded the fight to Sharkey. Some questioned why Kelly did not immediately and simultaneously call off the bets while ruling in Sharkey's favor, but rather did so in a separate subsequent ruling.

The Brooklyn Daily Eagle questioned Kelly's decision regarding the bets, because it appeared that Corbett could not have won anyhow. Thus, the referee unfairly saved Corbett betters from losses and prevented Sharkey bettors from obtaining their rightful winnings.

Some felt that Referee Kelly should have overlooked the ring entry and allowed the fight to continue. The entry had no impact on the bout and the fight could have just as easily been allowed to proceed. Professor Donovan believed that the referee's decision to stop the fight was premature. "I don't think any harm was being done and must differ with Mr. Kelly in acting as he did."

Technically, Kelly was within his rights to disqualify Corbett. Queensberry rules stated, "No seconds or any other persons to be allowed in the ring during the rounds." However, this was not the first time that McVey entered a ring during a Corbett fight. In 1894, when Corbett fought Charley Mitchell, Kelly had not disqualified Corbett when his seconds, including McVey, entered the ring. Back then, Kelly simply got them out and allowed the fight to continue. So, Kelly had acted inconsistently in the two Corbett fights that he had refereed. He probably should have allowed the fight to proceed.

Based on the Corbett-Mitchell fight, the *New York Clipper* rendered a scathing indictment and criticism of Referee Kelly's judgment, particularly in calling off the bets. It noted that John Kelly had refereed that earlier bout with a much different approach.

> Corbett not only deliberately fouled Mitchell, but in both the second and third rounds Corbett's seconds, one of whom was McVey, invaded the ring to prevent his further violating the rules. ... Mr. Kelly did not declare the result in favor of Mitchell, as in justice he should have done. Thus were the supporters of Corbett saved the loss of their money in that instance, just as those who took advantage of his unparalleled decision on Tuesday last, instead of in sportsmanlike fashion paying over money which they honestly lost. ... It cannot but appear strange, to say the least, to all persons of ordinary intelligence that a thoroughly fair and perfectly honest official should on two separate occasions take an entirely opposite view of precisely similar situations, and particularly when on one of these occasions he took no cognizance of flagrant fouling by one of the principals. In the former case the backers of Mitchell were defrauded of money fairly won by them, and in the latter case the partisans of the winner were by the previously unheard of, and utterly wrong, ruling of the referee rendered liable to the loss of their winnings. ... The referee had no more right, without convincing evidence, to assume that McVey's act was deliberately planned for the purpose of saving Corbett than has anyone to charge that Kelly was influenced in presuming to declare

bets off by a desire to defraud Sharkey's supporters of the fruits of their faith in the victor.[247]

Still, there were Kelly supporters, particularly those who thought the bout was a fake. Newspapers like the Pulitzer-owned *World* and the Hearst-owned *Journal*, both of which had a tendency towards the sensational, agreed that nefarious motives were at work behind McVey's ring entry. They felt that Corbett was winning at the time of the entry, and therefore there was no good reason for McVey to get him disqualified. They believed that McVey had been paid to let Sharkey win, and disagreed with those who felt that Corbett was being worn down. They supported Kelly's decision to call off the bets. "The decision of the referee, John Kelly, awarding the fight to Sharkey, but declaring all bets off, is the strongest possible corroboration of the existence of a conspiracy."

The Sun said that the decision to call off the bets was a popular ruling, for it would have been "manifestly unfair to decide away so much money on such a piece of unsportsmanlike behavior."

The World looked to the change in the betting. The odds had been 2 to 1 in Corbett's favor. However, Sharkey money appeared in such large amounts that the odds shifted to 10 to 7, 10 to 8, and even 10 to 9 in Corbett's favor. At ringside, there was so much Sharkey money that the odds fluctuated from 10 to 7 to even money, and between $30,000 and $40,000 was wagered.

The Herald echoed these suspicions about the betting.

> That there was a job and that some of Corbett's seconds were in with it, seems quite clear, in view of last night's developments. It is pointed out that all the wise gamblers and "sure thing" players bet on Sharkey, while the public form players wagered their money on Corbett.

However, there was no direct evidence of a fix.

The World summarized that for the first 2 rounds, Sharkey seemed to have things his own way. He floored Jim with a fierce right swing to the cheek. Sharkey impressed everyone with his tremendous improvement. He was very quick on his feet, and although many of his blows were wild, at least a quarter of them made their mark on Corbett's body. However, after the 2nd round, Corbett did better, taking the lead in the 3rd and 4th rounds, darting in and out and wearing Tom out by causing him to make many useless and exhausting leads. Sharkey often tired, but very quickly freshened up again. Corbett did not tire as often, but when he rallied, he did not seem as speedy as he had before.

The pace was fast and furious, faster than the Corbett-Fitzsimmons fight. "At times Corbett appeared to be mixed up by the fierceness of Sharkey's rushes, and mixed swings and body punches with him." Sharkey

247 *New York Clipper*, December 3, 1898.

had a tough time landing on the head, but landed a number of hot blows on the ribs and lower back.

In the 9th round, both were tired and holding onto each other. "When the referee stopped the contest both men were badly tired from their fierce and rapid exertions. It would be hard to say which was the more exhausted, although it is certain that when Connie McVey jumped into the ring Sharkey was hanging to Corbett just as hard as Corbett was hanging to him – possibly a trifle harder." *The World* saw no need for Corbett to be saved, and thus felt that the ring entry was corrupt and preconceived.

The Journal felt that Corbett had demonstrated that he was Sharkey's master.

> Corbett left the ring without a mark, barring a scratch or two about the body from the clawing and general roughing. Sharkey had an eye and was puffed about the face a bit. … Corbett had robbed Sharkey of his cleverness and had forced him to his old style. He was as strong as Sharkey and was doing the damage in spite of Sharkey's best efforts. The fight looked quite won.

In subsequent days, the *World* insisted that it was a fake fight. Even Corbett's supporters admitted that McVey's foul claim was ridiculous. Charley White heard Considine and McVey shouting "Foul!" but told them to stop. "I didn't see Sharkey foul once." It granted that there might have been such an excuse in the 2nd round or in one or two succeeding ones when Corbett was "up against it." However, in the 9th round, Corbett was getting better and Sharkey growing weaker, "and this is what the sports call inconsistency." It said that at the time of the stoppage, opinion was divided as to which fighter had the better end of the battle. "What he did was done deliberately, and he could have but one object. To all outward appearances Corbett was as strong as Sharkey in the ninth round. Therefore it would be absurd for McVey to claim he interfered for the purpose of saving Corbett from certain defeat."

Likewise, the *Journal* said,

> When it looked bad for Corbett, even in the 4th when Sharkey fouled him, McVey could see no reason why he should enter the ring. But in the ninth, when Corbett looked a certain winner, McVey saw fit to appear on the scene. … McVey knew what would happen.

Also, the fact that McVey made two attempts to enter the ring gave his actions an even odder appearance. Why did he enter twice? He could have made his protest from outside the ring. It seems clear that he was hell bent on getting into that ring. "It is hard to find a single man outside of Corbett and Considine who believe that the highest motives impelled McVey to climb through the ropes and so persistently disregard the commands of Chief of Police Devery."[248]

It had been 8 rounds of clever boxing on both sides, with probably the fastest fighting on record in a heavyweight contest, but the finale was unexpected and unsatisfactory. When Kelly announced his belief that the result was prearranged, "he dealt a deathblow to heavyweight boxing attractions in this city."

Bob Fitzsimmons claimed to have declared all along that the fight would be a fake. "Didn't I say it would be a fake? It was a big fake. McVey jumped into that ring on purpose to stop the fight, and it was all fixed for him to do it…. The whole thing was a put up job, and I tell you it was never on the square." He claimed that Corbett went down in the 2nd round intentionally.

Fitzsimmons perhaps had some ulterior motives in making such a declaration. He said that he would not pay attention to challenges from either fighter. Both of them being fakers justified his not fighting either one. Besides, he had already defeated both.

Most all of the newsmen were surprised and dumbfounded by McVey's ring entries, regardless of their opinions as to his motives. Many did not feel that he had a legitimate reason to enter or even to claim a foul. *The Journal* opined, "There was no foul to be claimed and Corbett was uninjured and giving Sharkey a beautiful tussle at his own game." *The Times* said that McVey had jumped into the ring without any apparent reason. "It was an uncalled for act, for Corbett had shown himself up to the time to have at least an even break, if not the best of the fight." *The Sun* said Sharkey had fought cleanly and fairly, and did not do the roughing or wrestling that he had done in previous encounters. *The World* said McVey entered the ring without provocation. *The Eagle* confirmed that when McVey climbed through the ropes and went almost to the center of the ring, Corbett and Sharkey were "hugged in a desperate clinch." Sure, they were technically violating the rules, but there was nothing so flagrant as to warrant a ring entry. Further, Corbett was holding his own at the inside game.

However, there was some support for McVey's protestations. Although entering the ring was a violation of the rules, in McVey's partial defense, Queensberry rules also said, "No wrestling or hugging allowed." Further, the men had agreed to no hitting in the clinches. Corbett had insisted on this term as a result of their first fight, in which Tom's wrestling had worn Jim out. The articles of agreement specifically said that Queensberry rules would govern, "except there shall be no hitting in the breakaway. Neither man shall strike with one arm free. No wrestling shall be allowed, and each man must step back after each clinch. Either man failing to comply with these articles his forfeit to be divided between the contestant and the club." The articles authorized the referee to disqualify any man not complying

248 *New York World*, November 27, 1898.

with these conditions. McVey was within his rights to protest the roughhousing, wrestling, and hitting in the clinches, in violation of the agreement and rules governing the contest. However, he should not have entered the ring to do so.[249]

McVey was quoted as saying that the sailor was not fighting according to the rules, that the referee was not on guard, and that he "slipped into the ring" to call the referee's attention to the fouls. He said that Sharkey first hit Jim low in the 4th round, but the referee did not seem to see it. In the 9th, Sharkey was hitting in the clinches, at least a dozen times.

> The rules under which the men were fighting did not permit hitting in the clinches, but just as soon as Sharkey got hit hard at the beginning of the ninth round he went in and fought, disregarding any rules and using his rough tactics. The referee paid no attention to my appeals for a fair deal. … I had repeatedly called upon the referee to break the men. …

> I jumped into the ring because I saw Sharkey hitting in almost every clinch and sometimes so low that anybody ought to have been able to see it. I called out to the referee time after time in the last round, and then I could stand it no longer and stuck my head through the ropes, but Kelly did not see me. Then I saw Sharkey hit him in another clinch. I guess I lost my head and put my foot over the ropes and they gave the fight to Sharkey.

He wanted to "get nearer" to Kelly to "explain my cause. I was excited for the moment, and did not realize that I myself had fouled until Jim was disqualified."

McVey was sorry for being the cause of Corbett's loss. He said that Jim would have won to a certainty. "He had Sharkey whipped, but I could not stand seeing Jim get fouled without making a protest." "The sailor can't lick Jim on the level and Sharkey knows it too." "My loyalty to Jim made me act the way I did." He was only looking for fair play, feeling that Jim's best interests were in his hands.

Perhaps McVey was just hotheaded and concerned for his man, knowing fully well that the Sharkey clinching and wrestling tactics were the very thing that had worn Corbett out in their first fight, and so he wanted it made clear that the referee needed to do his job and stop such actions, as required by the articles of agreement.

Both Corbett and McVey claimed that Jim had Tom at his mercy and would have stopped him. McVey said that Tom was growing weak, and that was why Sharkey resorted to foul tactics. Corbett echoed,

> I think that those who saw the fight will all agree that I had Sharkey whipped and would have had the decision in another round or two. I

---

249 *Brooklyn Daily Eagle*, October 12, 1898.

did not want to win a fight on a foul, and it was my misfortune that McVey jumped in the ring to call the referee's attention to Sharkey's foul fighting. He did fight foul; he hit me low, very low, once in the second round and again in the seventh. I did not see McVey jump into the ring. My back was turned to him, and when Kelly said, "You win," I thought he meant me, because I knew I had way the best of it.

With a cut lip, Corbett also said,

It is a shame that I was compelled to lose this fight on a foul. I was winning when this blockhead second of mine entered the ring and had the fight stopped. ... He evidently saw Sharkey hit me in the clinch in the last round when we were fighting at close quarters, and wanted to call the referee's attention to the breach of the rules.

Corbett said that he fought his best and had nothing to do with any crooked work. "A victory over Sharkey meant everything. It would restore me to the place which I formerly occupied and would give to me the opportunity of meeting Fitzsimmons." He even appealed to the referee to call off the bets in order to save those who had bet on him.

A day later, Jim said,

I lost, that is all there is to it. ... I cannot understand why the public should think my fight with Sharkey was a fake. If any one got the crack on the jaw which I did in the second round he would be quickly convinced that it was no rehearsed affair. I think that I ought to be congratulated for the fine display of generalship which I gave after receiving that blow on the mark and the way I pulled myself together.[250]

One woman who disguised herself as a man so that she could see the fight, which was the first that she had seen, said,

The fellow that got into the ring at the wrong time and stopped the fight should have been arrested. Corbett was whipping Sharkey fast and would have won in a few more rounds. ... It seemed to me they were holding and wrestling with each other most of the time. I'm sorry Corbett did not win, because he is much nicer looking than Sharkey and is not so rough.

The Sun agreed, "Corbett was not knocked out, nor was the bout stopped because of distress on his part." It said that it was the unanimous opinion that "either McVey lost his head or he made the break intentionally." There were rumors that the whole thing was preconceived by both sides before the fight, "but that is hardly probable."

---

250 *New York Sun*, November 24, 1898.

The Sharkey camp took another view of matters. They felt that Sharkey was winning, that Jim was tiring and would not last much longer, and so McVey saved him. Sharkey said,

> This man Corbett is just what I thought he was. He knew that I was going to give it to him and so he got McVey to jump into the ring and end it. McVey knows enough about the rules to keep out, and there is no doubt in my mind that he was instructed to get through the ropes and save Corbett. It looks like a case of 'quit' to me and I am disgusted. Corbett's punches never phased me at all. He had no steam in them, and I haven't a mark, and in fact I wouldn't know that I was in a fight unless some one told me…. I had Corbett going in the second round. … He fought himself out in the eighth round and he was tired. … I would like to say in conclusion that Fitzsimmons is a greater fighter in every way than Corbett and by far the hardest hitter I ever met.

Sharkey further said,

> I regret that Corbett's second got into the ring, for in a few more rounds, perhaps the next, I would have put him out. I fought fair. Corbett struck too low once or twice and I am a little sore below the belt now. … They say I am not clever and that I fight foul and that I lose my head, but here I stand to-night without ever having lost a fight on a foul, and having just stood Corbett off with all his much-vaunted cleverness, for eight rounds without a scratch on me. I can best any man in the world.

Sharkey manager Tom O'Rourke said,

> There was no job at all, except that Corbett was afraid of being thrashed in the presence of a big crowd and saw an easy avenue through which to escape. Sharkey would have put him out in a couple more rounds, as Corbett had fought himself out. McVey's argument that he got into the ring because Sharkey was committing fouls is laughable, for nobody saw my man violate the rules in the ninth or any other round. If notice was taken of it, Corbett could be seen hitting in the clinches and on the breakaways while his second was in the ring. McVey's deliberation in getting back into the ring after he had been ejected once appears to be additional proof that he was acting under instructions.

Interestingly, just a week or so earlier, on November 11, 1898 at the same club, George Dixon was beating up Dave Sullivan. During the 10th round, Sullivan's brother/second entered the ring, likely to save Dave from further punishment, and as a result, the referee disqualified Sullivan.

McVey used the Dixon-Sullivan fight as an example of how a second can sometimes lose his head and jump into the ring.

It was my anxiety for him to get a square deal that lost him the contest. It was an accident, and accidents are liable to happen at any time. It was not the first time a man has made a mistake. Why, was not Dave Sullivan's second accused of unfair methods when he went into the ring last week? Not a word has been said against that contest. I have been with Corbett for many years, have trained him for his important battles. I was behind him when he fought Mitchell at Florida and when he fought Fitzsimmons at Carson, but there was no occasion for one losing his head in those contests.

Of course, he was wrong about the Mitchell fight.[251]

Corbett trainer Charlie White said that it was all rubbish to say that there was a previous understanding for McVey to enter the ring. "He may have been rattled and lost his head. Why, the same thing happened in the contest between George Dixon and Dave Sullivan, when the latter's brother jumped into the ring."

Although McVey was using the Sullivan-Dixon fight to spin an argument in his favor, those who argued that the Sharkey-Corbett fight was a fake used that earlier fight as further evidence that the latter fight was fixed. Some thought that the Dixon fight gave the Corbett camp an idea.

It is said that the schemers were much perplexed as to just how the foul could be committed without being too glaring, until the Dixon-Sullivan bout ended so peculiarly at the Lenox Athletic Club a little more than a week ago. Dave's brother Jack climbed into the ring, Charlie White decided in the negro's favor, and the Sharkey-Corbett jobbers had an idea.[252]

Making matters more intriguing, Dixon trained with Sharkey, and White was a Corbett trainer. White had objected to the bets being called off, which some felt was evidence that he had bet on Sharkey.

Sharkey manager Tom O'Rourke said that if there was a fake, it had to originate from the Corbett camp. He said that Sharkey had Corbett beaten, and noted that the same course of action was taken the previous week by Dave Sullivan's brother in order to prevent a knockout. "The public believes the fight a fake, and it looks it."

Did the Dixon-Sullivan fight give McVey an idea as to how to save Corbett from being knocked out, so he could save face? Or was it his way of ending the fight so that he could win bets without Corbett having to be in on it, or having to fake a knockout loss if he was in on it? The circumstances surrounding that fight were an interesting harbinger of things to come in the Corbett-Sharkey fight.

251 *New York Journal*, November 24, 1898.
252 *New York World*, November 24, 1898.

The general feeling that ultimately prevailed was that McVey was trying to save Corbett from eventual defeat on the merits. *The Brooklyn Daily Eagle* said, "It was the almost unanimous opinion of the crowds that saw the fight that had the affair progressed it could only have ended in defeat for Corbett." Jim could not shake him, was knocked down, rushed to the ropes, was bleeding from the mouth and lips, and hurt by body shots. Despite his good boxing, Sharkey was gradually wearing him down. Hence, Jim could not move as much, and therefore, there was more clinching and infighting. It felt that Sharkey had the best of the contest, and that McVey got Corbett disqualified to save him from a more embarrassing defeat. "That Corbett's backers could not afford to lose on anything but a foul was apparent."

Professor Mike Donovan thought that McVey was simply trying to save Corbett from a knockout. "From the first Corbett displayed more science and a good deal more speed than Sharkey, but the latter is by no means the ignorant slugger that most people thought he was. He has plenty of science for a man of his build and style of fighting." He felt that Corbett could not have lasted more than 4 or 5 rounds before being worn out.

The Sun said the fight proved that Corbett was still the cleverest heavyweight in the world, for his dodging, ducking, blocking and side-stepping was marvelous. However, "when it came to real fighting Corbett appeared to be at a disadvantage." He had no power in his blows and grew tired after punching as hard as he could.

Although Jim had mostly outboxed Sharkey, the fight had been fought at Tom's pace, which from first to last had been exceedingly fast, as fast as ever fought by heavyweights. The question was whether Jim could keep it up for another 10 or 11 rounds, particularly after only a month and a half of training following a year and a half of inactivity. "As it was, after the eighth round, when he apparently fought himself out, he was not in the very best of shape. Some of the men who saw him at Carson City said that he began to look last night about as he did when he came up for the fourteenth round against Fitzsimmons." Having been in Jim's corner for the Fitzsimmons fight, perhaps McVey saw the signs and sensed that the end was approaching, despite Jim's superior points boxing. "There were rumors throughout the crowd and they would not down, that McVey's break was part of a scheme to save Corbett."

> The solution that seems most logical with a majority was that there was a fear in Corbett's corner that he might be beaten summarily, and that by breaking the rules in this way he could lose the fight in a manner that would not bring discredit upon his record. There was no doubt that in the nine rounds which were fought Sharkey was stronger, more aggressive and more powerful in action than Corbett. The latter boxed in the cleverest possible manner and scored repeatedly on Sharkey's face and body, but there was no steam in his

punches, and those who had seen him whip Sullivan six years ago said that he had gone back. ... In fact, after the fight had gone a couple of rounds there were many Corbett men in the house who feared the worst. All the punching that Corbett could give Sharkey had no effect on him. ... The latter, on the other hand, put in some tremendous smashes on Corbett's head and body, which undoubtedly made the latter fearful of the result.

It was in view of all this, that the impression gained ground that Corbett's handlers believed that he might be beaten. There is no question of doubt that he could not stop Sharkey inside the limit, for in the eighth round he fought himself almost out, landed the hardest blows of the fight, and yet found the Sailor bobbing up in front of him just the same. ...

McVey's assertion that the round was over was absurd. Corbett's action when McVey made this break was undoubtedly theatrical. He raged and stormed in the ring as if he was before a picture machine, and finally rushed at his old trainer, and tried apparently to punch him in the face. ... Corbett and McVey called each other names, made a show of fighting, and then McVey was thrown out bodily again by the Chief of Police.

It was interesting that the *Sun* described Corbett's actions as theatrical and that he and McVey "made a show of fighting." Was Corbett secretly happy that McVey got the fight stopped so that he could avoid being worn down and knocked out? That seemed to be the inference.

The Herald indirectly backed the idea that McVey wanted to save Corbett. It said that Sharkey had shown science in getting in close at every opportunity and replied to Corbett's light blows with sledge-hammer force. Jim attempted his hit and move tactics, but Sharkey was determined and successful at getting inside. After dropping Corbett, Sharkey won most of the subsequent rounds, but in the 7th, Jim landed some good shots that hurt Tom. Sharkey began clinching. Multiple mutual clinches occurred in the 8th and 9th rounds until the disqualification.

Although many yelled, "Fake," others said Corbett was growing weak, could not win, and that his cornerman's actions saved him the humiliation of being knocked out. "Corbett was not his old self in any of the eight rounds, and half a dozen times tottering knees, heaving chest, half power blows and feeble swings led the crowd to believe that the beginning of the end was near."

The New York Clipper summarized that the fight was even. The constantly aggressive Sharkey was stronger and the more powerful hitter, and had shown improvements in skill. Corbett was active on his feet, and clever and masterful in science, although not quite as fast or agile as he used to be. He never was a wonder in hitting power, and did little harm to his sturdily built opponent. Jim's most effective blows were landed in the 8th round, the only time he took the offensive, which raised the confidence of his friends, who were concerned by the easy manner in which Tom had been landing on him with effective blows, compared with the ineffectiveness of Jim's best punches.

However, Sharkey quickly recovered and resumed his attack. Corbett might have been fatigued by his hard-punching in the 8th. In the 9th, there were four clinches in rapid succession, the referee parting them each time. They were hard at it when McVey attempted to enter the ring, but the police prevented him from doing so. However, he again entered, claiming a foul.[253]

According to Corbett's autobiography, when Sharkey dropped him in the 2nd round with a right to the chin, Jim suffered an ankle injury. As a result, Corbett had to stand toe to toe for most of the bout. The fact that he used little footwork led some to think the fight was fixed, but he insisted that the injury was the reason he fought in an unusual manner. Jim admitted that he might have had to stop anyway owing to his ankle injury.[254]

However, at the time, Corbett never mentioned anything about an ankle injury, and most agreed that he was moving fairly well. He claimed that he would have won the fight had it been allowed to continue. Perhaps this was his way of saving face and maintaining his reputation and marketability.

In subsequent days, the analysis of the controversy continued. *The Sun* said that those in the know did not generally credit the charges that the fight was a fake. "The sailor worked hard from the start to score a knockout and showed that he was stronger and more aggressive than Corbett at every stage." Thus, it was not as if McVey had robbed Corbett of a certain victory, as some newspapers claimed. Club members had mostly bet on Corbett. Corbett's manager, Considine, had asked the referee to call the bets off, which was taken to mean that he did not wager on Sharkey. Corbett had done the same. Corbett trainer Charley White was said to have a sterling reputation, and he denied having any knowledge of a job.

Some felt that *if* McVey did it to save Corbett, that he did it too soon, because Corbett had several rounds of good fighting left in him. However, others felt that McVey could see the end, and wanted to stop it before the general public could realize it, which would further help Jim save his reputation.

> The majority of sporting men attribute McVey's action to an understanding with Corbett, not to be used to fleece the crowd, but more to protect Jim from defeat. … One prominent sport said: "Corbett knew that he was not in condition, but he needed money. … Corbett was to try Sharkey out and if he found that things were liable

---

253 *New York Clipper*, December 3, 1898.
254 Corbett at 271-273.

to go against him all he had to do was to give a signal to McVey. Then Jim was to make a great rally and in the midst of it his second was to leap into the ring, thereby losing on a technicality. That would allow Corbett to blow his trumpet again about how he could have easily beaten the sailor but for the stupidity of his second, and then, having received plenty of advertisement, both could resume their show business on the road. McVey and Corbett have been doing 'fake' fights as part of their theatrical shows for several years and they understand each other perfectly." ... McVey was with Corbett yesterday, as usual, and those who saw them said there was no ill-feeling manifested. If Corbett continues to keep McVey as a sparring partner on the road sporting men say that it will act as further proof of collusion. ... Corbett's inability to hit hard and Sharkey's skill in reaching him with his terrific smashers are thought to be the chief reasons why McVey was called into the ring to save the ex-champion.

Senator Tim Sullivan, who bet on Sharkey, said it was the greatest fight he ever saw, and that McVey should have known better. However, he also said, "My opinion of Corbett is that he has outlived his usefulness as a fighter. The young element now in the ring is too speedy for him, and Sharkey can whip him any time they meet."

Both Billy Edwards and Billy Madden said it was a grand fight, but that Corbett had gone back, and was not as quick and agile as he used to be.

Some felt that Corbett was taking the defeat almost too well. "Corbett takes his defeat with a good deal of fortitude. He does not seem to be very much concerned. In fact, he is rather indifferent, and his demeanor has called forth a good deal of adverse comment."

One reason why Corbett might not have been all that upset was because he had made a lot of money. The boxers allegedly met for a guaranteed purse of $20,000, split 75/25% ($15,000 winner, $5,000 loser), plus all money over $40,000 taken in at the door. "As the receipts were about $60,000, Corbett, although a loser, received a handsome sum for his services." But, Corbett might have made a lot more.

A *New York Journal* report said that despite public representations, there was no purse with a division based on a winner and loser, but rather an agreement for the gate receipts to be split equally three ways – between the club and the two principals. Therefore, Corbett would lose nothing by the contest's result. "The sporting men declare that if the public were deceived regarding the $20,000 purse, there remains not the slightest doubt that the fight was a fake, in which probably all hands were concerned." *The World* reported that the parties split up at least $50,000, which it claimed was further evidence of a fix.[255]

255 *New York Sun, New York Journal,* November 23, 24, 1898.

In June 1899, Corbett made further revelations about how they were paid. "It would surprise many persons…to know that the purse was divided before the fight began." Before even stepping into the ring, Corbett had received $16,000.

> I don't know what Sharkey got. It's none of my business. I had my money and then the only thing I had to look after was my reputation. It may be a very pleasing delusion to believe that two fighters are going to the trouble of training for many weeks and draw a large crowd and great gate receipts only to let the manager of the enterprise and the winner get all the money. Without the loser the fight could not go on. His reputation, especially before he loses, is a drawing card, so why shouldn't he get a division of the purse beforehand? They all do it. When I lost to Fitzsimmons at Carson City I came away with more money than Fitzsimmons made. Of course, had I won the battle, I would have won much more money, but I got the large end of the purse.

> In every bout which I have fought I have had it arranged so that I would have been well fixed, no matter which way the decision went. But, of course, I would make more if I won and then the incentive to preserve my reputation would make me fight my best.

At the time, this was practically considered blasphemy, because most sportsmen believed that the incentive to try harder was greater when the loser stood to make much less. Also, if a fighter knew he was coming away with a lot of money even if he lost, he would be more likely to quit if the going got rough. And someone like McVey would be less reticent to get his man disqualified, knowing that he would still be paid well. *The National Police Gazette* lamented, "Now, wasn't it real nice and 'clubby' of Corbett to tell that? And see how much the public is benefited by being so well enlightened." It believed that such terms were not good for the sport.[256]

As a result of the fight, the Police Commissioners were considering a proposition to revoke all boxing licenses granted under the Horton law. They wanted to prevent public swindles. Boxing was on the ropes.

A Board of Inquiry was set up to investigate, and it held hearings. The referee told them that he thought the fighters fought their best, on the merits, but that McVey acted by pre-arrangement, intentionally, and not on spur of the moment excitement. Referee Kelly said that there was nothing wrong with the fight up to the 9th round, and that it was an even thing at the time of the stoppage. He therefore refused to change his opinion that McVey was bought. He saw no other reason for him to stop it. He did not think Corbett was licked, and therefore did not think McVey entered the

.

256 *National Police Gazette*, June 24, 1899.

ring to save him from defeat. He said that if he thought Corbett was on the decline and getting licked, he would not have declared the bets off.[257]

Denny Sullivan testified that he was sitting in bookmaker Matty Corbett's box at the fight, and that just before McVey jumped into the ring, he heard someone in the box ahead of him, which was right near Corbett's corner, say something like, "Corbett was getting licked, and that now they would stop the bout." Sullivan also said that a number of men who sat in Corbett's box stated that the fight would be stopped if Corbett was getting the worst of it.

Although he would not reveal his source's identity, Bill Gray, Kid McCoy's manager, testified that a friend had predicted to him that the fight would end in the 9th round. However, a few days earlier, Gray was not that specific, but just told the reporters that he had heard that the fight would be stopped in Sharkey's favor, and would not last more than 12 rounds. *The Sun* said that Gray was unfriendly toward O'Rourke, Sharkey's manager, "and not much faith is placed in his charges."

In an interview, Corbett said,

> I don't blame any one for saying the fight looked like a fake, but I object to having it said that I faked. … If McVey did what he did out of friendship for me, fearing I was not getting a fair deal, all I can say is that he was hasty. He could have waited until I was groggy, for instance, or until I was down. … I had lots of money to bet on myself, but I couldn't place it. I told my brother not to bet on the fight at all. Now, if the fight was going to be lost intentionally, wouldn't I have told him and my friends to lay money on Sharkey? … I was the one who called out for Considine in the ring to have the bets called off. [258]

In his testimony before the Board, Corbett revealed some new information.

> I want to give you the reason McVey gave to my brother Tom privately just after the fight why he jumped into that ring … He said to my brother: "Tom, I could not see the big fellow licked, and that is why I got in there." I don't think I was licked. If he got in there to

257 *New York World*, November 26, 27, 1898. Referee Kelly denied that Corbett or Considine requested that he call off the bets. Charlie Harvey, the announcer, heard no one ask the referee to call the bets off. However, Considine and Corbett insisted that they did ask the referee to call off the bets. Corbett swore to it in an affidavit. This went towards showing that they were not trying to make money on some sort of a fix. Some support that someone convinced Kelly to call off the bets exists by reference to the fact that Kelly did not immediately call off the bets when he rendered his decision, but waited some minutes before doing so. Kelly later said that Considine only asked him to call off all bets three or four minutes after his decision had been announced. However, that supported Considine's version.
258 *New York Journal*, November 28, 1898.

save me he made a mistake of judgment. … I don't think McVey was bought.[259]

Ultimately, boxing was allowed to continue in New York, but incidents like this served to build momentum for the anti-boxing lobby, which wanted to see the Horton law repealed and boxing made illegal once again.

Corbett's skills and ability remained respected. However, Sharkey was the man of the hour, and as a result of the fight, his stock went up. New Yorkers wanted to see Sharkey again.

---

259 *New York World*, November 29, 1898.

CHAPTER 15

Road to the Crown

On January 10, 1899 at New York's Lenox Athletic Club, for a $20,000 purse, Tom Sharkey fought Kid McCoy, another well-respected rising contender known for his speed, skill, footwork, and punching power. In reaction to Corbett-Sharkey II, a term included in the articles of agreement stated that if a second entered the ring, he would be removed and the fight would continue.

Although McCoy dropped Sharkey a couple times in the 3rd round, Sharkey came back and used his superior strength, rugged constitution, and tremendous punching power during bull-like rushes to wear down the clever boxer-puncher and score a 10th round knockout. Once again, Sharkey impressed New Yorkers.[260]

On January 12, 1899, James Jeffries placed himself in William A. Brady's managerial hands. Brady, who had previously handled Corbett, advertised Jeff as the world's only undefeated heavyweight, who was willing to meet anyone, first come, first served.

Heavyweight champion Bob Fitzsimmons had not fought since winning the title back in March 1897. Instead, in late 1897, he went on a short exhibition tour. In 1898, he had been acting in a play with his wife.

Pressure was mounting for Fitzsimmons to defend his title. He had initially expressed his intention to retire, but found it more lucrative to call himself the reigning heavyweight champion. By early 1899, the question was whether and for how long Fitz could call himself champion without fighting. Relenting to the pressure, on January 14, Fitzsimmons said that he was willing to fight Tom Sharkey.

Jeff arrived in New York on January 29, likely to meet with Brady. He left that night, heading to Boston, set to exhibit there with Jack Jeffries.[261]

Jeffries (or Brady issuing statements on his behalf) lobbied for a title shot, noting that he was the only man to defeat Sharkey officially, as well as Peter Jackson, whom Fitz refused to fight. Jeff explained that his failure to knock out Armstrong was the result of a broken hand and the fact that Bob fought on the defensive.

---

260 Kid McCoy had been a very good middleweight, and had successfully moved up to heavyweight. His victories included: 1896 KO15 Tommy Ryan; 1897 KO1 George LaBlanche, KO2 Australian Billy Smith, and KO15 Dan Creedon; and 1898 W20 Gus Ruhlin and WDQ5 Joe Goddard. *New York Clipper*, January 21, 1899; Boxrec.com; *New York Sun*, November 3, 1899; *Brooklyn Daily Eagle*, December 9, 1898.
261 *Brooklyn Daily Eagle*, January 13, 14, 30, 1899; *National Police Gazette*, February 18, 1899.

Tom Sharkey's recent wins over Ruhlin (KO1), Corbett (WDQ9), and McCoy (KO10) made him a very strong contender. However, he had lost to Jeffries (and in truth, Fitzsimmons too), and given his history of fouling and the often tainted quality of his bouts, the undefeated Jeffries was probably a more befitting challenger.

However, after having seen Sharkey's strong winning performances against Ruhlin, Corbett, and McCoy, all of which took place in New York, and because of Jeff's lone less-than-impressive New York outing against Armstrong, New Yorkers most wanted to see Fitzsimmons fight Sharkey. And New York was where the biggest purses were to be obtained. Fitzsimmons wanted the biggest purse possible.

Therefore, on the afternoon of February 9, 1899, Fitz manager Martin Julian met with Sharkey manager Tom O'Rourke for the purpose of arranging a championship match.

CHAMPION BOB FITZSIMMONS AND HIS MANAGER MARTIN JULIAN.

However, interestingly enough, despite Sharkey's professed desire to meet Fitzsimmons, O'Rourke did not want the championship fight to take place until October. He had matched Sharkey to meet Charley Mitchell in England in May. Julian refused to wait past June. O'Rourke would not budge, and "thus the matter ended, with Julian having rather the best of the argument, as Sharkey had all along, until Fitzsimmons declared himself, manifested great anxiety to engage in battle with the kangaroo boxer, and four months is a pretty long time for training." Sharkey was not all that eager to get into the ring with Fitz again after all. It was said that not fighting Fitzsimmons would probably, in the end, prove to be a good thing for Tom - the suggestion being that Sharkey could not defeat him.

Therefore, Fitzsimmons went to Plan B. During the evening of February 9, Julian met with Bill Delaney and Joe Eagan (Bill Brady's representative) and made an agreement for Bob to defend his crown against Jeffries. The most relevant terms of the articles of agreement signed the following day said that the match would be to a finish or not less than 25 rounds, there would be no hitting in clinches or breakaways (a term Jeff did not want but Fitz insisted upon), neither could wear hand bandages (another term Fitz insisted upon), the gloves were to be 5 ounces, and the winner was to take the entire purse. At least that is what they told the public.[262]

Jeffries and Brady later explained how he obtained the title shot. Upon returning to Oakland after the Armstrong fight, Delaney received a telegram from William Brady saying that if Jeff would put himself under his management for two years that he would guarantee him a match with Fitzsimmons. They accepted. In order to induce Bob to make the match, Brady had to guarantee Fitzsimmons 65% of the purse, win or lose. According to Brady, he also offered Bob a 25% interest in the club with which Brady was associated (the Coney Island Club), which wanted to host the fight. It was an offer that Fitz could not refuse. Furthermore, Brady turned a negative into a positive by using the poor press surrounding the Armstrong fight to convince Bob that Jeff was just a dub and that it would be easy money for him. Fitz agreed, saying, "The bigger they are the 'arder they fall." Jeffries said, "He didn't know that I'd put in nearly a year studying the game and working up my speed."[263]

Initially, the deal to give Fitz the guaranteed lion's share of the money was kept secret from the public. Such an arrangement was considered a disincentive to give best efforts, because payment did not depend on success. However, fighters were well aware that future financial success depended on victory, so Fitz had a reason to fight hard. Plus, most champions have big egos.

Some believed (including Corbett), that Jeff's performance in the Armstrong bout is why Fitzsimmons elected to defend against Jeffries. However, what few realize is that Fitz was willing to fight Sharkey, "but the latter's refusal to fight forced him to accept Jeffries as an alternative." Economics was the biggest reason why Fitz took on Jeffries. Sometimes, when a contender wants to win a championship badly enough, he makes some concessions, as the Jeffries crew did.[264]

As a result of the notoriety Jeffries obtained by being matched to fight the champion, he was scheduled to appear in sparring exhibitions in order to make money and to allow the public to see the man set to fight for the championship. On February 20, 1899, Jeff opened his exhibitions at New York's Miner's Bowery Theater, sparring that week with his brother Jack, making a good impression.[265]

Regardless of the greater initial eastern interest in Fitz-Sharkey II, the Jeffries-Fitzsimmons fight wound up being a huge revenue generator anyway, in part because it would be Fitzsimmons' first title defense since

262 *National Police Gazette, New York Clipper,* February 18, 1899.
263 *My Life and Battles* at 29-30; *Two Fisted Jeff* at 94-99; Brady, *Life and Battles of James J. Jeffries,* at 16-17.
264 *National Police Gazette,* March 11, 1899.
265 *New York Clipper,* February 25, 1899; *National Police Gazette,* March 11, April 1, 1899.

winning the crown in 1897, and also because eventually, many suspected that the large, powerful, and durable Jeffries would put up a much better fight than some thought. Over the next several months, Jeff's appearance in training and in exhibitions bolstered the feeling that he was better than what the Armstrong fight had represented.[266]

On March 20, 1899, Jeffries began appearing at New York's Star Theater. He had previously been sparring with his brother Jack, but "his brother's nose has been hammered flat to his face and both ears have had to be lanced as a result." Therefore, Jim McCormick (a.k.a. Jack McCormack) took his place.[267]

The listed 240-pound Jeffries and the approximately 190-pound McCormick boxed 3 rounds. The forward-leaning Jeffries eluded most blows, lifted Mac's head with uppercuts, and displayed a very quick left that worked in a sort of lateral way, not straight. "It was give and take pretty hard, Jeffries punishing McCormick away hard each time they clinched."

Bill Delaney said that Jeff had been underrated because he was not able to show his best with Armstrong, owing to the broken hand and summer heat. Delaney explained that Jeffries does not perform well in the heat, and suffers terribly from it.[268]

Regardless, Delaney claimed that since the Armstrong bout, Jeff had improved his speed and defense. "He uses either hand like a flash. His trade has made him perfectly ambidextrous and he uses his knife and writes with his left hand as easily as he does with his right and with the gloves one is just as good as the other. He has a terrible straight jab with the left."[269]

On March 23, the parties accepted the Coney Island Club's offer to host the bout on May 26, 1899 for a $20,000 purse, the winner to take all, and for each pugilist to receive 33 1/3% of the money accruing from the picture machine exhibitions, with the club to take the remaining third. At least this is what they told the public regarding the purse split. It was also reported that Bill Brady, Fitz manager Martin Julian, and Senator Tim Sullivan (who had held the Corbett-Sharkey II hearings) were all given interests in the club. That is one way to guarantee that a championship fight will be held on

---

266 On March 4, 1899 in what some billed as being for the world colored heavyweight title, Frank Childs scored a KO6 over Bob Armstrong. Childs' record included an 1895 LKOby3 to Joe Choynski. Childs had lost an 1898 20-round decision to George Byers, which had also been advertised as being for the world colored heavyweight championship.

267 McCormick had been a Tom Sharkey sparring partner, helping Tom to prepare for the Corbett rematch. McCormick fought Sharkey in late January 1899 and Tom quickly knocked him out in 2 rounds.

268 Further bolstering that Jeff's handicaps in the Armstrong fight affected him; one can take a look at Bob's next several performances. In late August 1898, Armstrong fought a 6-round no decision with Joe Goddard, a man whom Jeff easily subdued in a few rounds. In December, Bob fought a 10-round draw against Ed Dunkhorst, and knocked out Mexican Pete Everett in 14 rounds, a man whom Jeff stopped in 3 rounds. Frank Childs stopped Armstrong in 6 rounds, a man whom Choynski stopped in 3 rounds.

269 *Brooklyn Daily Eagle*, March 23, 1899.

your premises. Both sides approved of George Siler, who had refereed Corbett-Fitzsimmons, to referee the fight.[270]

Tom Sharkey, who had initially turned down a Fitz fight, began saying that he wanted the fight, and withdrew from the Mitchell match. Jeffries responded "with all the force of a giant wielding a sledge. He did not hesitate to imply a cowardly motive on the sailor's part when he fell back upon his alleged match with Mitchell to evade Fitzsimmons." Jeff said,

> Mr. Sharkey (as the public well knows) had the best opportunity to meet Fitzsimmons, but he was too cowardly to do so. I was named as second choice because I had never been defeated, and because I thoroughly demonstrated my superiority over Mr. Sharkey in San Francisco, when I held a complete victory over him in a contest in which he refused to stand up and fight, but resorted to runaway tactics in eighteen of the twenty rounds we fought. I never faked a match in my life. I never depended upon a referee to win one for me.

Fitzsimmons too criticized, "Sharkey had his chance. For reasons, perhaps good and sufficient for his purpose, he refused to make a match with me."[271]

Jeffries went on an exhibition tour with Delaney, Kid Eagan, and former Corbett sparring partner Jim Daly. On April 4, 1899, Jeff exhibited in Dayton, Ohio, likely with Daly. On, the 5th, he exhibited in Kansas City, Missouri. "He considers himself just as quick and strong as Fitzsimmons, and thinks that he can hit as hard, if not harder, than Lanky Bob, and at the same time he thinks that he can take more punishment." At that time, Fitzsimmons was giving bag punching and sparring exhibitions with Yank Kenny, a very large heavyweight.[272]

Jeffries gave both afternoon and evening exhibitions at the St. Louis Standard Theater from April 6-8, 1899, sparring 3 one-minute rounds at each performance with Jim Daly. Jeff was described as a quiet, modest fellow standing 6'1" and weighing 225 pounds, although he expected to lose 15-20 pounds.

In his fast and scientific sparring with Daly on the afternoon of the 6th, Jeff made a favorable and surprising impression. He was very fast on his feet for a fighter of his size, and "the way he smothered Daly, who is a pretty fast boxer himself, was a treat. ... He used his left hand repeatedly in his exhibition, and landed with it on Daly's face and countenance with ease." Daly declared that Jeffries was as speedy as Corbett was, and could

---

270 *New York Clipper*, April 1, 1899; *National Police Gazette*, April 4, 8, 1899. On March 24, 1899, 160-pound Kid McCoy won a 20 round decision over 167-pound Joe Choynski. Choynski dropped McCoy in the 9th, but McCoy dropped Choynski in the 17th en route to the decision win. This made Sharkey's victory over McCoy more impressive.
271 *National Police Gazette*, April 4, 8, 1899.
272 *St. Louis Post-Dispatch*, April 5, 1899; Boxrec.com; *National Police Gazette*, April 8, 1899.

deliver a blow that would kill an ox. They repeated their performance in the evening.

At that time, Fitzsimmons said that he was not too far from being fit. "You see, I do not dissipate, and consequently I do not have to kill myself to be well for a mill." He would begin hard training in about two weeks, after his theatrical season closed. "I have no fear of the outcome. I have never met Jeffries as of yet, but I guess he is a nice fellow. There is one thing about him that I like. He can make a match without a lot of nonsensical talk and mud-slinging."[273]

On April 9, 1899, Jeff began his week of exhibitions at Chicago's Great Northern Theater. Sparring 3 rounds with Jim Daly, Jeff "shows up to advantage and is far quicker than most people give him credit for being. He boxes in a crouching position and is a hard man to reach." He looked good. "A better developed specimen of physical manhood would be harder to imagine."

Jeff had been privately sparring and training with Tommy Ryan. Delaney remarked that Ryan tried to hit Jeff, but found the proposition a hard one. Furthermore, "Jeffries is a tireless worker. ... He has wonderful recuperative powers, and no matter how tired at the end of the round, comes up comparatively fresh for the next. He is a hard worker and loves to train."[274]

Delaney, who had previously trained Corbett, told the *National Police Gazette* that Jeff was a more enthusiastic worker than Corbett ever was, "which is saying a great deal, for it is a well-known fact that the former champion never ceased training during the hours he was awake." Ever the advocate, Delaney further said,

This man Jeffries has what Corbett lacked – stamina. Hard labor in the boiler shop, coupled with the constitution of an ox, has given Jeffries the hardiest physique ever possessed by a boxer.... Jeffries'

273 *St. Louis Post-Dispatch, St. Louis Republic, St. Louis Daily Globe Democrat*, April 6, 7, 1899. Discussing his fight with Sharkey, Jeff said, "Sharkey ran away from me throughout the mill. Had he fought instead of indulging in a foot race, I would have stopped him sure."
274 *Chicago Tribune*, April 9, 10, 1899.

physical prowess is backed by cleverness with both hands and agility of foot. He has two good hands, and unlike the majority of big fellows, he doesn't bank entirely on his strength. He can hit straight out, like a shot from a gun, with both hands, and the straight right punch is safe and well-timed. At Carson City he would have beaten Corbett and Fitzsimmons in the same ring, and he's twice as good now as a ring tactician.[275]

After a week in Chicago, when Jeff arrived in Philadelphia with his vaudeville tour, he was billed as the coming champion and the world's only undefeated heavyweight. Jeff exhibited in Philly from April 17-22, boxing with Daly in "a most interesting set-to" in both the afternoon and evening.[276]

As of late April, the Police Commissioners had still not acted on the Coney Island Club's application for a license to host the championship fight. Local politics and competition with the Lenox A.C. were hampering matters. A local paper explained,

> The members of the Lenox Club, who have fought an element in the Legislature which has persistently tried to have the Horton law repealed, are not inclined to allow the Coney Islanders or anybody else to enjoy the results of what has been achieved through a great sacrifice of money, time and influence; and in this they are doubtless supported by the 'powers that be.'

The Lenox Club felt that since it was its influence that led to the passage of the Horton law legalizing boxing, and its monetary expenditures were used in fighting efforts to repeal it, that it should have the right to host the championship. It engaged its political influence to try to prevent the Coney Island Club from obtaining the required license, attempting to monopolize big fights in New York.[277]

Jeff began hard training on April 24, 1899 at Loch Arbour, near Asbury Park, New Jersey, the site of his training camp for the big fight. This was the same training quarters that Corbett liked to use. It had a

AMUSEMENTS

Thousands turned away in every city unable to gain admission to see the coming Champion.

SECURE SEATS AHEAD

THE LYCEUM

J. G. JERMON, Proprietor and Manager

Week Com. Monday. April 17th

FIRST AND ONLY APPEARANCE OF THE COMING CHAMPION

JAS. J. JAS. J. JEFFRIES

AND HIS
ALL STAR VAUDEVILLE CO.
DIRECTION ————— WM. A. BRADY

Mr. Jeffries is Matched to Fight

BOB FITZSIMMONS
MAY 26th FOR A PURSE OF
$20,000
And the Championship of the World

AN ALL STAR CAST
THE BROWNINS
GEO. BURRELL
GILBERT and TRIXEDO
WILLIAMS and ADAMS
CAMPBELL and BEARD
ROOKER and DAVIS
POST and CLINTON
JOHNSON, DAVENPORT
and LORELLO

—NEXT WEEK—
THE NEW BIG SENSATION

---

275 *National Police Gazette*, April 15, 1899.
276 *Philadelphia Inquirer*, April 16-18, 1899.
277 *National Police Gazette*, April 29, May 20, 1899.

handball court and a boxing room. Jeff's trainers were Bill Delaney, Kid Egan, and sparring partners Tommy Ryan, 190-pound Jim Daly, and 200-pound Jack Jeffries. James J. said he was weighing 220 pounds.

Fitz did not begin hard work quite as quickly, perhaps feeling that the New York authorities might prevent the fight. However, he was giving some bag punching and sparring exhibitions.

Although Fitz was the 7 to 5 betting odds favorite, Delaney opined that Jeffries had the edge in the upcoming fight. He was younger and bigger, but that was not all. "This boy is the best man I ever handled. He is a natural born fighter, can hit as hard as any man I ever saw in a ring and is a glutton for punishment. He has never been stunned and it seems impossible to knock him out." This was a high compliment, coming from a man who had handled Corbett. A reporter noted, "Those who witnessed his bout with Jim Daly, while he was in the theatrical business, were fairly astonished at the cleverness of the giant. He sends his ponderous arms to all parts of the body with lightning-like rapidity, and is as light on his feet as a dancing master."[278]

In his autobiographies, Jeff said that he told all his sparring partners to fight hard and try to knock him out. He mostly worked on his defense and hit his partners lightly, not wanting to disable them. Jeff knew that a crippled sparring partner was of no use.

He arose at 6 a.m., worked the pulley weights for ten minutes, and did 3-4 sprints from 25 to 100 yards. After breakfast, he would run 10-14 miles. In the afternoon, he would play handball, skip rope, punch the bag 10-20 minutes without rest, and then take on his sparring partners one after another, boxing anywhere from 8 to 16 rounds. Jeff said he boxed Ryan at least 4 rounds every day. Then he would throw the medicine ball for 15 minutes and shadow box. After dinner, he would take a long walk. Sometimes he swam.[279]

On May 15, as a result of political pressure from Brooklyn politicians, the Police Commissioners Board finally granted the Coney Island Club a license, "as in justice they were bound to do after granting licenses to rival organizations in the big city." It was thought that the fight would be delayed a couple weeks so that final arrangements could be made, including removal of the roof so that daylight could shine in to film the fight.[280]

Speaking of his fitness at that time, Jeff said,

---

278 *Brooklyn Daily Eagle, Asbury Park Daily Press*, April 25, 26, 1899; *National Police Gazette*, May 13, 1899.
279 *Two Fisted Jeff* at 94-100; *My Life and Battles* at 30-31. On May 2, 1899 at New York's Lenox A.C., Peter Maher and Gus Ruhlin fought a 20-round draw that was called the hardest heavyweight fight ever held. Both punished the other badly. On May 6 in Chicago, "Klondike" John Haines knocked out a 21-year-old black fighter named Jack Johnson in the 4th or 5th round. In 1900, Johnson would fight Haines to a D20 and KO14.
280 *National Police Gazette, New York Clipper*, May 20, 1899.

As a result of my few weeks of active training I am in excellent condition. ... I am just as confident as ever of defeating Fitzsimmons, and think I will be the next heavyweight champion without a doubt. Those who witnessed my performance with Armstrong, when I fought nine rounds with a broken hand, will see a new Jeffries.

Fitzsimmons was confident too, having been sparring with Yank Kenny and Dan Hickey. "I feel in better form now than ever before.... [I]t will be all over with him after our contest."[281]

Speaking of Bob's training methods, the *National Police Gazette* noted, "Fitz is a man who trains a little all the time and is really never out of shape." It observed a day of his training. In the morning, Fitz walked 2 ½ miles, and then ran back. After breakfast, Bob tossed the 15-pound medicine ball with Yank Kenny, who stood six feet and weighed 230 pounds. Fitz then did ball punching for 15 minutes. Following that, he hit the punching bag, which was three feet in diameter by four feet in length. Next, he worked the wrist machine. After that, Fitz sparred 4 rounds with Kenny. "Kenny, though a giant, in reality is no more than a boy in the hands of the champion, who spars, wrestles and literally roughs it with him in the course of the day." After sparring, Bob hit a baseball for an hour.

After a meal, Bob played a game called quoits for an hour, throwing a ring at a peg. Then, wearing 3-ounce gloves to prevent scratches, he and Kenny wrestled for half an hour, roughing it, pushing the head back, engaging in neck holds, and generally mauling each other. After a few minutes of rest, Bob hit a bag for 6 rounds while holding a pair of small dumbbells. He then wore 6-ounce gloves and exercised his legs, feinting, side-stepping, advancing, retreating, and ducking from little rubber balls thrown at him, this lasting 20 minutes. After an evening meal, Bob ran 7 miles with his dog.[282]

Fitzsimmons discussed his skills and strategies. He liked to bluff and lay clever traps in order to get an opening to knock his opponent out.

I guess I am the champion because I depend upon no particular blow and can drop my man with either hand. I know the spots on a man that are worth hitting. ... There was a day that I was the cleverest boxer in Australia, but I soon found that a man cannot be exceedingly showy and still punch hard. There is a difference between a boxer and a fighter. The boxer may be very pretty, but he is seldom capable of stopping things with a punch. A man who expects to beat the world must hit, and I have spent most of my time figuring how to do the most damage with a punch. ... When I enter the ring with a man I have no plans. After I shake hands I look him over in a friendly way, then I feint him. I try to figure what blow he wishes to use and which

281 *New York Evening Journal,* May 16, 1899.
282 *National Police Gazette,* June 3, 1899.

he thinks I will use. If he don't hit hard I won't mind being hit. I want him to keep working, for I am sure to find a chance for a good punch if he keeps coming. If he wants me to set the pace I crowd in with my jaw well shielded by my shoulder and jab his head back with the left. . … I have never yet got a man on the jaw fair that he did not drop and stay there for the ten seconds at least. … I do not know exactly how I will beat Jeffries, but I will certainly beat him. Furthermore, I won't let him hit me. He is a big, strong fellow and might do damage.[283]

When discussing his initial prediction, Jim Corbett said, "Fitzsimmons on form should carry off the honors. He is a great fighter and has experience in his favor." Bob was game and could take considerable punishment. However, Jim granted that Jeffries had a good chance.

Jeffries is a good, willing fighter, who can hit a terrific blow, and, should he get one of those punches in at any time, it will be all over with the Australian. Since I trained with Jeffries, over two years ago, he has improved wonderfully and may surprise his admirers. His contest with Armstrong, who he fought with a broken hand, can hardly be considered seriously.

Jim said that if Jeff won, he would return to the ring and fight him.[284]

Tom Sharkey believed that Bob would easily defeat Jeffries. "Fitz ought to win over Jeffries in jig time. He'll be an easy mark for Bob."[285]

Sparring with Tommy Ryan was of great benefit to Jeffries. Reporters who observed their sparring sessions were impressed with Jeff's improvement.

No man can box with Tommy Ryan and not learn something. … Jeff has with him a man who doesn't mind boxing in the least – a man who can be taught nothing about boxing or fighting by anybody. It is true that Jeffries outweighs Ryan by something like seventy-five pounds. He can certainly hit harder, and when it comes down to a rough-and-tumble affair he has him at his mercy, but they do not box rough and tumble, and Ryan is the hardest thing to hit good and hard that ever fought inside of ropes.

An unwritten law of training camps was that the sparring partner was there to take it and not to give it. However, Jeff allowed his trainers, including Ryan, to try to hit him as hard or as often as they could.

---

283 *New York Journal*, May 22, 1899.
284 *New York Journal*, May 17, 1899.
285 *National Police Gazette*, May 20, 1899. Sharkey continued claiming that he, not Fitzsimmons, was the champion. Of course, this overlooked the fact that Jeff had defeated him. Sharkey claimed that Alex Greggains had been paid $5,000 to give Jeffries the fight against him, a claim which no one gave any credence. "Shark has told that story about Greggains so often that he has begun to believe it himself."

He and Ryan box as if each were a champion, trying to show the other fellow things. They go it fast, Ryan shooting in and out with that marvelous footwork, with Jeff after him, hot-foot. It means speed to learn to catch Ryan, and it takes cleverness to corner him and put it on him without getting jolted. … Jeffries is getting fast, trying to reach Ryan. He is learning to smother up when he comes to him and hit without going any farther back than necessary for the punch. In spite of Ryan's size, he will make any one box, fight, work and figure to get a good punch home. Jeff is faster with both hands than the betting would indicate. He knows things about shifting a punch from the jaw to the body, then back, of blocking the right and middling his man, or ripping it up to the jaw, that make him dangerous even to the champion. That boxing is going to have an effect. Jeff is with the cleverest hard hitter that ever lived at the weight. He is growing better every day. … Jeff is learning during these weeks. He has got a man with him who is certain to improve his fighting, not make him careless. … This Jeffries is a strong, young, game animal. He is neither clumsy nor slow. He has a chance.[286]

As of May 23, the fight had been rescheduled for June 9. The roof was not being removed, because the fight was to be filmed indoors via several hundred electric arc lights.[287]

There was fear that the fight would be a hippodrome/fake. Some felt that the fighters would intentionally go rounds, because it was believed that the films for a short fight would have less value. Clearly, some were afraid of the effect that film might have on the sport. Fear of a fix was a common concern in boxing, but more often than not, such fear was due to pure speculation and paranoia.

One writer said that filming the fight would violate the Horton law, and therefore did not believe that the fight would be filmed.

With this machine out of the way, the public will have more confidence in the fight. … The management continues to announce, in a rather luke-warm manner, however, that the fight will be reproduced by a special photographic machine. … This is not so, and results will prove it.[288]

---

286 *New York Journal*, May 23, 1899. Since his last loss, an 1896 LKOby15 to Kid McCoy, middleweight champion Tommy Ryan had been undefeated in at least 23 bouts, if not more, including 1896 KO6 Joe Dunfee, W20 Dick Moore, and KO7 Billy McCarthy; 1897 KO18 Patsy Raedy, KO3 Paddy Gorman, KO6 Raedy, KO5 Jimmy Ryan, and KO6 Billy Stift; 1898 KO18 George Green, KO14 Tommy West, W20 Jack Bonner, and KO14 Dick O'Brien; and 1899 KO12 Tom McCarthy, KO8 Charley Johnson, and W20 Billy Stift. Boxrec.com.
287 *New York Journal*, May 23, 1899.
288 *National Police Gazette*, June 10, 17, 1899.

Despite being the underdog, Jeffries eloquently and confidently stated his belief that he would defeat Fitzsimmons, in addition to giving his assessment of fellow fighters:

> Oh, I don't think Fitz is the hardest man in the world, and if I didn't believe I could best him I wouldn't have made the match. I have thought so ever since he beat Corbett at Carson City. You know I helped to train Corbett for that fight. Corbett outpointed Fitzsimmons as a boxer, but his strength gave out. He had no force behind his blows.
>
> Fitzsimmons' strength is what I call natural strength. The work in his early days in a blacksmith shop gave him the foundation for a constitution which has stood by him in many a hard-fought battle. He could take a good, hard thrashing and turn around and beat a man of but ordinary strength, as he showed against Corbett at Carson.
>
> Corbett is what I call a manufactured gymnasium boxer, and I claim that manufactured strength gained in a gymnasium is not the real thing. It comes of training for an athletic event and comes out after a few hard knocks in the ring. The clever boxer with only manufactured strength has nothing to fall back on after his stamina has gone back on him....
>
> I am an admirer of the science of boxing, but science alone will not turn the trick when the scientific man is up against one who is twice as strong and only half as clever. Corbett whipped himself by punching Fitz, and after his wind and strength were spent Fitzsimmons finished him up....
>
> Sharkey is naturally strong, but loses his head entirely. He isn't half as good a man as Fitzsimmons, and never will be, because it isn't in him. ... We went twenty rounds, and during the entire journey I had him on the run. ... It's hard to whip a fairly strong fellow if he refuses to fight. I believe in clever footwork, but Sharkey wasn't clever on his feet. He simply refused to fight. ... I floored him at least ten times. Alex Greggains, who refereed the bout, asked Sharkey repeatedly to stand up and fight like a man, but the Sailor refused. As for Sharkey's hitting powers, they made no impression upon me. ... He can't hit straight to save his life. ...
>
> I can whip Fitzsimmons, because I will carry fifty more pounds of weight into the ring and have the benefit of thirteen years. He is thirty-six, and I am in my twenty-third year. I know I am as fast on my feet; yes, faster, and can avoid his swings. He is a wicked puncher and dangerous man, but I have studied his methods closely.
>
> I cannot see how he can spring any knockout surprise on me. I hold my right in reserve, and do most of my execution with the left. In

swinging with the right a fighter leaves an opening for a cross punch. Fitz won't surprise me with his long, sweeping right cross. Of course, I swing the right when I have my man in a position for a straight, right jab for the body or in swinging into a clinch at short range. I don't save a right swing for a knockout as a rule.

I don't want the newspapers to write me up as a swell chest or big head. I am asked an honest opinion. I give it without boasting, and it is my honest belief that Fitzsimmons isn't big enough, strong enough, or clever enough for me.[289]

Jeff's confidence got the boxing public excited. He told another local New York paper,

I certainly expect to beat Fitzsimmons on the evening of June 9, or I would not fight him. I do not think he is easy – far from it – but I believe in my heart that I can beat the man I saw beat Corbett at Carson. … I believe I know a few things about scientific fighting, in spite of the talk about being "just a strong, rough fellow." Fitz may know it all, but he will learn that I know a few things myself. … I am certain that Fitzsimmons will stand punishment. … He has got to be hit, and hit awful hard, to settle him. … As long as he is on his feet, no matter how groggy, he is always dangerous. … I must admit that Fitz, from his pictures, looks pretty hard to get at. Still, I will get to him. … I can stand a punch, and expect to have to take a few to get a few in. … I believe I know his tricks and how to discount them. … I am stronger, heavier, and can both give and take more punishment.[290]

The National Police Gazette noted,

It must not be forgotten that Jeffries is one of the greatest two-handed fighters of the age. Naturally he is left handed, but he has, owing to the requirements of boxing, been obliged to learn to use his right hand so that he can now use either one with equal facility and hits as hard with the right as with the left. …

The one thing that Jeffries needs to do, and I believe that is the reason why the services of Tommy Ryan were secured, is to get fast on his feet. If there is any man who can develop him in this direction it is Ryan, for he is the king at foot work.[291]

Some felt that Fitz's relative lack of activity for two years might affect his capacity for a sustained endeavor. Jeffries did not think it would last long, because neither of them was in the habit of running away.[292]

289 *National Police Gazette*, May 27, 1899.
290 *New York Journal*, May 26, 1899.
291 *National Police Gazette*, May 27, 1899.
292 *San Francisco Examiner*, May 30, 31, 1899.

Against common opponents, Fitzsimmons had the superior results. He had stopped both Choynski and Sharkey, while Jeff had only managed a draw with Joe and had won a decision over Tom. That said, Jeffries had never been down in a professional fight, while Fitz had been down and hurt on a few occasions, including against Choynski. Yet, Bob had stopped everyone who had hurt him. Both were punchers, having decked everyone they had ever fought, and both were fit.

> There cannot be the least doubt that both men are in as good condition as any two men who ever fought. The big fellow from California has done wonders in the way of work. … Still weighing in the vicinity of 210 pounds, he can do three miles at a speed which would bother a professional runner, and can tear off the last hundred yards in close to 11 seconds. He has improved in his general foot work and boxing to a startling degree. …
>
> Fitzsimmons, in turn, seems, like good wine, to grow better with age. He is a bit heavier than hitherto, and, in spite of the assertion that he will weigh but 158, it is likely he will be nearer 170. Fitz has always had people fooled on his weight.[293]

In late May, after sparring 6 rounds with Tommy Ryan, mostly working on his defense, Jeff again spoke of the Fitzsimmons-Corbett bout, which he had witnessed.

> Fitzsimmons didn't strike me as being particularly clever, and he certainly did not loom up as a terrible puncher in that go. He didn't knock Corbett down until the very last, and he didn't daze him. As for that famous solar plexus punch, it was simply a case of Corbett being fagged and going down from a light blow. I am sure that left-hander would not have hurt me. Poor Jim went all to pieces just as he did in his four rounds with Sharkey, and I knew that he was up against it long before that solar plexus crack came along…. I know that I have learned a whole lot about boxing, and all I hope is that Fitz will come at me the way he went at Corbett.[294]

Sizing up the men, the *New York Sun* said that Fitzsimmons had the experience, knew the scientific principles better than anyone, was one of the hardest hitters in the world, and possessed supreme confidence. "He has knocked out more antagonists with one punch than any other fighter and is a physical freak." Bob was not a showy boxer. "He is a fighter, pure and simple, but in addition is crafty, tricky and a quick thinker." He always demonstrated wonderful recuperative powers after being hurt. "Fitzsimmons declares that he will go into the ring not heavier than 156

---

293 *New York Journal*, May 27, 1899.
294 *San Francisco Examiner*, May 27, 1899.

pounds, but in the rival camp they believe that Bob will weigh close to 170."

A *Sun* reporter who had seen Fitzsimmons in training was impressed. He hit the punching ball and punching bag. Next, Bob boxed 24 minutes straight, alternating back and forth two minutes each with Yank Kenny and Dan Hickey, taking no rest. Bob showed his blocking and feinting, together with quick leg work, and was quick as lightning in all his movements. After 18 minutes, Bob rushed at the finely built and much larger Kenny. His left shot under the chin like a bolt of lightning, and Kenny fell against some pulley weights as if a mallet had struck him. Yank then ran away, but Bob was after him and nearly knocked him out with a jolt on the jaw. Hickey then went at Bob, who "could have put him to sleep at any moment." After the round-robin sparring, Bob worked the wrist machines and the pulley weights.

When the match was made, the general opinion was that Bob had picked out an easy mark. It was said that in the past, Jeff's chief weakness was slowness of foot, but that was allegedly due to the fact that he often weighed too much, up to 245 pounds. However, he had trained so hard and faithfully for the Fitz fight that he was down to around 205 pounds. "With decreased avoirdupois comes increased speed in attack and defense."

Jeffries was still the biggest fighter that Fitzsimmons had ever met in a professional contest. Bob had never seen him box, whereas Jeff had seen him in action. Despite Bob's powerful blows, Jeff could really take a punch. "He has never suffered a defeat, has never been knocked down and says that he does not know what grogginess means." Furthermore, Jeff had a "wonderful reach, great strength and endurance." It would not be easy to defeat such a man in a 25-round bout. Fitz would be meeting a very well-trained Jeffries.[295]

---

295 *New York Sun*, June 4, 1899, discussing Fitz's training the previous week.

On Wednesday, May 31, in the morning, Jeffries ran 7 miles with trainers Tommy Ryan, Jim Daly, and little Marty McCue, sprinting the last 500 yards. Jeff then skipped rope for five minutes "in a way that was surprising considering his task on the road, just finished." Jeff jumped "with the ease and grace of a school girl."

Jeffries told reporters,

> I may be able to keep Fitz away from me and just knock his block to pieces with my reach. I saw him fight Corbett and I got a fair line on him then. … I know that I can stand twice the punching that Corbett can and that I can also hit hard. I'll be fast, too, this time. When I fought Armstrong I weighed 235 pounds. … But this time I shall get into the ring in better shape than I've ever been before in my life. I shall weigh not more than 205 and I'll be just as speedy as Fitz.

When asked if he had ever been knocked down, Jeff responded, "Never in my life, and I've never been groggy, either. Choynski dazed me once with a right-hand swing on the cheek bone, but it only lasted a minute."

JACK JEFFRIES. TOMMY RYAN. BILLY DELANEY. JIM JEFFRIES. JIM DALY.

After the noonday meal, Jeff took a bike ride down to the railroad station. He got on a pair of scales wearing a heavy sweater, long trousers and thick-soled shoes, and tipped the beam at 221 pounds. He said that he weighed 210 pounds stripped, and would reduce to 205 by the day of the fight.

In the afternoon, Jeffries boxed 6 rounds with Tommy Ryan. Jeff was remarkably lively on his feet, "100 percent more so than when he met

Armstrong." He did not hit Ryan hard, content with trying to block his punches. Jeff said, "He's very clever, and keeps me guessing." James J. did his slugging with the punching ball, hammering it for 30 minutes without letup. "He used straight punches and great round-arm swings that almost exploded the leather object. Not a bit of puffing was discernible when Jeffries got through." Following that, Jeff engaged in another sparring bout, this time with Jim Daly. Jeffries also played three games of handball, threw the medicine ball, and worked the wrist machine.[296]

On Thursday, June 1, Fitz sparred 12 rounds with Kenny, Hickey, and "the other regulars in turn," including lightweight Jack Everhardt.

Jeffries was said to have been doing six hours of work every day. "It is doubtful if ever a heavy-weight was in as perfect physical condition as James J. Jeffries. ... It is wonderful the amount of work he does. ... He is better than any one believed he would be, as he has gained speed. He is fit and fast."[297]

On Friday, June 2, 1899, one week away from the fight, the hot weather had arrived. After Fitzsimmons boxed Kenny and Hickey 6 hard and fast rounds, alternating a round with each, the "spectators applauded vigorously, and declared the Australian to be the greatest fighting machine the world has ever seen." Kenny said, "I simply can't understand how a man of his weight can hit as hard as he does."[298]

Fitz claimed that he was weighing 160 ½ pounds and would weigh 158 in the ring. Jeffries questioned this weight and felt that Bob was fibbing, remarking, "He said he weighed somewhere about 156 pounds when he

---

296 *New York Sun*, June 4, 1899, in speaking of Jeff's training the week before; *New York Journal*, June 1, 1899.
297 *New York Journal*, June 2, 1899.
298 The 1st round with Hickey actually lasted six minutes. Hickey was pretty quick and unusually clever, but Bob handled him. Kenny, who was nicknamed "Jeffries" because of his size, did more slugging with Bob, but even he was about worn out at the conclusion of the 6th round.

fought Corbett at Carson, but I'd like to find some one who saw him on the scales." Delaney said Bob looked every bit as big as Corbett did. *The National Police Gazette* estimated that Bob weighed at least 168 pounds to Jeff's 213 pounds.[299]

It was at that time that the authenticity of Bob's reported age was also called into question. His birth certificate was found in London, and it placed him at 36 years of age, not the 37 that Bob claimed.[300]

Jeff was looking solid, allegedly 15 pounds below that which he had ever entered the ring before. "His weight is about 208 pounds...[I]t varies in a day from 207 to 211."[301]

Regardless of Jeff's good appearance, as the fight approached, Fitzsimmons moved to and remained the 2 to 1 betting odds favorite. This made sense because he had stopped Choynski, Sharkey, and Corbett. He had the lengthy impressive career, having knocked out every good fighter that he had ever faced. In fact, Fitz had never legitimately lost a fight to the finish. Americans had seen him score knockout victories over every opponent since his arrival in 1890, including: 1891 KO13 Jack Dempsey; 1892 KO12 Peter Maher; 1893 KO4 Jim Hall; 1894 KO5 Joe Choynski (although officially a D5 – police stoppage) and KO2 Dan Creedon; 1896 KO1 Peter Maher and KO8 Tom Sharkey (although officially LDQby8); and 1897 KO14 James J. Corbett.

Jeffries was a relative newcomer. He was criticized for not making sufficient use of his strength and weight in his fights, and therefore in a match of cleverness, it was believed that Fitz would win. It was said that Jeff lacked sufficient aggression, had an "absence of pugnacity from his temperament" and "hesitancy in mixing up." A San Francisco report said,

> When Jeffries fought Sharkey here he obtained the decision, and the award was no doubt, a just one. But in that contest Jeffries made but little use of his enormous strength and great weight. He seemed

299 *San Francisco Examiner*, May 28, 1899; *San Francisco Chronicle*, June 7, 1899; *National Police Gazette*, June 3, 1899.
300 *San Francisco Examiner*, May 30, 1899; June 5, 1899; *New York Journal*, June 5, 1899.
301 *New York World*, June 3, 1899.

content to stand off and swing his left in when he got a chance. From the two or three rallies that did take place, Sharkey emerged groggy. It was in these mix-ups that Jeffries showed how formidable he is when he fully exerts himself. Up to the time he met him, Sharkey had hussled every fighter he met about the ring as he pleased and worn them down by sheer brute force. In Jeffries' hands, even with his tremendous strength and desperate viciousness, he was a child.[302]

However, what his critics failed to realize is that the flip side to Jeff's cautiousness was that he knew how to pace himself and not wear himself out in a lengthy bout. He may have also believed that it allowed him to take care not to be hit with a knockout blow. Jeff adjusted his level of aggression based on his opponent's capabilities. Not everyone could be the vicious quick knockout artist that Sullivan was, although Jeff's size caused many to expect that of him. His occasionally more cautious, methodical style kept him in good stead in lengthy bouts.

Fitzsimmons's fighting style was sized up as well.

[Fitzsimmons is] purely and simply a fighting machine.... In action he is tricky to the last degree.... Every blow landed by Fitzsimmons hurts... He has one blow which is peculiarly his own. It only travels a few inches, and is made entirely with the forearm.... The champion's every effort is toward helping his opponent to beat himself out. He lays all sorts of traps to get his man in motion, so that he may catch him coming with a jolt.... Men have rained blows all over Fitz, and it looked that he must be dazed or at least confused, but it was only his way of finding a short route to the money and the championship. ... No one will question Fitzsimmons' shiftiness and pluck. Corbett, Maher, Choynski and nearly every fighter he has met has had him going at some stage of the encounter, but he has pulled himself together, and taken advantage of the critical moment to turn the tables. ... But Fitz himself says he does not fight two fights alike... It may be at long range fighting as he drove it into Corbett, or it may be close in with a short hook similar to the way he landed Maher. Fitz is cunning.... The faster the swings come the more closely he watches for a chance at the jaw. ... The faster his opponent goes the cooler Fitzsimmons becomes.... He will take punishment without a whimper or a sign of weakening. If his man is a mixer, he humors him into a close bit of work and drops him suddenly. If he is against a clever, elusive fellow he throws aside his caution and goes hunting him. ... That is what makes him so great. He adapts himself to his

---

302 *San Francisco Examiner*, June 2, 1899.

opponent's style of fighting and is so immeasurably superior that he bests the latter out at his own game.[303]

Another said,

[Fitz] knows when, where and how to hit. He has a proper conception of the value of timing a man…. Fitz has no particular style…. No two of his fights appear to be alike. To the uninitiated he seems to be awkward and shambling, but there is a purpose in every ungainly move.

This writer described Jeffries as a man who lashed out and was a "free-arm fighter of the dashaway school…. He is also very handy with his right at the ribs. He gets beneath a difficult lead remarkably quick for a man so big and ponderous."[304]

Another assessment of the two fighters said,

Fitz is like all great generals, as no two battles were ever fought exactly alike. … Fitz is a wonderful fighting machine, who is also shrewd to an unusual degree. He has a variety of shifts, which come perfectly natural to him, that fool the so-called clever boxers. …

Considered solely from the standpoint of physical construction, Jeffries is a marvelous man. … In fighting trim he strips at 220 pounds, and a more symmetrical man never got into a ring. … He has no hesitancy in expressing the opinion that he will win. He does it in no weak-kneed, half-hearted way, either; he says he will win in a manner which carries conviction with it. … Jeffries is a master of the left hand hook. … It is not generally known that Jeffries leads primarily with his left. His manipulation of that member is a study in itself. It is always ready and nine times out of ten when least expected. So deft is the Californian at left-handed punches that Tommy Ryan is often confused and seriously put out in his defense. … He has never known defeat. … He has never been hit with the right, or knocked down or fazed in the ring.

Although Jeffries would have a big weight advantage, Fitzsimmons was "just the sort of a puncher to check a big man." He had stopped Sharkey's rushes. Yet, "no one who has yet met the Los Angeles giant has succeeded in hurting him."

The writer also explained away Jeff's performance against Bob Armstrong by noting that a broken hand handicapped him. Also, Armstrong was a shifty and difficult fellow, and acted almost entirely on the defensive, making it difficult to knock him out in only 10 rounds. "Put Jim

303 *National Police Gazette*, June 3, 10, 1899.
304 *San Francisco Examiner*, June 9, 1899.

Jeffries in the ring for twenty rounds with Bob Armstrong, and the betting would be 5 to 1 in favor of the white man."[305]

On the morning of Monday June 5, Fitzsimmons hit the moving punching bag 9 rounds. In the afternoon, Bob boxed 12 rounds with Dan Hickey, Jack Everhardt, and Yank Kenny. After a meal, he ran 6 miles. "His condition is absolutely perfect." Fitz said, "I am now in better condition than I ever was before. My course of training has been thorough and systematic. … I expect to win in short order."[306]

Jeffries continued expressing confidence as well. On June 5, he walked 10 miles and also played handball. He worked with the punching bag, medicine ball, wrist machine, and jump rope, and he also sparred.

At one time, Professor Donovan had sparred with or seen in action all of the champions: Sullivan, Corbett, and Fitz. He was an excellent prognosticator and judge of talent. Donovan observed Jeffries in training that day and was very impressed. He concluded that Jeffries was fast, clever, and a "marvel of physical strength and endurance."

Donovan saw Jeff spar with his three strong, fast sparring partners for 30 minutes. Jeff's first bout was with Tommy Ryan, who was "about the fastest man of his weight in the world." Jeff's breathing was easy, and he showed a good ability to block punches, despite the fact that Ryan was clever and fast. Jeffries then sparred his 200-pound brother and Jim Daly, and although both were big and strong, Jeff tossed them around as if they were featherweights, "and could have put either one out at any minute he chose to do it." Donovan said,

> I have worked with and studied pugilists and pugilism since the time that big Mike McCool fought Joe Coburn for the championship, thirty-six years ago, and I don't hesitate to pronounce Jeffries the best, fastest and cleverest man of his size and weight I ever saw. … I had seen him once before when he sparred with his brother…and to compare the man as he was then with himself as he is now is to liken

305 *National Police Gazette*, June 17, 1899
306 *New York World*, June 6, 1899.

a dray horse to a thoroughbred. At that time he weighed 235 pounds, and was possessed only of the rudiments of boxing as a science. As he stands to-day, weighing 208 pounds, and stripped of every ounce of useless flesh, with the science of boxing drilled into him by capable instructors, he seems a perfect model of the heavyweight fighter. Next to McCool, I think he is the strongest man I ever saw in the ring.... [I]n this Californian great cleverness and speed are combined with the strength of a giant. Big men are generally slow...that is not the case here. ... From his actions in the bouts with his trainers he is a splendid judge of time and distance.

Donovan further said,

I had seen Fitzsimmons three days before, and had said that he was a fighting machine of the first degree...but with the ability of this man fresh before me I believe Fitz is lucky if he does not meet his Waterloo.... Fitzsimmons has no idea of what he is going up against. He imagines this fellow to be a big, unwieldy 210-pound man, totally lacking in science and one upon whom he can land when and where he chooses. He is mistaken, and...when he leaves the ring on Friday night he will be a sadder and a wiser man. I know size is not all, and that one punch in the right time and place will put the biggest man on earth to sleep, but this fellow has ideas of his own about avoiding those punches, and ideas just as good about giving them.

I had a long talk with Jeffries and was much impressed by his good sense and total lack of false pride. ... He showed his generosity by saving his sparring partners when he could have jolted them unmercifully. ... He is a plain, unassuming and sensible man. ...

Fitzsimmons's experience in his many years of fighting is a factor in his favor, but the youth and vigor of this young giant to some extent offsets that advantage. The undaunted courage and superb fighting qualities of both men will make this a battle worthy of the championship.[307]

Jeff opined that one of his famous left hooks would settle the champion.

As a novice I managed to land some good blows on Corbett, and Jim had no trouble getting in on Fitz.... My blows are harder than any Corbett delivered. ... Some people may laugh but I think I am just as clever as Fitz. They used to say I was slower than a truck horse, but I

307 New York World, June 6, 1899. Another observer of the sparring said, "He put up a stiff battle with all of his trainers, and they were knocked out one after the other by a left hook. Daly received a flat knockdown." According to Jeff's autobiography, on the Monday before the fight, John L. Sullivan came to camp along with news reporters. They watched Jeff box 4 rounds each with Ryan, Jim Daly, and Jack Jeffries. John L. apparently proclaimed Jeff the next champion and said that he was the fastest big man he ever saw. Two Fisted Jeff at 100-101.

think they will change their minds when they see me in action. My work with Ryan has made me fast. In fact I'm so speedy on my feet that Ryan can't hit me, and he is pretty fast.

Delaney said, "Every man who ever fought Jeffries with the exception of Peter Jackson, instead of fighting him ran away from him." Delaney said that if anyone was going to run, it would be Fitzsimmons.[308]

Referee Siler intended to meet with both pugilists during the week of the fight to discuss the rules. Siler noted that nothing in the Queensberry rules called for clean breaks. Straight rules meant hitting in the clinches and on the breaks. Hence the phrase, "Protect yourself at all times." However, the articles of agreement signed February 10 called for a fight under Marquis of Queensberry rules with the exception that there should be no hitting in the clinches or breakaways, and they were to break clean upon the referee's order. Neither man could wear hand bandages. The gloves each boxer chose to wear had to be given to the referee 24 hours in advance of the fight. Jeff had unusually large hands, and therefore was careful in selecting his mittens.

By the 5th, the odds in London were 3 to 2 on Bob, the favorite. He remained the 2 to 1 favorite in the United States.

Fitz's training on the morning of June 6 included running, boxing, and tossing the medicine ball. Bob hit the bag against the low board ceiling for 45 minutes, and his sparring partners went 3 rounds each. In the evening, he took the last of his long runs. Fitz was the biggest looking 158-pound man ever, if one believed he weighed that. "Nobody but Martin Julian has seen him weighed."

Julian said that Fitzsimmons was a pleasure to train, because he did whatever his trainers ordered him to do. "He says he is too wise a man to play the part of his own lawyer."

Fitzsimmons was "as sure of victory as if his adversary was already prone before him." He was "trained to absolute perfection, where exertion is a pleasure and fatigue next to an impossibility." One observer called Fitz a marvel of physical fitness. "No human fighting machine was ever geared in better trim than Bob Fitzsimmons is to-day." Bob said that he was tapering off in his work. The fight was only three days away.

After his training on the 6th, the confident Jeffries said, "Never for a second since I saw him win the championship at Carson City have I had the least doubt as to the outcome, should it ever be my fortune to meet him." Although Fitz had a reputation of being tricky, shifty, able to hit hard and take advantage of opportunities, Jeff still strongly believed that he would defeat him. Jeff was said to stand 6'1 ½" and weigh 206 pounds.

Analyzing the two combatants, the *New York Journal* said, "Both Fitzsimmons and Jeffries are fighters, pure and simple. They have science,

---

308 *New York Journal, San Francisco Examiner,* June 5, 6, 1899.

of course, but when it comes down to bedrock, they are both sluggers. They calculate upon taking a blow in order to give one."[309]

On Wednesday, June 7, Jeff just walked in the morning. The vitagraph machine filmed some of Jeff's afternoon work. He threw the medicine ball, wrestled a bit, skipped rope, swam, and hit the bag.[310]

During the evening of the 7th at Asbury Park, Jeff boxed Jim Daly 3 short rounds at the theater, between acts of "The Widow from the West." "[Daly's] 190 pounds counted for nothing in the hands of the young giant and at any moment Jeffries could have put him out."[311]

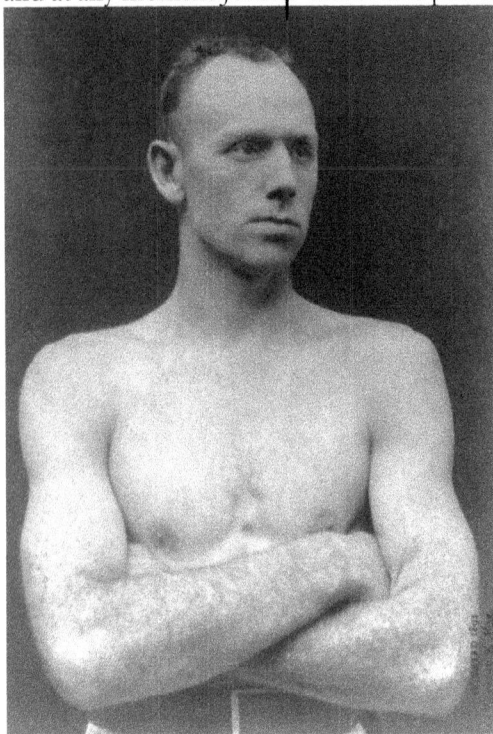

The heat and humidity caused Fitz to do very little on the 7th. In the morning, he worked with the medicine ball a few minutes and then punched the bag easily for several rounds. In the afternoon, Bob sparred 6 rounds in a half-hearted manner with Hickey, Kenny and Everhardt. Siler paid his official visit to Bob's camp to discuss the articles of agreement and the rules governing how the men were to fight.

On the 8th, the day before the fight, Jeff punched the bag for 20 minutes, skipped rope for a short while, and threw the medicine ball. He ran 2 miles, and then plunged in the ocean. It was the conclusion of six weeks of laborious exercise. "The heat has been intolerable at the respective training quarters during the past few days."

309 *New York Journal, New York World, New York Sun*, June 6, 7, 1899. On June 6 at the Lenox A.C., Bob Armstrong scored a KO2 over fellow black fighter Ed Martin of Denver. Both men were tall, splendidly built, and weighed about 190 pounds.
310 In throwing the medicine ball with Ryan, Daly, and Jack, Jeff successfully bowled them over like sticks, the big ball leaving his hands as if sent from a machine. Jeff engaged in a water fight with the hose with Ryan, which ended in an impromptu wrestling match in which Ryan was worsted. Rope skipping and a rubdown followed. Jeff, Daly, Delaney, Marty McCue, Jack Jeffries and Dick Toner all swam in the ocean for 20 minutes. A few minutes of bag punching ended the afternoon's work.
311 The first round was 1.5 minutes, Jeff tapping him on the head and body. The 2nd was stopped at 1 minute when a left uppercut on the chin rattled Daly's teeth. In the last round, Jeff knocked and tossed Daly about the stage as if he was a child. Despite his best efforts, Daly was unable to land.

That day, Fitz took an hour-long run. He then engaged in some light exercise, such as hitting the bag in a slow fashion, toying with the wrist machine, and sparring lightly with Hickey and Kenny. "The champion guards his weight with great secrecy, but his trainers think he will tip the beam in the neighborhood of 165 pounds."

Bob was wearing a bandage on his right arm, partly covering his elbow. "It will be remembered that this arm was injured in Chicago some months ago by Yank Kenny, whose powerful fist came in contact with Bob's elbow. …. Careful nursing and care have brought it into fairly good shape again."[312]

Responding to rumors that Bob was trained too fine, Martin Julian said that Fitz was in wonderful condition and "has never been quicker or stronger than now."

Fitzsimmons said,

> I can truthfully say that I was never in better condition. … I have worked as hard as I did at Carson or for any of my other important battles. … I was certainly never more confident or in higher spirits. … I am only thirty-seven years old, my habits have always been good, and I feel at least ten years younger than I am. … I advise my friends to bet on me…. They will see me at my best, and they know what that is.[313]

Likewise, Jeff said,

> I am fit to fight for my life. If I lose it will not be for lack of training. But I don't mean to lose. I am certain that I will defeat Fitzsimmons. I am faster and stronger than I ever was, and I am not afraid of those famous wallops. … All these other fellows Fitzsimmons has fought have hit him a good deal. Well, when I hit him I'll hurt him.

A *New York World* reporter who had observed Jeffries in Carson City in Corbett's training camp said that he was a much improved fighter.

> The Jim Jeffries of to-day and the Jim Jeffries of two years ago are as different as it is possible for two men to be. … He has gained in speed and cleverness. I watched him this morning with the especial object of seeing how he compared with the Jeffries of two years ago who helped to train Jim Corbett at Carson City. I found him a very different man – a new man so far as knowledge of the game of fighting is concerned.

---

312 *New York Journal, New York Sun, New York World, Asbury Park Daily Press,* June 8, 9, 1899.
313 *New York World,* June 9, 1899. Bob also said, "There has been much talk about the title of champion going to an American. I was not born in this country, but I have adopted it. I reside here, my children were born here, and all of my money is invested here. I am as good an American at heart as any man and a good deal better than a lot of cheap alleged sporting men who are continually harping on my nationality."

At Carson City Jeffries weighed 225 pounds and looked strong enough to push a house over – if the house would stand and wait to be pushed. He was brisk in his foot work without being fast. ... Of course, he was going against Corbett then, a man who could make any one on earth look slow. ... He could whip across a right or left hook with great looseness of elbow motion, but he never lunged out a straight left lead or counter. ...

Jeffries is a changed man to-day. He is down to 210 pounds and promises to go into the ring at 205. ... He used to look massive and burly. Now he looks big, strong and quick. Two years ago he was a bulky giant. To-day he is a trained athlete. It is doing him giant injustice to say that he is fifty per cent better than he was at Carson City. He is twice as good as he was on the night he fought Bob Armstrong.

This writer discussed his observations of one earlier day at Jeff's training camp for the Fitz fight. "Jeffries agility and judgment of distance in the handball court were revelations to one who remembered the heavy way he played at Carson City."

After handball, Jeff went to the barn where he sparred. "Against Ryan, Jeffries came in crouching with his head held well to the right and with his right hand open guarding the jaw. The clever style in which Jeffries came in was very different from the awkward trot he used a couple of years ago. His left foot steadily advanced, the right following it up step by step." Jeff blocked and countered blows nicely. "Jeffries's left shoulder was loose and easy – nothing muscle-bound about it." As opposed to just swinging, Jeff jabbed and lunged in with his left, "something he never did in any one of the sixteen days I watched him work at Carson City." Jeff kept coming in and never broke ground, reminding the writer of John L. Sullivan.

After sparring with Ryan, Jack Jeffries and Jim Daly took turns with Jeff for 3 rounds each. Neither could land, and Jeff just grinned, toying with them, except for one time when he landed a right under the heart which made Jack gasp and reel.

To sum up: Jeffries has a pretty good left anywhere and a mighty good right jolt for the body. His footwork is not brilliant but it is much improved over what it was two years ago. He seems quite as fast on his feet as Fitzsimmons is. He has an awkward head to get at. The way he carries it doesn't look pretty, but it is very hard to land there.

Jeffries's greatest quality is his strong, steady, patient courage. When he was Corbett's sparring partner at Carson City he never gave ground. Many a time I have seen Corbett left hook him on the jaw and send him reeling against the wall. Every time Jeffries pulled himself together, gathered his legs under him and rushed in on

Corbett, looking for more. That's the kind of man who cannot be beaten while he is able to move a hand. It seems to me that Fitzsimmons will find in Jeffries's youth, great size and strength, improved form, and dauntless courage a very hard combination to fight.[314]

The night before the fight, both men handed referee Siler their choice of 5-ounce gloves.

Bob was very reluctant to prove his weight. "It is a settled fact that Bob will not go on the scales at the clubhouse so as to let the public know how much he weighs. He contends that this is his own business, and as long as the fight is for heavyweight honors he is not compelled to announce the figures." Of course, if he was not willing to prove it, then the writers did not have to believe him either.

Regardless of size, Fitzsimmons remained a 2 to 1 favorite. Kid McCoy believed that Jeffries could not win. "Fitzsimmons is one of the greatest fighters the world has ever seen, and the man to get a decision over him must be a phenomenon." He said that as soon as Fitz landed a good blow, it would be the beginning of the end.

On the other hand, James J. Corbett, who could be fickle, switched his pick to Jeffries. He said that the odds were false, and that he would be betting on Jeffries. "Fitzsimmons is the best ring general, but Jeffries is the strongest man and should win."

> I honestly think Jeffries will win and win easily. He is a greater fighter than the public gives him credit for being…. Jeffries is remarkably fast for a man his size, and I know from experience he can hit as hard as any man in the world. If he ever lands on Fitzsimmons it will be all over, and it will only take one blow to do the trick. … The Californian is one of the most underrated boxers in the ring to-day. I believe he can defeat any man in the profession. … [W]ithin the last year Jeffries's improvement has been remarkable. He is exceedingly fast, has two good hands and is fairly clever.
>
> When I used to box with Jeffries he was a novice, but even then he showed signs of good foot-work. He is now a shifty fighter, capable of holding his own with any of the top notchers.[315]

The New York Clipper opined that Fitz would win.

> Fitzsimmons, on the strength of his greater experience, and series of uninterrupted and brilliant successes within the ropes, naturally enough has the biggest following among those who are putting their spare cash on the issue, odds of 2 to 1 having so far been easily

314 New York World, June 9, 1899.
315 New York Sun, New York Journal, June 8, 1899.

obtainable; nevertheless, there is considerable money behind Jeffries, and he will doubtless be well supported until after the battle is under way...for, with all his powerful physique, advantages in weight, height, and presumably in strength, it is pretty certain to be quickly seen that superior skill, generalship, experience, coolness and hitting power will combine to indicate the ungainly but ever-to-be-depended-upon Fitz as the eventual winner.[316]

Analyzing Fitzsimmons, another writer said that on several occasions, he had turned apparent defeat into victory, having kept opponents away when they might have finished him. Bob was a clever and dangerous man at all stages of a fight.

As the fight approached, further issues threatened the bout. Earlier, the Coney Island Sporting Club had struggled to obtain a license, which eventually delayed the bout from May 26 to June 9. Due to the inter-club inter-borough rivalry, forces were at work to frustrate and prevent the bout from taking place at Coney Island.

Despite the fact that Fitz was the odds favorite, on June 6, Police Chief Devery said that considering the weights of 210 pounds to 156 pounds, he believed it was impossible for them to carry out a lawful contest, and that if there was any slugging or heavy hitting, he would stop the bout and arrest them. The Horton Act had legalized boxing, but nevertheless the police could interfere. Devery also said that he would terminate the contest upon the first heavy blow struck.

New York had enjoyed all sorts of contests at the Lenox, Broadway, Greenwood and Pelican athletic clubs for two years without any police interference. Devery had seen many hard hitting boxing contests and had not interfered. Therefore, shock was expressed at his statements and inconsistent position. "Chief Devery saw the McCoy-Sharkey fight, which was one of the hardest and fastest battles that ever took place, and he did not interfere." Bill Brady said, "As the Police Board has licensed our club I expect the same treatment from Chief Devery as he has accorded to other clubs."

It was clear that Devery had ulterior motives. "Some such obstacle to the successful completion of this big match has been looked for by those who believe they are in touch with the 'inside situation' in local pugilism. ... There has been grumbling on the part of certain politicians interested in fighting at the Lenox and Broadway clubs" ever since the Coney Island Club secured the match. Thus, Devery, who had allowed a number of slugging matches to be fought without interference, was suddenly having a change in policy.

The press suspected Chief Devery was trying to use his power to have the fight transferred to the Manhattan Borough, where the police had

316 *New York Clipper*, June 10, 1899.

permitted several knockouts. Fitz's manager Martin Julian said, "It is very queer that Chief Devery should suddenly become so anxious about the law…. We expected something like this because of the effort that was made to prevent the Coney Island Club from getting a license."

One reporter noted that the Horton law was "a remarkably hard law to violate." It required that the boxers wear gloves weighing not less than 5 ounces, and the bouts had to be a limited number of rounds (generally 20 or 25). The statute did not put any check on brutality. However, the police, "having full power to preserve the peace…can do about as they please." Devery observed that the law allowed "sparring" matches, not slugging. However, "If Chief Devery lets fights proceed unmolested at the Lenox and Broadway clubs, there is no good reason why he should not follow the same policy toward the Coney Island Club."

It was thought that Brady's political friends in Kings County would be heard from again, as they had been with the license issue, and would see to it that Devery did not interfere. "The Brooklyn politicians say that if big fights are permitted by Devery in Manhattan there must be no discrimination against Coney Island."

In the end, on the day of the fight, "big guns" in Brooklyn political matters confirmed that only the referee would stop the fight. Apparently, Devery had been called off. It was noted that he had changed his tone a bit the day before the fight. The fight was on.[317]

Another aspect of the bout that bothered some was the fact that it was revealed that the purse split was agreed upon before the fight took place. Corbett noted that the purse would be divided between the combatants beforehand, as had been done in his own fights. Because the public might be upset and suspect a hippodrome, "The exact divisions of the purse can never be stipulated in the articles of agreement." Despite the articles of agreement saying that the winner was to take all, apparently the purse was $25,000, with 60% going to Fitzsimmons, win or lose. Jeff was initially reluctant to admit it, saying that it was nobody's business, Corbett should mind his own business, the purse was not being split, and the fight would be on the level. Of course, he later admitted to the pre-set purse split assuring Fitz of the big share of the purse, win or lose. It was a worthwhile investment.[318]

Despite his professed confidence, in his later autobiography, Jeff admitted that he placed a $5,000 bet on Fitzsimmons at 1 to 2 odds. He was just hedging, figuring that if he should lose by accident, $2,500 would look good, but if he won, then the loss of $5,000 would not hurt him.[319]

317 *New York Sun, San Francisco Chronicle, New York Daily Tribune, New York Herald*, June 7-9, 1899.
318 *New York Daily Tribune, New York Sun*, June 8, 1899; *New York Herald*, June 9, 1899; *National Police Gazette*, June 3, 1899.
319 *Two Fisted Jeff* at 100.

The National Police Gazette's writer offered a final analysis and prediction in Jeffries' favor.

In my opinion Fitzsimmons is not going to have such a walkover as the records of the two men would seem to indicate. He has the fight of his life on his hands this time, and although he affects to treat the Californian's pretensions with disdain he has reason to feel a wholesome respect of his opponent's ability... I am inclined now to favor the probability of Jeffries being returned a winner. I saw him at work the other day, a great, big, strong, healthy, ambitious fellow, who knows no limit of endurance, who labors earnestly, courageously and conscientiously... His confidence in himself impressed me. ... Argued from a rational, unprejudiced standpoint, everything is in his favor. He has youth, strength, height, reach, and pounds to his advantage. He may be a bit deficient compared with Fitz in knowledge of ring tactics, but it must be remembered that over two years have elapsed since Fitz has engaged in a fight, and a pugilist's knowledge of the requirements of his calling is not as keen after a long period of inactivity as it would be compared with that of a man who has had frequent opportunities to keep in practice. Jeffries has had eight fights in the interim since Fitz stood up in the ring with Corbett. ...

Jeffries is really a clever boxer and knows how to protect himself in a manner which will make Fitz wonder how to reach him with a damaging blow, while at the same time Jeffries, who hits equally well with either hand, and is quick, shifty and clever, may be depended upon to do his share of the fighting.

It is doubtful if Fitzsimmons will enter the ring as superbly trained as he was on that eventful day at Carson City when he wrested the championship laurels from Jim Corbett. He will have to be quite as good if not better than he was then, and that seems impossible in view of the long period in which he has been in retirement. Fitz has not been as abstemious in his habits, either, as he was before he donned Corbett's mantle. ... He has a big contract on his hands to defeat Jeffries, and as I said before nobody knows it better than himself.[320]

320 *National Police Gazette*, June 17, 1899.

CHAPTER 16

The Championship

On the eve and day of the championship fight, the newsmen, experts, and participants all rendered their final thoughts and analysis. Bob Fitzsimmons was certain that he would whip James Jeffries. He had never been given to excesses, and "I am in perfect shape." Bob said that if he could fight the version of himself which existed ten years ago, the version of today would defeat the version of yesteryear.

Jeffries said,

> That Fitzsimmons is the greatest fighter of years must be admitted. His performances warrant the belief that he is the hardest hitter that the fighting world has ever known. In his battles he has displayed remarkable skill and pluck, and for all of this I think he is entitled to great credit. At the same time I think tonight I will succeed where others failed. …
>
> Fitz can drop me with a punch on the jaw if it lands right. But when I get in the ring I'll do my best to keep away from such a punch and at the same time land a few hot ones myself. Other fighters have hit Fitz and had him groggy. Corbett had him going in the sixth round at Carson. I think I can put him out if I get over a good wallop and put it on right. Depend upon it that there'll be a real hot fight, no matter who wins. …
>
> I must say that I am not pleased with the rules. Straight Marquis of Queensberry would suit me better. But as I was anxious to fight for the championship, I accepted the changes on which Fitzsimmons insisted.[321]

Although straight Queensberry rules allowed hitting in clinches and on breaks, Fitz had wanted no punching in clinches and only clean breaks. Jeffries disliked the clause. However, as will be discussed, the rules were eventually changed on the night of the fight.

Analyzing Jeffries, on the day of the fight, the *New York Journal* said,

> Jeffries is today the fastest and most scientific fighter who ever entered the ring at that weight. He will weigh 210 pounds. That will be fifteen pounds lighter than he ever entered the ring before. He weighed nearly 230 when he fought Armstrong. … He has been

---

[321] *New York Journal, New York Sun,* June 9, 1899.

blessed with the handiest left hand ever hitched to a heavyweight. ... Jeffries's left hand knows the hooks, the jabs and the jolts perfectly. He feints savagely and with startling speed. His feet have improved until now he moves about like a shifty lightweight. His eye is wonderfully quick, and no matter how fast they come, he never blinks. His foot work resembles both Corbett's and Ryan's. He shifts about continually, is not obliged to set before he hits, and will never be caught flat-footed. ... Jeffries will likely have fifty pounds the better of the weight. He has never been knocked down or dazed in his life. He can stand more punishment than any man Fitzsimmons has ever fought, and he will give more. [322]

The fact that Jeff had handled the power of Joe Choynski and Tom Sharkey, and made these two fighters box and move when against all others they had usually attacked and mixed it up, was a sign that Fitz would have a tough time overpowering him. Jeffries had wonderful strength and stamina. Corbett again called the 2 to 1 odds in Fitz's favor ridiculous, saying that Jeff's chances were a lot better than that.

However, to most, it looked like a Fitzsimmons victory. He had a wonderful record of knockouts obtained by one terrific punch landed on a vital spot. He was rugged, powerful, and capable of standing any roughing Jeff could give him. He had done a lot of experimenting in sparring with Kenny, who weighed as much as Jeffries did. Bob was a great ring general, a schemer, quick-witted, shrewd, and full of tricks. "For this reason Jeffries will have to fight him warily until he believes he has the Cornishman's measure." Jeff would be able to do so because of his reach.

> Jeffries has such a tremendous reach that it will not be at all surprising to see him fight Fitz with left-hand jabs from the start, reserving his right-hand swings until later on. The boilermaker has been practicing defensive tactics more than attack, and believes that he can keep Fitz off. The latter is expected to force the fight from the start. In such an event it is believed that Jeffries will stand away and try to 'jab his block off.'[323]

Both were hard hitters, but Fitz had the superior experience. Both were clever, but Fitz was cleverer. He was shiftier and quicker. Jeff had advantages in weight, height, reach, youth, physical strength, and perhaps ability to absorb punishment, having never been down.

Although both were confident, neither took personal cuts at the other. "A satisfactory feature of the whole affair is the absence of mud-slinging." Fitz and Corbett had insulted each other, using such terms as "cur," "yellow dog," "quitter," stiff," "dub," and "hamfatter." Jeff had won friends by

---

322 *New York Journal,* June 9, 1899.
323 *New York Sun,* June 9, 1899.

refraining from indulging in the personal attacks. "It was that trait in Jeffries which helped to increase his popularity."

In his first autobiography, Jeff claimed that he was dried out and his weight lower than it had been for any other fight before or since. He had trained harder than ever, and had also dehydrated himself.

> When I came East to meet Armstrong I weighed just 245 pounds stripped to fighting togs in the ring. Now, ready to meet Fitzsimmons, I scaled exactly 204 pounds. I had run myself to a shadow. Two days before the fight I weighed just 206 pounds stripped, and let everybody around the camp see me on the scales. The day before the fight I went with a number of reporters to the baggage room at the railroad station. There on the baggage scales, in jumpers and a light sweater, I weighed an even 215 pounds. I never attempted to make such low weight again, as I know I'm stronger and have more endurance when I carry forty pounds more flesh on my bones.[324]

There is primary source support for Jeff's dehydration claims. In the days after the fight, Jeff told one reporter, "I can't get enough water. I haven't drunk any water for two weeks, and I could hardly sleep for my thirst. But they said it weakened me, and I was determined I wouldn't drink." Just imagine how much better Jeff might have been if he had not dehydrated himself and bought into the falsehood that drinking water hampered performance. Today, we know that quite the opposite is true. Lack of water adversely affects performance.[325]

The day before the fight, it was said that Jeffries would tip the scales at about 206 pounds. "In spite of the talk that Fitz will not be over 158 pounds, it is asserted that when the champion got upon the scales Wednesday [June 7] he weighed 170 ½ pounds. He has steadfastly refused to tell his weight and says he will not go on the scales to weigh in tomorrow." Usually fighters took on several pounds in the last couple days before a fight, because they did not train as hard. Therefore, both combatants were likely a bit larger.[326]

On the day of the fight, the *New York Herald* listed Jeff as 6'1½" and 206 pounds. Other local papers said Jeff weighed 215, while still others estimated that he would enter the ring weighing between 210 and 212 pounds. W.W. Naughton estimated that Fitz would be 165 pounds. *The New York Journal* listed the 5'11 ¾" Fitz's fighting weight at 171 pounds. Bob insisted that he weighed 158 pounds. However,

---

324 *My Life and Battles* at 31.
325 *New York Journal*, June 12, 1899.
326 *San Francisco Chronicle*; *New York Sun*, June 9, 1899. Another report said that "it is learned from a most trustworthy source that when the champion got upon the scales on Wednesday he weighed 170 ½ pounds."

This is not credited by the sporting fraternity. They believe he will weigh at least twelve pounds heavier. It was stated on reliable authority today that Fitzsimmons weighed 170 ½ pounds, and men in the know declared that Fitzsimmons's fighting weight would not be less than 171 pounds.

Jeffries was weighed in his clothes before he left his training quarters. He tipped the scales at 223 pounds. "I will weigh 215 pounds stripped," he remarked. ... Tomorrow morning I expect to be champion of the world.[327]

On June 9, 1899 at Coney Island, New York, over two years after he won the title, 36-year-old heavyweight champion Bob Fitzsimmons defended his crown for the first time, against 24-year-old James J. Jeffries.[328]

Tickets were $5 for the first-come first-served seats, reserved seats being $10, $15, $20, and $25, with boxes holding six persons each for $150.

That evening, those who could not afford tickets would be able to come to the Broadway Athletic Club, which would receive live telegraph wires during the fight. Two men would illustrate the bout, throwing the described blows at each other.[329]

A huge crowd of damp, steaming people stood in the pouring summer rain for hours to buy the high-priced tickets, demonstrating that "the boxing game is at its height in this country and that a set of boxing gloves and a 24-foot ring will not only get the dollars of the sporting men but the good coin of the day laborer, as well." Every large city from San Francisco to New York was represented. "It is safe to say that the assemblage was the most representative one which ever sat around a ring."

The "strangest thing of all was the great interest the women took in the affair, from the outside, of course." One-third of the crowd outside the arena was composed of women, "many of whom would have liked nothing better than to have paid some of their money as entrance fees." However, no women were allowed in, other than Bob's wife. "There was a great crowd outside composed of those who wouldn't or couldn't pay, and who were content, apparently, to be at least near the place where a great fistic battle was taking place."

At 6:30 p.m., the arena doors were opened. The $5 crowd rushed in, because their seats were first-come, first-served. The building was a large amphitheatre, "probably the largest of its kind in America." It was a "vast,

327 *New York Herald, San Francisco Examiner, New York Journal,* June 9, 1899; *New York Daily Tribune,* June 10, 1899.
328 The following accounts and quotes are the product of an amalgamation of the *New York Herald, New York Daily Tribune, New York Times, New York Journal, New York Sun, New York World, Brooklyn Daily Eagle, Asbury Park Daily Press, San Francisco Chronicle, San Francisco Examiner,* all June 10, 1899, as well as *New York Clipper,* June 17, 1899; *National Police Gazette,* June 24, 1899; *My Life and Battles* at 35-36. Jim Corbett wrote the *New York World* report.
329 *New York World,* June 5, 1899.

roughly finished building, destitute of interior paint or ornamentation; a mere great frame, which has been rebuilt for the purposes of ring entertainments." It was oblong in shape and located on the beach within 50 yards of the surf. Large windows around the sides and in the roof let in a cool breeze. The arena was well arranged, although some spectators were annoyed by being seated behind the machine erected for taking motion pictures of the contest. The telegraph operators sat in a gallery high above. The police were close to the ring.

High up above the ring was a scaffolding extending around the four sides. Upon this scaffolding were 24 electric calcium light reflectors, which would create a great glare of light into the ring. There were also 25 arc lights strung about in prominent places. All of these lights were designed to facilitate the taking of the motion pictures. Two film machines were shrouded in rubber covers.

At 7:00 p.m., all of the $5 seats were taken, and nearly all of the best reserved chairs had already been disposed of.

At 8:00 p.m., the electric reflectors were suddenly turned on, and the glare was so blinding that everyone shouted. One person said, "Put your hats on or you'll get sunstroke." The lights were quickly turned off, the operators pronouncing them to be all right.

By 8:30 p.m., there were easily 8,000 people present, and they were still coming. Although the seating capacity was 8,442, with the eventual overcrowding of the bleachers and those who jammed their way into the boxes and aisles, it was thought that 10,0000 were present by the time the boxers entered the ring. Every seat was taken, and all available space covered in humanity. Another 5,000 or more were unable to get in.

The gate receipts were the biggest of all time. Estimates ranged from $65,000 to $70,000 to $100,000 taken in. This beat Sullivan-Corbett, which was $52,000, Corbett-Sharkey II at $47,000, and Corbett-Fitzsimmons at $44,000.

Fitzsimmons had been sleeping from 7 to 8 p.m. at Bath Beach. Eventually, his team drove two and a half miles to the arena. He entered the building at 9:20 p.m. and went to his private room.

At 9:30 p.m., accompanied by his trainers, Jeffries entered the building. He was wearing a black-and-red-striped sweater and long trousers. His hair was long and uncombed, and his skin was well bronzed by the sun at the seashore. As Jeff passed by, Corbett shook his hand and wished him well. Jeff proceeded to his dressing room. Both Fitz and Jeff appeared confident.

By fight time, Fitzsimmons was the favorite at 2 to 1 and 5 to 3 odds. "That Fitzsimmons was a favorite with the majority was evident from the talk." He had a knack for winning battles against bigger men. Bob's strength, punching power, skill, experience and generalship were expected to win it for him. He was the real magnet, although the way that Jeff had taken off 30 pounds in training had won him a lot of public confidence.

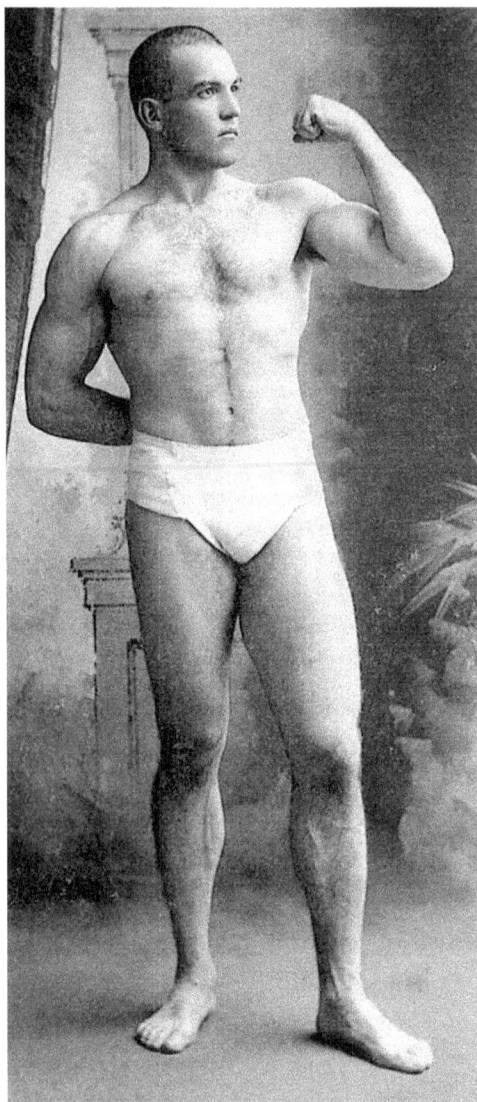

In his autobiographies, Jeffries claimed that on the night of the fight, Bill Brady told him that he wanted to try to shake Bob's confidence. Brady would intentionally get into a debate about the rules regarding clinching and breaking. He instructed Jeff to grab Bill, throw him aside, ask Bob how he wanted to fight, and then to grab Fitz and rough him a bit to show him just how strong he was, to intimidate him and shake his confidence. That evening, Jeff did just that. As they were debating the rules, he grabbed Brady by the collar and jerked him toward the corner of the room so hard that he spun around and fell. Jeff said, "You talk too much." He then asked Bob how he wanted to fight, and viciously shoved Bob back half way across the room. Fitz said, "Straight rules. ... We'll protect ourselves at all times."

Jeffries held contradictory opinions about the impact of their ploy. At one time, he said that although he believed that his display shook Bob's confidence, Bob still fought like a "cornered wild cat. He was the gamest man in the world. ... I learned to respect him as the best man I'd ever seen. It's a respect that lasts even today." However, Jeff later wrote, "Some thought that display of strength intimidated Fitzsimmons, but I do not. He was not that kind of a man. Nothing I ever saw bothered him excepting a hard punch on the jaw. But it caused him to change his demands regarding the rules."[330]

330 *Two Fisted Jeff* at 106-107; *My Life and Battles* at 35.

The primary sources support Jeff's version of events. A couple days after the fight, Jeffries said,

> Did you hear of the job Brady put up on Fitz? About twenty minutes before the fight Brady fixed it for me to meet Fitz face to face. The idea was for me to show him I wasn't afraid of his looks, or maybe to throw a scare into him, if you want to put it that way.
>
> We met in the dressing-room. I gave him a good, hard look. Brady said to Fitz: 'How do you want to fight?' Then along I came, as if by accident. 'Now, how do you want to fight?' I said to him, and with that I bumped up against him and shoved him clear down to the other end of the dressing-room.
>
> Well, you ought to have seen the look of surprise that lit on Fitz's face. He thought I would be paralyzed by one look at him. His eyes stuck out after he reached the other end of the room. I guess he was satisfied then that there was no scare in me.[331]

Both the *National Police Gazette* and the *New York Sun* discussed this pre-fight debate. It took place while various offers and challenges were being announced in the arena, just before the fight. In the dressing room at the back of the building, behind the bleachers, Fitzsimmons, Julian, Brady, and Jeffries indulged in an argument over the rules. Jeffries wanted straight Marquis of Queensberry rules, with hitting in the clinches and on the breakaway, while Fitz insisted on no hitting in clinches, and a clean break.

> This argument was kept up for more than twenty minutes, the crowd in the meanwhile stamping and whistling and calling for the fight to begin. … The wrangle between the fighters was finally settled in this way: If both men were holding, the referee was to go between them. If one man was holding with both hands, the other could fight himself free.

Hence, the rules were slightly modified. Ultimately, though, the fight descriptions gave the impression that the men fought with clean breaks and no hitting in the clinches.

At 10:10 p.m., clad from head to foot in a long blue bathrobe, Fitzsimmons appeared and walked toward the 24-foot ring. Martin Julian carried a six-foot-high floral horseshoe composed of roses, with the inscription, "Good Luck to the Champion." Dan Hickey, Yank Kenny, and Jack Everhardt also accompanied him. Julian held the horseshoe aloft inside the ring. Upon Bob's ring entry, Corbett said, "He looks about the same as he has always looked in the ring."

Only a minute behind Fitz, Jeffries, wearing a garnet sweater and dark trousers with suspenders, climbed through the ropes, and the house went

331 *New York World*, June 11, 1899.

wild over him. Bill Delaney, Jack Jeffries, Jim Daly, and Tommy Ryan attended him.

George Siler then entered, coatless and collarless, wearing a negligee shirt, with suspenders holding up his trousers. He was a small man, especially in comparison with the fighters.

As the boxers got ready, more challenges were announced. Kid McCoy challenged Fitz to a fight at middleweight, and Tom Sharkey challenged the winner.

At this time, with the men in their respective corners, the glaring lights were turned on with a great sizzle. "The ring fairly glistened from the rays." However, Corbett was the first to prophesize that something might be wrong with the lighting and filming process. "I wonder what's the matter with the photographing machine. Half the lights are out; still the ring is just as brightly lighted as if it was daylight."

Siler explained the rules and noted that it was a scheduled 25-round bout.

Jeffries was first to strip. "His magnificent physique was looked at in wonderment. He was a giant and no mistake. He was taller, bigger, heavier, and stronger looking in every way than Fitz." He wore white trunks. "His training at the seashore had bronzed him like an Indian, and his muscular development was wonderful." Corbett said, "By George, he has enormous legs! See how Fitz is looking over at him. … Great Scott, but he's enormous!"

Fitzsimmons removed his bathrobe. Corbett said, "He looks well. He looks great. He looks very big. I never saw him better." Bob wore black trunks with a belt of small American flags.

The fighters' weights were a point of some debate. *The Herald* said Jeff looked about 212. Corbett said Jeff weighed a trifle more than 200. One reporter said, "Fitz looked to be about 170 pounds in weight, while Jeffries was easily 206." *The Times* listed Jeff as 6'1½" and about 225. *The Sun* said that Jeff would tip the scales at about 206 pounds, the lowest he had trained down to in his career. Earlier that day, Jeff had admitted that he would weigh about 215 pounds in the ring.

One wrote, "Jeffries, judging by appearances, certainly weighed considerably more than two hundred pounds, while Fitz could not have weighed less than one hundred and sixty. Neither man wished the truth to be known." *The National Police Gazette* said,

> One thing which puzzled the sports was the respective weights of the men, and while it was confidently believed that Fitz would fight in the neighborhood of 170 pounds and Jeffries somewhere about 205 yet no one except the trainers knew what the weights really were. This was an item of interest which will probably never go on record, and all that will be known is that the men fought at their best weights.

In the ring, when Fitzsimmons claimed to weigh 157 pounds, Jeffries humorously/sarcastically replied, "If Fitz weighs 157, I weigh 148." In his autobiography, Jeff said that Fitz looked bigger and stronger than he did in Carson.

The boxers shook hands and began the fight at 10:24 p.m.

1st round

This was a feeling out round, with no damage done. They sparred cautiously, each feinting warily for an opening. Jeffries kept his position with his body bent towards the right, with his left held out, feinting often with the left. Corbett said, "Notice how low Jeff is crouching and how far out he has his left." Fitz smiled and backed away as Jeff approached, but neither led with any blows for a while. Neither was anxious to get down to business too quickly. They had 25 rounds.

Jeffries was more aggressive, but either his blows fell short or were blocked. Fitz was good at sidestepping, dodging, and moving away, coming back again, grinning. It was evident that Jeff's appearance made Bob respect him. Fitzsimmons was on the move, keeping out of harm's way, but the smiling Jeff did not run after him. Jeff followed him around and was quick to jump back at feints. When Bob punched, he found it difficult to penetrate Jeff's crouching defense. Both were cautious.

Fitz tried a light left but Jeff ducked and clinched. They broke and feinted again. Jeff kept trying the left jab for the body, but Fitz kept stepping back. Jeff threw a left hook, but Bob jumped away. Fitz blocked another hook and they clinched. Bob showed his strength by pushing Jeff away, even though he looked small next to the Californian. Both landed lefts to the nose. Fitz tried a right, but Jeff got inside of it very handily. Fitz stepped back and swung a left, but Jeff ducked and clinched, smiling. "Now you notice he throws Fitz away as easily as if Fitz was a boy." Bob's blows mostly missed or were grazing as Jeff ducked, but Fitz did land a few to the nose and mouth, which did no harm. Jeff landed one good left uppercut.

The Journal and the *Daily Tribune* called the round even. *The Examiner* said the round was a shade in Jeff's favor. Corbett said both appeared nervous, but felt that Jeff was doing well. *The Sun* said it was Fitz's round, as he landed the most blows. Outside the arena, when the mob asked how the fight was going, the answer came back, "Fitz is killing him." The crowd, which was mostly pro-Jeffries, became downcast. Of course, the report was in error, as the round had been fairly tame.

2nd round

Jeffries seemed more at ease, crouching low and hiding his face behind his guard arm. Fitz threw some lefts, but Jeff countered them by ducking and stepping in with heavy rights to the body. The crowd cheered with delight. When Jeff came in again, Bob clinched. Jeffries showed his great strength by pushing Fitzsimmons off with ease.

After sparring, Jeff landed a short right to the body, left to the ribs, then right to the body again. Corbett said, "Jeff is doing well." Fitz began making the pace, throwing some hard blows, but Jeff eluded them and kept Bob off. Jeff put in a left hook on the belly, but missed two lefts to the head as Bob jumped back. Fitz bluffed with his left and swung his right for the head, but his distance was off. Jeff rushed again and shoved Fitz fully 12 feet across the ring.

Jeffries became aggressive, landing a number of quick left jabs to the body and face in succession. A left to Bob's nose brought first blood, trickling down in a tiny stream. Bill Brady called out his claim of first blood, which was typically a betting point, and referee Siler nodded in acknowledgment. Jeff bluffed with his left at the head and instead landed a good right on the head. Fitz laughed.

Fitzsimmons feinted and advanced with a left, but Jeff immediately countered by dashing in with a perfectly timed quick and powerful straight left to the nose and jaw that caught Bob coming toward him and knocked Fitzsimmons down onto his back in his own corner. The excited crowd yelled like mad at the surprise knockdown.

The champion quickly rose after being down for only two seconds. He smiled and acted as if he considered it a joke. Mrs. Fitzsimmons said, "Corbett did that too, but he did not win. One knockdown don't win a fight. Just wait until the end."

After rising, the angered Fitzsimmons attacked and tried to mix it up. He forced Jeff back by swinging both hands, but Jeffries avoided him by dancing away and cleverly blocking the blows with his arms, smiling at the champion's unsuccessful efforts. The bell rang soon thereafter.

Bob looked to all four corners of the ring before locating his own. It was evident that the knockdown had dazed him a bit. He seemed unsteady when he went to his corner. It was a "decidedly bad round" for Fitzsimmons. However, Bob told his cornermen, "It's all right. I am not hurt."

In his autobiography, Jeff said that after dropping Fitz, although he thought of trying to finish, Jack told him to be careful. "That fellow is most dangerous when hurt. Look out for some trick." Jeff remained cautious, not wanting to fall into a trap.[332]

3rd round

In the corner between rounds, Tommy Ryan told Jeff to go for the body with his right, and to use the left at the head with jabs and hooks. Referee Siler later said that Jeff followed his corner's advice and landed often. "Some of course, were light, and Fitz, thinking he had no steam, did all the advancing."

332 *Two Fisted Jeff* at 108-113.

At the start of the round, Bob's nostrils were bloody. Jeff landed a left squarely upon the nose. Bob clinched, laughed and pushed Jeff away. The blood ran down from Bob's nose in a stream. Jeff laughed back at him.

Bob missed a left and right for the head because Jeff got away as quick as a cat. Jeff ducked under a left lead and clinched. After breaking, Jeff landed his left on the nose. They both rushed and landed lefts to the jaw. After clinching, Jeff threw Fitz away. Jeff rushed him and landed twice to the cheek. As Bob threw a right, Jeff stepped inside of it so that it missed. Jeff landed his left on the ribs and followed with his right on the other side. Bob landed a left to the body, but Jeff came back with a right on the ribs. To the body, Jeff landed a left jab and left hook. Fitz closed in but Jeff landed an awful right over the heart as they came to a clinch. In the clinch, some of the blood ran onto Jeff's shoulder. At that point, Corbett opined, "Barring accidents, barring a punch like I got, it looks as if Jeff ought to win inside of ten rounds."

Fitz looked a bit worried, and began forcing the pace. He tried to mix it, but Jeff blocked with both hands and clinched, smiling while there. After breaking, Fitz feinted Jeff into ducking and then hooked his jaw hard with the left. Jeff laughed as he straightened up. He rushed in and Bob clinched. After breaking, Bob struck Jeff's forehead with the same hook. Jeff coolly got to close quarters and landed a left and right to the stomach.

Fitzsimmons rushed in again with a very hard left hook. Bob tried rushing tactics, hitting his man hard and often, particularly with his left, but seldom without return. Jeff was very fast and seemed to land his left almost at will on Bob's face. He kept in a crouching position.

Both landed some hard blows to the body and head as they exchanged. Bob tried a left for the jaw, but was forced to clinch as Jeff rushed in like a tiger. They landed heart punches and rallied, fighting in exchanges all across the ring. Jeff landed his hook to the head and right to the body. "The men were now fighting very fast and both scoring effectively." Jeff landed with both hands to the body and sent Bob back with a left on the chest. "The fighting was of the hottest kind now, Jeffries forcing it, until Fitz caught him with a hard right-hander on the throat. Then Jeffries backed away, Fitz following with heavy swings and jolts which landed on Jim's head and made him take the defensive at the bell."

Jeff smiled as he walked to his corner. Bob seemed a bit concerned. Mrs. Fitzsimmons could not overcome her nervousness, and withdrew into a dark passageway, and then to her husband's dressing room. Corbett said, "This has been Jeffries's fight right through up to date, even on points." Kid McCoy said, "There was great fighting in this round, but Fitz was not showing his usual form." *The Herald* said, "The fighting in this round was fast and telling, with the honors, except for a short time, in favor of Jeffries." Outside the arena, the round was announced as being pretty even.

4th round

Thus far, the fighting had been remarkably fast. Jeffries was a big surprise. He was a bit slower this round, while Fitz was speedier than ever, strong and aggressive. Fitz rushed, but Jeff blocked beautifully with his elbow. Bob landed a long hard left on the jaw, but Jeff took it well. Fitz bluffed a left for the head and missed a right for the jaw. "Jeff waits and swings in a left hook that catches Fitz under the right ear and staggers him from head to foot." Although momentarily unsteady on his legs, Bob came in and sharp infighting followed. Jeff blocked him and landed a terrific right jolt under the heart. Jeff protected himself from a right to the head and jumped in with a right on the ribs. They clinched between exchanges. "Jeff was using his immense weight to advantage in the clinches and Siler had to force his way between them to break his hold." Jeff landed a left to the body, right on the ear, and a heavy left on the cheek bone. Still, "Fitz is a game old boy. He keeps coming right in for more of it."

Fitzsimmons seemed intent on landing a knockout blow with his right, but was unsuccessful in landing it, finding more success with his left. Jeff would duck the right aimed for his head and counter with a right to the ribs. Jeff smashed his right in on the belly twice more and drove Bob away. Jeff blocked some hooks, or took them with little concern, confident to a fault.

The fighting was terrific as they mixed it up in lively fashion, countering each other. Fitz landed multiple left jabs and hooks, but Jeff landed hooks and body blows. "The fighting during this round was very spirited and frequently worked the enthusiasm of the spectators to a high pitch." At the end of the round, Jeff chased Fitz, but Bob's side-stepping was too clever. "It was a terrific gait, and the crowd was howling."

The Tribune said the round was about even. Kid McCoy said Fitz was the aggressor and won the round. *The Examiner* said Jeff looked confident and by the end of the round had a shade the better of it. *The Asbury Park Daily Press* said it was Fitz's round. Outside the arena, the round was conceded to be in Fitz's favor.

5th round

Jeffries chatted with his seconds in the corner before coming out for the round. Corbett said, "I don't see how Jeffries can lose; he is the cleverer man by far. Fitz is coming at him, though, just as if he was right in it."

Jeff met him with a left on the sore nose that brought more blood. "Fitz dashes in with a right under the eye and raises a lump, but Jeffries meets him with a right jolt on the ribs." Fitz kept coming in, but Jeff stopped him with a left in the belly quickly followed by a right on the ribs.

As they stepped in to clinch, Jeff ducked into a vicious and quick straight left, which opened a deep gash in his forehead just above his left eye. The blood flowed copiously in a stream, running down Jeff's cheek onto his breast. Although he was not hurt, Jeff bent down low more.

The aggressive Fitzsimmons forced the pace and rushed in with rights and lefts, backing Jeff to the ropes, scoring with a left to the jaw. However, Jeff ducked under most of the leads or saved himself by clinching. Fitz laughed as Jeff was nettled and took the defensive. However, Jeffries then walloped Fitz on the jaw and over the heart. Bob again rushed him back to the ropes and landed a couple of swings on the head. Bob blocked a wild blow from Jeff, laughing. However, Jeffries landed a fearful left on the neck which made Bob's head wobble. Fitz landed a return blow which made Jeff stop his advance. Jeffries stopped him with a solid left on the bleeding nose and a driving right on the ribs. "They are mixing it up very fast."

Both went to the head and body. Jeff landed two lefts to the jaw and a right on the forehead. They slugged hard, and then took a rest for a few seconds until Jeff came in again with his left on the nose. Fitz then followed Jeff. "They are both looking for a chance to land a knockout."

The majority of sources agreed that as Bob was rushing in on the attack, he slipped or tripped, and as he was falling, Jeff hit him with a right to the heart (or elbow) that sent him down. Some simply said he fell down, and did not mention his being hit. In his autobiography, Jeff claimed that he hit Fitzsimmons in the ribs so hard that he went down for five seconds. Corbett backed Jeff's version. He said that Bob rushed in with two lefts and a right at the head, but Jeff drove his right into the ribs "that knocks him down on his knees hanging on the ropes." Bob took five seconds to get up.

After rising, Fitzsimmons landed a left to the neck and right to the body. As Fitz came in again, Jeff landed two straight lefts to the face. In the next rally, Bob landed several hard body blows, including a terrific right to the heart which made Jeffries grunt audibly.

Corbett said that both seemed a little bit tired. *The Examiner* called the round even. Kid McCoy said Fitzsimmons was fighting poorly. However, during the 4th and 5th rounds, Bob's corner was aglow. They declared that Fitz was wearing Jeffries down. They did not think Jeff could handle the pace, and felt that eventually one of Bob's sledgehammer blows would take him out. Certainly, the ever confident Fitzsimmons fought as if he believed that he would eventually land the knockout blow.

6th round

The Sun said, "Fitzsimmons would not sit down between the rounds." Corbett said that Bob was up first.

Fitzsimmons was fresher and on the aggressive, landing lefts to the head and chest. He appeared to be the more confident of the two. He backed Jeff to a corner, feinted with his left and landed a glancing right to the ear. Jeff clinched. Fitz did the forcing with considerable feinting. Jeff was more inclined to retreat, duck and clinch. Bob's rushing tactics slightly rattled Jeff.

A right to Jeff's throat could be heard throughout the pavilion. Bob also landed a left to the stomach. Bob jabbed his left lightly in the face and then landed a heavy blow that drew blood from the eye again. Jeff's cut was

227

bleeding profusely. Fitz played for the cut and hit it, but Jeff countered with a jab to the nose that again set Bob's blood flowing from it.

Corbett felt that Jeffries was resting and taking his time, mostly using his left jab. Jeff was slower, but came back occasionally with a surprising spurt when the champion did not seem to expect it. Whenever Bob would think that he had Jeff cornered and swung a blow, Jeff with surprising quickness sidestepped, ducked, or blocked, or struck out and hit Bob instead. Corbett said, "[Jeff] almost knocks his head off with a left hook." Every time that Bob led with the left to the head, Jeff stopped him with a right to the ribs.

Another writer said that Jeffries fought back wildly, missing with both hands. However, Jeff then used three left jabs, sending Bob's head back with each one. Although Jeff still hit him with some solid blows, he seemed to be a bit slower than before. On the other hand, "Fitz was faster than chain lightning."

The attacking Fitzsimmons was busier and landed more often. After Fitz caught him with a terrific punch to the jaw, Jeff clinched hard. After breaking, Fitz cut loose and rained the blows on Jeff's face. A left to the stomach made Jeff grunt again. Jeffries responded with hard blows, but Fitz landed two to his one, "which were frightful in force and made the crowd simply wild with excitement."

Mrs. Fitzsimmons returned in time to see Bob make a desperate rush that "but for a stumble might have ended the battle." Mrs. Fitz joyously said, "He's getting stronger, Watch him. He can't lose." Jeff's face was bleeding badly. Just before the bell, Jeff countered a left to the face with a hard punch to the body.

Almost all of the sources agreed that Fitzsimmons had the better of it in this round. John Kelly went so far as to say that it looked as if Fitz had merely to await his chance to land a knockout blow. However, the lone dissenter Corbett observed that both were tired and that Jeff's tremendous weight was telling on Bob.

After the round was over, Fitzsimmons said to his cornermen, "He is easy as sheckels," and told them to watch for a knockout.

7th round

Having recuperated wonderfully in the one-minute rest, Fitz seemed fresh as ever. He was the aggressor, doing the rushing, seeming confident. The fight had been one of the fastest ever seen between heavyweights. As Jeffries had been fighting very fast, he seemed to be taking a rest in this, as well as the previous round. Jeff was slow in getting to ring center, and walked backward around the ring.

Fitzsimmons took advantage of Jeff's slowing up by trying to keep the pace fast, advancing as Jeffries moved. Bob led with his left, and Jeff backed away. Bob missed a left swing and Jeff hit the body with his right as Bob was coming in. Fitz advanced and followed Jeff around the ring. Fitz was aggressive and appeared to be looking for an opening for his right.

Three times Bob came in and Jeff ducked under his attack and clinched, at the same time throwing his entire weight onto Fitz. Jeffries dashed in with a left on the belly, showing that he had faster feet than Bob. The next time Bob came in, Jeff landed his right to the belly. Corbett said, "That tires Fitz." However, Fitzsimmons kept coming.

As he was pressed, Jeffries landed some light lefts to the stomach and ribs, the left jab to the nose and mouth, and Bob laughed. A Jeffries hook to the jaw rattled Bob. Fitz grinned and shook his head. They exchanged swings, with Fitz ducking two or three and landing two or three himself. Fitz was faster and seemed at ease.

Fitzsimmons fought hard and went at Jeffries. As Bob was advancing, Jeff led with a left, but Bob stepped inside of it and countered Jeff with his hard left hook on the jaw, which appeared to shake Jeff up. Mrs. Fitzsimmons said, "Oh, that's it! I knew he would get it in." Bob missed a right but followed with a good left hook to the body. Jeff was busy blocking as Fitz threw hard blows. After a clinch and break, Fitz landed a left hook to the chin, but took a right on the ribs. Blood came from the corner of Jeff's mouth. Bob landed a right uppercut to the stomach and a left on the neck, both blows having tremendous power. He also nailed the eye with a right and split it open again. At the end of the round, Jeff landed a left on the cheek but Fitz came back with a hard thudding right to the heart that made a loud sound. Jeffries was doing his best to stop the assault when the bell rang. When Fitzsimmons was walking back to the corner, he looked back at Jeffries and smiled.

The local sources agreed that Fitzsimmons had the best of the round, particularly at the end, when he landed the most effective blows. Although Jeffries was still landing, his blows were not as hard or as effective as they had been earlier. His light blows did little or no apparent damage, and were not sufficient to keep Bob off. He failed to reach Fitz as well as he had in the previous rounds, and was doing most of the clinching. Fitz looked to have a chance to win. Even Corbett felt that Jeff appeared to be the more tired of the two.

8th round

Slow to respond to the bell, Jeffries looked puzzled as Fitzsimmons grinned and advanced confidently. Jeff backed away as Fitz pressed. However, as Bob moved in, Jeffries effectively countered him with lefts to the nose and mouth. Bob grinned and tried a left and right, but Jeff got inside of them, anxious to duck when Bob got close. Fitz's punches often missed around his neck. Jeff landed a hard right on the body, causing Bob to grit his teeth. Bob rushed the fighting, but did no damage. After a Fitz miss, Jeff landed a left swing full on Bob's neck and the crowd cheered. Jeff was as strong as when he began, and was going a little smoother than ever.

Fitz looked angry and went in with a wild rush, landing a couple of body blows and whipping up a jolt on the neck or jaw which made Jeff retreat.

Jeff met another rush with a left. James then rushed in and scored heavily to the body, but was hit in the bleeding eye. Fitz threw some hot jabs and the blood poured down Jeff's cheek. Jeffries seemed a bit slower, but was game and willing to fight, doing some rushing of his own. However, Bob was able to step back and smile. The champion still looked strong. Both landed left jabs. Fitz feinted with the right, trying to coax Jeff into a right lead. They exchanged blows for a while. Jeff mostly threw lefts at the body.

As Jeffries was rushing in, when they simultaneously threw straight lefts, Jeff's left jolt to the nose got there first and sent Bob reeling back to the ropes, acting as if he were groggy, leaning halfway over them. However, Jeff's second told him to look out, that Bob was only acting. Fitz was a master at bluffing grogginess in order to set a trap. Even when actually groggy, as fighters came to him, Fitzsimmons excelled at timing them perfectly with knockout blows. Referee Siler said, "[Jeff] kept away from Fitz in the same old cautious manner." Fitz came away from the ropes acting as if it had only been a joke and again bluffed with the right again. However, another reporter said Bob was momentarily dazed. Fitz grinned and rushed in. Like a flash, Jeff hooked a left, but Fitz slipped away from it.

As Jeffries came forward, Fitzsimmons missed a right but countered the advancing Jeff by catching him with a frightfully hard short left hook on the cheek. One said that although it was perhaps the best punch of the fight, it seemed to have no effect on Jeffries. Another said it was an awful hard punch, but it was too high to be effective, that if it had been a couple inches lower, it could have ended the fight. Still, one writer felt that it had to put some stars in Jeff's eyes. It was the best punch of the round, but overall, Jeff did the superior work.

After having lost the last two rounds, the local reports agreed that Jeffries had the better of it in this round. One said that Jeffries had rallied astonishingly. Another said that Jeff showed more strength and speed in this round. A third writer said that Jeff had the best of it at this point, and Fitz seemed to be growing desperate. Echoing this thought, one said that Fitzsimmons was trying to make a sensational knockout finish, but imprudently forced matters. Still, both smiled at each other after the bell. Corbett said Bob looked tired, puffing a little. "Jeffries had by far the best of that round. Look at the big boy smile as he comes back to his corner."

9th round

As usual, Fitzsimmons was first up and gamely went in to do or die, advancing to close quarters. He kept on top of Jeffries all the time. They mixed it and engaged in fast exchanges of heavy swings. Fitz seemed to pick out the marks with better judgment. He landed two solid body blows, then came in close again and punched Jeff on the bleeding eye.

Fitzsimmons was the aggressor, but Jeff countered frequently. Jeffries was stronger in this round, and by the middle of the round, it was anybody's fight. They were tired and clinched frequently. Bob looked for an opening, but Jeff ducked and threw his shoulder into Bob's chest. Jeff roughed it a bit. He sent Bob backward with a straight blow to the face. Fitz continued on the aggressive, but was sent back again with a left on the body. Two long jarring left smashes to the nose made Bob wince, and the crowd howled its approval. Fitz bled a good deal from his nose, the blood pouring down his chest. Later, a right to the heart had Fitz guessing.

Jeff alternated between jabs, hooks, and body blows, working up and down. After landing, Jeff would break away and begin feinting again with as much caution as in the 1st round. Bob was also bleeding from the mouth, and he spit up a considerable amount of blood. He landed a left swing on the cheek, but it was too high to do any good. When Jeff dashed in with his left and missed, he clinched. Bob spit out a mouthful of blood over Jeff's shoulder. The jabs smeared blood all over Bob's face. Fitz was a bit tired (his mouth was open) and probably wondering where all the blows were coming from. However, he kept forcing matters.

Jeffries occasionally smiled after landing. He knew what he was doing. However, Jeff did not get his full power into his punches because he was constantly getting away as he punched. Fitz treated his punches with disdain, constantly advancing and looking to land his power shots. However, Corbett said, "His swings are going wild. Jim is either a couple of inches away from them or else he steps in and lets the arm double around his neck."

Several times during the round, Mrs. Fitzsimmons exclaimed "Oh!" as Jeff's blows brought blood from Bob's nose or sent his head to the right or left. Jeffries suddenly made a savage feint as if to drive in the left jab, but whipped in a stiff arm swing across the neck, and then dug in an awful right to the body and roughed Fitz in the clinch. Regardless, Fitzsimmons continued infighting and leading until the bell, breaking no ground.

There was a difference of opinion regarding what this round showed. Corbett said, "Fitz is now much more tired than Jeffries. I think Jim has the fight now." *The Herald* presented different opinions. One said that this was a fierce round, and Jeff had somewhat the better of it. Another said that Bob was tired and unsteady with his movements, that it was a bad round for him. Jeff was comparatively fresh. Still a third opinion said, "There is no doubt that in the ninth round Fitzsimmons thought himself a winner as nearly as in the third. He looked it, and his backers believed that he had sized his man up and would soon land the decisive blow." *The Tribune* said Jeff clearly had the better of the round. *The Examiner* said that on the whole, it was Jeff's round. *The Sun* said, "The round was even, if not slightly in favor of Jeffries." Kid McCoy said that Fitz fought poorly and seemed a little weak. Referee Siler said that Jeff had the better of it, but there was still some hope for Fitzsimmons, as he kept smiling.

10th round

Although Fitzsimmons was a bit tired in the previous round, he appeared as fresh as ever at the start of the round. Corbett said of Bob, "He's a tough, game man." Jeff assumed his peculiar stooping position that he used throughout the fight, advancing cautiously toward Fitz. They exchanged blows, but Jeff landed the hardest and most effective punches, including his jab, a hard hook, and after ducking a left, a right to the body. Jeff dashed in, missed and clinched. Corbett said, "Fitz turns and looks to the referee for sympathy. He's getting done up, that's what's the matter, Jim hasn't done anything wrong." Apparently, Jeff was using his weight and strength in the clinches.

Jeffries landed a couple lefts on the nose. "They don't look hard, but they are rocking Fitz's head just the same." Fitzsimmons fought back hard and reached the face with the left, but his rights missed. No matter how quick Bob was, Jeff either blocked or stepped inside of the rights. Fitz backed Jeff across the ring. Just as Jeff touched the ropes, he used some neat footwork and slipped away.

After a few exchanges, Jeffries landed a right over the heart and straight left to the jaw that rocked Fitz's head. When Bob advanced again with a wild left hook lead, Jeff ducked and with lightning speed either swung his left hook or shot out his crushing stiff straight left (depending on the source), landing to the jaw with double force, dropping Bob backwards to the boards, his head striking the floor. As Bob lay motionless, Martin Julian tried to douse him with water. Siler quickly ordered him back to his place. Lying on his back, Bob rolled over as Siler counted four. Julian cried for him to get up. He slowly rose at eight in a dazed condition.

Jeffries, watching him like a cat, crouching low with his hands poised for instant action, crept steadily towards the groggy champion. Fitzsimmons tried to step in with a body shot and clinch, but Jeffries smashed him with another left hook to the neck and dropped him again. *The Journal* said, "Jeff caught him with a vicious left hook and nearly threw him on his head. But the blow was not as good as the other and Fitz came back quicker." Corbett said, "This Fitz is a game fellow. Those two knock-downs are enough to knock the life out of almost anybody."

Fitzsimmons rose in a moment and moved about the ring, hoping to recuperate. Jeffries was cool, not excited or overanxious to finish or leave himself open to one of Bob's desperate punches. Despite the roars of the crowd, Jeff began his feinting again. He was in no hurry. Referee Siler said that despite knocking Fitz down and Bob looking a bit dazed, "Instead of rushing him novice-like he restrained himself like an old-timer, and bided his time to lick him gradually but surely. … Jeffries was undoubtedly wisely coached. Instead of cutting loose and rushing at Bob…he fought just as carefully and cautiously as he had in the previous rounds."

When Bob saw that Jeff did not come at him, he gamely attacked again, still hoping to land a knockout blow. However, Jeff was able to avoid the blows, sending in rights to the body. Still, Fitz rushed Jeff to his corner. "His last mad rush was only a bluff, weakness was fast overtaking him, and the quivering of his legs was plainly visible to all." Corbett called Fitz a splendid bluffer, rushing Jeff into his own corner, "pretending he is trying to get in on him, and we, who are outside of the ring, can see that Fitz is too weak to do any real execution."

Jeff came back, and in a rush landed a left hook to the jaw, a left to the body, a left to the ear, followed by a right to the head, and Fitz wobbled like a dying top. Chief Devery was on his feet, waving his arms as if he wanted the fight stopped, but sat down again as the bell rang and saved Bob. Jeff had him pretty well used up.

Bob was practically a beaten man, weak, staggering, and reeling during the round and at the bell. He had managed to last the round through sheer pluck and gameness, but the end was near. The crowed was wild as Bob staggered to his corner. Fitzsimmons was clearly one of the pluckiest fighters ever, for even when he was hopelessly beaten, he once again refused to sit down in his corner during the minute rest.

11th round

Showing his gameness, Bob came out of the corner like a bulldog, seeming revived, fresh, and strong, advancing as willingly as Jeffries did. His wonderful recovery dumbfounded the crowd. Corbett said, "Did you ever see a man like Fitzsimmons? He comes out of his corner without a trace of blood on him, with his eyes bright and a cool, confident smile on his face as if he had just made up his mind to begin to fight." Fitzsimmons advanced quickly and aggressively. Jeff kept away, waiting for his chance. Fitz rushed in with a left and right but Jeff ducked under and landed his straight right jolt to the short ribs, "which stops Fitzsimmons dead and actually shoves him back." Corbett credited Jeffries for not taking a chance and rushing in, despite the crowd calling him to do so. "He knows enough not to take any risks." Jeff studied him for a moment.

Jeff hit the nose lightly with a left, then followed a second later with a stiff left on the nose that sent Bob staggering back. Jeff feinted his lefts, shifted to the left, broke ground, and then worked in again, drawing a left lead by Bob. Jeff blocked it, and coming into a clinch, landed his furious right over the heart. Jeff broke and feinted again. After some clinches, in close, a left to the body and right over the heart sent Fitz back. Bob did not like it, and made a desperate attempt to land a knockout blow with his right. Jeff dodged and laughed. He eluded or blocked Bob's right and lefts. Jeff landed two lefts solidly to the mouth and stomach. Corbett observed, "See how the flesh on Fitzsimmons's thighs is quivering? He is pretty nearly gone, but he is as game as a thoroughbred." The champion rushed in again with his right, but Jeff ducked low and landed his left straight into Bob's body.

Fitzsimmons rushed and fought recklessly, with Jeffries backing and getting out of harm's way before throwing some blows in return. "The game old champion is still on the rush and actually makes Jeff back away into his corner." Jeff was being careful, crouching with his body drawn in and both hands protecting his head, guarding against Bob's dangerous wallops. Fitz kept boring in, but Jeff stopped him twice with straight lefts on the mouth.

According to Corbett and the *Brooklyn Daily Eagle*, Bob kept rushing, while Jeffries quickly broke ground "as fast as an athlete can run." However, Jeffries suddenly stopped and shot out his straight left like a crowbar. Fitzsimmons ran his mouth right into it and went down on his face. Siler told Jeff to stand back. Fitz rolled over, and then arose.

Still game, Fitzsimmons rushed in but Jeffries met him with a piston-like hard left jab that stopped Bob in his tracks. Jeff then followed with a left hook hard as a mallet on the jaw that clearly dazed him. Bob's hands dropped to his sides. He stood still, but his limbs were wobbly. Jeff waited just an instant, but quickly realized the helplessness of Bob's condition, and raising his up his left arm as if to block, simultaneously shot out a thunderbolt sledge-hammer right squarely on the jaw and Fitz went down like an ox struck with an axe. Bob dropped backward, his back, shoulders, and head crashing to the ground with a thud. His outstretched arms flopped out beside him. He lay motionless as if sleeping. "No mortal physique could have withstood that blow." Corbett said, "It's all up with Fitz. He's gone. He'll never be able to get up." Referee Siler immediately knew that the fight was over, but gave him the full count. Jeff looked at him, and then stepped back over to the ropes, watchful as Bob was counted out. Fitzsimmons was motionless for a few moments, then vainly tried to rise, but sunk back into unconsciousness, the blood flowing out of his mouth and nose. He was out cold. After the ten-count, the referee waved his hands at one minute and 32 or 35 seconds of the 11th round. James J. Jeffries was the heavyweight champion of the world.

At first, there was silent amazement, but then the crowd came to life and there was wild excitement. They cheered the new champion. Men leaped into the ring from all sides and danced for joy. Many men tried to kiss and hug Jeffries, mobbing him. Brady, Delaney, and Jeff's brother hugged and kissed him too. The crowd was cheering incessantly and the big fellow looked over the ropes and bowed in response. Jeff's eye and nose were cut and scratched.

In the meantime, after being counted out, Julian and Kenny picked up Fitzsimmons and dragged him to his corner. Bob's eye was cut, his nose puffed, his mouth swollen, and there was an egg-sized lump on the back of his head. They wiped the blood from his face, gave him restoratives, and he came to within thirty seconds.

Police Chief Devery and his men hustled the crowd out of the ring and told Jeff to wait until they found out how badly Fitz was hurt. Back then, if a fighter died, manslaughter charges could be brought. However, when Bob got up and walked away, the new champion was allowed to leave too.

Fitz walked to his dressing room and lay down on the couch provided, looking like a broken-hearted man. His wife stroked Bob's forehead. Julian was crying. Some said Bob wept too. After about a half-hour, at 12:10 a.m., Fitz dressed and left, accompanied by his wife.

Praises were heaped upon both men. Although defeated, Fitzsimmons had "put up a game, hard, vicious fight against a man whom many will now regard as the greatest heavyweight in the world since the days of John L. Sullivan." Corbett said, "Well, the best man won. There is no excuse for Fitz. He was in splendid condition. Jeff was too big, strong and clever for him." *The Brooklyn Daily Eagle* said of Fitz, "He is certainly one of the gamest men that ever wore a glove." *The New York Journal* said, "James J. Jeffries is by long odds the greatest heavyweight fighter the world has ever seen. There is no man today who has a chance with him."

There were extensive post-fight summaries and analysis. *The New York Times* said that Jeffries was able to absorb Fitzsimmons' attacks and return his own powerful punches, launching counters from his famous defensive crouch which he had improved over the years. As the bout progressed, the attacking Fitz began landing more, but Jeffries' blows did more damage. Some experts thought that Jeff was done for at the end of the 7th round, but then his youth asserted itself and his reserve strength came to his rescue. The fight dispelled all doubts about Jeff's gameness and ability. He was clearly the best heavyweight that Fitz had ever met.

The New York Herald said that Jeffries "is not a finished sparrer, but he is wonderfully quick for a man of his tremendous size – the quickest big man, sporting men are saying tonight, just as they used to say of John L. Sullivan when he was in his prime." It also said, "Jeffries was simply tremendous. He is the ring giant, and, awkward as was his stooping position, he landed on the champion with an ease which surprised his warmest admirers." As often as Fitz landed, Jeff was never really groggy. Bob was "beaten down not alone by sheer weight and tremendous strength, but by a deceiving style of fighting which often led him to place his jaw in jeopardy."

The New York Daily Tribune said they had both landed savage blows "powerful enough to slay an ordinary man." Jeffries "showed himself a better boxer than he had been thought to be. He dodged with an agility wonderful for one of his size and weight. His punches in the stomach and his left-handed blows in the face were terribly effective."

The New York Journal said that Fitzsimmons had tried in vain to land his right on Jeff's jaw. Even when he did land some powerful blows, Jeff's iron chin held up. Conversely, Jeffries rarely used his right, except to the body. He fought cautiously, sliding back, but he did not run. The spectators shouted themselves hoarse watching them thump each other round after round, until the combatant's breasts were flecked with blood and shining with perspiration. Jeff's strength and youth told. Fitz weakened over time, but his courage never left him.

There was not a dull spot in it from the first clang of the bell to the last deadening punch. Fitzsimmons, in spite of the fact that it was going against him, came and fought. He proved himself as game a man as ever boxed and took his knock-out with as good a grace as he ever gave one.

It is likely he knew he was beaten after the second round. … He made a fight and had a chance to win all the way to the tenth round.

It is likely Jeffries has a respect for Fitzsimmons, for Fitz certainly landed him one or two terrific punches. Still, he out-feinted, out-boxed, out-generaled and out-fought the champion. He was as cold as ice from the beginning to the end. Never for a second did he show the least sign of stage fright, fear or hurry. Again and again, when half the spectators were howling for him to go on, he would lightly shift his position, feint and then break ground.

He was never in a hurry. … He had twenty-five rounds… Jeffries beat Fitzsimmons with his left hand. The right kept pounding away at his lower works and every time the jolt came it counted. But Jeffries's left hand work at the head and body was the feature of the fight. He knocked Fitz down, dazed him and all but put him out with the hand which Fitzsimmons never did know how to stop. Everybody who has ever fought Fitz has hit him with the left, but he finally induced them to use the right, then he won.

Jeffries was doing sufficiently well with his left to have no right-hand ambitions, and, in spite of Fitz's most tempting openings, Jeff never would let go. He used his right hand at the body and reached with an inside cross or two, but he never took a chance. When Fitz was all gone and did not have a punch in his right hand Jeff shot it over.

Further, the weight told. Jeffries had something between forty and fifty pounds in his favor. His rushes were savage, and whenever he came into collision with Fitzsimmons, it meant something. His quickness and ducking, his foot work and his general speed set all the wise people wondering. He was faster than Fitz. When he wanted to corner Fitz he succeeded, but had no trouble in slipping away from Fitzsimmons at will.

The New York Sun said that Jeff surprised the spectators the moment he put up his hands. He was cool-headed and looked so powerfully strong that everyone appreciated the fact that Bob had his hands full. Whenever Jeff got into a clinch, he pushed Bob off as if he was a lightweight. Fitz could not get to him as often as he liked, and when he did land to the jaw or stomach his punches had little or no effect.

Jeff was not only the biggest heavyweight in the world, but also one of the cleverest and fastest. He used his superior reach very well, mostly using his damaging left with wonderful speed, and only once cut loose a really hard right for the head at long range, for the knockout punch. "He watched out carefully for Fitz's hooks and kept away with religious care. He simply took his time, and with this powerful left of his swinging constantly in the Cornishman's face he slowly but surely battered Bob's countenance until it looked like a huge rosebud." Jeff worked his left hand so rapidly that at times Fitz, who did not block it, was dazed. Bob's nose bled profusely, although his nose had always been sensitive.

Fitzsimmons forced the fight, feinting, but Jeff was much cleverer than he had supposed, using excellent judgment, never losing his temper. His remarkable physique made it impossible for Fitz to hurt him. Jeff's left eye was cut, and it bled considerably, but he was never in serious trouble, despite the fact that Fitz worked at him like a demon.

> [Fitzsimmons] tried every known method of attack, and landed repeatedly. He got both hands to the big fellow's body, but it was backed up with a protection of steel which caused Fitz's blows to bound off as if his gloves were made of rubber. In short, Jeffries, while reasonably clever in defensive work, showed a wonderful amount of ability to take punishment without showing its effects. ... This ability was what helped to beat Fitzsimmons, for when he found that he could not affect the giant with his punches, he began to tire from the effects of his work.

> Jeffries was cautious to the end. There was just one period when he cut loose, but as soon as he found that Fitz was still dangerous, he let up. He fought the Cornishman at long range almost entirely, and when the end came he did not rush in close, but fired the left at Bob's head from a rather distant point, following with the right, which was a round arm swing delivered at full length squarely on the vital spot.

Fitzsimmons was called a great fighter whose blows would have knocked out anyone else in quick order, "but he can never defeat Jeffries, who is, in the estimation of every ring follower who saw him last night, a wonderful pugilist."

The fight was one of the fastest, considering the weight, ever seen. "There was no fiddling or fussing in trying, no light sparring of great length, and plenty of hard punching in every round. There was no faking, although the fight was photographed."

Although lauding his courage, the *Brooklyn Daily Eagle* was fairly critical of Fitzsimmons' performance. Every swing that Jeffries landed made it more and more evident that Bob had carried the pitcher to the well once too often. This writer opined that Fitz was not the same man that whipped Corbett and other top fighters, and was not even the same man seen in training the week before. "I am not trying to belittle Jeffries' victory. I think he is the greatest fighter breathing." However, "The Fitz I saw train and box during the six days preceding the fight seemed entirely different." In training, Fitz had shown "great cleverness, quickness, nimbleness and capacity for very severe exercise." The Fitz observed on fight-night "disgusted me with his lack of energy and style of fighting. He seemed stiff and stale. He lacked speed and generalship…. Perhaps his years had told against him."

In the 2nd round, the ease with which Jeff landed the blow to the nose which sent Fitz to the floor indicated to this writer that Bob had lost something. Jeff did not seem all that quick in his delivery, yet did not experience great difficulty in landing at least two out of five leads. "Fitz's once inimitable system of shifting, side stepping and blocking seemed to have gone somewhat wrong, for though he cleverly stopped many a vicious lunge, others found their way to his body and face." Bob showed a lack of energy and generalship by trying to block when he should have side-stepped or jumped nimbly out of harm's way. He was also unable to counterpunch "when Jeffries would give him a left hand jab on the face, which the latter used almost exclusively throughout the battle." Jeff landed those jabs with great frequency, some soft, some hard, but each blow brought Bob nearer to defeat. "Regardless of the weight of those terrible lefts of the Californian, Fitz kept wading in."

Occasionally Fitzsimmons would show his old form by ducking or jumping away or blocking, causing some to wonder whether Bob was only trying to draw Jeffries into a trap. However, Jeff continued landing his left jab or left hook with comparative ease.

Throughout the fight, Jeffries crouched peculiarly, "all doubled into a knot." Jeff's right was drawn up in front of his stomach. He straightened out his long and powerful left with a cat-like smack up and down at the stomach or nose, with a speed surprising in such bulk. It was this slightly bent blow that scored the knockdowns, and dazed Fitz in the 11th, setting him up for the right. Jeff also used the Tommy Ryan moves of "pushing in the face with the straightened left and right short arm jab in the wind. Another was the double blow, wind and then face with the left." Conversely, when Fitz landed on Jeff without telling effect, he worried.

However, despite all the criticism, throughout the fight, Bob was competitive, and "the fighting was but slightly balanced in Jeffries' favor, until the tenth round." This writer also said that it was all a surprise, for the crowd did not fully realize that Jeff was everything that he had claimed to be until Fitz was unconscious. "That I am amazed over the result is putting it mildly. I was certain Fitz would win."

In fact, even the odds remained in Fitz's favor throughout the fight, despite the fact that Jeffries had decked him in the 2nd and 5th rounds. *The New York World* said the odds remained 2 to 1 on Fitz until the fight was half over, then changed to 7 to 5, with Fitz still the favorite. Most believed that Bob would eventually manage to land the knockout blow, as he had always done before.

The Asbury Park Daily Press said that Jeff was never at any time in serious danger, and after the early sizing up, took the lead. They fought before a huge crowd in a great beam of blinding white light. It called Jeff a veritable giant, marvelously speedy for his immense size. It disagreed with the *Eagle's* assessment of Fitzsimmons.

> Less than a year ago [Jeffries] appeared in New York a great, awkward, ungainly boy. Today he is a lithe, active, alert, trained athlete. The men who prepared him for his fight worked wonders with him. They taught him a nearly perfect defense, instructed him in the methods of inflicting punishment. The transition since he appeared last has been little short of miraculous. ...

> The defeated man was just as good as when...he lowered the colors of the then peerless Corbett. He was just as active, just as clever, just as tricky and just as fearless of punishment.

The New York Clipper report summarized,

> It was a case of superior skill, experience, cunning and ring generalship, handicapped in a measure by advancing years, being pitted against great advantages in weight and muscular power, combined with the freshness of youth, and backed up with a fair amount of scientific knowledge and no end of laudable ambition. ...

> After [Jeffries] had sent the favorite to the floor in the second round, the first round having been without incident, he was regarded with greater favor, and as he continued to land on head and body with comparative ease, and his blows were observed to be full of steam, while those landed by Fitz seemingly were without effect, save at long intervals. ... [T]o the majority it was apparent that his triumph was simply a matter of time, provided Fitzsimmons did not manage to deliver one of those finishing punches for which he was famous. ... [T]he tactics employed by Jeffries when clinched, legitimate but very damaging, were clearly taxing Fitz's strength greatly. ... Nevertheless, [Bob's] courage never wavered, and he assumed the offensive round after round, always wearing a smile on his battered and bleeding countenance as he dashed upon his foe, who generally met him with more pepper than he was able to give. ...

Throughout it was a clean, satisfactory fight, unmarred by anything approaching foul tactics.... The fact that the victory of the brawny Californian was largely due, as above stated, to the manner in which he made his extra avoirdupois tell upon Fitz's strength when clinched, does not detract in the slightest degree from the credit due him; the weight of his tremendous blows certainly proved a most potent factor, while a great deal of his antagonist's strength was wasted in deliveries that either missed their mark or proved ineffectual when landed upon Jeffries' massive frame, so apparently impervious to injury. ... It may truly be said that after the opening Jeffries had the best of the fighting in nearly every round. He depended mainly upon straight left hits, with an occasional hook with the left, principally on the body, varied at intervals, when a good opportunity offered, with a swinging right, and he seldom failed to land, although, at times, his hits were light, but generally they were unwelcome guests. He certainly surprised his warmest partisans by the comparatively easy way in which he got onto his opponent.

The National Police Gazette called it one of the most viciously contested fights in pugilistic history, before the largest and most representative gathering of men ever amassed together in a pugilistic arena. Jeff was superior to Fitz in every round, demonstrating that he could reach him effectively with either hand. Bob fought courageously and gamely in the hope of turning the tide of victory in his favor, but never had more than a remote puncher's chance to win.[333]

A week later, the *Gazette* writer further analyzed the fight.

It's up to me I suppose to tell why I fancied Jeffries and ventured to express the opinion that he would win. ... His weight alone was an advantage.... The victor put this forty-pound advantage in evidence every time the two clinched and the lighter man was borne down and wearied beneath the ponderous load of flesh, muscle and bone which he was forced to support until Referee Siler pushed himself wedgelike between them and broke them apart. There is nothing in the rules which prohibited Jeff from doing that sort of thing as often as he could and he availed himself of the privilege much to Fitz's discomfiture and disadvantage. ... Jeffries' arms are so abnormally long that he found it a comparatively easy matter to...hit at the Australian without fear of counter blows. When his sturdy left landed full on Fitz's nose, Fitz's fist, with his arm fully extended, was a couple of inches away from the objective point of his return blow. It was only when the fighting was at short range that Fitz demonstrated that he was equal, if not superior, to his long-armed opponent. ...

333 *National Police Gazette*, June 24, 1899.

[Bob] was quick and resourceful in getting away from the Californian's punches during the earlier rounds of the battle, and really forced the issue until he began to grow weary from the impact of Jeff's ponderous rushes and clinches. ... Fitz tried every trick he knew to get Jeffries in position for one of his famous blows. ... He might as well have been punching away at the steel belt of an armored cruiser. ... When he subsequently tried and failed to reach Jeffries' jaw, owing to the ease with which the latter could block up and throw the blow off, he was utterly powerless, and was forced to depend upon a chance opportunity. ... Jeffries...was as firm and steady as the proverbial rock, fighting a carefully planned battle. He had demonstrated his ability to hit the champion and likewise demonstrated that he had nothing to fear from the latter's punches. ... He was as sprightly as a featherweight as he danced in and out, trying to draw an opening, or rushed into a clinch. Fitz was marvelously game and willing.... Jeffries never omitted a chance to rough matters.... By hanging his weight upon the Cornishman's neck and shoulders he was wearing him down. ... Jeff had been schooled to be wary of leaving an opening and he elevated his left shoulder and used a high right-hand guard to keep out of danger. ... He could wait, which was a great thing in itself; and he could afford to wait. ... He had been told that his opponent's only chance lay in a single blow and he guarded well against that. With his handy left and his strong guard he met the champion's rush and both punished him and hugged him into weakness. ... All the hard punching [Fitz] received only served to inspire him on to greater endeavor. He refused to believe that he was beaten. He fought heroically and well, and if I never had any admiration for him before, I had it then, when I saw him fighting so desperately, with defeat staring him in the face, to get in a blow that would turn the tide in his favor. ... Every time he was knocked down or dazed and tottering against the ropes he returned to the fray with a determination born of a fresh hope that the long-deterred change would come. ... Fitz certainly deserved the admiration of the mad thousands about him.[334]

The San Francisco Chronicle said Jeff "fought with the coolness and precision of a veteran and at no time was he in danger of defeat." "He was as lively as a lightweight on his feet and repeatedly ducked under the cutting swings of his opponent. ... He punches and hooks and swings with the precision of a finished boxer." Still, Jeffries was punished throughout, "for no man can engage the wonderful Australian...without being hit hard and often, but he stood up to it with lion-like courage and never faltered." Jeff was a finished fighter, alert for openings and swift to take them. His

334 *National Police Gazette*, July 1, 1899.

condition was superb and the fierce fighting did not affect him. Jeffries "showed himself a master at every point in the game and won as he pleased after he had taken the measure of his opponent."

Referee George Siler said it was one of the best fights he had ever witnessed, and that "if the fight had been stopped at any time previous to the knockout, the decision would have to have been in Jeffries's favor."[335] He said that it was the same old story of a man fighting once too often. Bob had met a younger, stronger, and faster man. "There was no time during the fight that Fitz looked as though he could win. Jeffries out-boxed and out-fought him from start to finish, having the best of every round." He also said, "In my opinion Jeffries had a shade the best of it for the last seven rounds. Jeffries is unquestionably a young man of remarkable strength. It was a good fight from start to finish and the best man won."

Siler believed that Fitzsimmons thought that Jeffries could not hurt him, because often Jeff would touch him only lightly with the left, and then Bob would smile and bore in. However, Jeff "avoided his swings in the easiest manner possible." Fitz was off in his judgment of distance, and probably should have utilized more straight blows. Jeffries was able to counter continually with his left and hooked him often without return.

Siler called Jeffries clever for his quickness on his feet and for his ability to duck Fitz's leads. "I knew that he was shifty on his feet, but did not think he was so clever with his head and hands, as time and again he ably ducked out of reach of Fitz's left and right hand leads." He thought that Bob should have used more uppercuts when Jeff ducked.

Siler felt that Jeff's crouched position gave him an advantage, guarding well against the right, with his jaw close to his shoulder. Fitz mostly missed his right crosses. A right did land to Jeff's left eye and caused a gash, but mostly the right went over his neck or landed on the back of the head.

Fitzsimmons was generally first up at the gong and went in on the attack. However, he did no damage. Jeff remained cool, whether being attacked, or after hurting Fitz. He took his time and acted like a master.

Another expert, John Kelly, said,

There is no similarity between the James Jeffries I saw attempt to knock out Bob Armstrong...in August, 1898, and the James Jeffries who put Robert Fitzsimmons to sleep.... One was a big, soft, painfully slow chap that didn't appear to know the first rudiments of boxing.... Last night he was big, strong, shifty, quick and scientific. A faster or a more scientific big man I have never seen. He hit like a battering ram and took hard blows in return without flinching. He used right and left hand with equal force, both hands seemingly being alike to him, and he wanted to fight all the time. His foot work was

---

335 Siler meant that if the police stopped the bout before its natural conclusion, he would then give a decision based on the merits up to that point.

simply a revelation, his improvement in this respect in less than a year being really marvelous…. Jeffries today is a great fighter. His youth, great strength, science, quickness of hand, eye and foot, and, above all, his fearlessness, make him a champion worthy of the title. He should be champion for several years to come.

Kid McCoy said that Jeff had shown wonderful improvement, and had proven to have more science, speed, and judgment than anticipated. "It was a magnificent battle and at the start it looked like Fitzsimmons would win it…. If I were asked what made Fitzsimmons lose, I would say, simply – Jeffries."

From San Francisco, Tom Sharkey was surprised at the result, for he thought that Fitzsimmons would win. He said that he could defeat Jeffries.

Bill Brady said,

I told you so! Jeffries is a corker and there is not a man on earth that can beat him. Jeffries is one of the greatest fighters the world has ever seen. He defeated a great fighter and only won the championship after one of the hardest fights witnessed in this country. He has a wonderful left hand that will defeat any fighter in the world. Jeffries will go on the road for a time.

Brady said that Jeff would be ready for Sharkey.

Bill Delaney, former Corbett trainer, said, "I have again brought a champion-beater from California and am naturally proud of it."

Yank Kenny said that Bob was in excellent shape, proven by the fact that he quickly recuperated from knockdowns and hard blows. However, Jeffries was a surprise.

Fitzsimmons gave multiple statements to different newspapers. He said,

I fully expected to win, but I didn't. Jeffries won because he was the best man. … He is young, strong, quick and clever. I have no excuse to make on the score of condition and over-confidence. I was in perfect trim, better, really, than I ever was before, and fought the best I could. … Jeffries is now the champion of the world beyond question, and is entitled to all the praise that may be showered upon him. He won the title fairly and squarely.

Fitzsimmons said that Jeffries was the best man he had ever met, and was too big and strong. "I fought my hardest, but he reached me in spite of all I could do. Jeffries made a great fight, far greater than I believed he could ever do. … I knew it was a hard game after the second round, and toward the last I was too much dazed to avoid him." Bob further said of Jeffries, "He's a hard hitter and clever. I did not seem to be able to get at him effectively. I was not prepared for his peculiar crouching style of fighting."

Mrs. Fitzsimmons claimed that Bob had gone into the ring with a bad right arm. Fitz said that he did not have excuses to make. "Well, I got licked, and what is the use of complaining now." However, Mrs. Fitz said that Bob's arm had been injured a year ago punching a bag and that it had never properly healed. Bob said, "My right arm was not in shape, but that is neither here nor there." Continuing to discuss the arm, Fitz said,

> [T]he result would not have been different had it been in good shape. Jeffries is a hard puncher, and I think he is fully as clever as Corbett. He may not be as quick, but he knows how to hit from the shoulder. … I did not weigh enough to have the strength to cope with this big fellow. My kidneys are sore and my stomach is badly used up.

Continuing, Bob said,

> My wife told me I would get licked, and as soon as I saw Jeffries in his dressing room I knew I'd have a good time. Jeffries was a hard man to get at. I sometimes think that if he had stood up I could have reached him better and the fight might have been different in its results. … I have no excuses to make. I forced the fighting, took my punishment like a man, got licked and that's all there is to it.

There were tears in Bob's eyes, and he seemed to be on the verge of breaking down.

> Jeffries is a wonder. I never saw a fellow get away so well from a punch or show so much speed on his feet. He was as quick as a flash, and his light footwork made me guess a great deal. … I made desperate leads; I tried every ruse at my command to beat him, but it was of no avail. He got away with such surprising skill that I wondered whether I was getting slow or whether I had before me a man whom I could not hurt. Jeffries's weight was against me. Every time we got clinched he fell against me and this impaired my chances. I don't want to have it inferred that he fought against the rules. … I got licked on the level. … My wife told me not to make this match…but I still clung to the belief that I was as good a man as I was two years ago and that my lay-off did not do me any harm, but now I realize that my wife was right. I know I must have been slow, for I could not use that speed that I used to have.

Fitz's face was considerably puffed up, and there was a large bump on the back of his head where his head had struck the stage floor. His eye was slightly cut, and his jaw was swollen.

Bob said that he would not bother Jeffries, and had not decided what he would do, but did leave open the possibility that he might one day ask him for another chance. However, when told of Kid McCoy's challenge for a fight at middleweight, Bob said that he was out of the game. "As for me – I will never fight again."

Discussing potential Jeffries opponents, Bob said, "No man in the pugilistic arena can stand against Jeffries. He is without a serious rival. In two punches Jeffries would kill Sharkey."

Jeffries said that he was never in danger or distress at any time, although Fitzsimmons hit him with some terrific blows. "Fitz fought a good and game battle and hit me harder than any man whom I have been up against." However, "Fitz never hurt me but once, and that was a hard blow in the left eye. His body blows did not have near the force they may have seemed to. In my estimation I had the best of every round." Jeff never had any real trouble landing his blows. "The fight was never for a moment in doubt so far as I was concerned. I had learned considerable since I fought Armstrong."

I have trained as few men ever trained for a fight. ... I expected to win. ... I gained a lot of knowledge from my connection with Tommy Ryan. He is certainly a wonderful fighter, and what he does not know about the game is not worth knowing. ...

In the first round I just sized my man up. ... I got many a good crack in the wind, but none of them even seemed to make me puff. ... In the second round, when I knocked him down, I felt more confident than ever. I was convinced then that my punches hurt. ... I thought I had him out. ... Fitz was extremely groggy, and only recovered because he was in such good shape. ... His vitality was too great and he fought as hard afterward as he did before. ... By the way, this fellow, Fitz, has a remarkable way of coming back, and this saved him many times. ...

As the fight went on I became more and more convinced that I would get him directly. There was not much time to think, but it did occur to me to be thankful for the hard work I had done and the good training. ... [I] give Fitz great credit for his splendid fighting ability. ...

Some of my friends say that my way of crouching my head to one side was somewhat instrumental in causing Fitz's defeat. Well, I puzzled him, to be sure, and I did the trick by playing for his wind...it was just the spot to play for. ... In the tenth, when I knocked him down, I knew I had him licked, for when he got up I could see that he was gone.

I did not care to take any chances, because he is noted for a foxy fellow who is liable to do some terrible damage with a chance swing. That is the reason why I did not go after him and settle matters then and there. As soon as I saw him standing up I realized that it was all over.... I defeated him with a left hook, which I followed up with a full right swing on the jaw.

Jeff had few marks of the battle. The skin over the left eye was cut up, but his body was not bruised. "One cut on the eye is all I got, but he opened that several times." Both eyes were slightly discolored with red within and with just a tinge of black and blue over the lids. "He laughingly pointed out on his head a few knobs about the size of walnuts – evidence of Fitz's prowess."

The next day, Jeffries was quoted as saying,

> The fight last night was the hardest I had ever had. It was a hard one from start to finish. Fitz never sized me up for a moment. I had him puzzled throughout. He could not reach my body because of my peculiar attitude. He reached my head often and heavily, but he did not jar at all. I did not feel his blows. I did not know that my eye had been cut until the blood came, but that blow was by long odds the heaviest that he gave me. … Fitzsimmons is a game man, a clever man and a good fighter. He could not understand my method. He expected me to do more right hand work. I fooled him all through, and I think he will admit that he was puzzled all the time he was in front of me. I owe my success, I feel, to Tommy Ryan. He put me through the paces that were fast and furious. I went through six tough rounds every day with him and you know what that means.

A couple days after the fight, Jeff said that his body punches licked Fitzsimmons, in particular his rights to the body. Delaney told him to use his right to the body, but not to the head, fearing Bob's counter right. Jeff granted that Fitz could punch hard. "He can punch…. Fitz was as strong as hades, I tell you. He's one-third stronger than Sharkey." He thought that Fitzsimmons could lick Sharkey.

Although Fitzsimmons hit him harder than anyone he had ever met, Jeff laughed at him every time he landed, just to discourage him. "I am not afraid of punishment in a fight. … I took all the iron out of him when he hit me hard and found it didn't hurt." Still, he did not allow Bob to reach his chin, effectively using his ducking. "I was always very handy at that. It comes natural for me to duck."

Jeff estimated that Bob weighed 180 pounds, while Brady thought he weighed about 170. "I weighed 210 pounds. Fitz refused to weigh. His people wanted to announce him at 158 pounds, I think it was, but Brady said if they did that he'd have me announced at 147, and they backed out." Because of his smaller size, "I was a little surprised at his hard hitting."

During the fight, Jeff took his time. He did not run, but he did not take undue chances either, employing Delaney's advice to be cautious and careful against a great ring general. Jeff said that Bob was good and strong right up to the very end.[336]

---

336 *New York World*, June 11, 1899.

Jeffries later gave his analysis of Fitz's style and fighting abilities from his first hand view:

He's a big, strong, healthy fellow, with a long reach, and is constantly coming. What I mean by coming is that he shuffles into his opponent and is on the advance much oftener than he breaks ground. I never did consider him a skilled boxer, because he swings too much.... But there is no denying his ability as a ring general. He is a deceptive feinter with his feet and hands. He pays little or no attention to his defense, but stands ready to take a chance at getting hit if he can return the blow. He figures that he can hit twice as hard as his opponent and can stand more punishment. He is always studying to locate a certain spot on which his terrific punch can find lodging.... I like the action of Fitzsimmons' feet better than his hands. While he is not shifty of foot, still he has an awkward and puzzling way of shifting about in sidesteps, this scheme having a knockout punch for its object. He is constantly sneaking to the right or left of his opponent, as he figures that by these maneuvers he can locate the jaw or body easier with his swings. He tried this dodge on me, but I was looking for it, and either blocked his swing or stepped inside of them, his arm and glove encircling my neck as I closed on him.... You probably noticed that I slammed against him without hitting a blow, allowing my weight to lean on his body. I could see that he was puffing from the effects of this collision, and this trick of leaning and slamming the body against him took the wind out of his bellows. I got a fair sample of his hitting ability when he copped me with a double swing in the fourth round. These blows jarred me for an instant, and I felt them more than any other punch delivered during the fight.... Even after I had floored him in the tenth round he was still as confident as ever.... After all, when you sum up Fitzsimmons you must give him credit for having the greatest powers of recuperation that were ever bestowed by nature on a boxer.... Combined with his cool head, ring generalship, punching powers and foot work, you have the qualities that make him a great fighter.[337]

A year and a half later, Jeffries discussed the effectiveness of his crouching position.

I adopted that crouching position for many reasons.... In the first place, it presents an almost perfect defense against body blows. It discounted Fitzsimmons' solar plexus, you remember. In the second place, it makes it hard for any one except a man with a very clever left to hit me in the face, and even then he can land only lightly. And in the third place, it gives me a longer reach.... I developed my left arm

---

337 *National Police Gazette*, July 1, 1899.

long ago, so I could hit very hard with it – harder even than with my right.[338]

Speaking of his future, multiple newspapers quoted Jeffries as saying, "I am an American born and bred, and as an American will defend my present title and honors of champion against all comers. ... I expect to hold this title many years."

The former champions all lauded the new champion. Jim Corbett said, "Jeffries possesses all the qualities of a great boxer. ... He does not lack ring science or generalship." Corbett won a bundle of money, supposedly $6,000 in profit by betting $3,000 on the underdog Jeff.

John L. Sullivan called Jeffries one of the greatest fighters that ever lived. He did not see how he could lose. John L. predicted that Jeff would defend the title for many years to come, and could be champion for ten years if he took care of himself.

Sullivan said that Jeff was wise to keep away early, confident that his opening would come later. "Jeffries took my advice. He played a waiting game, without losing any chance. He figured out Fitzsimmons in the first few rounds. Then he started in to worry him with that terrible left of his." Fitzsimmons simply went against too much weight and power combined with cleverness. "The talk about his being old is all nonsense. ... He has taken good care of himself and will be heard from again."[339] Continuing, Sullivan said,

> Never in my mind have I thought the Californian would fall. As I said some time ago, Jeffries is Fitzsimmons's superior in strength, and last night showed that he has skill as well. He displayed great head work throughout the battle and beat Fitzsimmons at his own game. That man Jeffries is a wise one. ... Jeffries relied solely on his left and a powerful left it is. It must have been a shock to Fitzsimmons when he first came in contact with it. All along I thought that the Australian underestimated the lad from the West. ... While I knew that Jeffries had improved wonderfully, I did not think he was as fast as he proved to be. He moved with the speed of an engine when he began to fight good and hard, and poor Fitzsimmons must have been sorely puzzled as the swings and jabs from the husky Californian began to shower on him. And Jim showed himself to be clever, too. From the time he began to stir things up in the fifth round he feinted and dodged and shifted like a veteran. It was this display of caginess that enabled him to first land on Fitzsimmons, and once he got in one or two, why the end was in sight. No man living, Fitzsimmons or any one else, can withstand the blows of that mountain of muscle. ... The young

---

338 *Louisville Evening Post*, January 22, 1901.
339 *New York World*, June 11, 1899.

American will be the champion for many years to come, or I am no judge.

There was a phenomenal amount of betting, one estimating at least $250,000. "Everybody bet on the fight." Another estimate of the betting claimed that $1.2 million changed hands. "Most of the talent wanted to see Jeffries win, but they could not figure out how Fitz was going to lose."

One said that Bob earned $25,000 to lose the championship and Jeffries $15,000 to win it. "Jeffries could not get Fitzsimmons into the ring except by agreeing to give Fitzsimmons the larger share of the money." However, "The real profit of a championship comes in the 'show' business, boxing tours and plays." Jeff's training expenses were $2,000.

They were also to split in equal shares the receipts accruing from the motion picture exhibitions. Unfortunately, although attempts were made to film the indoor fight, and at first, the films were reported to have been successfully taken, for whatever reason, the films did not turn out and were useless. The fighters lamented the loss of hundreds of thousands of dollars in potential profits.

However, promoters released fake films of the fight as being the actual films, and profited from them. Really, two actors put on a show, but most of the viewing public did not realize that the two were not Bob and Jeff. "Nobody who saw the actual fight could be misled or easily fooled by the fake exhibition, but unfortunately there are thousands of people who did not see the actual fight." This writer attended an exhibition of the fake pictures, and said, "Not an incident of the genuine fight was correctly reproduced."[340]

The Police Gazette noted a new tone of hope with the Jeffries era.

> When Sullivan was beaten a tidal wave of sorrow swept over the country…. Corbett's defeat was accepted placidly and philosophically. He had not wholly taken the place of the hero whom he had conquered. He was not a favorite with the masses. … Fitz when he came into possession of the coveted title made no effort to resurrect the sentiment which had been dormant through all the years since Sullivan was dethroned. …

> Jeffries gives every indication of being a people's hero, his personality being of a kind that wins the confidence and esteem of men. His victory was a popular one.[341]

---

340 *National Police Gazette*, August 5, 1899. Apparently, some of these fraudulent films still exist.
341 *National Police Gazette*, June 24, 1899.

CHAPTER 17

Exhibition Tour

James Jeffries' declaration that he intended to defend the title and take on all comers gained him much popularity. Regarding his future, Jeff preferred to face Sharkey, but "I'll fight anybody in the world; anybody. Depend upon it, I am going to take good care of myself. ... I don't intend to dissipate. I have never been what you'd call a drinking man. I don't care for drinking." However, he was not going to defend the title until the fall or winter, for Brady intended to capitalize on the crown for a short while with exhibitions and appearances.

The men clamoring for a chance at Jeffries were Sharkey, Corbett, and McCoy. McCoy was thought to be too small, strong and clever though he was. Tom Sharkey was generally conceded to be Jeff's most likely opponent. "He is as strong, if not stronger than the boiler-maker, has shown that he has almost superhuman endurance under punishment, and he is gaining quickness and cleverness every day." Sharkey had lost a decision to Jeff, but some felt that it was a close fight, and Tom had won significant bouts since then. Sharkey had knocked out Ruhlin and McCoy and had shown he could more than handle himself in his bout with Corbett.

Jim Corbett said,

> I would like to fight Jeffries...to see just what I could do with him. I don't want you to think that I regard it a 'cinch' to defeat him, for he is a wonderfully good man. He is a great, husky, strong, and for his build, remarkably clever boxer. He showed in his fight with Fitzsimmons that he has a cool head and can take and give punishment. I don't think anybody will doubt that he is a heavy hitter from now on. I am not satisfied with the ending of my career as a pugilist, and I would like to see just how good Jeffries is. ... If I fight again I will only fight for the highest honor. ... If Jeffries should not select me the only man that has any chance against him is Sharkey.[342]

Corbett could be an intriguing match.

> Two years ago in the training quarters at Carson, Corbett used to punch the burly boilermaker about like a meal bag and occasionally jar him with a punch on the jaw which came dangerously near putting

---

him out. That was two years ago. Whether he can do it now or not is a matter which can only be conjectured.[343]

Jeffries issued a statement directed at Tom Sharkey. He said that Tom knew in his heart that Fitzsimmons was his master and that he was a "party to a contemptible scheme" that robbed Bob. Jeff had accepted Fitz's terms in order to secure the championship. Now Sharkey would have to accept his terms. Jeff would fight him on or about September 15 for a $10,000 side bet, the largest purse a club offered, for the entire purse to go to the winner, no side or secret agreements, and with George Siler as the referee, because he "has demonstrated to the world that he is a fair man. I have no wish that you should perpetrate any Wyatt Earps on me." He also wanted the fight to take place in an 18-foot ring instead of the usual 24 feet, "so you cannot run away," with straight Queensberry rules, which meant hitting in clinches and on breaks.[344]

In the meantime, like other champions, Jeff would capitalize on his new popularity, giving boxing exhibitions and umpiring baseball games, often boxing during the 7th inning stretch or after the game. It was typical for new champions to give money-making exhibitions just after winning the crown, so the general public could see more of them. Everywhere he went, Jeffries was the center of attention.

On June 10, 1899, the day after winning the title, Jeff was given a reception in Philadelphia, and he boxed with Jim Daly at the Philadelphia Academy of Music. His knuckles were a little swollen, and there was a small strip of plaster on his eyebrow, "but the cut there didn't amount to anything."[345]

On the 11th, Jeffries was paid $500 to umpire a baseball game at Paterson, New Jersey before a crowd of 5,000.[346]

On June 12 at the Coney Island Sporting Cub, in the same ring that he had won the championship three nights earlier, before a crowd of 4,000 spectators, Jeff sparred 3 rounds of one minute each with Jim Daly. Although the crowd called for him to give a speech, Jeff was not big on public speaking, so he simply thanked them and told them that he would do his best to defend the championship. Jeff made $600 for his services.[347]

With Daly, and sometimes brother Jack, Jeff continued with his daily boxing exhibition and baseball umpiring schedule, exhibiting twice a day. He was scheduled to be seen over the next several days in places like Boston, Wilmington, Providence, Meriden, Hartford, Bridgeport, New

343 *National Police Gazette*, July 1, 1899.
344 *New York Clipper*, June 17, 1899; *New York Sun*, June 11, 1899.
345 *New York Sun*, June 11, 1899; *My Life and Battles* at 37.
346 *New York Journal*, June 12, 1899.
347 *National Police Gazette*, July 1, 1899; *Brooklyn Daily Eagle, New York Journal*, June 13, 1899. Jeff moved about with the activity and grace of a kangaroo, putting it all over Daly, who fled at the end of the bout.

London, Buffalo, Rochester, Syracuse (boxing Tommy Ryan), and again at Coney Island.[348]

Enjoying the fruits of his labor, when at a saloon, Jeff purchased drinks for himself and three friends. The bill came to less than $1. Jeff put down a $10 bill, and told the bartender to keep the change, in John L. Sullivan fashion. "A man who earns a thousand dollars in two days can afford to do this sort of thing." Jeff said that he did not drink much though. "I've never seen a man that it did any good." Jeff said that Sullivan was his ideal prize fighter, except that unlike John L., he was not a drinker, and would not allow alcohol to run him down the ladder the way it had with Sullivan.

One paper said, "Jeffries's tour is successful. His profits this week will exceed $7,000."[349]

Jeff's father, a preacher who was against boxing, wanted him to get beat. "When he gets licked he'll come to salvation. ... No man can come to salvation except through suffering. But Jeff's a good boy. He's no worse than the rest. He'll keep up his devilment until he gets licked, and then he'll quit." Still, his father also said that the Lord was in the Fitz fight and was with Jim, so of course he won. Mrs. Jeffries was happy that her son had won that which he had worked so hard to earn.

The Jeffries and Sharkey representatives were in ongoing negotiations, but it looked like the two would fight. Sharkey wanted a 24-foot ring rather than the 18-foot ring that Jeff wanted. Jeff wanted a small ring so that Tom could not run away from him as he did when they fought the first time. "If he had made as manly a fight as Fitzsimmons I would have knocked him out." Sharkey did not approve of a side bet because New York law did not allow it. Jeff wanted it to be winner-take-all but Tom wanted there to be a loser's share.

Everyone was excited about the prospect of a Jeffries-Sharkey title fight. "The general sporting public is unanimous in the opinion that Jeffries and Sharkey would furnish one of the greatest fights the world has seen."

Jeffries was complimented for being willing to defend his title so soon after winning it. No champion had done so since Sullivan, to whom Jeff was being compared. "The Californian in his pugilistic ambitions is very much like John L. Sullivan. He does not believe in taking a long rest after winning an important battle, but announces that he will meet all comers in the near future."[350]

On June 19, the Jeffries and Sharkey representatives (Bill Brady and Tom O'Rourke) signed articles of agreement for a 25-round fight to be held

348 *New York Journal,* June 10, 12, 14, 24, 1899; *New York Clipper,* June 17, 1899; *New York World,* June 11, 1899; *My Life and Battles* at 37. See Jeff's record for more on his exhibition tour.
349 *New York World,* June 16, 1899. Jeff was scheduled to eventually head west, to show on the Pacific coast and to spend a few weeks with his parents in Los Angeles. He would then tour Europe. "Engagements have already been arranged at the Alhambra, London, and in Paris. While abroad Jeffries may get a match with Charlie Mitchell."
350 *New York Journal,* June 12, 14-16, 1899; *Brooklyn Daily Eagle,* June 10, 1899.

on October 23. Both agreed that George Siler was a fair and honest referee, the best in the country, so they chose him to referee. Sharkey wanted to wear hand bandages. At first, Brady objected. Neither Jeff nor Fitzsimmons had worn them. However, Tom liked them. Brady relented when it was agreed that he would only wear soft cloth bandages which had to be approved by the referee and the opposing side. Although straight Queensberry rules were acceptable, Brady did not want Tom to be able to wrestle. They agreed to allow the men to fight with one arm free, but to immediately part at the referee's command, each to protect himself on the breakaway. They agreed to a 20-foot ring, or the regular-sized rings used by the Lenox or Coney Island clubs. Five-ounce gloves would be used, each to select his own pair to be provided to the referee the afternoon of the contest. Although the initial terms stated that the winner would take the entire purse, this later changed. Each side had to post a $2,500 forfeit, and the highest bidding club would have to post a $5,000 forfeit.[351]

Jeff was lauded for following the famous Sullivan example and not doing what Corbett and Fitzsimmons did. The latter two had sat on the title for years until their funds had dwindled, forcing them into the ring again. Within 10 days of wining the crown, Jeff had already scheduled a title defense against the next best man in the world. Jeff wanted to be a fighting champion. He said, "Before I met Fitzsimmons I declared that if I won I would fight any man in the world. … I am a fighter, not a talker. I plan to do just as John L. Sullivan did – meet any and all comers."

The National Police Gazette wrote,

> He is being compared with John L. Sullivan, and everybody seems willing to concede that he approaches nearer to the Sullivan ideal than any champion we have had since that famous old gladiator. … In proving his anxiety to fight Jeffries has earned the admiration of the sporting world. He wants to demonstrate that he is first, last and always a fighter, and if he continues to act in that manner his name eventually will be well placed beside that of the illustrious John L.
>
> Jeffries, like Sullivan, does not believe that success in the ring is won by newspaper controversies, and to him also the stage is a secondary consideration. I predict a popular career for the Californian. He is just the sort of a man the people can admire.[352]

Similarly, the *New York Journal* said,

> His decisive action has won for him many friends. The public is satisfied that he is a champion worthy of the honors. … The Californian's attitude since he won the championship recalls the time of Sullivan, when in the palmy days of his ring career Sullivan won the

---

351 *New York Sun*, June 18, 20, 1899; *New York Journal*, June 19, 1899.
352 *National Police Gazette*, July 8, 1899.

love of every true-hearted sport, owing to his willingness to tackle every one and everybody who desired a meeting with him.[353]

Brady booked Jeffries in cities all over the country to allow lovers of pugilism an opportunity "to worship at the shrine of the new champion." Everyone would pay to see the champ. Jack was with him as his sparring partner, "finding it harder than ever to be my brother." They exhibited in every big city in the U.S., sparring every day. With them were Charley Ross O'Neil and Kid Eagan. Daly did not join him on this trip because he was too used up from sparring Jeff for the Fitz fight. Jeff left for Syracuse on the morning of the 19th.[354]

Before heading west, Jeff met Admiral George Dewey. The world's greatest ring fighter wanted to meet the world's greatest sea fighter. "I always had a great admiration for the man who sailed into Manila Bay at night, over the torpedoes, and slammed the daylights out of the Spanish fleet lying at anchor there."[355]

On June 24 at Louisville's Macauley's Theater, before a small crowd, Jeff boxed 5 rounds with Jack Jeffries. The champion's form was admired. He was called a sleek, creamy-skinned panther, stepping light and noiseless on his graceful feet, always crouching near his opponent, edging away, and then sliding in to close quarters. The people who saw him were of the opinion that Jeff would remain champion until he was old, if he took care of himself. "He is a veritable giant and is as fast as the average lightweight, which is wonderful. ... He has reach, cleverness, foot work and the ability to punch." An ordinary man could go into the ring with a hammer and Jeff could still beat him. "If John L. Sullivan were in his prime again –ah! What a tug of war there!" Sharkey was said to be the only man left to give Jeff a challenge, although it was thought that Jeff would win.

Initially, Jeffries anticipated a lengthy reign in which he would bar no challenger, including blacks.

> I think I will be able to defend the title of champion for a long time. I am big and strong, and I know how to take care of myself. ... I am ready to meet any man of any color. No color line will be drawn by me. I can hit a black man a little harder than I can a white one, I think. They'll all look alike to me so long as I can make it profitable by fighting them.[356]

---

353 *New York Journal*, June 19, 1899.
354 *Two-Fisted Jeff* at 116-119. *New York World*, June 16, 1899. *New York Sun*, June 18, 1899. Jeff's itinerary included: June 19, afternoon, Utica, evening, Syracuse (boxing Tommy Ryan); 20th, afternoon, Rochester, evening, Buffalo; 21, afternoon, Scranton, evening, Wilkes-Barre; 22, Pittsburg; 23, Cincinnati; 24, Louisville; 25, St. Louis; 26, Chicago; 27, Omaha; 28, Kansas City; 30, Denver; July 1, Salt Lake City; 4, Los Angeles. Jeff would return east the second week in July, then set sail for Europe.
355 *My Life and Battles* at 37.
356 *Louisville Courier-Journal*, June 25, 1899.

Even the *National Police Gazette* later noted that Jeffries had said that he would defend against all comers. "I do not bar anyone, black or white, old or young."[357] However, later in his reign, Jeffries eventually did draw the color line.

During his exhibition tour, Jeff was often asked to discuss Bob Fitzsimmons and their fight. Jeff said that Bob was a good, game fighter who took many hard punches but kept coming up to the end, earning his admiration. Fitz could deliver a hard blow. "Ugh; you bet he can. I was sore for many a day after the fight." "He hit me harder than I was ever hit before – much harder – but they never hurt me at that. He can punch about three times as hard as Sharkey can." Jeff said that he took his time with him. He could have knocked Bob out sooner, but wanted to be careful. "There was no use in sticking my head out to get it punched off with a right." "I wasn't taking any chances with such a shifty man."[358]

Speaking of his wonderful improvement as a fighter, Jeff credited Delaney and Ryan. Sparring with Ryan was of great benefit, for Tom taught him many new tricks. He mastered the left hand feint for the body, which often set up his left hook for the jaw. Jeff attributed his success in part to his ability to anticipate and elude Bob's blows. "My crouching position was also the result of Ryan's tuition. My failure to fall a victim to Fitz's feints was also due to careful practice with Ryan." However, Jeff later said that he always had a crouch and knew how to duck, for it came naturally to him, but that Ryan helped him perfect it.[359]

On June 26, 1899, Jeff appeared in Chicago at Tattersall's before a crowd of 3,000. He sparred 3 short rounds with Jack. The champ was fast and clever, blocking and ducking in finished style, and was as light on his feet as a bantamweight. "Glimpses of Corbett's style were noticed." It seemed that a "large-sized edition of Tommy Ryan was at work." Jeff was called the largest boxer since Joe McAuliffe, the fastest since Corbett, and the strongest since Sullivan, "the whole combination going to make an almost irresistible fighting machine."

Following the 3 short rounds, they illustrated the 11th round of the Fitz fight. Jeff hooked his left on the jaw, Jack dropped his hands, Jeff put his right across, and Jack feigned the knockout. Referee Siler, a Chicago resident, counted him out. After Jack rose, Jeff walked up to him and gave Jack a playful kick to the back side. This was the routine which they repeated in their travels from town to town.[360]

---

357 *National Police Gazette*, August 12, 1899. Speaking of potential contenders, Jeff said, "The most promising man I know of is this fellow, [195-pound] Joe Kennedy, of San Francisco, who beat [190-pound] Gus Ruhlin there last night [June 23, via a 20-round decision]. Kennedy is a good man. I have seen him fight, and I believe he is a comer." However, in late September, Peter Maher would knock out Kennedy in 2 rounds. In early 1900, Kid McCoy would knock out Maher in 5 rounds.
358 *National Police Gazette*, August 5, 1899; *Louisville Courier-Journal*, June 24, 1899.
359 *St. Louis Daily Globe-Democrat*, June 25, 26, 1899.
360 *Chicago Tribune*, June 26, 27, 1899.

In Salt Lake, it was noticed that on the lapel of his coat, Jeffries wore an emblem of two tiny gold hammers, crossed and surrounded with a diamond. This was the badge of the Boilermakers' union, of which he was a member.[361]

The Jeffries party reached San Francisco on July 6. When his ferry arrived at the docks at 2:30 p.m., 5,000 people were on hand, as well as a band, which played the Star Spangled Banner, a reminder that the championship was in the hands of a native-born American again. Everyone wanted to see the champion, and crowds of people followed him about. Jeff's father was expected to be amongst the spectators at the exhibition that evening, "and will see his son in action for the first time."

That night, at Woodward's Pavilion, before a crowd of 4,000, Jeff boxed 3 rounds with Alex Greggains and then 3 more with brother Jack.

After meeting with his son, the Reverend Alex Jeffries said, "I'd rather have my son an honest prizefighter than a hypocritical preacher. I know he doesn't drink, neither does Jack; and they'll both behave themselves, even if they have to be fighters." Jeff's father thought his son looked thin. James told him, "Why father, I weigh 240 again. I'm all right." However, he usually said that he was weighing around 220 pounds.[362]

Many in San Francisco wanted the Sharkey fight to be held there, but the question was whether they could offer the largest purse. New York had a much bigger and richer population, which meant more ticket sales at potentially higher prices.

On July 9 at San Francisco's Glen Park, 5,000 watched Jeff spar Jack 4 rounds. Jack did not land a clean blow. "In fact, the champion played with him as a cat does a mouse. His ducking and marvelous quickness were astonishing."[363]

Jeff arrived in Los Angeles on July 10. A brass band, members of the local athletic club, and his former fellow employees from the Lacy pipe works in East Los Angeles greeted him. Jeff wanted to visit his mother.

On the 10th at the Burbank Theater on Main Street in Los Angeles, under the auspices of the Los Angeles Athletic Club, before a large crowd which included the local Mayor and county officials, as well as 68 women, one black, Jeff boxed Jack 4 one-minute rounds. Jeff's boxing showed "that the reports of his cleverness have not been exaggerated. He is beyond doubt the fastest big man ever seen in the ring, and his footwork was a marvel." Jack was unable to land, even when Jeff kept his hands by his sides, ducking and dodging. They ended the show with the usual demonstration of the Fitz knockout, with Jeff giving Jack his kick in the rear afterwards.

361 *Salt Lake Tribune*, July 4, 5, 1899.
362 *Los Angeles Express, San Francisco Call*, July 6, 7, 1899; *Los Angeles Herald*, July 7, 1899.
363 *San Francisco Call*, July 8, 10, 1899.

Even Jeff's father was there, having "ceased his crusade against the devil in San Francisco, in order to be at the homecoming of his son whose career he does not approve, but whose manly straight success he can but take pleasure in, and find a source of unacknowledged satisfaction."[364]

After his home visit, returning back up north, on July 14, 1899, a thousand enthusiastic men cheered Jeffries when he entered the ring of Oakland's Reliance Athletic Club for its benefit. As usual, he sparred 3 rounds with Jack, with an additional round in which the Fitz knockout sequence was demonstrated. Everyone noted Jeff's remarkable improvement in skill and speed. The bashful Jeffries gave his usual short speech in which he thanked everyone for their kindness and said that he would do all that he could to keep the championship in America. The crowd cheered, and followed him about town even after he left the exhibition. "It was a case of hero worship."[365]

Jeff headed back east, arriving in New York on July 26. He was to set sail for Europe the following day. He was scheduled to return to the U.S. about September 15, when he would go into training for the Sharkey bout. Jeff said, "Sharkey is a big, strong fellow and has a chance to defeat me, but I think I will get the decision when we meet."[366]

On July 27, 1899, Jeffries sailed for Europe on the Fuerst Bismarck, in company with brother Jack and Ross O'Neil, who would look after business matters on behalf of Brady. At the shore, when Jeff was about to leave,

> Several women acquaintances outdid each other in their efforts to kiss and hug him. One woman particularly occupied the attention of the champion above the others. She was said to be Jim's sweetheart. Although she knew the crowd was staring at her, she boldly encircled her arms around the big fellow's neck and kissed him passionately.[367]

Jeff was scheduled to exhibit in London, England, Paris, France (a week at the Foiles Bergere), Ireland, Scotland, and Wales.

It was not anticipated that Jeff would have many legitimate bouts, if at all, in England. "The number of first-class men in England now might be counted upon the fingers of one hand." Such would also be the case in France. "Pugilism is not popular in France."

---

364 *Los Angeles Express, Los Angeles Herald*, July 10, 11, 1899. It was at that time that Jim Jeffords began making his claims that he had once bested Jeffries in a 4-round draw bout, but newsmen did not believe him. *National Police Gazette*, July 29, 1899.
365 *Oakland Tribune, Oakland Enquirer*, July 15, 1899.
366 *San Francisco Call*, July 27, 1899. Regarding Kid McCoy, Jeff said, "McCoy is a good, clever middleweight, but has no chance against heavyweights."
367 *New York Sun*, July 28, 1899.

However, Jeff was willing to box anyone. "While I am on British soil any heavyweight pugilist in Europe can secure a match with me. I do not bar any one, black or white, old or young. They all look the same to me."[368]

Jeffries arrived in London on August 3. He commenced his engagement at London's Royal Aquarium on Friday, August 4, 1899, and "had a big reception." A *Police Gazette* report said he "sparred four rounds with his sparring partner and made a favorable impression." In his autobiography, Jeff said that he sparred his brother Jack 4 rounds, although Jack went on with a different name.[369]

Discussing his stay in Europe, Jeff said, "My manager has secured several profitable engagements for me in London, Paris, Liverpool and Dublin. I am very anxious to make a match in England, but, from the little I have already heard, no one seems inclined to stand up against me." Jeff noted that despite some negotiations to box Charley Mitchell, the match had fallen through. In his autobiography, Jeff said that the Mitchell challenge was thought of as ridiculous, and did not take place because no one would pay to see it. At the time, Jeff had hoped that Jem Smith would be one of his sparring partners, but "I understand now that that is out of the question, as he has not been training for some time. Beyond the exhibitions I am engaged to give, and provided none of the English champions care to take me on, I intend to devote my time to sightseeing."

A few days later, a local paper said, "To those interested in the noble art of self-defence the splendid exhibition sparring of Jim Jeffries, a heavy-weight boxer of high ability, in contest with an opponent worthy of his skill, proves a great attraction." Jeffries was boxing nightly at the Royal Aquarium with Jack.[370]

An American dispatch indicated that on August 7 at London's Royal Aquarium, Jeff sparred with George Chrisp and "Ed Dunkhorst" before a warm and large crowd which appreciated him. In his autobiography, Jeff said that Chrisp was the first Brit who went up against him. Chrisp knew that he had no chance, but needed the money. So Jeff just worked with him, and after 2 rounds, finished up with brother Jack.[371]

---

368 *National Police Gazette*, August 5, 12, 1899. There was some talk of a potential match with Charley Mitchell. "This bout I look upon as a foregone conclusion. Mitchell is a 'has been'.... To tell you the truth, I don't look on it in the light of a fight." He would also possibly have a match in Paris with Jem Smith. "Smith is also a dead one, and I anticipate little trouble in putting him out. If any of the younger crop of English heavyweights desire a match I will accommodate them." Jeff said that he currently weighed 224 pounds.

369 Jeff was advertised to appear at 9:45 p.m., set to box "v. recognized Ex-Champions." This is what the daily advertisements said. Perhaps because they were just exhibitions, and boxing was not the most popular sport in Great Britain at that time, the local papers did not provide much detail. The newspapers typically discussed actual fights only, not exhibitions.

370 *Pall Mall Gazette* (London), August 4, 5, 8, 1899; *National Police Gazette*, August 26, 1899; *New York Clipper*, August 12, 1899; *My Life and Battles* at 38.

371 *San Francisco Call*, August 8, 1899; *My Life and Battles* at 38. George Chrisp was a British fighter whose experience included: 1893 L20 Ted White (English middleweight title); 1895 LKOby17 Charley

Despite reports that Jeff was boxing "Ed Dunkhorst," who was an actual fighter, the reality is that for whatever reason, Jack Jeffries was boxing under this assumed name. Jeff said that Jack "went on with me under some other name." Jack Jeffries was going by the name of Ed or Jack Dunkhorst, as he was also called.[372]

The ad for the August 14 show said that Jeff would box "Bendoff, Champion of Africa, and Dunkhorst, Ex-Champion of America." Of course, neither "Dunkhorst" nor Jack Jeffries had ever been an American champion, and Bendoff was not the African champion, so they were clearly fudging on the facts for promotional purposes.[373]

The ad for the 15th again said that Jeff would box with Dunkhorst and "another."[374] In America, it was reported that on August 15, Jeff boxed 3 rounds with Jack Scales, who put up a creditable showing. *The London Sporting Life* was quoted as saying,

> In his own particular class Jack Scales is a pretty useful customer.... The Londoner, a tall, wiry youth, treated the spar as purely exhibition and he twice led with taps of the lightest possible description. Jeffries paid little or no attention to his defence and by this means Scales was enabled to visit the face several times.
>
> Adopting more business-like tactics, the champion gave glimpses of the lightning left hand work for which he has achieved so much distinction in his own country. This is about the first occasion he has assumed this style of work since his sojourn in this country, and his efficiency is most marked. Scales throughout the second round was of course nonplussed, but his sharp movements brought to light Jeffries's acknowledged cleverness.[375]

The London advertisement for the August 16 show said that Jeff would box Jack Walsh and Dunkhorst (Jack Jeffries).

On the 17th, first up was Arthur Morris. In his autobiography, Jeff said that he was told that Morris was a stone mason who had one-punch knockout power. Morris alternated between swinging hard and missing, and backing away and covering up. Jeff blocked a punch and countered with a right to the body that doubled Morris up. Arthur clinched and would not let

Johnson; 1897 WDQby5 Jem Smith (heavyweight) and WDQby12 Ed Starlight Rollins; and 1898 KO8 Jim Richardson and LKOby13 Frank Craig (heavyweight).

372 There was no mention of Dunkhorst having journeyed to Europe with Jeffries, and Jeff never mentioned sparring with him in England.

373 The U.K.'s Wolf Bendoff was an old-timer who had been boxing since the early 1880s. His career included: 1884 LKOby13 Jem Smith; 1888 D6 Jack Burke; 1889 LKOby27 James Couper (South African heavyweight title) and LKOby2 Peter Jackson; and more recent 1898 LKOby2 Gus Ruhlin. Bendoff weighed about 190 pounds for the Ruhlin bout.

374 *Pall Mall Gazette* (London), August 14, 15, 1899; Boxrec.com.

375 *New York Sun*, August 27, 1899. In November, Scales would score a KO2 over Tom Lees, but in 1900, would be knocked out in the 1st round by Dick Burge, and in the 3rd round by George Gardner. Boxrec.com.

go, so Jeff threw him against the ropes. He bounced off and swung a couple times. Jeff nailed him with a left in the ribs that lifted him through the ropes onto his back. Jeff pulled him into the ring again and helped him up. Arthur tried to sneak a swing on Jeff, but another punch dropped him across the ropes, and then the bell rang. Once more, he brought Jack Jeffries in to spar a couple of rounds.[376]

The 18th was Jack Scales (again) and Dunkhorst/Jack Jeffries. The advertisements over the next couple days just listed Jeff's name or said that he would be boxing recognized ex-champions. The 21st said he would box Arthur Morris (again) and Dunkhorst, while the 22nd said Jeff would box Wolf Bendoff (again) and "Jack Dunkhorst." The 23rd was Jack Walsh (again) and Jack Dunkhorst, while on August 24, only Dunkhorst was mentioned as the opponent. Ads thereafter provided no opponent information.[377]

The last advertised Jeffries appearance at London's Royal Aquarium was on August 29. Thereafter, he toured Paris, and later the other provinces of the United Kingdom.[378]

According to his first autobiography, after England, Jeff crossed over to Paris. "The Frenchmen didn't know anything about boxing at that time." He sparred with Jack. The spectators knew so little of boxing that they squeaked and thought they were killing each other. "It was a great joke to us." In a much later autobiography, Jeff claimed that he boxed every night, "meeting the French champions and allowing them to fight any way they pleased." Jeff said that he easily defeated everyone that they put in front of him. After seeing Jeff easily handle one man, the French champion declined to meet him, saying that he was too big and fast.[379]

In America, it was reported that Jeff did no serious boxing while in Europe, mostly sparring with his brother Jack. According to Jeff, he sparred in Paris, London, Scotland, Wales, and Queenstown.[380]

Jeffries left Europe on September 15, leaving from Queenstown (likely Ireland), and arrived back in the U.S. in Boston on September 22, 1899. A

---

376 *My Life and Battles* at 38-39. Back in America, on August 18, 1899, 180-pound Jack McCormick, who had once sparred with Jeffries, scored a surprise 1st round knockout over Kid McCoy. Tom Sharkey had scored an 1899 KO2 over McCormick. *National Police Gazette*, September 9, 1899. McCoy would eventually avenge the loss to McCormick with a 9-27-99 KO8 over him.

377 *Pall Mall Gazette* (London), August 16-18, 21-24, 1899. Although Jack Jeffries' name was never used, the fact that the name "Jack" was now being associated with the name Dunkhorst gives the impression that Jeff called his brother "Jack," although they had been using the last name Dunkhorst for him.

378 *Pall Mall Gazette* (London), August 29, 30, 1899; *London Daily News*, August 29, 30, 1899.

379 *My Life and Battles* at 39; *Two Fisted Jeff* at 120-125. Jeff said they toured England, Scotland, France, and Ireland.

380 *National Police Gazette*, September 23, 1899, October 14, 1899. Speaking of the failed Mitchell match, Jeff said that Charley was willing, "but what was the use of arranging a match with him? They would not pay a shilling apiece to see him box. I did well in England and Paris." Jeff did not do any real fighting while abroad, because Mitchell and Smith were the only ones who could have made "even a mild bluff" at competing. *The National Police Gazette* reported that Mitchell and Smith both demanded 50% of the gross receipts, and demanded that Jeff agree to box them to a draw. "Brady wisely declined to meet the demands of this precious pair of worn-out has-beens."

260

brass band and thousands of fans welcomed him on the docks. Jeff was accompanied by brother Jack and a trio of English boxers: Ben Jordan, Harry Ware and Will Curley.[381]

Jeffries returned to New York on the 23rd. Speaking of England, Jeff said that they made plenty of money, about $10,000. "At first the English folks did not take kindly to me. But I soon got into their good graces and they came to the Royal Aquarium in droves every night." Jeff was not impressed with the English fighters, "and thinks there is not a man in Great Britain whom Tommy Ryan could not whip." Jeff said,

> Boxing is at a low ebb in England. The absence of a good heavyweight is the cause of this. I toured the Provinces and the principal cities of England, Scotland, Wales and Ireland. There are many big fellows in Ireland who like to fight and I expect to see some of them develop into champions. Dublin is a great fighting town. But the spot of all spots is Paris. The Frenchmen dote on pugilism and it's a pity some of them are not taught to use their hands instead of their feet. … The Frenchmen treated me nicely and wanted me to stay two weeks longer.[382]

Jeff told another paper,

> I enjoyed my trip immensely. … I was treated royally on all sides. … The only thing I regret is that there was not any pugilist abroad that was capable of giving me an interesting bout. I had to confine the greater part of my exhibition sparring to bouts with my brother Jack.
>
> In Paris I sparred several times and gave like exhibitions in London, Scotland, Wales and Queenstown. That was the last place I visited before I sailed for home. On the eve of my departure I was requested to try conclusions with an Irishman named Hennessey, but I was unable to take him on, owing to my agreement with Sharkey.
>
> From a financial end our tour was a big success, and every time we appeared it was before crowded houses. Boxing is practically dead in England.[383]

Jeffries was set to leave on September 24 for Allenhurst, New Jersey, just north of Asbury Park, to start training for the late-October Sharkey fight, one month away.[384]

---

381 *New York Sun*, September 22, 23, 1899; *National Police Gazette*, September 23, 1899.
382 *New York Sun*, September 17, 24, 25, 1899. Jeff and Jack appeared at Ulmer Park on the 23rd for the benefit of the Boilermaker's Union, of which Jeff was a member.
383 *National Police Gazette*, October 14, 1899.
384 *New York Sun*, September 17, 24, 25, 1899.

CHAPTER 18

A Snag in Preparation

James J. Jeffries would defend his crown before the year 1899 concluded. To his credit, he took on the recognized top contender. Three months after losing a 20-round decision to Jeffries in 1898, Tom Sharkey knocked out Gus Ruhlin in 1 round. Concluding 1898, Sharkey defeated former champion James Corbett via 9th round disqualification, dropping him in the process. Sharkey also had a January 1899 10th round knockout victory over Kid McCoy, important because McCoy had a W20 over Ruhlin and later defeated Joe Choynski via 20-round decision in March 1899. Sharkey had clearly established himself as the most deserving contender.[385]

Sharkey and Jeffries did not like each other, and frequently exchanged harsh words in the newspapers, even before Jeff fought Fitzsimmons. Jeffries almost immediately agreed that his first defense would be against Sharkey.

On September 1, 1899, the Coney Island Club secured the fight by outbidding the Lenox Athletic Club. It agreed to give 66 2/3% of the gross receipts to the fighters, and guaranteed a $30,000 purse. The fight was to be filmed. The bout was originally set to be held on October 23, but it was moved to October 27. Sharkey insisted that there be a 25% loser's share, and agreed not to wear hand bandages in return for the concession.

Jim Corbett also wanted to fight for the title, and said that he would fight the winner. "He has taken the best of care of himself, and looks better than ever before. …. He believes he can defeat either Jeffries or Sharkey, and says he will show that he has lost none of his old-time form."[386]

Jeffries had returned to the United States from Europe on September 22. He arrived at his training quarters, the Brady cottage at Loch Arbour, on September 24, 1899. He began training the next day. He walked, ran, and jogged to Long Branch and back (about 11 miles). He was weighing 235 pounds, but expected to reduce to 208. His training would consist of handball, skipping rope, running, wrestling, boxing, punching the bag, and various other exercises.[387]

Tom Sharkey said that strength and grit were much more important than science in a fight, and one good swing was worth many jabs. Tom had met many "so-called scientific men" and defeated them all. He did not

---

385 *Brooklyn Daily Eagle*, June 10, 1899.

386 *New York Sun*, September 2, 1899; *National Police Gazette*, *New York Clipper*, September 16, 1899.

387 *New York Sun*, *Asbury Park Daily Press*, September 25, 1899; *National Police Gazette*, October 7, 14, 1899. On September 27, 1899, Kid McCoy avenged his loss to Jack McCormick with a KO8 victory.

mean to imply that science was not important, but if that was all a fighter had or relied upon, he would not defeat someone like Sharkey.[388]

Sharkey began his hard training on October 4, 1899 at New Dorp, Staten Island, New York. His chief sparring partner would be big Bob Armstrong, who had gone 10 rounds with Jeffries. Although in his other fights he usually weighed 185 pounds, Tom expected to take on flesh for this one, so that he would weigh over 190.

Tom·Sharkey·sparring·with·Bob·Armstrong·:·
PHOTO TAKEN ESPECIALLY FOR THE WORLD BY MARX

Jeff said that training at this time of year was a pleasure, because the cold suited him. He had developed a plan of defense which would more than counteract Sharkey's rushing tactics. He did not think Tom was as dangerous as Fitz was.[389]

The reported daily training regimen of each fighter included:

<u>Sharkey</u>: 6 a.m. 10-mile run and walk, occasionally swim, 8 a.m. breakfast, 11 a.m. dinner, 1 p.m. 5-mile bicycle ride, then nap, 3 p.m. gymnasium

---

388 *New York Journal*, October 2, 1899.
389 *New York World*, *New York Journal*, October 5, 1899.

exercises – skipping rope, wrist machine, dumbbells, medicine ball, punching bag and sparring Armstrong, then rub down, then supper, 7 p.m. stunts on his wheel, 8 p.m. bed. In sparring, "Sharkey goes at Armstrong like a house afire, and Armstrong has all he can do to come back for the next round."

Jeffries: 6 a.m. 10-mile run and walk, then rub down, then breakfast, 10 a.m. croquet, 11 a.m. handball, then dinner, 1 p.m. handball again, 2 p.m. gymnasium work, 3 p.m. throw medicine ball and wrestle with wrestling champion Ernest Roeber, then rub down, 5 p.m. croquet, then supper, then short bicycle ride, 8 p.m. sleep.[390] Sharkey was sparring 6 rounds daily with Bob Armstrong, with as much zeal as if the purse depended upon his knocking him out there and then. George Dixon, the world featherweight champion, who was the first black world champion, was also training and sparring with Sharkey. Although Tom would not fight blacks, he would train with them. It was predicted that October 27 would see "a meeting of muscle and brawn never equaled in ring history." Weighing in at 185 pounds, Tom said he never felt better in his life.[391]

It was said that roughing and wrestling would be a more important factor in Jeff's training this time because of Sharkey's known propensity to rough it in the clinches. That was why Ernest Roeber's services were obtained, because he was the strongest and most scientific Greco-Roman wrestler in the world. Roeber, along with Jack Jeffries, would rough it with Jeff.

At some point during the week following October 5, Jeffries' training befell a set-back that could have and probably should have derailed the fight. Jeff was throwing the 8-pound medicine ball with Roeber. He missed the ball and it struck his forearm, badly wrenching and straining both the forearm and his left elbow. At first, the seriousness of the injury was not

390 New York Journal, October 24, 1899; National Police Gazette, November 11, 1899.
391 New York World, October 8, 1899; New York Journal, October 12, 13, 1899.

realized. However, within the next few days, it became so inflamed and sore that he could not box, and needed to see a doctor.[392]

The October 14 edition of the *New York Journal* said Jeff was suffering from a severe strain of the left arm. "The matter has been kept quiet in the hope that the strain would pass away, but it gradually became worse." His arm was so sore and stiff that he could barely move it.[393]

The October 16 edition of the *Asbury Park Daily Press* said that Jeff sprained his left arm sometime last week while practicing with the medicine ball. His arm was bandaged. A physician who examined it said the injury was not serious. However, there was some uncertainty as to whether the fight would need to be postponed. Sharkey's team said that Jeff would have to fight or give up his $2,500 forfeit money.

After his usual run to Long Branch on October 15, Jeff removed the bandage on his wrenched left arm. "The swelling has disappeared and the pain is not as severe as it was a few days ago." Jeff said that if the arm continued to improve as it had for the last day or two that the fight might not be postponed. "I am bigger, stronger and faster than ever before in my life, and do not see how I am going to lose the fight. Except for my injured arm, it would be impossible for any human being to feel better than I do."[394]

On October 16, Jeff ran and played handball, but "avoided using his injured left arm as much as possible and in one game never used it at all." He also skipped rope and performed some light leg exercise. He was still bandaging his arm from shoulder to wrist. Jeff said that he would not go into the ring unless he was fit to do so.

Unfortunately, Jeff was left handed. He used his left much more than his right, standing in the orthodox position. Therefore, having a handicap in that arm would be even more problematic, not only for the fight, but for his training. His arm was still a little stiff. He was going to have a New York doctor look at it again the following day.[395]

---

392 *My Life and Battles* at 40; *National Police Gazette*, November 11, 1899.
393 *New York Journal*, October 14, 1899.
394 *Asbury Park Daily Press, New York Sun, New York World*, October 16, 1899.
395 *New York Sun, New York World*, October 17, 1899.

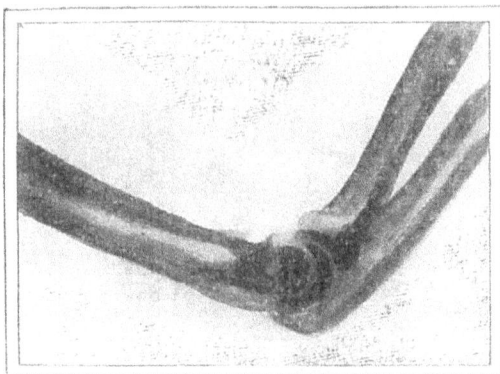

JEFFRIES'S ARM THAT POSTPONES THE FIGHT.

After examining the arm on the 17th, a doctor said, "The arm is badly strained, there being a bad wrench at the elbow. … An X-ray photograph of the arm was taken. … It shows no bones broken, but it shows plainly the dislocation at the elbow." The synovical membrane was inflamed and/or ruptured. His muscles were strained and still swollen. The doctor was also quoted as saying that the tissues of the left arm were lacerated. The doctor told Jeff that he would be very foolish to use his arm on the 27th, just ten days away. He re-bandaged the arm and put it in a sling.

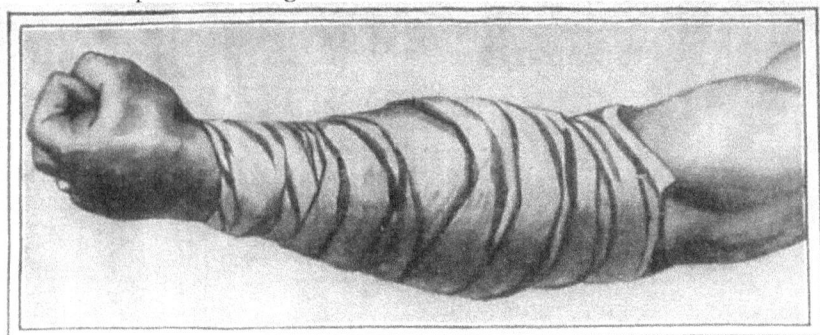

JEFFRIES' ARM IN ITS ARMOR OF BANDAGES

As a result, Sharkey manager Tom O'Rourke agreed to a one week maximum postponement without taking the forfeit money, although Brady had wanted fourteen days. The fight would come off on Friday, November 3. Jeff said, "I will be there no matter what happens. I regret the accident which caused the postponement and appreciate the generosity of O'Rourke and Sharkey in refusing to claim the forfeit."

That afternoon (the 17th), after returning to his training quarters, Jeff ran 4 miles and did a little gymnasium work. He had to rest the left arm and do no sparring. Still, Jeff remained the 10 to 8 favorite.[396]

Although the Sharkey crew initially wondered whether the injury was a subterfuge because Jeff was not in good shape and required additional time to train, the opposite was found to be true.

---

396 *New York World, Sun, Journal,* October 18, 1899; *New York Clipper,* October 28, 1899.

On the contrary, Jeff had been doing too much work, and was, if anything, trained down finer than he really should be. Instead of weighing 215 pounds, his best weight, he had allowed himself to go down as low as 205 pounds, and against the urgent advice of his trainer, Billy Delaney, he seemed intent on reducing still lower.

Jeff listened to Ryan more than he listened to Delaney, which caused a lack of harmony in the camp.

In the meantime, during the time that Jeff was unable to spar or hit the bags, Sharkey was sparring with Bob Armstrong. The Sharkey-Armstrong sparring sessions were described as "bruising" and worth the price of admission. Tom went at him viciously for 6 rounds. Sharkey was in superb condition, and demonstrating improved skill. "Sharkey is no longer the rough, slugging type of a fighter that he was when we first saw him in the East. He has acquired a lot of knowledge about the finer points of the boxer's art."[397]

On the 18th, Jeff had his left arm steamed with hot air, which he said helped. He planned on undergoing such treatments on a daily basis. "I can notice great improvement already. The only bad feature is that I am deprived of much good training." It was lamented that without the use of his arm he "cannot indulge in the exercise which will do him the most good." Unfortunately, "The spot where the medicine ball struck it is badly swollen and each effort to raise the elbow is accompanied by a shooting pain." Jeff had mostly been confining his labors to road work and working his right.

In his second autobiography, Jeff said that Ryan wanted the fight to be called off, but Delaney and Brady wanted it to go on for financial reasons, and he gave in to them. Jeff at least wanted a longer delay, but for whatever reason, the November 3 date remained firm. "Jeffries, it is known, would rather forfeit $2,500 and have the battle put off at least four weeks hence." Still, Jeff remained a 3 to 5 favorite.[398]

---

397 *National Police Gazette*, November 4, 1899, November 11, 1899.
398 *New York Sun, New York World*, October 19, 1899; *Two Fisted Jeff* at 127-129.

After his steam treatment on October 19, Jeff took his long run to Long Branch and back. In the gymnasium, he punched the bag moderately for 15 minutes. In the afternoon, he took a bike ride and played two games of handball.

On October 20, Jeff ran 6 miles, 3 of which were run at a fast gait. In the afternoon, he spent two hours in the gym, wrestling with Roeber and Jack Jeffries, jumping rope, punching the bag, and playing handball. A doctor who was present advised Jeff to be cautious, and would not permit him to toss the medicine ball.[399]

Jim Corbett predicted that Jeffries would have a tough time with Sharkey, and that it would be one of the most closely contested fights ever. He had bet on Jeff against Fitz, but would not bet on either man for this one for the simple fact that he had no idea as to who would win.

> It is one of the most difficult fights in which to predict the winner. I have met both men and have no choice so far as the outcome is concerned. I believe it will be a question of condition and endurance, and the one who can stand the gaff, will, in my opinion, be the victor. … Sharkey, from his recent fights, showed ability to take considerable punishment. … Whether Jeffries will be able to stand the grueling in such a contest remains to be seen. … Sharkey is a different man from Fitzsimmons. The sailor is built more on the lines of his opponent, Jeffries. He has the strength, endurance and vitality. Of course, Jeffries will have the advantage in reach, weight and height, but these handicaps in a fight do not always mean victory for the man who possesses them. What Sharkey lacks in weight, reach and height he makes up in quickness. Sharkey is a remarkably quick man on his feet and may surprise many of the wise ones who believe he has not a chance. … I would not be surprised to see the bout go the limit. It makes little difference to me who carries off the honors. I have posted a forfeit and will fight the winner for the championship.[400]

Corbett later said of Sharkey, "I never met a man that had such an appetite for hard punches. The more you give him the more he laughs and runs in."[401]

As of the 22nd, Jeff was the favorite at odds of 10 to 8. The injured arm had not shaken the gamblers' confidence in him. Authorities declared that Jeff was a much cleverer infighter than Sharkey and could stand rough-and-tumble punishment much better than the sailor could. However, Corbett and John L. Sullivan liked Sharkey's chances.[402]

---

399 *New York World*, October 20, 1899; *New York Sun*, October 21, 1899. Jeff was set to second featherweight Marty McCue in a fight the following night, on the 21st.
400 *New York Journal*, October 21, 1899.
401 *New York World*, November 4, 1899.
402 *New York World*, October 22, 1899.

Jeff had allegedly gotten his weight down to 206 pounds, less than what he weighed for the Fitz fight. "Jeffries is taking flesh off at a rapidity that is not at all pleasant to his backers." They wanted him to weigh more. However, Jeff said that he felt just as strong as ever, and could work hard all day without feeling fatigue. As of the 23rd, "His injured arm seems to be all right again."

On October 24, Jeff reduced his morning run by several miles. In the afternoon, he tested his left arm in sparring for the first time, boxing Tommy Ryan 6 rounds. "Jeffries used his left arm freely and punched hard with it. At the end he said he did not suffer any inconvenience and was surprised at the strength of it." Jeff declared that he did not expect to be handicapped any further. Still, he would only get to spar for a little over a week. Also, the question was how well the arm would be over the course of 25 rounds, punching really hard with it rather than more lightly as Jeff was compelled to do against the middleweight-sized Ryan.[403]

On the 25th, Jeff went running with Ryan in the morning for several hours. After breakfast and a rest, he played handball. Jeffries next sparred 6 lively rounds with Ryan. He then did some wrestling with Roeber. Jeff said that he never felt stronger in his life. Roeber corroborated the statement, saying that he never tackled a stronger man. Jeff appeared to be in good condition, looking lighter than when he won the title.

Sharkey was tapering off in his training. "The unanimous opinion was that the sailor was never in such excellent condition for a fight." Tom's weight vacillated between 185 and 187 pounds.

On the 26th, Jeff ran 5 miles, sparred 6 rounds with Ryan, and wrestled Roeber. He also played handball, skipped rope, and punched the bag. Roeber discussed Jeff's training.

Every day I spend a short session with Jeffries, trying to tire him. We wrestle about fifteen minutes. ... Honestly, I try hard, but up to date I welcome the end of the bout more than Jeffries does. And that is only

---

403 *New York Sun, New York World*, October 24, 25, 1899. That same day, Sharkey reveled in his dumbbell exercise, and boxed 4 rounds with Jeff Thorne.

one portion of his daily plan of campaign. He runs, walks, plays handball, slams the bag, thrashes his brother Jack, gives Tommy Ryan a thump or two and leaves the medicine ball alone.

However, another report said that Jeff had a stiff neck, and so he let up on his training on the 26th, only running, playing two games of handball, bag punching, rope-skipping and engaging in a light tussle with brother Jack. It claimed that he did no sparring owing to the stiff neck.

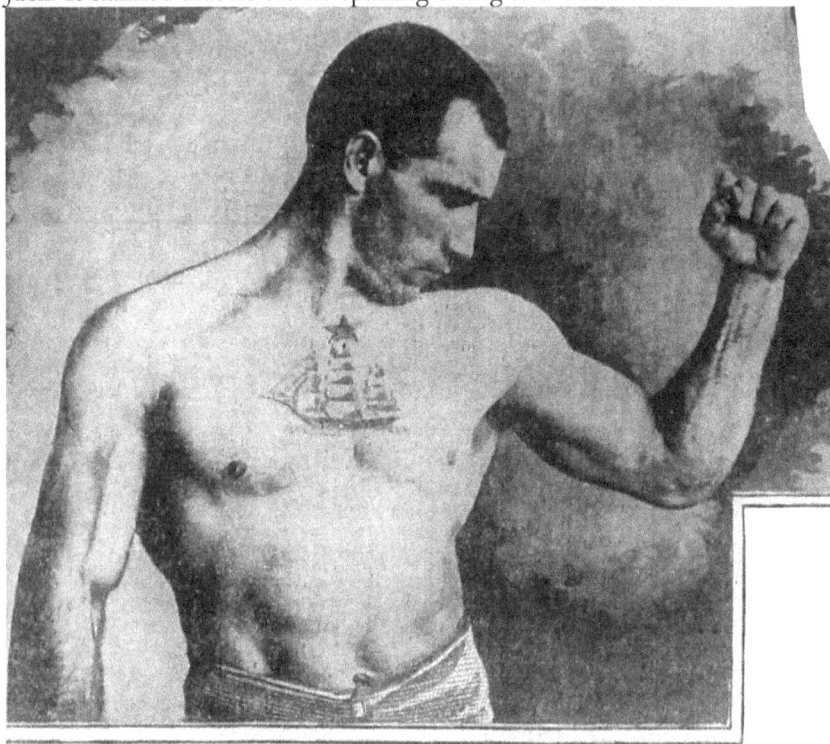

"I JUST FEEL SORRY FOR JEFFRIES, THAT'S WHAT I DO."

Bob Armstrong said that Sharkey was better than Jeffries. Armstrong said, "Some of the sore spots on my body and the lumps on my face remind me of that." Bob and Tom were boxing hard together daily.[404]

On the 27th, Jeffries did his customary morning spin along Shore Road. His arm was said to be in excellent condition and did not show the slightest evidence of being out of order. "Jeffries employs it as much as his right to play handball, box with Jack and Tommy Ryan and punch the bag." Jeffries discussed his feelings, condition, and training.

My injured arm having yielded to medical treatment, I am now almost in perfect physical trim.... While I admit that the bruise caused me considerable inconvenience and compelled me to let up in my training

---

404 *New York Journal, New York Herald, New York Sun, New York World,* October 25-28, 1899.

for a week, it has in no way militated against my chances of success. Not that I believe Mr. Sharkey to be a cinch, but because I think I am his superior.

The extra week allowed me has helped me greatly. It has given me an opportunity to do considerable boxing and sparring, which, to my mind, are most necessary to a pugilist…. My bouts with Ryan during the past week have done me a wonderful lot of good. As matters stand now I believe I will win sure. …

It is true that I do not look so heavy as when I fought Fitzsimmons, but in reality I weigh more. I now weigh 215 pounds. … When I first began training my legs and body appeared fat. Today there is no unnecessary flesh on any part of my anatomy. This is the result of hard training, and any reports to the contrary are false and circulated to influence the betting. …

In addition to sparring bouts, I play considerable handball, wrestle and take a little road work. … Every morning I am up at 6 o'clock ready for business. I first go on the road for a short distance. … After breakfast I play a game or two of croquet. … I then take to the road again, running short sprints, say about 100 yards at a time, and covering the intermediate distance at a brisk walk. On arriving home I have a salt water bath and then a stiff rubdown. The afternoon is generally given up to gymnasium exercises. I go to the handball court for fifteen minutes, playing with my trainers. Bag punching follows, and finally I conclude with six hot rounds with Ryan. The evenings are given up to pleasure, such as playing cards or going to see some show.[405]

John L. Sullivan watched Jeffries box with Tommy Ryan on the 27th. Jeff impressed John L. with his strength, quickness, judgment of distance, and hitting abilities. John said that Jeff was a mighty clever fighter and one of the most active big men he ever saw. "He gets away from Ryan's leads in clever fashion, and Ryan is a pretty good one, too. It proves Jeffries is far from a slugger." John L. said that Jeff looked to be in great shape, that both he and Sharkey were great fighters, and that it would be a grand battle.

Another report of that day's sparring with Ryan said that in the 2nd round, Jeffries "accidentally clouted Tommy on the jaw very much harder than was intended, and Jack Jeffries was called in to take the vacant place." Jack roughed it and fought 3 fast rounds, and James displayed cleverness that surprised the onlookers.

On the 28th, Tom Sharkey did his morning run, hit the bag for a half hour, and sparred 4 rounds with Bob Armstrong, "who has all of Jeffries's weight and reach and more." When Sharkey read that Sullivan pronounced

Jeff to be in good condition, he said, "I am glad to hear it. Now the champion will have no excuse to offer if he is beaten."[406]

On October 28, 1899 in Chicago before a crowd of 6,000, Bob Fitzsimmons knocked out Jeff Thorne, the English (or South African) middleweight, in 1 minute and 10 seconds of the 1st round. Fitz had feinted with his right, and as Thorne ducked, Bob landed a left hook to the jaw which dropped him for the count. Thorne had recently been sparring with Tom Sharkey, who had predicted that Thorne would put up a good fight against Fitzsimmons. He was wrong.

In an interview a couple days after the fight, Thorne remarked, "You know I didn't see much of Fitz," which brought laughter. "Say, but can't he hit? That was the worst punch I ever got in my life. Why, that man Fitz is as far above me as a fighter as I am above a blind cripple. He is so blooming fast that I couldn't tell whether he was leading at me with his hands or his feet. … He'd whip McCoy easily."[407]

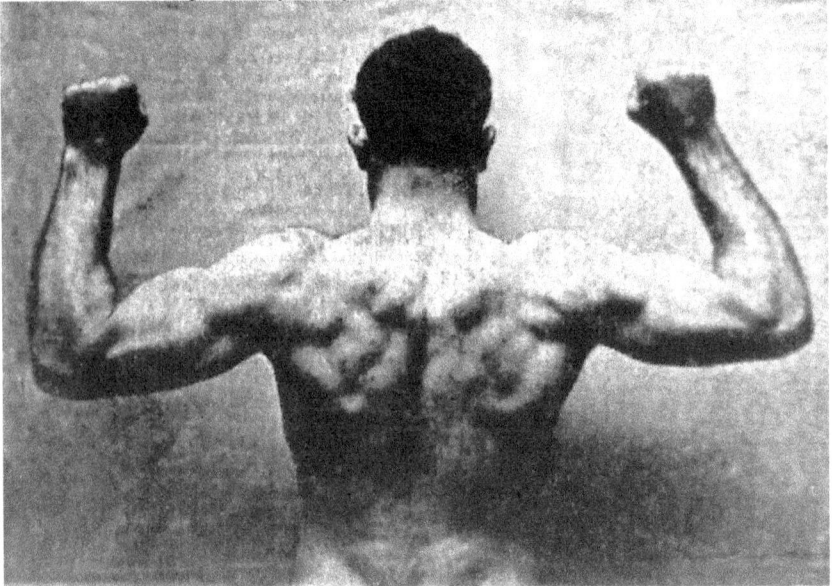

Jeffries shows off his back muscles

On the 29th, Jeffries punched the bag, skipped rope, and went through his other exercises. Brady said that there was no doubt about the fight.

---

406 *New York Sun, New York Journal, New York World,, New York Journal,* October 28, 1899. As part of his training on the 28th, Jeff ran a two-mile course, doing short sprints throughout.

407 After the fight, Fitzsimmons told Thorne, "You see, I had to beat you more quickly than McCoy did, for reasons you yourself can figure out." In early September, Kid McCoy had knocked out Thorne in the 3rd round. *New York Clipper,* November 4, 1899; *Chicago Tribune,* October 29, 1899; *New York Sun,* October 30, 1899; *New York World,* October 31, 1899.

Although the odds were 10 to 7 in Jeff's favor, many shrewd judges of boxing thought that Tom had a fine chance to win.[408]

On the 30th, Sharkey boxed 4 rounds with Armstrong, 2 rounds with George Dixon, and then went at the punching bag and did his other gymnasium work.

Sharkey was a favorite with the women. Nearly every day there were from one to five women around the training quarters trying to get a peep at him while he was at work. Women would often waive their handkerchiefs at him.

That same day, the biograph filmed Jeffries going through his regular training. After his road work, he sparred Ryan and Jack, and wrestled with Roeber. In his 6 rounds with Ryan, Jeff looked faster than ever, and

Bill Delaney, James Jeffries, and Tommy Ryan

his defense appeared to be far better than it was for the Fitz fight. Jeff jumped rope a thousand times and punched the bag for 15 minutes. He also played handball. "His wind is good, and he was not fatigued in the least."

A 4-year-old little girl took a prominent part in one of the scenes filmed. She boxed with Jeff, knocked him out with a punch on the jaw, counted him out, and declared herself the winner.

The afternoon was taken up

by a short run and a spin on the bicycle. "The big fellow weighs about 210 pounds, having gained a little of late."

Jeff said that if Sharkey defeated him it would be because he was the better man, not as a result of lack of condition. "I defeated him once, and since that contest have improved fifty per cent in every way. I am feeling

---

408 *New York Sun, New York World, New York Journal,* October 30, 1899.

much better physically, and am considerably faster on my feet than ever before." He said his hands were in good shape, and he was stronger than when he won the championship.[409]

After seeing Sharkey train on the 31st, including boxing 4 rounds with Armstrong, punching the bag and skipping rope, Mike Donovan said, "No man could be in more perfect condition." He also said that there could be no finer physical specimen than Sharkey.

> He is as supple and quick as if he was on springs. He is as fast on his legs as any clever featherweight. Anybody who thinks Sharkey isn't a clever boxer will be surprised when he sees him fight. ... His footwork is fast. He isn't afraid of a punch or two. He dashes in, protecting himself well even in his rush, then cuts loose both hands with terrible speed. He is chain-lightning at infighting. He is able to throw the whole weight of his body into a short jolt that will knock out any man it lands on. ... I think that any man who will mix it up with Sharkey will be sorry for it, for he is one of the hardest half-arm hitters I ever saw.

Donovan analyzed the matchup. Jeffries had very good defense and a long straight left that Fitz could not get inside of. The question was whether Sharkey could get in on Jeff. "Bob Armstrong is as tall as Jeffries and has just about as long a reach, yet Sharkey got in on him when he liked. I don't write this to compare Armstrong with Jeffries, but to show what Sharkey can do against a big man six inches taller than himself and twenty pounds heavier." Sharkey was "clever and strong enough to get to a big man." His tactics were to get close and batter his man to pieces with both hands. Despite the size disparity, Donovan said, "Jeffries has no advantage over him in strength. In fact, I think Sharkey is the stronger man of the two for his weight. The height of Jeffries won't be so great a handicap to Sharkey as people think." Sharkey knew how to get in. "Watch Sharkey on Friday night, and you'll see one of the greatest infighters that ever got into the ring. He has wonderful strength, and he can throw it all into a short punch." Donovan noted that Tom improved in each fight, and was displaying more quickness and a better knowledge of the game than ever before. "His headwork has improved as well as his footwork. His defense is clever. He can block as well as anybody I ever saw." Summarizing, "If Jeffries whips Sharkey he will have to fight harder than he ever fought before, for Sharkey no doubt is one of the hardest pieces of humanity that ever went into the ring. There is no man in the ring today who can stand as hard a blow and come back as strong from it as Sharkey."[410]

On the 31st, Jeff walked to Deal Lake, and rowed across the lake to a friend's house, a distance of about 3 miles. His schedule called for a stroll

---

409 *New York Journal*, October 30, 31, 1899; *New York World*, *New York Sun*, October 31, 1899.
410 *New York World*, November 1, 1899.

for several hours. Later, Jeff went at the punching bag with vim, and worked the wrist machine. He boxed Ryan 6 rounds in no tame affair. Jeff cut loose at him more than usual, forcing Ryan to hustle to get away. "Ryan was surprised, for it was the first time since he has been with the boilermaker that the latter has cut loose. When it was over Ryan remarked that Jeffries knows more about boxing than he cares to let his friends believe." Then Jeff sparred Jack. "It was not very long before his brother measured his length on the floor in temporary slumber. A left jab settled him." He also likely wrestled with Roeber.

Jeffries said, "That injury to my arm…was only a trifle that passed away completely in a couple of days. It interfered hardly any with my training." Jeff again confirmed that he was in better shape than he was against Fitzsimmons. His sparring was done, and he would only skip rope and hit the bag over the next couple of days. He did no evening road work, owing to the rain.[411]

Jeff gave manager Bill Brady $8,000 to wager on himself. "It is the first time in his ring career, Jim says, that he has bet on his chances." Tommy Ryan bet $500 on Jeff. Ryan had boxed with both men [having boxed Sharkey in a Feb. '99 6-round exhibition], and felt that Jeff was superior. "Jeffries's muscles are pliable and looser than Sharkey's. He is a

JEFFRIES AND RYAN PLAYING HANDBALL.

straight puncher, while the Sailor depends upon…heavy swings."[412]

On November 1, Jeff did several long sprints on the road with Ryan, from 3-5 miles. He would sprint 100 yards, then slow down for a like distance and sprint at the end. After a rubdown and a meal, Jeff skipped rope, punched the bag, and sparred some fast rounds with Ryan for the edification of Mike Donovan, his last sparring before the fight. Jeff later played some croquet, and punched the bag for 15 minutes.[413]

---

411 *New York Journal,* October 31, 1899; *New York World,* November 1, 1899.
412 *New York Sun,* November 1, 1899. Police Chief Devery announced that he would not interfere with the fight, and denied rumors to the contrary.
413 *Chicago Tribune,* November 2, 1899. On November 1, Sharkey walked and sprinted alternately over about 4 miles.

Jeff said that it did not matter what tactics Sharkey employed, whether rushing in or running away, for he was prepared to either rough it or take the aggressive.[414]

Mike Donovan said that although Jeffries was in good condition and strong, he felt that Jeff was not quite as good physically as he was when he fought for the crown. He saw Jeff in the morning after a 3-mile run. Jeff's face seemed to be drawn and worn, his eyes not very bright, and he did not seem as big and robust as when he fought Fitzsimmons. However, Jeff stepped on the scales for Donovan, and weighed 210 ½ pounds, and that was after the run. Despite weighing more than he did in June, Donovan said that he appeared smaller. However, Donovan said the rumors of poor health were untrue.

Donovan contradicted himself a bit by saying that in Jeff's sparring with Ryan; Jeffries was just as clever, faster, and better than before. The champion could alternate between a crouching position and standing upright. "This is a distinct improvement in his boxing since he fought Fitz." His left arm appeared to be strong, flexible and as good as ever. "Jeffries uses it as feely as if nothing had ever gone wrong with it." Jeff was very quick on his legs, rushing in and getting out as fast as a small man. He also had a good defense, ducking and bringing in the elbows close to the ribs. That said, although Ryan was the cleverest and quickest man in the world for his weight, Sharkey was thirty pounds bigger, stronger, and just as quick. "Jeffries is full of confidence and quiet courage. He isn't as brisk and merry as Sharkey; but then he isn't an Irishman and lacks the mercurial spirit of that race. ... I think the battle ought to be the finest in the history of the ring. No one ever saw such a speedy and powerful pair of men face each other."

Although there was some debate about Jeff's condition. Jeffries claimed, "[M]y condition is as perfect as it is possible for it to be." He said that he was stronger and quicker than Sharkey, had a longer reach, was just as good on the inside, had greater weight, and could stand punishment without flinching.

Tommy Ryan said that Jeffries was as fit as any man who ever wore gloves. He was game, able to stand punishment, as handy with his right as with his left, and was faster, stronger, and more scientific than the sailor. He also had the reach, extra weight, and harder punches, both at long and short range.

Sharkey said that he was 100% better than when he had met Jeffries in San Francisco. He claimed to be faster with his feet and hands than Jeff was, and could hit just as hard a blow. His manager, Tom O'Rourke, said that Tom was in better shape than Jeffries was. O'Rourke bet $1,400 on Tom, and Sharkey bet $5,000 on himself at 10 to 7 odds.

---

414 *New York Journal,* November 1, 1899; *New York Sun,* November 2, 1899.

The day before the fight, on November 2, Jeffries biked to a barber shop and got a shave. He later punched the bag and skipped rope, and possibly worked the pulley machines a bit. Jeff again said that he was better prepared for battle than ever before and was confident of victory. Sharkey "has repeatedly said that I received an unjust decision over him in 'Frisco, and I am glad that the time has come when I can prove to the world who was entitled to the referee's verdict. I defeated Sharkey once and am confident that I will defeat him again."

With wagers coming in on Tom, the betting odds were 10 to 8. Sharkey's muscles looked larger and stronger than ever before. One local paper said that Jeffries was weighing 216 pounds to Sharkey's 185 pounds. Another said he was 210 ½ to Sharkey's 195 pounds.

James J. Corbett ultimately picked Jeffries to win, although he felt that the champion would have a hard fight on his hands. Basing his prediction on his experience with both, Jim said that he had bet $1,000 on Jeff. However, "I do not underestimate Sharkey's ability as a fighter nor overlook his strong points." Jim wanted to fight the winner. "I am far from a dead one and still believe that I can regain my lost laurels. I have been promised a match by both fighters and am taking daily exercise in anticipation of a match in the near future."[415]

W.O. Inglis predicted, "It seems to me that Jeffries will win…not by any such comfortable margin as the odds of 8 to 10 would indicate, but after the hardest kind of a fight." He said that pound-for-pound, Sharkey was stronger than Jeff was, but that Jeff's bigger overall size gave him the strength edge. Jeff was nimble, with fast legs, and could rush in or dart away as briskly as a middleweight could. He knew how to use his weight to advantage. He could also use his height and reach. Although Jeff's stooping

---

415 *New York World*, November 2, 3, 1899.

position was awkward looking, it was effective as a defense, particularly in the Fitz fight. No one had yet been able to penetrate his crouching defense. The question was whether Jeff could stand off Sharkey and wear him down with repeated left jabs. It was quite possible, for "no man living can take many of these left jabs from Jeffries and keep awake." Both were good at infighting, although Sharkey had a slight edge there. Sharkey had the power to rally after being hurt and fight as hard as ever. He had wonderful vitality. Ultimately, though, Inglis favored Jeff.

Jeffries said that both of them had improved since they last met, but felt that his own improvement was greater. He had better knowledge of the science of boxing, was faster on his feet, and in better condition than when he won the title. Both men were confident that they could knock the other out.

Sharkey said that Jeff's crouching position would mean nothing, and that Jeff would stand straight up after the 1st round or not be standing at all.

Jeff's mother thought he would win, and wished him well, although still insisting that boxing was the "devil's work."

The Sun's analysis said that Jeff's speed, ring tactics, generalship, and strength during the fight with Fitz stamped him as one of the cleverest heavyweights in the world. His science, headwork and terrific hitting power had knocked Fitz out. Jeff was surprisingly shifty for a big man, and "has a wonderful left hand." It was the left that repeatedly went into Bob's face and set him up for the final right. "Jeffries showed that he could take Fitz's hardest blows, whether on the jaw or in the stomach, without flinching."

Regarding the first Sharkey fight, there were all sorts of versions. Sharkey maintained that he was robbed, but of course, he said that about every fight he had lost or drawn. "But on the other hand persons who saw the fight with unprejudiced eyes, state with emphasis that Jeffries was far and away the better pugilist." However, both had improved since then.

In an interview, Sharkey said that he should have gotten no worse than a draw in their first fight.

> If there is any difference in strength it is in my favor. ... When it comes to speed, hitting power, ability to go a long distance at a killing clip and aggressiveness, the advantage is all on my side. ... As regards hitting powers, you need look no further than our respective battles with Gus Ruhlin. Jeffries boxed him a twenty-round draw. When I met Ruhlin we had only boxed a minute or two. It was all done with one ponderous punch. ... If I could accomplish in a minute what Jeffries failed to do in twenty rounds, it bears me out in a measure when I say I am 'there' with a harder wallop than the Californian. ... I have fought...Ruhlin, McCoy and Corbett. ... I have improved many per cent since meeting Jeffries. I study the game closer than people

imagine, and I acquired considerable additional knowledge of the boxing game in those three bouts.[416]

Sharkey was a rusher and a heavy hitter at close range with both hands, to both the body and head. "He is game beyond a doubt." He was able to stand punishment without showing its effects. He had more brute strength than Fitzsimmons did. "If Sharkey forces the fight, it will not at all surprise the talent to see Jeffries shift about on his feet and work the left into the face as he did with Fitz." Jeff's reach would likely help him at long range.

The Sun said that in training, Jeffries had reduced from 240 to 210 pounds. He had not trained for quite as long as Tom had, but was in good trim. Jeff currently weighed 212 to Tom's 185 pounds, having gained a couple pounds as a result of letting up on his training the last few days. "Jeffries says he feels as strong as a bull, but fancies that the lay off from now until the battle will add several pounds to his weight." Sharkey's manager said that Tom would likely weigh 190 pounds on the night of the fight.

Jeffries said, "Although I have been so unfortunate as to meet with an accident at this important moment, I hope my injury will have no effect on my coming contest.... My arm, while quite painful at the time, has come around all right in time to prevent any further postponement. ... I have no doubts about the outcome."

Sam Austin said that taking everything into consideration, "the fight is about as even a proposition as I have ever seen." Jeff had the facility of using his arms as quickly and as dexterously as a featherweight. "For a big man he is phenomenally light on his feet." Sharkey was marvelously quick and clever at getting in and out.

As for Jeff's condition, Austin opined that he was in good shape, but not the shape that he was in when he fought Fitzsimmons. Bill Naughton of the *Examiner*, who had observed Jeff at his training quarters, said, "But, truth to tell, it is not only a twisted arm that ails Jeffries. He has all the earmarks of a man who has taken off weight in too much of a hurry." Austin agreed. Regardless of the arm, he felt that Jeff did not allow himself sufficient time to get into perfect condition.

> While he was sojourning abroad he did no training, loafed around London and Paris, ate and drank of all the good things set before him, and accumulated so much fat and flesh that when he arrived here he resembled a prize beef and looked as if he needed at least six months of steady, methodical training to fit him for the ring.

Instead, he had only given himself five weeks of work, and during part of that time, an injured arm hampered him. He had only sparred for nine days before the fight.

---

416 *National Police Gazette*, November 11, 1899.

Compounding matters was the fact that there was dissention in the training camp. Although Bill Delaney had been the chief trainer, it appeared that Tom Ryan was more and more gaining Jeff's ear, and Delaney and Ryan did not agree on the proper training methods. Jeff had previously acquiesced to Delaney, but "the fact of the matter is Jeff is not as compliant or as easily handled as he was before he reached the pinnacle of championship fame. He undertook to dictate how he should be trained and was at variance all the time with the man who brought him from obscurity into the limelight of public favor."[417]

Bill Delaney issued a statement indicating his dissatisfaction with how things had gone. He felt that Jeff had overtrained.

> Jeffries has trained in opposition to my wishes. I have objected to his continual running and sweating. He would not have worked as hard as he has if I had more to say about it. Jeffries was advised by friends, who believe in his methods, which were those adopted by Corbett, and over which we had a row. In the last ten days Jeffries has stopped his foolish practice of sweating and running and has since worked in a moderate manner.
>
> The question is, has he stopped in time? I don't mean that he is not physically fit or that he is unable to beat Sharkey, but there is a limit to everything, and I have objected all along to the severe method of training adopted this time by Jeff. He goes ahead and works like a steam engine, almost killing himself on the road by running and sweating. He is not moderate in his work.[418]

Bill Brady, Jeff's manager, was astounded when he read Delaney's statement that Jeff had worked too hard and overtrained himself. He said that Jeff was never in better condition, and that statements to the contrary were due to jealousy between Jeff's trainers. "Jeffries has prepared for this fight in his own way, and I don't think he has made any mistake. Jeffries is intelligent and knows better what is good for himself than any one else does. ... I am perfectly satisfied with the champion's condition."

On the morning of the fight, November 3, Jeff took a 2-mile walk. He said, "I wish to say...that I never was in better condition for a battle than I am now. I feel that I can do better work than I did when I fought Fitzsimmons. If I do not win the fight tonight I do not feel that I can beat Sharkey at all."

Sharkey too said that he was in perfect shape, that he would have no excuses if he lost. "If Jeffries beats me he will be entitled to all the credit in the world."

Bob Armstrong said that Sharkey would win easily, in a walk.

---

417 *National Police Gazette*, November 11, 1899; *New York World*, *New York Sun*, November 3, 1899.
418 *New York Journal*, November 3, 1899.

CHAPTER 19

Reaching Deep Into the Inferno

On November 3, 1899 at the Coney Island Athletic Club in Brooklyn, New York, in the same arena that he won the title, a 210-215-pound James J. Jeffries first defended his title against 185-195-pound Tom Sharkey in a scheduled 25-round bout. Jeffries was 24 years old to Sharkey's 25 or 27 (depending on whether you believe Sharkey was born 11-26-71 or '73).[419]

A few hours before the fight, a *World* reporter asked Bill Delaney if he had said that Jeff was not in good condition. Bill replied,

> No, I did not say that Jeff was out of condition, for I think his condition is plenty good enough for him to win this fight. I believe, however, that his condition could be better, and had he trained as I thought best he would be in better fix now. I was opposed to such hard work in the latter part of the training. I was afraid he would get too fine, and I wanted him to weigh, stripped, 216 or 218 pounds when he left the quarters yesterday. I know that a man must have some weight to lose in a hard and bruising contest, and if he hasn't got it to lose there will be trouble. For that reason I would have had Jeffries weigh more than he does, but at his present weight and condition he can win anyhow.

Some sports said that Delaney was simply getting ready to save his reputation as a trainer in case Jeffries was licked, wanting to be able to say, 'I told you so. If Jeffries had trained according to my ideas he would have won.' Others said that he was merely bluffing and generating rumors about Jeffries being overtrained in order to affect the betting odds.

Jeffries was a 10 to 7 odds favorite at ringside, and it was estimated that $200,000 had been bet over the last week, with Jeff at 10 to 8.

When the arena doors opened at 6 p.m., there was a wild rush for the bleachers because the $5 seats were first come, first served. "Hats were lost, clothes torn, and occasionally an unfortunate would fall and be walked over. No time was lost in picking up clothing. Getting a good seat was more important." Eventually, about two-hundred policemen were on hand

---

419 The following pre-fight, fight, and post-fight discussion and analysis is taken from *New York World, New York Sun, Brooklyn Daily Eagle, New York Herald, New York Times, New York Daily Tribune,* November 4, 1899, and *National Police Gazette,* November 18, 25, 1899. Subsequent analysis is also taken from *Asbury Park Daily Press, San Francisco Chronicle, San Francisco Examiner,* November 4, 1899, and *New York Herald,* November 5, 1899; *New York Sun,* October 31, 1899. Corbett wrote the *World* account of the fight.

to ensure order, including Chief Devery. Some spectators grumbled about the no-smoking rule.

Ticket prices for the box seats were $20, $25, $30, and $35. Every box seat had been sold, which in itself represented at least $25,000. The rest of the seats were $5, $10, and $15. Eventually, there were about 10,000 people present.

The same scaffolding suspended above the ring and used for the lights for the unsuccessful attempt to film Fitzsimmons-Jeffries was still present. However, this time, suspended below it was another more massive scaffolding, from which a canopy of 400 electric arc lights and reflectors, yielding 400-candle-power each for a total of 80,000 candle power, hung so closely to the ring that "a good high jumper might have broken the globes." There was a platform on the massive framework where electricians and a switchboard were located.

Once turned on, the power of these lights was so strong that the heat would be intense. "This is probably the strongest artificial light that has ever been brought to bear upon any stage. It is better than sunlight." An electrician said, "Wait until the lights are turned on. Those lights are the most powerful group ever put together and they will make that ring sizzle." The light would be almost blinding. It needed to be extremely bright in order to allow the indoor filming.

At 8:40 p.m., for a preliminary fight, only 17 of the arc lights were turned on, and the "light was so dazzling that the eyes of the spectators blinked." Three electric fans, one in Jeff's corner and two in Sharkey's, were hanging half-way down in order to cool the men off during the minute's rest.

The American biograph film device was located 25 yards away from the ring on a big stand.

> The biograph uses a film 2 ¼ x 3 inches in size, which runs through the cameras at a rate of 340 feet a minute. This film is much larger than that commonly used and its speed is three times faster, making its exposure at the rate of thirty a second, while the so-called standard gauge machines run at about twelve exposures a second. Four cameras were ready for use, each loaded with film long enough for a round and the usual minute's rest, which was 1,280 feet. ... This would mean 37,400 feet of film for the fight.[420]

When the preliminary was over, the building was crowded from pit to dome, not a seat left. Some who wanted to buy tickets were turned away. The bleachers were filled so tightly that it was impossible to move. Jim Corbett and John L. Sullivan sat close to the ring.

---

420 Successful tests had already been conducted by filming the Dixon-Bolan and Mysterious Billy Smith-Jim Jeffords fights.

Most spectators ignored the no-smoking rule. "The smoking rule was a dead letter. Cigars were lighted all over the house, in spite of the efforts of the police, and the atmosphere was soon heavy with tobacco. The sports could not be happy without cigars." Even a local judge was smoking.

There was concern that the smoke might interfere with the filming process. At 9:40 p.m., the master of ceremonies got into the ring, and, using his megaphone, asked the crowed to stop smoking. There was so much noise in the house that he could not make himself heard at the extreme end. Those near the ring who heard him simply laughed and "went on curling the blue smoke roofward."

Although it was cold and raining outside, inside the ring it was quite the opposite, owing to the intensely hot lights. It quickly became evident just how hot the overhead lights would be. "As the electricians turned on three complete rows of lights, which was about a fourth of the entire number of blazers, the heat around the ring became uncomfortable." As the other lights were turned on, "The heat in the ring gradually became so intense that some people believed that the fighters would kick like steers when they got into their corners. Several of Jeffries's friends said that he never could stand summer heat, and that if these lights were permitted to burn during the contest that he would suffer."

At 9:55 p.m., there was an outburst of applause and everybody stood up as Sharkey left his dressing room and approached the ring. He wore a brown bathrobe. George Dixon, Bob Armstrong, Tim McGrath, and manager Tom O'Rourke led the way. Once he entered the ring, Sharkey bowed in acknowledgment to the crowd, and then sat down. Two electric fans hung in midair over Tom's head to cool him off. "He needs them under the fierce electric lights. They are as hot as the mouth of a blast furnace."

One to two minutes later, Jeffries entered the ring. He too was generously applauded, but not wildly. He wore a bath robe and neatly creased trousers, which he intended to pull off later. Tommy Ryan, Bill Delaney, brother Jack, and Ernest Roeber accompanied him. Jeff sat down in the same northeast corner that he occupied for the Fitz fight. He then got up and met Sharkey in ring center. They shook hands, both smiling. Tom said, "May the best man win." Then the usual challenges to fight the winner were announced, including those by Corbett and Fitzsimmons.

The electric fans were running to cool the men off, and their seconds sponged their heads. "All of the lights were turned on now and the heat was oppressive." It was so hot and bright that the spectators around the ring were putting newspapers over their eyes and also fanning themselves. "The glaring light overhead was almost blinding."

> The battle was fought under unfavorable conditions for both men. The intense white lights directly over the heads of the fighters produced a temperature that must have been easily a hundred in the

ring, possibly more. It was almost unbearable for those who occupied the seats at the immediate ringside.

It was estimated that Jeff would weigh 212 to Sharkey's 195 pounds. The day of the fight, Jeff said he weighed 212. He said that was four pounds more than he weighed against Fitzsimmons, although most were saying that he looked even thinner and smaller than he did against Bob. Sharkey was listed as standing 5'8 ¼" to Jeffries' 6'1 ½".[421]

In the ring, the weights were announced as Jeffries, 210, Sharkey, 185. Corbett estimated that Jeff weighed 211 or 215 pounds, with Sharkey at 187 or 190. *The Brooklyn Daily Eagle* said that Jeff admitted to 212 pounds, "but was heavier." Sharkey claimed he was "about 187." *The Sun* said, "In appearance Jeffries did not look as powerful as when he fought Fitzsimmons." *The Eagle* agreed. On the other hand, "Sharkey was the picture of physical perfection He was bigger than ever and in superb shape."

It was announced that the men would fight under Queensberry rules, which meant that they would be permitted to fight with one hand free in the clinch, and would also protect themselves on the break.

Sharkey removed his robe. He wore green silk trunks with an American flag for a belt. O'Rourke sponged him off with water. Delaney gave Jeff a douse as well. Jeffries wore black trunks. They shook hands at 10:10 p.m. and the men returned to their corners to await the gong of the bell. Referee George Siler of Chicago was the third man in the ring.

1st round

Jeffries crouched as he came in, with his long thick left arm sticking out in front of him, his jaw crouched down behind his left shoulder, and his bulky right arm hugged tightly to his ribs and breast. His "queer crouching position" brought Jeff down so low that he did not stand more than an inch

---

421 *New York Herald*, November 3, 1899.

or so above the sailor. "There is a great difference in their blows. The Californian lunges or wallops with his big arms as if they were enormous clubs. Sharkey runs up close and explodes his blow as if it were a 6-inch shell."

Throughout the round, Sharkey rushed in, missed a wild punch, and they clinched. Tom threw Jeff off to show his strength. Tom missed some more blows. As Jeff came to a clinch, he shot in his hard right on Sharkey's ribs. "They are going as fast as bantams." The sailor made a fierce rush

SCENE IN CONEY ISLAND CLUB-HOUSE WHILE THE FIGHT WAS IN PROGRESS.

and they clinched, and again Tom pushed Jeff off. Jeffries blocked a wild lead, then stepped away and laughed at Tom. Sharkey came in with a left that only landed on the shoulder, but he then pushed the heel of his left glove up against Jeff's chin in the clinch, already using his rough tactics.

Sharkey rushed but was met with a heavy left swing that sent his head back. Jeff danced out of harm's way, landed a right to the ribs, smothered a counter and clinched. Jeff would duck and clinch. Sharkey's right eye was reddened from the left-hand punch that he got.

It was evident from the start that as he had done with Fitzsimmons, Jeffries had chosen to allow Sharkey to set the pace. Jeff backed away and shot out his left jab when Tom rushed, occasionally timing him on the way in and landing, but often Tom would duck while advancing. Jeff either blocked, ducked or used his legs to elude many blows, and would then fire back his own punches or clinch. Occasionally Tom feinted, rushed in and landed his left on the cheek. Jeffries frequently used clinching to stop Tom's rush and to neutralize him at close quarters. In the clinch, Jeff would lean his weight on Tom. He seemed cool and calm, laughing at Sharkey's efforts. Sharkey kept up his rushes, but was over-anxious and wild. The crowd, "with its usual ignorance of Queensberry rules," hissed when Sharkey fought himself free from the clinches. Immediately after the bell, Tom threw and landed a blow.

2nd round

Jeffries dropped Sharkey in this round, each local New York source providing a different version of the knockdown(s).

Times: Jeffries dropped Sharkey with a left on the chin.

Herald: A left to the jaw dropped Tom.

285

Corbett (writing for the *World*): Sharkey rushed, missed, and they clinched. Tom hung onto Jeff's neck. Jeff pushed him backward to the ropes and gave him a short right jolt in the ribs, and Sharkey went down on his knees (This is the version Jeff used in his first autobiography). He stayed down 8 seconds.

Sun: Sharkey slipped a Jeffries left lead and landed a right to the body. Jeffries rushed, and Sharkey countered on the stomach. Jeff forced him to a corner and dropped Sharkey with a left and right to the head. Tom rose after six seconds. He was not exactly groggy, but his pins were weakened.

Brooklyn Daily Eagle: Jeffries met Sharkey's rush and backed Tom into the northwest corner. Sharkey mixed it up and received a right on the side of the head while off his balance and he went sprawling. Jeff backed away while Tom took nine seconds to rise.

New York Journal: Jeffries forced the sailor into the corner. A right swing staggered Tom, and a follow-up powerful left dropped Sharkey. Referee Siler stepped in between them and pushed Jeff back while he administered the count.

National Police Gazette: Jeff came forward in a crouching position. Tom's blows went over his shoulder and they clinched. Sharkey rushed and Jeff met him with a straight left on the face that carried him back to the corner, sending him down on his haunches.

After rising, Sharkey quickly went down again, some saying by throwing himself off balance with a punch, while others said Jeffries dropped him a second time.

Herald: Another Jeffries left scored a second knockdown.

Corbett: Tom got up with a rush and lunged so fiercely that he fell on all fours. "Now he sticks out his tongue to show that he does not care."

Sun: Tom rushed and in missing a double swing, fell upon all fours. Jeff stepped away and laughed at him.

Brooklyn Daily Eagle: Upon rising, Sharkey rushed and Jeff side-stepped and the sailor went down on all fours.

New York Journal: Another Jeffries left-hand swing sent Sharkey down.

After Tom rose for the second time, as they came together again, Jeff hit him with a terrible right smash under the heart. "Jeffries is laughing all the time." Sharkey threw heavy swings, but Jeff blocked most of them with his solid guard. "He would not set the pace, however, and simply waited for Tom to come in." Sharkey was willing and strong, as usual, fighting like a demon, driving in smashes with frightful force. In a clinch, Sharkey dashed his right into Jeff's ribs. "That was a terrific punch, enough to knock a hole in a stone wall." Sharkey liked throwing rights on the breakaway, as he had a right to do (although he sometimes drew hisses), and he occasionally landed to the ear or jaw. Jeff smiled and caught him with heavy punches in the heart or stabbed his mouth with a left. "Jeffries finally rushed his man to a corner and as Sharkey fell the champion toppled over him and grabbed the ropes." They were exchanging swings at the bell, both having about equal strength.

Jeffries later claimed to have re-injured his left arm when punching Sharkey hard in this round, which thereafter affected how hard and how often he could throw the left.

3ʳᵈ round

Corbett said, "This is the fastest, hottest, heaviest fight I ever saw." Sharkey attacked with a flailing left and Jeff ducked and landed a right to the ribs and left to the belly. "This is the sort of thing that will weaken Sharkey if it happens to him very often. Tom is hanging on hard in the clinches." They came together like freight trains, exchanging hard blows. Sharkey rushed and missed and Jeff caught him with a right down swing on the jaw that staggered Tom. Sharkey rushed in and landed a blow "way down below the waist line. The crowd hisses him." Sharkey kept up the attack until Jeff shook him hard with a left jolt on the jaw.

The Eagle said that Jeff used the "right jab" to the body and Sharkey ran into some hard ones. Some have taken this to mean that Jeff occasionally stood in the southpaw stance, which might have been the case, although not necessarily. Sometimes a right jab was meant as a straight right lead, not in swinging fashion. However, as a result of his injured left arm, Jeffries might have sometimes stood in the southpaw stance so that he could use more right leads.

Twice Tom rushed in, but each time he ran into Jeff's solid and crushing right under his heart, the last one staggering and driving Sharkey almost half across the ring. Jeff laughed and made a face. Corbett said, "They are awful blows. … Sharkey has endured terrible punishment from this round." Tom still seemed strong at the finish though. Both were blowing a trifle, affected by the intense heat.

Although Corbett was impressed with Jeffries, the Sun was critical of his style. Jeff was not setting the pace "as champions usually do," but instead depending upon heavy counters. "The fight was even and Jeffries had not come up to expectations. He was fighting on the same lines used in his battle with Fitzsimmons." This was an odd critique given that said formula had worked against Fitz and appeared to be working in this fight thus far.

4ᵗʰ round

Jeff came out quickly, crouching over in his famous attitude. Tom rushed in with a left and right, clinched and hung onto Jeff as if he was a buoy, resting himself. Twice Sharkey rushed in, only to meet with a right to his ribs, one of Jeff's favorite punches. Sharkey had absorbed awful body punishment up to this point.

Tom came in again, and getting under Jim's left, landed a right to the heart. It was the best punch he had landed thus far. When Tom tried it again, Jeff straightened him up with a stiff straight left. In another clinch, Tom hit Jeff's ribs with his right. Tom darted in again, clinched and threw a right which only grazed the back of Jeff's head. Jeffries tried to counter another rush with a left uppercut, but Tom blocked it with his right arm. Tom guarded his face well. They continually clinched between exchanges. Sharkey looked serious, while Jeff was grinning.

Jeffries rushed, but Tom side-stepped and got under him. Sharkey was surprisingly shifty and got away from two leads. He came back again and mixed it, with Jeffries clinching. Tom was lighter on his feet than Jeffries, and when he ducked the left, he grinned. When clinched and trying short inside blows, Jeffries laughed at Tom, and Sharkey returned the smile. Tom rushed again, but ran into a right uppercut on his jaw. Both were a bit wild, but Jeffries landed some heavy blows on the chest. A right to the heart and left to the jaw sent Sharkey reeling momentarily, but he was right back on the attack. Tom's leads were blocked, and he would tumble into the big fellow's arms. Tom struck after the bell.

5ᵗʰ round

Sharkey was still rushing, throwing, and clinching. His rights missed over Jeff's head or grazed the back of his neck. Jeff would often meet his rushes with a hard right to the ribs. Tom clinched, and as he stepped away, pushed Jeff's chin with the heel of his glove. Sharkey attacked, and getting Jeff near the ropes, landed a heavy right on the ear and a left as well. Jeff hit the ribs with another powerful right and followed it with straight left jabs that rocked Tom's head. Sharkey kept coming, which was his best style of fighting, but Jeff had warmed up and found that he could reach the body with his right. He kept driving it in. Tom rushed and swung wildly. The men mixed it and fought themselves free from the clinches. Jeffries "did some terrible execution on the body."

Sharkey took to wrestling. He dashed in time after time and hung on, for "he was only a block or two from Queer street." One of Tom's tactics when hurt was to rely on his wrestling skills. However, Jeff was careful, not rushing in, but waiting.

Sharkey finally recovered his wind and attacked with many heavy left hooks on Jeff's neck and chin, which hurt and made Jeff retreat. Corbett said, "This is the fiercest fighting I ever saw. Now it is Jeff who is clinching and resting." Sharkey landed some hard lefts to the body which made Jeff grunt and clinch. Sharkey never let up, although Jeffries eventually countered fiercely on the stomach with terrific blows.

The Eagle said Tom again struck Jeff after the bell had rung. Brady claimed a foul, and Siler warned Sharkey. Corbett agreed, "This is the third time this has happened and it ought to be stopped. This was Sharkey's round at the end." However, the *Sun* said Sharkey landed one punch as the bell rang and Brady claimed a foul. "There was nothing to it and it was an absurd claim." Still, between rounds, the referee warned Sharkey.

6th round

Sharkey ran out of his corner and landed a left hook squarely on the jaw, but without effect. Tom was the aggressor, rushing in, but Jeff ducked under him, clinched and threw all his weight on Sharkey. Jeff feinted and missed, and Tom laughed and stuck his tongue out. Tom came on again and Jeff met him with a short, straight right on the ribs. In a clinch, Sharkey hit the kidneys with his free hand. On the break, Tom landed a left on the chin. Again, the sailor came, and Jeff landed a left on the abdomen which stopped him. Jeff ran in with a left uppercut on the ribs.

Sharkey was still strong, forcing the fight and punching without any sign of weakening. He repeatedly landed his left to the neck hard enough to knock out an ordinary man, but Jeff took the blows wonderfully well. Tom rushed continually, using straight lefts and uppercuts on the body. Jeffries steadily countered with plenty of power in his punches, but Sharkey was on top of him so frequently that the champion's blows were ineffective.

Sharkey had the better of the infighting. A heavy left cut Jeff's lip and drew a little blood. A Sharkey left swing shook Jeff. Jeffries replied with a terrific right over the heart, but received a left swing on the jaw which hurt and caused Jeff to clinch. Jeffries repeatedly rested on the sailor in the clinches, and the referee had to pull him away. Tom continued attacking the body and head and was the fresher of the two. At the close of the round, Jeffries was bleeding from the mouth and ear. *The Sun* said, "The round was Sharkey's, and Jeffries looked surprised." *The Eagle* said that from this point on, Sharkey's aggressiveness gave him a decided advantage.

7th round

Blood was coming from scratches on the right side of Jeff's neck. There was a lump under Sharkey's right eye. Sharkey came in, missed two left leads and clinched. Generally, Jeff would get inside the blows or duck and then counter. Jeff drew back and smashed Tom's belly with a very hard short right. "Jeffries is very sure with his right jolt on the short ribs." Jeff came in and they clinched. Sharkey held on to get a rest. After breaking,

Tom ran in with a left swing on the ribs. Jeff countered hard on the ear with a left hook. Tom forced, and as Jeff ducked a left, Tom gave him a right uppercut. With terrific power, Jeffries pounded the stomach with his left. Jeff was slower, but had enough strength to floor a bull. Sharkey took the punches well though. Jeff ran into a right on the body that jarred him, and he rested on the sailor. As they backed away, Tom missed a left swing that just grazed the top of Jeff's head, making the champion laugh. "Sharkey lands a regular Sullivan swing with his left arm, the forearm itself banging in on Jeffries's neck."

Sharkey was very aggressive and cut out the pace, frequently scoring to the body and head. He focused more on the head, while Jeff focused more on the body. Three times Tom rushed in with left and right swings, landing one blow out of three. Jeff clinched and hung on to rest himself, leaning his weight on Tom. The referee was compelled to push him away on several occasions before he would break. Sharkey kept forcing and leading, landing two lefts to the jaw. Jeff rarely led. The locals agreed that it was Sharkey's round.

8th round

Sharkey was again active. As Tom came in, Jeff clinched and rested his entire weight on him, causing the crowd to hiss. As usual, Jeff was on the defensive, waiting for Sharkey to come. Tom rushed again and Jeff met him with a right on the ribs. Sharkey rushed in and landed a straight left on the chest that forced a grunt out of Jeff. Tom rushed again, but Jeff met him with a left in the pit of the stomach, causing Tom to grunt. In a clinch, Sharkey twice smashed the ribs. Sharkey came in again and again with his left on the body, landing tremendous body blows.

Still, Jeff cut loose at close quarters, and for a while, both did an equal amount of effective work. They mixed it up roughly, and Tom's left eye was slightly bruised. A Jeffries right swing split Tom's cauliflower left ear open and caused it to bleed profusely. Each took turns leaning on the other in clinches.

Eventually, Tom landed a vicious left swing that dazed Jeff, who clinched and refused to break until the referee pulled him away. Hot infighting followed and Sharkey scored the greater number of blows. Jeff clinched and pushed Sharkey across the ring, half-way through the ropes, which drew some cries of foul from the spectators. Jeff seemed weary. Corbett said, "This is clearly Sharkey's round." *The Eagle* said, "The sailor's aggressive tactics won him many friends."

9ᵗʰ round

Sharkey was again the aggressor. The defensive-minded Jeffries used his feet and circled around, jumping away from leads or ducking under them. When Jeff ducked again, Tom squeezed his neck under his arm. Siler warned Sharkey not to "throttle" when he had Jeffries' head "in chancery," which often happened when Jeff ducked. Sharkey was steadily fighting, but Jeff's footwork and ducking served him well. Jeff blocked his rushes and clinched. Jeffries pushed Tom around again in a clinch. Tom shook him up with a left on the chin, and followed it up with a hard right to the ribs that made Jeff hug. Upon another rush, Jeffries met him with a left on the belly. Jeff hugged for a moment to rest, but Tom broke away, stepped back and jumped in with a Sullivan swing.

Jeff seemed tired. His blows were not quickly delivered and his left seemed to be losing its effect. Sharkey stuck to him. His condition had to be wonderful to continue such an incessant attack without visibly tiring. He was in and out of clinches, and kept coming.

However, Jeff steadied himself and did good execution with both hands, catching Tom on the head and ribs as he rushed. Both landed lefts as the bell rang, and Sharkey laughed. *The Herald* said that Sharkey won this round, as Jeff kept moving out of range and clinching. Tom had landed frequently to the body.

10ᵗʰ round

SHARKEY MASHES JEFF WITH A VICIOUS LEFT.

(Copyright, 1899, by the American Mutoscope and Biograph Company.)

Tom rushed in, and Jeff met him with a terrific left counter on the belly. Jeff blocked a left and Tom clinched and roughed it, getting his right around the back of Jeff's head and dragging him across the ring. Tom kept charging in, and Jeff clinched and pushed Tom half-way across the ring, lying on him on the ropes for a few seconds until the referee stepped in. "The men were inclined to hang on and wrestle, and the referee separated them several times." They again clinched. "Now they are both hanging upon each other, each one trying to tire the other out with his weight. Sharkey will be the loser at this game." Sharkey kept up his assault, landing to the head at close quarters. "He was delivering two blows for one by Jeffries, and the latter was putting up a fight inferior to that which beat Fitzsimmons." In a clinch, Jeffries laughed at Tom O'Rourke. "There was clinching galore." The pace slowed. "The heat from the lights was telling and the fierce rays had both the principals and the spectators near the ring in running sweats."

Sharkey rushed in again, but ran into a powerful right cross which landed on the left eye and split open the flesh above it. The cut bled in streams, down the sailor's neck and onto his breast. Jeff did not follow up, and Tom rushed in fiercely again. "Jeffries was evidently playing a waiting game with the idea of having Sharkey tire himself out with his hard work."

When the round ended, the men stood still for a moment, grinning at each other.

11ᵗʰ round

During the rest, Sharkey's eye was fixed up. At the start, he rushed into a clinch. As they broke away, Jeff took a chance with a rush and landed a lead to the chest that sent Tom back across the ring. "Jeffries was cutting loose now and fighting in his best style." He landed the right to the body repeatedly and hooked a left into Sharkey's face. Jeff also landed some jolty lefts to the head. Tom's left ear was swollen to the size of a tomato. Tom rushed in and Jeff continued holding in the clinches. Jeff blocked some attempted hooks to the body, and then smashed his right to the wounded eye with staggering force. Jeff was grinning, while Tom was serious and apparently puzzled, for he momentarily looked over to O'Rourke. Tom stepped in again, but Jeff clinched.

Jeffries then rushed Sharkey across the ring into his own corner and "sends him into a half-sitting position on ropes with a right jolt on the belly. Tom comes up weary but still aggressive." Another version said Tom slipped and overturned a pail of water onto Jeff's seconds. A third said Jeff shoved Sharkey back into a corner and nearly lifted him from his feet with a hard left on the chin. They sparred until time was up. As Tom went to his corner, his eye was bleeding. He shook his head and laughed.

12ᵗʰ round

Corbett opined and observed, "It is anybody's fight yet. Both men rally well." Jeff met Sharkey's rush with a right to the body. Tom's ribs were showing the effects of the blows. Jeff ducked a left, but Tom repeated the left and landed it to the body. Jeff jumped back from another swing and clinched. Jeffries blocked many of Tom's body blows with "beautiful skill." Jeff was cool and collected, not taking any chances, and simply countering whenever the opportunity offered.

Tom landed his right to the body. He rushed again, Jeff clinched, and Tom sent in a hard right on the jaw that made Jeff hug hard. Jeffries rushed Sharkey a few times and swung his right for the neck, landing once. Sharkey continually swung his left forearm like a club on Jeff's neck or jaw, which drove Jeffries away. The crowd yelled "Oh!" in unison when Sharkey landed a hard left, but Jeff showed no signs of dizziness in the clinch that followed. Jeff returned with a heavy left in the stomach. Sharkey kept the pace up, outpointing Jeff. Tom was like a cyclone with both hands.

Jeffries began fighting more openly and they mixed it until the crowd was wild. They exchanged blow for blow, the fighting being very fast. *The Sun* said, "It was anybody's fight and the man who could get in first punch in the right place would probably win it. Sharkey had done the better work so far without doubt." *The Eagle* said that Sharkey increased his lead and tore the champion's right ear. Still, Jeff laughed and winked at the bell.

13th round

At the bell, Jeff waited for Sharkey to come to him, as usual. Sharkey landed a double left, first to the neck, and then to the jaw, both tremendous punches, but they did not seem to affect Jeffries, who pounded the body with the right and hooked the left to the head. Tom was just as willing as ever, and some awful blows were exchanged. Tom landed a left to the ear. Jeff landed a right but received a jolting overhand right in return. Sharkey landed a clean and loud-sounding left on the ear and again the crowd yelled. Jeff took the offensive and dashed in with hard rights to the body which did not faze Sharkey, who kept rushing in and scoring with the left on the head and body. A Sharkey left down chop to the chest slammed Jeff back to the ropes. Tom came on and Jeff put his left on Tom's throat.

Sharkey missed some blows and Jeff rushed, pushed and rested himself on the sailor. Some cried foul. Tom landed low and Jeff protested mildly. Shark landed a left on the neck, tried again but missed, but on the recoil landed a backhanded left on the ear. Brady was screaming foul. Jeff grinned. Again, Tom came in working both hands, landing a left to the face, but Jeff punched the body solidly with the right. In ducking some of Jeff's lefts, Sharkey seemed to butt Jeffries in the body with his head. Jeff grinned and complained to the referee. One said that both were tired, but Sharkey appeared less so. Corbett said, "This has been Sharkey's round clearly, but both men seem to be equally tired."

14th round

In the corner, Delaney put ice on Jeff's neck. As Jeffries came out of his corner, he looked up at the round number on the bulletin board. Clearly, he was pacing himself for the long haul. Sharkey did all the leading and at close quarters landed a left swing to the jaw. Jeff was on the defensive and Tom was all over him, outfighting him, landing five blows to one. Jeff was still using counters, but they were not as effective as expected. Tom did the better work with the free hand.

Sharkey rushed, clinched and landed a right in a short up-hook on the jaw. Tom kept coming. Jeff hugged in the next clinch. A left under the chin lifted Jeffries up, and as the champ clinched, Tom hooked him again with a powerful punch. Tom roughed it a bit. At the break, Sharkey landed a hard left hook on the jaw, but Jeff shifted his head away and went with the force of the blow to diminish its power. Tom rushed but Jeff met him with a right on the ribs. Tom rushed in with a straight left on the nose that shook

Jeff's head. He rushed again, but missed, and Jeff rushed him and pushed Tom to the ropes.

Jeff clinched often, doing more clinching than Sharkey did, and also resorted to the old trick of bearing his weight down on the sailor. "They hugged and swayed and hung together and Siler pulled them apart fully half a dozen times. Once or twice Jeffries' head went into chancery and Sharkey made vain attempts to uppercut his man." *The Sun* said, "Sharkey outfought his man without cessation, and when the bell rang he had the round."

15th round

This was a fierce round. Sharkey's aggression was limitless and Jeff hugged to stop him. Tom landed a terrific left hook squarely on the chin that momentarily shook and staggered Jeff back. However, Jeffries had wonderful vitality and quickly countered sharply on the eye. Tom countered with a right to the ear. Jeff's left ear was bleeding a trifle. After some swings and misses, Sharkey rushed and landed a terrific straight right smash on Jeff's nose that split it open. However, both the referee and Jeff later said that it was a head butt that split Jeff's nose. The flood of bloody gore flowed in streams from Jeff's nose and mouth. Brady, now anxious, called out to Jeffries, "Keep your left out." Jeff stooped over as he did when he met Fitz.

Jeffries rallied, fighting briskly, landing rights and lefts to the body and head. There was a frightful mix-up, with both landing, causing the crowd to jump to its feet. Tom rushed again, but Jeffries sent his right across in a short hook that caught Sharkey on the point of the jaw, staggering and nearly dropping him. Tom rushed again, only to be met with a left on the throat. Sharkey kept jumping at him and pounding on the side of the neck with short left swings. Jeff blocked a right and landed a big body punch. Sharkey hustled harder than ever and reached the point of the jaw with straight lefts. Jeff clinched and hung on so hard that the referee had to get in under the clinch and pry upward with his shoulders to get them apart. Jeff's face was covered in blood. The locals agreed that Sharkey won the round.

16th round

In the corner, they sponged off Jeff's seemingly broken nose. Sharkey resumed his attack, which Jeffries blocked and countered on the stomach. As Tom came in again, Jeff met him with a left hook high on the cheek. Tom stuck to him, and did some clever ducking which surprised Jeff. Tom's left was as effective as Jeff's was, and he reached the jaw without much trouble. Sharkey's lefts drew blood from the nose again. On a break, Tom landed a right to the jaw that sent Jeff's head back. "Jeffries was taking these blows in a way that astonished the onlookers."

Jeff collected himself and blocked the next rush. Jeffries began crouching more than ever. He met Tom with a right on the ribs that caused

Sharkey to grab around the neck. They hauled and mauled each other in the clinches. Although Sharkey was rushing, he was not leading, but rather guarding himself from Jeff's blows as he came in. A right opened an old gash on the side of Tom's eye. By the end of the round, both were too exhausted from the heat and the terrific pace to do much damage. *The Eagle* felt that Sharkey won the round. "Siler took some stimulants."

17th round

In the corner, "They have given Jeffries champagne to drink to brace him up." In a lengthy fight in hot conditions, water is what the human body needs. Alcohol was more likely to dehydrate and have a detrimental effect.

Sharkey forced matters, but Jeff blocked and clinched. Jeff crouched in a tricky way, waiting with arms bent and still. Tom twice rushed with lefts on the neck and nose. Jeff broke ground, clinched and held. Tom sent in a left and right to the head. Jeff pounded the body and landed on the left eye. Sharkey had little trouble landing with his left, and threw it often. Several times Jeff ducked at a feint, and the crowd jeered him. Jeff's face was a "nasty sight." His punches were slow, as was his footwork.

Sharkey kept Jeff in a corner for a good portion of the round. Tom kept leading and fighting into continual clinches. After one clinch, Tommy Ryan yelled, "Push him off!" Sharkey, while hanging on, turned to Jeff's corner and yelled at Ryan, "I'll make a sucker out of him and then I'll make a sucker out of you." Sharkey kept on with his left and paid no attention to any blows Jeffries landed on him, including some good body shots and a right to the jaw that sent Tom's head back. Despite Sharkey's relentless attack, Jeff kept hitting him.

Jeffries rallied and the last half of the round was his. Jeff rushed in and landed a left uppercut high on the belly. He again rushed and repeated this punch. After clinching, Tom tried to show his strength by pushing Jeff away at the break. Jeffries landed a left hook in the face. At the end of the round, Tom missed as Jeff ducked and then Sharkey got his head under his arm and tried to wring it. The crowd hissed these tactics and the referee cautioned him. The bell rang and Sharkey swung and landed a right on the shoulder as Jeff walked away.

18th round

As soon as they came together, Sharkey landed a left swing on the back of Jeff's head. Jeffries jumped away from a left hook for the belly. Tom bore in, but Jeff clinched and hung onto him. At the next rush, Jeff clinched and rushed the sailor back to the ropes, resting on him. After another clinch, Jeff met Tom's rush with a left swing to the chest. Tom rushed and Jeff landed the same punch again. To a large degree, it was a hugging match. They would clinch after each lead. Jeff landed a body punch and then clinched. Tom landed a left to the body. Jeffries looked to the referee as if it had been low.

Sharkey forced so much that Jeffries was compelled to mix it up. Jeff landed a hard right to the ear. Sharkey staggered just a bit, but he ran right back at Jeff, landing a left in the face, drawing the blood again from the nose. Sharkey's left was far better than Jeff's left now, for it was landing with better effect and with better steam. Sharkey rushed in and landed two left hooks to the cheek, one of which seemed to shake him. At the next rush, Jeff landed two left jabs on the nose and mouth, but Tom twice landed his right to the body. With mouth open, Jeff clinched to rest himself, puffing away. After breaking, Jeff rushed and Sharkey caught him with a left swing on the back of the head.

Tom came on again, but Jeff met him with a straight left hard on the chin that made Tom hang on wearily to save himself. Sharkey clinched and dragged Jeff across the ring by the neck, punching him in the face all the while. Tom seemed tired. Jeff smashed him on the face and body, and Sharkey kept reaching out to clinch. As they separated at the bell, they both winked and grinned defiantly at each other.

The Sun said, "Sharkey had more steam in his punches, and so far had scored the points, also doing almost all the aggressive work." *The Times* and *Herald* agreed that it was Sharkey's round.

19th round

Twice Jeff clinched as Tom rushed in with left swings. Jeffries suddenly rallied, though, and darted in with a left uppercut squarely in the pit of Tom's stomach, one of his best punches. They clinched. Tommy Ryan yelled, "Punch him in the belly!" Sharkey held tightly and winked at Ryan. In another clinch, Sharkey twice hammered Jeff's kidneys with rights. Sharkey landed two terrific clubbing lefts to the side of the face and neck that rocked Jeff, who clinched.

Jeff pulled himself together and rallied, landing his right on Tom's ear. Sharkey rushed in swinging wildly, his left ear almost dropping off, but as Jeff walloped it with the right, Tom showed what he was made of by grinning. Sharkey's ear began to swell, and blood ran from it in streams. Sharkey came in again and Jeffries banged him squarely on the nose with a straight left that had the force of a mallet. "This blow shakes up the Irishman like an electric shock."

Both had marks of the fray. Jeff's shoulders had a blood color and his nose had lost a strip of skin. Sharkey's eye was cut and his left ear looked like a small-sized tomato.

20th round

Between rounds, Jeff's cornermen iced his neck. Jeff hit Tom with a body punch which made Sharkey clinch. "Tom shows how tired he is by telegraphing ahead of his left swing." As Sharkey rushed in, Jeff smashed him with a straight left on the nose that sent his head back. Tom shook his head, rushed in and forced Jeff to the ropes and pushed Jeff's head back with the heel of his fist on the champion's chin. The crowd hissed. Brady claimed a foul, which was not allowed. Sharkey ran in with his lefts, missing most of them. Once he ran into Jeff's straight left on the cheek.

Jeffries was fighting with better judgment. His nose was bleeding freely, but it made no difference, as he did not keep away. Sharkey came out of a clinch with gore trickling from his ear. Jeff mixed it and used his right on the body and on the neck. A right to Sharkey's jaw dazed him and he clinched to avoid punishment. He recovered and fought back well. They engaged in several spirited rallies. However, Jeff could not beat the sailor off. Sharkey led with a short left, and overbalanced, Jeff picked him up with a vicious left uppercut under the chin. Tom landed a left hook on the nose. At the end, Tom was smiling. *The Eagle* felt that Sharkey did the better work, but some felt that Sharkey was tiring and the tide shifting.

21st round

The glistening sloppy pair fell together at the start. Sharkey ran across the ring and Jeff put in a right to the body. Sharkey attacked again and Jeffries held. Tom pounded the kidneys with his right. Jeff laughed at his efforts, even when Tom swung his flair-like left on the neck. Sharkey led twice with his left and landed a hook on the ribs, only to be countered each time with a short straight left on the cheek. Tom followed up with a left that shook Jeff's head, and he also drove it into the stomach. Jeff countered as usual with both hands, but did little leading. A straight left made Tom's head shake, but it did not drive him away. Sharkey rushed in a couple times, only to be clinched. In the clinches, both landed kidney blows.

On another Sharkey rush, Jeff met him with a left hook on the jaw that wagged Tom's head. Sharkey pulled himself together and came in gamely again as if nothing had hit him, showing his wonderful vitality. Tom swung his left for the head but received a cross counter to the mouth. Jeff landed a long left to the mouth. He steadied Tom with a straight left to the nose, a wicked right to the ribs, and a left swing. Sharkey clinched.

The Eagle said that although Sharkey had done the better overall work in the fight, the worse he made Jeff look, the more Jeffries improved. "It appeared at this time as if a draw would result."

22nd round

Jeff waited on Sharkey's attack. Sharkey came in and Jeffries landed a solid left to the neck. Tom ran into Jeff's clinches a couple times without doing any damage. Tom came in again and landed a powerful left hook on the jaw, hard enough to knock out any man, but Jeffries only laughed. Jeff met Tom's next rush with a right that opened the cut over Tom's eye and made it bleed afresh, yet Jeff hung on hard in the clinch that followed, and rested himself on Tom for eight seconds. The blood poured down from Sharkey's eye onto his cheek. Jeff clinched again on Tom's next rush, and referee Siler had to separate them. Sharkey's left ear was swollen so badly that it was nearly as big as a baseball. Still, he refused to break ground, and he kept up the pace. Jeff landed many left uppercuts and rights to the body on the bleeding Sharkey.

Towards the end of the round, Jeffries landed a fearful right uppercut on the jaw that shook Sharkey up and made him stagger. The crowd yelled for Jeffries to do it again. On Sharkey's next rush, Jeff whipped up another right uppercut full on the chin "that would have killed an ordinary man." Sharkey was dazed and clinched

for dear life. Tommy Ryan jumped on the outer edge of the ring and wildly begged Jeffries to cut loose and finish him. Sharkey was unsteady and wobbling perceptibly. However, Jeff backed away and waited for a few seconds, sticking to his usual style for the fight, looking to counter. Tom revived, rushed in, clinched, and shouted over his shoulder to his manager, "I'm all right." Tom continued forcing, only to run into a right, or to duck into uppercuts, which were landing and hurting him. When the bell rang, Sharkey was hugging to save himself, "for he was surely going."

The Eagle said that Sharkey was winded, and "from that moment the battle was lost to him." Jeffries had clearly turned the tide in his direction. *The Sun* said, "It was Jeffries's round and Sharkey must have felt the force of these blows if he did not feel the ones he got before. He went to his corner in rather poor shape." *The Gazette* said that Tom seemed listless and the blood pouring down his face gave him a woe-be-gone appearance. Jeffries was showing his ability to close a fight well.

23ʳᵈ round

In the corner, Jeff took a couple more swallows of champagne, but waived the bottle aside when Tommy Ryan urged him to take more. Perhaps he realized that it was not doing him any good.

Jeffries began the round by landing a terrific left on the chin, which ordinarily would have produced a knockout. It took a lot of steam out of Sharkey. Jeff did not follow it up enough and Tom recovered and forced the fight again.

Jeffries' hard left jabs to the face staggered Sharkey. Tom clinched and pushed Jeff's head back with his right arm up against the throat. Jeff laughed at him and made some remarks. Sharkey had a habit of fouling and wrestling when hurt. Tom hung on hard with his left and threw his right down on the kidneys. Jeff clinched harder. Tom roughed it in a clinch and worked the elbow across the face.

After the break, Sharkey rushed twice and Jeff met him each time with hard right counters on the chest and cheek. Sharkey was shaken up a bit, but they did not stop him, and Jeff clinched and rested his chin on the sailor's shoulder. As they swayed over towards Tom's corner, Jeffries, with his chin resting on Tom's shoulder, passed joking remarks with O'Rourke. "Jeffries's stock was booming, and his seconds were begging him to hurry the fight." When Jeff rushed in and missed a left jab and they clinched, Sharkey again put his right arm against the throat to push Jeff's head back. They indulged in a good deal of standup wrestling. They clinched so hard that the referee had to go between them.

At the break, Jeff missed his left lead but landed the right on the cut eye. This caused some of the medicine on the cut to trickle down into the eye, half blinding Tom. Sharkey plucked at the eye multiple times with his left hand, but Jeff did not immediately attack.

Jeffries landed a left and right on the jaw and Sharkey wobbled. Jeff then landed a terrible left swing on the jaw which staggered Sharkey. "For the twentieth time the Irishman clinches, hangs on hard and saves himself." Jeff began throwing right uppercuts, some being blocked, but some getting in which drove the sailor back. Jeff was able to block Tom's blows, and landed a right to the jaw that made Tom groggy. He reeled toward the ropes and clinched to save himself. There was such an uproar from the crowd that neither fighter could hear the bell. Jeff landed a light punch on the head after it had rung, and Sharkey broke out of the clinch and swung his right hard on the back of Jeff's head.

The Herald said that Jeff was strong and fighting fast. *The Times* said that Jeff was decidedly better at this point, landing hard and effective blows, as Tom clinched more.

24th round

They dashed at each other, exchanging hard lefts on the body and following up with a clinch. Tom rushed, but Jeff clinched and threw his weight on him. Sharkey missed a right and Jeff missed a counter. Jeff's left shot out onto the mouth. Sharkey missed a wild right and Jeff landed a left under the chin. Jeff used his reach and stood away and pounded Tom's face with the left as Tom forced his way in.

Sharkey feinted a lead left, and before he could throw his right, Jeff shot in a wicked right hook on the jaw that staggered Sharkey. The crowd roared with delight. Jeff then landed a right over the heart that made Tom unsteady, "and the crowd is roaring so loudly that I don't suppose you could hear a cannon if it were fired off before the door." Sharkey was in trouble and clinched to save himself. However, Tom kept coming in, even landing a right. He was mostly only throwing wild clubbing rights at this point, which left him open to counters. Jeff nailed him again and again with the right. Jeffries landed two hard right uppercuts that nearly closed Sharkey's left eye. Tom staggered about and resorted to foul work in the clinches, using his elbow and grabbing hard. He refused to break.

Both cut loose a volley of body punches, about one-third landing. Sharkey backed away looking weak. Jeffries saw victory before him. "Jeffries rushes at him, swings his right on the chin and nearly sends him down." However, Tom lunged forward, grabbed Jeff around the neck, and clinched desperately. After a few seconds, the game Sharkey broke away and dashed in with a left swing which landed high on Jeff's breastbone. Despite unsteady legs, Sharkey was still willing to mix it, and rushed in again, but Jeff planted a right uppercut on his jaw. Sharkey was being outfought. Jeffries cut loose, slugging with right and left swings which put Sharkey on the defensive, clinching often. "The Irishman is very weak, groggy, staggering." Sharkey ducked, clinched, and held on "like grim death," trying to save himself from defeat. The gong rang before the referee could pry them apart.

The Gazette said that Sharkey "was in a bad way when the round ended." *The Eagle* said that despite continuing to attack, Sharkey was wild and weak, while Jeff was much stronger. *The Times* said that Jeffries again did well in this round and had Sharkey clinching frequently to save himself.

25ᵗʰ round

They shook hands at the start of the final round, smiling. Corbett said, "The Sailor knows that while he has been on the aggressive during most of the fight yet not enough of his blows have landed to give him the victory unless he knocked his man out, so he rushes fiercely at the champion, and the big fellow clinches to keep him off."

Jeff led with a left over the eye. Sharkey was active again and ran in with a right that was stopped. They followed with a lot of clinching and roughing. With a free right, Jeff punched the wind and also hooked it up under the jaw. Sharkey kept swinging and countering. After a couple clinches, as Tom rushed again, Jeff threw up his left arm and smashed his right straight on the ribs.

As Sharkey started another rush, Jeff rushed in too, and met him with a terrific right uppercut on the point of the chin that sent Tom's head flying upward and backward. Sharkey threw both hands around Jeff's neck and hung on for five seconds. It was an awful smash that was hard enough to knock out an ordinary man for half an hour. *The Gazette* said that Jeff timed Sharkey with terrific right uppercuts, "and any other man but the sailor would have gone down and out." While Sharkey was holding on with his left around the body, he landed his right three times on the back and the back of the head until Siler parted them. Both of their mouths were open.

Suddenly, Jeffries closed his mouth and jumped forward with a terrific straight right that crashed on the chin and drove Sharkey backward, shaken up perceptibly. Once more Jeff leapt forward and dashed in the same right to the chin. "The force of it hurls Sharkey against the ropes so hard that one foot slips out beneath the lowermost rope and the sailor saves himself from falling by a sudden jump forward and a clinch."

After the referee parted them, Jeff leapt in again and smashed Tom on the jaw with a right and then a left, staggering him. Sharkey held Jeff's left, and Jeff half punched and half pushed him on the chest with his right and Sharkey went down in a sitting position on the floor. However, during Sharkey's fall, in his efforts to hold himself up, he had ripped off Jeff's left glove. He jumped up quickly and darted back towards Jeffries into a clinch. Jeff called Siler's attention to the missing glove, so Siler shouted to Sharkey to keep back and pushed him back. Tom walked off, looking anxious.

Siler tried to put the glove back on, but the laces could not be untied and he could not get the glove back on for fully fifteen seconds. Tom could no longer stand the suspense, so he rushed at Jeff, running around Siler's elbow. Jeff shook his head and waved his bare left hand, but Tom dashed in anyway. Jeff either met him with a straight bareknuckle left on the neck and clinched (Corbett's version) or simply reached out with his left and held Tom. The popular version is that Jeff struck him. However, the *Eagle* said, "Jeffries made no attempt to use his bare hand."

Siler jumped in to push Tom away, and the gong rang. As Jeff turned to walk away, Sharkey whirled around and swung his right hard, but it only landed on the shoulder. "The greatest heavyweight battle ever seen in the world is at an end."

Referee Siler awarded the fight to Jeffries, and the crowd cheered. *The Herald* said, "The decision was received with cheers and was evidently a popular one." *The Times* agreed that although the bout was close, the crowd approved of the referee's decision for Jeffries.

However, Sharkey went wild and jumped out of his corner, but O'Rourke held him back until his senses were restored. Corbett said, "The decision, I think, is a fair one. Sharkey, it is true, has done most of the leading, but the majority of his blows were wild, while Jeffries hit straighter and had the best of it all the way."

Even the *Sun*, whose description of the fight gave Sharkey the most credit, said, "The decision was considered just in view of the unsteady condition of Sharkey in the last five or six rounds. It was the consensus of opinion, if the fight had gone on to a finish, Jeffries would have won with a knockout."

Both men's friends congratulated them for the wonderful fight which they had put up. Delaney hugged Jeffries and tied a silk American flag around his neck. Brady, wild with joy, shook Jeff's hand. Jeff went over to shake Tom's hand once more.

Both had marks of punishment on their faces, but Sharkey was the more severely bruised. His ear was swollen so badly that it had to be lanced. O'Rourke said that two of Tom's ribs were fractured.

They had been in the boiling hot ring for about 1 hour and 40 minutes. Excluding the rests, they had been fighting for 1 hour and 15 minutes. That is a little more than twice as long as one 12-round championship bout in the present day. Imagine some of these fighters today having to fight two 12-round fights in a row and not collapse from exhaustion. It was still 10 rounds more than the old 15-round distance popular throughout much of the mid-20th century. Then factor in the extremely hot lights that made the inside-the-ring temperature over 100 degrees Fahrenheit, the fact that they were getting hit with five-ounce gloves, and not wearing mouthpieces. To say that these two men were tough and well-conditioned is an understatement. Furthermore, Jeffries was given alcohol between rounds, rather than water, and was fighting with a hurt dominant left arm, which hampered him in training and in the fight. No one can question his championship heart and toughness.

The local papers summarized the fight. *The Times* called it the "fiercest that the American fight-going public ever witnessed." The fighters, with their gigantic physiques, were game to the core. *The Sun* said, "The fight was one of the fastest for the weight ever seen in America." Both were wonderfully conditioned, and they threw "blows hard enough to have felled an ox." Sharkey was the aggressor, set the pace and did most of the leading, but Jeffries counterattacked well and had Tom almost out at the finish. "Not that last night's battle was devoid of the element that boxing instructors define as the science of self-defense but it was essentially a slugging match." The more critical *Asbury Park Daily Press* said that the battle was 25 rounds of "rough thumping, hugging, rubbing and wrestling," and "more like a succession of railroad collisions than a fist fight."

The Brooklyn Daily Eagle said that neither man could be called a clean fighter. Jeffries used his great weight around Sharkey's neck. He also leaned heavily on him and bore Sharkey into and once almost over the ropes. Sharkey used his elbow in clinches and roughed it at all times. Sharkey never complained, although Jeff called Siler's attention to Tom's tactics on several occasions.

They battered each other to the body and head throughout, each taking turns staggering and hurting one another, both bleeding about the face. *The Times* said, "Both men were badly punished - Sharkey showing a cut ear and a badly cut eye, while Jeffries was pounded on the neck with Sharkey's vicious left hand until the flesh there was as raw as a piece of beef." *The Sun* said Sharkey split Jeff's nose, but Jeff knocked him down in the 2nd round, broke his ribs, and outfought Tom towards the close, weakening him with terrific blows.

The Eagle said that Jeffries had the fight of his life.

> It is a certainty that in no twenty-five round fight ever seen before was there such terrific punching, from start to finish, combined with an ability to take it as fast as it came and go back for more.

> Jeffries was rarely the aggressor, save in the last five rounds of the fight, yet the mere fact that Sharkey followed the big champion around the ring for round after round did not argue that he was giving Jeffries a beating. The sailor was running into punches as often as he landed them and Jeffries seemed to be content to let the fight go that way.

> Both men undoubtedly can endure more pounding than any two pugilists in the ring today. Some of the blows that Sharkey landed on Jeffries' jaw would have put an ordinary heavyweight out of the game…while, on the other hand, the sailor seemed possessed of an iron jaw and a mail clad body. Heart blows that left their telltale marks did not seem to weaken his vitality.

Despite the intense and almost unbearable heat, "Sharkey and Jeffries stood it for an hour and forty minutes of the hardest kind of slugging." No one could question either man's gameness.

Summarizing the rounds, Tom rushed so much that Jeff made no effort to attack and mix it up. He waited for Tom to come after him. His unwillingness to take a chance surprised everyone.

Jeffries had the edge in the first 5 rounds, including decking Tom in the 2nd, but from that point on, Sharkey's incessant fighting caused the tide to turn in his favor. In the 7th, Tom had Jeff guessing. Jeffries began improving in the 11th round, and in the 12th, he mixed it up with Sharkey. However, Tom was so strong that Jeff did not think it advisable to keep up this plan.

In the 13th and 14th rounds, Tom had a marked advantage, and in the 15th, one of the fiercest in the fight, Sharkey almost broke Jeff's nose with a left hand smash. The blood spread all over Jeff's face. However, "blood does not always mean distress in a prize fight." Jeffries was not weakened.

In the 16th, Jeffries fought well, but still refused to set the pace. Jeff felt confident that he could land just as effectively with the sailor coming to him as he could by chasing him around the ring. In the 17th and 18th rounds, Sharkey had an advantage because he kept on with the leading. Jeff could not block or punch him off, and took many hard knocks.

In the 19th and 20th, Sharkey was perhaps a bit tired. During the 20th round, Jeff began to take advantage of his long reach, and with well directed smashes, he had Sharkey in trouble.

After the 20th round, Jeffries discovered that he had "a right hand that could deliver effective jabs and upper cuts." It was the same thing in the 23rd and 24th rounds. Somewhere late in the fight, Jeff cracked one or two of Sharkey's ribs on his left side, which made it difficult for him to throw lefts. In various interviews, Tom also claimed that a left hand or a left shoulder injury hampered him.

Still, the *Sun* said that Tom broke no ground, manfully stood the gaff and showed wonderful pluck. Despite being hurt, Sharkey was still strong and dangerous, and Jeffries, perhaps realizing this, refrained from letting himself out too much. In the 25th round, Jeff maintained his advantage. Sharkey was staggering, and he pulled off Jeff's left glove when he fell to the floor. Some said that Jeffries' losing his glove helped Sharkey, because at the time Tom was in dire straits.

The Eagle said that the last few rounds were a steady chopping process that told heavily on Sharkey. The blows took the steam out of him and left him groggy at the finish, "with a good prospect of being knocked out had the fight been prolonged. In fact, it seemed in one round that only the bell saved the sailor." Regardless, the *Sun* said the fight established the fact that 25 rounds was too short a time for Jeff to finish Sharkey.

Jeffries had a much tougher time with Sharkey than he did with Fitzsimmons. Jeff's long left was not able to keep Tom off of him. Whenever Jeffries hit him, Sharkey took the blows and kept coming, showing that he was a "glutton for punishment."

Sharkey had won numerous admirers by his plucky showing. He was credited for being tough beyond belief. It was his nature to keep fighting as long as there was "a breath of wind or a spark of sensibility. Sharkey will be knocked out only when he is as unconscious as a stone." At all times, he was willing to take two to give one in return.

> Sharkey is probably the most wonderfully aggressive man in the ring today. Whether he is fresh or groggy, he follows his opponent around the ring ceaselessly, taking his punishment with a lion's heart and landing his blows with a speed and brute force that make him at all times a dangerous man.

Sharkey not only forced the fight, but also fought with "splendid judgment," showing wonderful improvement over the last year. Tom demonstrated that he had a great left hand. "Sharkey developed a left that was phenomenal and landed on the big fellow's neck and jaw repeatedly round after round."

Jeff's plan was to stay away until the sailor tired himself out. "Jeffries was the same cautious, careful fighter and took no chances until he thought he had his man where he wanted him. He did very little leading in the first twenty rounds." Tom made things warm every minute.

When Jeffries did cut loose, "he made Sharkey have visions of Queer Street, although he was not squarely knocked down at any late stage of the fight." Sharkey's wonderful condition kept him in the fight at the end, for Jeffries hammered him with all his might during the last five rounds.

> Sharkey tested Jeffries's strength, too, and it was remarkable. The sailor rushed incessantly during the greater part of the fight and had very little trouble in landing his left hand on the champion's jaw. He swung repeated jolts that were powerful enough to knock an ordinary pugilist out in jig time, but beyond a slight rocking of the head Jeffries did not show any sign of pain.

Jeffries eluded Tom's blows with good head movement, countering with rights to the body in almost every round. "These blows undoubtedly weakened Sharkey but they were not as effective as the left-handers which Tom received on the jaw during the last stages."

The Sun criticized that Jeffries did not look to be in the same fine shape that he was in when he beat Fitzsimmons. He did not have the steam in his punches in the early part of the fight, and did not do the same clean work. "The fight showed that Jeffries is not the knocker out that John L. Sullivan was." However, his faults were overlooked when he cut loose in the last part of the fight. Furthermore, Sharkey looked like the loser. "His face was pretty badly battered and his eyes were swollen."

In Jeffries' defense, he did knock Sharkey down early, punched hard enough to break ribs, and had enough steam and endurance to hurt him late and almost take him out. In his autobiography, Jeff said that when he saw that he had a really tough customer in front of him, he decided to pace himself. After the fight, Jeff also said that the injury to his left arm that he suffered in training bothered him during the fight, and as a result, he could not punch as hard or as often with his left, and had to rely primarily on his right. This explains why Jeff relied on his right so much, when ordinarily he mostly used his left.

In one interview, Sharkey said that he had fought the last five rounds with two broken ribs. In another interview, Sharkey said it happened in the 24th round. Tom said, "I felt the rib go. It jumped in, and then I thought it would jump out of my skin. It happened in the twenty-fourth round. Jeffries did it with a right-hand hook." According to the *World*, Sharkey received a blow to the ribs in the 15th round that crippled him more than the spectators realized. "Two of his left ribs were broken, and the Sailor sank as if he were about to fall." At the end of the round, when he went to his corner, he grabbed his left side. A doctor examined Sharkey on the following morning, and he confirmed that there was a fractured left sixth rib. He said there was no truth to the report that two ribs were broken. He said only one rib was fractured.

Tom also said that he was further handicapped by an injured left arm. He had wrenched it trying to swing for Jeffries' jaw. "I was using it nice and strong until the accident. Without the use of it I was like a fellow with only one shoe." Owing to the injury, Tom was not able to use his left hand with any effect, and it was almost useless during the remainder of the fight. The day after the fight, he carried it in a sling. A doctor confirmed that Sharkey's arm was dislocated. This, combined with the rib injury, explains why at the end of the fight Sharkey only used his right.

Sharkey was very unhappy about the decision, saying that he outpointed Jeffries. He felt that the worst he should have received was a draw, but that if anyone won, it should have been him. Still, Tom Sharkey had a habit of crying robbery when he was not declared the winner. "Sharkey, had he been groveling upon the floor, would have still claimed that he was robbed of a decision."

Discussing the fight, Sharkey said, "I was never groggy, although I will admit he gave me a hard thumping. He is not as clever as he has made the public believe, but he is strong and when it came to wrestling he seemed like a stone wall."

> At times, the strong light which flooded the ring made my sight bad. The heat was intense, and I perspired more than I should. When we fought in San Francisco he did not crouch as low as he did tonight. This puzzled me to some extent and I could not get away from those smashes in the ribs. Two of them caused me to feel a shooting pain. Some people thought I was foolish to rough it. That is the way I fight, and nothing could keep me from going in. … If I had not hurt my left hand I would have copped him. … The weight was against me in a way, but that does not cut any ice.

Sharkey responded to Jeff's claims that Tom butted him during the fight. "Well! If the truth be known he shouldered me and tried to get square." Tom also said that Jeff had no right to complain about fouls, for Jeffries butted, shouldered, and did everything he could to win by unfair means.

Sharkey said that Jeff would have to fight him again. "If my shoulder had not let down on me I would have whipped Jeffries. I still think I can whip him and want another chance. … If he don't fight me I will hunt him up in the streets, and we will have it out." He felt that Jeff would be reticent to do so, because Jeff realized that Sharkey was his master. Tom said that he would fight him again in six weeks time. However, that was just promotional talk, because it would require a fair amount of time for him to heal all of his injuries.

Tom was aching from many bruises to his body. He had a black eye and a face which "looked as if it had passed through a thrashing machine." His left ear was puffed up to twice its natural size, his fractured left rib was in excruciating pain, and his left arm was supported in a sling.

The Sharkey supporters voiced their displeasure at the decision. Sharkey manager Tom O'Rourke called the decision a barefaced robbery. He said that Sharkey had the better of the first 22 rounds, and that what Jeff did in the last few rounds did not overcome all of Tom's work. Sharkey sparring partner Bob Armstrong thought the fight should have been a draw. George Dixon said that Sharkey led all the way and should have won.

Jeffries said that he was in great shape. "The talk that I was in bad shape was absurd. I fought as good as I ever did tonight, in fact better."

However, a couple factors which hampered his performance were the intense heat from the electric lights and his injured left arm. Jeff no longer wanted to have his fights filmed because the heat bothered him considerably. The lights indeed made the ring as hot as a furnace. Jeffries was well known for hating the heat.

In *Two Fisted Jeffries*, Jeff said that the lights hung so low that he could have reached up and touched them. "I did not think it possible for lights to make so much heat. It was like standing at the mouth of a blast furnace, and hotter than the blast from a locomotive when the fire door is open." He claimed that it was so hot that he lost 20 pounds during the fight, and that some spectators and reporters passed out.[422]

Jeffries was reported to have injured his left arm, somewhere in either the 2nd or the 4th or the 7th rounds, depending on the source. This was in part his explanation for why he did not knock Sharkey out, and why he primarily relied on his right. "My left arm troubled me a great deal and I did not attempt to use it very often. When I did use it, it pained me a whole lot." This was a big problem for a left-handed fighter. In *Two-Fisted Jeffries*,

422 *Two Fisted Jeffries* at 127-136.

he claimed that his left arm was in a cast for three weeks after the fight. The day after the fight, his left arm was slightly swollen.[423]

The following year, in 1900, Jeffries said, "The stories about my left arm were true, and after two rounds it was absolutely helpless. Why, I couldn't even shove him away with it. ... Fitzsimmons would have won from me that night." Still, he knew that Sharkey could not defeat him in a week. "The only thing that could have beaten me in the ring with [Sharkey] that night was the heat from the lights. It took all the strength out of me."[424]

Jeff also claimed that Sharkey had fought foul, and felt that it was a wonder that Tom was not disqualified for his head butts and use of elbows. "Sharkey fouled me on several occasions." "The only evidences I bear of the fight were given by foul blows. Sharkey butted me repeatedly with his head during the clinches. All the injury to my face was done by his head." He also said, "The only evidence that I have of having met Sharkey is this split between the eyes, where he bucked me, and the swelling which you see on my chin, where he pursued the same tactics. He constantly gave me the heel, which is not according to Marquis of Queensberry rules. In a perfectly fair fight...I know I can put the sailor out."

Jeff was aware that he was being criticized for not rushing things. However, he knew that it was Sharkey's tactic to rush, and so he restrained himself, wanting to use intelligent counterpunching and show his staying ability. "I knew him of old and was prepared for his rushing tactics. ... I did not exert myself until the finish."

Jeffries justified the decision by saying that he had knocked Tom down twice, and despite the hard blows Sharkey landed, he was never hurt. Jeff had done most of the clean hitting, and knew that his blows hurt. On the other hand, Sharkey's blows rarely landed squarely, "except one I got in the left eye and made the blood appear. Of course it bothered me but did not weaken me in any respect." "I am surprised that the decision of Mr. Siler should be questioned. I know that I beat him fairly."

> Never at any time during the contest was I in the slightest danger of defeat. I followed my instructions implicitly and didn't let myself out until the latter part of the contest I deliberately acted on the defensive in the first part. ...
>
> I feel that I could have stayed fifteen rounds more and have gained strength with every round. ... Anybody who was near enough to us at the end of the twenty-fifth round could see at a glance who was in the better condition to continue the fight. I did not settle down to real fighting until the fifteenth round. I felt sure that Sharkey had killed, through his foul tactics, whatever chance he might have had of winning on points. Sharkey was game and awfully strong, and, at

423 *Two Fisted Jeffries* at 142.
424 *Detroit Evening News*, April 6, 1900.

times, forced me to keep up a terrific pace. There was not a minute, however, when I was not getting the best of it. Perhaps it was a mistake to have adopted waiting tactics, for the result was not entirely satisfactory.

Jeffries responded to Sharkey's claim that he would fight Jeff on the street if he did not give him another bout. "He had better not go looking for me in the street, because if he does, I'll knock his head off." Jeff said, "In my opinion, Sharkey is not entitled to another fight." He had twice defeated him. However, he was willing to fight him again if that was what his manager wanted.

Jeffries did give Sharkey credit. "Sharkey is the hardest and best man I have ever met. ... It was a hard fight from the start. ... He has improved a great deal since I met him on the coast, but he can never beat me."

Jeff felt that he deserved credit for doing all that was asked of him and having been an active fighter. "Within six months I have met and defeated the best two men in the world and will now take a long rest." He noted that no other champion in recent years had done what he had.

In Jeff's first autobiography, he admitted that it was a close fight, but justified Siler's decision. "Sharkey had fought aggressively all the way, but many of his swings were wild, while my blows seldom missed the mark. I came through the fight very little damaged, while Sharkey, with his broken ribs and battered body, never reached the same fine fighting trim again."[425]

Tommy Ryan was perfectly happy with Jeff's performance. He said,

> Jeffries had the better of the fight from beginning to end. He just waited for Sharkey to lead and countered. Sharkey led often, but never reached the spot; Jeffries was the better man all through. ... He outfought and outgeneraled Sharkey. ...
>
> I told him to fight just the way he fought. He could have forced the battle if I had desired…but I was reserving his strength for a final rally, and you know the result. Jeffries, in my opinion fought better tonight than he did with Fitz. He was never in distress. In the fifteenth round, when I told him to take things easy, he kicked. Jeffries is a wonderful fellow, and the reason that he did not knock Sharkey out is because the latter fouls him, and he did not want to take any chances. Jeffries is improving right along and a year from now will be invincible.

Ryan claimed that Jeff was in finer shape than he was against Fitzsimmons, that if he was not so carefully trained that he could not have withstood 25 rounds of roughing against a naturally strong and aggressive man. "If Sharkey ever fights Jeffries again, which I doubt, judging from the beating Tom got, there will be another story to tell."

---

425 *My Life and Battles* at 41.

Bill Delaney said, "Although Jeffries made a good showing, he was not himself. The light under which he fought was too hot for fast work." Delaney also said that the sailor was a foul fighter and repeatedly used unfair tactics.

Those in Jeffries' camp argued that in a few more rounds the big fellow would have knocked out Sharkey with those terrific right uppercuts. Jeff let out in about the 23rd round and did terrible execution with his right to the head. Sharkey went in with his head down, and instead of clinching as usual, Jeff whirled his massive right in a semi-circle squarely up into the sailor's face. He repeated this again and again. This caused Tom to stop ducking, and to keep his head up. Then, while dazed, he received the left jabs that earlier he had escaped by ducking. Jeff landed multiple right uppercuts, as well as his hard jabs, leaving Tom groggy. On the other hand, Jeff took Sharkey's blows and laughed. Sharkey had broken ribs, a bloody ear, blood pouring into his swelling left eye, and his body was black and blue, covered with blood bruises.

Referee George Siler afterwards said, "It was a great fight, and one of the hardest to referee I ever saw. Both men were so large and so active that I had constantly to go between them. … I decided in Jeffries's favor because he won on points. His blows were more effective and he did the better work." Furthermore, Tom "roughed it" and frequently employed foul tactics, and therefore could not be given credit for the results of such work. He essentially backed Jeff's version of the fight. Describing the fight and explaining his decision, Siler said,

> To begin with, the fight was the fastest I have ever seen. I thought when it began that it would not go over six rounds. The slugging was simply terrific. Jeffries started in with terrific right-hand body blows hard enough to stop an ordinary man, or any fighter not as tough as Sharkey. It was simply remarkable that he stood it without giving way under them. … Jeffries…devoted all his time to Sharkey's body, landing hard and often with the right. Sharkey seemed to be all abroad in regard to his leads, going over Jeffries' shoulder repeatedly. … In the general mixup for the first three rounds Jeffries had all the better of it.

> Sharkey began roughing matters in the third round [sic – it was the 2nd] and banged Jeffries pretty hard in the clinches, hitting him with his right and forcing him into a corner with his forearm across his throat. In the mixup which followed, Jeffries, who had shoved his right up under Sharkey's guard, caught him under the chin and dropped him.

> The sailor remained down, partly dazed for the first few seconds, until I had counted nine, when he arose and stood looking a bit queer. He rushed to clinch as quickly as possible and was met with another

stiff right-hander over the heart. It looked bad for Sharkey for two or three rounds after that, Jeffries' heart blow beginning to tell. He stuck gamely to his work, however, roughing it repeatedly, forcing his elbow across Jeffries' throat, getting his arms around his head and choking him, and running his head into his body. Jeffries' seconds claimed foul repeatedly and I was compelled to caution Sharkey quite often.

It seemed that every time he was hit hard he went into it bulldog fashion, banging any old way and roughing it as much as possible in the clinches. Several times during the fight he hit Jeffries alongside the head after the bell had sounded.

He seemed to become stronger after about the tenth round, and Jeffries, it seemed to me, was becoming weak. Still, there was not much force in the blows of either one. Sharkey swung his left at Jeffries' head time and again and landed across his neck oftener with his forearm than he did with his glove. While he was doing this, Jeffries kept sticking out his left into Sharkey's face. These blows, it appeared to me, were overlooked by the spectators. They seemingly only appeared to see Sharkey's swings. Sharkey, it struck me, was the stronger of the two along the fourteenth or fifteenth round and had a shade the better of the fight. I thought, though, that Jeffries might have been holding back, as he would come with a spurt, quite often landing hard.

Along about this time Jeffries' nose was cut. No doubt, a number of the spectators, especially Sharkey himself, thought he did it with a blow, but it was done with his head. Jeffries stepped in to avoid a blow and at the same time went in head first and struck him on the nose. During these rounds he laid on quite often, but Sharkey offended also by roughing it, butting his head on Jeffries' body and getting the strangle hold on him, using the latter to good effect.

The fighting up to this time, considering the advantage that Jeffries had gained in the early part of the fight and the margin in Sharkey's favor after that, was about equal, with, of course, Sharkey receiving the most severe punishment. After that it tamed off a bit, both leading with their left, Jeffries making good use of his long left.

It was still anybody's fight. Jim braced up after the twentieth round, and had a shade the better of it for two rounds, although Sharkey would slam on occasionally. The last three rounds were all in favor of Jeffries, who came with a rush, peppered Sharkey severely, uppercut him repeatedly with his right, and had the sailor looking a bit queer.

The twenty-fourth round was all Jeffries'. He went at Sharkey heavily and did the most execution with his right on body and head, although he did not overlook letting the left go now and then. Sharkey, in the meantime, was not idle. He kept close to his man and, while he did not land often, avoided a great number of blows by keeping inside of Jeffries' left and right. It looked bad for Sharkey about this time, and here is where stamina and endurance showed. He stuck to his work gamely.

In the twenty-fifth round both came up fairly strongly and both went at it hard. Jeffries continued his upper-cutting, but unfortunately towards the end his glove came off and before I could replace it the gong sounded, calling the end of the round and the fight.

Summing the fight up as a whole, I consider that Jeffries did the cleaner work, while Sharkey roughed it, hit low repeatedly, besides fouling by hitting several times after the bell had rung.[426]

In another interview, Siler also said,

Throughout the fight, Jeffries did the clean punishing, his blows landed fair and square, while Sharkey's swings to the head were delivered with the forearm, the glove often failing to counter at all. Jeffries certainly had the better of the first six rounds, and from then on till the tenth it was fairly even. Sharkey had a trifle the better of the next seven rounds, but Jeffries continued to improve and the last five rounds were all his.

Sharkey was foul at times. He hit low at different times and hit in the clinches while holding. He twisted Jeffries' neck several times and cut Jeffries' nose with a butt, not with a punch. His head was constantly thrown into Jeffries' body and he roughed it almost throughout.

All of this I took into consideration in making the decision, for clean and fair tactics are what count. Sharkey was knocked down clean and was groggy at several stages. I gave what I think was an honest decision and was upheld by the crowd, and feel satisfied with my work.

There was some controversy regarding the decision. Sharkey was more badly punished, but he had been busier and more aggressive. Some felt that he had won the majority of the rounds. Others felt that Jeff had landed more cleanly and done the more effective work. Each local paper offered various opinions of the decision.

The New York Herald said they displayed ring generalship early, but eventually brutality supplanted cleverness. Jeff took the early lead, but Tom's brute courage and willingness to take punishment was impressive. Some argued that Tom should have at least received a draw.

---

426 *Chicago Tribune*, November 4, 1899. Siler was from Chicago.

Before the last round began hats and coats were put on, for it was thought it was going to be a draw, but the referee had a different opinion.... [T]he house was equally divided upon the merits of the men, and while the referee was pointing to Jeffries as the winner at least half the house was pointing to Sharkey as the winner on the ground that he led oftener and was always on the aggressive.

However, the *Herald* agreed with the decision. "To some it may have seemed that a draw would have been more in keeping with the work done by the two men, but the decision given by Mr. Siler was undoubtedly the one that should have been given." That said, Tom's defeat had been "none too decisive" and at "all times he had a chance to win. He was outpointed, to be sure, but his ability as a fighter and his willingness to take punishment stood him in such good stead that more than once his admirers were confident that he would be returned a winner." It noted that Sharkey preferred to fight foul.

The New York Daily Tribune said Jeff clearly had the better of it in the first two rounds and the last three, but the other twenty saw Sharkey forcing the fighting. In those twenty rounds, Jeff's weight and brawn helped him hold off Sharkey. Jeff often threw himself on top of Tom, but Sharkey did his share of the clinching as well. It favored Sharkey's aggressive tactics.

The New York World called it the fastest and hardest heavyweight fight ever fought. It was a marvelous display of endurance. It felt that Sharkey had the better of most of the fight until the end. "It was only in the last few rounds that Jeffries evened up matters."

The Asbury Park Daily Press claimed that the majority of those at ringside thought that Sharkey would get no worse than a draw.

The New York Sun's headline said, "The Verdict Considered a Just One." However, Jeff was "not considered the world beater that he seemed to be when he knocked out Robert Fitzsimmons." Sharkey was groggy several times during the last five or six rounds, as Jeff cut loose his attack and landed tremendous blows on the jaw and stomach. It was this marked advantage at the end that earned Jeff the decision, which "was considered fair by a majority; still there were those who thought that as Sharkey forced the fight in almost every round, and during the first half of the encounter had a pronounced advantage on work, blows landed and strength he might have received a draw." Continuing, the *Sun* said,

His victory over Sharkey last night was not clean-cut and caused many of his supporters to feel chagrined. He out weighed Sharkey by twenty-five pounds, was taller, had a longer reach, and was supposed to be stronger. Yet in twenty-five rounds he could not stop the sailor and received the referee's decision solely by a phenomenal rally in the last few rounds, during which time he made up for most of the lost ground. There is no doubt that when the fight ended Sharkey could have gone on and probably could have fought with as much strength as he did at any stage of the fight. His recuperative powers showed that to be a possibility for him at any stage. For that reason and for the additional reason that he forced the fight and landed almost as many blows of effect during the mill as Jeffries, his friends believe that he should have been named the winner.

Still, the *Sun* agreed that the majority considered the verdict the proper one, particularly in light of Sharkey's unsteady condition over the last five or six rounds and at the end. Most thought that Jeff would have eventually knocked Sharkey out had the fight continued.

The Brooklyn Daily Eagle agreed with the decision.

> Siler's decision seemed to be an eminently fair one. Sharkey would probably have had a draw out of it if he had been able to keep away from Jeffries' right in the last few rounds. But, aggressor to the last, he ran into jabs and uppercuts that even he, with his iron jaw and muscle clad body, could not withstand. He was in poor shape when the final tap of the gong came.

According to the *New York Journal*, there was a big debate as to whether Sharkey won or at least earned a draw. Jeffries won the start and finish, but Sharkey had the middle. It was generally felt that Tom forced the action and secured the most points for most of the fight, that Jeff did less work, but was more effective. Jeffries did the most damage at the end of the fight and finished strong, which usually counted big-time in referee's decisions. Historically, championships changed hands in fights to the finish. It appeared to most that Jeff would have won a finish fight, for even though Sharkey was the more active, Jeff's blows did the most damage and he appeared to be wearing Tom out at the end.

However, aggression also counted a lot with most referees, and Sharkey was the aggressor. The scoring of fights at that time was not so much done round by round as much as it was an overall impression as to who did the better work and effective damage, and who would have won by knockout had the fight come to a natural termination. Jeff dropped him early and had him looking bad at the end, so he got the nod.

Still, there was a "generous sprinkling of those who thought the decision should have been a draw." Some questioned the logic of Referee Siler's statement that Jeffries had fought the cleaner fight, and that Sharkey had been guilty of fouling. The opinion was that if Sharkey had fouled, then he should have been disqualified. If not, then the fight had to be decided on points, and Sharkey's supporters felt that he had outpointed Jeffries. Perhaps Siler simply meant that only the blows that Sharkey landed fairly would count, not those which were facilitated by fouls. Any damage Sharkey did as the result of fouls would not inure to his credit. Certainly also, fouling in order to avoid or deter Jeffries when the going got tough for Tom could legitimately count against him in the scoring.

Either way, Siler was considered a fair man. "Certain it is that Siler's opinion was based upon his honest convictions, for Tom O'Rourke, the manager of the loser, is Siler's closest friend." Some who had money on Sharkey said that they had lost fairly, while others who had bet on Jeffries admitted that Tom should have had a draw. From Chicago, Bob Fitzsimmons, who had not seen the fight, said he knew that Siler was a good and honest referee, and would back any decision he made. "He knows the game, and if he said Jeffries won – why Jeffries did win."

The San Francisco Chronicle was most critical of the decision, saying of the referee that "neither his fairness nor his honesty has ever been questioned, but it would be very difficult to attempt an explanation of his decision tonight." Sharkey made the pace for 20 rounds and was at least even in the matter of effective work, but then Jeff assumed the lead and held it to the end. Still, it questioned whether this was sufficient for a victory. It called Jeffries' performance disappointing and the exhibition unsatisfactory. Jeff seemed to be holding back with his offense and clinching often. Sharkey's condition and speed of foot was complimented, but he remained a foul fighter, particularly losing his head when under fire. Jeff did most of his effective work with his right instead of left (perhaps owing to his injury) and was more erratic in his performance than against Fitzsimmons. *The Chronicle* felt that it should have been decided a draw.

The San Francisco Examiner provided different views. One said the majority felt that the referee's decision was fair. Another said,

> It is sufficient to say that the award was a surprise to most of the spectators and disgusted many. For twenty rounds Sharkey did nearly all the leading, forced the fighting and drove Jeffries all over the ring. In the last three rounds Jeffries certainly made the better showing, but he would not have done so had he fought freely and openly during the earlier part of the fight.

It too was critical of Jeff's performance, saying that he gave ground, clinched often and bore his weight on Tom, and did little clean hitting. "Plainly, I think that his decision was all wrong, and that Jeffries only won a draw by a very close shave."

Another writer for the same paper said that Sharkey was ahead early, but after the 20th, Jeff "took a decided lead and did work that rather more than offset the advantage held by the sailor prior to that. It was a grinding, jarring, wearying fight."

The National Police Gazette called it a marvelous battle. Sharkey fought wondrously well and had the better of it during the earlier stages. Jeffries was more effective at a distance, but Tom was better at close infighting. Jeff won in the stretch, for up to the end of the 20th round, Tom was the aggressor and based upon a comparison of scientific work, leads, counters, etc., would have been entitled to the verdict. Jeff was mostly on the defensive, allowing Tom to wear himself out. He then called upon his reserve strength late in the fight. It too noted that Jeff did not fight as well as he had against Fitz. Neither demonstrated cleverness, throwing science to the wind. However, it was a "terrific volley of blows" in a "murdering battle."

Various experts and boxers rendered their opinions of the decision. Former champion James Corbett felt that the fight up to the 20th round was pretty even, but after that, Jeff grew stronger, and deserved the decision. Peter Maher thought Sharkey won. Jim Kennedy said the decision was a good one, for Sharkey was too anxious and forgot the rules in his desire to do damage. Kid McCoy thought Sharkey won. He said, "Sharkey had the best of the fight up to the twentieth round. The other rounds from the twentieth on were Jeffries's. Sharkey was not knocked out and should have had a draw at the very least." Jack McCormick said, "I think it should have been a draw. Jeffries outpointed Sharkey on body blows and possibly he got the decision on that." Ernest Roeber said that Jeff would have finished Tom off in the last round if his glove had not come off. "The referee's decision could not have been otherwise." Al Smith said that Jeff could have fought many more rounds without getting tired. Jim Carroll said that Jeff was in better shape at the finish. Mike Donovan felt that the two men were even on points, and it should have been a draw. Sam Austin, who often wrote for the *Police Gazette*, said the decision was fair.

Ultimately, it was noted, "Referee Siler's opinion is generally favored among the men who see many or all of these big battles and who are not prone to miss any points of superiority in either man, regardless of their betting." Another paper said, "Naturally there was some discontent over the verdict ... Jeffries's victory, in the opinion of good judges, will not add to his reputation." However, the "better class of sports," who often went to boxing matches, made no complaint about the decision.

The crowd of 10,000 had generated $66,848 in reported ticket sales. Some estimated that the receipts must have been close to the $100,000 mark. According to Brady, the fight receipts were $80,000. If true, this would be the richest fight in history.

There were varying reports regarding what the fighters were to make. One said that the winner was to receive 75% of a $30,000 purse ($22,500), plus 50% of every dollar in excess of $40,000. Another account said that according to the articles of agreement, the fighters were to receive 2/3 of the total gate, or $44,564. The winner was to receive 75% of that amount, or $33,423. Sharkey's share was the remaining 25%, or $11,141. "Jeffries's share of the receipts is the largest ever received by a prize fighter for winning a battle." Plus, Jeff and Tom each had a one-third interest in the fight pictures, which could potentially add many thousands of dollars to their purses. Another said that each man was to get 15% of the fight film receipts.[427]

The top challengers made known their desire to fight Jeffries. Peter Maher said he could whip Jeff. Bob Fitzsimmons believed that he could defeat Jeffries, and wanted another chance. "I have been training lightly for several weeks in anticipation of a match with the winner, and you can bet I will be better prepared for a battle next time I enter the ring." Jim Corbett said that before the fight, Jeffries agreed to take him on next.

> I think there is no one capable of battling with the champion but myself. ... I am in good shape. ... Jeffries is a big, strong, clever fellow, but I think I can defeat him in a bout. Having been assured of a match with the champion several weeks ago, I have been training daily and as a result of the light exercise, I am in shape for another hard battle.

Regarding his future, Jeff said that he was going into the theatrical business for a while, and would not fight again until the following year. "I have several engagements. Tomorrow night I will appear in Philadelphia and meet Joe Goddard. On Monday night I will show at Koster & Blals [in New York] for a month or so." The day after the fight, on the 4th, Jeffries left for Philadelphia, where he was set to give an exhibition that night.

Jeff said that he was willing to fight anyone in the world, and "I don't bar anybody." Although he was willing to fight Sharkey again, "I really ought not to give him another chance, for I have beaten him twice." He also said, "Sharkey will never meet me again. He will now go around the country and say that he was robbed. He did the same thing in San Francisco after we fought. But it did not avail him anything."

Jeff also said that he had won about $5,000 in wagers, gave $1,000 to Ryan for training him, as well as something to his other sparring partners.[428]

When asked about his reaction to trainer Bill Delaney's statements about his condition, Jeff said, "I was all right. Perhaps I could have been better."

Bill Delaney again reiterated his pre-fight criticism of Jeff's preparation, in harsh terms. "He was stale, worn out and slow. ... He worked too hard and did nothing to give him any strength." Delaney said that despite reports that he weighed 210 pounds, Jeff was actually only weighing 204 pounds. "He should have carried at least 220 pounds." It was reported that as a result of Delaney's statements, Jeffries might get rid of Bill.

Jeffries returned from Philly on the morning of the 5th with Ryan and brother Jack. When asked about Delaney's further statement, Jeff said,

> That was a nice thing for him to say, wasn't it? I would never have believed it of him. Why, it looks as if he wanted to see me licked. ...

427 *New York Herald, New York Sun*, November 5, 1899; *New York Journal*, November 7, 1899.
428 *New York Sun*, November 5, 1899.

Had there been any ground for such remarks, which he knows in his heart and soul that there wasn't, he ought to have kept it to himself. ... Well, I might as well say right here that he and Ryan don't pull very well together. He is sore because I engaged Ryan. Well, what was I to do? Ryan is a fast, clever fellow and I have learned a lot from him. If I had taken Delaney's advice I would never have known as much about the game as I do. He wanted me to work with slow men, but I refused to do it. ... If Delaney says I was not fit he is telling an untruth. How could I have stood twenty-five rounds and allowed Sharkey to butt and rough me the way he did? ... You can gamble that if I thought I was 'wrong' I wouldn't have entered the ring. ... He received $100 a week, and got several thousand dollars from me when I won. That was fair, I think.

When asked whether Delaney would train him again, Jeff said, "I don't think he will." However, he would discuss the matter with his manager, Bill Brady. Ryan said,

Delaney is jealous of me, and Jim did not like it. Jeffries followed my advice throughout the contest and never consulted Delaney. This angered Billy. ... When he says that Jeffries did not weigh more than 204 pounds he is 'kidding' himself. Jeffries entered the ring at 215 pounds, and when the battle was over he only tipped the beam at 206 pounds.[429]

Jeff and Delaney eventually met to discuss their differences over a drink. Jim said, "I have nothing against you. I think the world of you, but I don't think you treated me justly by saying I did not train properly." He asked Delaney to retract his statement. Delaney responded, "I won't take back what I have said. I'll stick to every statement I made. You worked too hard, Jim, and you know it. You was not in shape, and you know it. ... I still think you are a great pugilist and can beat any one in the business." *The Sun* opined in support of Delaney, "No man who has the courage of his convictions ever gets the worst of it in this world."[430]

As of Monday, November 6 at Koster & Blal's music hall, Jeffries began performing in a new burlesque show, "Around New York in Eighty Minutes." "Jeffries gets $2,500 for his theatrical debut." He would be paid that amount for every week that he performed there.

After Jeff's performance on the 6th, he, his brother Jack, and manager Robert Blal were arrested for violating the law regulating boxing exhibitions. Jeff and Jack had exhibited as part of the theatrical performance, which the police felt was not within the requirements of the Horton law, which required a permit for a bout at a regular athletic club.

429 *New York Sun*, November 6, 1899.
430 *New York Sun*, November 9, 10, 1899.

They were charged with engaging in a boxing exhibition in a public place of amusement. Captain Price said that they would be arrested again if they repeated the performance. As a result, on the following night, a wrestling match between Jeffries and Ernest Roeber was substituted until the legal business could be settled.

On November 9, a judge heard evidence in the case, and then discharged the accused, deciding that they had not violated the law by engaging in a sparring bout which formed a part of a dramatic production. Jeff could continue with his exhibition as part of the theatrical performance.[431]

Tom Sharkey wanted another fight in two months and said he was posting a $5,000 forfeit. Tom O'Rourke said, "If Sharkey committed fouls, as Siler says he did, why didn't he disqualify him then and there?" Of course, reporters then asked, "Did O'Rourke want Sharkey disqualified?" It seemed that Siler had given Sharkey a break and cut him slack by not disqualifying him. However, certainly his fouls were considered as factors in Siler's decision. O'Rourke also criticized that Siler should have sent Jeffries to his seconds to replace the glove when it came off, and then continued the round for its full length.

Jeffries said that he was entirely in Bill Brady's hands, and that if he wanted him to fight Sharkey again, he would. Again responding to the criticism of the decision, Jeff said,

> Now, about that decision. This talk of its being wrong is perfect nonsense. Why, if ever a man was whipped it was Sharkey. Look at our condition when we left the ring. Look at it an hour after that and look at it today, and any impartial judge could tell who landed the blows and who did the damage. This stiff arm…was caused by ripping in blows that would have knocked out any other man on earth. There are two scratches on my body caused by his fists, and he butted the skin off my nose and forehead with that hard head of his.
>
> I jumped out of the ring, dressed myself and left the club-house, while Sharkey almost collapsed after the fight. Does that look like I was whipped? I have not seen him, but I am told that one of his eyes is cut, discolored, and almost closed, that his shoulder was dislocated and two of his ribs were broken. … Sharkey's strangle holds and butting tactics were foul all through.

Confirming Jeff's statements, it was said, "Save for a slight scratch over the nose there is no marks to show that the champion was a principal in one of the hardest fist to fist fights ever recorded."

Bill Brady said, "Well, we'll fight when we get good and ready and not before. It's all bluff on their part. We've licked him twice and my man is

431 New York Sun, November 8, 1899; New York Clipper, November 18, 1899.

champion, and we intend to take advantage of that fact. ... Jeffries needs a rest. ... I think it will be next August before Jeffries has another fight."

Jeff confirmed that he would not do any fighting for several months at least. His left arm was in pretty bad shape and needed rest. He did not want to engage in any vigorous exertion with it. Furthermore, "He thinks that to win the championship and then defend it against as good a man as Sharkey inside of five months entitled him to a year's rest, especially as the champions who immediately preceded him took even longer rests."[432]

Regardless of how long Jeff's layoff would be, Jim Corbett again said that he was sure that he was Jeff's next opponent, for he had been so assured before the Jeff-Sharkey fight.

> I believe I can regain my lost laurels if given an opportunity, and nothing would suit me better than to fight the Californian. ... I am far from being a has been, and if I meet Jeffries I will surprise many of the wise ones. For some time past I have been following a light course of training. This I will continue until a match is arranged, when I will then go into active training. Jeffries may be a big strong fellow, but I do not believe the fighter lives today who can defeat me.[433]

432 *New York World*, November 6, 7, 1899.
433 *New York Journal*, November 6, 1899.

CHAPTER 20

The Impact of Film

The Jeffries-Sharkey fight was the first heavyweight championship successfully filmed *indoors*. Interestingly enough, it was actually filmed by two companies. The American Mutoscope and Biograph Company took the official authorized films. They had made the financial investment in all of the necessary lighting.

However, another company, by stealth, smuggled into the building several film machines. Joe Howard of the Howard & Emerson vaudeville troupe had used Edison moving picture machines to make the films. Howard and six confederates each strapped a device to his waist and concealed it by wearing a mackintosh with a white cape so they could smuggle the devices into the building. The operators had purchased $15 seats on the mezzanine floor. They worked their machines with hand cranks, each taking turns filming one round. One operator would signal to another to take up the work for the next round. Each man wore a bright new Fedora hat. If caught, the operator was to throw up his hat to signal the next operator to start at that point. These pictures were developed in a hurry, rushed to Washington, and copyrighted prior to the official Biograph films.

Initially, the Biograph Company said it was not worried about the fact that rivals had taken moving pictures. They were going right ahead and developing their fourteen miles of film. Bill Brady said,

> Mr. White or his friends who claim to have taken the pictures of the fight may have a few rounds, but that is all. The machine was carried into the clubhouse under a mackintosh, and, from what I understand, only ten rounds were taken. This whole thing looks like a blackmailing scheme, but it will have no effect on our pictures.

A lawyer for Joe Howard of the Howard & Emerson Vaudeville Company, the one which had surreptitiously secured the fight pictures, said that the pictures taken by his client had already been copyrighted at Washington and would be produced very soon.[434]

A mere six days after the fight, on November 9, 1899 at Sam Jack's Theater on Broadway near 29th Street, Joe Howard exhibited his fight pictures reproducing the battle between Sharkey and Jeffries. Howard claimed that 18 rounds were secured, "but there was no semblance of this

---

[434] *National Police Gazette*, November 25, 1899; *New York Journal*, November 7, 1899.

fact last night. The pictures are indistinct and were apparently photographed under difficulties." The films were of poor quality and not of the duration claimed.

Bill Brady purchased a ticket to see the films, along with members of the press and paying public. An announcer enumerated the rounds for the audience's benefit. When he said that there would be a ten-minute intermission, Brady stood up and yelled in the darkness, "Ladies and gentlemen, this exhibition is a fake. The pictures were stolen from the biograph company, who paid a large sum of money to get them up. You will see the original ones at a show in this city in one week from next Monday." Brady then left the theater. He came across Sharkey, and asked him not to go inside, that if he did; a crowd would follow him in, which would mean more money for the competing interest. The Sharkey and Jeffries teams stood to make money from the Biograph films, not the bootlegged Howard films.[435]

On Saturday, November 11, Tom Sharkey saw himself fight in a private exhibition of several rounds of the authorized pictures taken by the American Mutoscope and Biograph Company. The private screening utilized a 9-foot screen, but for the public showings, a 20-foot screen would be used. The fight as projected on the screen was perfect, or as near perfect as the photographer's science could make it.

> There are none of the shadows or annoying flutterings noticeable in the other pictures that have been shown of fights, and except when an occasional cloud of smoke crosses the camera the pictures are as clear as a time exposure. When the pictures are shown in a theater the spectators will be able to see everything that those who were in the Coney Island Sporting Club the night of the fight saw. There will be nothing missing but the sound.[436]

Watching the films, Sharkey was at times "pleased, bewildered, angry and disgusted." The rounds shown "were all in favor of Sharkey, and naturally the sailor was very well pleased with them." Tom said, "They are the greatest pictures ever taken." He also said, "It's the first time I ever saw myself fight, and I'm glad to see how well I do it." Bill Brady said, "Jeffries shows to great advantage. They show a clean, scientific bout on his part resulting in a brilliant victory." Sharkey and O'Rourke said they would leave it to the public to decide who won.[437]

Joe Howard was working with the Edison Manufacturing Company, and they engaged the American Mutoscope and Biograph Company in an advertising war. Edison took out an ad in the *New York Clipper* informing readers not to be fooled by fake pictures, that they had the real films taken

---

435 *New York Sun*, November 10, 1899.
436 *New York World*, November 11, 1899.
437 *National Police Gazette*, December 2, 1899; *New York World*, November 11, 1899.

under the direction of Messrs. Howard and Emerson, which were copyrighted, and that they and would protect their rights against all fake exhibitions. To say that they had nerve, chutzpah, audacity, is an understatement.[438]

The following week, the American Mutoscope and Biograph Company took out its own ad in the *Clipper*. It informed readers that it would give $5,000 to the Edison Manufacturing Company if it could prove that its films were anything more than fragments of a few rounds taken by cameras smuggled into the club and worked secretly, the view of the ring being often obscured by movements of spectators and interrupted by fear of detection, the results being wholly without completeness or continuity. "It was this exhibition that closed after one night at Sam T. Jack's. It was made to last 15 minutes by repeating films." The Biograph Company claimed to have the only complete and accurate fight pictures, taken without a break. "The authentic representation of fight and preliminaries occupies 2 ¼ hours."

There was light enough to illuminate a city of 50,000 inhabitants concentrated beneath the reflectors over a 24 foot ring. To operate the lights eleven electricians were stationed over the ring. To work the four cameras 12 skilled operators were kept on the keen jump, one camera taking up the pictures as another left off. The disbursements included: $3,200 for 400 arc lights, $1,200 for wiring, $800 for carpenters, $850 for current, $250 for reflectors. Thus, at a total cost of $6,300 were taken 7 ¼ miles of film, from which have been developed 216,000 distinct pictures. Vividly representing every move

---

438 *New York Clipper*, November 11, 1899.

in the 25 round contest, rendering recognizable the faces of well known men who were at the ring side, and requiring in representation 2 ¼ hours. These films are the largest ever made (2 x 2 ¼ inches), and the result is the most marvelous ever known in the history of moving photography.[439]

The ad also said that an S. Lubin of Philadelphia was putting forth total and complete fakes of the Jeffries-Fitzsimmons fight, "of which no pictures were taken, owing to a failure to secure satisfactory results by electric light. The people know this." The fakes were simply similar-looking actors posing in a make-believe contest.

Despite claims that it had the complete Jeff-Sharkey fight, the Biograph version was missing a large portion of the 25th round. As a result, Jeff and Sharkey met on November 16 to reproduce the final round, "which it appears, the camera did not catch clearly." "Both were in ring costume, Jeffries's glove came off in a clinch, and with the exception of Billy Brady's presence in the ring as the referee in place of George Siler, who could not be found, the original round

JEFFRIES-SHARKEY PICTURES

Under the direction of WM. A. BRADY & THOS. O'ROURKE.

The Greatest Motion Photographs ever taken by the

AMERICAN MUTOSCOPE AND BIOGRAPH CO

Showing every move from start to finish of this, the greatest battle of modern times.

was followed closely," or so they claimed. Naturally, Sharkey was not going to be willing to act in a groggy fashion as had been described on the night of the fight. Thus, film spectators would not get an accurate view of the last round.[440]

The Biograph Company scheduled the first public exhibition of its films for Monday, November 20. However, at a New York theater on the afternoon of November 19, about 100 invited guests watched an early showing of the Biograph films. Those present included Sharkey, as well as managers O'Rourke and Brady, but not Jeffries. The films were projected onto a white sheet of canvas. *The Sun* observed,

The pictures are clear and distinct. Of course at the finish there were many different comments as to what the verdict should have been, but no one who viewed the pictures from an unprejudiced point

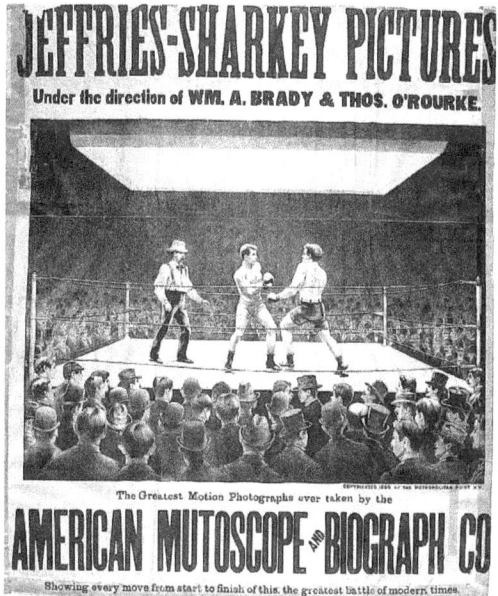

439 *New York Clipper*, November 18, 1899.
440 *New York Sun*, November 18, 1899.

could say that the fight was not on the square and that Jeffries is not a wonderful exponent of the manly art.

The film began with scenes before the battle, the men in their corners receiving instructions. Siler stood against the ropes. Sports around the ring were drinking, smoking, and talking. Some held newspapers above their heads to shade their eyes from the strong light. Others could be seen mopping the perspiration from their brows, looking rather uncomfortable in the face of the intense heat. Waiters rushed up and down the aisles. Policemen and ushers stood against the posts with their eyes riveted on the fighters.

Announcer Dunn moved around the ring, waving his hands and moving his lips, as an occasional cloud of cigar smoke wafted above the ring. The fighters went to ring center with their seconds, and it is evident that the crowd applauded and cheered, despite the films being silent. The fans were spellbound with interest.

Of course Jeffries crouched low, as he did in the fight. Not many blows were exchanged in the first round, but in the second, in which Sharkey took to the boards, a left hook on the jaw was accurately shown. When Sharkey himself observed this punch, he said to a few friends: "Well, there I go. That was nice, wasn't it?" The third showed Sharkey rushing, while Jeff met him with body blows. The fourth showed Sharkey rushing again, but not landing to any extent. The fifth was hot, and some of the sports in the pictures were seen to arise and cheer. Sharkey missed a lot of swings in the sixth and seventh rounds, while Jeff landed. The eighth was very vicious, while the ninth was made up of clinches.

The tenth reproduced Sharkey's damaged left eye, the result of a jab, with the blood streaming down his cheek bones. In the next Jeffries could be seen beating the sailor's face. Nothing daunted, Sharkey was aggressive and Jeff appeared to take his chair very tired. Sharkey rushed with a vengeance in the thirteenth round, and almost fouled the champion after missing a swing and spun around coming back with his elbow close to the boilermaker's jaw. The fourteenth and fifteenth rounds were hard ones and full of action. In the sixteenth Sharkey staggered the champion and his left swings seemed to nettle Jeffries in the seventeenth and eighteenth rounds, for he retired to his chair rather dejectedly. Sharkey's left eye was bleeding again in the twentieth. In the twenty-second interest flagged for a while, but Jeffries had Sharkey going in the twenty-third. Jeffries prodded Sharkey's ribs quite hard and the gong seemed to save him.

At this stage the pictures seemed to lose their charm, for only one minute of the last round and the action where Ryan and Delaney tie the American flag about Jeffries' neck are displayed. O'Rourke said that the films ran out at this crisis and that the remaining two minutes were lost. The incident, where Jeffries' glove comes off, had to be taken over again at Coney Island the other day. As shown yesterday it was quite funny. Brady, wearing a hat many sizes too large for his head and made up to resemble Siler as closely as possible, acted as referee. Brady's antics were ludicrous and the spectators had to laugh. Otherwise the pictures are a marvel of photographic skill. There is no strain on the eyes, and when the machine finally stopped everybody applauded.[441]

Sharkey claimed that the Biograph films showed that he had won.

You can see by the pictures that this fellow never hurt me. ... In the fourteenth round I broke one of my ribs and a few rounds after that my left hand was disabled. Still I had the better of the contest. The worst I should have got was a draw. ... Everybody can see for himself who was entitled to the decision. The public's decision I am sure will be in my favor and that is all I want. ... I fought on the aggressive all the time and I was as strong in the final round as in the first. I was a mile ahead on points. Jeffries may have had the best of five rounds, but then that was when I had only one hand to fight with.

The New York Journal said that those who saw the pictures were of the opinion that a draw would have been a popular decision. Bob Hilliard, the actor, who lost money betting on Sharkey, "said he thought Jeffries was entitled to the decision the night of the fight, but now that the excitement had passed away, a review of the pictures shows that the fight should have been a draw."

However, the *Journal* noted that one reason why many who viewed the films thought it should be a draw was because they did not see the complete final round, which possibly would have cemented the victory for Jeffries in their minds.

The entire twenty-five rounds are shown in the pictures, with the exception of the incident in the last round when Jeffries's glove was removed from his hand. That incident was lost by the machine while the operators were changing films. It is due to this incident that many who see the pictures will believe that a draw would have been a just decision, as Sharkey was distressed and all but out at the time.

The last three rounds do not give Jeffries the advantage he appeared to have after the twenty-second round. Sharkey appears to hold his own on every point up to the finish.

From a spectacular standpoint the pictures are probably the best of their kind ever produced. The fighters appear of natural size, and the

---

441 *New York Sun*, November 20, 1899.

surroundings would make one believe that he was witnessing the real thing in the Coney Island Club arena.

The second round shows Sharkey going to the floor twice from left-hand swings, but he comes back strong. The fifth is a hot one, the men continually mixing it up. Jeffries draws the blood from Sharkey's ear with swings, and the crimson can again be seen to flow down the sailor's cheek in the tenth round from a deep gash over the eye.

Jeffries has a decided advantage of Sharkey in the fifteenth, and the remainder of the fight, according to the pictures, is a pretty even thing.[442]

The National Police Gazette subsequently wrote that Sharkey's pride would boom if he watched the fight pictures a few more times, for the films "emphasize the fact that the giant annihilator of boiler iron got a shade more than was a comin' to him when George Siler frantically grabbed him by the mit and proclaimed him the winner of the greatest heavyweight championship battle that was ever fought." There was a "uniformity of sentiment" in that regard amongst those who did not see the fight, but only witnessed the film reproduction. Sharkey was "reveling in the admiration of an appreciative public which chooses to differ with the judgment of the famous referee."[443]

Still, there were plenty of those who witnessed the films and felt that Siler was correct in his decision. One Louisville report in late December said that the 25 rounds plus preliminaries would be exhibited there. They had just been shown in Chicago, where they generated $16,000. "The pictures are life-size, and are thrown on the canvas devoid of much of the flickering and lapses that have hitherto been so annoying in the presentation of moving pictures." The films were also called "a vivid, realistic representation of the whole, reeled off in exactly the time taken up by the fight itself."

The time consumed in presenting this moving show is two hours and a half. Every one who has seen the exhibition says it is the most marvelous and realistic piece of mechanism ever presented to the public in the way of moving pictures. Every detail of the great fight is accurately depicted.

Some of the few people in Louisville who have seen the genuine pictures say that Siler, who has been so severely criticized for his decision by the Sharkey followers, was correct in his decision, and the pictures justify his verdict. Others claim that Sharkey should have been the winner. A local sport who was a visitor in New York some

442 *New York Journal*, November 20, 1899.
443 *National Police Gazette*, December 9, 1899.

few days ago says that he saw the pictures while he was there, and that while they show Sharkey doing most of the leading in most of the rounds that the latter rounds of the battle, especially the last three, show that Jeffries was easily the winner.

The lights used for filming clearly impacted the fight. Referee Siler observed that a part of the ring which the overhead lights did not reach left a cooler zone. Jeffries backed up to that part of the ring quite often in order to avoid the intense heat. Siler said, "I have never been so hot in all my life as I was during that fight. The 800,000 candle power of the lights made the ring a place to remember." And this was coming from the referee, who was not exerting himself the way that the fighters were. This explains why Jeffries was subsequently not too eager to have his fights filmed, despite the fact that films generated huge revenues, of which Jeff got a cut.[444]

Jeffries was later quoted as saying,

> Had I known how intense the heat was going to be I would not have left my dressing room on that evening. ... It was something terrible, and I thought I would fall down from exhaustion. As I went to my corner in the fifth round I said to Tommy Ryan, "If I go down it will not be from Sharkey's blows, but from the awful heat." I wouldn't fight under similar circumstances again for all the championships and money in the country.[445]

Sometimes art imitates life, but sometimes it also affects it.

Apparently, very little of the official superior Biograph films still exist, and, after over a century, they are mostly disintegrated, of poor quality, and projected at the incorrect speed. Longer portions of the Howard/Edison version still remain. Unfortunately, these films are even more difficult to view, due to the fact that they were bootlegged from a distant hidden camera in the crowd, are of poor quality, and have been projected and transferred at the incorrect speed, making the punch sequences occur too fast to view critically. The speed problems are in part due to the fact that the films were hand cranked when created, causing an inconsistent rate of filming.

Excepting the difficulties of viewing the limited existing footage, the bout appears to have been fought mostly in close, with a great deal of clinching. Jeffries dipped slightly to the right, with his left arm in front, but fairly low. He would step back a bit and allow the shorter Sharkey to advance. Then, just when Sharkey got in range, both would flurry with punches and clinch. The footage is poor, so it is difficult to see who did better. It seemed to be a fairly even fight. Both fighters appear comfortable fighting at close range, even fighting in the clinches a bit. Neither seemed

444 *Louisville Courier-Journal*, December 24, 29, 1899.
445 *Louisville Courier-Journal*, June 11, 1900.

interested in boxing at long range very much, although the taller Jeffries was more comfortable stepping back and playing the counter puncher and using his jab. However, Jeff did not move a great deal.

In the wake of the decision controversy, the way referees arrived at and should arrive at decisions was discussed and analyzed. It reveals that the way fights were viewed and decisions generated was quite different than today. Referees awarded fights based on an overall impression of who had done the most effective work and damage, not so much on a strict round by round system. Thus, just because a boxer slightly edged more close rounds did not mean he was the better fighter if his opponent did more overall damage. Scoring today often excessively rewards one fighter over the other for winning close rounds or rounds that probably should be scored evenly, while under-rewarding one fighter for more clear-cut and damaging rounds. At that time, aggressiveness also generally counted more.

Many criticized Referee Siler for failing to consider what Sharkey had done early in the bout. *The National Police Gazette* opined, "It would be difficult indeed to find a single unprejudiced spectator who wouldn't declare that an injustice had been done Sharkey, and that a rational, fair and carefully considered decision should have been a draw."

To decide a fight on scientific points, so called, requires exceptional judgment, coolness, mental caliber and memory on the part of the referee. It is not customary for him to keep on record in tabular form the points scored by the men engaged in the fight. ... It is impossible for a referee to "biograph" twenty-five rounds in his mind and it is only by making a general recapitulation of what has occurred is he able to arrive at a conclusion which enables him to decide the fight. In a fight of limited duration credit must be given a boxer for what he does in the earlier rounds irrespective of his condition at the end of the fight. His aggressiveness must be taken into consideration also, whether he does the leading or simply blocks and counters - the man who does the leading is favored from a point of scientific judgment, for he leaves himself open and unguarded and at the mercy of a counter fighter.... Sharkey forced the battle from the beginning...led five times to his opponent's once...landed the most number of punches by a goodly margin and had the best of the battle for at least twenty rounds. His own exertions weakened him and if Jeffries did have the better of the final rounds Sharkey, himself, contributed more to his own physical disintegration than his opponent's punches possibly could have done, considering the few that were delivered. ... In the face of these facts it is difficult to find a standpoint from which Referee Siler could justify giving his decision to Jeffries.[446]

---

446 *National Police Gazette*, November 25, December 2, 1899.

The Gazette noted that Siler pointed to Sharkey's condition after the fight, including his broken rib, injured arm and gashed forehead. However, it claimed that he did not know these things until later, and that the cut was from a butt. It also felt that "Sharkey was not helpless, as Siler tries to make it appear." Although Siler observed Sharkey's fouls, the *Gazette* felt that Jeffries had fought foul also, citing his wrestling tactics, pushing Tom back up against the ropes a half dozen times, and holding Tom in a vise grip and laying his weight on him. It felt that a draw would have been appropriate. "This would have given Sharkey credit for his work at the beginning, and justice to Jeffries for equalizing matters at the end. The margin in Jeffries' favor, as Siler must have figured it to justify his action in discriminating between the two men, was not sufficiently pronounced, according to my judgment, to warrant it."

Some called for a round by round scoring system. However, John L. Sullivan said that there was no need to change the way fights were scored.

> This proposed system of awarding a bout according to rounds amounts to nothing. ... What advantage is it to insist on a separate decision after each round? ... Only one thing is needed for a fight. That is an honest referee. And from my observation the referees of the present day are honest as a rule. ... If ever there was an honest referee it is Siler, and his decision was just.

Despite many feeling that the recent championship should have been a draw, Sullivan felt that draws should be abolished, that every fight should have a winner, and that extra rounds should be authorized if needed to determine a definitive winner.

> There should be no draws. There should be a winner in every fight. ... If that plan was followed out the scrapping would be more lively, as the uncertainty of the result would force both men to try for a knockout. If two men should be so evenly matched that a referee could not choose at the end of a certain number of rounds, the referee ought to ask them to continue until he is able to say whose fight it is. All of which goes to show how far from right it would be to have a point system. A fight is not decided that way. A referee takes so many things into consideration that he could not award points every round and still give a decision that was at once satisfactory to the spectators and just to the principals.[447]

Perhaps those are wiser words than we might have realized, especially when juxtaposed against so many dissatisfying decisions over the years in this sport under the newer round by round judging system, particularly under the 12-round distance. Boxing fans want decisive results, which is why most pure fans wanted fights to the finish.

---

447 *New York Evening Journal,* November 16, 1899.

Sullivan opined that if fights had to be of the limited round variety, the referee should be empowered to allow a close fight to continue until a decisive result is achieved, so that there would not be dissatisfaction over a decision.

The Police Gazette echoed Sullivan's sentiments, feeling that the way to prevent dissatisfaction was to invest the referee with the power to order additional rounds until a satisfactory and decisive result was reached. It suggested authorizing the referee to order increments of 5 additional rounds "until it is apparent beyond all question that one of the two men engaged is hopelessly beaten." Of course, most agreed that even under that system, Jeffries would likely have knocked Sharkey out or more clearly defeated him.[448]

448 *National Police Gazette*, November 25, 1899.

CHAPTER 21

A Thriving Sport Under Attack

In anticipation of a title shot, prior to the early November 1899 Jeffries-Sharkey fight, Jim Corbett had been "quietly undergoing a light course of training for the past two months." Corbett was confident that he could defeat his former sparring partner.

Bob Fitzsimmons also made a challenge and posted $2,500. Martin Julian contended that Fitz was not in shape when he met Jeffries. In support of the argument, he noted that Sharkey made a much better showing against Jeffries than he did against Fitzsimmons when Bob was sharp.

Jeffries was perfectly willing to fight Fitzsimmons again, provided that "I receive the biggest end of the receipts, win or lose, as I was forced to give him when we fought before." Jeff noted that after Fitz beat Corbett, everyone challenged him, but he did not fight for over two years. One writer opined, "Fitz has no good excuse for complaining because Jeffries chooses to give him a strong dose of his own medicine."

Gus Ruhlin wanted to fight Jeff to a finish, and posted $1,000 for his challenge. He believed that the recent dissatisfaction over Jeff's last fight proved that "a knockout is the only real decisive method of ending a pugilistic conflict when so much is at stake." Many agreed. Gus suggested Carson City. "There are many who think Ruhlin will give Jeffries a better fight than the erstwhile boilermaker would bargain for."

Jeff said that Corbett was next, but all those who wanted to fight him would get their chance. "I promised Corbett I would take him on before I defeated Sharkey, and I will keep my word. ... Jim is a clever boxer. He may be the one who will beat me. I don't think he will."

Since Corbett was next up for Jeff, some felt that Fitzsimmons and Sharkey should fight each other for the next opportunity. Jeff said, "It is only right that these two should have it out before coming back at me. I defeated them both, and am now ready to meet whichever one is the better. I don't care which one it is."[449]

Unfortunately, it was rumored that New York Governor Theodore Roosevelt, via assemblyman Lewis, was going to initiate legislation to repeal the Horton law, which would once again render boxing illegal in New York. The pro- and anti-boxing factions were gearing up for a potential legislative

---

449 *New York Journal,* November 11, 11, 1899; *New York Sun,* November 12, 1899; *New York Clipper,* November 18, 1899.

battle. Jeff said that if fighting in New York was stopped, he would fight in Carson City, Mexico, or anywhere else.[450]

However, New York was where the money was. It had a big population base that could afford to pay high prices to see the fights. According to the 1900 census, the U.S. population was 76.2 million for the 45-state union. The largest population in the United States was in New York City, which contained 3,437,202 people. The next closest were less than half as big - Chicago at 1,698,575 and Philadelphia at 1,293,697. After that, no U.S. city broke the 600,000 mark. San Francisco was the 9th most populous city in the U.S., with only 342,782 people. Jeff's hometown of Los Angeles only had 100,000 people.

What was so wrong with boxing? After all, football was gaining increased popularity, and was very big in major colleges. Jeffries saw a football game on November 11, 1899. He commented,

> I never looked at so much lively slugging and roughing in all the years I've been in the fighting business. ... If I had to take my choice between having a man punch me as hard as he could or run ten yards and jump on me with his shoulder against my stomach I think I'd take the punch. ... But I don't kick about it as lots of these football supporters kick against fighting.

Jeff said that boxing was not one-half as rough as football.

> I notice that under these football rules they give a knocked-out man three minutes to recover and get into the game. Do you know what that means? It means that he has a chance to get hurt eighteen times as much at football as he has at fighting. Under Queensberry rules a man who can't go on fighting within ten seconds after he is knocked down is out of the game. That's a merciful rule. But at football they give a fellow three minutes and he can come back and get knocked out half a dozen times in a game. ... Next time the good people make a roar about prize-fighting I'll know what is their idea of a pleasant, easy, safe sport.[451]

Still, by the end of 1899, seven men had perished in the ring that year. John L. Sullivan said that rules should be adopted to reduce the killings. He felt that a physician should examine a fighter a week or so before the fight, and on the night of the fight. Referees should stop a fight when it was evident that one boxer was unable to defend himself any more. Seconds or club doctors should not be allowed to give "dope" to a man when he is almost out. "Whiskey or brandy is all right, but strychnine and such drugs make the knockout a lot worse when it comes." Ring floors should be

---

450 *New York Journal*, November 11, 1899.
451 *New York World*, November 12, 1899.

padded. However, he did not want to see the sport tinkered with too much.[452]

Regardless of the legal wrangling about boxing's future, the next big fight on the minds of boxing fans was Jeffries-Corbett. In an interview, Corbett, who had just posted his $5,000 forfeit, said,

> I believe I can whip Jeffries, and what is more, I think I am the only man in the world that can do it. No big, clumsy fighter can do it, no matter how strong he may be; no middle-weight can do it, no matter how clever. It will take a heavy man and a clever man to do the trick. I have both the requisites and intend to be champion again. I want to fight in less than six months, and will be ready when Jeffries is.[453]

As of November 17, Corbett said, "I have been training for some time in a gymnasium in Twenty-seventh street, and will continue to do so." He promised to "be in such shape as I never was before." Corbett was expressing nothing but confidence. "I will win without a doubt."

Bill Brady said to Jim, "I admire you for your confidence, but I don't think you will have a chance with Jeffries." When asked when Corbett and Jeff would fight, Brady was not sure. "Jeff wants to make some money on the fruits of his victory over Sharkey, you know."[454]

Initially, Jeffries-Corbett was not anticipated to take place until the following September 1900. Jeff said that although almost a year was a long time to wait for a fight, "in view of the fact that Fitzsimmons and Corbett only fought once in two years I think I should not be criticized because I don't fight every month. I have met both Sharkey and Fitzsimmons inside of six months, which is quite a task, I think."

As a general rule, it paid to have periods of time between fights. It allowed fighters to exhibit and earn easy money based on the fame they obtained from their prior fight, and gave them time to build up anticipation and interest for their next bout. "There is no denying the fact that a very extensive road tour has been mapped out for Jeffries. Billy Brady thoroughly recognizes the value of his attraction and intends to realize all he can out of it. ... Brady is shrewd enough to make money with a champion without letting him fight too often."

In this instance, a respite would also allow time for the Sharkey fight films to circulate and generate their full revenue stream before another fight took place. "Jeffries will take a long rest; possibly a year – to give the pictures a chance." Bill Brady said, "We want to give the pictures of the Jeffries-Sharkey fight a chance to be shown, and I think Jeffries is deserving

452 *New York World*, December 16, 1899.
453 *New York World*, November 14, 1899.
454 *New York Sun*, November 18, 19, 1899; *New York World*, November 18, 1899. Brady said that Fitzsimmons had insisted on 65% of the gate receipts, win or lose, when Jeff fought him for the championship, and would have to accept those terms for a rematch. Instead, Fitzsimmons and Sharkey verbally agreed to meet in their own rematch the following summer.

of some consideration, and he wants to make what money he can by touring the country." It was later reported that both Jeff and Sharkey were raking in the money from the picture exhibitions, which had "become a permanent amusement feature all over the country."[455]

On November 21, 1899, Corbett and Jeffries signed articles of agreement to fight on September 15, 1900. Corbett said to Brady, "Well, Billy, you helped to make me champion, and now you are trying to get me licked." Bill replied, "Yes, and I learned a trick or two about the game from you that will stand me in good stead now." Everyone laughed.

Regarding the terms, Corbett wanted clean breakaways and to be allowed to wear soft hand bandages. After some negotiation, it was agreed to allow the referee to decide the hand bandage issue, but there would be clean breakaways. The fight was to be 25 rounds or to a finish, depending on the laws of the jurisdiction where the club was located which made the highest bid to host the fight. The purse was to be split 75% to the winner and 25% to the loser.[456]

It was noted, "Now that Jeffries is signed to meet Corbett, the other heavyweights will have to fight it out among themselves. Fitzsimmons and Sharkey will in all probability be matched in the near future, and the winner of this bout will be matched to fight the champion."[457]

Martin Julian claimed that the only reason for putting off the Corbett fight for so long was to stall off other heavyweights. He said that Jeff caught Bob when he was not right, that Jeffries recognized the fact that he was lucky, and was loath to take another chance with Fitz, "whom he knows in his heart is the best in the business." This was the kind of talk that managers engaged in so that they could advertise their man and obtain another lucrative fight.

Fitzsimmons was in training again, and said,

> When Jeffries fought me at Coney Island he did not meet Bob Fitzsimmons; at least, not the same Bob Fitzsimmons that he will face in another contest. I was not myself. ... My senses seemed to have failed me and I am sure that all this was not from a blow. I don't believe Jeffries can hit hard enough to defeat me when I am in my proper shape.

The dissatisfaction over the Jeffries-Sharkey decision caused many to wish that Jeffries was facing Sharkey again, rather than Corbett. However, Jeffries wanted to defeat the two men who had once held the crown, and noted that he had already twice defeated Sharkey. It made a certain amount of sense to require Fitzsimmons, Sharkey, and Ruhlin to battle it out to determine who was best entitled to face him after Corbett.

---

455 *National Police Gazette*, November 25, December 9, 16, 23, 1899.
456 *New York World, New York Sun*, November 22, 1899.
457 *New York Journal*, November 22, 1899.

Bill Delaney maintained that Jeff would have performed better against Sharkey if he had not overtrained. Even so, "I am of the opinion that Jeffries is the greatest living prize fighter, and have not the slightest doubt but that he will whip Corbett. ... Jeff is young, and is improving every day. With Corbett it is quite the opposite."[458]

As of December, Jeffries had been appearing at Koster & Blals Music Hall for several weeks in a theatrical engagement.

Jeffries planned to visit his folks at Los Angeles. "He will work his way West, showing on the road." Speaking of his parents, Jeff's mother was pleased that he had defeated Sharkey, but prayed that her son would give up boxing and direct his energies to the pulpit and follow in his father's footsteps.[459]

On January 1, 1900, 163-pound Kid McCoy scored a 5th round knockout over 172-pound Peter Maher. McCoy outboxed, outgeneraled, and outfought Maher, dropping Peter in the 1st round with a left hook, and using that same punch to finish him in the 5th round.[460]

Less than two weeks after defeating Maher, on January 12, 1900 at New York's Broadway Athletic Club, McCoy fought a controversial rematch with Joe Choynski. Choynski had not been defeated since losing an early 1899 20-round decision to McCoy.

This time, Choynski dropped McCoy four times in the 2nd round. When McCoy rose the last time, the bell rang after only two minutes and 20 seconds had elapsed. The timekeeper said that he rang the bell to signify that the fight was over and that McCoy had been counted out, being down for 12 to 15 seconds. A debate ensued regarding what should happen. This took up 1 minute and 40 seconds, until the referee decided that the fight would continue, which it did. Just as the bell rang to end the 3rd round, McCoy dropped Choynski with a right. Choynski's camp claimed the punch was thrown was after the bell, but the referee did not recognize the claim of foul. When the 4th round began, Joe remained unconscious in his corner and the sponge was thrown up. McCoy was the official winner, but not without some debate. Some reporters said it was a robbery that would lead to boxing becoming illegal again.[461]

When New York Governor Theodore Roosevelt in his annual message to the legislature recommended the repeal of the Horton law, it instilled fear

458 *National Police Gazette*, December 16, 23, 1899, January 13, 1900.
459 *New York Sun*, November 21, 1899; *New York Journal*, November 4, 1899; *New York World*, November 6, 1899.
460 *National Police Gazette*, January 20, 1900. Boxrec.com. McCoy's victory was significant, because Maher had not been defeated since 1898, when Goddard stopped him, but Peter had avenged that loss. Prior to that, Maher had not lost since 1896, when Fitzsimmons stopped him. Over the intervening years, Maher had such results as: 1896 KO4 Frank Slavin, KO6 Joe Choynski, and KO1 Steve O'Donnell; 1897 D7 Tom Sharkey; 1898 LKOby1 and KO8 Joe Goddard; May 1899 D20 Gus Ruhlin (exciting war), and September KO2 Joe Kennedy.
461 *National Police Gazette*, February 3, 1900; *Louisville Evening Post*, January 16, 1900.

that soon New York boxing would be illegal, ending the "generous inducements which are only to be had in the East."

Fearing the end of boxing in New York, the Corbett-Jeffries fight was quickly moved from September all the way up to March (although it was subsequently moved to April, and then to May 1900). Ironically, the fear that boxing would be banned stimulated the making and hosting of even more boxing matches. Everyone wanted to earn their coin while they still could. "I shall not be surprised to see several very important matches made within the next few weeks, owing to a desire to get a number of fistic arguments...settled before the anti-boxing element gets a crack at the Horton law." Hence, there was an explosion of matches being made.

Roosevelt's announcement was something of a bombshell, because he had previously been a supporter and exponent of boxing. Roosevelt had boxed at Harvard University, and had attended many boxing matches. He had frequently visited the Broadway Athletic Club on boxing nights when he was the president of the New York Police Board. He had once said, "There is nothing brutal about boxing; it is a manly sport, and ought to be encouraged." His tune had oddly changed. A politician making an about-face?[462]

The Amateur Athletic Union urged the legislature not to repeal the Horton law. There was great fear that if the law was repealed that boxing all over the country would receive a setback.

Upset that his fellow legislators were looking to do away with boxing, Assemblyman Tim Sullivan "handed back a hot one to the anti-boxing element" by introducing a measure intended to put an end to football. "From an array of statistics he is prepared to show that football is more brutal than boxing and is responsible for more casualties in the way of deaths, broken limbs and other injuries." He was essentially calling attention to the legislators' hypocrisy in supporting football but attacking boxing.

On February 8, 1900, the state capital at Albany, New York was the scene of a debate about the potential repeal of the Horton law. A large delegation of ministers and representatives of law and order leagues backed Assemblyman Lewis, who had proposed an anti-boxing bill. The lawyer for the opposition noted that since the Horton law had been in effect, over 600 contests had been pulled off without difficulty, few injuries, and under the supervision of the police in a lawful and decorous manner.

The Lewis bill, as amended, proposed that the repeal go into effect as of September 1, 1900. Thus, even if the bill was passed, boxers would have until then to complete whatever fights that they wanted.

As it became clear that Jim Corbett had been training diligently over a lengthy period of time, and was taking the match very seriously, intrigue developed for the bout. Corbett was already at Lakewood, New Jersey,

---

462 *National Police Gazette*, January 20, 1900.

actively preparing for the battle, "training like a race horse." "He says Jeff never was able to hit him when they were training together and does not understand how he can have improved sufficiently to do it now."

When analyzing the upcoming fight, one writer noted that Corbett used to wear Jeff out when he had been Jim's sparring partner in early 1897. "Jeffries was leaning against the side wall of the court, completely fagged out, and Jim was standing in the centre as unconcerned as could be." When Jeff recovered his wind, they went at it again. Corbett only cut loose on him occasionally, to let Jeff know he was still in the game. "But that was almost three years ago."

Corbett was managing to convince some reporters that he had a good chance to defeat Jeffries. "Time and again I have listened in a confidential way to Corbett's arguments until I found myself sharing the belief and confidence in him against what, perhaps, my own better judgment seemed to dictate." Corbett had "analyzed the possibilities of a match with Jeffries to the smallest detail." Not only had Jim sparred with Jeff, but also he had seen him fight Fitz and Sharkey. Jim was known to have keen analytical skills, and was able to map out a way to defeat opponents.

Regarding Corbett, even Jeffries said, "I fancy he is a tough proposition. He is shifty, clever, and a great general in the ring. He may not punch so hard as either Fitz or Sharkey, but he knows the game though like a book."

Although Corbett had already been training, Jim Jeffries went to Hot Springs for a rest and some treatment for a while, prior to going into training. Apparently, Jeff was a bit ill, with a slight blood disorder, but nothing serious. More importantly, the tendons in his left forearm, which was his best arm, "as he is left handed," had drawn up considerably and the arm was noticeably crooked. It was the result of the medicine ball injury prior to the Sharkey fight and its subsequent reinjury during that fight. He was still healing.

The Corbett-Jeffries fight was eventually set for May 11 at Coney Island. Corbett took a brief training hiatus, but planned to return to Lakewood about March 15. Jim said that when he entered the ring on May 11, he expected to be in better shape than when he fought Fitzsimmons.

As of mid-March, Jeffries had returned to California from Hot Springs. He expected to remain in Los Angeles for a couple weeks before returning to Asbury Park to train. "He hopes to start in on April 1, and that will give him six weeks at the Jersey quarters."[463]

In the meantime, Bob Fitzsimmons came out with an announcement claiming that he was drugged when he fought Jeffries. It was an "eleventh hour excuse which excites ridicule among the followers of ring happenings." One opined that it was a little late for Bob to be making excuses. Still, Fitz claimed that after the 2nd round, "I took a long drink of

463 *National Police Gazette*, February 10, 17, March 3, 10, 24, 1900.

mineral water, and following that I have only a hazy recollection of one or two incidents of the fight." A *Police Gazette* reporter responded, "My opinion is that the wallop on the head in the second round which landed him upon his back in the southwest corner of the ring was hard enough to make him forget he was alive." No one gave Bob's claim any credence. Even Martin Julian did not back him.

Fitzsimmons posted $5,000 and challenged Jeffries, Sharkey, and Kid McCoy. Eventually, on March 5, Fitz and Sharkey met and agreed to box on or about August 1, 1900, to settle which one was best entitled to another crack at Jeffries. Fitz was happy to prove that there was something crooked about his first encounter with Tom.

Although Fitzsimmons thought that it was a "cinch" to beat Sharkey, many experts felt that he was underestimating Tom's improvement. "He has become a really clever pugilist." Either way, it was good that Bob was becoming an active fighter again. "Only fighting can keep a man at the top notch. Exhibitions are all right and practice sparring serves its purpose…but the real thing is what is wanted, even if the man in front is a sucker of the greenest type. A fighter realizes that his mission is to beat him and he throws his heart and soul into the proceedings."[464]

On March 27, 1900 in Philadelphia, Bob Fitzsimmons fought Jim Daly in a scheduled 6-round contest. Daly had sparred hundreds of rounds with both Jim Corbett and Jim Jeffries. It did not help him. As soon as the bell rang, Fitz attacked and never permitted Daly to move more than ten feet from his corner. Bob missed a left and they clinched. He then landed a left on the wind, and Daly missed a similar response. Bob landed two lefts on the face that dropped Daly. After Jim rose, Bob feinted a right, and then whipped his left to the belly, and Daly went down again. From that point on, Fitz landed as he pleased, although he did not appear to be putting his full force into his punches. Just before the gong, Bob landed a left on the jaw which dropped Daly for the third time in the round.

Although the bell saved Daly, the referee wisely and properly declined to permit the bout to continue. If he had not stopped it, they would have needed to call in the coroner. Daly was game but overmatched. With little exertion, Fitz had punched him into partial unconsciousness in 1 round.[465]

On March 28, the New York Senate passed the bill repealing the Horton law by a party vote, 26 to 22. The Republican majority were against boxing, with the exception of only one senator, who voted with the Democrats against the measure. Governor Theodore Roosevelt subsequently signed the bill. The repeal would go into effect on September 1, 1900. Therefore, anyone who wanted to fight in New York needed to do so before then.

---

464 *National Police Gazette*, February 17, 24, March 3, 10, 17, 24, 1900. Fitz and Sharkey agreed to box 25 rounds, to wear no hand bandages, and for the winner to take the entire receipts.
465 *Philadelphia Inquirer*, March 28, 1900.

The National Police Gazette lamented, "The action of the Legislature in its illogical view of the boxing situation means the loss of a large revenue to local promoters of the game, and will incidentally curtail the coming into the Metropolis of a vast amount of money which was put into circulation by visiting sporting men, who were prodigal in leaving it behind them." An unhappy Senator Tim Sullivan said, "It required a special messenger from the governor, the calling of a Republican party caucus and an exhibition of treachery which was justifiable under the pressure brought to bear to pass the Lewis bill and to practically eliminate professional boxing from this State." Still, boxing would be hot until the repeal went into effect.

Jim Jeffries said that all of the top fighters were afraid of Fitzsimmons and dodging him. "To tell the truth, I would rather fight ten Sharkeys, a dozen Corbetts and all the McCoys you could bring before me than fight Fitz again. … They do not think they can beat him, and have a fear that he may wind them up in a hurry, as he can do." In response, Gus Ruhlin also made a match with Bob. So, Fitzsimmons had potential summer matches with both Ruhlin and Sharkey. If they wanted to fight in New York, boxers needed to fight before September.[466]

THE JEFFRIES BROTHERS.
(1) TOM. (2) JACK. (3) JIM. (4) JOHN. (5) GEORGE F. MILLER.

---

466 *National Police Gazette*, April 21, 1900. Fitz and Ruhlin agreed to a 25-round contest, which was to be filmed, for the fighters to receive a 67% share of the gate with a like share of the picture receipts, with 75% to the winner and 25% to the loser. They agreed to George Siler as the referee.

CHAPTER 22

The Road to Corbett

Preparing for the upcoming Jeffries fight, Jim Corbett was looking well and talking confidently. "I know Jeffries is a big ox, hard to hurt and with a destructive, dazing punch. But, as every one will admit, I'm clever with my hands and feet, and I think I can jab this husky mountain of brawn and muscle into wonderland. ... It's a business with me. There's money in it, and I'm after the coin."[467]

In late March/early April, Jeffries had been doing some training with Tommy Ryan and Jack Jeffries at West Baden, Indiana. Before returning east to train for the Corbett fight, Jeffries stopped off in Detroit, Michigan. Five months after his Sharkey defense, on April 6, 1900 at the Light Guard Armory under the auspices of Detroit's Cadillac Athletic Club, Jeff took on Pittsburg's "Irish" John/Jack Finnegan. Although it was only scheduled for 10 rounds, and appears to have been a non-title-bout tune-up in preparation for the Corbett title fight, Finnegan had some fair experience, including: 1899 D20 Jack Bonner, D20 Jimmy Ryan and KO18 Jack McCormick. However, on January 31, 1900, Gus Ruhlin stopped Finnegan in the 4th round. For the Jeffries bout, Finnegan had been doing a great deal of roadwork in preparation, running from 12 to 20 miles a day, in addition to hitting the bags 10-15 rounds.[468]

---

467 *National Police Gazette*, March 31, 1900.
468 Boxrec.com. *National Police Gazette*, April 28, 1900. *Detroit Tribune, Detroit Evening News*, April 5, 6, 1900. Two of three local newspapers called him John Finnegan, while a third used the first name Jack.

Finnegan was shorter, lighter, and less experienced, but was known as an aggressive fighter who could take punishment. "Finnegan gave Jack McCormick a good drubbing early in the winter."[469]

Finnegan said,

> Jack McCormack, of Philadelphia, is almost as big as Jeffries and has fought all of the prominent heavyweights in the country, yet I had McCormack whipped all the way in our fight last winter, the referee, Tim Hurst, stopping the fight in the eighteenth round…. I never saw Jeffries fight but have seen him in exhibition bouts and also saw the pictures of his fight with Sharkey. I do not care to say anything about the decision that was rendered by Referee Siler at that time, but will say that if Jeffries fights me that way, I'll surely be there at the end of our ten round bout. …

Finnegan also spoke about the color line and other bouts in his career.

> I see that they think, over there in Chicago, that Frank Childs, the colored heavyweight, is very close to the championship throne and I know that several of the prominent big fellows have refused to meet him in a limited round bout. It is very convenient for them to draw the color line – if he was a white man they would have to fight Childs…. Only recently Childs was stood off in two six-round bouts by 'Mustard' Jack Bonner, a draw being the decision in each instance and I fought a 20 round battle with Bonner in Wheeling last November, the majority claiming that I was clearly entitled to the decision…. When I fought Gus Ruhlin, he happened to land a blow on the body early in the first round that took all the steam out of me…but even then it took him four rounds to knock me out.[470]

In the dressing room that evening, there was an argument over the gloves. Finnegan would not allow Jeffries to wear an old pair that he had. However, the new gloves were too small for Jeff's hands. They finally agreed to put on a set that had been used in other contests.

Jeffries claimed to weigh 220 pounds, although during the day he said he weighed 221. One paper said his weight was so well distributed that in street clothes he did not look that big. However, when seen bare-chested, some said he looked fully 10 pounds bigger. Others felt he appeared to be closer to 250 pounds. Finnegan was announced as weighing 180 pounds, but looked like a boy beside Jeffries.

Jeff's seconds were Jack Jeffries, Tommy Ryan, and manager William Brady, who sat on an overturned pail quietly smoking a cigar.

Referee George Siler told them that each man should protect himself in the breakaway.

---

469 *Detroit Free Press*, April 1, 1900; *Detroit Evening News*, April 6, 1900.
470 *Detroit Free Press*, April 2, 1900.

At the bell, Jeffries hurried to ring center, crouching, with Finnegan dancing about. Finn threw a right that just grazed the champ's face. Jeff feinted a couple times with the left and followed Finn around. Finnegan was quickly sent down, each local paper giving its version:

Detroit Free Press: Finn threw a left that was blocked, and Jeff countered with a left to the body and they clinched. After breaking cleanly, Jeff rushed in and dropped him with a left hook to the side of the head.

Detroit Tribune: Jeff straightened his left out and it landed on his opponent's neck. Finn was immediately jarred, and before he could recover, Jeff landed three more times to the same spot and Finnegan went down.

Detroit Evening News: Jeff blocked a swing and then countered with a left to the face, followed by two more to the same place, the last one sending Finnegan down in a tangle with the ropes.

It appears that Jeff's left was launched differently than most, causing some to call it straight, while others described it as a hook.

Finnegan rose quickly, at or before the count of three. Jeff immediately attacked and in an instant sent him down again with another left hook or straight left to the head. The Irishman took another short count, but came up a little wobbly.

Jeffries gave him no rest, quickly attacking again. Finnegan missed a wild desperate swing, and Jeff beat a tattoo on his jaw and wind, the same left to the head dropping Finnegan hard for the third time.

This time, Finnegan did not rise so quickly. When he got up, Jeff rushed to close quarters. Finnegan raised his hands to guard against the hook, but this time Jeff whipped in a short left uppercut to the pit of the stomach, lifting Finn off the floor, dropping to his hands and knees. It was the fourth knockdown. Finnegan struggled to rise at nine, but immediately sunk and fell back to the ropes, partially down again "with a look of agony on his face." Siler stepped in and held Finn, preventing him from going down fully to the floor. It was over after only 55 seconds had elapsed. Siler held him until Finnegan's manager picked him up in his arms and carried him to his corner, where he was revived in a few moments.

The locals summarized that Jeffries was purely aggressive, and struck Finnegan with a bombardment of rapid-fire lefts to quickly dispose of him. Jeff was "not only fast, but he can hit like a mule kicking, and knows how to take care of himself." He had earned $1,200, or $21.82 per second of work, which ranked him amongst the Rockefeller class in terms of earnings per second.

Jeffries waved his hands to the crowd, laughing as he pushed towards his dressing room. While getting into his street clothes, Jeff said,

> I wouldn't have rushed him like that if he hadn't made me mad. He was too fresh about the gloves, and I didn't like his sass. I told Brady

I would knock him out inside of a minute. If he had been a decent fellow I would have allowed him to stay a while and done some boxing. Maybe he'll behave next time.[471]

Jeffries arrived in New York the following evening, on April 7. He would begin training for the Corbett fight without delay at his usual training quarters and facilities at Allenhurst and Asbury Park, New Jersey. Jeff said the trip out West did him much good.[472]

Jeffries knew that Corbett was no easy task. He said that Jim was very clever, shifty, deceiving, and hard to hit cleanly. Therefore, it would not be easy to take him out. Still, Jeff was very confident that he would stop him before the fight was over.

> Mr. Corbett is pretty, or thinks he is, which is just as good, so far as he is concerned, and he has a holy horror of having his beauty warped. You may have noticed this if you ever saw him fight. He turns his face away from a blow, like a schoolgirl when her first sweetheart says things to her. … I'm not a matinee idol by any means, and I don't care any more about the displacement of my face than I do about the discovery of the North Pole. … I'll just rush and smash. Corbett's guard against the rush and the smash will vanish like a puff of cigarette smoke before the business end of a cyclone. Nor will he be able to avoid me. I'll nail him at the ropes and by my superior strength and weight just beat his head off.
>
> I'm bigger and stronger than any man in the prize ring today. I can punch harder than any of them. It is almost impossible to hurt me, and I don't care whether I get a wallop or not, so long as I can land. … I'll beat Mr. Corbett by fighting him. He'll have no chance to do any grand stand sparring. I'll simply go at him, biff, chug from the bell, and he'll never be able to stand the racket.[473]

Jeffries had been running 10 miles a day, but on April 16, he added two miles to his run, going 12 miles in all. That afternoon, after Jeff had boxed with Jack Jeffries and Tommy Ryan, he began working with Ed Dunkhorst (who weighed 260-300 pounds), doing some roughing with him.[474]

Absent from Jeff's training camp was Bill Delaney, who had not been with him since the Sharkey fight. Apparently, there was still some bad blood. Delaney was clearly upset by Tommy Ryan's more prominent role in

---

471 *Detroit Free Press, Detroit Tribune, Detroit Evening News*, April 7, 8, 1900. Many consider Jeff's 55-second knockout over Finnegan the fastest heavyweight championship win, but in 1884, John L. Sullivan knocked out Sylvester Le Gouriff in 20 seconds, and had several other knockouts faster than one minute. Some might question whether the title was actually on the line in any of these bouts.
472 *New York Clipper*, April 14, 1900; *National Police Gazette*, April 28, 1900.
473 *New York Journal*, April 14, 1900.
474 *New York Journal*, April 16, 1900.

Jeff's training, for he and Ryan did not agree on how Jeff should prepare. For the time being, Jeff favored Ryan, so Delaney was out.

Corbett explained why he would defeat Jeffries, saying that it was the one ambition of his life to win back the title.

> Of course he is a big and ugly customer to tackle, and he is no slouch at the game, but I am his master in the art of hit, stop and get away, and can outgeneral him. His size and weight do not make me doubt for a minute. He can hit a stiff punch, but he cannot land it effectively on me. I'll feint him into a fit, and when I get his eyes wandering I'll get in a rip to some finishing spot. ... It isn't always size and strength that win fights. Skill and science and a knowledge of the most effective way to avoid attack and at the same time be on the aggressive are the most important factors in getting the referee's verdict. I don't think Jeffries is as well up in this part of the programme as I am, and on this fact I am banking.[475]

In his autobiography, Corbett said that he had been secretly training for the past year in anticipation of a Jeffries match. He sparred with contender Gus Ruhlin for three weeks prior to the fight, paying him $100 per week. Corbett claimed to have handled him.

In his autobiography, Jeffries said, "Corbett really thought he could beat me, and for a year he trained on the quiet and got into great condition." Jeff said that Corbett trained and sparred with Ruhlin for ten weeks.[476]

A top contender in his own right, Gus Ruhlin was an excellent sparring partner for Corbett. He was big and muscular like Jeffries, weighing over 200 pounds of solid muscle. He was good enough to have fought Jeffries to a 20-round draw, and like Corbett, knew a few things about Jeff's style.

Corbett was also regularly sparring with "Stockings" Conroy.[477] He even sparred 3 rounds one day with Kid McCoy. Clearly, Corbett had dedicated himself to training harder and longer for this fight than he had in quite some time.

Corbett said that he was better at this point than he ever was at any time in his life. "If Jeffries can beat me in my present condition, why, he could have beaten me at any time in the past." He predicted that he would whip Jeff without even getting a black eye.[478]

Again speaking of how he would fight Corbett, Jeffries said,

> I will have him beaten on size and weight and strength. I'll go in to smash him from the sound of the bell. ... It won't be a case of his

---

475 *New York Journal*, April 21, 1900.
476 Corbett at 284-288; *My Life and Battles* at 41.
477 Conroy's record included: 1897 L10 Dunkhorst; 1898 WDQ17 O'Donnell, L6 Armstrong, WDQ2 Dunkhorst, and L6 Childs; 1899 LKOby7 Maher, D6 Childs, L20 Armstrong, and LKOby7 Ruhlin; 1900 KO4 McCormick, WDQ5 McCormick, LDQby5 Maher, and LKOby2 Sharkey. Boxrec.com.
478 *National Police Gazette*, May 12, 1900.

going the limit as with Sharkey. Corbett can box and has a good head on his shoulders so long as he is not stung with a hard rap. He can't stand for a grueling. Hit Corbett and he is all at sea. I'll hit him hard enough. It will be only a question of getting to him, and I don't think any one doubts but that I can do that.

I can box a little myself and know a few tricks of the trade as well as Mr. C. When he rushes I will let him come and meet him with a stab or two to the wind or heart that will make him pause.

I suppose he will fight me at long range if I will let him, but I won't. … I don't underrate Corbett at all. I do not think he has gone back, as some people say. He is probably as good, if not better, today than ever he was, but he is not good enough to take the championship away from me. [479]

On April 24, visitors to Jeff's training quarters were impressed with his wonderful improvement in form and science. Jeff sparred 10 total rounds – 3 with brother Jack, 3 with big Ed Dunkhorst, and 4 rounds with chief trainer Tommy Ryan.[480]

Jeffries again spoke highly of Fitzsimmons, and also claimed to be badly injured and ill-prepared going into the Sharkey fight.

I think Fitz is one of the hardest men to beat the ring ever knew. … If Fitzsimmons had caught me in the same shape Sharkey did, he would have beaten me. When I fought the sailor at Coney Island my left arm was bad – much worse than many suppose, and if I were to tell just how bad it was people would not believe me. I was not up to the standard… I have no hesitancy in saying that it was a lucky thing for me that I was not in the same condition when I met Fitz as when I met Sharkey. My left arm has mended nicely and is as good as ever. The trouble I had with my blood is also a thing of the past. Do I look like the poor, broken down, emaciated boxer the papers painted me a month or two ago? I never was better in my life, and when I fight next month I will prove it most conclusively.[481]

On April 28, during Jeff's 6-mile spin on his bicycle, he found himself pocketed between a carriage and a stage coach going in opposite directions, and in an effort to avoid running into the carriage, Jeff made a sharp turn to the left and ran into the stage coach. He was thrown head first and slid for 20 feet. His left hip was bruised and there was a contusion of the left forearm. Still, Jeff continued his training at the gymnasium.[482]

479 *New York Journal*, April 21, 1900.
480 *New York World*, April 25, 1900. At around that time, when Jeff's grandfather died, his father inherited part of a $20,000 estate left at Lancaster, Ohio. *National Police Gazette*, April 28, 1900.
481 *National Police Gazette*, April 28, 1900.
482 *New York World*, April 29, 1900.

On April 29, 1900 at New York's Madison Square Garden, 6,000 fans attended a benefit held in John L. Sullivan's honor. Tom Sharkey, Gus Ruhlin, and Peter Maher all participated in separate sparring exhibitions. Bob Fitzsimmons boxed Jeff Thorne 3 rounds.[483]

The main event was a friendly sparring exhibition between Sullivan and Jeffries. The 41-year-old Sullivan was very fat, while Jeff was trained to the hour, his muscles evident everywhere. They boxed 3 tame half-minute rounds with two minutes of rest in between. The crowd applauded.[484]

The next night, on April 30, 1900 at New York's Hercules Athletic Club before a crowd of 3,500 to 4,000, Bob Fitzsimmons took on the very experienced and durable "Human Freight Car," Ed Dunkhorst, in a scheduled 25-round bout. Most recently, Dunk was a Jeffries sparring partner, taking a brief hiatus to go box Bob.[485]

JEFFRIES GETS DUNKHORST READY FOR FITZ

Champion Is Putting on the Finishing Touches.

How the Big Fellows Spar While at Practice.

What most distinguished Dunkhorst was his durability and massive size. Estimates of his weight ranged anywhere from 225 to 260 to 300 pounds. Jeff thought he was about 287. Given that the 215-pound Jeffries looked much smaller than Dunkhorst in photographs of their sparring, it is probably safe to say that Dunkhorst weighed in the uppermost range of those estimates. Dunk "looked three times as big as the lank Australian." Fitzsimmons likely weighed at least 170-180 pounds. Dunkhorst was so big that he "looked like a week's output of a sausage factory rolled into one convoluted and corrugated gigantic link." However, Dunk could fight. Regardless of the fact that he was the heaviest and fattest fighter in the business, "he has shown considerable agility and also plenty of punching power."

---

483 Bob was in total control for the first two rounds, but in the 3rd, Thorne dropped Fitz twice, Bob dropped him once, then Bob got decked again, and then both went down at the same time and both were counted out. "Then for the first time did some of those present realize that they had been witnessing a really clever fake." Fitz and Thorne popped up and shook hands. They had just pulled a goof on the crowd, which loved it anyway, applauding and cheering.
484 *New York World*, April 30, 1900.
485 Significant Dunkhorst bouts included: 1897 D15 Jim Hall; 1898 D10 Bob Armstrong, LKOby22 Gus Ruhlin, W20 C.C. Smith, D10 Armstrong, L6 Peter Maher, and L6 Joe Choynski; 1899 KO5 Charley Strong, L8 Frank Childs, LKOby6 Joe Butler, L25 Yank Kenny, D6 Jim McCormick, LDQby7 Peter Maher, W10 Bob Armstrong, and D20 Jack Stelzner. Boxrec.com.

Upon his ring entry, Dunkhorst received little applause, while Fitzsimmons was cheered. Ernest Roeber, Dan Hickey, and Jeff Thorne, the English middleweight whom Bob had stopped in 1 round but had taken on as a sparring partner, seconded Fitz. Dunk's seconds were Tommy Ryan, Jack Jeffries, and Dan Johnson.

Fitzsimmons was stripped to the buff, only wearing his white knitted breech clout for trunks and an American flag for a belt. Dunk work blue trunks that reached half-way down his thighs. Fitz was a 4 to 1 favorite. It was even money that the bout would not last 10 rounds. They shook hands at 10:20 p.m. Charley White refereed.[486]

1st round

Dunkhorst was several inches taller, but crouched down in Jeffries style. After some sparring, Fitz shot his left hook to the ear with jarring force. Bob feinted swiftly and played for Ed's head. "He wanted to get Dunkhorst's hands up about his face so that he would protect it and forget that he had any lower works." Bob strategically set up debilitating blows. He landed a heavy right to the ribs and a hard left jab. It was mostly a feeling out round, but Bob hooked him on the jaw with lefts whenever he wanted and landed the right with equal ease, causing Dunk to retreat. Fitz followed, forcing Dunkhorst to mix it until the bell rang. However, Dunk never landed. Although experienced, Ed was a like novice in Fitz's hands.

2nd round

Fitzsimmons was grinning, and started in to end the fight. Bob sent his stinging stabs to Dunk's face, causing Ed to protect there. Dunk landed a left on the nose. Bob jabbed him on the eye and ducked a right swing. He went in close and missed an uppercut. Fitz then poured in body blows and drove his right to the jaw.

Grinning, Fitzsimmons feinted his right for the head, and then ripped the left into the stomach. The glove dug into the fat until it disappeared to the wrist. The surprised Dunkhorst cried out with pain and hugged with both arms. After being separated, Bob once again hit the wind with the left, which sounded like "a pig of lead striking a ton of lard." Bob quickly followed it with a tremendous left hook to the chin that dropped Dunk to the floor on his face like a log. He "wriggled about on the floor like a huge jellyfish. His motions were convulsive." However, he soon became motionless, stretched out. Fitz wore a broad grin and circled around until the referee counted Ed out. The crowd heartily congratulated Bob.

One source said the fight was over at 1 minute and 45 seconds of the 2nd round, while another said that the time of the round was 2 minutes and 45 seconds.

---

486 The fight account is taken from *New York Journal, New York Sun, New York World, Philadelphia Public Ledger,* May 1, 1900.

Stopped only twice before, this was the first time in Dunkhorst's career that he was put to sleep, out cold. With a huge effort, his seconds lifted and dragged him to a chair. As usual in a Fitz fight, it was at least a minute before Ed came to. They poured water on Dunkhorst in order to revive him. When he awoke, he put his hand to his right jaw and groaned. He asked, "What happened?" His cornerman, Tommy Ryan, said, "Why, the roof fell in." With a far-away look in his eyes, Dunkhorst replied, "Then it must have hit me."

Thought the Roof Had Fallen on Top of Him.

ROBERT FITZSIMMONS.   EDWARD DUNKHORST.

One newspaper said that Fitz was far from being a "dead one," that he had accomplished a feat which others and bigger men had found impossible. Bob's "wonderful hitting powers have not forsaken him, and he was as lively on his feet as ever." Another said that Fitzsimmons was in prime shape, fast and clever, and "best of all he hit with all of his old-time vigor."

As of May 3, it was said that Jeffries had been doing a prodigious amount of exercise every day, and had an increasing appetite for more and harder work. As of the 4th, Jeff said, "I never felt better in my life. … I don't care how clever the man might be." As of May 5, Dunkhorst was back sparring with Jeff, along with Tommy Ryan and Jack Jeffries.[487]

Jeffries said,

> It will be a matter worthy of a boast to have whipped Fitzsimmons, Sharkey and Corbett in the same ring in less than twelve months' time. The scalps of a champion, a former champion, and one of the burliest, huskiest fighters in the world will be trophies of my strength and skill when I have finished with Corbett. I have no doubt about beating him. I will not be able to hit him as often as I did Sharkey, but I won't need to. One of the blows that shattered the Sailor's ribs will

---

487 *New York Journal*, May 3, 4, 1900. Jeff's daily training included rowing 4 miles on Deal Lake, running 10 miles, punching the bag, boxing with Jack Jeffries, Tommy Ryan, and Ed Dunkhorst, tossing the medicine ball, jumping rope, and working the wrist machine and pulley weights.

settle Corbett's aspirations for the championship, or one of the wallops that I gave Fitz in the jaw will serve the purpose just as well.[488]

JEFFRIES
LANDS
A HARD ONE

Corbett's training on May 5 was quite intense. After walking 2 miles, he then sparred Gus Ruhlin, with no spectators being allowed. However, from outside, the newsmen could hear the call of time for each round and the sounds of the men shuffling about and exchanging blows. From what could be heard, the men had sparred 23 rounds. That was an interesting number. The crowd was admitted to watch Corbett wrestle with Leo Pardello.

Corbett said,

> I know my condition and my capabilities and I also know what Jeffries can do. Since the days at Carson City I have followed closely his every movement, have watched his improvement – and he has improved wonderfully.... I have the speed and skill, as everybody knows, and if there is doubt in any minds concerning my stamina and condition they will vanish before we have fought five rounds on May 11.

488 *New York Journal*, May 5, 1900; *New York World*, May 6, 1900.

I have trained with one end in view – to gain strength sufficient to enable me to use my science to advantage against a man very much slower than myself – and the result has been even better than I expected. I will win the championship as sure as the fight comes off.[489]

Corbett also said that he had not trained properly for some of his former bouts, but he had sacrificed for this one.

As usual, the legal authorities tried to hinder boxing, and there had to be yet another legal dispute. In the wake of the new Lewis law, the Police Commissioners decided to stop granting boxing licenses, which would stop clubs from hosting boxing matches prior to September 1, the date the Horton law ended. However, the clubs took them to court and won. The Jeff-Corbett fight would go on as scheduled.

On May 6, while riding his bicycle, Jeffries heard a snap as the bike broke, and he went flying ten-feet forward on his hands and knees. Given that it was his second crash, Jeff stopped bicycling for the remainder of his training camp. He was tapering in his work anyhow.

Jeffries said that he was not overconfident, feeling that Corbett was a better man than Fitz or Sharkey, "and his ability to sidestep, together with his fine generalship, makes him a hard man to reach." However, he still felt that he would knock him out within the scheduled 25 rounds.

Jim Corbett was the "personification of perfect health." His step was light, his eyes bright, and he seemed to have a youthful and merry heart. "I will win," was Jim's simple statement of sincere conviction. "He works like a whirlwind. From medicine bag to punching bag, from pulley weights to a hot set-to with Trainer Ruhlin, he flees with the speed of lightning."[490]

Perhaps either wanting a psychological edge or just trying to promote the fight, Corbett, always the master of head games, began bragging to the press about how he had easily handled Jeffries in sparring, knocking him about, and once even knocking him out, which may or may not have been true.

Jim had sized up Jeffries in Carson. He recognized that Jeff was powerful and remarkably quick for a big man. He had seen Jeffries against Fitzsimmons and Sharkey, and was not afraid. Corbett said of Jeff, "He has more confidence and he hits cleaner. Otherwise he is the same old Jeffries. I tell you he can't do any damage unless you go to him…. I'll make him come to me."[491]

[Jeffries] sparred with Corbett every day. He was so willing and hardy that these sparring bouts ofttimes culminated in downright battles. The champion would go at young Jeffries like a whirlwind and Jeffries

---

489 New York World, May 6, 1900.
490 New York Journal, New York Herald, May 7, 1900; New York Sun, New York World, May 8, 1900.
491 San Francisco Examiner, May 7, 1900.

would stay there and fight like a wild-cat. But the champion, with confidence and prowess, born of an unbroken string of victories, was too much for the young Californian. These fast set-tos would end with Jeffries 'all out,' as the vernacular of the 'squared circle' puts it.

In discussing one of those sparring sessions, Corbett said, "As I planted my right he was coming toward me and when he went 'out' lurched forward. He would have fallen flat on his face if I had not caught him in my arms. He was 'out' clean as a whistle and it took several minutes to bring him around." Jim asked, "And why not again?" Certainly, Corbett's past sparring with Jeff gave him confidence. Whether or not he told the truth, Corbett was up to his old psychological and promotional gamesmanship.[492]

An upset Jeffries said that Corbett's claim that he knocked him out in their early 1897 sparring sessions was a lie. Jeff said that he could have defeated Jim on his best day. "I have made my record fighting men in their prime. Mr. Corbett, in his five years as a champion, fought two old men – John L. Sullivan and Charlie Mitchell – both of whom were not fit to enter a ring…. When he did meet a live one – Fitzsimmons – he was defeated." Sharkey, who had fought both, said Corbett had no chance to win.[493]

Leading up to the fight, the betting was not very vigorous. Still,

> On all sides glowing reports of Corbett's condition are heard. Many of those who have seen the ex-champion work lately declare that he is in better fettle than he has been since he defeated John L. Sullivan at New Orleans in 1892. Jeffries is in fine trim, too, and is not taking any chances, as he realizes that Corbett will give him a hot tussle for supremacy.[494]

492 *New York Journal*, May 8, 1900.
493 *San Francisco Examiner*, May 9, 1900.
494 *New York Sun*, May 8, 1900.

Corbett called Jeffries a slow cart horse, whom he was positive would be unable to hit him in 25 rounds. He said it would be an easy fight. Jeffries replied that Corbett could not hit hard enough to do him any harm, and by keeping after him, he was bound to win at some point.

A few days before Jeffries defended against Corbett, on May 8, 1900 in Chicago, a 185-pound Tom Sharkey fought a third match with 165-pound Joe Choynski. Sharkey attacked in a ferocious nonstop fashion and pounded on Choynski. At the end of the 2nd round, he dropped Joe with a right. When Choynski was still groggy and unable to answer the bell for the 3rd round, Sharkey was awarded the fight. It was Sharkey's fifth knockout victory in a row since February 1900.[495]

Also on May 8, an expert for the *New York World*, W.O. Inglis, watched Jeffries train, and rendered his assessment that Jeff was quite fit. "I never saw him look so well. … He is stronger, huskier and younger looking than I ever saw him before. … He is full of energy and high spirits." Jeff was allegedly weighing 208 pounds, and stood a trifle over 6'1".

When Inglis told Jeff that he looked like a new man, he responded,

> I feel like one too. You know when I trained before I didn't take enough time for it. I did all my work to get ready for Sharkey in about three weeks. I worked too hard and I was bilious. This time I went to Hot Springs more than two months ago and boiled out. Then I went home and visited my family and went out shooting and got fat. Then I went to Baden Springs and drank the water and got my stomach right. After that I came here, worked easy for two weeks and then settled down to slugging. The result is that I feel better now than I ever felt before. All my work has been like play.

Jeff and Ryan said that Corbett expected to meet the same man that he had sparred, and the same slow man that fought Sharkey. "Well, he has a surprise coming to him, all right," Jeff said.

Jeffries played two games of handball with Inglis, and then sparred him 2 rounds.

> In these two rounds the first thing that appeared was Jeffries's great improvement in foot work. He slipped in and out of hitting distance without the least exertion. Last year he made work of it. Even then he was fast for a big man. Now he darts in or sidesteps or backs away as lightly as a feather whirled by a breeze. He crouches so low and sticks his left arm out so far that no ordinary big man can spar within hitting distance of him. … He blocked everything and always handed out a counter or a return, even though in this case they were only taps. … Afterward, when the champion boxed his brother Jack, I could see

495 *New York Journal, San Francisco Examiner*, May 9, 1900.

that he is faster than ever. He is a great deal quicker than he was last year.

There was some debate regarding who would referee. Corbett claimed that Brady had agreed to Sam Austin. Jeffries and Brady actually selected Charley White. Jeff said, "My choice of referee is Charley White. He is a friend of Corbett and nobody knows better than Corbett himself that White will give a decision absolutely free from any bias or prejudice whatever. The public knows this, too." Corbett admitted that White was a friend and was all right, but made an issue out of it simply because he claimed that he had been told that Austin would referee. Brady asked, "Didn't White help train him at Carson City and has he ever had anything but friendly feelings for Corbett? Is there anything the matter with his record?" Brady said that Corbett had no problem with White, but was just being a pain because that is what he liked to do. "You tell Corbett I taught him all these little tricks, and they won't go with me – not a minute." They eventually agreed upon White.[496]

Corbett had not fought in almost a year and a half, since being disqualified in the 9th round against Sharkey in late 1898. He had lost his championship in early 1897, after having won it in late 1892 at age 26. Still, he was not exactly old and over the hill. Having fought few battles in recent years, the 33-year-old was still physically fresh. Most importantly, he had trained steadily and consistently during the past year, something he had failed to do before the Fitzsimmons and Sharkey bouts.

Corbett expressed nothing but confidence and said that he was perfectly satisfied with his condition. He believed that he was Jeff's master in generalship and could hit hard enough to put him out. According to the *New York Journal,*

> He looks as strong as at any time in his career. He walks with a springy step, and his eyes are bright, the latter the surest indication of an athlete's good condition. … It must be remembered that Corbett has been training for this battle many months. He began to take care of his physical condition fully a year ago. He worked hard in old John Wood's gymnasium and the result is that he seems to be again the speedy, shifty fighter who sent the redoubtable Sullivan into retirement.[497]

The New York World's W. O. Inglis said that after six months of quiet, steady training, Corbett was like a new man. Inglis said that there was a revelation in store for the sporting world when they saw how big, rugged, and robust Corbett had become. They would wonder how he was a 2 to 1 underdog. He looked like he should be even money.

496 *New York World, New York Sun,* May 9, 1900.
497 *New York Journal,* May 10, 1900.

I have seen Corbett during his training and in his battles with Sullivan, Mitchell, Fitzsimmons and Sharkey, and I never saw him so well and fit, so rugged and strong as he is now. He looks as young today as he did in 1892, when he fought Sullivan. Every New Yorker who knows Corbett, and a few thousand others who think they know him, will laugh at this statement. Let them. They won't laugh tomorrow night when they look at him.

This man has accomplished a revolution. … How has he done it? Simply by long, patient, faithful training, by living outdoors…and by not grinding the vitality out of himself with overwork, as he did in his training for other battles.

Corbett said that he was not well in Carson for the Fitz fight. He had come into camp from the road of acting, and tried to make up for years at the theatrical life by working himself to pieces in six weeks, doing enough work for three men. This time he had better sense, keeping good hours and living regularly for a year. "During October, November and December I worked hard every day in Wood's Gymnasium in New York." He came to his training camp in January and had been working there ever since, except for a couple weeks in March, but even then, he kept up light exercise and his regular way of living. At his training quarters, he had been running long distances two or three days a week, and never working more than an hour and a half a day in the gymnasium. He avoided handball so that he would not overwork.

As he had done with Jeffries, Inglis sparred a couple of rounds with Corbett.

It was like chasing a shadow. … His footwork, always superb, was as easy and swift as ever. His rugged arms looked strong enough to knock his opponent's head a mile off. His feinting and incessant play of the fists worry a man tired. It is impossible to spar with him without getting angry at the impossibility of landing a blow anywhere near him. Meantime, he is dancing about, never within your reach, but always near enough to throw in a hook or a jab or a swing heavy enough to drop an ox.[498]

Corbett also punched the "lively bag" 20 minutes, the 65-pound bag 15 minutes, and then wrestled 20 minutes with 190-pound Leo Pardello. Corbett said he was weighing 183 pounds, but looked 185 and "strong enough to outslug any man he meets."

Regarding the rules, both men agreed not to hit in clinches and to break clean at the referee's order. The experts and writers agreed that the barring of hitting in the clinches was a condition in Corbett's favor, for he preferred outside boxing and was the lighter man. "He can hit, jump away and not be

---

498 *New York World*, May 10, 1900.

compelled to fight his burly rival off when embraced. On the strength of this the impression prevails that the contest may be prolonged unless either pugilist gets home a quieting knock in the early rounds." Hand bandages were also authorized if either one desired them. Corbett especially liked bandages.

Many top fighters and experts thought the bout would be competitive and that Corbett had a good chance to win, given his cleverness and current state of condition. Gus Ruhlin said, "Corbett is in magnificent condition and I expect to see him champion again." Kid McCoy picked Corbett "because he is better than people think he is." Bill Muldoon said if Jeff failed to get a knockout in the early rounds that Corbett would win. Dave Sullivan said that in his present condition, Corbett could defeat any man in the world, and would defeat Jeffries easily. Bob Fitzsimmons said, "Jeffries looks a shade the best, but Corbett is apt to surprise him."

Honest John Kelly said that Jeff would be too strong for him, despite Jim's cleverness. Tom O'Rourke, Sharkey's manager, said, "It will be a hard fight. On form Jeffries should win, but I understand Corbett is better than he ever was. Jeffries is a hard man to beat." Tom Sharkey said, "If Jeffries makes an aggressive fight he will win. He generally makes the other man do all the fighting, but he will have to work harder with Corbett to get the decision." Bob Armstrong said, "Jeffries will win. Any man who can get a decision over Sharkey will defeat Corbett."[499]

Corbett said,

JACK JEFFRIES.   TOMMY RYAN.

JEFFRIES Does TRICKS Like THIS WITH An EASE THAT Is WONDERFUL

---

499 *New York World, New York Sun,* May 10, 1900; *New York Journal,* May 11, 1900.

If I don't beat Jeffries for the championship on Friday night I'll take off my hat to him and say he's the greatest man I ever fought. … Of course, he has improved since he was my sparring partner at Carson. I'm not making the mistake of thinking he is a cinch.

I am as confident of winning as I am sure that I'm alive. I was never so well and big and strong in all my life. Three months' work in the gymnasium last winter, followed by three months of hard work, most of it outdoors, here in Lakewood, have made a new man of me. I am rugged. When I strip in the ring Friday night I will laugh to hear the exclamations of surprise from my kind friends who think I am a dead one. I have endurance to burn.

Jeffries said, "I can truthfully say no man was ever more fit for a long and fast battle, and for Corbett's sake I hope the favorable reports sent out from his camp are true. The victory, which I fully expect to win, will then be all the more decisive. When I enter the ring tomorrow night I will weigh between 210 and 212 pounds." Tommy Ryan said the fight would be easy for Jeff. Jack Jeffries said Corbett would be quickly knocked out.[500]

Giving his final analysis, W.O. Inglis, who had sparred with and observed both men leading up to the fight, said that it was youth and strength against experience and speed. The question was, "Will Corbett's superior speed hold him safe from Jeffries's attacks and keep him free to jolt the champion now and then with a fierce blow when it is least expected? The answer to this is: Yes, as long as Corbett's strength lasts." Jim would have to be able to keep up with Jeff for 1 hour and 40 minutes, or 1 hour and 15 minutes of actual fighting. Still, Inglis felt that Corbett was in good enough shape to make the fight of his life in the large 24-foot ring.

I have seen Corbett every time he trained and fought since 1891, and I have seen Jeffries in all his big fights since he was Corbett's sparring partner at Carson in 1897. There has been some dispute, by the way, as to whether Corbett used to punch Jeff hard out there. On at least two occasions at Carson I saw Corbett shake Jeff up with left hooks to the chin. No one who saw it can ever forget the indomitable courage with which Jeff rallied from these attacks and charged at Corbett like a tiger. In those days Corbett was so much faster than Jeffries with feet and hands that he easily kept out of his way and popped in jolts now and then which startled the big boilermaker.

Since that time Jeffries has fought his way up the ladder to the championship. At Carson he never tried to lunge long, straight blows with either hand, nor did he ever use jabs or jolts, but simply whipped the fists across in short swings. He was slow on his feet. He is as much improved today as a trained four-year-old is better than a raw

500 *New York World*, May 10, 1900.

yearling. Tommy Ryan's coaching and his own active intelligence have made a new man of big Jeffries. He can jab, jolt, lunge, swing or hook as occasion requires. He knows how to get in and out of hitting distance. ... Jeffries hits with tremendous power. He has also developed a good defense – a low, crouching guard with his left arm far out in front and his right well up, which makes it almost impossible for a man even as big as Corbett to get in on a vital point. ...

I may not have been explicit enough as to his hitting power. It is well to remember that he knocked out Fitzsimmons with comparatively few blows; also that he is the only man who ever succeeded in mauling Tom Sharkey so that he had to be helped out of the ring and kept in bed for several days. If he ever lands one of his hard smashes on Corbett the fight will end right then and there.

Can Jeffries land such a blow? The problem is fascinating. At first he won't be able to get within gunshot of Jim. Will he wear Corbett down? He certainly will do so unless Jim's stamina is far greater than it was at Carson City. We are sure that Jim is stronger than he was out there. But how much stronger?

It seems to me that the issue is much in doubt; that 2 to 1 betting is ridiculous and that Jeffries ought on form to win the fight. But no one should be surprised if Corbett goes the distance and wins on points.

Corbett told Inglis,

[Against Fitzsimmons], you saw how tired Jeff got in the fifth and sixth rounds; how his legs gave out and he had to clinch to save himself, grabbing Fitz around the neck and throwing all his weight on Fitz's shoulders. Well, he can't do that with me. The agreement we made stops all those clinches right at the beginning. ... He hits harder than I do, but I know he isn't half as fast. I'll keep out of his way and occasionally throw a hot one into him.[501]

Bill Brady said that the fight would be easy for Jeffries. "Jeffries could have beaten Corbett the best day he ever lived. ... The first time he lands on Jim with a left-hand hook, either on the head or stomach, the end will be near. ... Rumors to the effect that any former friendship I may have had for Corbett may tend to save him tomorrow night are the purest rot." Brady said it did not matter how good Corbett's condition was – he would lose just the same.

Jeffries said,

Corbett is, of course, the cleverest man I have ever met, and I don't suppose I shall ever meet a cleverer one. But you can bet that if I hit him I'll hurt him. He's clever, but he can't keep away from all I send at him. … When I trained for Fitzsimmons and Sharkey I didn't take enough time to do myself justice. I was not half as good as I am now.

Corbett thinks I am slow. I know I may not be as fast as he is, but I also know that I have always been quick enough to protect myself and to land on any man I ever fought.

Corbett said,

If I don't beat Jeffries tomorrow night I will be the most surprised man in the world. We won't be in the ring very long before he will think he is back in Carson getting some of the same old medicine. … No matter how powerful the big gun is it won't do any harm unless it hits what it aims at. Jeffries can't get at me, and I am strong enough and clever enough to keep landing on him. There is the whole battle.[502]

Their results against common opponents were: Joe Choynski – Corbett KO27 ('89), Jeff D20 ('97); Peter Jackson - Corbett NC/D61 ('91), Jeff KO3 ('98); Bob Fitzsimmons – Corbett LKOby14 ('97), Jeff KO11 ('99); Tom Sharkey – Corbett D4 ('96), LDQby9 ('98), Jeff W20 ('98), W25 ('99).

The New York Sun said that Corbett's principal weakness was his inability to punch his opponents into dreamland. Both Fitz and Sharkey were heavier hitters than Corbett was, and they had failed to render Jeff groggy. Conversely, Jeffries knocked out Fitz and "met Sharkey with such terrific right hand body blows that the sailor was in trouble on several occasions and finished fit for the hospital." The question was how Corbett could hurt Jeff or expect to outpoint him without being hurt. Corbett opined that Jeff would not go forward and that he could dance circles around him. However, the *Sun* believed that Jeff did not go to Fitz and Sharkey because he did not need to – they came to him. Furthermore, Corbett did not hit like those men, so Jeff could attack with less fear of running into something. Also, Corbett had never shown himself the equal to Fitz, Sharkey, and Jeff in the ability to receive punishment. Jeffries was stronger, bigger, hit harder, and was not devoid of science.

Still, respected men such as Billy Madden said that he had never seen anyone as lively or as quick on his feet as Corbett, that he had shown great form in his sparring bouts with Ruhlin, was in splendid shape, and expected him to win. The general feeling was that Jim's only chance was to evade Jeff, show his superior skill, and hope to win a points decision.[503]

502 *New York World*, May 11, 1900.
503 *New York Sun*, May 11, 1900.

CHAPTER 23

Trial of Will

On May 11, 1900, six months after the Sharkey fight, at Coney Island's Seaside Athletic Club in Brooklyn, New York, James J. Jeffries defended his world heavyweight championship against former champion James J. Corbett in a scheduled 25-round bout. It was the first time under Queensberry rules that a former champion fought to regain the title.

The men were battling for 60% of the gross receipts, with 75% of that share going to the winner and 25% to the loser. Tickets were anywhere from $5 to $25, in $5 increments.

The day of the fight, Corbett said that when he met Sharkey a year or so ago he was not in condition, but that fight made him realize that if he wanted to regain his lost laurels he would have to engage in an extended course of training, which he had done for the Jeffries fight. "Never in my life did I feel better than I do today. I am like a new man." He was in perfect physical condition, and expected to surprise everyone. "Jeffries will be a lucky man if he can put a glove on me. I'm too fast for him."[504]

> For nine months I have worked to get myself into such condition that I will excel even the Corbett who defeated Sullivan in 1892, and I believe that I have succeeded. I have the endurance and vigor, am stronger and faster than I ever was in my life and feel confident that I know how to fight Jeffries better than either Fitz or Sharkey did.
>
> Jeffries is big, awkward and slow. He is a dangerous hitter and a hard man to hurt, but this contest is a battle for scientific points, and that is where I expect to come in. ... I do not believe that he can hit me enough times to make me stop, whereas I think that I may be successful in jabbing him into a rather battered shape. ... I think people will admit that I can hit. I have never been a slugger, but, as Fitz can tell, I gave him a pretty severe beating and had him licked in the sixth round.[505]

Bill Brady said that Jeffries was the greatest pugilist in the world and would quickly win by knockout. "It makes little difference to me how finely trained Corbett is, for Jeff has prepared himself for this encounter with even more care than he did for Fitz and Sharkey."

---

504 *New York Journal*, May 11, 1900.
505 *New York Sun*, May 12, 1900.

Jeffries said that he had trained harder for this fight than any previous encounter. He felt better than he did before meeting Sharkey and about the same as he did before battling Fitz. "I will enter the ring weighing very close to 210 pounds." Jeff had nothing personally against Corbett, except that "his statement that he knocked me out in Carson City when I was his sparring partner is a lie. He will have a chance to eat his words, however, later on this evening."[506]

The general opinion amongst experts was that Corbett would outclass Jeffries in point of rapid scientific boxing and showy work early in the fight, but that Jeff would slowly wear him down and finally, having tired him out, stop Corbett with one of his tremendous smashes, in about 15 rounds.

Regarding the rules, Referee Charlie White said,

> There should be no clinching and there will be no holding. In the natural course of the fight the men will come together and their arms will become entwined. Each is to step back immediately of his own accord. If either does not step back, I will tell him to do so, and if he does not do so then I will separate them by force. Holding at all is positively against the rules, and as to holding and hitting, that is a breach that will not be tolerated.[507]

However, one source said that hitting with a free hand and on the breakaway was permitted.

Estimates of the crowd size ranged anywhere from 8,000 to 10,000. Betting was light, with Jeff a 100 to 40 favorite. Another said that Jeff was a 3 to 1 favorite.

Jeffries approached the ring first, wearing a blue sweater and long black trousers. He received a cordial greeting, but it was nothing in comparison with the ovation tendered to Corbett when he followed a few moments later.

According to Kid McCoy, Corbett actually entered the ring first, followed by mascot Frank Dwyer, and his seconds, George Considine, Billy Madden, Leo Pardello, Stockings Conroy and Gus Ruhlin. Corbett was wearing a long gray bathrobe and smiled pleasantly as the crowd cheered wildly and waved hats.

Ed Dunkhorst, one of Jeff's seconds, jumped into the ring ahead of Jeffries. Just after Corbett entered, Jeff got into the ring, along with Bill Brady, Tommy Ryan, and Jack Jeffries. Noticeably absent was Bill Delaney.

Fitzsimmons noted that the fight would not be filmed. "Corbett...looked up regretfully at the scanting where the verascope used to be. No pictures."

The two boxers smiled pleasantly and shook hands. New sets of gloves were thrown onto the floor. Corbett selected his desired pair, while Brady

506 *New York Sun*, May 12, 1900.
507 *New York World*, May 11, 1900.

picked up a pair for Jeff. Jeffries would wear new yellow gloves laced with bright red ribbons.

Jeff stripped first, and looked as big as a house, like a rugged bear. "I never saw him look so well as he does tonight. He looks as strong as a big stone wall. His skin is as brown as an Indian's." Jeff wore black trunks and a silk American flag around his waist. His white socks were rolled over the tops of his black fighting shoes.

Corbett stripped, and he too was in fine trim. He looked smoothly modeled. "His flesh is as white as marble except where the hot sun of Lakewood has tanned his face and neck. Every move he makes is a picture of ease and grace and power." Despite his 33 years of age, "he doesn't look more than twenty-six." Corbett looked every bit as big as his listed weight, if not more. His muscles were hardened. He showed a thicker upper body than usual, and his legs appeared stronger than previously. Altogether, he looked quite fit, "a picture of a man in perfect condition." His hair was parted down the middle and his eyes were bright. He wore a white breech cloth.

In point of physique though, 25-year-old Jeffries was far superior in every way. His body was covered with steel muscles. He looked strong enough to pick Corbett up with one hand and pound him with the other. However, the agreed upon rules did not allow that. "That was a wise movement of Corbett's to make the agreement which prevents holding and clinching. It reduces the fight to a simple matter of hitting, blocking and footwork."

Jeff sat in his corner quietly waiting, his hands stretched out on the ropes. He wore no bandages, while Corbett had both hands encased.

The day of the fight, Corbett self reported his weight as being anywhere from 182-185 pounds, which looked about right. In his autobiography, Jim claimed that he weighed 188 pounds. Jeffries was listed as weighing either 210 or 212 pounds. Corbett claimed that Jeff weighed 218 pounds. *The World* said Jeffries looked closer to 225. *The Sun* said, "Jeffries told Announcer Humphreys that he tipped the scales at 200, but in this he was joking. He was at least twelve pounds heavier." Kid McCoy called Jeff the perfect model of the gladiator, "except that he is a little too heavy." He said that Jeff was nearly 6'2" in his fighting shoes, but was so thickly built that "he doesn't look his height until another man stands near him." Corbett, whose body was modeled like a race horse, looked like a boy next to him.[508]

There was some delay, because Referee Charley White was missing. There was some trouble about his fee. The management wanted to pay him $250, but he wanted $500. Another said that the management wanted the fighters to pay him. The club felt that the fighters had to pay the referee because they had selected him, as opposed to the club. After a ten-minute delay, Jeff and Corbett both agreed to give him $250 each. White entered the ring at 10:33 p.m.

Brady came over and objected to Corbett's soft hand and wrist bandages. "That is just a game to try and worry Corbett, because the bandages were agreed upon in the articles when the match was made." After a minute's talk, Corbett agreed to remove one outside layer of each of his elastic tape bandages. Corbett, who generally had hand problems, had insisted on wearing hand bandages under his gloves. Fitz said, "I never wore a bandaged hand in my life, so I can't tell what advantage it might be."

They shook hands and the fight started somewhere between 10:36 and 10:40 p.m.[509]

1st round

Jeff came in crouching, while Corbett met him half-way and feinted. Jeff started to attack, but Jim ran away. Jeff feinted and stepped forward, while Corbett moved and danced about with his lively and shifty ways, tantalizing his opponent with his clever footwork. Jeff followed and rushed Jim to the ropes, where he landed a left to the ribs and right to the top of the head. Jim clinched. After breaking, Corbett landed a left chop to the cheek and got away. As Jeff advanced, Jim landed a quick left hook. Jim got away from another lead and shot a quick sharp left to the eye. He danced away from a heavy swing for the neck. Jeff calmly chased him around the ring. Corbett worked his left rapidly to the head, always dancing away afterwards.

---

508 *San Francisco Chronicle, New York World, New York Sun, New York Herald,* May 11, 12, 1900.
509 The following round by round account and follow-up analysis is an amalgamation of multiple local primary sources, including the *New York Journal, New York World, New York Sun, New York Tribune, New York Times,* and *Brooklyn Daily Eagle,* May 12, 1900. Bob Fitzsimmons wrote the round by round report for the *Journal.* Kid McCoy wrote the rounds account for the *World.* Also amongst the spectators were Tom Sharkey and John L. Sullivan.

Jeffries was not in a hurry, but when he eventually got to close quarters, he drove the left to the stomach and followed with another left on the head. Jim broke ground with both blows and then ran around and clinched as Jeff approached. The referee went between them. Jeff was crouching low. He swung but Jim clinched again. After breaking, Corbett was standing with his hands wide apart, bluffing at Jeff. They both missed some blows. Jeff chased Corbett across the ring and Jim clinched just as he got to the ropes. Jeff eluded two hooks to the head. Corbett hooked again and landed on the mouth. He followed it up a moment later with a hard hook on the jaw, but it was a little too far back to do damage.

Corbett kept at long range, putting in jabs and running around as fast as he could, with Jeff following. When the round ended, the crowd cheered Corbett's splendid cleverness. *The Tribune* said it was Corbett's round. Kid McCoy opined, "Corbett had a little the better of the first round." He felt that both were a bit nervous. Bob Fitzsimmons said, "This fight demonstrates one thing so far, and that is Corbett's cleverness. It is surprising how little he knows about actual hitting."

2nd round

Corbett landed a light left hook on the cheek. Jeff swung his left hard on the chest. They both missed a couple blows. Jeff rushed in, but was so excited that he missed wildly with both hands and they clinched. Jeff came after him but Jim landed a corking left to the cheek.

Corbett was using his wonderfully quick footwork, and continued his jabbing tactics, landing squarely on Jeff's mouth. Jim landed a sharp left on the eye, but Jeff rushed him across the ring and landed a frightful left to the belly which drove Corbett back and jammed him up against the ropes. Jim clinched. After the break, Jeff tried a right for the ribs but Jim ran away. Corbett came back again with a left hook on the jaw. Jeff followed him around, patiently waiting for an opening, but could not get to him.

Jeff rushed at Corbett, who ran away, but then Jim suddenly stopped and planted a right high on the cheek. Jeff jumped at Corbett but Jim swung his left on the belly and pushed Jeff up against the ropes. Jeff sent his head back with a left on the head. Corbett landed his left, but Jeff ripped in his hard right solidly on the body. Jeff kept crowding in and landed a left to the body. Still, Jeffries could only land the occasional punch. Corbett's wonderful footwork puzzled him. Jim's right sent Jeff's head back. Corbett then danced away. Jeff laughed good-naturedly and was still patiently following him.

With rapid leg work and swift movements with his arms, Corbett kept Jeffries moving, unable to get set. His feinting and jabs were very fast. Corbett landed his left to the face almost at will, but his punches had little power. In spite of all the blows landed, there was not a mark on Jeff's face. Jeffries was smiling as if amused by the way that Corbett ran around him.

The Sun said that Corbett made the crowd stand up and cheer during the first two rounds. They appreciated his scientific boxing. "On points so far Corbett had an easy thing." Summing up the significant punches of the round, Fitzsimmons said that Jeffries landed a good stiff punch on Corbett's ribs, but received three wallops on the jaw from Corbett. Again discussing what he felt was Corbett's lack of power, Bob said, "Now, as a matter of fact, any one of them should have put him out had they been properly delivered." Of course, the hard-punching Fitz had also hit Jeff without having an impact. Kid McCoy said, "Thus far Jeff has done most of the following up, but Corbett has landed five blows to Jeff's one." Corbett was successfully using his hit and run-away tactics.

3rd round

Corbett backed and danced around with fast leg work. Quick as a flash he landed his left to the nose. Jeff grinned and came running in with heavy swings, but Jim was not there. Jeff blocked Jim's left hooks for the face. Jeffries whirled around as if on a pivot while Corbett danced easily around him. Corbett was at long range, shuffling, sidestepping, backing around and at times running at full speed. Jeff was patient, until finally with a rush he drove Corbett to the ropes for a clinch. Jeff made another rush and Jim ran away and laughed. Jim landed some light jabs to the body. He often clinched if Jeff got too close.

Jeffries ran in again, missed the left to the body but drove in a heavy right to the ribs just as Jim backed up against the ropes, which clearly distressed him. It was a corker, and according to the *Sun*, Jeff's first effective blow of the fight. Jeff's punching power was strong enough to make it clear that if he properly landed his punches, he could drop the pompadour boxer some time before the limit. However, Corbett was doing all that he could to ensure that Jeffries did not land often or solidly. Jeff took his time. He had plenty of strength.

As Jeffries came in again, Corbett landed a left swing on the jaw and followed with a right on the cheek. Jeff pursued him across the ring and lunged with his left for the head, but Jim ducked. With another swing to the jaw, Jeffries shook Corbett a trifle. Jeff rushed, but Jim was able to keep away. As Jeff advanced, Corbett jumped in and landed a heavy left on the ribs. Jim continued feinting and shuffling until Jeff chased him into a clinch.

Kid McCoy said, "I never saw Corbett so fast and so good." There was not a mark on his body or face. Jim was very clever. *The Tribune* said that in this round, Jeffries was cool and deliberate in his movements, focusing on the body. Fitzsimmons said that Corbett picked up confidence and toyed with Jeff's stomach, while Jeffries pasted in a hard left to Jim's wind.

4th round

Jim feinted, but Jeff ignored the feints and followed him into his corner. They rushed into a clinch. Jim missed some lefts to the body. When Jeff rushed, Corbett clinched and laughed. However, Jeffries was beginning to show his weight in the clinches. When Corbett tried to side-step out of the way at the ropes, Jeff slammed in a good left on the ribs. He rushed Corbett to a corner and Jim clinched again. Jeff chased him from one corner into another corner, but Jim once again showed his wonderful cleverness by ducking, moving away, or clinching without being touched. In one clinch, Jeff swung his right on the cheek, which brought a good deal of hissing from the crowd.

Corbett was very cautious, still sparring, using his legs, but Jeff followed rapidly, rushed Corbett into a corner and landed a tremendous right on the ribs. Jim backed away and Jeff rushed him to another corner, where he pounded Jim's ribs again with a right and left. Jim retreated as Jeff chased him around. When Jeffries got to close quarters, he hammered him on the head and body with frightful force. Jim clinched, but when they broke, Jeff was after him with a great rush and landed heavily wherever he struck.

Corbett began looking a little bit tired. His speed was leaving him and he could not keep away as well as he had done before. Jeff was still attacking, and just as Jim rushed into a clinch, Jeff caught him with a left hook on the jaw. Corbett hung on. Jeff rushed again and Jim met him with a left on the cheek. Jim tried a right for the body and ducked under a heavy left swing. Jim tried right and left and Jeff countered hard on the ear with a right. Jeff rushed into a clinch, with the referee breaking them. Jeff landed a left in the stomach and right that grazed the jaw. Jeff's attack and strong rushes seemed to be wearing him down.

During this round, Jeffries landed a number of lefts to the body that had Corbett looking worried. Jeff paid more attention to the body, likely in his desire to slow Corbett down. Some terrific rights and lefts to the head also jarred Jim. However, Kid McCoy said, "They are both pretty tired now, for it has been a very fast fight thus far."

5th round

Both were cautious. Corbett fiddled with his hands, but did not run as much as before. He shuffled around rather slowly in comparison to his previous work. His blows were not hard enough to hurt the champion, but he landed.

Jeffries did some long-range sparring of his own, and made a face at Jim which brought a laugh from the crowd. Jeff was in no great hurry. He was no longer running in, perhaps pacing himself, or perhaps frustrated by the fact that all his energy-sapping rushes had born little fruit, given that Jim usually clinched, ducked or moved away when Jeff got close. In one clinch, Corbett laughed as the referee told Jeff to step back. The referee would occasionally pass between them after breaking them. Jeff came in again, and Corbett met him with a right to the short ribs and a left swing on the eye. Jim scooted away as Jeff bore in with swings.

Jeffries clearly realized that in order to deal with Corbett's clever footwork he had to do something, and so he focused hard on the body, hitting it with lefts. For a time he made Jim slow down a bit. Still, Corbett continued to move around and jab him in the face. These blows, while not powerful enough to hurt or put him down, over time banged Jeff up perceptibly.

After a clinch, Jeff got in his hard left to the body. Jim did some more jabbing, but Jeff rushed Corbett to the ropes, again ripping in his left hard to the body. Jim clinched again and gritted his teeth. After the referee parted them, Jeff rushed and threw with both hands for the body, but Jim blocked them with his elbows. Jeff swung a short left hook on Corbett's jaw that moved his head and nettled him. Jim clinched hard. Jeff crowded in and Corbett followed his leads with clinches. Jeff forced the fighting and sent the left to the face and body with telling effect at the bell.

Fitz said that Corbett seemed a bit worried. McCoy said, "Honors are easy thus far in the amount of damage done, although Corbett has landed by far the greater number of blows and the cleanest blows." Still, both had landed some good punches in the round.

6th round

Jeff did not seem quite as fast at this point. He occasionally rushed Jim to the ropes, but Jim would duck, block, and/or clinch. Jeff blocked and ducked some blows as well. Corbett moved out of his reach in a flash. He shifted continually to avoid leads, and used his legs for safety, without scoring any blows.

Still, one said that as a result of the hard body blows, Corbett lost some of his speedy maneuvers. Thus, he relied more on clinching. After another clinch, Jeffries asked the referee to make Corbett stop holding. He rushed Jim to the ropes, but Jim clinched just as his back grazed the ropes. "Corbett has held his man very safe thus far." Corbett's clinching worried and bothered Jeffries. At that point, Jeff had slowed down a great deal.

Jim again used the entire ring, dancing around in lively fashion. Jeff followed with a laugh on his face and terrific power in his punches. Jeffries chased him into a corner, hit Jim over the eye with a left, and also drove a right to the heart. Corbett used his skill and sidestepped another rush, drawing applause from the crowd. He was still fast in getting away, but Jeff did not seem to mind and was continually forcing.

Although Jeff did not land many blows, whatever he did land were sledgehammers compared to Corbett's "tack-hammer taps." Jeff made Jim break ground, and all of his rushes were backed up with tremendous strength.

The Sun said Corbett seemed to be tired at the end of the round. Fitz said that it was a fast fight. He felt that Corbett seemed to be getting a little weak. Jeff was solid on his feet, but too solid to shift quickly. "His opponent has plenty of time to duck Jeffries's unscientific swings."

7th round

Jeffries picked it up, looking as if he wanted to knock Corbett out quickly. Jim immediately clinched. Corbett swung a right and left for the head, with Jeff countering on the body. Jeff blocked a couple more lefts and landed some hard body blows. Jeff rushed again and Jim met him with a left hook on the jaw. Jeff kept rushing into clinches.

Kid McCoy said Jeffries lost his temper over the fact that he could not land. He was coming with persistence all the time and drove Jim around the ring until Corbett stopped in a corner and clinched again. Corbett met him with two lefts on the jaw and then ran away. Jeff was infuriated and sent in right and lefts for the body in short hooks, but Corbett evaded them.

Jeffries went after him hard, and sent in powerful and effective rights and lefts to the body. Jeff bore in like a bull, chasing Jim around until they had a terrific exchange of swings. Jeff reached the jaw squarely with the left. Jim was not fazed, but mixed it warmly until they clinched. Fitz said, "Corbett is pretty cagey in the clinch and roughs it in a mix with his old mate. Is he getting tired? Well, it certainly looks this way." Jeff continued his attack until Jim clinched. Corbett went to his corner slightly leg-weary. His speed was leaving him and he was puffing slightly.

The Sun said this was the best round thus far. *The Tribune* said it was clearly Jeffries' round. Fitzsimmons said the round featured feinting, ducking and sprinting by Corbett, who was growing fatigued from all his hard work and Jeff's body shots, so he was forced to stand and fight more.

8th round

As he came up, Jeffries had a slight swelling under the right eye. Jim landed a left on the body and right to the ear. Jeff blocked a left hook and they clinched. Jeff came in with a left to the body that made Jim clinch. Corbett blocked some more body shots. Jim landed a light left on the mouth, a light right on the neck, and a left hook. Jeff forced him to the ropes with a right to the chest and sent his left to the ribs, but Jim reduced the force by putting his forearm in the way. He got away and landed two rapid lefts to the eye.

Jeffries kept forcing the pace, but Corbett effectively dodged blows. Jeff got him to the ropes again and as they clinched, he threw his weight on Corbett. Jeff chased him to another corner, and Jim blocked a left for the jaw.

After a clinch and break, Corbett landed a fierce right on the jaw, and Jeff looked mad. With Jeffries in full pursuit, Jim retreated and ducked a terrific left. Corbett came up with a jump and landed a right to the jaw. He also landed a light left hook on the mouth.

Corbett occasionally stepped inside and landed body shots of his own. Jeff kept coming with ponderous blows which were meant to do harm. Instead of sprinting, Jim stood up to him and landed a right on the body.

Corbett finished the round with a fine rally which set his friends wild. He also rushed in at Jeff with a left on the jaw, but it was light.

The Sun said Corbett rallied in grand style and had the round. He seemed to have recovered his speed. Jeff was more awkward, but stronger. Fitzsimmons said Jeffries "handed the pale face a skyrocket" at the start of the round, but "took a bunch of tickles in the jaw." Kid McCoy said, "Jeff still looks tired, and Corbett is pretty good still. He is in great condition." He said that Corbett was landing at will.

9th round

Corbett rushed in with a left to the belly. He landed a hard right and left hook on the jaw, and followed with a terrific right cross on the chin that staggered Jeff and set the crowd hollering with delight. Jim followed up, rushing in and cutting loose with an auxiliary battery of fast right and left swings, landing and making Jeff retreat to the ropes. Jim had suddenly become a fighting machine, looking to knock Jeff out. He rained in blows with lightning rapidity, bewildering Jeffries, who looked a bit wobbly. Corbett was cleverer in the exchanges and landed his left with regularity.

Despite the many hard and speedy blows that Corbett landed, Jeff recovered fairly quickly and came back rushing in like a bull with lots of strength. Having thrown a number of hard and fast punches, Corbett looked to take a momentary rest. Jeff smiled at Jim and kept forcing. Jeffries occasionally landed tremendous blows to the chest and stomach. Jeff came in without throwing, and Corbett met him with his left shoulder, allowing Jeff to run into it. He kept doing this.

Corbett kept outlanding Jeffries. After a clinch and breakaway, he landed a right to the jaw, but this time it did not jar Jeff. After a few seconds, Jim went in again with left and right swings before they clinched. Fitz said, "If Corbett could only punch hard." Corbett would occasionally time Jeff on the way in with a right or left hook to the jaw. Jeff rushed in with a left on Corbett's stomach. He rushed again and they clinched. Corbett was puffing, but in a moment landed a hard left on Jeff's head. Jim let up his attack, probably because he was rather tired, and Jeff laughed and finished the round with a hard rally to the body.

Because of Corbett's remarkable work in this round, the crowd's wild cheering was deafening and nearly raised the roof. Everyone agreed that this was a big round for Corbett. McCoy said, "This was all Corbett's round. He is doing magnificent work, and twice he had Jeff badly shaken up. Jeff's youth will bring him back in great shape." The Sun said that Corbett had the round "with plenty to spare." The Tribune said it was the best round of the fight up to that point. By Fitz's way of thinking, the real fighting started in this round. Corbett had decided to cut loose with a succession of hard and fast punches in an attempt to hurt or knock Jeff out.

10ᵗʰ round

Corbett continued showing his cleverness, landing straight punches to the face. After each man landed light left chops on the jaw, they clinched. The referee had to tap Jeff on the shoulder and tell him to let go. Jeff rushed and clinched. Corbett missed a right for the jaw, but followed it up with two left hooks, one of which landed on the jaw, and a right which caught Jeff on the cheek. McCoy said, "I guess that Jeff doesn't think that Corbett is a dead one now."

Corbett danced with plenty of life and landed a couple of punches to Jeff's left eye. Jeffries swung wildly and Jim ducked and came up into a clinch. Corbett was just as fast on his feet now as he was in the 1ˢᵗ round. However, he did not move as much, but stood up and fought more. Jim whipped in the blows right and left to the face so rapidly that the champion did not know from where to expect them. Jeff rushed into a clinch.

Jeffries looked slow and sluggish, but he was still very strong. He was on the aggressive, but Corbett, quick as lightning sent in left and right to the face and had Jeff guessing before he knew where Jim was. Jeff came all the time. However, Corbett sparred with confidence and skill. He blocked several body drives and used his feet in getting away from hard blows.

Just as Jeff started in, Corbett landed a fierce left uppercut to the jaw. Jeff clinched and threw his weight on Corbett. White tapped him on the shoulders and half pushed him away. Jeff swung left and right to the stomach, but Corbett blocked him. Corbett was laughing and appeared to be playing with him. The crowd was howling and jumping up and down and clapping. McCoy said, "This is Corbett's round too. In the last clinch, he yanked Jeff around the neck and whirled him half way around him. The veteran seems to be in great shape and he's got Jeffries well measured and worked down so that his 27 pounds' extra weight are not doing him any good."

At the bell, the crowd again wildly cheered Corbett, who had won this round as well. *The Sun* said that Jim's science was magnificent, and it seemed that if he could keep it up to the end, he would win on points. Fitz said, "And still the champion comes up for more. It begins to look considerably better for Corbett, and if he is careful he has more than an even chance." Jeff was no longer attacking as much, sparring more from the outside, which was to Corbett's liking.

In his second autobiography, Jeff said that after the 10ᵗʰ round, when he had lost his wager to knock Corbett out within 10 rounds, he slowed up. Instead of chasing him, he started to follow Jim in his own way, slower and without a rush, but pressing after him steadily.

11ᵗʰ round

Corbett jumped out of his chair and landed a left in the face with great speed, then ran away from a rush which sent him to a corner, but Jeff could not land. However, Jeffries ripped in a left hook under the ear that took some of the smile off Jim's face.

Jeff ran into a left jab, which drew first blood from his lower lip. Corbett landed two more jabs to the mouth which raised Jeff's temper. His lip bled freely. Twice Jeff rushed into a clinch and neither landed. Corbett landed a left hook under Jeff's right eye and made it swell some more. Jim landed several hooks throughout the round.

Corbett's left jabs also brought some blood from Jeff's nose. He landed his left at will. He also continued slipping under Jeff's lefts and hit the body. The puzzled Jeffries swung wildly. Corbett rushed in with a left on the nose and Jeff spat out blood as he clinched. Jeff rushed again with his left on the body, and Corbett hooked his left on the sore mouth again. Corbett ducked a left, but Jeff pulled it back and swung it again in uppercut fashion to the breastbone. Jim smiled at the end of the round.

Everyone agreed that this was Corbett's round. *The Sun* said that the former champion did so well that the crowd went wild. Corbett rained the blows in so fast with both hands that they could not be counted. McCoy said, "This was Corbett's round, too. He had Jeff very weak in the middle of the round. All those hooks he is planting on Jeff's jaws are shaking him up and making him very tired. Thus far Corbett has not received a single severe blow. He is altogether too fast for Jeff and will win if he can keep this up."

12th round

Corbett blocked a rush with great cleverness. He ducked a heavy left and then whipped in his own left to the mouth. In a clinch, both used their free hands. Jeff landed heavily on the ribs. As they rushed together again, Corbett landed a left uppercut. There was another rush and clinch. On the breakaway, Corbett landed a left hook to the jaw and a right to the mouth. Jeff rushed him into a corner but Jim hit him with a right to the lips, which swelled up again. Jim landed his left to the face whenever he let it go. Jeff rushed in and Jim jabbed him on the nose, bringing blood. Jeff crouched more, but Jim straightened him up with a right on the nose that brought the blood flowing more freely.

Corbett was cool and confident, while Jeffries seemed somewhat puzzled because of his inability to land an effective punch. Three times Jeff rushed into clinches without striking a blow. He hung onto Corbett for at least eight seconds. White could not tear him away. McCoy said, "This is Corbett's fight now if he takes it easy. He has Jeff all doubled over, clinching every time he makes a lead. Jeff's face is all red and his right eye is frightfully swollen."

Corbett landed more chopping lefts to the face, which was now spattered with gore, but Jeff was just as strong on his legs as ever. He got close and drove the left into the body. Jim grabbed Jeff's left arm. He drew him in and tried to uppercut him. After that, from the outside, Corbett poured in the jabs and continually hung to Jeff's left with his own right when Jeffries drew close. Jeff was tired, although he made a terrific dash at Jim a moment before the gong.

McCoy said, "Corbett is fresh and cool. He is winning easily bar accident. Jeffries is tired, but he is strong yet and will recuperate." *The Sun* agreed that Corbett continued his remarkable scoring of points, and had a clear advantage in the fight up to this time.

13th round

Corbett blocked a rush and then played with Jeff, using his outside boxing and footwork. Jeff ran into a clinch. After breaking, leaning far over, from that position Jeff threw and badly missed three punches, seeming to have "lost all judgment of distance." At last, he landed a left hook, but it was high on the breastbone and glancing. Jim partially blocked with his elbows a right and left to the ribs. Jim easily ducked another left swing, and then a right. Corbett coolly backed away from a rush, kept out of trouble, and they clinched. Upon another clinch, Corbett accidentally butted Jeff under the left eye with the side of his head. Jim smiled and apologized. Jeff smiled too.

Jeffries rushed Corbett over to the ropes, landed a right over the heart, and left near the solar plexus which made Jim more serious. Jeff went in with determination, but Jim ducked away from the left and blocked the right. Jeffries was forcing the fighting, lunging repeatedly with the left. He was looking for a knockout and rushed Jim to a corner, but Corbett hit him with a right to the cheek. Jim took no chances. He did some clever body checking and laughed good-naturedly whenever they came together. However, Jim was a trifle slower than usual.

Jeffries drove Corbett across the ring in a tremendous rally. *The Times* and *Tribune* said that Jeff landed a left to the body and right to the head that sent Jim staggering back to the ropes. However, the *Sun* said that although the blows were fearful, somehow Jeff could not land any of them to a vital spot. He was as strong as a bull, but Corbett had the science and knew how to avoid him. At the bell, according to McCoy, Corbett walked briskly to his corner, while Jeff sank into his chair.

14th round

Both rushed to a clinch and hung on to each other. Jeff threw a chop, but it only landed on the shoulder. As they were breaking, Jeff swung a right to the eye and Corbett countered sharply on the mouth. After another clinch, in the breakaway, Jeff sent his right in a hook blow on the jaw. Corbett responded with a right, but Jeff ducked and Jim clinched. Jeff was constantly coming in and trying to wear Jim down.

As Jeffries came crouching in, Corbett jabbed and hooked him with his left on the mouth and nose, causing them to bleed again. Jeff rushed in fiercely, swinging left and right, but only landed on Jim's arms as he danced away. Jeff swung for the body, but Jim blocked with his forearm. Jim blocked some tremendous blows. As Jim ducked a right, Jeff chopped down viciously on the back of his neck. The blow jolted Jim for a moment, but it did not slacken his speed, for he came back with a fierce left jab on Jeff's mouth, causing it to bleed profusely. As they clinched, Kid McCoy made signs to Corbett to rip his right over to the jaw, but Jim smiled, laughed, and shook his head, as if to say, "No, I'm going to take my time."

According to the *Sun*, Jeffries paid no attention to the left jabs shot rapidly into his face. He was fighting to wear Corbett into a state of submission. He kept boring in and finally landed a left that slightly shook Jim, forcing him to clinch. Jeff forced the pace faster than before and barely missed a hard right.

The majority gave this round to Corbett. McCoy said, "This was Corbett's round by long odds." *The Tribune* agreed that Jim won the round. One *Sun* writer said that Corbett continued scoring, and his condition was remarkable. However, another *Sun* writer said, "This round was in favor of Jeffries, who did the bulk of the work."

15th round

Jeff rushed fiercely, swinging both hands, but Jim easily slipped away. Corbett used his fast stepping and sprinting, but Jeff rushed with vigor and got him to the ropes, hitting Jim heavily with the right to the neck. Corbett escaped and resumed his jabbing. Jeff came in again and Jim met him with a left jab on the cheek as he was backing away. Jeff rushed, clinched, and hung on so long that White had to go between them to push him off. It was unclear as to whether Jeff was tired or trying to lay his weight on Jim in order to wear him out.

Jeffries was aggressive, while Corbett seemed to be throwing and landing fewer blows. However, Corbett's defensive skills kept Jeff from doing any significant damage, while Jim mostly landed what he threw. Jeff fired a left for the body and then whipped it up for the neck, but it struck the shoulder and slipped lightly over the neck, doing no harm. They exchanged some swings, but Jim was not fazed. Jeff, with his sheer weight and strength, almost pushed Jim over with his left to the jaw, but Jim grabbed him around the neck and kept his feet. McCoy said, "Corbett has got to take it easy, because there is always a dangerous punch in a big man."

Corbett ducked, blocked, and moved away well. Jeff was aggressive all the time but not doing anything effective. Corbett was laughing, and when he took his corner at the bell, he told his seconds that he could stay the limit without any trouble. He was successfully keeping Jeffries on the outside, and tying him up when he got close.

McCoy said, "Corbett is taking his time with him, because he knows he has a sure thing unless some accident happens." *The Tribune* said, "Corbett's work is wonderful, and the Jeffries people look worried." *The Sun* said that the round was about even. However, Corbett was still looked upon as a probable winner.

16th round

Once more Jeff rushed into a clinch. After the referee ordered them to break, Corbett said with a smile, "Why don't you break, Jim?" The referee pushed Jeff away and both boxers smiled at each other. Corbett used his rapid lefts to the face. Jeff paid little attention to the blows, wading in trying to land a knockout punch. Jeffries came in with an infuriated rush, but Corbett laughed as he held him so that he could not hit. Jeff leaned over on Jim, trying to make him carry his weight and not get a rest.

Jeffries was rushing fiercely, but Corbett danced away, exhibiting fine footwork which kept him at long range. "Corbett jumps around as lively as a cricket." As Jim was moving about, he swung left and right hooks on Jeff's jaw, which caused the crowd to break out into cheering. When Jeff got close, Corbett ducked and clinched. Jeff looked tired. He was trying, but Corbett was much quicker and cleverer. Corbett beat a tattoo on Jeff's mouth and nose with his left jabs, but the champion was not bothered. Jeffries kept forcing the fight and eventually reached the body with a couple of heavy lefts and a right. Jeff chased Jim to the ropes, but Corbett held. Jeff swung terrific blows which Jim ducked. He narrowly escaped hitting the referee with one of them. Jeff said, "Excuse me," to White.

The Sun said that the round was even up. Fitzsimmons, who had not chimed in for a while, said that it had been a fairly dull fight from the 12th through the 16th rounds. "I honestly expected more good fighting. … When I say fighting I don't mean boxing. There is nothing really exciting at this juncture." It had mostly been an outside boxing match.

As will be discussed, it was later revealed that late in the fight, possibly after this round, or possibly after the 19th round, Tommy Ryan was no longer in Jeff's corner. He had been advising Jeff to box Corbett at long range, to use his left jab. However, Brady thought his plan was all wrong. Jeff had attacked, but not enough, to Brady's way of thinking. He wanted Jeff to rush savagely and consistently. He therefore ejected Ryan from the corner, as a manager had the right to do.[510]

17th round

Between rounds, the crowd was howling, "Corbett, Corbett, Corbett." Jeff looked desperate and rushed wildly. Jim met him with jabs. Despite throwing many punches, Jeff only landed a right to the ribs. As Jeff rushed in, Jim whipped in the left to the nose and right cross to the jaw, but Jeff

---

510 Some sources say this took place after the 19th round, but they might be wrong. Based on the round by round accounts, it likely took place after the 16th round, because from the 17th round on, Jeff rushed and attacked more consistently. However, the *Police Gazette* later claimed that it was after the 19th round that Ryan was deposed. Sources often got details such as this wrong. The next-day reports failed to mention this incident, but the *Gazette* and Jeff later did.

kept rushing. He mostly missed, but crashed a right to Jim's ear. After a clinch, Corbett darted in with a hard left hook on the mouth. Jeff rushed in with a right on the belly that lifted Corbett up on his toes, but Jim seemed to have gotten away from most of the force of the blow. Although Jeffries swung many terrific smashes, he could not land them, except for the occasional shot, usually to the body.

Corbett's exhibition of skill was beautiful. He backed away and bounded off the ropes. Corbett hooked in his left to the mouth and jaw. Jeff was puffing hard, while Corbett was laughing.

Eventually, Jeffries swung a terrific left on the jaw that shook Corbett to his toes. He followed with a right to the body. Jim clinched, and Jeff slowly pulled his right arm back and pounded Corbett over the kidneys. Many in the crowd howled "Foul!" After breaking, Jim feinted fast. Jeff made a feint, Corbett ducked, and Jeffries swung a terrific uppercut on Jim's breast which almost took him off his feet. Jeff rushed in and missed some left swings, but landed one on the chest. Jim stood up to his attack well by moving, ducking, and clinching. Jeff was just starting a rush as the bell rang. Corbett stepped back and laughed mockingly at him.

McCoy summarized, "For the first time since the early part of the fight Jeff has shown a desire to fight instead of trying to spar with Corbett. But even at that he has done very little." Still, Jeff seemed to be catching his second wind and fighting better. Fitzsimmons said, "Jeffries has discovered the value of velocity and is hurling himself into the fight." *The Sun* said, "Jeff had the round on work." It further said that starting in this round; the pace began to tell on Corbett. Jeff's attack had become more ferocious. Jeffries rushed harder, faster and more consistently in each subsequent round.

18th round

Between rounds, Jeffries was instructed to go right after Corbett, and he did so. He rushed with a left to the body, but Jim countered to the mouth. Jeff was full of fight. He came in fast and strong like a mad bull, with punches that were bound to do damage if they landed. However, Corbett displayed splendid judgment, looking out for the hard punches. Jim blocked and clinched three times. Just as Jeff was getting ready for a rush, Corbett stopped him with a left hook under his swollen eye. Jeff rushed again, but ran his chest into Jim's shoulder. As he set up again, Jim met him with a left swing on the jaw.

Eventually Jeffries got to the neck and body with effect, ignoring the jabs that Jim was raining into his face. Jeff rushed with a left chop which caught Jim on the side of the jaw and neck and jarred him considerably. Jeff rushed again and landed a left on the body, but Jim turned his side away and reduced the force as it glanced off. Corbett backed away from another fierce rush, Jeff being puzzled as to how to hit him. Jeffries chased him all the way over to the ropes, but Jim covered up and blocked the attempted body shots. Jeff rushed in with a left to the pit of the stomach and landed another to the head. Jim stood up to the blows, but did not do much countering because Jeff kept him too busy defending himself.

Corbett landed a left on the jaw and Jeff countered with a right swing for the head which Jim ducked. Each landed a left hook on the jaw, and as they clinched, both seemed tired. As Jeff rushed in Jim sent in a light left swing on the throat and ducked Jeff's swing. Jeffries ended the round with a left in the body and a terrific right over the kidneys.

The Sun said, "This round belonged to the champion on work." Fitzsimmons said that Jeff's confidence had returned, and "Corbett's coy tactics diminish considerably. He has already taken more punishment than I thought him capable of. It is beginning to be a great fight." Still, Kid McCoy noted that Jim was smiling during the minute's rest, with not a mark on him.

19th round

From the start, this round was full of desperate Jeffries attacks. Jeff rushed, but Corbett stepped back and clinched. Also, when Jeff came at him, Jim would turn and stick out his shoulder so that Jeff would run up against it. Jeffries rushed several more times, but Jim side-stepped or blocked the blows. Jim stepped back and landed a left on the mouth and a light chop on the eye, but had little effect. Jeff kept advancing, and rained in the punches so hard that Jim clinched again.

Corbett went down in this round, each source giving its own version.

Tribune/Times: Jeff rushed and forced Jim to the ropes, sending a left to the body and right to the neck. Jeffries scored a knockdown "with a right smash to the ear. Corbett got up like a flash as if the fall had not taken any of the steam out of him."

Fitzsimmons: "Jeffries downs him with a right and left."

Sun: Jeff piled in with tremendous vigor and knocked Corbett down with a right swing on the jaw.

Kid McCoy: Jeffries rushed Corbett into a corner, swung his left on the jaw and staggered him, and followed with a right swing on the neck that jarred him. Jeff rushed and swung his right, but Jim ducked. His foot caught over Jeff and Jim slipped down to a sitting position. He jumped up immediately and rushed at Jeff. "You can see that he has not been knocked down, as he rushes at Jeff as lively as a cricket." However, twice Jim rushed in and clinched.

They all agreed that Corbett rose quickly. Jeff was after him fast and Jim had to clinch. Corbett began to look tired. He countered with some jabs, but was punching less often. According to the *Sun*, Jeff landed a right swing over the ear and brought a little drop of blood from it. Jim danced away as best as he could and landed a few jabs.

Jeffries had the power and strength to keep up his attack, which perceptibly weakened Corbett and took away much of his speed. Fitz said that Jeff severely punished Corbett about the body. "I tip my hat to his gameness." In a clinch, when Jim held onto Jeff's left hand, Jeffries twice pounded Corbett's kidneys with his right. There were some cries of foul. *The Sun* said the punches were legitimate, while McCoy said it was a violation of the articles of agreement.

Jeffries had clearly won the round. McCoy said that Corbett went back to his corner looking very tired for the first time. He was rapidly fatiguing. "Jeff has shaken him up very considerably. Now it will be just how much stamina Corbett has in him." *The Sun* said that it was the beginning of the end. "This round was Jeff's, and Corbett finished very tired."

20th round

Corbett clinched as Jeff rushed and drove his left into his ribs. Jeff rushed again, but Jim glided away. Corbett continued side-stepping and slipping away as Jeff attacked "under full sail." Jeffries mostly missed, for Corbett was elusive again. Fitz said that Corbett needed the rest that "his long distance tactics enable him to enjoy." *The Times* said, "Jeffries rushed at his man like a mad bull, but Corbett side stepped and sprinted out of harm's way…. Corbett's footwork was extremely clever in this round and he surprised everybody who watched him. Jeffries seemed disgruntled at not being able to land a telling blow."

After moving and eluding blows, Corbett came in with a left hook on Jeff's mouth. Jeff chased him half-way around the ring until Jim suddenly stopped and jabbed the mouth. Ruhlin kept crying, "Watch him, Jim!" Corbett was very careful. "He knows he has no strength to waste." Jeffries slowly walked around the ring after him with his left stuck out, but Corbett would not stand still long enough to let Jeff get set for a blow.

Eventually, Corbett began running around so much that for the first time in the fight, the crowd hooted and hissed at his purely defensive tactics. Corbett had made up his mind to keep away even if he did not land a blow, intent on lasting to the end. Sometimes he walked about; sometimes he sprinted, with Jeff always following. He finally stopped and put in a light jab to the face, stepped back, and then came in again with a left hook on the belly. Jeff rushed in at him at top speed, landing a left hook on the neck which jarred Jim for a moment, but he nimbly danced away again, and then clinched when Jeff got close. After breaking, Jeff came forward crouching with his tongue stuck out. Corbett used his generalship and speed to get away. *The Sun* said, "It was Jeffries's round on work."

21st round

Jeffries was out to end matters, boring in all the time. However, Corbett's ability to keep away, block cleverly, and clinch made it difficult to accomplish his desire.

Jim immediately began dancing away as fast as a racehorse. He hooked Jeff on the jaw with the left. Jeffries followed as fast as he could and finally drove Corbett to a corner, and as Jim clinched, Jeff sent in a right to the jaw. After breaking, Jeff came after him with persistency, but not much success. He rushed but Jim easily slipped away. Corbett danced in again and threw his shoulder out as Jeff came at him.

According to Fitzsimmons, Corbett acted as though he wanted to stave things off for 25 rounds, while Jeff acted as though he was afraid that Corbett would do it. "Jeffries has a very bad habit when chasing a man of stopping short with an uncertain movement when he catches up to him. He should punch in flight and upon arrival."

Finally, Jeff landed a couple hard lefts on the jaw, which worried Corbett. In the next rally, Corbett hooked his left and right to each cheek, but Jeff jolted him on the jaw with a left and Jim clinched, momentarily shaken, but not seriously. Jeffries chased him around the ring, only to run into that shoulder once more and a clinch. Jeff hooked his left on the breastbone, then clinched, and smashed Jim in the middle of the back with his right.

On the inside again, Jeffries landed a right to the stomach. *The Sun* said, "Jeff was doing the real fighting now, and whenever he landed a punch Corbett weakened." Jeff missed a right and chased Jim around, only to be clinched. Jeff landed to the body and kidneys at the end. "It was the champion's round." McCoy said that both were tired, but Corbett was still twice as fast as Jeffries. It was a fight between a bear and a panther.

22nd round

Jeffries was out to end matters. He rushed across the ring and landed a left to the stomach that almost sent Corbett down. Fitz said that Jeffries staggered Corbett severely with the first punch, and Jim's legs quivered violently. Jeff then cut loose and with frightful smashes that nearly lifted Corbett off the floor. Jim clinched and used his legs in defense. Jim also drove in the left to the face, but Jeffries came all the time with remarkable strength. Jeff landed a right over the heart that did damage, but Jim ducked a left. Jeff landed two more punches to the stomach, and Jim clinched.

Jeffries would not allow Corbett to run, keeping on top of him with tremendous blows. A right to Corbett's shoulder sent him down to one knee. Jeff's punches were so powerful that even landing on the shoulder could knock a man off balance.

Corbett jumped up immediately and went right at Jeff. The constant pressure had forced Corbett to fight back. They mixed it up in close with right and left jolts on the body. They fought themselves apart from a clinch. Jim landed a left swing on the jaw, and Jeff soaked a heavy left hook on the short ribs. Jim hooked Jeff's sore mouth lightly with the left. They rushed together and Jeff swung his right hard on the kidneys. Jeff twice rushed but hit nothing.

Jeffries never let up in his attack, but Corbett's left counters drew blood from Jeff's mouth and nose once more. The crowd was with Corbett whenever he landed his versatile left. Still, Jim was visibly worried and clinched at every opportunity. Jeff worked his left, and a right to the stomach made Jim retreat. Corbett looked tired as he clinched. On the break, Jeff swung his right on the neck. Then he rushed with a left jab to the stomach. Corbett backed out of range. Jeff rushed in with a short left jolt on the jaw. He rushed madly, landing a left to the head and right to the body.

Jeffries continued forcing matters, landing hard lefts to the neck. Corbett moved well, but Jeff eventually landed a left and right, followed by a left to the body that "jarred Jim considerably. Jeffries was very strong at the end of the round, while Corbett seemed to be weakening." Jim finally recovered his equilibrium and finished the round exhibiting solid defense. Corbett's ability to keep away made it difficult for Jeffries to stop him. Still, Fitz noted, "Jeffries had him to the bad toward the close." *The Sun* said, "The round belonged to Jeffries on work."

23ʳᵈ round

At the opening of the round, Jeffries rushed at Corbett like a bull, but Jim clinched. Corbett blocked some lefts to the body. Jeff landed a couple rights to the jaw, rushed Jim to a corner and Corbett hung on to save himself. Jim blocked a left to the body. Corbett threw jabs and hooks which landed on the mouth and nose and started the bleeding again. Jeff rushed and they both landed left hooks on the neck. Jeff jumped in once more with his left on the belly. Corbett danced away from a rush and came back with left jabs on the mouth, eye and nose, and landed a right to the neck. Jeff blocked a hook.

Each local source gave its version of how the fight ended:

Times/Tribune: Corbett hooked twice to the face, "sending blood spurting again from Jeffries's face. Jeffries threw two hard lefts into the body and smashed his left again on Corbett's face, sending Corbett's head back. Then Jeffries crowded him to the ropes and, with a full swinging left, smashed on the jaw and sent Corbett rolling down and out." Corbett's head struck the floor heavily. He rolled over in a vain attempt to rise, but was too far gone to recover in time.

Kid McCoy: Jeff rushed at Jim "in his clumsy way and seemed just as uncertain as ever where he was going to hit him." Corbett backed away, and Jeff swung his left for the body, but the blow traveled upward, landed obliquely under Corbett's chin, and sent him up in the air so that he fell down in a sitting position. He rolled over on his right side and lay there with his right elbow under him. He struggled to get up, but fell flat and rolled over onto his back. He lay there dead to the world while Charley White counted to ten.

Sun: Jeff rushed him toward the ropes and landed a couple light taps to the jaw. Jim retreated, but Jeff drove a left to the stomach. He followed it with a heavy right high on the ribs and then shot the left straight out from the shoulder "with the force of a hundred-ton weight. The punch caught Corbett squarely on the point of the jaw. He reeled a moment and fell over backward, his head striking the ropes." Jim tried to rise, and for a moment seemed as if he was about to do so, but then his eyes rolled and he sank back down. He was out cold when the referee finished the count.

Fitzsimmons: "Bang, a left on the jaw swung like a catapult. Corbett had made the fatal mistake of overconfidence. He is down and out. He should have won. The cart horse wears the smile again."

Brooklyn Daily Eagle:

> Corbett while full of steam had evaded the massive left. … Time and again he ducked it or blocked it or jumped back from it, but now he was too tired. Jeffries rushed him to the ropes and hit him a right on the body, hooking his left for the face viciously. Corbett drew back from it, but Jeffries repeated the blow very quickly. The ropes were behind Corbett; he could not get away the second time, and he sank down, almost knocked through he ropes by the force of the blow that landed fairly on the point of the jaw.

Police Gazette: Jeff cornered him on the ropes by the southwest corner. Jeff drove a left to the face, feinted a right to the body, and then shot up the left to the jaw with terrific crushing force. Jim fell as if struck by an axe, and his head hit the floor and bounced up. He lay prone and rigid.

As Referee Charley White was counting over Corbett, Jim's manager and second George Considine ran along the edge of the ring, outside the ropes, and tried to use a sponge to sprinkle water on Corbett to revive him. However, Jeffries, who was standing alongside the ropes, quickly moved towards him and swung his long left arm over the ropes to wave him off or shove him back out of the way. They exchanged angry words, but no blows.

Time of the round was 2 minutes and 11 seconds. "It was a clean, decisive and well-earned knockout." The crowd wildly cheered the fight, which they had immensely enjoyed.

After the referee concluded the count, Corbett's seconds picked him up and carried him back to his corner. They placed him in his chair and then put a bottle of ammonia under his nose. After a few moments, he revived, but was still badly dazed. He looked around in apparent astonishment. He wanted to continue fighting, but was very disappointed when told what had happened.

Jeffries approached and said, grinning, "It was a good fight, Jim." Corbett responded, "I don't remember anything about it." After resting in his chair for a while, Corbett revived, stood up, and tottered over to Jeff's corner, still a bit unsteady on his legs. With a smile, Corbett shook hands with Jeffries and congratulated him.

As Jeff left the ring, the crowd cheered him. However, their cheers were even louder when Corbett left. The crowd wildly applauded him for his superb exhibition. He had gained a lot of respect, even in a loss.

Corbett bore no marks save a slight cut over the left ear. Both of Jeff's eyes were black and swollen. His right ear was badly swollen, and his lips were bruised and puffy, almost level with the end of his nose.

Jeffries was highly complimentary towards Corbett, saying that Jim gave him the best fight of his career. "Corbett is the best man I ever went up against." "Corbett is a wonderful fighter, and I give him credit for troubling me more than any man I ever met." It was a much harder fight than he had expected. "Corbett was really a revelation to me and I did not look for such a battle from him." "I was never so surprised in my life as I was at Corbett's boxing."

Jeffries felt that Corbett was in far better shape than he had been in against either Fitzsimmons or Sharkey. "Sharkey and Fitz were easy compared to him." Jeff had been warned several times that Corbett was still clever and one of the most dangerous men in the ring. "I will say that if it had not been for this repeated warning I might not have trained so diligently for this fight and the result might have been different."

Jeff said that early in the fight, he hurt his left arm, the injury initially caused when training for Sharkey. It disturbed him quite a bit during the fight. "Still I kept on with it for I knew it was the only hand I could use with effect, as Corbett got away from the right by wonderful ducking." He felt that he could have ended the fight sooner had it not been for the hurt arm. Subsequent reports backed up Jeff's injury claim.

However, Jeff missed the left as often as the right. "I tried at least a hundred times a certain blow, a left hand hook, and missed each time until the last, and that put him out. He got under my hand repeatedly even when I aimed low to catch his duck. The best I could do was to cut his back up." The reality was that despite being injured, Jeff's most powerful arm was his left, and because he stood in the right-handed stance, his left was closest to Corbett and therefore most likely to land against the retreating dancing master.

Regardless of his misses, Jeffries was convinced that he would eventually land well and knock Corbett out. "The result I at no time felt doubtful of, for I knew I would eventually land the blow that I had been looking for all along."

Jeff was in great shape, and although Corbett's punches did superficial damage, they did not hurt him. Thus, he was confident that he could attack and eventually catch up with him. "I was not in the least bit tired, and although I received many cracks in the face, none of them seemed to hurt me." "I believe I could have fought along for twenty-three rounds more."

The only time that Corbett caught Jeffries with an effective blow was in the 9th round, with a right, but Jeff was more careful after that.

> This was because I made up my mind to knock him out and got a good rap in the jaw because of carelessness. I wanted to keep forcing it for I realized that I could win if I did not let up. I won the fight because I forced it and then tired the other fellow out. ... It was a little slower in coming than I thought it would be, but I never had a doubt that I would land the finishing blow at last.

When he felt the final punch land, he knew it was all over.

Speaking of a potential decision, Jeff said,

> Some of the friends tell me that I would have been licked had the battle gone the limit. That would have been unjust, because I was cutting out the pace and Corbett was running away. Neither Sharkey nor Fitz did this. I guess Corbett was anxious to stay the twenty-five rounds, for he thought he would receive the verdict on points.

Although Jeffries agreed that Corbett had never fought better and was very fast, he felt that he had done more effective work than Jim had. "Corbett is still the shifty man of old, but agility and cleverness are not all in this game. I am not slow by any means, but I rely far more on my ability to administer severe punishment than on showy side-stepping and jabs that have not got the strength to back them."

The day after the fight, Jeffries was bruised and cut up. Court plaster concealed an ugly cut just above the right eye. Below the eye was swollen and discolored. His nose was scratched and his lip was cut. However, his jaw was free of marks. Jeff said,

> These little things don't hurt. Why, those little jabs were just hard enough to break the skin and get my fighting blood up. As for knocking me out there is not power enough in Corbett's left hand and arm to do it. His can hit hard enough with his right, but in order to do so he must set himself for the swing and that makes him as slow as anybody else. I could see when his right was coming over with force behind it and each time but one I got away. Once he landed fairly on my cheek and it shook me worse than all the rest of his blows combined. I saw to it that it did not happen again. ...

> [W]hen round after round went by and Corbett's bewildering speed continued and the expected collapse didn't come, I began to think that there was something in the story that he was rejuvenated. ... I knew I would hit him at last. He could not duck just at the right

moment all night long, and I was so sure of it that I would not adopt any other style.[511]

Jeff admitted that Corbett gave him a "surprise party" and was very clever and shifty, but also said that Jim could not hit as hard as either Sharkey or Fitzsimmons. Still, he said that Jim knew more about the game than Fitz or Sharkey. "If he fights Sharkey the same way he did me last night he will cut Sharkey all into ribbons."[512]

Regarding his future, Jeff said, "I will continue to defend the championship against all comers."

In his second autobiography, Jeff said that he had to time the knockout blow just right, because usually Jim pulled his head back and away from his blows. After he finally landed it, "White could have counted forty before he could get up." Ultimately, Jeff said, "There is no doubt in my mind but that Corbett was the fastest and the cleverest man that ever stepped into a ring, and probably the best timer and judge of distance."[513]

After the fight, Corbett said,

> Well it's too bad. I did the best I could and have no excuse to offer. … When I entered the ring I was confident that I would win and up to the time I received the fatal punch I thought I would carry off the honors. … I was in great shape and but for the final blow I would have easily gone the limit.

Corbett had been so concussed that he did not even remember the knockout punch. "How I got the knockout blow I don't know. I have no recollection of it landing. It must have been a corker, however, to have put me out." When told that it was a left to the jaw that had knocked him out, Corbett replied, "I tried to avoid that all night, but it seems that he caught me."

Unlike most of those who felt that Jeffries had finally worn him down, Corbett's version was that he was not tired, was doing well right up to the end, and was simply caught with a lucky punch.

> I would surely have won, for I had things all my own way. … Jeff did not hurt me as much as some people thought. He got to my body quite often, I'll admit, but the punches were more of the glancing order and did not do so very much damage. Up to the time I was knocked out, I would not have sold my end of the purse for $50,000. I saw victory within my grasp and that is all there is to it.

He further said,

---

511 *Brooklyn Daily Eagle, New York Journal, San Francisco Examiner,* May 12, 1900; *San Francisco Chronicle,* May 12, 13, 1900; *New York World,* May 13, 1900.
512 *New York Sun,* May 13, 1900.
513 *Two Fisted Jeff* at 155-162.

I had the fight won until in a moment of carelessness I left my jaw exposed to a left hook. The same blow had passed harmlessly over my head so many times in each of the previous twenty-two rounds that I had begun to pay very little attention to it. I had him whipped to a standstill, and but for a piece of rare luck on Jeffries's part, would have won the fight.

Giving Jeff some credit, Corbett said, "Jeffries' strength is marvelous. I cut the pace and he followed." He had erroneously figured that Jeff would be the same man whom he had sparred. He found him to be cleverer, and a man who "though not unusually agile, yet more than made up for his lack of speed by powerful blows. For he does strike a fearful blow."

Still, without a mark on his face, Corbett said that he felt good up until the final punch, and wanted a rematch. "I can whip Jeffries. ... I want another go."[514]

The day after the fight, Corbett said that he felt as good as he did ten years ago. He intended to remain in good shape. "It is a great thing to be well and healthy and no one appreciates this fact now more than I do." He again insisted, "I was not badly hurt at any stage of the combat and I think I would have won had it gone the limit."[515]

Referee Charley White said it was a grand, clean battle, and that one like it was seldom seen. "The winner had an uphill fight all the way and the loser deserves all the praise that can possibly be given him. His footwork was simply perfect and he is to be congratulated on his return to his old time form." White said that Corbett never put up a better fight in his life, and that if he had fought that way against Fitzsimmons, he would not have lost the title to him. "The blow that knocked Corbett out was a terrific punch, and I thought it was over when I saw him fall. They are both wonderful fighters, and I dare say everybody in the house was surprised by the stamina displayed by Corbett."

Experts and writers unanimously agreed that everything said about Corbett's wonderful training and magnificent condition proved to be true. He surprised everyone by successfully regaining his old-time form. He was a new man to those who had seen him fight Sharkey. Corbett was pronounced to be in the finest shape of his career since he fought Sullivan. "Last night he was the Corbett who beat the great John L. Sullivan."

Bill Brady agreed that Jeff had fought a Corbett at his best. Considering the fight that Corbett made, Brady was even more satisfied with Jeffries' showing. Jeff had defeated a very sharp version of Corbett, which meant that the victory would earn Jeffries even more credit. Experts agreed. "With all his cleverness and wonderful ring tactics he was not able to offset the

---

514 *New York Journal, New York Sun, New York World, San Francisco Chronicle, San Francisco Examiner,* May 12, 1900.
515 *New York Sun,* May 13, 1900.

terrific rushes of James J. Jeffries, the most muscular and hard hitting champion since the days of John L. Sullivan." Continuing, Brady said,

> Corbett's performance was a big surprise to me. I did not really think it was in him. He was a better man last night than when he fought Fitzsimmons at Carson. He took more punishment and put up a gamer fight. Jeffries was never in danger. He took things easy until the opportunity arrived, and then finished his man.

Corbett's performance was not a surprise to Tommy Ryan, who said that he knew that Corbett was one of the most wonderful men in the ring. However, Jeffries proved to be the strongest, "and in a few years he will be absolutely unbeatable."

Despite Corbett's excellent superior outside boxing, the newspapers' round by round accounts noted that even in many early rounds, Jeffries landed strong body shots, and at times, hurt Corbett with these blows, including in the 4th, 5th, 7th and 8th rounds. When Jim was briefly in distress in the 5th round, Kid McCoy yelled to Corbett, "Punch him in the jaw, Jim!" and like a flash, Jeff squarely landed a right to the jaw. The bell rang "not a moment too soon for Corbett." McCoy said, "I forgot there were two Jims in it." He had meant to encourage Corbett.

Overall, though, Corbett boxed and countered well, landing punches to the body and head, outpointing Jeffries. In the 9th, Corbett came out of his corner full of fight and for the first two minutes landed a bunch of left jabs to the face. On the inside, Jim landed a hard right to the jaw, and followed it up with a grand rally of blows that caught Jeff on the jaw and had him hurt and staggering for a short time. It was the only point in time when Corbett made his blows tell and he came near winning outright. But Jeff recovered quickly, for he could take it. "Jeffries was not hurt worse than a temporary shock…for Corbett's efforts did himself as much damage as they did the big gorilla like man in front of him. Jeffries is like no animal so much as the biggest of the ape tribe." Trying to finish Jeff caused Corbett the expenditure of a great deal of energy. Jeffries recovered and gave a grand exhibition of rough fighting that put Jim on the defensive. Jeff tried to throw his weight upon Jim in the clinches, to wear him out, and the referee warned him against roughing it more than once.

After the 9th round, Corbett did not use his right very often, except in the clinches. Some wondered if he had hurt it, but he made no such claim afterwards, so "it must have been that he was afraid to risk it, his left hand doing all the execution."

One writer said, "Corbett retained a shade the best of the fight during the next six rounds." Another said that Jim's left jabs were able to stop Jeff short in his rushes, enabling Corbett to have things his own way from the 9th up to the 16th rounds. A third noted that Corbett made Jeff's nose bleed in the 10th and his lips bleed in the 11th, landing at will. He outpointed the champion in subsequent rounds.

It seemed that Corbett had studied Jeff so well that he knew just how to fight him. He danced around him rapidly and threw in left-handers that made Jeff blink and shake his head. Jim weaved in and out, avoided great rushes and heavy blows, blocked drives that might have broken his ribs, and showed wonderful defense. For 15 rounds, Corbett was confident of victory, and his face showed it, laughing at Jeff and toying with him as if he were a sparring partner. Corbett was still fresh in the 16th round.

However, from the 17th round on, Jeff's staying powers began to turn the tide of battle in his favor. Jim's blows did not have enough steam to deter Jeffries, who started rushing desperately. When Jeff began to get to Corbett with his terrific body punches, the pompadour pugilist's face gradually assumed an ashen color. He became more and more apprehensive. Although Jim was game, he knew full well what to expect if Jeffries landed one of his big fists upon the proper mark. Still, Jim took a hard punching without quitting. Up until the 18th round, most thought that Corbett would get the decision on points at the end of 25 rounds.

However, one said that Corbett fell off very badly in the 19th round. "Jeffries came from his corner with instructions to finish his man, and from the way he mauled and pounded Corbett around the body made it appear that Corbett could not stand the round out." Jeff knocked Corbett down with a right. Still, Jim showed great judgment when in danger, for he ducked and blocked, and finished the round smiling.

Corbett used his footwork and blocking ability to escape in the 20th and 21st rounds. He was in distress and devoted most of the time to sprinting, only occasionally landing a snappy left to the nose. "Jeffries continued to rush and bore, to throw his weight into the collision and to do anything, to hit anywhere, just so it was a shock."

Jeff jarred him with some head and body shots in the 22nd, and Corbett was weakening, while Jeff was still strong.

Jeffries finally caught up with him in the 23rd. Corbett was so tired that he could no longer run, but was still trying to evade. Jeff rushed viciously and threw quick blows. Corbett mixed it up, ducked, and smiled, still hopeful that he would last it out, but in the next rush, he backed to the ropes, and that time, there was no escape from the left hook to the jaw.

There was some later criticism of Tommy Ryan as a cornerman, while Bill Brady was complimented. Ryan had Jeffries stand at a distance and try to spar and box with Corbett. Apparently, he had persuaded Jeff that he could box Corbett into submission, "and the absurdity of his advice was apparent every time he tried to engage in an exchange of long arm hostilities."

> The plan of battle outlined by Tommy Ryan, who was the chief adviser in Jeffries' corner, would have caused the shifting of the coveted title to Corbett had not Brady, at the end of the nineteenth round, ordered Ryan from his lofty position in Jeffries' corner.

"Come down out of there," ordered Brady, pulling at Ryan's leg in a nervous manner. Ryan crawled through the ropes and Brady mounted the platform, pulled off his coat and began advising the champion in an earnest manner. Ryan had advised Jeffries to meet Corbett at his own game. He made the big boilermaker believe he could outspar the scientific Corbett.... Brady immediately changed the plan of battle when he entered the champion's corner, and he told him that his only chance of winning was in landing a knockout punch. Brady was worked up then. He saw the game slipping away from him. "Go in and slug," said Brady, with emphasis. "Never mind sparring. He's too clever for you. Don't attempt to outpoint him." Jeffries followed these instructions to the letter. From that time on he took every possible chance and suffered great punishment. ... In the final rounds Jeffries made a furiously aggressive effort. He constantly hurled his huge body against the comparatively slender Corbett and threw in volleys of crushing blows with force enough to fell an ox. ... A less nimble and agile man would have found it difficult to elude his giant pursuer as long as Corbett did. ... The success which accompanied Brady's instructions now make pugilistic history. This is the second time that defeat has been turned to success by Ryan being deposed and his plan of battle reversed.[516]

In his autobiography, Jeffries said that Brady told him after the fight that Ryan's advice made him suspicious. Brady thought Ryan was trying to make Jeff lose. He felt that Ryan had Jeff spar and box with Corbett too much, that Jeff should have been attacking and pressuring a lot harder and more consistently. Brady eventually kicked Ryan out of the corner, but the two men exchanged harsh words before Ryan relented. Brady told Jeff to attack and knock Corbett out or else he would lose a decision. "Your only chance is to knock him out. Forget everything about boxing and go out and fight." From that point on, Jeff attacked and never gave Corbett any rest. He noticed that Jim was wilting and could not stand the pace or his powerful body shots.[517]

Although a slight majority felt that Corbett would have won a decision had it lasted the distance, there was no consensus. Some said that Jim could not have obtained better than a draw, while others said that Jeff would have earned the decision given his strong finish, aggressive tactics, and more

---

516 *National Police Gazette*, June 2, 1900.
517 *My Life and Battles* at 42-43. After Brady mounted the apron and told Ryan to get out of the corner, Ryan responded, "Get down or I'll bust your head." Brady jumped down and got two policemen with clubs. He then ordered Ryan, "You get away from this corner." Ryan replied, "Get away yourself before I take a punch at you." Brady insisted, "This is my club and I'm Jeff's manager. ... If you don't get back there and keep still I'll hand you to those two cops, and they'll rap you over the head and throw you out." Ryan gave in.

effective blows. Ultimately, it did not matter, because Jeffries had finally caught up with him and ended matters.

One writer said, "Up to the twenty-first round Corbett would have won a draw in all probability." However, in the 21st round, Jeff had the upper hand. The next two rounds were all one way in Jeff's favor. Hence, Jeff was on his way to a victory.

The Journal said that up to the 20th round, no one in Jeff's corner thought that he would win. "Brady was nearly crazy." They all thought that they would go broke losing their bets on Jeff. "None of Jeffries's friends deny that they are glad the fight did not go to the limit, as a decision on points must have been against their man."

The World said that Corbett fought a wonderful battle and for more than half the distance had the champion at his mercy. With cat-like agility, he was able to step in, deliver a blow, and then get away cleanly. Jeff swung time and again with force enough "to break iron," but Corbett kept away. Corbett hit him at will, landing four to one. His cleverness amazed everyone. However, it also said that up to the knockout it was anybody's fight.

The New York Sun said, "Had the bout gone the limit the decision would have been a draw with fairness to both men. But because of Jeffries's superior strength, his incessant leading and his marked advantage in the last half of the fight it would not have been fair to have given the decision to Corbett."

The Brooklyn Daily Eagle said that if the fight had been scheduled to a finish, no one would have ever doubted that Jeff would eventually win, but at times during the limited rounds contest, it looked like Corbett might last the distance and win on points. However, Corbett's science finally succumbed to brute force.

> Had the battle ended as the men stood from the fifth to the sixteenth or eighteenth round Corbett would have been entitled to the decision on points for he punched and stabbed Jeffries in the face until the champion's countenance looked like a raw hamburger steak. ... But from this point the one time champion began to tire, slowly at first and then became so weary that it was work for him to hold up his hands. ... Corbett was spent. The body blows that he had received had destroyed his scant supply of reserve force and he began to lag dreadfully. His fast foot work weakened.

Once he was too tired to avoid Jeff's blows, the end was near, and the knockout blow eventually landed.

Another *Eagle* writer opined that "barring the knockout blow, it was a certainty that Corbett would receive the decision. He out-fought and out-boxed and showed more ring generalship than Jeffries from the very beginning and at times made him look like a cheap amateur." However, Jeff's constant rushing and boring tactics finally worked. He had shown his bulldog tenacity and perseverance. "The fight proved that the skillful light-hitting boxer cannot cope with the rugged heavy hitter who is willing to take all kinds of chances to land a knockout blow. Not being able to hit hard showed Corbett's one weakness and lacking this important feature cost him the fight."

The National Police Gazette said that Corbett "gave the most marvelous exhibition of scientific pugilism ever witnessed in the annals of fistic history." He had "demonstrated beyond question that so far as the scientific quality of his work is concerned he is the peer of any fighter, living or dead, the world has ever seen." It felt that up until the time of the knockout, no one would dispute that Corbett had the best of the battle on points.

However, it also noted, "Jeffries' superior weight began to tell a couple of rounds earlier, and he was gradually wearing Corbett down." The blows that Jeff landed to the body were hard and effectual. Although earlier Jim had recovered quickly as a result of his fine condition, he was gradually broken down. Summing up, "the battle was simply a contest between a boxer - the best in the world from a scientific point of view – and a fighter with weight, strength and gameness, a combination of qualities which Corbett simply could not overcome."[518]

The New York Tribune said Corbett had an excellent chance of winning if it had gone the distance. Jeffries "was clearly outboxed."

However, the *Tribune's* round by round account made the bout sound more competitive than the overall analysis would lead one to believe. The description gives the impression that it was competitive early, that Jim took over through the middle rounds, but that Jeff kept pressing and hitting the body, with his strength, willpower, and conditioning taking over late as Jim became fatigued and worn out. *The New York Times* agreed that Jeffries "showed bulldog determination that was unwavering."

The New York Clipper said that Jeffries was aggressive, "caring nothing for the ineffective punches landed by Corbett." Although Jim did no material qualitative damage, he appeared to better advantage with his astonishingly clever, quick and shifty points boxing style. It said that had a decision been given on points, Corbett would in all likelihood have received it, "for he did almost all the leading, planted innumerable hits that were perfectly clean, if lacking in steam and punishing power."[519]

The New York Herald said, "Corbett is endowed with more gray matter than two ordinary pugilists…. He is the master of masters in cleverness and defensive work, but he cannot deliver a knockout blow…. But Corbett should have assured himself at least a draw."[520]

A couple days after the fight, the *World* said that opinions differed markedly regarding who would have won had the fight gone the distance.

518 *National Police Gazette*, May 26, 1900.
519 *New York Clipper*, May 19, 1900.
520 *New York Herald*, May 13, 1900.

"Some declared for Jeffries because he was aggressive and his face was always to the enemy. Others thought Corbett because he landed oftener, and others thought that White could have called it nothing but a draw."[521]

The post-fight analysis was quite mixed. In general, the newsmen were high on the fight and complimentary towards both fighters, perhaps even more so towards Corbett, who had rejuvenated himself and fought masterfully. Various newsmen alternately emphasized the strong and weak points of both fighters.

The New York Tribune said everyone agreed that Corbett had fought a remarkable battle, showing his old form, employing his strategy of jabbing and getting away. His defense was almost perfect.

Jeffries showed his ability to set the pace, take a punching, and go any distance and still punch hard, showing strength and vitality up to the end. That said, the fight "showed that a fast man can reach him and get away without a return. If that fighter of the future happens to be strong and rugged in addition to being fast he will take the honors." Of course, the flip side of this argument was that Corbett was able to get away better because of the fact that he was not punching as hard. To punch hard would mean that he would have to sit down on his feet more, which would also mean that he would be in Jeff's range longer and more often, which could have meant that he got hit more often and more cleanly, and possibly knocked out sooner.

The Sun said that the fight demonstrated that Corbett was the most expert boxer in the world and game to the core. However, Jeffries' indomitable will, strength and condition were able to overcome a Corbett at his best.

> In point of boxing skill, generalship, blows of every description and speed, Corbett while he lasted made Jeffries look like a lumbering amateur. But Jeffries had the strength to stand all the rapid jabs that were fired into his face even though they drew the blood from his nose and mouth, and when Corbett began to tire, the big boilermaker with tremendous rushes wore him down and finally dropped him with a left-hand punch on the jaw.

> The knockout came unexpectedly. It was the result of constant boring tactics. Jeff had tried for twenty-two rounds to get in just such a blow and had missed his man time and time again. But with bulldog tenacity and perseverance the champion finally succeeded and when Corbett got this blow he was put to sleep beyond any question of doubt.

> It was the old story of a magnificent boxer meeting a rugged, muscular, heavy hitter capable of taking all kinds of punishment in

---

521 *New York World*, May 13, 1900.

order to get in a decisive smash. Corbett showed one weakness. That was inability to hit with the power of Fitz and Sharkey. He got to Jeff oftener and better than either of these pugilists did, but his blows, beyond bruising the champion's eyes, nose and mouth, did not beat him down.

Jeffries had shown his versatility from fight to fight. He had been more defensive-minded against Sharkey and Fitz, allowing them to force the fight, carefully picking his punches, but he was more aggressive against Corbett.

> Had he remained on the defensive as he did with the Cornishman and sailor, Corbett would undoubtedly have won hands down on points. When the fight was half over this was appreciated by Jeffries's seconds who saw that Jeff, though he had forced the fighting from the start, had not forced it hard enough to make an impression. Then it was that [Jeff's corner] sent him out to beat Corbett down by sheer strength and resistless rushes, which proved to be the winning combination.

Although outclassed in science by a man of remarkable ability, "Jeffries showed once more that he is a fighter pure and simple, that he can take punishment and give it."

The Brooklyn Daily Eagle said of Corbett's tactics,

> His plan of battle was to stay away, to protect himself always and not take any chances with a counter, to keep his right hand until absolutely, positively certain that he could use it safely and to be content with an occasional left to the face. That was all that he did or tried to do during the whole journey.

Corbett used his clever footwork, darting in and out, ducking and blocking, clinching when necessary, and stabbing away with a "nasty tantalizing left."

Despite its criticisms of him, the *Eagle* granted, "Jeffries is more clever than most people who saw last night's battle think; he looks clumsy because he was shown in contrast with the fastest boxer in the world." "Jeffries took the offensive from the start, and whatever his other failings he must be credited with great patience and good control of temper. His favorite blow was a left swing that Corbett ducked so cleverly that Jeffries actually became bewildered." The right to the body that Jeff had often used against Sharkey did not land as often on Corbett because Jim blocked it with his left arm. "Nevertheless, Jeffries put in several very handsome body blows and it was these beyond doubt that weakened the ex-champion to the fatigue stage."

According to the *New York Journal*, from the start of the fight, Corbett backed away, sidestepped, laughed, ducked, blocked, clinched, circled and shifted about in every direction, and once in a while stopped to feint or punch. "But there was just steam enough in the blows to break the skin of the champion's lips and puncture the membrane of his cheeks with the loosened teeth." His boxing was not powerful, but beautiful. "Taken all in all, there has not been such an exhibition of scientific boxing since the days when Corbett graduated from the gymnasium of the Olympic Athletic Club." In boxing skill and finesse, Jim had proved himself Jeff's master.

However, Jeffries hit the body, and showed that he always had reserve strength to use at the end of fights. "Once again Jeffries came out of a state of lethargy with the bound of a great chunk of rubber, even as he did in the Sharkey fight." After the 20th round, the time was ripe for vicious rushes.

> Jeffries had faith that sometime, somehow or other, one of those cruel, ram-like left swings would strike the frail mechanism of the boxing master before him and fell him. And so it happened. … Fifty times, or perhaps seventy-five, Jeffries had tried that left swing, now for the jaw and now for the abdomen, before the chance befell when it landed.

> Corbett was not careless at the moment. He was not stunned from the repeated collisions with the rushing form of the giant who came at him like a stampede of prairie bulls. His eye was clear as in the first round, and his ankles and arms as shifty as human joints are made.

It apparently disagreed with the majority of those who felt that Jeff had gradually worn Corbett down.

Summarizing his round by round report of the fight for the *World*, Kid McCoy wrote,

> Jim Corbett lost…but he made a magnificent struggle, leading all the way until he was suddenly dropped with a left upper cut on the jaw after 2 minutes and 11 seconds of fighting in the twenty-third round. He showed that he was just as speedy and as clever as ever and he made a show of Jeffries right up to the last two rounds. He was fighting the big fellow carefully and made him look like a novice for an hour and twenty minutes. What beat him was Jeffries's youth and strength and heavier weight.

> If Corbett should meet Jeffries again I would not be a bit surprised to see him win, although he would always run the risk of being knocked out just as he was tonight.

> There is no denying the fact that Jeffries is fully entitled to his championship honors. He won them honestly, and he is wonderfully clever for such a big man. He took a good deal of jolting and jabbing from Corbett and had enough recuperative power left to finish him at last.

Regardless of the victory for Jeffries, "no vanquished gladiator ever received such attention." The press gave much of the glory and credit to

Corbett. The fight proved that Corbett "told the truth when he said that while using Jeffries as a training partner at Carson City he was able to hit him when and where he pleased."

Still, the *Police Gazette* complimented Jeff's determination and said that his victory was a great one, "the greatest he has ever won." He left the ring with his eyes puffed, lips cut and bleeding, and nose battered, proving his courage.

> Jeffries deserves much credit for his gameness, which undoubtedly helped him more than anything else to win such an up-hill contest. He never lost confidence in himself and did not overlook an opportunity to get in a telling blow.... [H]e did not get rattled and stuck to his job until he finally won out. Had he gone to pieces when he realized he had the Corbett of old before him there might have been a different story to tell. But he didn't. When he saw that he had a tough time on hand he settled down to win out like a champion, and that's what carried him through. It was the most interesting battle in the history of the ring and reflects credit on the man who so fairly won and the man who so gamely lost.[522]

Several days later, "Right Cross," writing for the *New York Journal*, gave Jeffries his just due credit. He said that Corbett's fancy boxing, with all his blocks, slips, and side-stepping, was pretty to look at, but the real fighter needed a wallop in order to take home the money. Big Jim Jeffries might not have been pretty, but he had the punch.

> While the stabber is playing a quick-step on his face and body, [Jeffries] manages to keep all vital spots free from the tattoo and, through the rapid fire of his antagonist, he sends in a heavy solid shot that does more damage in an instant than the scattering grape would in twenty-five rounds of battle.

> It is this ability to stand jabbing without being jolted off his feet or even budged from the set of his own lead or counter that has won victories for the champion. ... Jeffries is clever enough to mix it and win by the superiority of his crushing punch.

He said that Corbett's concern was too much on the lines of self-defense, rather than what he was going to do to the other fellow. "When Corbett lands a punch, the uppermost thought in his mind is to get away from the return." Therefore, he did not have the same power behind his blows because he was looking to get away. Fitzsimmons occupied a middle ground. He was able to give a punch and take one. He had stamina and cleverness, and probably the best "ring head" around. Summing up, "The cleverest blocker at the game must take the loser's end when opposed to

---

522 *National Police Gazette*, May 26, 1900, June 2, 1900.

the man who has the knockout blow." This was especially true in a long fight when the puncher had the stamina to keep punching hard, and could avoid damaging blows while attacking. That is why Jeffries won, and it did not matter how many rounds it took him to do it.[523]

Regarding the financial result of the fight, "It was said that Jeffries had won $33,900 and Corbett $11,300." *The World* said the gate receipts were $34,000, with the winner's share being $15,300, and the loser's share $5,100. Tom O'Rourke said the receipts were a trifle over $33,000. Half went to the club and the remainder to the fighters, to be split 60/40 winner/loser. "This would make Jeffries's share about $9,900 and Corbett's about $6,600. The impression prevails, however, that the receipts were nearly $40,000 and that the fighters received a guarantee of $10,000 each."[524] Some later said the receipts were closer to $60,000. As was often the case, the true numbers and split were not necessarily revealed.

Jeffries was complimented for having defeated the three cleverest, toughest, and greatest fighters in the world – Fitzsimmons, Sharkey, and Corbett, all within one year. Very few heavyweights throughout history, including up to the present day, could say that they fought the three best men in the division in the span of one year. Jeff had put three very big names on his resume, which earned him a lot of respect and admiration. It was natural that the division's best would give him tough fights, but he had come through them all with victories. In doing so, he had proven that he could defeat multiple styles, and adapt to them.

The fight showed both the good and bad of Jeffries. He was not the polished quick outside boxer that Corbett was, but at that time, strength and stamina were often more important because the fights were of such a great duration. A strong fighter who could take it for a long time could eventually break his man down and land a big one against the tiring boxer, as was the case in this fight. Despite being outboxed, Jeff demonstrated unbelievable will, determination, a good chin, and excellent conditioning, maintaining his punching power even late into fights. Jeffries was well suited to a championship system where bouts were quite lengthy. He was about long-term effectiveness rather than points, and he knew how to pace himself accordingly. He was a fighter.

Another way to look at it is that Jim Corbett's speed, footwork, and relaxed punches would have given anyone trouble. Sullivan was an aggressive burst fighter who wasted energy attacking Corbett too much early on. Jeffries was not as quick or as ferocious as Sullivan was, but that helped him set a more even pace and gradually break down an opponent like Corbett, who was not easily caught in the early rounds. By keeping himself in reserve more, the very thing that brought him a great deal of

523 *New York Journal*, May 16, 1900.
524 *New York Sun, New York World*, May 12, 13, 1900.

criticism actually helped Jeffries remain strong in the later rounds so that he could attack when he had Corbett fatigued. Fitzsimmons had shown that a consistent, determined attack was the way to defeat Corbett. Jeffries had to face an even better conditioned version of Corbett.

So, the question was whether Tommy Ryan's more deliberate strategy was the correct one. He probably should have had Jeffries press more. Jeff might have caught up with Corbett sooner if he had been attacking more ferociously and consistently earlier in the fight. However, Jeffries also could have drained himself missing Corbett and using too much energy early in the fight, when Corbett was fresh and his defense at its finest.

Another thing to consider is the fact that Corbett stunned Jeffries in the 9th round. Attacking could cause Jeff to run into Corbett's punches, doubling their power. This is how Corbett had allegedly hurt Jeff in sparring. Perhaps this is the real reason why Jeff grew more cautious and took his time more, not wanting to run into a punch and give Corbett a chance. Jeff was more willing to attack hard later in the fight, after he had Jim a bit more fatigued. Ryan might have factored this into his strategy of advising Jeff to take his time and box on the outside with his jab, to pick his moments of attack, to press calmly but not to rush in recklessly.

However, it is also clear that the strategy that Brady had Jeffries employ late in the fight was successful, and the correct and necessary one for that point in time. Brady felt that Ryan was trying to make Jeffries into too much of a cautious, outside boxer, as Ryan was, rather than maximizing Jeff's strengths.

After the Corbett bout, Brady got rid of Ryan, brought Delaney back, and had Jeff fight more aggressively. They had seen the Ryan style lead to a close one with Sharkey, and put him in jeopardy until late against Corbett. That was enough for Brady.

Ryan might argue that his style - use of counters, the crouch, more of an outside game, sliding back, allowing opponents to come to him, kept Jeff defensively sound, efficient, and always finishing strong. The more aggressive, attacking and leading, upright style led to Jeff getting hit more. However, he also got more knockouts, and got them faster, which actually gained him more credit for his ability as his career progressed. Regardless, James Jeffries could employ either style.

CHAPTER 24

The Bevy of Battles
as the Horton Era Ends –
Ruhlin, Sharkey, and Fitzsimmons

Following the Corbett fight, James Jeffries said that he had done a great deal of fighting in the past year, and wanted a rest. He needed time to heal his left arm properly. Jeff had earned some time off. Excluding exhibitions, in the span of one year, from June 1899 to May 1900, he had fought 60 professional rounds. In today's terms, that is the equivalent of five complete 12-round title fights.

A few days after the fight, the *World* reported that Jeff's left arm was in very bad shape and might need elbow surgery. "The injury lies in the elbow at the junction of the three bones of the arm. One of three bones, the doctors say, has been torn from its socket and has slipped down about a quarter of an inch. Its point presses against one of the others and prevents the arm from being straightened out."[525]

On May 17, just a week after the Corbett fight, Jeff umpired a game at Reading, Pennsylvania. Afterwards, before a crowd of 2,000 in the local auditorium, despite his injured arm, Jeffries gave a 4-round exhibition with Jack McCormick, the trial horse whose record included 1898 LKOby8 Gus Ruhlin; 1899 L6 Joe Choynski, L6 Ruhlin, and LKOby18 Jack Finnegan; and 1900 LDQby5 Stockings Conroy, LKOby1 Tom Sharkey, and LKOby7 Jack Johnson.[526]

So, how hurt was his arm? Within a few weeks, the *National Police Gazette* reported, "Jeffries now says there is nothing the matter with his left arm, and he is willing to fight any man in the world, giving Corbett the preference." In response to Corbett's claim that he lost by accident, Jeff said, "I am quite sure I can bring about the same kind of accident if we come together in the ring again." It is possible that Jeff's manager Bill Brady issued these statements.[527]

All of the managers wanted to make matches before September 1, because after that, the big New York purses would be a thing of the past.

---

525 *New York World*, May 14, 1900.

526 *Philadelphia Public Ledger*, May 18, 1900; Boxrec.com.

527 Corbett needed time to nurse his hands. Furthermore, his rejuvenated popularity was enabling him to make $1,200 a week making appearances. "He now intends to take advantage of the situation and is booking himself for a tour which will extend well into the summer months."

Brady said that following September 1, Jeff would start with a theatrical company and not put on the gloves again until the following May.

In the meantime, Jeffries was making money touring around umpiring baseball games. He had been showing people his damaged arm, which was now encased in plaster of Paris. So, the arm was indeed badly hurt.

Owing to an injury to his left hand, Bob Fitzsimmons required a postponement of his scheduled bout with Gus Ruhlin. His hand had been hurting since the Dunkhorst bout.

Tom Sharkey had been scheduled to fight a rematch with Kid McCoy on June 26, but McCoy pulled out for dubious reasons. He said, "I called the fight off because I think that training hard in the summer time throws a man into consumption." The truth was that after already having been knocked out by Sharkey, McCoy knew that he could not defeat Tom and did not care to try again. McCoy would eventually make a summer fight with Corbett instead.

Both Ruhlin and Sharkey were looking for opponents, so they agreed to meet each other. Ruhlin always contended that his 1-round knockout loss to Sharkey was a fluke, and wanted another try. Plus, that was two years ago, and Gus had improved since then.

Corbett said that Ruhlin had made marvelous improvement in his boxing ability since sparring with him, and was one of the world's most proficient exponents of the fistic art. "Corbett is very enthusiastic in his admiration of him and predicts that he will not alone beat Fitzsimmons but will eventually take Sharkey's measure and also defeat Jeffries."[528]

Since the Jeffries fight, Sharkey had been on a six-fight win streak, all of them by knockout, including: 1900 KO4 Joe Goddard, KO2 Jim Jeffords, KO1 Jim McCormick, KO2 Stockings Conroy, KO3 Joe Choynski, and KO1 Yank Kenny.

Ruhlin's record included: 1897 D20 Jeffries; 1898 L20 Kid McCoy, LKOby1 Sharkey, ND6 Joe Choynski (but Gus apparently had the best of it); 1899 D20 Peter Maher (brutal war) and L20 Joe Kennedy.[529]

Subsequent to the Kennedy loss, Ruhlin had been on an 8-0, 7 KO win streak that included: 1899 KO7 Jack Stelzner, KO5 Jim Jeffords, W6 Jack McCormick, and KO7 Stockings Conroy; and 1900 KO4 Jack Finnegan and KO6 Yank Kenny. He had been getting plenty of good press from sparring Corbett, who lauded his improvement. Naturally, the fact that

---

528 *National Police Gazette*, June 2, 9, 16, 23, 30, 1900.
529 *National Police Gazette*, March 25, 1899, April 8, 1899, May 20, 1899, October 14, 1899. On May 2, 1899, Ruhlin and the hard-punching Peter Maher fought a 20-round draw in what was called the hardest heavyweight fight ever. From the beginning, it was a war, and both were badly punished. Gus was dropped in the 1st, but both went to their corners bruised and wobbling. Ruhlin staggered Peter in the 2nd. Gus took the lead in the 5th and backed Maher up. From the 10th to the end, Ruhlin was the aggressor, but Maher countered hard and took punches well. Recall that Maher and Sharkey had fought to a 7-round draw. On September 26, 1899, the 175-pound Maher scored a KO2 over the 190-pound Joe Kennedy. However, in January 1900, Kid McCoy knocked out Maher in the 5th round.

Ruhlin had once fought a draw with Jeffries also put his name in the spotlight. He was a big, strong, muscular 200-pounder who looked the part.

On June 26, 1900 at Coney Island's Seaside Athletic Club, "Akron Giant" Gus Ruhlin fought "Sailor" Tom Sharkey. Manager Billy Madden and James J. Corbett seconded Ruhlin. George Dixon and manager Tom O'Rourke were amongst Sharkey's seconds. Johnny White refereed.

From the beginning, it was a fast-paced, exciting battle, with Sharkey boring-in trying for a knockout, as usual. However, Ruhlin boxed very well, using his reach and good defense. It was a hot fight, each giving and taking strong blows. In the 6th round, Ruhlin's left cut Tom's right eye, and the blood affected his vision. At times, Sharkey was staggered and hurt, but he always recovered and came back fighting hard.

In the 8th round, after landing a dozen jabs, Ruhlin landed a right to the jaw that staggered Tom. The next blow dropped him. Tom attempted to rise, but fell backwards into the ropes. However, he managed to beat the count and was fighting hard and roughing it at the bell.

In the 9th, the blood was spattering from Sharkey's bruised face, as Ruhlin seldom missed a blow, while Tom missed most of his. Sharkey roughed it in the clinches, but Ruhlin looked to be an inevitable winner, barring fatigue or one of Tom's haymakers landing and doing the trick. Ruhlin was successfully outboxing him and beating him up.

In the 15th round, Ruhlin landed a right to Sharkey's jaw "with force enough to topple him over on the ropes." Tom rose and Ruhlin hammered him down flat onto his back. He rose at nine and was hardly on his feet when Ruhlin uppercut him and Tom fell against Gus and held on. When Ruhlin pulled away, Sharkey fell to the floor. "Five times in all the game sailor regained his feet, only to be beaten flat the next instant." Finally, after the sixth knockdown in the round, Sharkey could no longer get up. Sharkey was counted out at 2 minutes and 55 seconds of the 15th round.

Ruhlin had shown "that he had improved considerably both in skill and in ring generalship." Acting on the defensive throughout, he allowed Sharkey to fight in his usual aggressive, vicious, determined fashion, but met him with straight right and left handers. "His blows were delivered straight from the shoulder." Gus was a cool, careful master of the art and his persistent endeavors gradually wore Tom out while at the same time cleverly avoiding Sharkey's bombs. "He used his reach to excellent advantage and time and again stepped in after the chunky Irishman had swung at him and made his blow count." Sharkey contributed to his own defeat, for by rushing into Ruhlin's blows, he doubled their power. Ruhlin gave Sharkey an awful beating.

It was an unquestionable and decisive victory, leaving no doubt regarding who was the superior man. "Ruhlin won by a steady volley of terrific punches, terminating in a clean knockout in fifteen rounds." Sharkey's face was badly battered and his body bruised, but still he showed gameness, rising from each knockdown and fighting hard. "They are both giants in strength and their contest was worthy of the arena."

This victory instantly made Ruhlin a top contender. He was the man of the hour. Ruhlin had decisively beaten Sharkey, the man whom Jeffries could not stop in two fights. As a result, it was said that Ruhlin was likely to be Jeff's next opponent. A *Police Gazette* writer said, "Ruhlin, in my opinion, is just the man to defeat Jeffries. He has size, bone, substance and gameness, and under Corbett's tuition has improved in boxing ability, and is the boilermaker's master in matters of ring technique. He is unquestionably more clever than the present champion."[530]

However, it was subsequently reported that Jeff's hurt arm was worse than previously believed, and would likely keep him out of the ring for quite some time. "The injury to his arm has been of such an aggravating character that he has had to carry it in a brace ever since he fought Corbett, and there is no indication that it will be all right for some time to come."

Even as of late July, Jeff's left arm was still badly injured.

It begins to look as if Jim Jeffries' career of usefulness in the ring is ended. His arm, which was injured in the fight with Corbett, is still in a bad way, and gives no indication of ever becoming entirely right

530 *New York Clipper*, July 7, 1900; *National Police Gazette*, July 14, 1900; *Louisville Evening Post*, June 27, 1900.

again. The most eminent specialists have had it under treatment with indifferent results, and its present unsatisfactory condition necessitated his declining offers to fight Fitzsimmons and Ruhlin. This is unfortunate, perhaps, for it cuts him out of a chance to participate in the distribution of public money which will be made next month when the fighting game in the Metropolis threatens to be hotter than hades.

However, in early August, it was reported that Jeffries wanted to make some money before the Horton law went out of existence. Although he allegedly said that he was willing to fight prior to September 1 and would be able to do so, "it is hardly likely that he will be." It was wishful thinking.

> Just at present he is in a bad way. His mighty left arm…has only just been unharnessed from a steel and leather device which has for weeks kept the injured member almost continually bent. For a month before the harness was put on the arm was in a plaster paris cast. This allowed no movement whatsoever. … The big fighter was only the other day permitted for the first time in weeks to remove the device. …
>
> According to the doctor, the synovial membrane between the joints of the elbow was injured. It is not necessarily a serious injury, but it is very painful and demands careful treatment.
>
> Absolute rest is also advised, and by September 1 the champion expects to be as good as ever. He will then issue a sweeping challenge. He has gone to Mount Clemens, Mich., where by well-timed work he hopes to get his arm back to its original shape.[531]

Since Jeffries was out of the game for a while, in the mad rush to make big fights prior to boxing going out of business in New York, Bob Fitzsimmons made two matches – one with Ruhlin, and another with Sharkey, both fights to be held in August. The press opined that Ruhlin "will give him a better fight than he bargains for. He is cleverer than Sharkey, with youth and physical advantages which will be a factor in determining the outcome of his battle with the Australian." Fitzsimmons was called courageous for taking on such a tough fighter.

Sizing up Ruhlin and Fitzsimmons, one writer noted that Fitz had Sharkey in a state of total collapse in 8 rounds, while it required Ruhlin 15 rounds to stop Tom. However, Ruhlin drew in 20 rounds with Jeffries, whereas Jeff stopped Bob in 11 rounds. Ruhlin's "experience with Corbett was invaluable; he has a better knowledge of scientific fighting than he ever had and is able to execute blows with rapidity and effect." "He will give a

531 *National Police Gazette*, August 4, 11, 1900.

good account of himself in the ring, and I certainly believe he has the best chance of winning."[532]

Since his loss to Jeffries in June 1899, Fitz had boxed in three bouts: 10-'99 KO1 Jeff Thorne, 3-'00 KO1 Jim Daly, and 4-'00 KO2 Ed Dunkhorst. Although the fights were short, by staying in active training and having legitimate contests, Fitz got himself fight sharp and maintained his fitness.

Training at Bergen Beach, Fitzsimmons was "in as fine fettle as any man I ever saw." On the morning of August 7, three days before the fight, he ran 6-7 miles, alternating between brisk walking and sprinting. In the afternoon, first he boxed 6 rounds with Bob Armstrong, the big 6'4" black fighter who once went 10 rounds with Jeffries and had often sparred with Sharkey. During the 6 rounds of sparring with Armstrong,

> Fitz did not strike a single blow. He simply stepped in and out of hitting distance and feinted Bob into leading. Then Fitz started a blow for the opening thus obtained, but stopped it before it landed. Ordinarily this sort of thing would be very dull entertainment, but with Fitzsimmons doing the work it was very exciting. He sidestepped around…. He bluffed him again and again into awkward dilemmas, so that he created a chance to put in one of his famous little knockout punches as Armstrong laid himself open by an unprotected lead. Fitz is one of the greatest men living at this sort of thing. To see him putting it all over a clever big fellow like Armstrong was a treat. The black man tapped him with his left on the cheek now and then, but Fitz always shifted his head and let the blow glance off harmlessly. Often he worked Armstrong into such a position that it would have needed but half a second of time to throw in one of his bombshell punches that are always fatal. This is the sort of battle that Fitz always fights. A great test awaits Ruhlin on Friday night. If he ever lets Fitz step around him and feint him into a tangled position or an unprotected one he will vanish from the scene with awful rapidity. Of course Ruhlin is preparing to avoid the calamity, but he cannot be too careful, no matter how good he is.

Fitzsimmons showed himself to be in fine condition, while Armstrong was puffing and often asking if time was up. "Fitz's footwork was of its former quality, awkward looking on the surface, but wonderfully effective in taking him just where he wanted to go."

After sparring Armstrong, Bob boxed in a similar manner for a couple of rounds with Jeff Thorne, his other sparring partner. After that, Bob

---

532 *National Police Gazette*, July 28, August 11, 1900. Fitz-Ruhlin was scheduled for 25-rounds to be held August 10. Madison Square Garden had the winning bid to host the fight, offering the fighters 50% of the gate receipts, which was to be split 75/25% winner/loser. Soft bandages were to be allowed, and Charley White was to referee. The Fitz-Sharkey fight was scheduled for August 25 at Coney Island.

practiced clinching and breaking from clinches for five minutes each with both Armstrong and Thorne. Fitz appeared to be about 172-174 pounds.

W.O. Inglis opined, "Ruhlin will have to fight the keen, shrewd, calculating, puzzling fellow who beat Corbett, and not the cocky, overconfident champion who quickly fell beneath the fist of Jeffries. So it appears that not only is Fitz's bodily condition perfect, but his mental attitude is perfect, too."

Back in April, speaking of his then future summer fight with Ruhlin, Fitzsimmons said, "I will not fight Ruhlin as I fought Jeffries. He, like Jeff, is bigger than I, and I'll have to be careful not to let his weight tell. I'll just smash and bang him from a distance, safe from hugging."

James Jeffries, who had been doing some light training in Atlantic City for the past two weeks, came to New York for the big fight. Jeff said, "I find that my arm is improving steadily." However, he was still nursing it. "I have been advised by my physicians not to take a chance until they declare it has completely recovered." Regardless of that advice, Jeff still wanted to fight, and initially said that he was willing to take the risk and fight despite doctors' advice not to do so. "I now stand ready to make a match for the world's championship with the winner of tonight's battle, the bout to be decided in or about New York City before Sept. 1." If Fitzsimmons won, Jeff was ready to give him a chance only if Fitz accepted the same financial terms that Jeffries had accepted when he obtained his title shot. Jeff also said that if Fitz or Ruhlin did not meet him prior to September 1, they would have to wait at least six months, for his time would be occupied with other matters until May 1. "I defeated Fitzsimmons in a most decisive manner, and therefore do not consider myself bound to meet him again, but will give him another chance if he agrees to box before September 1."[533]

Heading into the Ruhlin fight, Fitzsimmons was confident, as always.

> I am as good a man as I ever was. I am certain I will whip Ruhlin, and I expect to defeat him before the limit. He is a good, strong, clever fighter, but he will surely be added to my list of victims. I think that a lot of people will be surprised when they see me in action. It's all very well to call me an old man, but when I land a couple of good ones on Ruhlin they will see that I have lost none of my speed or hard-hitting powers. As Jeffries has promised to meet the winner of this fight, I can almost see myself the world's champion again.[534]

Ruhlin was positive that he would defeat Fitzsimmons. "I am in excellent condition, and if I don't knock Fitzsimmons out I will be able to go the whole twenty-five rounds at a fast gait and will win on points." Ruhlin also said that he would be world champion before the end of the

---

533 *New York World*, August 8, 10, 1900; *New York Journal*, April 21, 1900; *National Police Gazette*, August 25, 1900.
534 *New York Journal*, August 10, 1900.

year; for he was sure that he could defeat Jeffries. "In fact, I consider Fitz harder game."

As usual, the experts made their predictions. Jim Corbett said that Ruhlin should win easily, and would end the fight within 10 rounds. "Ruhlin should stop any heavy weight in the ring today." He said that Gus was faster, stronger, more scientific, and had youth on his side. Kid McCoy agreed that Ruhlin would win. However, John L. Sullivan said, "Fitz ought to win. He has the experience, and is a hard hitter." Jimmy Carroll, George Siler, and Tom Sharkey (who had fought both), all picked Fitzsimmons.[535]

The day of the fight, the *New York World's* W.O. Inglis picked Ruhlin to defeat Fitzsimmons. Gus was about 30 pounds bigger (165 vs. 195), significantly younger (28 vs. 37), had the height advantage (6'1 ¾" vs. 5'11 ¾"), 4 inches of reach advantage, and was coming off his biggest victory, in which he had shown improvement as a technician. Ruhlin had shown great ability at blocking both in sparring Corbett and in the Sharkey fight. "Tom Sharkey, who is as fast as any fighter that ever lived, rushed at Ruhlin like a whirlwind, but Gus coolly stuck out his left time and again and uppercut the Sailor with his right until he stopped him. Certainly he showed coolness."

Still, Fitzsimmons "undoubtedly knows more about ring generalship than any other fighter in the business." He had the superior experience, and had taken care of his body, making it younger than his chronological age. Although Ruhlin had been defensively sound against Sharkey, it was quite another thing "to hold that form in a fight with a man of Fitzsimmons's terrific punching ability."

Summarizing, Inglis said,

> It seems to me that the issue comes down to whether or not Ruhlin will be able to keep cool and avoid being flurried by Fitzsimmons's great name and foxy tactics. If he can do this he is certainly big enough, strong enough and fast enough to win the battle. I think it is reasonable to believe that Ruhlin will keep cool and take care of himself. I expect to see him win.[536]

One source said Fitz was a close 6 to 5 odds favorite. Another said that Bob had been the betting favorite at 8 to 10 odds, but on fight night, so much money came in on Ruhlin that he wound up being the slight favorite.

On August 10, 1900 at New York's Madison Square Garden, Bob Fitzsimmons fought Gus Ruhlin before a huge crowd (estimates of 10,000, 12,000 or 15,000). Jim Jeffries was in attendance. Tickets sold for $3, $5, $7, $10, $15, and $20.[537]

---

535 *New York Journal*, August 10, 1900; *New York Sun*, August 11, 1900.
536 *New York World*, August 10, 1900. Results against common opponents included: Maher – Fitz KO12 and KO1, Ruhlin D20, Sharkey – Fitz LDQby8/KO8, Ruhlin KO15, Jeffries – Fitz LKOby11, Ruhlin D20, Dunkhorst – Fitz KO2, Ruhlin KO22, Choynski – Fitz D5/KO5, Ruhlin ND6.
537 *New York Herald*, August 10, 1900.

It was a hot, humid day, the thermometer reaching 105 degrees, and it was still hot in the evening. A howl was made for more air from the fans, but they were already working at their limit, so the crowd had to stand the heat.

A picture machine was at one end of the building, and it was understood that an attempt would be made to film the fight.

At 9:45 p.m., Fitzsimmons entered the ring wearing a light bathrobe. Ruhlin followed a moment later, his shoulders covered with a towel. Gus wore a canvas breechcloth. Upon removing his bath robe, it was seen that Bob was wearing a pair of pink trunks and a belt made of American flags.

The Herald reported that Fitz weighed 168 pounds to Ruhlin's 190. Bob claimed to weigh 162 pounds, but the *Sun* said it was a good bet that he really weighed about 172. It said that Gus tipped the scales at 194. *The Eagle* said Ruhlin admitted to 195, but it felt that he weighed at lest ten pounds more. Their size difference was most noticeable. "He was bigger than Fitz in every way. He towered above him half a head and looked powerful enough to twist the Cornishman in two in a wrestling match."

Fitz's seconds were George Dawson, Jeff Thorne, Bob Armstrong, Dan Hickey and Percy Williams. Jim Corbett, Billy Madden, Charley Goff and Matty Matthews attended Ruhlin.

Fitz had brought his own gloves, and took them over to Ruhlin's manager Billy Madden for inspection. Jim Corbett insisted on putting on Fitz's gloves for him, "a proceeding which the Australian didn't seem to relish."

The bout was scheduled for 25 rounds. Charley White refereed. They were ready to go at 10:10 p.m.

1st round

Early on, it looked as though Fitzsimmons would be an easy victim. Ruhlin forced matters and landed a number of hard jabs, as well as a left to the body and a right to the jaw. Fitz seemed asleep and some wondered what was wrong with him. Ruhlin landed straight punches as well as hooking blows. One particularly hard jab shook Bob considerably. "There's nothing to it. The old man is all in." Gus was very fast and tried to stay close.

However, Bob suddenly came to life and landed a couple rights to the jaw that slightly staggered Gus. Fitz mixed it up with a left and right to the jaw. Gus came back with a straight left to the nose and right to the jaw. Bob landed a hard left uppercut to the body that made Gus grunt, but Ruhlin with his great strength rushed Fitz to the ropes and smashed him with both hands to the face and body. Blood "spurted from Fitz's face." His left eye had been cut. They mixed it hotly, and both landed heavy smashes on the head. Gus staggered Fitz with a left, but Bob feinted and landed a good counter wallop to the mouth that drew blood.

Gus landed a left hook to the jaw and Fitz clinched. Either Bob slipped down or Gus wrestled him down, depending on the source. Blood was flowing from Bob's left eye. There was something wrong with the bell. It was barely audible, and when it went off as Bob rose, Fitz stopped fighting, but Ruhlin hit him with a right before the referee intervened. The spot over Fitz's eye where Ruhlin had landed his jabs became blue and swollen as big as an egg.

Most thought that Ruhlin would defeat Fitzsimmons in the same way that he had done with Sharkey. Bob had been clearly jarred by several lefts. One gambler offered 5 to 1 odds, with Ruhlin the favorite.

2nd round

Ruhlin immediately went in with rapid swings, and cut open Fitz's eye again. However, Fitzsimmons had woken up. After taking a jab, Bob stood in close and landed a terrific right to the jaw that staggered Ruhlin. "A shift with the left and a hook on the nose and the lower part of Ruhlin's face was a splash of blood." The blood poured out of Ruhlin's mouth and nose in a stream, smearing his chest with huge red patches.

Fitz hurried maters and a left to the stomach made Gus back away. Bob was quick and strong, his blows falling with the rapidity of an avalanche. He feinted often and crashed his gloves to the face, sending the blood flying. Gus was surprised, and seemed tired and dazed by the fast pace and hard blows.

Bob rushed and they mixed it up, both landing terrific punches to the head. Bob landed a hook that made Ruhlin tumble back into the ropes. Gus responded with jabs, but "he might as well have tried to stop the coming of tomorrow as make any halt in the now fighting Fitz. Old man, eh?" Both were bleeding, but Gus was backing away. Fitz rushed and with left and right on the head made Gus stagger. When Bob came in, Ruhlin lowered his head and clinched. Fitz landed a short stab in the ribs, which caused Gus to bend forward. Bob then straightened him up with an uppercut to the chin. Gus missed a wild right and clinched. Bob shook him off.

Both seemed tired. Ruhlin landed some light jabs and hooks to the face. "He landed them so easily that Bob looked silly." Fitz was not trying to block or evade Ruhlin's punches at all.

However, Bob rained in the blows again and a left on the jaw knocked Gus against the ropes, and he staggered away dazed. Bob landed a left and right. When Gus threw up his guard to block a hook, Bob shifted his feet and "for the first time Ruhlin knew what a Fitzsimmons shift and solar plexus blow meant. It landed fairly and solidly, sending Ruhlin to the floor." Another version said Bob bluffed the right, landed the left hook to the head, and then dropped the left hook down to the body. Ruhlin went down on his hands and knees, doubled up like a jackknife, with a look of agony on his face. Fitz smiled as he walked away. After Gus rose, Bob went to finish him off, but the bell saved Ruhlin. "If there had been a half a minute left to this round Ruhlin would have surely been put to sleep, for when he got to his feet he was scarcely able to stand and was about to pitch forward on his face when the bell rang and his seconds caught him."

The body punishment had taken all of the steam out of Ruhlin. It seemed as if it was just a matter of time before Fitz ended matters.

3rd round

Bob Armstrong, Fitz's sparring partner, said that between rounds, in the corner, a Fitz handler who was very nervous got ammonia into Bob's eyes. It nearly blinded him and he was almost beside himself with pain. After boxing a little at the start of the round, Fitz managed to come around all right before anyone realized that something was wrong.

Ruhlin recovered fairly well from the previous round, and opened on the attack, mixing it blow for blow, but Fitzsimmons got the better of it. Bob's terrific smashes beat Ruhlin back and had him in trouble. Fitz's punches raised a lump over Gus's left eye. Bob landed a number of short heavy hooks that had Ruhlin's nose and mouth bleeding again. Gus used his left jabs to the mouth and eye, drawing blood, but Bob never weakened and kept smashing the big fellow on the head and body. Gus grew fatigued and began clinching. Bob showed some signs of weariness, too. They clinched and wrestled around.

Gus jolted Bob's eye with a left, but Fitz responded with a left hook to the jaw that sent Gus staggering across the ring. He followed with a left to the stomach that caused Gus to clinch. Ruhlin landed a right but Bob responded with a left and right to the head that made Gus stagger. In close, Ruhlin landed a blow to Bob's neck with his left elbow. The referee briefly stepped in to warn him. Both were tired at the bell.

4th round

Fitzsimmons tried to end matters, forcing the fight. Willing to take chances, he held his face out and let Ruhlin hit him at will. Bob never broke ground. He took punches, either to show Gus how weak they were, or to allow Gus to wear himself out, or, by allowing Ruhlin to punch, Gus would expose himself to one of Bob's brutal counterpunches. Perhaps Bob was just resting. Corbett and Madden warned Ruhlin to be careful, feeling that Bob was faking in order to set a trap.

Eventually, Fitzsimmons retaliated and again put it all over his man, landing a number of hard smashes to the head and body. Ruhlin jabbed, but had little effect. Bob chased him around. Ruhlin was unsteady, but in the clinches, he laid his weight on Bob. Fitz took his time, appearing to be tired. "He was faking, however, for the next moment he let loose a left for the stomach that made the big man retreat." Gus was slow with his punches and seemed to be weakening.

Fitzsimmons rained in the blows and knocked Ruhlin down again with right and left smashes to the body and head. Particularly effective were the right to the jaw and the left to the body. After he rose, a right split open Ruhlin's eye. "Corbett made a demonstration in his corner and was warned by the police to keep quiet." Some feared that he would try to enter the ring to lose the fight for Ruhlin on a foul, to save him from punishment.

> Just what Corbett's idea was nobody could tell, for Referee White thoroughly understood that no foul would be allowed should a second enter the ring during a round, as Corbett's handler, McVey, did when Jim was 'getting his' from Sharkey at the Lenox Club last year. But a cool-headed policeman prevented any possible unpleasantness by reaching over and shaking a club in Corbett's face with the remark, 'Don't get gay or I'll throw you out of the building!'

At the bell, Ruhlin was in bad shape, bleeding, groggy, and weak.

5th round

Ruhlin was still groggy and had no strength in his punches. Fitz was strong. He walloped Gus with a double left, first to the jaw and then down to the body. Gus hung on. After breaking, Ruhlin tried his left with all the force that he could, but Bob ignored it and sent in smashes to the face that left Gus covered in blood. Ruhlin had a lump on the right eye the size of a hen's egg.

However, once again, Fitzsimmons allowed Ruhlin to hit him. Gus landed half a dozen blows to Bob's face. All those hard punches that Bob was throwing had to tire him. However, Ruhlin's blows did no damage. Fitz took matters very coolly, and after they clinched, Bob laughed at the spectators over Ruhlin's shoulder. Corbett gave constant frantic advice from outside the ring, and upon one occasion, the police had to suppress him. Jim wanted Ruhlin to watch out for one of Bob's smashes.

Fitzsimmons took his time, stalling for a while, but then finally hurried matters with body blows and facers that made Gus clinch hard. He again slugged him into a groggy state. With a right on the jaw, he made Gus drop his hands and lay against Bob's breast.

Ruhlin rallied gamely, but his blows missed, and at the end of the round, Bob was once again punching him into a state of distress. Ruhlin walked unsteadily to his corner, his face covered with bruises. Both of Bob's eyes were swelling.

6ᵗʰ round

Fitzsimmons came out briskly and drove a left to the stomach. Ruhlin responded with a left and right to the body but Fitz ignored them and landed a left hook to the mouth that opened up "the floodgates of blood again." Gus ran away, but Fitz followed and hooked him hard in the stomach. Gus came back with a stiff jab to the nose and short jolt to the chin.

Ruhlin was awkward and wobbled around. Bob followed, and in an unconcerned manner, took all the face punches Gus threw. Ruhlin's punches had little force, while Bob hit like a trip hammer. Fitz simply slugged Ruhlin about. Gus did not have enough strength to hold up his hands and was blind from the blood that flowed from his eyes, nose, and mouth. Fitz got him to the ropes and shook him up with a right smash to the jaw. Gus clinched to stop the follow-up onslaught.

After breaking, Bob rushed and knocked Ruhlin down with a storm of blows, including a right to the jaw and left in the stomach. He rose at nine, reeling about. Fitz threw caution to the wind and went after him. He almost dropped Ruhlin with a left to the stomach, but Gus held around his neck.

After breaking, Fitzsimmons put on the finishing touches. He cut loose with a succession of punches that landed all over the head and body. Ruhlin tottered, and Fitz landed a left hook to the body that caused Gus to pitch forward. Bob followed with a final tremendous left hook/uppercut under the chin which raised Ruhlin off the floor and made him drop heavily on his head, limp and lifeless. He was knocked out so cleanly that the count was not even necessary. Gus was out cold.

Ruhlin's seconds dragged him into his chair in an unconscious condition. After getting to his corner, Ruhlin vomited blood, and because he was bleeding from his ears as well, his handlers were concerned. They feared fatal results. His eyes were closed. His face was very badly bruised and his body severely punished.

Fitzsimmons came over to his corner and, taking Ruhlin's head in his hands, he turned up his face and said in a low voice, "Brace up, old fellow, I didn't mean to hurt you so bad!" But the moment Fitz let go, Ruhlin's chin fell to his heaving bosom, and there was no response. "Ruhlin was too far out to know where he was." It took Madden and Corbett five to ten minutes to bring him out of unconsciousness.[538]

Fitzsimmons greeted Jeffries, who came over to congratulate him. Bill Brady asked Bob if he would fight Jeff. Fitz said that he would after he was through with Sharkey. Brady said, "Jeffries will meet you before the 1st of September, on the same terms which characterized the battle which you indulged in at Coney Island last year."

When speaking with a reporter, Jeffries said,

> It was an easy victory for Fitzsimmons. The result was just as I expected. Fitz simply waited for a chance to send in his good left. Ruhlin's blows did not seem to have any effect on Lanky Bob. I am ready to meet Fitz to arrange a match at any time. If he wants the championship he can fight for it, but he must accept my terms.

Jeffries went to visit Ruhlin in his dressing room. Ruhlin's right eye was nearly swelled shut, and his left eye was badly discolored and swollen. "His face was the color of uncooked liver." His mouth so swollen that he could not be understood, and he could hardly speak above a whisper.

When Jeff left the Garden, he said with a gleeful smile, "I am still champion, and what is more, I know I can beat those two fellows who fought tonight."

Ruhlin was in a bad way. While in the dressing room, he passed out and lay unconscious for an hour. When Gus finally left his dressing room, two men supported him by the arms. He could hardly walk and twice staggered as if about to fall.

Even into the early morning hours, Ruhlin's situation was precarious. "Ruhlin talked incoherently and lapsed occasionally into unconsciousness." A doctor said that Gus was in a state of total physical collapse. He was fearful that Bob's blows had caused a blood clot to form on the brain. Physicians worked over him all night, and it was not until 3:30 a.m. that full consciousness returned.

When the doctor tried to examine his body, Ruhlin winced with pain. His breathing was irregular. After about an hour, Gus vomited and said that he felt better. He then went to sleep. "Both of his eyes were almost closed and his face appeared as if he had passed through a threshing machine. His

---

538 *New York Sun, Journal, Tribune, Herald, Brooklyn Daily Eagle,* August 11, 1900; *National Police Gazette,* August 25, 1900; *New York Clipper,* August 18, 1900; *New York Sun,* August 12, 1900.

right arm is all black and blue where Fitz's gloves landed, and his breast is one mass of bruises." Despite the concern, by the next morning, Gus was all right.

Jim Corbett said that Ruhlin made a great fight, but was not himself. After the 2nd round he was all out and no longer had the steam in his punches. Jim claimed that Gus was not in the condition that he was for the Sharkey fight.

Ruhlin's manager, Billy Madden, concurred, claiming that Gus was stale and sluggish, but game, for he took ferocious punches. "The smashes which Gus received in the body did more damage than anything else. It made him forget his cleverness and he started in to slug. That was just what Bob wanted and you know the rest."

Ruhlin had hurt Fitzsimmons with lefts in the 1st round, but Bob's shift and tremendous left hook to the body in the 2nd that dropped Gus essentially won the fight and took Ruhlin's strength. After that, Ruhlin had no more steam and forgot about his science and the instructions that he was receiving. In the 6th round, Ruhlin "received a body punching, together with a series of jaw breakers that has seldom been seen."

> The blow that put Ruhlin to sleep was a left hook that might be called a half swing. It shot in under the chin and ear and reached the jugular. Had Fitz used a big mallet he could not have administered a more tremendous blow. Though Ruhlin said he weighed 194 pounds, and he was probably heavier, he was lifted off his feet as he fell head down, it is a wonder that he did not break his neck, as his head bent under him. The Akron man was unconscious, however, before he reached the surface of the ring, as the hook acted like an electric current of high voltage.

Ruhlin did not remember much after he received the heavy blow in the stomach in the 2nd round. "I didn't know what was the matter with me. I could not hit hard enough to kill a flea. I must have been stale." Gus thought he might have been fighting and training too much over the past year. "The hot weather hurt me. After the first round, I gave out. I was like a dead one. Why, in the sixth round I hit Fitz four times and he never put up his guard. I couldn't move him. That shows how weak I was."

> I did my best, but Fitz proved too much for me. I looked for an early victory from the start and thought I had my man beaten several times, but he came back strong. Fitzsimmons is unquestionably the greatest fighter in the ring today. He is a cool, calculating proposition, and despite his years had a punch – well, everybody knows when it lands.

Ruhlin said that Bob was the hardest hitter on earth and was just as clever as ever. This was coming from a man who had fought both Jeffries and Sharkey. Often during his career, Bob Fitzsimmons did not simply knock his opponents down for ten seconds; he knocked them out cold, quite often for substantial periods of time. To say that he had freakish power is an understatement.

Ruhlin felt that Bob had fought a better battle against him than he had with Jeffries. Tom Sharkey agreed, saying that Fitz would defeat Jeffries in his current shape.

John L. Sullivan said, "Fitzsimmons is still a great fighter. He can defeat a whole lot of these good fellows yet." Sully said that Ruhlin put up a good fight, had the making of a great fighter, and might do better later on.

Honest John Kelly said, "Fitz is generally a safe fellow to bet on. The fight by the way, was one of the best I have ever witnessed."

It had been a ferocious, exciting, and damaging battle. *The New York Journal* and *New York Sun* agreed that in terms of punishment and slugging, it was the fiercest and bloodiest fight between prominent members of the fistic arena ever seen in the east since the Horton law went into effect.

Fitzsimmons literally beat Ruhlin into a state of unconsciousness. Bob showed that he could take any kind of punches without weakening, and although cut and bruised, was never anxious to retreat. He forced the fight from start to finish, and sometimes rushed in with blows so quickly delivered that they could not be counted. Fitz alternated between vicious punching and sometimes appearing tired, perhaps bluffing, but he always quickly recovered after stalling for a bit. Ruhlin's cornermen at times yelled, "He's fakin', Gus! Look out for one o' them quick swings or a drive in the body!" Regardless of the blows that Bob took, "Fitzsimmons inevitably cut loose all of a sudden with some kind of a smash that had danger in it." Fitz's sudden recovery with quick advances and fearful belts led some to believe "there was no doubt about the fake."

The Brooklyn Daily Eagle said that given their huge size disparity, Fitz's victory was even more creditable. "To mow down such a giant, the victor needed his claim to being the hardest hitter in pugilistic history and last night he added a strong claim to being able to stand as much punishment as anyone." Fitz willingly allowed Ruhlin to hit him with the same punches that Gus used to beat Sharkey down, took them well, and landed vicious punches in return that sent Ruhlin down and out.

On all sides, Bob was given "unlimited credit for his remarkable showing," for stopping the man who had drawn with Jeff and knocked out Sharkey. Bob demonstrated beyond a doubt that he was not played out as a fighter, and was a "pugilistic phenomenon." He had retained all of his hitting powers, was young in point of strength and condition regardless of his numeric age, and "stripped in magnificent shape, never having looked better in his life."

Amongst the sports, "there was a prevailing impression that had Champion Jeffries been in Ruhlin's place the Cornishman might have regained the laurels lost."

Against Jeffries it will be recalled that Fitzsimmons was slow, and used only one style of assault, a rush with double swings. The latter was whipped chiefly because he continually ran his head into Jeffries' stiff left hand, which went to the mark repeatedly with damaging effect. But against Ruhlin Fitzsimmons was as fast as chain lightning and varied his style of attack so much that he had the Akron man puzzled.[539]

The victory put Fitzsimmons next in line to meet Jeffries. "Fitz showed that a man must not always be a giant to whip another."

Interestingly enough, Bob's success also "served to boost Jeffries quite a bit." Jeff had already defeated Fitz convincingly, so the fact that it had become clear that Bob wasn't old or shot made Jeff's victory over him all the more impressive. He was the only man to have knocked Fitz out, besides having defeated both Corbett and Sharkey. Ruhlin had defeated Sharkey, and Fitz had defeated Ruhlin, as well as Corbett, and, for all intensive purposes, Sharkey too. That "makes Jeffries a real champion. But Fitz's return to earth has caused a universal demand for another fight between the Cornishman and Jeffries."

Fitzsimmons spoke with difficulty, owing to the fact that his larynx was badly swollen due to blows and elbows. "My throat hurts and my left hand will not close tight, but beyond a pain in my 'Adam's apple,' I feel all right."

Bob complimented Ruhlin. "That fellow is a terribly hard puncher and he is clever, too. ... It was the hardest fight of my career and I think it was the greatest and fastest that ever took place." Bob said that Gus was a wonder who put up a game fight from the start. "He gave me lots of trouble in the first round – I don't know how, but he did." "He hit me repeatedly in the early rounds, but I was willing to take his punch for an opening to send a good one in. I was never in danger."

Fitz's left eye was badly swollen and blackened and his right eye was marked. Speaking of the left eye, Bob said, "I got that from Ruhlin twelve seconds after the bell rung at the close of the first round. Ruhlin probably didn't hear the bell." That punch hurt, and Bob admitted to being shaken up by it. Fitz said that other than that punch, Ruhlin's blows did not hurt him, but admitted that Gus's punches made him tired, so tired that he did not know what to do for a minute.

As I stood there and let him swing on my jaw, I thought to myself, 'what a fool I am to do this,' but I wasn't a bit frightened and I did not feel that he could hurt me. I had my wits all of the time and heard all of the bells, even when Ruhlin didn't. He was worse than I at every

---

539 *New York Sun*, August 12, 1900. Also, against Jeff, Bob did not attack the body consistently or use his shifts, but "went after the head with wild swings, after the style displayed by Sharkey against Ruhlin." Of course, Jeffries had a harder punch than Ruhlin, better defense, and apparently could take it better as well. Forgotten was the fact that Jeff used his crouch and tight guard to make it difficult for Bob to land his body shots, all the while nailing Fitz with his long and powerful lefts.

stage and I knew it. …. His blows were so hard that they took some of my steam in the first round, so I went in to store up enough for the rally. …

After the first round tonight I had no fear of the result. Ruhlin was a very fast fellow. He landed very often on me, but his knocks lacked steam and force. In the opening rounds I took things decidedly easy, doing this to size my man up. I made it look as though I was slow and heavy, but it was just the manner in which I mapped out the contest. The bell hampered me more than once. The sound was too faint for any one to hear it. For this reason I had to be very careful at times. Ruhlin is a game fellow, but he was susceptible to my body blows. These punches really licked him.

As soon as I realized that I could get to him with my left shift and right cross I knew I had him. … Only once in the fight did my right arm hurt me. That was in clinches, for Gus is very strong and roughed it with all his might. …

That blow I landed on his solar plexus at the end of the second was a corker and Ruhlin never got over it. He is a monstrous big fellow, but you know the old saying, 'The bigger they are, the further they have to fall.' Yes, he is a good man, better than I thought, but he isn't good enough to do the old man yet awhile.

If I had fought like that with Jeffries I would never have lost the championship, for this fellow is a better man than the champion and can lick him any time they meet.

The next day, Bob said,

My throat bothers me a good deal and I still feel the effect of some of the blows I received. Ruhlin caught me in the neck several times with his elbow, but he could not help it. It happened, you know, in clinches. I could not swallow very well last night, but I'm all right this morning. I got a couple of smashes on the Adam's apple, and I tell you it hurts when you get struck there. …

Billy Madden states that Ruhlin was stale, and that he was overtrained. I don't think so. Any man who can stand the smashes which I gave him must have been in good and sound health. He got to me pretty often, and in the first round I was a bit unsteady; but I was in fine condition. In fact, better than when I fought Jim Jeffries or Corbett.

Bob spoke of his improved sharpness, how some underestimated him after the Jeffries fight, and how he wanted another title shot, feeling that he would do better in a rematch. He asked, "I'm too old, am I? Well, I guess I am young enough to make things hum for some people. … I was not in good trim when beaten by Jeffries. To tell you the honest truth, I took things very easy in that mill and had to pay the penalty."

Bob's plan was to go after Sharkey next. He would rest for about a week, and then return to training. "My ambition is to regain the championship. I have no doubt as to my chance with Sharkey, and if I defeat him Jeffries cannot fail to give me first chance."

One report said that Fitzsimmons had earned $15,750 and Ruhlin $5,250 (75/25% split of the $21,000 fighters' 50% share of the $42,000 generated). However, it was also learned "on good authority" that the boxers had agreed to split $20,000 evenly, $10,000 each.

Bill Brady said that if Fitzsimmons failed to make a match with Jeffries before September 1, when the repeal of the Horton law went into effect, he would have to wait at least a year. However, such a match seemed unlikely, given that Bob had a late August match with Sharkey already scheduled. Both Bob and Tom had already posted forfeit money. Plus, Jeff's arm status was questionable, and certainly he could not be put into championship condition in such a short period of time.

Having attended the Fitz-Ruhlin fight, Jeffries returned to his training quarters, where he was doing some conditioning work. Jeff said,

> Robert Fitzsimmons, who demonstrated last night that he is a wonderful pugilist, and for whom I have an intense admiration, has often stated, since I defeated him, that he would sacrifice anything for another chance to regain the championship. When I fought him his manager forced me to give Fitzsimmons 65 per cent of the purse, win or lose, and in order to obtain the chance I agreed to this unheard of arrangement. Since that time I have held that I was entitled to a similar division of the purse, if I agreed to meet him again, as there can be no question that my victory over him was clear and decisive.[540]

However, Jeff (or Brady on his behalf – managers often spoke for their fighters) also said that if Bob fought him before September 1, he would agree to either a winner-take-all fight, or a division of 75% to the winner and 25% to the loser. Furthermore, if Bob called off his fight with Sharkey, Jeff would agree to fight both Fitz and Sharkey before September 1 – Fitzsimmons on August 25 and Sharkey on August 31. This way, Sharkey would still have a match and not be harmed by Bob pulling out of his bout with him. "If by Tuesday [August 14] I have received no favorable answer from Fitzsimmons I shall discontinue training, and refuse to meet any one until on or about June 1, 1901."

Quite frankly, this sounded like a bluff. Jeff knew fully well that he was not going to fight either of these two men in the next two weeks, and the fact that he was not going to fight again until the following year

---

540 *New York Sun*, August 12, 1900.

demonstrated that he really had other plans in mind. He was not in fighting shape, and his arm was still recovering.

J.C. Kennedy, the Twentieth Century Athletic Club's manager, said he thought that Jeff's proposition was spectacular and impracticable. Charley White recalled the time when Jeff was set to box two men, broke his hand, and was unable to fight the second bout. He said that Jeff's posting a large forfeit could offset such a contingency.

Perhaps to call his bluff, Fitzsimmons immediately said that he would fight Jeff. He had posted $2,500 to meet Sharkey on August 25. He said that he would honor his contract to fight Sharkey and then fight Jeff the following week. He would allow Jeff whatever terms he wanted, "he to take 65 per cent, win or lose if he is afraid to meet me winner to take all. I know I can beat him."[541]

However, Jeffries insisted that Fitz and/or Sharkey immediately post a $5,000 forfeit or he would cease training and not resume. He did not want to train for a fight that might not take place if one boxer was injured in the Fitz-Sharkey fight. He wanted them to demonstrate their sincerity with money.

The Police Gazette opined that it was Jeff's way of getting out of a possible fight. "A blind man could see that this was only a subterfuge to evade the issue, and it is not surprising that both Fitz and Sharkey laughed at this unreasonable proposition and questioned Jeffries' sincerity." It called Jeff's demand "preposterous."[542]

On August 13, while riding from his training quarters at Loch Arbour, Jeffries fell off his bicycle again and wrenched an ankle. It was painful, but after Jack McCormack attended to it, Jeff declared that the injury would not seriously interfere with his plans. However, "shortly after the mishap Jeffries was in bathing, his ankle swathed in as many bandages as a baby in Iceland." Some questioned whether it was a genuine injury, or whether Jeff was seeking a way out of a fight with Fitzsimmons, surprised that Bob accepted his offer.

> There are skeptical folk hereabout who hint that Jeffries will next be taking milk baths or discovering live sea serpents in the ocean off Bradley's resort. Others, also unbelievers, wish to know if Jeffries's manager, Brady, whose theatrical methods are known, has been in the vicinity lately.

One report said that Fitzsimmons was disgusted with the off-and-on hot-and-cold Jeffries. Bob said that Jeff was crawling out of a match that Jeff offered and he accepted. "The truth of the matter is that Jeffries is afraid to meet me again." Bob said that each time that he had accepted an offer to fight Jeff, "he has made some silly excuse to get out of the match."

---

541 *New York World*, August 12, 1900.
542 *National Police Gazette*, September 8, 1900.

Jeff or Brady should have known that they were going up against a master of the mouth. When he wanted, Fitzsimmons could match even Corbett went it came to a sharp tongue.

The Journal said that Jeffries, or his manager Brady in speaking for him, was "as coy and uncertain as the sun in April. Jeffries says he will and then he says he won't. From his lofty perch he can dictate terms, and he knows it." It felt that Brady did not want to risk a loss, and wanted to capitalize further on Jeffries before taking another risk. With Jeff's arm troubles, and being less than perfectly trained, going against a sharp Fitz with such little time to train was a risk that Brady did not want to take.[543]

The Police Gazette said that Jeff was not going to fight the winner of the Fitz-Sharkey battle before September 1. "I never believed he had any such intention, but he had to do something to pose before the public, and the effort he was compelled to make to keep from being lost in the shuffle was really pathetic." No one believed in Brady's proposition to have Jeff meet the winner of Fitz-Sharkey six days after their fight. "Jeffries conveniently came to the aid of his embarrassed manager with a notification that he was not satisfied with the conditions demanded by Fitzsimmons and Sharkey for a meeting with him, and he did not wish to lose time training for an uncertainty." The real "fact of the matter is that his injured arm will not stand the strain of training again and he isn't going to take any chances of losing his title. . . . And nobody can blame him."

The Gazette also opined that Brady simply wanted to keep Jeff's name in the newspapers so that he would not be forgotten. It sarcastically remarked, "Two whole days have gone by and Jim Jeffries, the champion prizefighter, has not sprained his leg, fallen off his bicycle, captured a runaway horse or snatched a beautiful young woman from a watery grave. There'll be a press agent out of a job if he doesn't get a hustle on himself pretty soon!"[544]

Amazingly, Bob Fitzsimmons was scheduled to fight Tom Sharkey just two weeks after defeating Ruhlin. Sharkey said that he was in great shape, that Fitz would meet the same Sharkey that Jeffries met. Bob said that a victory would surely entitle him to another fight with Jeffries. "Both are as fit as two men ever were, and each is supremely confident of success."[545]

On August 22, 1900, a couple days before the fight, Fitzsimmons wound up his training at Bergen Beach, exhibiting before a paying crowd that included 100 women. Bob punched the bag 3 hard rounds, and then sparred with Bob Armstrong and Professor George Dawson. Armstrong "slugged, sprinted and feinted for three rounds, and Fitz caught him unawares a number of times. Once Armstrong was punched over the heart and he almost fell." The "women spectators were fairly beside themselves

543 *New York Journal*, August 14, 16, 17, 1900.
544 *National Police Gazette*, September 1, 8, 1900.
545 Kid McCoy, Jim Corbett, Jim Wakely, John Kelly, Jimmy Carroll, and John Considine all picked Fitz to win. Tom O'Rourke, Sam Fitzpatrick, and Spike Sullivan picked Sharkey.

with delight. They stood and applauded vigorously." After sparring George Dawson, Bob wrestled for 13 minutes with Jack Neary. Following that, he tossed the medicine ball with Neary and Joe Knipe, the amateur champion.[546]

Bob's three sons, Bob, Martin, and Charles, and Bob Armstrong, watch him make horseshoes.

Assessing the rematch, the *New York Sun* said that Sharkey's chances should not be held too cheaply, given his improvement over the three and a half years since Fitz stopped him in 8 rounds, and given how well he did against Jeffries the previous year. However, against Jeffries, "Sharkey received a pretty severe grueling from which it took him a long time to recover." He had once stopped Ruhlin in 1 round, but got handled and knocked out by him in the June 26 rematch, two months earlier. Some wondered whether the beating Tom had absorbed against Jeffries had taken something out of him. Still, Sharkey said that he had not trained properly for Gus because he thought Ruhlin would be easy. He was taking Fitzsimmons seriously.

Sharkey argued that he could take a lot more punishment than Ruhlin could, and would be able to exchange with Bob longer and with better results. "There is no doubt that Sharkey is a more rugged fighter than Ruhlin both in physique and in punching power. It has been said of him that barring Fitzsimmons he has no equal as a hitter."

Regarding Fitzsimmons, the *Sun* said that as far as physical strength and speed were concerned, judging from his work in training over the last ten days, he had not gone backwards at all.

> Fitz's habit has been to go to a man, mix it up and beat him down as quickly as possible. He relies almost wholly upon his craftiness and his heavy hitting. He can take punishment and a lot of it, and still come back with blows that cannot be resisted. Sharkey, while not so clever, is just as willing and just as game. Against Ruhlin, Sharkey

546 *New York World*, August 23, 1900.

could not get to the big man because the latter was too shifty on his feet and too quick with his defence. Ruhlin also met the Sailor's advances with a remarkably fast left hand, which had power enough in it to not only shake the Sailor up, but put him down when he had lost much of his vitality.

Fitzsimmons has a better left hand than Ruhlin, but he does not use it in the same manner. Fitz seldom adopts a straight jab for the face as an opponent comes in, but he hooks that hand or swings it for the jaw or body with a shift that has been widely talked about. … Fitz is one of the quickest fighters in the world in changing the course of his blows. He may start a left apparently for the body and yet shift it so that it will land upon the jaw in the twinkling of an eye. He does not have to swing a punch…but he can use a six-inch jolt with just as much effect because of the accuracy with which it is landed. Fitz has an eye for openings that cannot be excelled.[547]

The World said it was a match between the world's greatest ring general (Fitz) and the world's most courageous and aggressive heavyweight (Sharkey). Describing Fitzsimmons, it said,

His pose and motions in the ring are awkward and seemingly slow. His long strides and shambling gait draw the attention of spectators from the lightning swings and jabs of his arms and hands. In each of his fights he appears at one time or another to be groggy, but many good heavyweights say that right at that time he is most dangerous. As he reels around about to fall any opening left by the other man revives Fitz more than a five-minute rest. More than one ambitious fighter has rushed into a hook that put him out because he foolishly thought that old Fitz was gone.[548]

On August 24, 1900 at Coney Island's Seaside Sporting Club, Bob Fitzsimmons took on Tom Sharkey in a rematch scheduled for 25 rounds for a $25,000 purse, with 50% or $12,500 going to each, win or lose. Seats were $3, $5, $7, $10, $15, and $25. Estimates of crowd size ranged from 4,000 to 5,000, relatively low given the two combatants' popularity. The crowd gave a great reception to John L. Sullivan. Corbett was also present.

Some thought that Fitzsimmons would weigh about 170 pounds to Sharkey's 185 pounds. *The Journal's* day-of-the-fight report said that Fitz was 175, while Sharkey was 190. Jeffries thought Bob weighed about 170 pounds. *The Eagle* said Sharkey was about 190 pounds.

At first, there was a big delay, because referee Charley White refused to work until he received payment. After that was settled, at 10:40 p.m., Sharkey entered the ring wearing an elegant and expensive-looking blue

547 *New York Sun*, August 24, 1900.
548 *New York World*, August 24, 1900.

bathrobe. Because it was hot, he immediately pulled it off. His seconds fanned him. Tom wore green trunks. His hands were well protected with bandages. According to Jeffries, who was reporting for the *World*, Sharkey looked first-rate and strong as a bull. Still, Fitz was the 10 to 6 and 10 to 7 favorite.

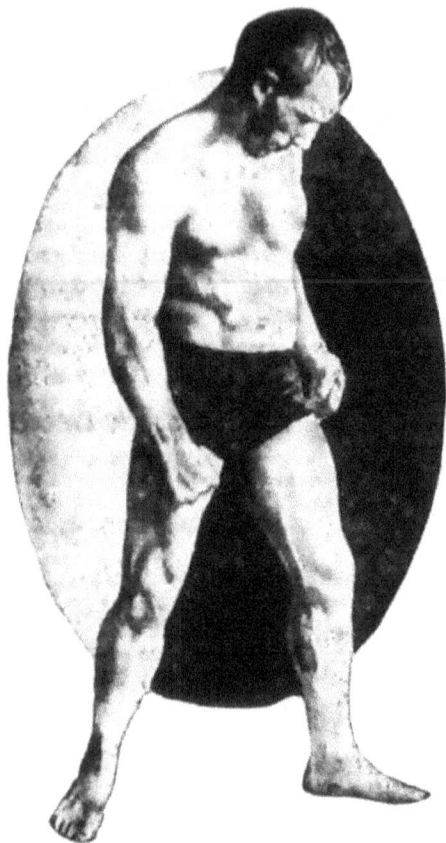

There was yet another lengthy delay because Fitz also wanted to be paid before he would enter the ring. The sweating crowd fumed. Finally, after receiving payment, Bob approached the ring at 11:05 p.m. to a great number of hisses, jeers, and groans. The crowd was angry with him for having made them wait in the heat.

Bob removed his long white bathrobe, looking very confident, ignoring the hissing and hooting, which then turned to cheers and applause. He wore white trunks with an American flag belt around his waist.[549] He brought his own gloves with him. Like Sharkey, his hands and wrists were wrapped in bandages. Jeff said, "Fitz's hands are thoroughly bandaged, and even the fingers are wrapped in adhesive tape."

Sharkey manager O'Rourke examined the gloves and bandages and pronounced them to be all right.

With Bob were Bob Armstrong, Dan Hickey, Jeff Thorne, and Jack Neary. Sharkey had Tom O'Rourke, Spider Kelly, Jim Buckley and Jack Sullivan.

Fitz walked over to Jeff and told him, "I got my whack before I went on," meaning that he got his money. Jeffries said that Fitz was "the coolest, shiftiest fighter that ever got inside the ropes and he has the hardest punch of the whole lot."

---

549 Another source said that Fitz entered the ring wearing a pale lavender robe and pink tights.

Sharkey remained seated while Tom O'Rourke sponged and rubbed him down with a towel and gave him a lemon to suck. Tom's seconds also fanned him. Bob remained standing.

The men shook hands at 11:12 p.m., ready to begin the fight.[550]

1st round

Typical of his style, Sharkey ferociously attacked Fitzsimmons, rushing in with swings, but Bob was able to hit and move, back away and sidestep to avoid him. Tom did the rushing, while Bob was feeling him out, taking his time.

Eventually, Fitz held his ground more. They went at it, but Fitz seemed too clever for him, showing his craftiness and generalship. Timing Tom on the way in, Fitz would dip, step inside of Sharkey's hard rushing wallops and counter, or he would use his nimble footwork to evade him altogether. Bob landed relatively easily, mostly with hard rights and right uppercuts to the ribs, focusing on the body.

Bob landed powerful blows, but Sharkey remained anxious to mix it up. Fitz backed out of reach whenever Tom rushed, but always came back with solid punches to the head and body.

Sharkey kept swinging, and amongst their mix-ups, landed a number of hard blows to jaw, nose, and ribs. However, Fitz's right was like a triphammer, and he landed his hard left shift to the solar plexus, as well as a left uppercut. Fitz landed a right to the stomach and Sharkey began backing away.

Perhaps as a result of his ability to land so easily, Fitzsimmons grew even more aggressive. However, in a careless unguarded moment, Sharkey knocked him down, each local source giving its own version.

Eagle: Fitz pressed Sharkey back to the ropes and missed a vicious right uppercut. Sharkey countered with a terrific left jab in the mouth that sent Bob's head back, and followed it with a powerful right to the shoulder that dropped Fitz. He went down on his back and Tom fell and rolled over him from the force of his own blow. Fitz essentially backed this version.

Journal ('Right Cross'): Tom became wild and Fitz ducked a left smash, but Sharkey followed fast with a right to the jaw that staggered Bob. Sharkey shot another punch to the same place, Fitz toppled over onto his back, and Tom fell over him from the force of his own blow.

James Jeffries (for the *World*): "Sharkey lands a wild left swing on the jaw and sends Fitz down backward and falls down over him." Jeff also said, "It was a holy terror – that left swing on the nose."

Sun: Tom went in to mix it and Fitz slugged him right and left until Tom clinched. As they broke, Tom landed a terrific left on the jaw. Another

---

550 The following account and post-fight discussion is taken from the *New York Journal, New York World, New York Sun, New York Herald, New York Tribune, Brooklyn Daily Eagle*, August 24, 25, 1900.

punch knocked Fitz down, but before he rose, the bell rang. "The Cornishman was unquestionably in some distress from the effects of that punch, but the bell came to his rescue."

Gus Ruhlin (reporting for the *Journal*): "It was all Bob's round up to the very last, when Sharkey put him down."

Fitz rose and the bell rang. Neither man heard it amongst the roars of the crowd. Sharkey attacked and they both threw punches and clinched. Their seconds, who had heard the bell, entered the ring and brought their men to their corners. After a few seconds in the corner, Bob looked as well as ever, having quickly revived.

2nd round

Encouraged by his round-ending knockdown, Sharkey again attacked like a bulldog, rushing in. Fitz backed up, blocked, and clinched. However, Bob was "as fresh as a rose," clever and cunning, and had gauged his man.

After breaking, to the sailor's surprise, Fitzsimmons began to do some rushing of his own. He sparred and feinted, got within distance and then landed awful uppercuts. Fitz stepped inside a Sharkey left swing and shot a right to the lip that drew blood. Fitz feinted a left for the head and then shot a right to the body. Sharkey's rushing wallops were in vain, as Fitzsimmons easily avoided them, sending in the uppercuts to the body. Bob sidestepped and counterpunched hard, jolting Tom with his short shots. Fitz caved in his body with ripping blows, and then straightened him up with a few lefts and rights to the chin.

They went at it, both landing good blows, but Fitz had the best of it. Ruhlin said, "Look at the way he is lacing it into the sailor's ribs. That was a nasty uppercut, too, wasn't it?" He staggered Tom with a right smash to the heart, catching Sharkey as Tom was advancing. Tom threw his arms around Bob's neck.

After that, they both mixed it up, swinging right and left heavily for the head and body until Fitz landed a right to the jaw which made Tom hang on. Sharkey kept throwing wild and inaccurate blows, while Fitz piled in with short effective jolts that made the sailor reel backward to the ropes.

This time it was Fitzsimmons who knocked Sharkey down.

Journal: Tom rushed in, but Bob dropped him with an uppercut to the wind. Ruhlin: Fitz kept hitting him and Sharkey seemed all at sea. Bob landed another hard shot to the body and Sharkey went down.

Eagle: Fitz dropped Sharkey with a left hook on the chin.

Jeffries: Sharkey missed a left for the head but sent in a hard right to the body that shook Fitz. Sharkey rushed in and ran into a right hook on the jaw that shook him up. He rushed in again and Fitz landed left and right hooks on the jaw that sent Tom to the floor.

Sun: Tom fought desperately until Fitz landed a heavy right to the jaw which knocked him down.

Some said the blow that dropped him was a left hook to the head, some a right to the head, while others said it was a body shot. Another local account said Fitz dropped Tom with a series of rights and lefts to the body and head, which appears to have been the case.

Sharkey showed his toughness by rising. Fitz then finished him off.

Journal: Tom rose and missed a right. Bob ended matters by using his shift, bringing his right foot forward, sending the left to the stomach and then shooting his left up to the jaw, twisting his left leg into the punch. "No one of that big crowd who saw it will forget that punch." Tom's head dropped forward as if his neck had been suddenly broken. His legs bent and he sank to the floor on his hands and knees.

Sun: After he regained his feet, Tom swung away again. Fitz brushed aside the blows and dashed in with a volley of smashes that blinded the sailor. Bob landed all over until Tom's hands dropped. A double body punch almost ended him as Tom groaned. In another mix-up, Bob landed a close in left swing that did not travel very far, landing on the point of the jaw and sending Tom down on all fours, the blood running down his mouth. Fitz had a little blood trickling down his lips too.

Ruhlin: Ever the finisher, Fitz was on top of him, reigning in the blows, forcing Tom to hold. Bob landed another stunning left. Fighting like a demon, Bob landed terrific lefts and rights to the face and body. One landed square in the solar plexus, and then the left crashed to the jaw and Tom went down and out.

Jeffries: Sharkey rose after eight seconds. Fitz rushed at him with left and right hooks on the jaw four or five times in succession and Sharkey fell down on his face.

Eagle: After Sharkey rose, Fitz bore down upon him. Tom threw blows hard enough to turn the tide of the battle, had they landed. Fitz was merciless, landing right and left to the face, and Tom hugged. Bob pushed him off and threw in the finishing blows. Bob hooked the left to the jaw and right to the temple. Before Tom fell, another left hit him, but it was not necessary.

Sharkey's efforts to rise were in vain. He could not lift his head. He swayed as his hands felt about on the floor as if looking for something he could not find. One supporting hand gave way and his shoulder bumped down to the canvas. He drew a leg up as if to get it under him, but it slid back. The instinct to rise was there, but it was only a flicker, and it went out. Referee White counted him out at 2 minutes and 6 seconds of the round.

Ruhlin said, "Just look how Fitz wins. He's a wonder, isn't he?"

Fitzsimmons walked over to Jeffries at ringside and said, "Get up, Jeff, and shake hands." They shook cordially. The crowd cheered Fitzsimmons, who had squared accounts with Sharkey.

After Tom was brought to his senses, Bob walked over and they shared some water from the same bottle.

The Sun said that Sharkey grew too confident after dropping Fitzsimmons. Fitz once again showed his tremendous hitting powers and his science in avoiding many dangerous smashes. He stepped inside of Tom's swings with short, accurate hooks to the head and body. "It is safe to say that there was not a punch delivered by Fitzsimmons that did not take effect." Whether it was a right or left, to the body or head, "there was enough power behind every punch to take away the phenomenal strength of the muscular Sailor, who was outclassed in headwork, generalship, speed and hitting." Fitz literally beat him down as if he had a hammer in each hand. In every respect, Fitz was Sharkey's master. *The World* said Fitzsimmons had landed three blows to Sharkey's one.

The press complimented Fitzsimmons for knocking out in the span of two weeks two men whom Jeffries had failed to knock out. It stood to reason that Bob was in better shape to take on Jeff than he was the previous summer. "Fitzsimmons stands today as the only rival to Jeffries. There is no other pugilist in his class." He had fought his way to the top again and had earned his shot. Bob "clearly proved his right to another chance at championship honors, the lines of parallel being shortly drawn."

Fitzsimmons told the *Sun*,

> In the first round he caught me lightly on the jaw and knocked me down. It was not exactly a hard blow, but it was enough to jar me. The punch that did the business was the left. I made a feint with the right and as he came forward I nailed him with the left.

> I observed as soon as my glove landed that the smash had dazed Sharkey, for he began to sway back and forth like a drunken man. Quick as a flash I hit him on the jaw again, and this was the knockout.

In other interviews, Fitz claimed to have slipped down in the 1st round. He agreed that Tom hit him hard once or twice, but that was before he got going. Bob told the *World* that he hit Sharkey whenever and wherever he pleased.

Fitzsimmons said that Sharkey was not as good a man as Ruhlin, for Gus was shiftier and cleverer. The only thing Tom did better than Ruhlin was hit harder. "Tom certainly can hit a terrible wallop." However, in another statement, Fitz gave Sharkey more credit. "I was lucky to defeat him in two rounds. He was cleverer than I ever saw him, and far and away better than when he fought Ruhlin." "Sharkey blocked and ducked better than I thought he could, too." Either way, Fitz said that the fight proved conclusively how affairs really stood when they had fought the first time in San Francisco in late 1896.

Sharkey took his defeat good-naturedly. He had a puffed lip and a bruise over the left temple, but otherwise was unmarked. He said,

Fitz surprised me. I thought I had him sure in the first round, but he came back strong and beat me out in the lead. Fitz is a great fighter. He has a wonderful punch and can inflict great punishment. I hit him repeatedly in the opening round and felt confident that I would end matters in the next. Although defeated, I have no complaint to offer. I was beaten fairly and squarely in a hard battle. I may have been a trifle careless after I thought I had Fitz going, but that was my own fault. …

I made a mistake in mixing it up. If I had followed the advice of my seconds and fought the second round the way I did the first everything would have been all right, but I thought otherwise and I was licked. Fitz is a wonderful fighter for an old man. Why Jeffries is not in it with him, and if the two ever meet I will put my money on Bob. He is the greatest hitter in the world. When he landed on me I did not know what hit me. The blows came so fast that I did not know how to fight him at all. … Fitz is the toughest customer I ever faced. He has two good hands; you don't know which one is going to land first. … I simply wish to say that Fitz can beat them all and is really the champion. He'll whip Jeffries as sure as you live, if they ever meet.

Sharkey further said, "I never knew anybody could hit such blows." "As a marksman Fitz is without an equal in the world. He can hit straighter and harder than any man I ever fought. Every blow he hit hurt me. They did not seem to come hard, but they fairly lifted me off the floor and took the life out of me."

Referee Charley White said,

The fight, though short, was the best I ever saw. Both men displayed great gameness. Each man had a hard punch. It was a hard, fast, furious fight from the first tap of the bell. … Sharkey landed a heavy swing on Fitz just as the gong sounded at the end of the round. The blow knocked Fitz down, but it was a trifle too high to be effective.

Fitz and Sharkey mixed it up from the opening till the finish of the second and last round. Fitzsimmons got in a number of hard punches on Sharkey that would have knocked out a less courageous man than the sailor. When the end came Sharkey stood the rain of blows like the stoic he is. When nearly gone Fitz got in his famous left hook to the jaw that won the fight.

Fitz proved by his fight that he is a clever, shifty man with a hard punch. No man in pugilistic circles has anything on Fitz in any shape. He is right in line for a return match for the championship. Should he and Jeffries come together again in the squared circle the sport-loving people of this country will have a chance to see the greatest fighters of the age struggle for supremacy.

White was also quoted as saying,

> Fitzsimmons is a great fighter, and a battle between him and Jeffries would be the best fight ever seen. Sharkey did well in the first round and seemed to have a chance, but when Fitzsimmons got in that stomach punch it was easy to see that the fight was almost over. It was the same punch that beat Ruhlin. No man can take it and still fight.

Discussing Fitzsimmons, James Jeffries wrote, "He is the best man of all of them that I have met. I like Fitz and I'm perfectly willing to fight him within six months before any club in this country offering the greatest amount of money." "I hope Fitz will be as well when he fights me as he is tonight. It ought to make an interesting contest."

When asked what his future plans were, Fitzsimmons said, "I'm going to take a rest. I think I need one. I have engaged already in two battles inside of two weeks. ... I am not as young as I used to be, but I am as strong as I was when I was 21 years old. I took care of myself, and that is the secret of my success." However, Bob also said that he wanted to become world champion again, and after his time off, he wanted to fight Jeffries.

> He whipped me once, but I don't think he will do it again. When we met I had not fought in a couple of years, and naturally I was not in the best of condition. But I am in great form now and really think that if we were to meet again soon I would come out on top. In fact, I held Jeffries too cheap. I learned a lesson and will not be caught napping the next time. If they give me enough money I guess I will be ready to fight Jeffries some time inside of the next six months.

Bob's hands were tender. His knuckles were a little swollen and bruised. He did not remove his hand bandages until the following day. He had a couple body bruises, a tiny scratch under the right eye, and a little abrasion of the inner lip. Bob also claimed that he hurt his right arm in the fight. Therefore, it made sense to wait the six months that Jeff wanted.

Still, Fitzsimmons issued conflicting statements. In one interview, Bob said, "I'm not yet ready to say what I'll do in regard to a fight with Jeffries." However, Fitz was also quoted as saying, "I stand ready to meet Jeffries before September 1, but he does not seem to want any of my game." This sounded like promotional talk rather than a genuine desire to fight again in a week.

The Sun wanted Fitz and Jeff to fight the following week, and said that it was up to the boxers to prove whether they "prefer the pleasantries of a theatrical tour to a mix-up inside the ropes." However, Jeff said the fight could take place in about six months.

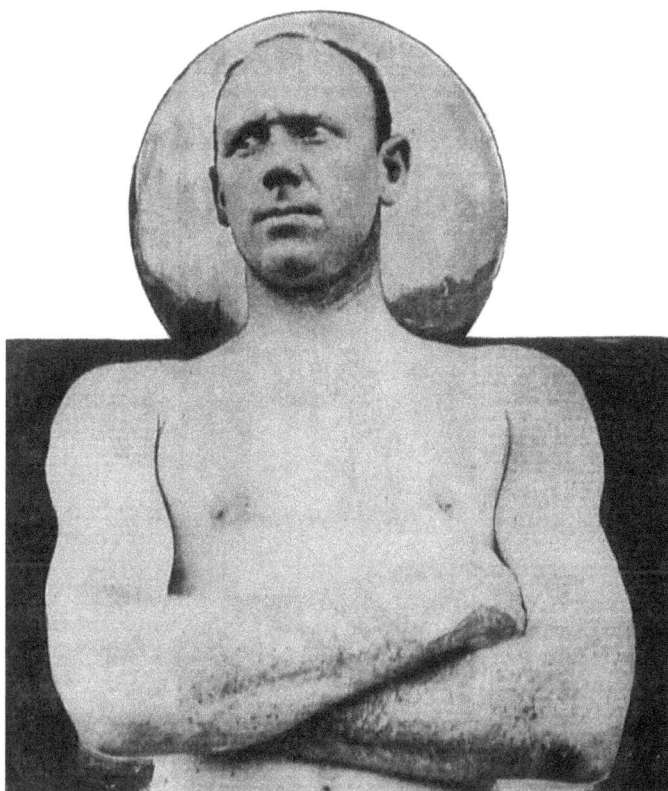

Jeffries had a tour scheduled and was not interested in fighting any time soon. Therefore, the day after the fight, perhaps for show, aware of the fact that Jeff was not ready or really interested in fighting that quickly, Fitz signed a contract with the Twentieth Century Athletic Club for a fight with Jeffries in one week. Bob said, "I've changed my mind about not fighting again in six months, and if Jeffries is satisfied I will meet him next Friday night." He also said, "I had serious intentions of quitting the ring, but as I have a good chance of becoming the champion again I want to fight Jeffries." Of course, he could afford to seem courageous, given that he was well aware that Jeff was not going to fight him in a week.

A battle between them so soon was "rather improbable." It was said that Bob's willingness to fight again so quickly was a surprise, given that he too had said that he would not fight again for six months. Both Jeff and Fitz intended to make money in theatrical tours.

Bill Brady responded,

> Fitz can make all the bluffs he wants to now. He has the upper hand, but Jeffries is the champion and will dictate terms. Jeffries quit training about ten days ago, and is in no condition to meet anybody next Friday night. Why didn't Fitz give us his assurance about two weeks ago when we asked him, that he would take on the champion?

No, he did not care to because he did not mean to fight. Now that Jim is in no condition and would be at a decided disadvantage if he agreed to battle with Bob inside of a week, Fitz tries to make a grand stand play. ...

He can have a mill with Jeffries, but it will not be next week. There are plenty of places outside of this State where the pair can settle their grievances. And what's more the world is not coming to an end right away. When Fitz was the champion he only fought once in two years. Jeffries on the other hand has met two men sine he knocked Fitz out. And what's more Fitz can thank Jeff for his victory over Sharkey. The boiler maker gave the sailor such a hard beating that he has not recovered from it to this day. Sharkey before Jeffries met him and the Sharkey of Friday night are two different individuals as far as physical condition is concerned.

If Fitz is so desirous of meeting the man who licked him so squarely last year why does he not post a forfeit? It will be covered in a hurry.[551]

Fitzsimmons responded to Brady by saying that he would post a $2,500 forfeit to fight next Friday night. When told that Jeff would not be ready by then, Fitz replied, "Well, then he can't get on a scrap with me." When asked about Carson City as a possible location for a later fight, Bob said, "The devil with that. The East is good enough for me. Brady told me to put up my money, didn't he? It's up." Of course, Brady was talking about a forfeit for a fight in the next six months.

Some thought that Fitz did not really want or need to fight Jeffries, because his popularity had boomed owing to his recent performances, so he, like Jeff, could make money on a theatrical tour. However, by seeming more willing to fight, he could gain an upper hand over Jeffries in public opinion, and perhaps in future financial negotiations.

Jeffries was in Norfolk, Virginia on August 27. That afternoon, he umpired a baseball game, and might have sparred 3 rounds with Jack McCormick. Jeff said that he would not recognize Bob's challenge for a fight within one week, because he was making money on an umpiring tour. "I will, at the proper time, give him ample opportunity to redeem the drubbing I gave him." Jeff planned to return to New York in a couple days to spar at Sullivan's benefit on the 29th, and then witness the scheduled August 30 Corbett-McCoy fight. He was willing to negotiate a Fitz fight to be held later in the season. "Pugilism needs a rest at present."[552]

Interestingly enough, Fitzsimmons said that if Jeff did not consent to a fight the following week, before the Horton law was repealed, that he

551 *New York Sun*, August 26, 1900. As time passed, the point of view that Jeff had softened Sharkey up for others gained greater acceptance.
552 *New York Journal*, August 28, 1900. Cyberboxingzone.com.

would retire from the ring for good and not fight any more. Fitz again claimed that Jeff licked him because he was doped. Brady responded that the dope was in Jeff's fists.

Brady noted that if Fitz was really anxious to regain the title, he would consent to a later meeting. "The world is not coming to an end next week. There are plenty of other places where we can fight. Jeffries is in no condition to fight on Friday next." Jeff was weighing over 250 pounds and not ready to fight immediately. On Jeff's behalf, Bill was willing to post a forfeit and sign an agreement to hold the bout within six months' time. Brady felt that Carson City or San Francisco would be suitable locations.

Brady also argued that the deluge of recent bouts meant that the public needed a rest. Fitz-Sharkey did not have the hoped-for attendance, and the club actually lost money. The market had been flooded. Corbett-McCoy was already scheduled for the 30th. He felt that waiting to fight would mean more money for everyone. Further, "Suppose something happened at the Garden on Thursday night when McCoy and Corbett meet, would it not hurt the attendance the following night?" That was an interesting thought.

Fitz responded, "I will not go in the ring with him within six months' time. It is now or never. It is no use of talking any further on the subject." Bob said that he was going out of the business along with the Horton law, and was retiring. Brady said the fact that Fitz was retiring demonstrated that Fitzsimmons really had no intention of fighting Jeffries, because Bob did not want any more of the Californian's smashes.[553]

Opinions varied as to whom had the best of the argument, if one did. *The National Police Gazette* harshly called Jeffries discredited and meriting disdain for failing to take on Fitz the following week. It said that such an astute manager as Brady would not allow him to risk losing his title in another fight until he had been exploited as a theatrical star. It argued that the original offer to fight the winner of the Fitz-Sharkey fight a week later was an unadulterated bluff, "made for no other reason or purpose than to obtain the usual cheap notoriety which prize fighters are prone to seek." To make the offer in a face-saving way, so that he would not actually have to fight, Jeff "arbitrarily fixed a certain day when the $5,000 forfeit must be posted, announcing his intention to quit his training camp if this extraordinary condition was not complied with."

However, those were Jeff's terms, and when the forfeit was not posted on time, Jeff ceased his training. When the forfeit was later posted after the deadline, it was less than the required amount, something the *Gazette* failed to acknowledge. Still, the *Gazette* felt that Jeff's refusal to fight immediately, after initially making the offer to do so, had brought him some humiliation. It noted that Fitz did much better against common opponents: Sharkey, Ruhlin, Armstrong, and Corbett. "While Fitz never actually fought

---

553 *New York Sun*, August 28, 1900; *New York World*, August 25, 1900.

Armstrong, what he did to him in training bouts every day demonstrated his ability to beat him in short order any time they started."[554]

The argument in Jeff's favor was that Fitzsimmons had the opportunity to fight Jeffries within the next six months, and declined, choosing to retire instead. This made it seem that he did not really want to fight Jeffries. Jeff had already defeated Fitz, Sharkey, and Corbett in the span of a year, so it was a bit of a stretch to imply cowardice. This was the type of gamesmanship that Fitzsimmons had engaged in with Corbett for years prior to their fight. Fitz was also repeating a pattern that he had established after defeating Corbett – win a big fight, capitalize on his popularity with a theatrical tour for a lengthy period of time, and then come back and make big money with another huge fight when public demand was at its zenith.

The truth was that Jeff was still nursing his injury and was not in shape to fight on such short notice. Further, he was looking to make easy money in a theatrical tour. Fitz had just fought twice and was nursing bruised hands, and did not really want to fight any time soon either, given his booming popularity and ability to make money on the road as well. It was in both of their financial interests to wait and build the fight, particularly since there was a glut of New York bouts leading up to the Horton law's termination.

On August 29, 1900 at New York's Madison Square Garden, a benefit for John L. Sullivan generated $15,000 in ticket sales. About 5,000 to 6,000 were in attendance, including a dozen women. In separate 3-round exhibitions, Gus Ruhlin, Tom Sharkey, and Peter Maher all sparred. The most popular fighter who attended was Fitzsimmons. He engaged in a 3-round comedy with Jeff Thorne, each mock dropping the other several times each round. "It was the best fake fight in many moons, and the crowd laughingly enjoyed it." The two "showed how easy it is to fake grogginess, falls and knockdowns." "It was the cleverest kind of a fake."

Jeffries sparred 3 friendly rounds with former champion John L. Sullivan. Sully, wearing black trunks (instead of his usual green), was gray, fat, and out of shape. The announcer said that Jeff was ready to defend his title at any time, which statement was met with mixed applause and hisses. Jeff looked to be no more than 220 pounds, much less than his manager claimed. None of the 3 rounds lasted even a minute.[555]

554 *National Police Gazette*, September 15, 1900.
555 *New York Journal, Sun, Herald*, August 30, 1900; *National Police Gazette*, September 15, 1900.

CHAPTER 25

Hell Hath No Fury...

The final fight held under the Horton era was Jim Corbett vs. Kid McCoy. There were some rumors before the fight that it had been fixed, but both combatants denied it. Some subsequently questioned the fight's sincerity, while others thought it was on the up and up.

To make the match, or generate publicity for it, McCoy spread the word that Corbett was afraid to meet him. He also said that if Corbett should say things about him that Jim had said of others that he would break his jaw. McCoy went to Corbett's café. Perhaps not so coincidentally, Jim was there with several newspaper men, "apparently with no very definite purpose in view, but it was in the air maybe that something might come off." The two pugilists engaged in insults and threats, and eventually they decided to meet on August 30 to settle things. This was the type of publicity stunt for which Corbett was famous.

Kid McCoy had victories over Ruhlin, Maher, and Choynski, amongst others. His real name was Norman Selby, and he was also known as the Corkscrew Kid. Corbett was coming off his impressive performance in a loss to Jeffries months earlier, in May.

The fight was considered a competitive and even matchup in its inception, anticipated to be the "greatest scientific battle ever seen." Corbett had a size advantage, while McCoy perhaps had a punching power advantage, but both fighters were "conceded to be the two cleverest boxers in the world." They both knew all of the tricks of hitting, stopping, and getting away.[556]

Sharkey, who had victories over both, believed McCoy would win because he was just as clever and hit harder. Tom later changed his pick to Corbett (a typical Sharkey trait), saying that the Corbett that fought Jeffries ought to win easily.[557]

Fitzsimmons thought Corbett would win because he was taller, heavier, stronger and cleverer than McCoy, and the theory that Corbett could not punch was erroneous. Given that Jim was used to fighting big, strong men like Jeff and Sharkey, it would be a welcome break to fight someone smaller.

---

556 *National Police Gazette*, August 18, 25, 1900. McCoy career highlights included: 1896 KO15 Tommy Ryan and KO3 Jim Daly; 1897 KO1 George LaBlanche and KO2 Australian Billy Smith; 1898 W20 Gus Ruhlin and WDQ5 Joe Goddard; 1899 LKOby10 Tom Sharkey and W20 Joe Choynski; and 1900 KO5 Peter Maher and KO4 Joe Choynski.
557 *New York Sun, New York World*, August 30, 1900.

When assessing McCoy before he was supposed to fight Corbett back in 1898 (before Jim's father's homicide/suicide), one said that the Kid was the "epitome of all styles." He was quick, could punch, attack or retreat.[558]

Prior to the fight, the *National Police Gazette* reported a quote from the *Exchange* speculating, "If Jim and the 'Kid' fight on the level it will be a fight that will be a fight." Sam Austin questioned the rumor.

> Just why there should be any doubt about the fight being 'on the level' I am at a loss to comprehend, but perhaps the talented young person who penned the above for the edification and enlightenment of the readers of his column has reason to believe that all fights are prearranged affairs nowadays.

Austin felt that victory would mean a great deal to either fighter in terms of securing a match with Jeffries, so both would try their best to win.[559]

The day of the fight, Corbett was the favorite. The talent believed he would win owing to his superior weight, height, and ring experience. Although the Kid took hard punches from Choynski, Ruhlin, and Maher, he "has often shown that he cannot stand the slugging of a heavier man." Corbett was the quickest puncher in the ring and threw more punches than the Kid did. "Those who think Corbett should win say that Jim will be fast enough to put it all over McCoy and that the Kid will be knocked out or outpointed because Corbett will land two blows to the Hoosier's one." However, McCoy hit harder, having twice decked Sharkey in the 3rd round before succumbing to him in the 10th. Further, the Kid was very clever and much faster than Jeffries was.

On August 30, 1900 at Madison Square Garden, James J. Corbett took on Kid McCoy. 8,500-10,000 spectators paid $5, $10, $25, and $35 to witness the fight.

The considerable pre-fight talk of a potential fake influenced the betting. Most of the money came in on Corbett, such that the odds gradually shifted from 10 to 8, to 3 to 1, with Corbett the favorite. Not much money was placed on McCoy.

558 *New York World*, August 1, 1898.
559 *National Police Gazette*, September 1, 1900.

It was reported that the two agreed to split the purse evenly, win or lose, although Corbett later denied it. Generally, sporting men did not favorably look upon these purse splits, feeling it was a disincentive to give best efforts. The boxers would be splitting 60% of the gate.

Wearing white trunks and no robe, McCoy entered the ring at 10:20 p.m. His brother Homer Selby, Philadelphia Jack O'Brien, and Harry Harris seconded him. Corbett followed a few minutes later, wearing a long robe covering his black trunks. When Corbett offered, McCoy refused to shake hands with him, turning away. Corbett bandaged both of his hands before putting the gloves on.

Writing the report for the *World*, Jeffries said that both men appeared to be in good condition.

> I like Corbett better than I do McCoy. I think Corbett looks just about as well as he did the night he fought me. He is too big for the Kid. It's going to be a great deal harder for McCoy to hit Corbett than any other man he ever fought. Corbett is not only too big for the Kid, but he is too fast. It is a case of class.

The *World*'s day-of-the-fight report said that Corbett would weigh about 183 pounds to the Kid's 172 pounds. It also estimated 186 to 170 pounds respectively. McCoy had said that he expected to weigh 175 pounds, ten more than he had ever fought at before. Some reported that Corbett weighed 190 pounds, his highest fighting weight up to that point.

The night of the fight, Corbett refused to give his weight. Jeffries estimated Corbett's weight to be 183-185 pounds. McCoy claimed to weigh 170 pounds. Jeff said the Kid weighed at least 170 pounds. "It looks like solid stuff, too; no fat or useless flesh." Jim was 6' ½" to McCoy's 5'11".[560]

They were scheduled to box 25 rounds. Charley White refereed.

1st round

Both were too anxious and nervous to do any harm, neither landing a hard blow. However, their sparring was clever and interesting, one of the prettiest exhibitions of feinting and footwork ever seen. Jeff said, "When you get two such clever men as these together you can't expect much damage right away."

2nd round

McCoy started as the aggressor, but as the round progressed, Corbett grew more confident and aggressive. McCoy then backed away, although he occasionally rushed in with an attack. They threw and landed some head and body shots, but none seemed particularly effective, because they were both very cautious. Corbett did land one good left to the body that

---

560 *New York Herald*, August 29-31, 1900; *New York Daily Tribune, New York World, New York Sun, Brooklyn Daily Eagle, New York Journal*, August 31, 1900.

produced a red mark. The round was essentially more fancy sparring. Jeffries said,

> They are both sparring very hard, but neither is doing any damage when the round closes. I suppose this is just about as scientific as any bout that was ever fought, but thus far neither one has shown any advantage over the other. Each one has taken the lead and made the pace for a few minutes. Corbett seems to me to be the most anxious to get at close quarters, but the Kid keeps slipping away from him.

3rd round

Throughout the round, Corbett was the more aggressive fighter. Jeff said, "He is cutting out the pace most of the time. He is too big for the Kid." In general, they engaged in very fast work, but without much harm done. Jim advanced and feinted, but the Kid escaped with clever footwork. At one point, Corbett started a hook for the head, but shifted it down to the ribs, where it landed. "That blow hurts more than you'd think." Corbett won the round with some uppercuts.

The first 3 rounds featured clever sparring by both boxers. Some felt that McCoy had not fought up to his previous form, for he was mostly cautious and defensive.

4th round

Corbett took the aggressive again. He feinted rapidly and gradually forced McCoy to the ropes, where he rained blow after vicious blow on McCoy's body and head. McCoy clinched and then retreated. Corbett was confident and determined, and he dashed in with a storm of blows. A right to the mouth made the Kid spit out blood. Corbett rushed in and they engaged in what Jeffries called "the fastest infighting I have ever seen between big men." Jim landed a left hook on the short ribs and right on the jaw. As they broke away, Corbett rushed in with "a perfect storm of lefts and rights to the body and jaw and dazes McCoy. It is so fast that no man living can follow all the blows. Corbett has all the best of it and rushes McCoy to an off corner, punishing him badly." McCoy blocked some and clinched repeatedly to save himself. His legs were shaky.

Corbett was all over him with tremendous speed, rushing the Kid across the ring, landing with rapid jabs, hooks and uppercuts, to both the body and head. "He had received a punching that was entirely unexpected and was too fast for him to escape from." McCoy was in trouble, staggering around and looking like he was about to be knocked out. Jeff said,

> McCoy is very weak and clinching to save himself as the gong rings for the end of the round. I never saw greater speed than this, and Corbett's punishing power is tremendous. ... I tell you, the Kid isn't in Jim's class. The bell just saves him. He goes staggering to his corner, with blood flowing from his mouth.

McCoy had failed to fight back in the way that many had expected he would. What blows he did throw either missed or landed without effect. He was in against a bigger, stronger, and faster scientific master.

5th round

The round started slowly and cautiously. Corbett was a bit winded from all of his exertions in the previous round. Eventually, McCoy threw a left jab, but Jim stepped in to meet him with a left uppercut on the body and right to the jaw, driving McCoy back. Corbett followed up with a very short but heavy left hook on the belly. "Corbett has been practicing those fierce short blows for a month and he gets tremendous power into this one." He pressed the Kid about the ring. McCoy was so weary that his mouth was open, but he used some feints, footwork and clinching to escape.

When McCoy clinched, Jim threw him off and hammered the stomach and face with rapidity. The faster the Kid retreated, the faster Corbett followed. Corbett pounded McCoy half a dozen times in the wind. The Kid showed some fight, but Corbett beat his guard down with vicious uppercuts and body blows that weakened him. McCoy's legs grew heavy and his blocking was ineffective.

Corbett smothered and knocked McCoy out, each local source giving its own version of the end.

Sun: Corbett belted him a left in the stomach and made McCoy visibly weaken. Jim whipped in three or four uppercuts, and as McCoy was gradually sinking, Corbett drove in a corking left smash to the pit of the stomach which doubled the Kid up in a heap on the floor. McCoy groaned in agony.

Eagle: The Kid backed away again, but Corbett caught him and sunk in a left to the body that doubled him up. McCoy grabbed Jim's left, but Corbett drove him away with a right in the stomach, and then floored him with another left in the pit of the stomach. He squirmed about as Referee White counted ten. McCoy rose just after the count had concluded.

Journal (Right Cross): Jim landed a left to the body, and then followed with two more to the same place that dropped the Kid.

Journal (second version): Corbett landed two lefts to the stomach that made McCoy wince with pain. A right to the heart then sent him down, and he did not beat the count.

Jeffries: On a break, a left jolt to the ribs made the Kid open his mouth even wider and he clinched again. Jim pushed him away with his right and followed with a terrific hook to the belly. "It is a tremendous blow. McCoy staggers three or four steps to the left, completely knocked out, and as he falls, Corbett hooks him rapidly with lefts and rights on the body and jaw." McCoy went down and out.

It was that heavy left in the belly that did the business. He makes faces and squirms and grimaces, and holds his hands low, as if he had been hit in the groin. That won't do. The blow that knocked him out was a perfectly fair punch in the belly. There is no question of a foul about it. The Kid is fairly and decisively defeated on his merits.

The fight ended at 2 minutes and 3 seconds of the 5th round. "Corbett has shown his superiority to McCoy all the way through this fight. He has completely outclassed him in cleverness, strength and speed. The Kid was no match for him at any stage of the game."

Jeffries said that Corbett was in better condition for this fight than he was at Carson City. "I helped to train him out there and I know what I am talking about. At Carson City Jim was run down by too much work until he was a mere shadow of himself." Jeff said that Corbett was still one of the best men in the ring. Clearly, he had maintained the form that he had shown against Jeffries in May.

The World said the two masters had given a wonderful display of cleverness and science, the cleverest ever seen in New York. The fans yelled themselves hoarse as the men feinted, side-stepped or attacked. Although McCoy kept away by fast footwork and ducking, he was eventually beaten to the floor.

Some called it a very scientific fight, while others called it a fake. Those who said that it had been a pleasing demonstration of science, cleverness, and ring generalship countered those who questioned the bout's sincerity. The conclusion arrived at was that Corbett was capable of a hard blow once he was not in fear of one in return. He had taken McCoy's measure, solved him, and then pressed matters with hard punches. He had done the same thing years earlier with Charley Mitchell. Jeffries said McCoy had no business mixing it up with Corbett.

The experts did not think it was a fake. Tom Sharkey said Corbett won on the merits. Fitzsimmons said Corbett was too heavy for him and was as fast as ever. Gus Ruhlin said he knew Jim's weight would tell in the fight and thought he would win easily. Corbett won on his merits by superior cleverness. The Kid appeared slow and uncertain in his attacks and his punches without the same power shown in the past. The way that Jim went after him was enough to take the steam out of anyone. The solar plexus punch did the trick. "They say that Corbett cannot punch. Just put that query to McCoy."

The Brooklyn Daily Eagle rendered its opinion that the fighting was on the level and that McCoy had met in Corbett a man whose feinting, blocking, side-stepping, footwork and punching was superior to his own. Those who saw Jim's left to the solar plexus revised their opinions of his punching ability. It had been a most scientific bout, but once they decided to mix it up, Corbett was the stronger fighter.

The crowd was satisfied that the rumors of a fix were without foundation. The only real criticism lodged against McCoy was that some felt that although he was clearly a beaten man, he could have risen. Some said that he had quit, but "it is a fact that McCoy never did show any too great a liking for punishment." *The Eagle* felt that he was legitimately hurt, and that even had he risen, Corbett would have knocked him out for good soon thereafter.

Referee White, "whose honesty has never been questioned," believed that "McCoy was whipped simply because he had met his master."

> The work of both men was wonderfully clever and fully bore out all that has been said of them for some years past. Any one, no matter how big or strong, would have gone down from those last three blows that Corbett landed, as they were full of strength and were planted in the proper spot. ...

> It was the fastest and cleverest fight by heavyweights that I have ever seen. Corbett outclassed McCoy in every respect. His feinting was wonderful and he simply made a monkey of the Kid. When Corbett got to fighting at his best there was nothing to it. His blows were so fast that McCoy was blinded. The Kid was fairly smothered with the punches and was knocked out with a left-hand blow in the stomach which was a beauty. He was on his knees when I counted ten and was beaten then and there under the rules, though he got up a second later. But he did not have a chance to stay the round out, for Corbett would have finished him with another punch if he had been called upon to land one. Corbett won on the level, in my estimation, and I feel quite sure that the fight was an honest one.

White was also quoted as saying,

> I am satisfied that the contest was strictly on its merits. It was a good, clean, hard, well-fought fight, and I think the best man won. The men put up the cleverest exhibition of feinting and boxing that has ever been witnessed in the ring. I was on the look-out for any wrong-doing. McCoy's showing in the early part of the fight was a revelation. He held his own with Corbett, so far as science was concerned, but when it came to fighting, Corbett put it all over him.

Those who questioned the bout mostly did so based on the pre-fight rumors. *The National Police Gazette* noted that suspicions of a fake were based on several things, including rumors circulated in betting circles the afternoon of the battle that McCoy had agreed to be knocked out, that Corbett's friends offered to wager at most inconsistent odds, the fact that little money was wagered on McCoy, and some claims that McCoy did not fight up to his best form during the bout. "At any rate there was no fake in the manner in which McCoy's defeat was accomplished. He got a terrific solar plexus punch which he told me afterwards was the hardest blow he ever received." As a result of that punch, McCoy was so sick that he was unable to leave his dressing room for almost an hour after the fight.

Ultimately, the *Police Gazette* writer, who saw the bout, did not believe it was a fake.

> I am not prepared to believe that any prearranged understanding existed. It was as fine a display of boxing as I ever witnessed…. It was artistic in the extreme, and the participants deserve to be commended for the manner in which they performed, but while I ain't "from Missouri," some stronger evidence will have to be adduced before I will believe that the bout was anything but a fairly contested affair, in which the best man won.[561]

The New York Sun said the results refuted the rumors that the fight would not be genuine. "As far as the fight itself is concerned, it did not look like a fake for the reason that Corbett clearly outclassed McCoy in every way and gave a sound licking to him in the bargain." It was a grand exhibition of science on both sides, but McCoy weakened under heavy punishment. "Just as many persons predicted, McCoy demonstrated an inability to take grueling punishment." Corbett put forth such a marvelously swift assault "that nobody who saw the fight believed that it was anything except on the square."

Corbett feinted McCoy until he was all tangled up, and then cut loose with one of the fastest assaults ever seen, literally beating the Kid down and out with a storm of all kinds of blows, and "it was the power of the punches which undoubtedly puzzled McCoy more than anything else, for he had been led to believe that Jim could not punch." His punches came so rapidly that McCoy did not know how to ward them off and was completely puzzled. Conversely, McCoy could not hit Corbett at all.

Kid McCoy said that Jim Corbett was too fast for him, had great defense, and hit harder than most realized. "I never got hit as hard in my life as I did tonight." "Corbett may not knock a man out in a punch, but he has a blow with great force. It is a stinger. Corbett evaded my blows with ease." A left to the pit of the stomach (or ribs, depending on the quote) defeated him. "It took the wind out of me and made me gasp for breath."

> It was an awful blow and I felt myself sinking to the floor immediately after I received it…. I was not unconscious, but I could not regain my feet. It seemed as if my legs weighed a ton. …

> Corbett is certainly a clever fellow. He puzzled me at every stage. He sent the punches in with speed and accuracy and at times it seemed as if his glove was coming in all directions. … He was too quick and shifty for me. His weight was an important factor against me. …

---

561 *National Police Gazette*, September 15, 22, 1900.

I tried to clinch with Corbett to save myself, so as to recover my strength and continue. While I was attempting to embrace Corbett he hit me hard on the ribs. The blow knocked all the fight there was in me out and I fell to the floor.

Corbett said that he was a trifle nervous at the start, and did not care to mix it up too much in the early rounds, using them to figure out McCoy. However, once he had him measured, and realized that he could get to him easily, his confidence came to him and he knew it was all over. It was then that Corbett decided to rush in and slug him out.

Corbett admitted that McCoy puzzled him a little bit, but said that the Kid was not as fast as he thought he would be. Jim wanted to knock him out with a punch to the jaw, but the Kid protected his chin so well that he went for the body instead. "He was a very easy mark."

Of the finish, Corbett said, "He was tired and tried to fall on me for a clinch. I jumped back and let fly my right and left. Both landed in his stomach. He doubled up like a jack-knife, and I knew it was all over for him. I aimed a left for his solar plexus. It landed true, and my old friend, the Kid was lying sprawled upon the floor."

One paper estimated that 10,000 people generated $60,000 in gate receipts. Corbett told a *Sun* reporter that the receipts amounted to $72,000 and that his share was a bit over $31,000.

Although it was reported that the two pugilists split the boxer's end of the purse, Corbett denied it, saying that he always knew he would win, so he insisted on receiving a winner's share. However, McCoy did not exactly back Corbett's version. He "made an evasive reply, when asked if the purse was cut in two. All he would say was, 'I got what was coming to me, and that's all there is to it.'" McCoy's manager would neither confirm nor deny that the purse was evenly divided.

Corbett believed his showing entitled him to a rematch with Jeffries. He said that Jeff was easier to get at than McCoy, but was stronger and could stand punishment better.

Bob Fitzsimmons visited Corbett's café to congratulate him. Bob said, "You're the cleverest man in the world." Corbett replied, "Yes, and you are the hardest hitting fellow in the world." Of course, Jeffries had defeated both, so what did that make him?

Jeffries was anxious to arrange a match with Fitzsimmons, or at least eager to show that Bob was not really interested in meeting him. He offered to cancel all of his theatrical dates to take Bob on at either Carson City or San Francisco. All he asked for was a month's time for training. However, Bob responded, "I have retired and will not fight any one. ... I have all the money I want. I am going to be an actor and star in a play called *The Honest Blacksmith*." Fresh off the Ruhlin and Sharkey victories, Bob had plenty of money in the bank, a booming reputation, and could make more easy money on the stage, without having to worry about losing to Jeffries.[562]

Two days after the Corbett-McCoy bout, on September 1, 1900, the repeal of the Horton law went into effect and a new anti-prize-fight law (the Lewis law) made boxing illegal in New York. Boxing was dead in the most populous state in the nation. Cities like Chicago and Philadelphia only allowed 6-round bouts, too short to determine a champion. Nevada and California were on the other side of the country, in less populated areas. The large New York purses had spoiled boxers, and they feared that they would never see such bounty again.[563]

Jeffries was scheduled to umpire baseball games until September 20. "He is Jeffries, and that draws the crowd." After that, he was set to tour with the play *The Man from the West*. Fitz was going on the road with *The Honest Blacksmith*, and Corbett with *A Naval Cadet*.

Jeffries had also taken to weight lifting, and impressed everyone with his strength. Jeff said, "It's as easy as rolling off a log for me to push up a hundred and fifty pound dumb bell over my head ten times with one hand, and this only gives me an appetite for more." For his most miraculous feat, he took a 160-pound man and, "standing the man on his wrist, raised him from the floor to a level with his shoulder and then held him out at arm's length, keeping the man balanced there for fully a minute." No one ever said Jeff lacked for strength.

On September 5, 1900 at S.S. Lubin's laboratory in Philadelphia, Corbett and McCoy reproduced their battle for the *Evening Journal* cameras. They wanted to make some money with fight films. That idea had been abandoned for the real fight because the lighting was so poor. Therefore, they essentially acted out their fight again.[564]

Although the fight itself had satisfied the majority that it was legitimate, what really stirred up the speculation about the Corbett-McCoy bout being a fake was when the recently estranged wives of both Corbett and McCoy claimed that they both knew the fight was fixed. The sensationalist newspapers could not resist any controversy that would sell more newspapers, and so they went wild.

Jim Corbett was having marital problems with his wife of five years, Vera Corbett. They had a number of recent spats, and for the past six months, Jim had been an unhappy man. Apparently, unbeknownst to his

562 *New York Sun*, September 1, 1900.
563 *National Police Gazette*, September 22, 1900. It was estimated that during the Horton law's existence (Sept. 1896 - Sept. 1900), 1.76 million boxing patrons at New York clubs paid nearly $3 million dollars ($2,657,800) to watch 3,350 fights. 1898 and 1899 were the banner years, with 900 fights taking place each of those two years. The fighters' share of the purses was $998,186, while the promoters made $1,677,120. Sharkey cleared the most, at $92,000, with Jeffries coming in second at $90,000. The largest gate receipts were for Jeffries-Corbett, which brought in $60,000. Corbett-McCoy was said to have generated $55,310.
564 *New York Journal*, September 3, 6, 7, 1900.

wife, on or about September 8, Corbett sailed for Europe, possibly with another woman. At that point, his wife filed divorce papers and made some harsh allegations.

Mrs. Corbett alleged that the recent fight was fixed, and told her version of events. There were several secret meetings between the boxers' representatives. The first plan was for Corbett to throw the battle. Mrs. Corbett claimed to have written a check for $2,500 to square McCoy. Of course, it is unclear as to why she would need to pay McCoy if Corbett was going to be the one doing the lying down. At the last moment, Corbett decided that he could not afford to lose. "When it came time for the men to enter the ring Corbett told McCoy's representative that he would not lie down, but wanted the Kid to do it." This also did not entirely make sense, because the whole purpose of fixing a fight was so that certain persons could make a killing off wagers placed on the fight. To alter the fixed result at the last minute would have cost those in on the scheme the money they had already bet on McCoy. She said that McCoy kicked because he had not trained any. Of course, if one of them was going to throw it, it would not have mattered who trained or did not train, and so it would not make sense that his objection was based on his condition unless Corbett wanted the fight to be on the square. Regardless, Mrs. Corbett claimed to have in her possession proof that would show that the battle was not a square one.

When told of her claims, Kid McCoy responded,

> The woman does not know what she is talking about. What, me lay down? And to Corbett too? Why, that is one of the best jokes of the year. She is sore because he left her and is trying to square herself and get the sympathy of the public. As to my not being in condition, why it's a rank falsehood. Do you mean to say that I would throw my friends for $2,500. A million dollars might tempt me. But such a paltry sum, why never. The fight was an honest one. I lost because Corbett was the better man.[565]

A few days later, Mrs. Corbett's allegations grew, claiming knowledge that the Corbett-Sharkey rematch was also fixed. She said, "What would they say if I were to produce the check for $2,000 which I drew in favor of poor McVey, who jumped into the ring to stop the [Corbett-Sharkey II] fight?" She claimed that George Considine was the one who was supposed to jump in, but at the last moment grew too cowardly to do so, and got McVey to do it and bear the brunt of the criticism.

Things really heated up when Kid McCoy's wife backed Mrs. Corbett's claims. Coincidentally, the Kid was having marital problems as well, and had decided to sue his wife for a divorce. What horrid timing! Mrs. Selby (McCoy's real name) alleged that the Kid had acquired $100,000 by entering

565 *New York Sun*, September 9, 1900.

into a conspiracy to allow himself to be defeated. She claimed that McCoy was required to deposit $10,000 as a guarantee that he would throw the fight. She said that the purse was equally divided, with her husband receiving $22,000. McCoy was also to receive a $1,500 weekly royalty from the fight films.

Mrs. Corbett then claimed to have knowledge that the McCoy-Sharkey and McCoy-Choynski fights were fixed as well, and that Mrs. Selby should know this if she knew as much about her husband's dealings as she did about Jim Corbett's. It is unclear how Mrs. Corbett would know all of this.

Kid McCoy denied his wife's charges, and alleged that his wife had recently obtained $600 worth of diamonds from a local jewelry firm on false pretences. Mrs. Selby countered that she had the Kid's permission to make such purchases and that he always paid the bills.[566]

McCoy further answered his wife's charges by giving permission to the telegraph companies to publish all dispatches sent. His wife had alleged that he used a cipher code to inform his friends that the fight was to be a fake. The Kid said that since he had gone into training, he had only sent one telegram to one person wherein he said that he was in good condition and expected to win in ten rounds. He publicly offered to pay $1,000 for every telegram, except that one, shown to be sent by him. "No such dispatches can be produced. It will be found that my wife did not think of this charge of fake in connection with my fight with Corbett until after she saw how much notoriety Mrs. Corbett got by trying to ruin her husband's reputation." The McCoy team challenged Mrs. Corbett to produce the $2,500 cancelled check that she allegedly wrote to McCoy. He also asked for proof that he had posted $10,000.

McCoy said that there was not one word of truth to his wife's story. He claimed that it was all "silly rubbish invented by a woman for revenge." The Kid claimed that his wife had been unfaithful, and she countered with the same allegation. Mrs. Corbett in her divorce suit also claimed that Jim had been unfaithful. McCoy said, "I don't believe that the charge of two hysterical and jealous women is going to ruin my reputation." McCoy said that he had made the decision to sue for divorce three months ago, but waited so that it would not interfere with his upcoming fight. "Is it likely in the face of this that I would have let her in on such a secret? No businessmen will believe such an absurdity."

The Sun said there was a wide difference of opinion as to whether the women's charges were true.

> Taking the battle as it was fought and as it resulted, it looked all right and was considered by a majority to be one of the best contests seen in any American ring for years. If Corbett and McCoy really did fake the fight…then they acted with extreme cleverness. … Men who

566 *New York Sun*, September 12, 1900.

believe the fight was on the level use as argument that McCoy never was in Corbett's class as a boxer; that Corbett had a big advantage in weight; that the Kid had previously shown inability to receive body blows; that there was bad blood between the men, due to a fight between them in the Gilsey House several years ago in which Corbett was kicked in the groin and had to go to bed for a week; that McCoy was in much pain when he went down…there was no betting to speak of on the fight, and that as yet no big poolroom keepers in any of the big Western cities have let out a roar to show how they were fleeced. …

On the other hand men who have all along regarded the fight as crooked say that McCoy didn't put up anything like his best efforts; that he purposely missed swings…that he wasn't hurt enough when he went down…that the betting was suspicious in that it opened at 10 to 8 on Corbett and finally was lengthened to 3 to 1 in his favor as the surprising scarcity of McCoy money was discovered…that certain well-known 'sure-thing' gamblers …were loaded with Corbett money and wanted to get it down at any old price. As a matter of fact when Corbett and McCoy were matched there were rumors of fake.[567]

The Sun noted inconsistencies in the charges of fake. "Mrs. Corbett, who first made charges of crookedness, has told several stories since Saturday which do not agree."

On September 13, McCoy went to his home to pick up some items, but his wife would not allow him to retrieve them. They got into a spat and she threw a whiskey decanter at him. It struck his arm, glanced off and smashed against the table. The liquor and glass scattered all over the room and cut one of Mrs. Selby's fingers. The Kid pushed his wife away, and in doing so, she claimed that he struck her on the nose with his fist. Speaking of the incident, the Kid said,

> I have a perfect right to enter my own home. She is still my wife until the courts separate us. I called to get some of my clothes and other effects. She would not let me take a portrait of myself and this led to a tilt. She broke a decanter over my arm, but I did not punch her on the nose as she says. If I did there would be a mark to show for it.[568]

From London, Corbett said that the allegations that his Sharkey and McCoy fights were fakes were too ridiculous for discussion. He said that he wanted to meet Jeffries again, "but I think he's a dead one. His left arm is gone." Jim said that his wife's divorce suit was news to him.[569]

567 New York Sun, September 13, 1900.
568 New York Sun, September 14, 1900.
569 New York Sun, September 16, 1900.

Jim Considine, Corbett's manager, said there was not a scintilla of truth to the allegations. He said that on the night of the McCoy fight, Corbett and his wife had a quarrel, and her last words to him before he left to go to the arena were, "Jim, I hope McCoy will knock your head off tonight!" Considine argued, "Now, that remark shows conclusively that at that time Mrs. Corbett knew of no deal for McCoy to lose. She thought that the fight was to be on its merits, and in her anger at her husband she hoped he would be defeated."

The Police Gazette said that when the allegations first came out, there was "a general disposition to attribute it to being enraged at her husband's departure, and in her anger, willing to say or do anything which might show Corbett up in an unfavorable way." However, when McCoy's wife made the same allegations, even though they were having marital discord as well, the fact that both wives made the allegations shifted the public's opinion towards the belief that the allegations were true.

McCoy continued denying the allegations. "This story is made out of whole cloth by two hysterical women, who have fancied grievances against their husbands." He said that the big fighters were too much for him, and wanted to return to fighting as a middleweight.

Some believed the wives, while others felt that they were simply fabricating the stories as a result of their ire against their estranged husbands. One *Gazette* writer said,

> I have no knowledge that a fake was perpetrated and am only prepared to believe what I saw, five rounds of clever boxing and a knockout which terminated the contest. Nobody can deny that the bout, as far as it went, was clever, and nobody who saw the punches which Corbett landed in McCoy's stomach and subsequently on the jaw can question their efficacy in lulling the recipient to sleep.

Many were willing to believe that the fight was not on the level. However, the chief element missing was proof. The women had not produced cancelled checks, dispatches, or anything to substantiate their allegations. Some chalked it up to jealousy. "Revenge is sweet and hell knows no fury like a woman scorned." Still, "human nature is not always discriminating, and the public, keen in its appreciation of new sensations, is disposed to believe the stories told by the two wives and point to it as corroborative support to the general belief that the affair was prearranged."

Despite the allegations of a fake, "it is extremely difficult to impress some of the most expert judges of pugilism in the country that it was." *The National Police Gazette* and Bill Naughton both still felt that the fight was on the level. Naughton wrote, "If Thursday night's fight was a fake it was the acme of faking. Ring followers were never before fooled with such a realistic display." There was no fake about the vicious punches that Corbett landed, nor the howl of pain that McCoy made when struck. If it was a fake, then the boxers were both the "most accomplished exponents of the art of ring acting the world has ever seen." They wanted more proof.[570]

Sensational developments were constant. Mrs. McCoy issued a statement claiming that the only Kid McCoy fight that was square was the one with Sharkey. She said that McCoy carried Choynski 20 rounds in March 1899 because they all bet that the fight would go the limit. She said that the Corbett fight was a fake from the start, for Corbett would not fight unless McCoy would agree to lay down to him. She quoted Jim as saying,

> Now, Kid, I'm getting along in years. This will probably be my last fight. I've got this show on my hands for the winter, and can't afford to lose. Let's have a fight before the Horton law goes out of effect and arrange it so that both can make a barrel of money. Then, when my show goes on the road, you can come along with me and spar with me in the scene where there is a sparring match.

She claimed that their refusal to shake hands on fight-night was all part of the game. The true evidence that there was no ill-will was the fact that Corbett and McCoy had gone out together the next night. However, the *Gazette* writer disagreed. "I have reason to know for a fact that the last statement is incorrect, for the reason that during the night after the fight I was with Corbett a good part of the time and can positively assert that McCoy was not in the company."

One other point worth mentioning is that the two wives' stories did not match. Mrs. McCoy said Corbett was always to win, whereas Mrs. Corbett said that the initial agreement was for McCoy to win. Mrs. Corbett said McCoy-Sharkey was a fix, whereas Mrs. McCoy said that was the only McCoy fight that was legitimate.

From London, Jim Corbett sent his wife a telegram saying, "Stories about woman false. Come over here quick, darling. Will prove it. Love you only."[571]

Again responding to the situation, Jim Corbett said, "It would be madness for anyone to think that if I would try to throw the McCoy fight I would make such an arrangement in the presence of my wife or any other outside party. Things of that kind, if done, are not done in the presence of third parties."[572]

Corbett returned from Europe on September 30. He and his wife had reconciled. Jim said, "Every one will admit that my fight with McCoy was a good one. … The battle was on the level and I won because I was the better man. She is sorry now for what she has done. … My wife knows that I have not done anything wrong."

---

570 *National Police Gazette*, September 29, 1900.
571 *National Police Gazette*, October 6, 1900.
572 *National Police Gazette*, October 13, 1900.

At that point, Mrs. McCoy said that Mrs. Corbett was only retracting her statements because she was allowing her affection for her husband to get the better of her. "She knows as well as I do that the fight was fixed. I do not know a great deal of the lady, but I doubt if she has any backbone or she would not allow that man to come back and get her to accept his story."

Some did not believe the retraction, and actually felt that by reconciling with his wife, Corbett was seeking to suppress the truth.

> Corbett came back, the well-spring of knowledge was closed, and now the impression is a pretty well founded one that some great truths had been spoken and that fearing a further expose which had been threatened, Corbett resolved to return to the arms of the deserted one with apologies and pleadings for forgiveness and secure a retraction of the things she had said about him.

> This is the public's view of it, but having reiterated my opinion that there was nothing wrong in connection with the McCoy fight I am surprised that Corbett has not made a more determined effort to establish the fact and demonstrate that he was guiltless of any participation in a scheme to swindle or defraud the public. Thus far he has contented himself by making a simple denial which was of little or no use in allaying public suspicion.[573]

Of course, that argument puts the burden of proof on the accused. How could he prove that something did not happen? It was the duty of the wives to prove that it did.

In November 1900, the *Police Gazette* reported that Corbett and George Considine, his partner and manager, had parted ways. At that point, Considine declared in writing that the fight was pre-arranged, and that both McCoy and Corbett had admitted it to him.

> Considine, in his rather lengthy statement, denies that he was personally cognizant of this, but was only apprised of it when Kid McCoy, whom he met in London, admitted the truth of the statement about the match being faked and said that McCoy told him he left New York because the downtown people were 'sore' on him for his 'throw down.' …

> "McCoy also made the statement," says Considine; "that he had the right to get the money any way he could. And he got it, he added, by laying down to Corbett as per agreement. …

> "On my arrival in New York and before making any statement I called on Corbett and accused him of having a part in a fake fight. This he denied, but I caught him in several misstatements… He then

573 *National Police Gazette*, October 20, 1900.

admitted that he knew that McCoy was going to lay down and I said to him: 'Why didn't you tell me…to which he replied: 'What for, so you could tell Tim Sullivan, who would make McCoy fight on the level as you did in the McCoy-Maher fight? I didn't know that I could lick McCoy on the level and I was glad to know that he was going to lay down.'

Corbett responded by saying that Considine's story was a complete fabrication. "I never was and never will be a party to such a detestable piece of infamy as Considine avers. Considine and I had a quarrel in London, and his statements are due wholly to his ill feeling toward me and his desire to do me an injury." Regardless, increasing numbers of folks began believing the fight was a fake.[574]

In his autobiography, Corbett said he was aware of the rumors that the fight was fixed, but did not believe them, and denied that it was fixed. "I had bluffed my opponents sometimes, but it was beyond me ever to descend to *fixing a fight*."[575] Still, the rumors persist to this day.

Regardless of whether or not the allegations were true, Corbett and McCoy's reputations took a blow. McCoy would not fight again for over a year, and only then boxed in England starting in December 1901. He did not fight again in the U.S. until May 1902. Jim Corbett would not fight again for three years. Of course, legal impediments played a factor, as well as the fact that Jim said that he did not want to fight again unless it was for the championship.[576]

---

574 *National Police Gazette*, November 24, 1900.
575 Corbett at 296-300.
576 Although there was some discussion of Tom Sharkey fighting Kid McCoy in San Francisco, the authorities there in February 1901 said that they would not license any bout involving McCoy. *National Police Gazette*, February 9, 1901.

CHAPTER 26

Boxing's Old Nemesis

In late September 1900, following his baseball umpiring tour, James Jeffries made his debut as the star in a drama called *The Man From the West.* Jeff played a sheriff. He admitted that the play and his acting were both bad. Still, it was a financial success, for no apparent reason "beyond perhaps a desire to see me."[577]

The National Police Gazette, always wanting battles to take place, began urging Jeffries to schedule a title defense. Billy Madden, Gus Ruhlin's manager, posted a $1,000 forfeit for a fight with Jeffries, noting that tradition dictated that a champion must defend his title within six months of a challenge and posting of a forfeit. *The Gazette* said, "Gus Ruhlin believes, and very justly, too, inasmuch as he fought Jeffries a draw in twenty rounds, that he is entitled to another crack at him."[578]

Bill Brady, still hopeful that Fitzsimmons would agree to fight Jeff after all, said that he would give Bob until December 1 to accept Jeff's challenge. Brady declared that Jeff's arm was back in shape and well enough again to stand vigorous training. Fitzsimmons responded by saying that Jeff and his manager could not use him for advertising purposes. Bob still claimed to be retired.

Ruhlin was next in line after Fitzsimmons. Although Ruhlin said that he would claim the championship if Jeff did not accept his challenge within six months, "claiming a championship for a man does not make him a champion."

> It's all very well for the rules to say a champion must defend his title every six months if he is challenged, but that rule is regarded more in the breach than in the observance. The holder of a title is a dictator, so to speak, and the public supports him on the ground that he has a right to suit his own convenience about fighting.[579]

Jim Corbett deposited $2,500 for a Jeffries fight. "I gave him the hardest battle of his career, and I am sure that my showing entitles me to another fight. With Fitzsimmons out of the game there is no other legitimate opponent for the champion to meet." Tom Sharkey also wanted consideration, although he had been knocked out in his last two bouts.[580]

577 *Two Fisted Jeff* at 165, 187-189; *National Police Gazette*, November 10, 1900.
578 *National Police Gazette*, September 22, 1900.
579 *National Police Gazette*, October 13, 1900.
580 *National Police Gazette*, October 27, 1900.

Jeffries said that the Corbett and Sharkey challenges were insincere and merely issued to boost their businesses. He alleged that these men did not really think they could defeat him, but just wanted to make money by fighting him, inspired by a desire to obtain half of the receipts. Jeff would not go for such a proposition.

> I don't think there is one of them really anxious to fight. ... If I thought for a moment that those heavyweights were sincere in their declarations I wouldn't hesitate in making a match, but just as soon as you consent to fight the first thing they will propose to you is that the money be split, or else they will not fight. This proposition alone is enough to convince one that they are not anxious to fight. If they were do you think that they would ask for such a thing? ...

> At the present time, as every one knows, I am tied up with theatrical engagements and will be for the next six months. When that time expires I will make these same men fight or else prove conclusively that they were only bluffing. When I am ready to take on these fighters, the one condition I will fight under is that the winner take the entire purse. ... This is no 'stage money' talk either, for I firmly believe I can beat every one of those big fellows. ...

> I am tired of splitting the money with my opponents. In my fight with Corbett I was compelled to consent to split the money with him before he would enter the ring. Before the match was made he said he only wanted one-third of the money, but when it came time for us to enter the ring Corbett sent for Brady and told him that unless he got half the money he wouldn't fight. I don't intend to ever fight again under those conditions unless, of course, I should be successful in getting on a fight with Fitzsimmons. If Fitz will only agree to fight I will make an exception in his case and box him on terms of 75 per cent to the winner.

> If Fitz continues to refuse my offer then it is open to Gus Ruhlin, who I think is the next man entitled to a fight with me. Ruhlin beat Sharkey in as decisive a manner as ever a man was beaten, and he has a draw with me, too.

> As for Sharkey and Corbett the only chance they have of getting on a match with me is by agreeing that the winner shall take the entire purse. Sharkey was beaten twice in succession only recently and I have beaten him twice. I can't see why he should get a chance, anyway.

> In regard to Corbett, I knocked him out completely and when he says I must fight him he doesn't know what he is talking about. Corbett has done more to kill boxing than any other fighter living. No one can

ever say that I was mixed up in a fake fight. When I fight I do my best.[581]

Responding to these statements, Corbett unleashed his usual mouthiness, saying that Jeff's victory over him was the greatest fluke of the age. Corbett called Jeff an accidental champion, and if he had not grown careless and overconfident, he would have defeated Jeffries. Of course, he also said that about Fitzsimmons' knockout victory over him as well.[582]

Finally taking Jeff's side, the *Police Gazette* said that instead of talking and acting like a bunch of "braying jackasses," making challenges at Jeffries when they knew that he was tied up with theatrical engagements for six months, the top contenders – Ruhlin, Corbett, Sharkey, and Maher – should fight each other to determine who should first be entitled to challenge Jeffries.

At that point, there appeared to be too much suspicion surrounding Corbett. Jeff said that his reputation would be sullied if he mixed it with him again. "I haven't a word to say in Corbett's behalf regarding the McCoy affair. The stench is as offensive to me as it is to anybody else." It was later said that both McCoy and Corbett had become objects of ridicule and disgust and that Corbett realized that he was regarded with suspicion. The next best option appeared to be Ruhlin.

Despite having resolutely refused to enter the ring again, a published statement said that Bob Fitzsimmons was willing to fight Jeffries at the close of his theatrical season.

However, fickle Fitz again changed his mind. "Several days ago Fitz startled the sporting world with a statement declaring that he would re-enter the ring and if possible get on a match with Champion Jim Jeffries. Now Fitz, with his customary inconsistency, makes another statement." Bob again claimed that he had no intention of returning to the ring, and was retired no matter what. "Fitzsimmons, by his refusal to fight again, has injured himself to an immeasurable extent in the estimation of the public."

Fitz claimed that he had never changed his mind, that the statement issued claiming that he was willing to fight was unauthorized, false, and likely put forth by Brady. Bob said it was just another way for Brady to advertise Jeff and his show. "Jeffries isn't drawing very well on the road, and Brady wants to get the people talking fight to advertise his champion. … Jeffries wasn't so anxious to fight me last August, was he?"

In late 1900, a Mr. Witte from Cincinnati, on behalf of the Saengerfest Association, offered $15,000 for a 20-round bout between Corbett and Jeffries. Brady informed Witte that Jeff would not fight Corbett because of the McCoy scandal, but would consider a fight with Ruhlin. Witte offered 60% of the receipts for a Ruhlin battle.

---

581 *National Police Gazette*, November 3, 1900.
582 *National Police Gazette*, November 10, 1900.

On December 8, 1900, an agreement was signed for a 20-round fight between Ruhlin and Jeffries to be held in Cincinnati on February 15, 1901. The fight was contingent upon Ruhlin's not losing to Peter Maher, whom he was scheduled to box in mid-December.[583]

On December 17, 1900 in Philadelphia, Gus Ruhlin and Peter Maher boxed a 6-round no-decision bout (all that was legal there). "The consensus of opinion was that Ruhlin had the better of the fight, although Maher put up a game battle and made a splendid showing." Ruhlin won the newspaper verdict. Since no official decision could be rendered, other than a knockout or disqualification, the newsmen generally rendered their own verdicts, upon which the public relied.

The Jeffries-Ruhlin contract called for a $2,500 forfeit by which the promoter guaranteed that neither the mayor nor the governor would prevent the fight. Cincinnati's mayor said that a license would be granted. It was assumed that Ohio's governor would not interfere.

However, it was subsequently reported that the governor was going to be a problem. "I am in a position to know that Gov. Nash of Ohio, is very much incensed at the unwarranted assumption that he would take no official cognizance of the contest." Governor George Nash said that he had not been consulted, and that prize fights were a felony in Ohio.[584]

Nevertheless, Jeffries and Ruhlin began preparing for the fight as if it would take place. Both began training on January 7, 1901, Jeff at Loch Arbour/Allenhurst, New Jersey, and Ruhlin at Bath Beach. Gus soon transferred to Ohio.[585]

On January 14 in Cincinnati, Gus Ruhlin gave a lively 3-round exhibition with his sparring partner, "Denver" Ed Martin, a black fighter. Martin weighed over 200 pounds and stood at least 6'3", if not more. Manager Billy Madden said that he would make Martin the colored heavyweight champion before long. In June 1899, Bob Armstrong, who was currently Jeff's sparring partner, had knocked out Martin in 2 rounds.[586] Since then, Martin was undefeated in seven bouts, and would later be prominent on the heavyweight scene. For now, he was Ruhlin's sparring partner.

---

583 *National Police Gazette*, November 17, 24, December 1, 8, 15, 29, 1900, January 19, 1901. The contract that Brady signed said that he would receive 70% of the gross receipts – to be split between the fighters via whatever agreement they came to. News reports said the split of the fighters' share would be 75%/25%.

584 *New York Clipper*, December 29, 1900; *National Police Gazette*, January 5, 12, 1901.

585 *National Police Gazette*, January 26, 1901.

586 *Cincinnati Enquirer*, January 15, 1901; *San Francisco Chronicle*, June 7, 1899; *National Police Gazette*, June 24, 1899. When Denver Ed Martin challenged Tom Sharkey in late 1900, Sharkey responded that had "never barred nobody outside of a nigger. I will not fight no nigger. I did not get my reputation fighting niggers and I will not fight a nigger. Outside of niggers, I will fight any man living." *National Police Gazette*, January 5, 1901.

The 240-pound Jeffries was reunited with and trained once again with Bill Delaney, as well as brother Jack Jeffries and former opponent Bob Armstrong. Tommy Ryan had been dismissed after the Corbett fight.[587]

Unfortunately, Ohio clergymen were united in their efforts to try to prevent the fight. Jeffries, whose own father was a minister, said that the churchmen were overstepping their bounds.

> Why don't those ministers mind their own business and not interfere in a matter which does not in any way concern them? Ever since pugilism was introduced in this country these clergymen have always been opposed to it, and have never missed a chance to hurt it. Their repeated attacks on the sport have not brought them any good results. On the contrary, their attacks have boomed the sport instead of helping to kill it.

> These church people preach from their pulpits about pugilism being a brutal and disgraceful sport, and demand that it should be prevented, but they seldom say a word against such real brutal sports as football, dog fights, chicken fights and other similar events put down as pastime.

> Why, the members of their own congregation are the persons who support the game, and whenever a championship battle is fought they don't hesitate to pay for a seat.[588]

The National Police Gazette also noted the ironic inconsistency of the legal treatment between football and boxing.

> Although football is encouraged and upheld by the best classes of American society, and all attempts to even modify the rules have proven futile, it has been four times as fatal as boxing, a sport generally reprobated by the hysterical enthusiasts of the gridiron. In ten years forty-seven men have met death in all parts of the world as the result of engaging in boxing contests. That is less than an average of five per year. On the basis of fourteen men killed in football in America alone in one season, a very modest estimate, by the way, the total in ten years would be 140, as against forty-seven in boxing. That is conclusive evidence of the relative roughness as to the two branches of sport. There never has been so much boxing as in the past ten years…. There may be, as the football enthusiasts assert, deliberate intention to injure in the game of boxing, but the fatalities in football are four times as great. If football is a gentle game, injuries

---

587 *Cincinnati Enquirer*, January 20, 1901; *National Police Gazette*, February 16, 1901.
588 *Cincinnati Enquirer*, January 16, 1901.

being entirely due to accident, it is the most unfortunate sport on the face of the globe.[589]

This argument still holds true. For whatever reason, this illogical, irrational discrimination has continued to this day. Despite the fact that football statistically has more injuries and deaths per participant, we have colleges and television wholeheartedly promoting it, while at the same time shunning boxing. Federal and state legislators and athletic commissions hinder and regulate boxing to death, while leaving football alone.

The local Cincinnati businessmen wanted the fight. They were fully aware of the positive economic impact that boxing would have on their town. They argued that although Ohio law made prizefighting a felony, it was perfectly legal for an incorporated athletic club to host a public boxing exhibition if the mayor granted a permit. They argued that no one had a legal right to interfere.[590]

It was said that Jeffries would probably retire if he defeated Ruhlin. He believed that boxing was dead in the big cities where large purses were once obtainable.[591]

On January 26, 1901 at Jeff's Price Hill training quarters in Cincinnati, James Jeffries and Bob Armstrong put up a good 4-round sparring bout. "Armstrong showed up very well, but it was plainly evident that Jeffries was his master at all stages. Armstrong is quite clever with his hands and feet, and also a stiff puncher." Jeff also jumped rope, punched the bag, worked with dumbbells and the rowing machine, and ran 4 miles.[592]

On January 28, Jeffries injured his kneecap when he fell during a handball game trying to make a difficult return. The knee became inflamed and he walked with a perceptible limp. The following morning, Jeff skipped the run and just did a short walk. He punched the bag for 20 minutes without rest. He also worked the rowing machine.[593]

Discussing the matchup, Corbett advised Ruhlin to fight at a slow pace at long range. If he rushed at Jeff, it would be a short fight in Jeff's favor because he could beat anyone who rushed at him. He was so big and strong that it was difficult to hurt him. Corbett said that Jeff liked to wait and have the fight brought to him. Jeffries was slow but sure. Jim had made Jeff

589 *National Police Gazette*, December 29, 1900. "Every sporting writer in the country has had his say about the injustice of the authorities in discriminating against boxing in favor of football, which is conceded to be more dangerous to life and limb and responsible for more injuries and fatalities than any other game in the category of sport." *The Police Gazette* said that the many fatalities and injuries resulting from football demonstrate that prize fighting, by comparison, was mere child's play. *National Police Gazette*, November 29, 1902.
590 *National Police Gazette*, January 19, 1901.
591 *Louisville Evening Post*, January 22, 1901.
592 *Cincinnati Enquirer*, January 23-27, 1901. The typical Jeffries day was said to include a 2-mile walk, boxing with brother Jack and Bob Armstrong, rowing and bag punching, pulleys and rope skipping, dumbbells and wrist machine, short run, 10-mile run, and more machine exercises. Sometimes Jeff rode his bicycle as well.
593 *Cincinnati Enquirer*, January 29, 31, 1901.

come forward, and gave him a difficult time of it. Of course, even he could not escape when Jeffries turned up the aggressive intensity late in the fight.

Tommy Ryan said the two men were well matched, that the fight might go the limit and be decided by a close margin. He felt that Jeff did his best work when allowing opponents like Fitz and Sharkey to come to him. Ryan said that Fitzsimmons might defeat Jeffries if they fought again because Bob would fight a different kind of fight.

Some criticized Jeff for not rushing and forcing fights more. Folks wanted a return of the Sullivan style. Jeff was big and strong, with a good chin and defense, and a strong punch, such that many felt that he would be better off forcing fights more. "Jeffries would satisfy his admirers considerably more if he would indulge in rushing, just as John L. Sullivan used to do. They say that the champion, with his weight, strength and agility, ought to beat down quickly some of the men who have stayed before him for more than twenty rounds." To date, against the best opponents, Jeff had a more methodical style, and was not afraid to allow his opponents to rush at him, or run from him.[594]

Unfortunately, Governor George Nash, a former civil war veteran and former state Supreme Court justice, instructed his attorney general to find a way to stop the upcoming contest.

On January 30, 1901, the police arrested Jeffries, who was upset at having to suffer the ignominy of arrest for a crime that he never committed. However, it was practically a champion's right of passage. Sullivan, Corbett, and Fitzsimmons all had to deal with serious legal hurdles and arrests when making their fights. The law was rearing its ugly head once again.

Apparently, though, the promoters caused his arrest for the purpose of having a friendly magistrate adjudicate the question of the contest's legality. It was said that this tactic did not fool the Governor.[595]

The Police Gazette reported that the opposition to the fight was growing stronger every day. Even the mayor was backing down, having been told that he might be compromising a chance to one day be governor.[596]

594 *National Police Gazette*, February 2, 16, 23, 1901.
595 *Cincinnati Enquirer*, January 31, 1901; *National Police Gazette*, February 23, 1901.
596 *National Police Gazette*, February 2, 1901.

On February 2, Governor Nash declared that the bout would not be allowed to take place in Ohio, and that the entire power of the state would be used to prevent it. [597]

Instead of simply attacking boxing's legality, the State via its attorney general attacked the sport as a public nuisance and sought an injunction against it on that basis, a novel tactic. The promoters (the Saengerfest Athletic Association) spent a great deal of money on attorneys' fees in order to fight the State quite vigorously. They would also be subject to paying the fighters $2,500 each if they failed to bring off the fight for any reason. Six law firms argued for the Defendants. Seven separate attorneys argued on behalf of the State. The pleadings and arguments required 186 pages to transcribe.

A statute passed in 1868, before gloved boxing existed, section 6888, prohibited prize fighting, making it a felony punishable by imprisonment from one to ten years. Historically this meant a bareknuckle contest for a prize. A subsequent statute passed in 1880 and amended in 1888, section 6890, made it a crime to fight or box or engage in any public sparring or boxing exhibition with or without gloves, punishable by a maximum fine of $250 and up to three months of imprisonment. However, like the Horton law, the statute had an exception which stated, "nothing in the foregoing shall apply to any public gymnasium or athletic club, or any of the exercises therein, if written permission for the specific purpose shall first have been obtained from the sheriff…or…the mayor…."

The State argued that the Saengerfest was not a legitimate athletic club, but rather its sole purpose in regard to athletics was to bring off this one fight. Even if it was a legitimate athletic club, the mayor had no authority to issue a permit for a prize fight, but only for an exhibition. A fight would defy peace and good order, impugn the state's good name and the general welfare, endanger the lives of the participants, bring to the state a lawless, violent, turbulent, idle and dangerous assemblage, incite quarrels and breaches of the peace, and the exhibition of brutality would have a demoralizing and pernicious effect on the good order and well being of the community that would endanger life and property generally unless restrained by an injunction.

The Defendants argued that boxing exhibitions were legally permitted by statute when an athletic club secured a permit from the mayor, that they were a properly incorporated athletic club, were acting pursuant to a permit granted by the mayor, and that exhibitions of boxing skill were frequently given in all of the larger cities in Ohio without objection, and without any argument that they created any nuisance. The mayor had exercised his judgment in issuing the permit, which was entitled to respect. The fight would attract many professionals and would mean an economic boom for

597 *Cincinnati Enquirer*, February 3, 1901.

the city, and help the Saengerfest Association pay off a large sum of indebtedness that they had incurred. All reasonable precautions would be taken to secure good order, and there was no proof that the audiences for boxing were any less orderly than those who attended the theater or other large assemblies such as political conventions.

The Defendants also argued that injunctions could only be granted when it was shown that property rights would be injured. There was absolutely no evidence placed into the record to demonstrate that this fight or boxing generally would constitute a nuisance that would injure personal or property rights. Contrary to the anti-boxing morality arguments, boxing was an original Anglo-Saxon form of amusement that had been encouraged because it increased and maintained the courage and pluck of the race. English troops around the world were learned boxers. There was evidence of boxing matches taking place in nearly every state in the Union. The only difference here was the celebrity of the boxers. When the boxers were lesser-knowns, the State and ministerial community had no concern and allowed it to go on in Ohio, without problems. Under the Horton law, New York had held boxing matches for four years, four or five nights a week, and the police were able to maintain order and control.

Further, the Defendants argued that if boxing was a crime, there were adequate alternative remedies via the criminal laws, which perpetually enjoined such acts with harsher penalties (and allowed a trial by jury), and therefore a court of equity had no jurisdiction. This fight also did not fit the definition of a public nuisance because there was no ongoing perpetual act, typically required in a nuisance suit.

The State argued that every state in the Union of 45 states had put the seal of disapproval upon prize fights. Any time two men engaged in combat competing for a prize, they were engaged in a prize fight. A prize fight was illegal, and the mayor could not issue a permit for an illegal act. Reading the two existing statutes together, the one prohibiting prize fights, and the other authorizing boxing permits, the mayor could only issue a permit for pure exhibitions of skill with no prize involved.

After the case was submitted on February 11, on February 14, 1901 the judge agreed with the State and enjoined the fight. He held that if a prize is offered for a fight and the men fight for that prize, then it is a prize fight. The Jeffries-Ruhlin contest was a prize fight regardless of whether it was called a sparring or boxing exhibition, whether there were a limited number of rounds, or whether there was any ill will or intent to do harm. Either way, it was in the pecuniary interest of a boxer to knock his opponent out. Therefore, a permit for such a contest was illegal and void. Further, a public gymnasium had to be organized not for the singular purpose of avoiding a statute, but a more permanent purpose to serve in encouraging healthful and manly exercises.

The judge noted that the law only required the fighters to put up a total of $20,000 as a bond guaranteeing that they would not fight ($10,000 each). He held that given the vast sums that the fight would generate, the bond amounts would be insufficient to prevent the fight. They could take their chances on forfeiture and still reap great rewards. Further, the municipal powers would not stop the fight because they were "in league with evil-doers." Because there was no adequate remedy under the current statutes, an injunction was appropriate.

Although a court of equity would not enjoin the commission of a crime unless it also constituted a public nuisance, the judge agreed that there would be incidental evils attendant to a prize fight which implicated the honor and good name, peace and dignity of the state, the morals, welfare and happiness of the people, their property, and progress of civilization, which made the fight a nuisance. The judge said that boxing was an animal and brutal competition, with no self-respecting women amongst the crowd, but harlots and gamblers and persons with deadly weapons, persons constituting the idle and vicious elements in society, whose lives and conduct degrade a community, and therefore constitute a riot. They would remain after the contest and be a blight upon the community, requiring additional expenditures for police and courts of criminal jurisdiction. "But, more than that, the affair will be demoralizing and pernicious in its effect on the good order and well-being of society. Such an assemblage is an offense to every good citizen." The judge called boxing a disgrace to the community, affecting the fair name and honor of the state, making the city a less desirable place to live. He used strong words like "humiliating," "evil," "degrading," "corrupting," and "a moral stench."

The judge was convinced that the fight would be injurious to public morals, affect the welfare, safety, comfort, peace and happiness of the citizens, and that there was no adequate remedy at law, for the mischief which flowed from the fight would be irreparable. Therefore, the court had jurisdiction in the face of an emergency to resolve any doubts in favor of law and order and decency and the well being of the state, in the interests of good morals and public righteousness. Yes, those were his words. Welcome to the views of the anti-boxing establishment.[598]

Additionally, Governor Nash was instrumental in sanctioning the adjournment of the State Supreme Court until after the bout's date in order to block a timely appeal. Once again, the law and politics had quashed the sport of boxing.

Jeffries said that he was not surprised, but was disappointed at not being able to defend the title in his birth state. All of his training and preparation had been for naught. "For the time being I shall go from the science of

598 Special thanks to Clay Moyle for providing me with the entire transcript of Ohio, ex rel. Attorney General vs. Hobart, et al. See prizefightingbooks.com.

boxing to the art of acting." The big fighters were disgusted with the whole affair and were determined to sidestep the fight game for the more lucrative and enjoyable occupation of acting. Jeff returned to performing in *The Man From the West*, traveling around the country.

The Gazette reported that there was some discussion of having the fight transferred to San Francisco, but for whatever reason, "They found to their chagrin that San Francisco did not want the match and they abandoned training." For the time being, boxing was in a post-Horton blue period.

The Gazette also speculated that Jeff was not all that disappointed that the fight was called off, because his knee was still in a bad way. He was afflicted with what was termed a floating cartilage, or water on the knee.[599]

On February 25, 1901 at Galveston, Texas, before the Galveston Athletic Club, 32-year-old Joe Choynski knocked out 22-year-old Jack Johnson in the first few seconds of the 3rd round of a scheduled 20-round bout. "Both men showed up well, but it was apparent from the very

---

599 *Cincinnati Enquirer*, February 15, 1901; *National Police Gazette*, March 2, 16, 30, 1901.

beginning that Johnson was outclassed." In the 3rd round, "Choynski caught him on the jaw with a right hook and he went down and out like a log."

After the fight, a squad of Texas Rangers under Captain Brooks dashed into the ring and arrested both pugilists, charging them with violating the state law against engaging in a prize fight, the penalty for which was 2 to 5 years in the penitentiary at hard labor. This was the law that Governor Charles Culberson had facilitated in order to prevent the Corbett-Fitzsimmons fight. "The arrest was made at the instigation of Gov. Sayers." Many governors enjoyed the cheap notoriety they obtained when they attacked high profile fights and fighters. Both Johnson and Choynski were required to post a massive bond of $5,000, without which they would have to remain in jail pending trial. Neither could pay, and so they remained incarcerated. All of this was illustrative of the reinvigorated legal trend against the sport.

Governor Joseph Sayres was persistent in his efforts to punish Choynski and Johnson. When a Grand Jury failed to indict them, he immediately telegraphed Captain J. H. Brooks of the State Rangers, asking him to re-arrest them and to hold the boxers until another Grand Jury could be empanelled and the case again considered.

The Gazette noted that Texas had a new way of dealing with boxing, as illustrated by the Choynski-Johnson situation. Rather than preventing the bout, they simply allowed the fighters to fight and then arrested and held them afterwards. "The mere matter of arrest will serve as a salutary warning to all fighters that they are not wanted in Texas. Thus will the object be served, and the end justify the means."

Having been arrested on February 25, Choynski and Johnson were not released from jail until March 23, when the Court of Criminal Appeals mandated that they be released from incarceration on a bond of $1,000 each. Eventually, the second grand jury failed to indict the boxers, and so they were free once and for all.

The Grand Jury felt that too much importance had been attached to the fight, "and that the moral and religious element in the State has been unduly excited by sensational and exaggerated enlargement of what otherwise, to this Grand Jury, appears to be a small affair with no motive, intent or fact to show a violation of the law." Still, the boxers had been in jail for 29 days, and were not likely to attempt to box there again. The message had been sent and received. Legally, most of the country remained against boxing, despite its popularity.[600]

---

600 *New York Clipper*, March 16, 1901; *National Police Gazette*, March 23, 30, April 13, 27, 1901. *The New York Clipper* reported that a "right hook square on the jaw put the darkey to sleep."

CHAPTER 27

Getting Sharp Again – Griffin and Kennedy

As of April 1901, James Jeffries and Gus Ruhlin were continuing their discussions with San Francisco clubs for a fight between them to be held there. Jeffries wanted the fight to be held later rather than sooner, because his two-year contract with Bill Brady was about to expire. "Jeffries' insistence about naming the date is probably actuated by his desire to get rid of Billy Brady so that the latter will not have a finger in the pie, or in other words, take fifty per cent of the fighters end."

The boxers did not want too much publicity to surround the match; fearing that politicians would seek to prevent the granting of a permit. It was thought that the pre-fight publicity in Ohio had garnered the anti-fight lobby.[601]

The Police Gazette reported, "The boxing game is staggering under the effects of a knockout opposition in some parts of the country but shows signs of reviving despite the hard knocks administered in the past few months. San Francisco, Denver and other Western cities are holding big contests."

On May 3, 1901 in Denver, Colorado, in his first fight in about eight months since Fitzsimmons knocked him out, Tom Sharkey knocked out Fred Russell in the 4th round.[602]

Four days later, on May 7, 1901 at Cripple Creek, Colorado, Sharkey was disqualified in the 2nd round against "Mexican" Pete Everett when Tom floored him, but then punched Pete while he was down.[603] It was typical Sharkey. Tom would not enter the ring again for a serious fight until 1902.

In his second autobiography, Jeffries said that he closed his theatrical season in Pittsburg on May 15, 1901. When his two-year management deal with Brady expired in early June, Jeff severed relations with him and decided thereafter to be guided by Bill Delaney.[604]

---

601 *National Police Gazette*, April 13, 27, May 18, 1901.
602 Boxrec.com. Russell's career included: 1899 WDQ4 Theodore Van Buskirk and L20 Joe Kennedy; 1900 L6 and L10 Frank Childs, KO9 Mexican Pete Everett, and LDQby4 Joe Choynski; and 1901 KO1 Jim McCormick. After the Sharkey loss, Russell's results would include: 1901 LDQby10 Denver Ed Martin; 1902 KO3 John Klondike Haines, D6 Joe Walcott, KO14 Hank Griffin, LKOby5 Sam McVey, and LDQby8 Jack Johnson.
603 *National Police Gazette*, June 1, 1901.
604 *Two-Fisted Jeff* at 190-191.

Jeff wanted a rest after a tiring theatrical season on the road. He said that the Ruhlin fight would not take place until the fall. He was willing to fight Gus in San Francisco for 65% of the gross receipts. "I am not as much in love with this fighting business as some persons believe I am. There does not seem to be much money in the game anyway at present, but I am always ready to defend my title."

Jeffries also said that he only planned on having a few more fights before retiring undefeated. He had been giving some indications that he was growing tired of boxing. *The Police Gazette* reported, "It is a positive fact that Jeffries would retire from the ring on small provocation."

The Gazette sarcastically remarked, "Too bad about them great big husky guys who are so affected by two hours work a night that they have to rest six months to recuperate." It opined that "the champion's waning glory demands something more of him in the way of professional activity than masquerading as an actor."

The Gazette felt no sympathy for Jeff's claim that boxing was financially struggling. Sure, the legal restrictions hurt the ability to hold matches in places where huge purses could be obtained, but there was still plenty of money to be made. "If he had never aspired to the ring and remained steadily at his trade he would be making $2.50 a day as a boilermaker." There were not many college presidents who were clearing the $500 to $1,000 a week that Jeffries was. Although the boxer's career did not last as long as many of the learned professions, the boxer "makes a whole lot more money in his few brief years of glory than the college professor does in a life of slavery to books and classes." Still, Jeffries had been spoiled by the huge New York purses. When you have done something for $30,000 or $40,000, you are not as thrilled about doing the very same thing for $10,000 or $20,000.

When Jeff returned to Los Angeles in June, a large crowd royally received him. He wanted to see his folks and rest a bit before becoming active again. "I will be gone about six weeks, during which time I will go hunting and at the same time put in three weeks of training."

Subsequently, Jeff was reported to be feeling well and ready to get back into the ring. He said that he was weighing about 235 pounds in his street clothes, and never felt better. His left arm was back to being as good as ever. "You know I always did use my left a great deal in fighting and so I would not take any chances with Ruhlin or any one else unless I thought it was good again."[605]

In the meantime, although Bob Fitzsimmons was still officially retired, in May or June, he had been doing some sparring with the very large 220-pound Sandy Ferguson. However, Sandy soon quit. "While boxing the other night Sandy started in to mix it up with Bob. The result was a

605 *National Police Gazette*, June 1, 8, 22, 29, 1901.

smashed ear, a bloody nose and several other catastrophes for Sandy, followed by his sad departure for his home in Boston."[606]

Because the boxing business was in a lull (and mostly illegal), Fitzsimmons was considering taking up wrestling. In fact, engaging in wrestling bouts was a way that boxers could perform in places like New York and make some money without worrying about legal impediments. Eventually, a wrestling match was made between Fitz and Ruhlin.

On July 9, 1901 at New York's Madison Square Garden, Gus Ruhlin defeated Bob Fitzsimmons in a Greco-Roman wrestling match. They were scheduled to wrestle the best two out of three falls. In their first bout, Ruhlin got Bob on his back in 12 minutes and 45 seconds. After a 15-minute rest, Ruhlin defeated Bob in their second bout in 12 minutes and 24 seconds, to win the match with two falls. Fitz was much better at punching and fighting than at wrestling. Ruhlin simply had too much brute strength for him.[607]

Ruhlin was hoping for a Jeffries boxing match. Reporters opined that a fight between the two would be quite interesting, given that Gus had youth, strength, height, reach, skill, and gameness.

Jeffries was spending a few days fishing at Catalina. When asked if he would fight Ruhlin in San Francisco, Jeff said that he would, but

> I don't propose to fight him for fifty cents. They must show me the money. You know it costs me a great deal of money to train for one of these big fights, and I don't propose to make this outlay and enter into a hard contest and get nothing for it. ... I am not going to throw away my money and put in five hard weeks at training just to please some fight promoters. ... It is simply a question of dollars and cents.

It was said that at present, San Francisco "looks to be the only place where a fight between two big fellows for championship honors can be held without conflicting with any State or local laws." Unfortunately, San Francisco did not have the affluence of the much more populous New York, and therefore, much to Jeff's chagrin, "the days of $60,000 gates is a thing of the past."

Eventually, it was announced that Jeff and Ruhlin would box 20 rounds in mid-November in San Francisco in a fight sponsored by the Twentieth Century Club. It agreed to pay the fighters 62 ½% of the gate receipts, but refused to pay them anything for training expenses. Once again, Denver Ed Martin would be Ruhlin's sparring partner. Jeff would train at Harbin Springs.[608]

---

606 *National Police Gazette*, June 15, 22, 1901. Fitz and Ferguson had given a 4-round exhibition in Boston.
607 *New York Clipper*, July 27, 1901; *National Police Gazette*, July 6, August 3, 1901. In Philadelphia, Tom Sharkey wrestled Peter Maher. After each won a fall and the tame match disgusted spectators, the bout was declared a draw.
608 *National Police Gazette*, August 10, 1901, September 14, 21, 1901.

The San Francisco Board of Supervisors quickly issued a permit for the bout, and there were no protests.

In September, Ruhlin and Denver Ed Martin began sparring and training, occasionally exhibiting. "He and Martin are in the habit of mixing it up rather lively at times for the amusement of the spectators."

Tom Sharkey, who wanted to fight the winner, predicted, "Jeffries will lick the big Dutchman in jig time. He will punch so many holes in him that Gus will look like a bit of ancient swelter cheese."[609]

In his second autobiography, Jeff said that he was in good shape due to constant boxing with Jack, but had been idle from serious competition for well over a year. He knew what happens to boxers who stay long out of the ring, and so he was anxious for some tune-up matches to help prepare him for Ruhlin.[610]

On September 3, Jeff offered to stop any heavyweight on the west coast in 4 rounds or forfeit $100. Jeff went on an exhibition tour of Southern California. Joe Kennedy, who had once won a 20-round decision over Gus Ruhlin, accepted the offer, but wanted enough time to get into condition. They agreed to box later in the month in Oakland.[611]

In the meantime, black heavyweight Hank Griffin also agreed to take up Jeffries' offer to stop any heavyweight in 4 rounds or forfeit $100, the match to take place on the 17th at Hazard's Pavilion in Los Angeles.

In meeting all comers on his western exhibition tour, Jeffries was "emulating the example of the champion of all champions, John L. Sullivan." Jeff said that he was simply doing it as a way of making some extra money and getting into condition for the Ruhlin championship fight.[612]

On September 6, 1901, while standing in a receiving line at the Buffalo Pan-American Exposition, an anarchist named Fred Nieman shot U.S. President William McKinley twice. He died eight days later, on September 14, from complications related to the gunshot wound. On that day, Theodore Roosevelt became President.

On September 15, 1901 at a benefit for striking machinists held at San Francisco's Armory Hall, both Jeffries and Ruhlin appeared in separate sparring exhibitions and had the opportunity to see each other in action. In boxing 3 fast rounds with brother Jack Jeffries, the champ devoted most of the time to ducking and side-stepping. "His footwork is a revelation in quickness when his great bulk is taken into consideration." Ruhlin, weighing 203 ½ pounds, boxed with Denver Ed Martin, "a likely man himself." They "gave a pretty exhibition of hitting and stopping, which showed both off to

---

609 *National Police Gazette*, September 28, 1901.
610 *Two-Fisted Jeff* at 190-191.
611 *Oakland Tribune*, September 4, 11, 1901.
612 *Los Angeles Herald*, September 16, 1901.

advantage." Jeff took the train to Los Angeles, set to box Griffin in two days.[613]

The next day, on September 16 at Oakland's Dewey Theater, the "Akron Giant" Ruhlin boxed 3 hard rounds with Denver Ed Martin.

> It was a display of science and it was also a display of strength and a capacity to give and take punishment. ... Blows were struck strong enough to fell a horse, and both the pugilists felt their effects, Martin going to his knees several times. Ruhlin, of course, was the more scientific of the two, but Martin was sufficiently skilled to make the contest a most interesting one.

They repeated their performance there on the 17th, again boxing 3 rounds.

> Ruhlin is a magnificently-formed man and for a man of his weight is light and shifty on his feet and clever with his hands. He forced the play last night and dealt blows which were not intended to be taps. Martin is a boxer of considerable ability and helped to make the bout an entertaining one indeed.

Ruhlin and Martin continued sparring 3 rounds there nightly until Saturday the 21st. It was said that Ruhlin "is in every way a foeman worthy of Jim's renown."[614]

In the meantime, Jeffries boxed Hank Griffin in Los Angeles. Griffin was a solid fighter with plenty of experience. Therefore, when the match was made, it was immediately said, "There are many who believe that Jeffries has taken a big contract on his hands in attempting to stop Griffin in four rounds, for the husky heavyweight is very shifty and has a good defense." Griffin also had a knockout blow. He was no easy task. In fact, "some local people think Jeffries cannot make Griffin quit in four rounds."

Although Jeff was weighing around 230 pounds to Griffin's 180+ pounds, Hank was in good shape, having been training faithfully, looking good when boxing and wrestling in intense sparring sessions with Billy Woods (the black middleweight) every day. Although no one thought that he could actually beat Jeff, many felt that Hank was good enough to stay the 4 rounds and pick up $100.[615]

Jeffries knew that he had a good fighter before him because he had fought him before; having stopped Griffin in about 14 or 15 rounds in Jeff's first pro bout, somewhere around 1893-1894. Griffin had fought an 1893 20-round draw with Frank Childs. He had an 1897 KO4 over Dan Long. More recently, from 1900-1901, Griffin fought Jack Munroe 20 rounds (either a win for Griffin or a draw), was stopped in 11 rounds by

613 *San Francisco Call*, September 16, 1901.
614 *Oakland Tribune*, September 17, 18, 20, 1901.
615 *Los Angeles Express*, September 12, 1901; *Los Angeles Times*, September 16, 1901.

Bob Jones, and fought Joe Kennedy to two 20-round draws. Obviously, going rounds had never been a problem for Griffin, who was more than a fair fighter. In fact, Griffin had only been stopped twice, by Jeffries and Jones, and neither one of those knockouts came until after the 10th round, so stopping Griffin in 4 rounds was not likely to happen.[616]

Jeffries said of Griffin, "I guess I know about as much as anybody; I fought him once. He is a big fellow, and very strong…. If I cannot knock him out in four rounds I will not kill myself or tear my head off trying to." Jeff was just using the bout as a money-making tune-up, and did not necessarily mind if Hank lasted the distance.

Jeff offered another, less generous assessment of Griffin, saying,

> They think a lot of Griffin here, I can see, but he did not succeed in whipping Joe Kennedy, and Jack Root used to do that every day when he was training for his fight with Kid Carter. Root is a light heavyweight, and if he could put it all over Kennedy, and Griffin could not whip him, it seems as if Griffin wasn't any wonder.[617]

Still, Griffin was the favorite to make it the full 4 rounds. *The Los Angeles Herald* said,

> Griffin has never disappointed an audience that assembled to see him fight, and while he has not always been proclaimed the winner he has never quit for a little punishment. The proposition in which Griffin is the favorite does not mean that he shall defeat Jeffries, but that he shall be on his feet at the end of four three-minute rounds, with the usual one-minute intermission.[618]

The Los Angeles Times said that the big, shifty colored fighter was going to make the effort of his life to last and earn a reputation. Gamblers were offering even money that Jeff would not stop Griffin. Jeffries was reported to be weighing 220 pounds to Griffin's 180.[619]

Technically, it was not a bout to be fought on the merits, with an official decision rendered. Rather, it was essentially an exhibition in which Griffin would endeavor to last 4 rounds, and if he did so, he would be paid a bonus.

The Jeffries-Griffin exhibition took place one year and four months after the Corbett fight, on September 17, 1901 at Hazard's Pavilion in Los Angeles. The pavilion was packed, with every seat on the floor, balcony, and gallery filled. *The Call* said Hazard's contained fully 5,000 people.[620]

---

616 Cyberboxingzone.com; Boxrec.com. *Los Angeles Express*, September 17, 1901; *National Police Gazette*, November 1, 1902.
617 *Los Angeles Daily Times*, *Los Angeles Express*, September 17, 1901.
618 *Los Angeles Herald*, September 17, 1901.
619 *Los Angeles Times*, September 17, 1901.
620 The following account and post-fight discussion is taken from the *Los Angeles Daily Times*, *Los Angeles Express*, *Los Angeles Herald*, *San Francisco Call*, September 18, 19, 1901.

1st round

Griffin was obviously afraid. Jeff pursued him about the ring. After a clinch and break, Jeffries rushed in hooking short lefts to the jaw, and knocked Griffin down with a "half-arm swipe on the side of the head." Another local source said the knockdown came from a right half-hook to the head. Hank took a nine-count. When he rose, in order to survive, for the remainder of the round, Griffin ran around and clinched often.

Another local source said Jeff was too fast, and dropped Griffin every time he landed, though Hank did not seem to be hurt. A non-local source said that Jeff got him down simply by pushing him over. Griffin was fine though, and landed some inside blows to Jeff's chest.

2nd round

Griffin continued running and evading until Jeff dropped him with another half-arm overhand blow or hook to the jaw. Griffin tried to clinch, but received many hard punches. Hank tried to mix it a little bit, but Jeff smiled whenever Griffin landed, and responded with rib shots, which made Hank change his mind and run again. Griffin's agility amused the crowd. Another left counter to the ear, although light, gave Hank an excuse to drop and take another nine-count. He was smart enough always to take the full extent of the count in order to kill time. Hank did little except try to move and hold.

3rd round

Jeff rushed and Hank ran, dodged, and clinched. In the rare mix-up, Griffin hit him in the mouth, but Jeff just laughed again. Jeffries hooked lefts to the ribs and head. However, "Griffin's defense in the clinches was remarkably clever." In another clinch, Hank punched Jeff a number of times in the stomach, but Jeffries responded with harder blows. Jeff landed right and left hooks to the head, dazing Hank, but Griffin clinched and blocked some punches.

When they broke, Jeff went at him, doubled his left to the head and jaw, dropping Griffin to a knee again for a nine-count. After rising, a Jeffries left dropped him for eight seconds. Another light left sent him down for nine seconds. The crowd hissed Griffin for not fighting, but apparently voluntarily going down to avoid punishment and to kill the clock. Hank made a running race of it, occasionally stopping to tap Jeff lightly.

4th round

Jeff kept after him, but Griffin survived by mostly clinching and running, only occasionally striking back and mixing it up. Jeff once threw Griffin halfway across the ring and down. Griffin survived to the final bell.

According to the *Los Angeles Times*, Griffin lasted, but barely attempted to fight, being more concerned with survival.

As a "fight," there was nothing to it, for Griffin made a foot race of it almost every minute of the time, and ran so fast around the ring that the mighty slugger couldn't catch him. He varied his hot-escape act several times by kneeling to keep from being hit, and clinched at every chance. 'De Champ' knocked him down several times with half-arm jolts, and Hank never forgot to take the full count.

Griffin was only concerned with trying to stay the 4 rounds, and did not have the ghost of a show with Jeff. "He hit Jeffries three or four times, twice on the face, but Jim only gave him the laugh and kept on trying to catch his long-legged antagonist. His only lead at Griffin was a left hook, but he jarred him hard a number of times in the stomach in the clinches." Jeffries charged at his man like a bull, crouching with a short guard, but did not extend himself as much as he might have, perhaps concerned about injury or giving the Ruhlin folks too much of a line on him.

The Times concluded, "Griffin is a good man at his weight, but has no business, of course, with the champion. Had he stood up and fought he would not have lasted two rounds, but he did not go in the ring to fight, as the crowd knew." Griffin was Jeffries' Tug Wilson, who had survived against John L. Sullivan in a similar manner.

The Los Angeles Express applauded Griffin as being clever for not leading, fighting a smart defensive fight, and utilizing good ring generalship. Although Jeff's "speed is remarkable for a big man," his showing was disappointing to many because he did not stop Griffin. Still, the paper felt that Jeff's performance was creditable enough under the circumstances.

The Los Angeles Herald reported that despite the fact that Jeff was from Los Angeles, the immense crowd rooted for Griffin to last, and was strong on his side. This was perhaps natural given his underdog status, and the fact that Griffin had actually fought more often in Los Angeles than had Jeffries.

The Herald was critical of Jeffries, and unfairly said that the bout "showed conclusively that he is not a champion of champions, such as John L. Sullivan was, but that he is such a big, powerful fellow that nobody in the ring today can dispose of him." It opined that although Jeffries was "marvelously fast for a big man," the bout was not to his credit. He was not in condition for a hard fight, while Griffin was, and Jeff either underestimated Griffin or did not care to extend himself trying to knock him out. It applauded Griffin for avoiding the knockout punch.

> To be sure he went to his knees several times, but throughout the four rounds there was not a blow delivered which constituted a clean knock down. In the first and second rounds Jeffries had a seemingly good chance to put his opponent away, but he always hesitated with an apparent idea that the negro had something up his sleeve. ... Jeffries is far from being a Sullivan. He is more shifty, perhaps, and has learned the science of foot work and defense more thoroughly,

but he is not the possessor of a decisive blow which made the name of Sullivan a terror to all aspirants to heavyweight honors.

Griffin's ribs had suffered from the effective body blows, but he was ready to go on had it been necessary, while Jeff's breathing was labored. Of course, Jeffries had done a lot more punching. Still, Griffin had effectively managed to elude all of Jeff's attempts to put him away.

> The bout, as it was fought, was a distinct triumph for Griffin. Jeffries' blows were all delivered at short range, and while they outnumbered the punches of the colored man five to one, they lacked the force expected of them. In return Hank caught the champion a few blows which left their mark.

This analysis completely overlooked the fact that it was not easy to look tremendous when in against a highly defensive fighter who rarely opened up, and who moved, clinched, and dropped to the canvas.

Noted was the fact that the articles of agreement did not call for a decision in Griffin's favor if he lasted the 4 rounds, and that the general impression to the contrary was in error. "Instead of this the articles merely called for a forfeit of $100. ... The victory for Griffin could not be proclaimed by Referee Harry Stuart because the articles forbade." Nevertheless, the *Herald* opined that Griffin was victorious for lasting the 4 rounds.

Clearly though, this was just a money-making tune-up exhibition bout designed to get Jeff some work and generate some additional money, which it did. Griffin got some unofficial accolades by merely surviving, but there was no decision on the merits.

The Oakland Tribune's report said, "The colored man put up a sprinting game that Jeff could not beat," and therefore Jeffries had to give him $100 for lasting the 4 rounds. Of course, $100 was a paltry sum compared to the receipts of a full house, of which Jeff was to receive 65%. Therefore, the fear of losing $100 was not much of an incentive for Jeff to do his best or risk injury, particularly with the more lucrative Ruhlin bout on the horizon. Quite frankly, the survive-and-earn-money offer sounded more like an effective marketing ploy.[621]

Quite a number of blacks attended the match, many of whom were concerned about Griffin's welfare, and early on, they told Hank to stay down and forget the money, for Jeffries might kill him. However, at the end, they celebrated his ability to avoid being knocked out.

The National Police Gazette reported that the result was not a surprise to Eastern followers of the game who had seen the champ in action. "Jeff is not a quick finisher. He has never won a fight in short order. That is not his

621 *Oakland Tribune*, September 18, 1901.

style. He depends upon his wonderful endurance, and wins after having worn the other fellow out gradually."[622]

In his first autobiography, Jeffries said that he when he first knocked Griffin out, he was a novice. He did not train much for their 4-round bout, "regarding it as a workout with a fast man." He had been out of the ring for a long time, and wanted a couple of tune-ups before taking on Ruhlin. Jeff called the Griffin bout comical. He could not get much of an opportunity to hit him, because Hank sprinted about as fast as he could. When Jeffries did get into range, Griffin would either clinch or flop down without being hit, "so of course he lasted the four rounds."[623]

Following the Griffin exhibition, Jeffries, who was a trifle fat, remained in Los Angeles for several days, and then gave exhibitions with Jack Jeffries in some of the Central California towns such as Fresno and Visalia.[624]

A week after the Jeffries-Griffin bout, on September 24, 1901 at Oakland's Reliance Club, Jeffries took on Joe Kennedy in a bout of some significance. The 6'2" Kennedy, who generally weighed at least 190-195 pounds in top condition, had been a sparring partner for Pete Everett (1898), Tom Sharkey (1898), and Jack Root (1901). Kennedy had some good experience, including an 1898 W20 Jack Stelzner, and more importantly, a June 1899 W20 over Gus Ruhlin, a fight in which Joe acquitted himself well. After that bout, Jeffries said, "The most promising man I know of is this fellow, Joe Kennedy, of San Francisco, who beat Gus Ruhlin…. Kennedy is a good man. I have seen him fight, and I believe he is a comer." However, in September 1899, the hard-punching Peter Maher stopped Kennedy in the 2nd round.

The following month after the Maher bout, in October 1899, Kennedy fought colored heavyweight champion Frank Childs to a 6-round draw.

---

622 *National Police Gazette*, October 12, 1901.
623 *My Life and Battles* at 43-44.
624 *San Francisco Call*, September 22, 1901.

Kennedy could hardly have been in condition, yet they say it was a rough, bruising fight all the way after the first and the Westerner had the big negro guessing time and again with those hard left jabs of his. Childs got in some of his swings occasionally and put Kennedy to the bad and each had the other groggy a couple of times. Malachy Hogan called it a draw and the crowd left well satisfied with the decision.

In December 1899, Kennedy scored a KO4 over Soldier Walker and won a 20-round decision over Fred Russell. In May and July 1901, Kennedy fought Hank Griffin to two 20-round draws. Joe Kennedy was no dub.[625]

Jeffries withdrew his offer to forfeit $100 if he failed to stop Kennedy in 4 rounds, but said that he was still going to try to do so. Jeff wanted the 4-round fight to be on the merits, so as to incentivize Kennedy to try to fight to win, rather than just survive as Griffin did. Thus, there would be an official decision rendered.

> Kennedy thinks he will be not only able to stay the four rounds but he says he firmly believes he will get the decision as he intends to fight the champion from start to finish. Kennedy says he does not intend to adopt Hank Griffin's tactics simply to stay as he does not see how such a contest could help him. If, however, he could get the decision on points he would then be in a position to take on some of the heavy-weights who have heretofore given him the go by. Kennedy is in excellent condition and his friends are confident that Jeff will have a big contract on his hands if he figures on putting the big fellow out in four rounds.[626]

Another local Oakland paper said,

> Having had a month in which to get into good condition Kennedy has succeeded in getting into fine shape. As this will be a four round contest for a decision Kennedy announced his intention of fighting Jeff every inch of the way in the hope of getting the decision. … Jeff's friends think that he will have a better opportunity to put Kennedy out of business than he did Griffin as they all believe Kennedy will try to out point the champion.[627]

So, it appeared that Kennedy's goal was to win rather than merely survive, which actually made it more likely that he might be knocked out. The fact that Kennedy had once defeated Ruhlin lent additional interest to the bout.

On fight-night at Oakland's Reliance Athletic Club, shortly after 10 p.m., Kennedy entered the ring first, to the cheers of the crowd. According to the semi-local *San Francisco Call*, which appeared to have a reporter on-

625 *National Police Gazette*, November 4, 1899; *Los Angeles Daily Times*, *Los Angeles Express*, September 24, 1901; *Louisville Courier-Journal*, June 25, 1899; *New York Clipper*, July 1, 1899: Boxrec.com.
626 *Oakland Tribune*, September 23, 1901.
627 *Oakland Enquirer*, September 23, 24, 1901.

scene, Kennedy was actually more than 30 pounds above his normal fighting weight (currently weighing 220-225), but did not show it, wearing the weight well.

A few seconds later, James Jeffries entered, followed by Jack Jeffries, De Witt Van Court, and Billy Delaney. Upon seeing upcoming opponent Gus Ruhlin at ringside amongst the reporters, Jeff walked over and said, "Hello, Gus." Ruhlin responded in kind. For whatever reason, the attendance was disappointing, the gymnasium being hardly more than half full.

Two judges were appointed, and Ed Smith refereed. The fact that there were two judges further confirms that this was a bout to be fought on the merits, and not a mere exhibition. The men agreed to fight according to the Marquis of Queensbury rules.[628]

1st round

After both sprang to ring center, Jeff landed lightly to Joe's jaw, and again on the body. They mixed it up in lively fashion, with honors even. Jeff hit Kennedy's wind, but Joe countered heavily on the stomach. It was give and take for a while, with Kennedy making a surprising stand against the champion. He stood his ground and gave blow for blow. Joe often led each time they came together, and usually landed, but received Jeff's right on the ribs in return.

Upon a Jeffries rush, Kennedy side-stepped and landed a hard swing to the nose, knocking Jeff's head back. Jeffries retaliated with a right on the ear. Joe landed a left to the jaw and right to the eye and the crowd cheered him. Jeffries did not seem to mind the punches. He landed heavily on the stomach, but Joe countered with both hands to the body. The pace was very fast and the hitting of the cleanest kind. As the gong sounded, the crowd was cheering. Both men still seemed fresh.

2nd round

From the start, Jeffries took the aggressive and went in as if determined to finish the contest. He had learned that Kennedy could not hit hard enough to hurt him, so he changed his style of fighting. Jeff did not use his crouching attitude, but rather stood up, advancing quickly and irresistibly upon his opponent like a bear, giving him no rest. They went right at it.

Jeffries landed a left to the stomach, but Kennedy countered with a left to the body and right to the nose. Joe was game and ready to mix things, but the champion's speed soon began to tell, while Kennedy's blows lacked effectiveness. "The champion showed himself to be very shifty and clever and remarkably fast on his feet for a man of his weight." Jeff seemed to have absolutely no fear of his opponent and made little attempt to guard himself as he kept boring in and crowding Joe to the ropes.

---

628 The following account and post-fight analysis is based upon the *Oakland Tribune, Oakland Enquirer,* and *San Francisco Call,* September 25, 1901.

Jeffries kept coming all the time and for every blow that he received, he landed two. His favorite punch was a right to the body just before they clinched. It was a powerful blow, seemingly propelled by the force of a battering ram, looking as though it would go through Kennedy.

After they exchanged a few blows, Jeff landed a hard left to the solar plexus and right to the jaw, staggering Joe. Jeff pressed him back to the corner and, with the full force of the body behind it; Jeffries landed a very short, hard left hook to the jaw that put Kennedy down for the count, ending the contest. Immediately after the ten-count passed, Joe scrambled to his feet. The round had lasted 2 minutes.

Kennedy showed no marks. The crowd vigorously cheered him for his gameness, as well as Jeffries for his victory. The end had come unexpectedly after one of the prettiest exhibitions of boxing ever seen.

The Oakland Enquirer said that Jeff had quickly disposed of Kennedy, but that Joe had shown much gameness. *The Call* said that Kennedy simply could not withstand Jeff's powerful onslaughts. "It seemed nothing human could stop Jeffries. He was as lithe and as active as a cat." Having determined that Joe could not hurt him, Jeff took chances that he might not have otherwise done.

Gus Ruhlin, who had been present at all of Jeff's championship fights, said that he never before saw Jeff perform so well. Jeffries usually approached his opponents slowly, but against Kennedy, he walked briskly up to him each time and exchanged blow for blow. As would be seen in his subsequent fights, this was Jeff's new style.

Jeffries acknowledged that he had met a clever and hard-hitting antagonist. In his autobiography, Jeffries called Kennedy a big, strong, willing fellow. He thought that Kennedy would make a first-class sparring partner, so the following year, he invited him to join his training camp.[629]

---

629 *My Life and Battles* at 44.

CHAPTER 28

The Road to Ruhlin

After completing his exhibition tour with Jack Jeffries, boxing in places like Stockton and Bakersfield, in early October 1901, champion James J. Jeffries started training at Harbin Springs for the November 15 Ruhlin title fight. He sparred with brother Jack as well as Bob Armstrong. Gus Ruhlin prepared at Blankin's Six-Mile House, near San Francisco, sparring regularly with top black fighter "Denver" Ed Martin. Both Jeffries and Ruhlin were said to be training very hard, as if their lives depended upon winning. Ruhlin was weighing 203 pounds and looking strong and fast.[630]

Born of Swiss and French descent (not German), Gus Ruhlin was 29 years old. Noted for his strength, it was said that Ruhlin's weightlifting feats overshadowed the great Sandow, the former strongman.[631]

Ruhlin's career included: 1897 D20 Jeffries; 1898 L20 McCoy, LKOby1 Sharkey, and ND6 "win" Choynski; and 1899 D20 Maher and L20 Kennedy. After losing to Kennedy, Ruhlin went on a nine-fight win streak, including 1899 KO7 Jack Stelzner and KO5 Jim Jeffords; and 1900 KO4 Jack Finnegan. Ruhlin had been a Corbett sparring partner prior to Corbett giving Jeff hell over 23 rounds.

Most importantly, in 1900, Ruhlin scored the KO15 over Tom Sharkey, who had given Jeffries a tough and close battle at the end of the previous year and was coming off a KO3 over Joe Choynski. In his next fight, Bob Fitzsimmons stopped Ruhlin in 6 rounds in an exciting hard-fought battle. Gus subsequently boxed Peter Maher to a 6-round no decision, although most felt that Ruhlin had the better of it. Gus had also defeated Fitzsimmons in a wrestling contest.[632]

On October 2, 1901 in Los Angeles, Ruhlin sparring partner "Denver" Ed Martin took on Hank Griffin, less than a month after Griffin had boxed Jeffries in a 4-round exhibition. Martin was superior from the start. He dropped Griffin four times in the 6th round and knocked him out in the 7th round with a right to the jaw. *The Police Gazette* said, "There doesn't seem to be any real reason to question "Denver Ed" Martin's claim to the title of

---

630 *National Police Gazette*, October 12, 1901; *Los Angeles Daily Times*, September 17, 1901; *Los Angeles Express*, September 28, 1901.
631 *National Police Gazette*, April 8, 1899, February 3, 1900.
632 Ruhlin was viewed as a good opponent because of his 20-round draw with Jeffries and his knockout victory over Sharkey. Corbett and Kid McCoy were out of the running because of the controversy surrounding their fight. Fitz was not willing to fight. That left Ruhlin as the next best contender.

colored heavyweight champion. The manner in which he disposed of Hank Griffin the other night at Los Angeles settled all controversy on the subject." After the bout, Martin returned to training with Ruhlin. Gus had a quality sparring partner.

Jeffries paid tribute to Ruhlin as a fighter, saying, "Don't let any one tell you that this fellow Ruhlin can't hit hard. When Ruhlin and I met for the first time, at San Francisco several years ago, we were both new at the business, and of course did not know the ropes very well. Ruhlin got in a punch on that night that I never shall forget." Jeff said it was a punch delivered after the bell, after he had begun to return to his corner and was off his guard, so it jolted him.[633]

As of October 26, Bill Delaney said that Jeff was a glutton for work, in great shape, and using more judgment in his training than at any time in his career. Jeff's training included handball, medicine ball, pulleys, rowing machine, dumb-bells, rope skipping, bag punching, wrestling, and sparring. In his free time, he enjoyed baseball, billiards, croquet, horseback riding, and shooting game.

Jeff was weighing about 214 pounds, but Delaney felt that weighing too low hurt him. Bill wanted Jeff to go into the ring weighing 225 pounds. "Honestly I never thought he would recover from that crazy course of training he went through for Sharkey. Now, however, he knows himself. Too much road work is not beneficial." This would be Jeff's first title fight without Tommy Ryan's influence. Ryan liked Jeff low in weight, but Delaney wanted him bigger, and did not want him doing many long runs. Still, it was difficult to control Jeffries, who loved to train long and hard.[634]

Jeffries felt that the press did not give him the credit that he deserved. Clearly, he was motivated to have a dominant performance.

> He has the championship title, but he thinks he has not been given the same amount of pugilistic honor that has been thrust upon other champions. His long fights with Sharkey and Corbett made it look as if he won the championship on endurance, rather than science and hard hitting.[635]

Jeff liked taking the occasional 3-4-hour hike and run. On October 31 at Harbin Springs, Jeffries took a 20-mile jaunt over the hills. He later played a game of baseball.

In the afternoon, Jeffries and the 207-pound Armstrong went at it briskly, neither man sparing the other's feelings. Observers noted that Jeff had discarded his use of the crouch. At times he would use it, but most of the time he was upright and seemed to do better with this stance. "He showed his tremendous strength by the manner in which he tossed his

---

633 *National Police Gazette*, October 26, November 16, 1901.
634 *San Francisco Bulletin*, October 27, 1901. See Appendix for more detail on Jeff's daily training.
635 *Louisville Evening Post*, October 31, 1901.

heavy sparring partner around. He roughed it. Armstrong landed some heavy blows on Jeff's stomach, but this did not stop the champion. He was always boring in and would take a blow for the sake of landing a pet blow." Near the close of the 4th round, Jeff told Bob to let loose, which he did, slamming in an assortment of hard blows. However, Jeff only smiled, coming back for more even when his head was once rocked by a right. After it was over, Jeff said, "It is hard work following a man around." Armstrong replied, "It's just as hard work running away."

Jack Jeffries then took on the champ for another 4 rounds in lively fashion. They hammered each other. James landed a stiff one on the neck that nearly stopped his brother. The champ was looking strong and extremely fast for a big man.

After the sparring, Jeff vigorously hit the bag for 10 minutes. He then worked the rowing machine for a couple of miles. The usual rubdown ended the day's work.[636]

The Police Gazette opined that Bob Armstrong would be valuable to Jeffries, for he was "unquestionably one of the best sparring partners in the business today."

> Although Armstrong has been unfortunate in his ring engagements, it is a well known fact that there are few of the heavies who can outpoint him in private. Armstrong fights his battles in training and shows himself a 50 per cent better man than when he appears in a public exhibition. He has in turn trained Sharkey, Fitzsimmons, Ruhlin and Jeffries for important battles. Armstrong is a six-footer and weighs more than 200 pounds. He has a terrific punch and is credited with flooring Fitzsimmons in a hot mix-up with a single swing.[637]

It was suggesting that Armstrong was a "gym fighter," or someone who looks great sparring in the gym, but is not necessarily able to shine in actual combat on a consistent basis. Still, Bob had good results too, and was always competitive. Armstrong had scored an 1899 KO2 over Ruhlin's sparring partner, "Denver" Ed Martin, although Martin went 6 rounds with him in a 1900 6-round no decision bout.[638]

Jeffries had a badly puffed lower lip from a collision with his brother's head, which a doctor treated. When asked about all the hard blows dealt his way in training, Jeff said that he did not take punishment like other fighters, and though he had often been hit hard, it was seldom with force enough to worry him. The doctor said that Jeff's activity, quickness, and agility were truly phenomenal, especially when considering his great size.

---

636 *San Francisco Call*, November 2, 1901.
637 *National Police Gazette*, November 2, 1901.
638 Armstrong's record also included: 1898 L10 Jeffries and D/W10 Ed Dunkhorst, KO14 Mexican Pete Everett; 1899 LKOby6 Frank Childs, KO2 Denver Ed Martin, W10/20 Stockings Conroy, L10 Dunkhorst, KO3 Jim Jeffords; and 1900 ND6 Ed Martin. Cyberboxingzone.com; Boxrec.com.

While his capacity to receive and assimilate punishment is great, his power and ability to inflict it is terrific. … He revels in hard work. The harder it is the better he likes it and it does not seem to tire him. … He is even-tempered, good-natured and as frolicsome as a schoolboy on a vacation.

Ruhlin hauls a heavy load as part of his training.

On November 2 in Redwood City, Ruhlin went through dumbbell exercises, jumped rope, punched the bag, and sparred Ed Martin, Charley Goff, and the veteran heavyweight Joe McAuliffe, who was Jeff's size.

Jeffries was looking good in his daily sparring. "Judging from the manner in which Jeffries handles Bob Armstrong…it is doubtful if the pugilist lives who can get the better of him at the roughhouse game."[639]

On November 4, Jeff played three fast games of handball and showed his wonderful speed. He then sparred 4 hot rounds with Armstrong. "They did not do any love-tapping. Jeffries sailed into the big colored boxer and had the latter pinned to the wall in every round. Bob landed some stiff punches to let Jim know that he was in the game." Without rest, Jeff then took on Jack and mostly played defense, working on blocking and side-stepping. He was not bothered even when Jack went at him hammer and tongs. Jeff then tossed the heavy medicine ball with Armstrong, skipped rope, and worked the rowing machine.

Reports from the training quarters indicated that both pugilists were "indefatigable workers," training hard and ready to fight the battle of their lives.

639 *San Francisco Call*, November 3, 4, 1901; *San Francisco Examiner*, November 4, 1901.

Ruhlin was confident. "Ever since I fought Jeffries in this city I have always felt that he was one fellow in this business that I can trim. ... I can honestly say that I would sooner fight Jeffries than almost anybody in our class. I'll wager that I am stronger and quicker and cleverer than Jeff."[640]

Jeffries believed that he represented a modern improvement over old methods, and felt that his skill was underrated.

> I don't mean to say that I can't be hit... I believe, though, that my system of defense prevents me from receiving the full force of a blow. Armstrong is under orders to punch away at me to his heart's content, and he gets home pretty often, but he has yet to land a smash that amounts to anything.

Jeff took pride in his short range power as well. "All I need now is a few inches leeway and I'll go pretty close to knocking my man out if I land."[641]

Jeffries was looking good. "The big fellow could not possibly be in better fettle. He is hard and as strong as an ox, and feels that he is going to win early in the game."

Gus Ruhlin's sparring sessions with Ed Martin were fierce. Martin was a good-looking fighter and might have been a contender in his own right, but "white champions are more profitable as show cards than the colored variety, and goodness knows what might happen if Gus and Martin locked horns in a regulation Queensberry engagement." The following year, Martin would officially become the colored heavyweight champion.

The San Francisco Evening Post opined that although Ruhlin had a punch, was strong and confident; his best chance of victory would be to box at a distance and use his jab. By quickly stopping Joe Kennedy, who held a 20-round decision victory over Ruhlin, Jeffries proved that "the man who attempts to outslug the big fellow is taking mighty chances." Ruhlin was a 5-2 underdog, because even if he boxed from the outside; Jeff was likely to catch up with him. Jeffries was faster on his feet than Ruhlin, and even Jim Corbett, "the fastest heavy-weight that ever donned a glove," failed to escape being cornered and taken out by Jeffries.[642]

---

640 *San Francisco Call*, November 5, 1901.
641 *San Francisco Examiner*, November 5, 1901.
642 *San Francisco Examiner*, November 7, 13, 1901; *San Francisco Evening Post*, November 6, 1901.

Also on November 4, 1901, in Bakersfield, coming off the KOby7 loss to Martin, Hank Griffin won a 20-round decision over Jack Johnson.

On the 5th, Ruhlin trained in front of the Edison Company's movie cameras, showing all of his training stunts for 2 hours. Ruhlin boxed with Goff and Martin for 1 round each. Against Martin,

> They pummeled each other hard and often, and in this bout Gus exhibited a remarkable improvement. Those who have not seen the big Akron fighter handle his mitts since he fought Joe Kennedy here two years ago would be surprised at his rapid strides toward perfection. His delivery and defense have been strengthened and he looks every inch a match for Jeffries.[643]

Jeffries put in a hard day's work on the 5th. He went hard at his brother in sparring 3 rounds. He next took on Armstrong,

> The two big men were slamming each other in a manner that signified that something was doing. In a mix-up Bob shot his right across and caught the champion flush on the mouth. Jeff's lip was badly cut by the blow, but unmindful of it, he bored right in. He retaliated by giving Armstrong a short arm blow in the ribs that made Bob gasp for breath. Bob was too foxy a ring general to show he was in distress. He stepped back and began to feint until he recovered his breath. Then he went in again, but Jeff made him retreat all over the gymnasium. At the end of the third round Armstrong was blowing and tired.

After Jeff's one minute of rest, he skipped rope. Then he worked the rowing machine for 10 minutes, followed by bag punching for 10 minutes. "His blows were powerful and rapid." He wrapped up the morning session by tossing the 20-pound medicine ball for 15 minutes. In the afternoon, Jeff ran 4 miles to Middletown, and then, on the return 4-mile journey, he spurted all the way. Following this, Jeff hit a nearly 200-pound bag of sand for 15 minutes.

Jeffries was very happy with his training, and felt much better than he did before he fought Sharkey and Corbett. He recognized Ruhlin's ability, but remained very confident. "I am satisfied Ruhlin has greatly improved since our last meeting. I can safely say I have also improved."

Jeff also said that he was in the business for money, and realizing that Fitzsimmons would be the greatest draw, he wanted a fight with Bob. Jeff was concerned that Fitz felt there was more money in the theatrical business than in boxing. If Bob was not willing to meet him, Jeff was ready to meet Sharkey instead.[644]

---

643 *San Francisco Call*, November 6, 1901.
644 *San Francisco Call*, November 6, 7, 1901; *San Francisco Bulletin*, November 10, 1901.

Jeffries and Armstrong

On November 8, for his final days of preparation, Jeffries moved his training camp from Harbin Springs to Oakland's Reliance Club, where he had trained for previous fights.

No police or political interference with the fight was anticipated. *The Police Gazette* said, "Out on the Coast they are by no means as squeamish as they are here in the effete East, and the thought of a fistic battle between two well-trained athletes does not fill them with the horror that the prospect of such a thing does our law makers and law enforcers."

The Gazette called Jeffries and Ruhlin scientific and experienced giants of the prize ring. It was impressed by Gus's victory over Sharkey. "Sharkey has gone back, and may not be the fighter he was a few years ago, but when Ruhlin defeated him he was an opponent to be feared." However, unlike Sharkey, who just rushed into Ruhlin's punches, Jeffries "is an extremely cautious fighter," and was faster on his feet than Gus, which were amongst the reasons why Jeff was a strong favorite over Ruhlin.

Gus intended to enter the ring at his current weight of 200 pounds. He was confident in his strength. "I don't think Jeffries will be able to blanket me at close quarters the way he did Sharkey. In every clinch he leaned his entire strength on the sailor and had poor Sharkey's knees sagging. I think I'll be able to straighten him up if he tries any of those dodges with me." Billy Madden said that his protégé had never looked so well nor been in better shape than at present. Ruhlin said, "You can say for me that I am fit to fight the battle of my life. … If I had been in this condition when I fought Fitzsimmons there would be a different story to tell of the outcome."

The San Francisco Evening Post said that Jeffries "has proved himself a great pugilist."

His work in the ring has never been of the spectacular order. He is a cool-headed fellow, one whom the hottest part of a combat will not rattle, and to this fact more than any other he can ascribe his success. He boxes crouched down, leaving but little of his burly body open to the caresses of an opponent. His long left arm waves in front of him like a foot-racer getting ready to start, but encased in that gigantic arm is the power that an Ajax might envy. His right hand he uses freely, but generally for protective purposes or for body punching, and when he drives it with all the cruel force back of his massive body the blow can be heard for some distance. The man is not alive and in ring work who equals Jeffries in natural strength. He is big in hard flesh and muscle, and can be depended on to go the route, whether it comes his way or not.

Even when the honors look darkest for him, when defeat seems to be hovering nigh, as in the Corbett contest, Jeff still keeps pegging away as cool as an iceberg, and success generally rewards his efforts.

He is the best money carrier we have had in the ring. His coolness gives him an advantage hard to discount, and, knowing that he is fighting for life as it were, he will wade through gore to win the present combat.[645]

Their respective sparring partners gave their opinions regarding the upcoming fight. Bob Armstrong said,

Jeff is big and strong, besides being fast... I don't know of a fighter who has improved more than Jeffries has since he has been in the business. He has the best defense of any heavyweight I know, and, barring accidents, I don't see how he can lose. I boxed with the champion for all his previous fights, and it's dead right when I tell you he's 50 percent better than he ever was before.

Denver Ed Martin said of Ruhlin,

If anyone can lick Jeffries, it will be Ruhlin.... I have been with Gus a year now, and I know that he is faster, stronger and more clever by far than I have ever seen him. ... [S]hould Jeffries lick Gus he can then go down the line among the other big fellows like breaking sticks.[646]

George Siler visited Ruhlin's training quarters. He thought that Gus looked bigger, stronger, and better than when he defeated Sharkey, and was big and strong enough to make it a hard fight, or at least interesting for Jeffries.

---

645 *San Francisco Call*, November 10, 1901; *Oakland Enquirer, National Police Gazette, San Francisco Evening Post*, November 9, 1901.
646 *San Francisco Examiner*, November 11, 1901.

Former lightweight champion George Lavigne (who held a knockout win over Joe Walcott) said that although he liked Jeff in the fight, and considered him a great fighter; Ruhlin was the picture of the well-trained athlete and would put up a good fight. He predicted that the fight would be a "corker" and that the winner would know that he was in a scrap. He said that Ruhlin was a

Ed Martin, Gus Ruhlin, George Siler, Billy Madden

second Sharkey when it came to taking punishment.[647]

Jim Corbett said that Jeff had a hard battle on his hands, that Ruhlin would not be a cinch, but still felt that Jeffries would win in the end.

At the Reliance Club on November 11, in the morning, Jeff punched the bag and then boxed 8 fast rounds with Armstrong and brother Jack, alternating a round with each. Jeff tossed the husky Armstrong around "like a sack." He then skipped rope and worked with the rowing and wrist machines.

In the afternoon, Jeff performed before the moving picture machine. Some of that training footage still exists. In it, Jeffries appears quick, agile, and active on his feet, especially for a big man. He moves around holding hand weights as he shadow boxes and feints. As he jumps rope, Armstrong can be seen in the background. In sparring (likely his brother or another white boxer), Jeff is very lively with his footwork and head-movement, showing that he knew how to step in and out, lift his hands to block, lean his head back, dip off to the side, or duck and weave around under blows, a precursor to the future famous Jack Dempsey head movement. He throws light counter shots, mostly with his stiff-arm left, either jabbing or hooking with it, but not really attempting to put too much power behind the blows, not wanting to hurt his sparring partner. Jeff seems to be mostly playing defense, working on his timing and distance, able to elude blows while in range. Neither man wore headgear.

George Siler, who observed Jeffries in training, said, "I have seen Jeff in all his big Eastern engagements but I must confess he never looked the

---

647 *San Francisco Call, San Francisco Bulletin*, November 11, 1901.

physical wonder he is today. He is faster and surer in his work and has not an awkward movement. There never was such an ideal boxer of his weight and inches. He is a wonder." The champ was much faster on his feet. Further, "Jeff has changed his position. He used to spread in taking his attitude. He now keeps his feet closer together and as a result he springs quickly and carries all his weight with his blows."[648]

On the 12th, Jeffries exercised for 2 hours at the Reliance Club. "Every one who has seen him exercise marvels at his swiftness. He is extremely fast on his feet and never tires. That he is hitting with great force was evidenced by the manner in which he punched the bag." In the evening, he went to the theater and laughed at the comedians.

Jeff said that his hard work was over. He would do just enough to keep sharp. "You can rest assured that I will win as soon as I can without exposing myself to any great danger of getting licked myself. Really, I don't think it will be a long fight." Still, he gave Gus his just due credit. "Ruhlin is a big, strong fellow, very game and fairly clever. ... I know I have improved since I fought him here but he has improved as well."

Gus was said to have improved in his speed and footwork. He was running 8 miles every morning with sparring partners Ed Martin, Ed Smith, and Charley Goff.

Ruhlin said that although he was a long odds underdog, the odds did not win or lose a fight. Champions were generally top-heavy favorites. He was ready. "I never felt like I do now in all my life. I simply can't express the improvement I feel the last six months' work has made in me. ... I am trained to perfection."[649]

Jeffries said that after he defeated Ruhlin, he was willing to take on either Fitzsimmons or Sharkey before the holidays. Sharkey was willing to take on the winner in late December.

At the conclusion of his training on the 13th, Jeffries weighed 208 ½ pounds. Jeff felt that he fought better when lighter. He said that when he fought Fitzsimmons, he weighed 207, was fast as chain lightning, and could have fought all night. However, Delaney said that he preferred Jeff to weigh 215-217 pounds. He was sure that Jeff would enter the ring at about 215 pounds. "The reason he is down to 208 is because of the heavy work he did today. He will rest tomorrow and will take on a few extra pounds." Bill was satisfied with Jeff's condition.

Speaking of his motivation, Jeffries said, "I fight for money. Well, of course, there's glory in it, too – when I win." When asked if he would be content with glory without the money, Jeff responded, "Would those prima donnas over at the Grand Opera House sing for glory – or dollars? Boxers and prima donnas are alike in their professions – it's glory and dollars. They

648 *Oakland Tribune, San Francisco Call*, November 12, 1901; *San Francisco Bulletin*, November 11, 1901.
649 *San Francisco Bulletin, San Francisco Call*, November 13, 1901.

go together. Of course Ruhlin will get dollars and no glory – but he'd win more dollars if he could collar the glory."

Jeffries was the embodiment of confidence. When asked if he ever got nervous in a fight, he responded that he had once been nervous, "but that was when I was new and raw." When asked what he thought of when fighting, Jeff responded, "I'm thinking of only one thing – how I can land to put the other fellow out."

Lou Houseman called Jeffries "the most formidable monster" that ever donned the gloves. Ruhlin was actually more experienced, having had more bouts. However, he was known as an inconsistent performer, or an "in and outer." He had fought some great battles, and some poor ones.

Ruhlin's manager, Billy Madden, did not believe the reports regarding Jeff's weight. He said that Jeffries would enter the ring weighing close to 225 pounds. Ruhlin was weighing 201 ½ pounds. He was going into the fight in the best possible shape and very confident. Gus said, "I firmly believe I will win, and if I don't it will be because Jeff is a better man. I am in shape to fight the battle of my life."[650]

Jeffries was certain of victory.

> I will defeat Ruhlin and you can bank your money on it. He is a good man, but I think I am his superior in strength, science and punching power. ... I feel stronger than I did when I met Fitzsimmons. I expect to enter the ring weighing about 212 pounds. I am faster than I ever was and I feel strong. I think I can punch harder than ever before in my career. . ... [W]hen I defeat Ruhlin I will be ready to fight any man in the world. I prefer to meet Fitzsimmons, but if he does not like my game Sharkey will do.[651]

Like Jeff, the day before the fight, Ruhlin was claiming to be in the best shape of his life, faster, stronger, and more confident than ever. "I feel confident I can beat Jeffries because I subdued Sharkey in less time than he could ever do. It is true Fitzsimmons defeated me, but those who saw that battle will attest I gave the blacksmith a beating he will not soon forget." Plus, Gus said he was in better shape this time and much improved. Ruhlin had fought Jeff before and knew what he had. "I don't see anything in Jim Jeffries to scare me. ... I put up as good a fight as Jeffries when I fought him to a draw and I think I've improved as much as he has since that fight." Both men could dodge, guard and feint, and both could strike powerful blows. The press expected a competitive fight.[652]

650 *San Francisco Call, San Francisco Evening Post, San Francisco Bulletin*, November 14, 1901.
651 *San Francisco Call*, November 15, 1901.
652 *San Francisco Call, San Francisco Evening Post*, November 15, 1901.

CHAPTER 29

Ruling Ruhlin

On the day of the Jeffries-Ruhlin championship fight, November 15, 1901, Billy Madden was confident that Ruhlin would win. "Ruhlin is faster now than he ever was in his life. That fellow, Denver Ed Martin, is a wonder for speeding a man up, and when a big man like Gus can cut out a pace with him I think he is pretty good, don't you?"

Bill Delaney was just as proud of Jeffries' condition. "I think Jeff is better prepared to meet Ruhlin than he has ever been during his career for a battle." The champ had followed his instructions, and they had gotten along well. "I have seen the best of the fighters when they were in the greatest days of their strength, and never one of them equaled this man Jeffries. He is a marvel and there's no mistake about it." He felt that Jeff would win quickly.[653]

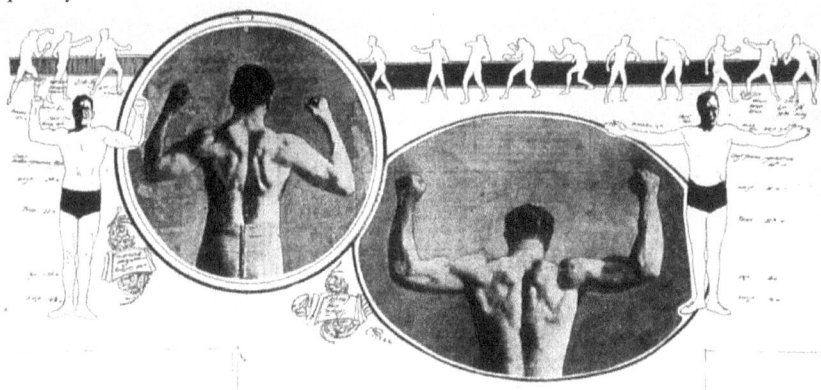

Ruhlin photo on the left, Jeffries photo on the right

Harry Corbett, Jim Corbett's brother, was selected to referee the fight. Referee Corbett declared that the men would have to protect themselves in the clinches. However, he would not permit holding and hitting.

Sam Austin, writing for the *National Police Gazette*, opined that Ruhlin's biggest weakness was that he was a slow starter, usually beginning fights nervously and cautiously for a few rounds until "a sudden metamorphosis occurs." Austin heard from an inside source that Jeffries intended to exploit that weakness, to force the pace from the start and try to knock Gus out quickly. Jeff could hit harder and was game enough to go in and take a

653 *San Francisco Bulletin*, November 15, 1901.

chance. However, Sharkey had attempted the same tactic, and Ruhlin outboxed and knocked him out. Austin opined that Jeff would try to use his superior weight by leaning and bearing down on Ruhlin in the clinches to wear him out. The rules allowing hitting in the clinches would favor Jeff, because he was the better infighter. Ruhlin's forte was long range work.[654]

The sporting fraternity and experts were mostly solid for Jeffries. He had superior ring knowledge, combined with better fighting instincts.

In his interviews, Jeffries confirmed his intention to attack Ruhlin from the start, to force the fight and end it quickly. He wanted to show his versatility. He had already won fights backing and countering (Fitz and Sharkey II), as well as boxing and attacking (Corbett). He could fight in any manner that he desired. His left arm was in good shape, and he wanted to silence critics who said that he was not the aggressive knockout artist that Sullivan was.

Before consenting to allowing the bout to be filmed, Delaney and Jeff required assurances that the apparatus used would not create the same oppressive and intense heat as had been the case for the Sharkey fight. Delaney was promised that a different system would be employed, one which used half the number of lights. Furthermore, the lights would be higher up, with holes cut in the reflectors to allow the heat to escape and rise to the ceiling. As a result of these assurances, the fight would be filmed.

Ticket prices ranged from $2 for gallery admission to $20 for choice box seats adjacent to the ring. Good seats could be obtained on the floor for $5 and $7.50. "These prices strike the casual San Francisco fightgoer as a trifle high, perhaps, but compared to the prices charged for the championship goes of the East, they appear reasonable." Seats for Jeff-Fitz were $5 all the way up to $35. Corbett-Fitz seats were $10 up to $40. Tickets for most championship fights were generally $10 to $50. Of course, this was why the fighters lamented the fact that boxing was no longer legal in New York. The purses would not be as big in San Francisco.[655]

Estimates of crowd size varied from 6,000 to 10,000. The Twentieth Century Athletic Club said 6,000 people were in the building. One local paper reported that there were 6,610 paid admissions. 3,680 were on the main floor and the rest were in the gallery. 250 tickets were given away to city officials and others. Other reports said 10,000 were present, with every seat in the immense structure filled. However, yet another said, "There are few people who can estimate anywhere near correctly the number of people in an audience, and invariably when they try they guess about twice as many as are really present."

At 8:30 p.m., Jeffries entered San Francisco's Mechanic's Pavilion. He watched a round and a half of one of the preliminary bouts, and then went

654 *National Police Gazette*, November 23, 1901.
655 *San Francisco Evening Post*, November 5, 13, 1901; *National Police Gazette*, November 23, 1901.

to his dressing room. Ruhlin entered a few minutes later and went straight to his dressing room. Ringside betting was 2 to 1, with Jeff the favorite.

When it was time for the fight, Jeffries walked down the aisle first, wearing a bright red sweater and black trousers. He entered the ring at 9:30 p.m., holding his hands over his eyes to protect them from the glare of the kinetoscope lights. A frame suspended over the ring held a number of arc lamps which threw a total of 80,000 candle-power light upon the ring. Despite the glare, the heat was not noticeable.

Jeff received a warm ovation as he leaned against the ropes, smiling. His seconds were Billy Delaney, Bob Armstrong, Jack Jeffries, and Eugene and De Witt Van Court. Jeff strolled about, testing his shoes on the new canvas.

A minute later, Ruhlin entered and sat down. His seconds were Charlie Goff, Young Gibbs, Billy Madden, and Denver Ed Martin.

Ring announcer Billy Jordan introduced Ruhlin first. Jeffries followed, introduced as "the only champion of the world." Jordan announced that the fight was scheduled for 20 rounds.

Referee Harry Corbett examined the gloves, as did Delaney, Madden, and Police Captain Wittman. At 9:35 p.m., Referee Harry Corbett called the boxers to the center of the ring and gave them their final instructions.

The men then stripped and gloved up, this being completed by 9:40 p.m. Jeff wore black trunks with an American flag around his waist. Before the fight commenced, he removed the flag and attached it to the ring post in his corner. Ruhlin wore closely knitted white trunks.

A few days before the fight, Jeffries did not think he would weigh more than 215 pounds in the ring. The day before the fight, Jeff said he expected to weigh 212 pounds for the fight. Madden thought he was really weighing around 225. Ruhlin was said to be weighing about 201 pounds.[656]

1st round

Jeffries took the aggressive. He discarded his crouching pose, walking straight into Gus with his head slightly bent forward. Ruhlin broke ground when he saw "that ponderous piece of machinery moving toward him." Jeff hit the body, but the blows landed as Gus was moving away, so they did little damage. As Jeffries crowded in, Ruhlin fired jabs at him. Jeff was utterly confident, and did not even try to evade some of the blows. Gus landed jabs to the mouth and some rights to the head and body, but the rights did not land very squarely.

After some exchanges and clinches, Jeffries landed a right to the body which Ruhlin later said shook him up. Gus kept backing and punching. Jeff momentarily forced him to the ropes with a left and right on the body.

Ruhlin broke ground all the time, rapping Jeff with his left. Jeffries rushed in with a left on the body. He was smiling as Gus backed away and

656 The fight account and analysis is taken from the *San Francisco Examiner, San Francisco Chronicle, San Francisco Evening Post, San Francisco Bulletin, San Francisco Call,* November 16, 1901.

peppered him with blows. Jeff was throwing harder, but Gus was busier and landing more. Ruhlin's body shots caused a red mark to show on Jeff's side. Jeff landed a left on the jaw and they clinched.

On the inside, in the clinches, Jeffries was the stronger man and pushed Ruhlin about at will. Gus complained to the referee that Jeff was hanging on to him, but it soon became evident that it was Ruhlin who was clinching. Jeff tried to discourage Gus from grabbing by bearing his weight on him and wrestling a bit so as not to allow Ruhlin to get a rest. When the gong sounded, Jeff was smiling, while Gus was complaining to the referee. He looked far from being happy, while Jeffries was not even breathing hard.

Summarizing the round, a couple local sources said that Ruhlin had outboxed Jeffries. "Perhaps Ruhlin scored more points in the first, but they were points that did not hurt." Jeff's left eye was already red, but the blows had done him no internal harm, only leaving superficial wounds. He appeared unphased by Ruhlin's blows. Another local paper said that the round ended with honors about even. Jeff had forced the action, throwing fewer, but harder blows.

2nd round

Ruhlin outboxed Jeffries, making his best showing. He was faster, and landed jabs to the mouth, hard rights to the ribs, and occasional rights to the mouth. When Jeff's lips began bleeding, Ruhlin was awarded first blood, and the spectators cheered. It was a fast round.

However, although Ruhlin was landing his right to the body and head, Jeffries took the blows very well, leading some to wonder whether Ruhlin lacked force behind the blows or whether Jeff just had a wonderful ability to assimilate punishment. "Jeffries, who is a battleship for taking punishment, shook them off so unconcernedly that it made the jolts seem light and easy to take. Jeffries' wonderful ability to assimilate punishment undoubtedly had a dire effect upon Ruhlin's courage." Still, Gus outpointed him, which made the crowd look forward to a great battle.

Mostly, Ruhlin danced, landed on Jeff, who ignored his blows and stepped in, and then Gus clinched as Jeff would hit his body and head with short shots with both hands once he got close.

With a tiny stream of blood running from his mouth, Jeffries kept on working, coming in with his head and body low, forcing his way into Ruhlin. Gus landed rights to the body and head and backed around as Jeff chased him. After Gus landed a right on the ribs, Jeff rushed and landed a right to the body and left to the face. Ruhlin stumbled and nearly fell in one of his efforts to get away. Jeffries cut loose but missed as Ruhlin broke ground and countered with hard jabs and jolts in the body.

Referee Corbett warned Ruhlin for roughing in the clinches. Jeff was a bit riled and landed some jolts in the stomach. After another clinch, Jeff landed a left uppercut. Ruhlin complained that Jeffries was hitting in the breakaways and leaning on him. The referee told Gus to let go and that he would make Jeff back away.

All agreed that Ruhlin won the round on points. However, one source said, "In this round Ruhlin scored the most blows, but they were not effective."

3rd round

The tide suddenly turned. Jeffries got going and turned loose his battering-ram hooks to the head and body. Ruhlin was likely discouraged when he saw what little effect his blows had. Jeff followed him leisurely as Gus moved about. Ruhlin "broke ground continually, with the champion walking after him, head down, partly unguarded." Jeff took Ruhlin's rights with a smile. "He moved, cat-like, after Gus and by getting him in a position where he could not squirm out, managed to land several hard left jolts on the body and a right on the neck."

A Jeffries counter left hook to the jaw and hook to the ribs staggered Ruhlin to the ropes and took the fight out of him. According to Referee Corbett, during this round, Jeff sent Gus back towards the ropes with a straight left in the eye followed by a smash in the stomach. "Ruhlin backed further up against the ropes and murmured something about the blow being foul, but I had my eye on both punches and the last blow was well above the stomach. Ruhlin complained several times about Jeffries boring in after the breakaway, but this to my mind was perfectly fair." Jeff had a perfect right to bore in as long as Gus broke ground. "If Ruhlin objected to Jeffries' methods in this respect he should have held his ground."

Each time Jeffries landed the left to the stomach; Ruhlin winced in excruciating pain and clinched. Jeff shook him off as he would a small boy and repeated with rib roasters that nearly lifted Ruhlin off the floor. "Jeffries' blows were short, but terrible force was behind them." His body blows would have killed an untrained man. They sapped Ruhlin's strength and gave him a wholesome fear of the relentless man in front of him. On the other hand, Jeff was totally unconcerned by Ruhlin's blows.

It looked as if Ruhlin lost heart. Another hook caused the challenger to clinch. "He wore Gus down systematically and flogged him into submission in a workmanlike manner." Ruhlin staggered and wobbled around the ring. He ducked a punch and clinched. He seemed weak and frightened as he moved and punched with little force. Jeff smiled at his blows. Ruhlin's finish was already in sight, for his strength was fast leaving him.

One of Jeff's great lefts to the face sent Ruhlin staggering across the ring, and only the ropes kept him from falling off the platform. Jeffries continued landing flush shots to the body and head while Gus would move and clinch.

Ruhlin finished the round with a nasty cut under his right eye, which was puffed and bleeding badly, and his body was pink all over.

4th round

The round was all in Jeff's favor. Jeffries was fighting steadily, going right at him with great determination, full of confidence. He paid no attention to Ruhlin's seemingly weak punches, but merely laughed and advanced. Jeff hit the body often, particularly with his left, and gave Gus a dreadful beating.

Ruhlin landed a right to the body, but Jeffries beat a tattoo on his bad eye and was all over him. Jeff landed a left to the wind. He rushed Ruhlin to a corner and landed a stiff left to the jaw. He landed another such punch and Ruhlin was rattled. Gus missed a swinging left, while Jeff landed a right to the jaw which caused the challenger to clinch.

Referee Corbett said that Ruhlin landed a hard right to the body, but Jeff countered on the jaw and dazed him. Gus clinched and then revived. "He fought like a man whose head was alternately befuddled and clear." Ruhlin came back with a right to the head and heavy smash over the kidneys. Jeff roughed him in the clinches.

Jeffries took several blows in the face without flinching. Afterwards, Jeff said he knew there was no danger because Gus had no force in his blows at that point. Ruhlin backed away and Jeffries caught him a hard right to the head and left to the body, which hurt considerably. Gus clinched. Jeff continued landing body blows, paying no attention to Ruhlin's taps. Jeffries hurt him with several punches to the body and head. A right and left to the body made Gus double up and clinch.

Ruhlin went down from either a left to the jaw, a left to the body, or both in quick succession, or a combination of rights and lefts to the body and head. Each local source had a slightly different version of what had caught their eyes. *The Evening Post* and the *Chronicle* said Jeff dropped Ruhlin with a short left on the jaw. *The Examiner* basically agreed, saying that it was a snapping left uppercut on the chin. *The Bulletin* said, "It was a blow on the jaw coupled with the body blows that took his steam." Jeff landed a right on the body, and, in forcing Gus to the ropes, landed a left to the wind. Jeff then whipped in a straight left to the body and Ruhlin went down on his knees. "A blind man could see that the blow was painful and took about all the fight out of him that was left." *The Call* said Jeff landed rights to the head and body. "He then brought his right to the body after a pretty movement, in which he shifted suddenly from left to right, the blow knocking Ruhlin down."

Referee Harry Corbett later said that he knew it was all over when Jeff dropped Ruhlin with a hard right and left. "When he went down and I began to count off the seconds I felt that Ruhlin's chances for lasting out the round were very slim. The blows were terrific."

On his knees, Gus took his time in getting up from the first knockdown of the fight, waiting to rise until the count of eight. He appeared weak, and fell into a clinch as Jeff tried to follow up his advantage. In the clinch, Jeff roughed him a little and calmly untangled himself, but the gong sounded, saving Ruhlin. Gus returned to his corner groggy and tired. George Siler said that Ruhlin still had the overall margin in the number of blows landed, but it was obvious that he would not last.

5th round

Although Ruhlin had gone to his corner in a weakened condition, the minute rest revived him. This might have been due to the fact that between rounds, Ruhlin's seconds put smelling salts under his nose. Jeff sat in his corner appearing to be the most unconcerned man in the house.

During this round, Jeffries hit the body frequently. He willingly took Ruhlin's blows with a smile and kept at him. "The almost imperceptible jar of Jeff's punches told on Ruhlin." George Siler said that Ruhlin still landed as often as Jeff did, but Jeff's punches had the force, every blow being meaningful. He drove Gus about with both hands. Ruhlin made a faint show of fighting, but Jeff followed him around the ring and landed a good right to the heart that hurt. After that, Gus's movements were noticeably slow. Jeff forced the fighting and pegged away at the body.

Jeffries landed left and right short-arm jolts to the head. Gus landed a right to the body, but Jeff simply smiled and pushed him away. Gus missed and they clinched. A Jeffries left on the body followed by a left to the ear drove Ruhlin back. They tussled against the ropes and Jeff landed a left to the body. He then landed a right and left on the jaw and another left that sent Gus onto the ropes. Jeff forced him into the corner, paying no attention to Ruhlin's blows, smiling as he advanced. Jeffries was slaughtering him, particularly with the left to the body.

Jeffries dropped Ruhlin for the second time in the fight, each local source giving its version of how it happened. *The Chronicle, Evening Post,* and Referee Corbett all agreed that a vicious left uppercut or hook to the solar plexus dropped Ruhlin to the floor, wincing in pain. He took 8 seconds to rise. *The Bulletin* version said that Jeff continued working his left to the body and Ruhlin went down coming out of a clinch. He took a seven-count. An *Examiner* reporter said that Gus went down from a left uppercut on the chin. George Siler said, "Jeff waded in, caught Ruhlin a hard one on the neck, and as the latter pitched forward into a clinch, ripped him up in the body, and from the look of agony which came over Ruhlin's face it was apparent that the jig was up." The films show a double left, first to the head and then to the body, both very short and compact.

After rising, Ruhlin moved about and clinched, but Jeffries caught him with more body shots. A solid left to the neck made Gus groggy and he again clinched. Jeff kept at him, landing hard blows until the end of the round. Ruhlin mostly moved and clinched to avoid punishment. When the gong ended the round, he was wobbly and dazed.

The fight was filmed, but apparently, only part the 5th round still exists. The footage shows that Jeffries walked toward Ruhlin with his chin down, with a slight dip to the right, but much more upright than prior accounts of Jeff's style would have led one to believe. The newsmen noted that Jeff was more upright in this bout. He kept his right hand up a bit, but left down, somewhat cocked to the left. Jeffries was aggressive, simply walking in on his opponent, keeping the pressure on, launching one or two-punch bombs at Ruhlin, mostly left hook leads to the head or body. The punches are obviously hard with a fair amount of speed, but with pretty good, controlled form, particularly the short hook to the body. Ruhlin mostly clinched, punching little. Late in the 5th round, a hook/left uppercut to the head followed by a very short, likely more damaging hook to the body dropped Ruhlin. Gus survived the round by grabbing and moving.

Between rounds, the men had been in their corners for about 30 seconds when Billy Madden saw that his man was beaten and had enough. Therefore, he threw up the sponge into the ring to retire his man and prevent the inevitable knockout. *The Bulletin* said that Madden "wisely threw up the sponge, though there were many who thought he ought to have let his man take a knockout."

There was some chaos amongst the audience, which was surprised that Madden was stopping it. They were asking what the matter was, and what happened to Ruhlin. Referee Harry Corbett stepped to ring center and asked Madden, "Is this right? Do you want to do this?" Billy nodded his head and said to Corbett, "Harry, there's no use letting him stand up there and take all that punching for nothing. He can't win." De Witt Van Court, one of Jeff's seconds, said, "They've thrown up the sponge." Jeff looked surprised. The spectators hissed and jeered Ruhlin. Some rushed the ring, but Police Captain Wittman and his men stopped them.

Jeffries went over and shook Ruhlin's hand. While putting his hand on his own abdomen, Gus said, "You hurt me. That welt you gave me in the fourth round in the wind and then that one on the jaw took all my steam. I knew that I couldn't go on and do any fighting. You fixed me so I couldn't protect myself."

The retirement was a hot topic. *The Call* said, "Some held that, being a championship fight, Ruhlin owed it to himself and to his future career to have toed the mark until the decisive blow had been delivered." Referee Corbett said it was a bad ending, even though he agreed that Ruhlin was very groggy. "Of course Ruhlin was out for all fighting purposes…but at that it were better for all parties concerned…had Gus Ruhlin been allowed to toe the scratch for the sixth round and face the inevitable knockout." He said that Gus was wobbly, but not badly punished, and could have continued. However, the body punch ended Ruhlin's desire for any more of the fight.

The majority condemned Ruhlin for not taking his medicine, which would have been more satisfactory to the crowd. They had paid to see a decisive knockout. Still, everyone knew that Ruhlin could not win and that Jeffries would have knocked him out in the next round.

Despite the criticism of Ruhlin, the *Bulletin* felt that Madden threw up the sponge on his own, not at Ruhlin's request. Billy simply felt that his protégé was beaten. Ruhlin seemed surprised when he saw Corbett motion to Jeffries, have him walk to the center of the ring, and declare him the winner.

> Madden recognized that Ruhlin was hopelessly defeated, and to save him from a brutal beating terminated the contest when he did. Any intimation that Ruhlin quit or displayed any streak of cowardice is an injustice to as brave and true a fighter as ever went into battle. If permitted Gus would have gone on and received his punishment until he was hammered into insensibility.

The Examiner agreed that Ruhlin could not have lasted another round. It believed that a left to the body just before the bell ending the round was the blow that did him in. Siler agreed that the knockout was inevitable.

Although Billy Delaney agreed with the stoppage, he also felt that it would have been better for Ruhlin to have been cleanly knocked out. "On account of the crowd I would like to have seen a few more rounds, but Gus was licked when Madden threw up the sponge, and it would have been brutal to have punished him any more." He said that Ruhlin fought a game fight, but was clearly outclassed. "Jeffries' body punching did the work. Ruhlin could not stand the terrific pounding of Jeff's lefts in the stomach. I saw in the second round that Ruhlin could not last long."

Still, Delaney was sorry the contest had ended the way it did. Folks expected combatants fighting for the richest prize in sports, the heavyweight championship, to fight to the bitter end and not retire. He told the *Call*,

> Although the man was punched harder than the spectators appreciated, still it would have been better if Ruhlin had been counted out. It gives the people a chance to talk, and this has a bad effect upon the fighting game. Jeffries cannot be blamed. He did all the forcing, and followed his opponent all over the ring from bell to bell. … Not a blow that Ruhlin landed caused him any bother. He had not begun to fight. … He has a punch that hurts when it lands. … When he went to his corner at the close of the fifth round I knew that Ruhlin was beaten. It therefore did not surprise me to see Madden throw up the sponge. … [Jeffries] was as cool as a cucumber, and fought just as I wanted him to fight. He did not hurry, because he had plenty of time before him.

Billy Madden explained his reason for throwing up the sponge. He said that Jeff was a big, strong fellow with a terrific punch, and in the 3rd round landed several stiff raps to the jaw, which dazed Ruhlin and left him open for left and right jolts in the stomach. The body blows did the trick. After the 3ʳᵈ round, he saw that Gus was out of it. Jeff slugged him all over the ring in the 5ᵗʰ and he knew it was no use in letting him go on, for Ruhlin was almost defenseless. He did the humane thing. "There is no use letting a man stand up and take punishment simply because the audience wants to see a man knocked out."

> What was there to be gained by letting Gus get beaten to death? He was cut all to pieces by Fitzsimmons, and after that fight I said I would never let him be punished like that again. He was clearly defeated and might have lasted another round, but it would only have been a slaughter. Ruhlin never asked me to throw up the sponge. I did it on my own responsibility. Jeffries was much better a man than I thought he was, and the best man won.

Madden noted that Ruhlin landed several hard jolts in the ribs in the 1ˢᵗ round, and landed a straight left to the mouth which drew blood. He felt that if Jeff had not landed the left hook to the body in the 3ʳᵈ round, there might have been a different story to tell.

When asked what he thought of the stoppage, Jeffries said, "He did the best thing he could. What was the use of him going on to slaughter? The next round would have finished him, and he didn't have a chance in the world."

> If he had gone on another round he would have got an awful walloping. I think I would have knocked his block off. He didn't have a punch in him, and I hurt him pretty badly. He wouldn't fight because he was damaged so much, but I don't want to say that he is a quitter, because he isn't. I just bored into him, watching carefully to bring my right above and below his guard.

Jeff felt that he had landed some awful body punches on Ruhlin. Although Gus landed some hard body blows of his own, Jeff proved that he could take them, and was not bothered in the least. Ruhlin landed some head shots, too, but "he never hit me flush because my head was always low down."

> It was no kind of a fight. He hit me a few punches, but did not do any damage. I always let my opponent get in a few blows anyway – that's the way I get a line on what sort of a fight I have got to make. I certainly had the best of it from the start…. I took all the steam out of him in the first two rounds, and the job was done with a few punches…. I hit him hard and often, and he could not stand it. …
>
> I saw Ruhlin fight Fitzsimmons, and I knew then that I could take his measure…. I was as strong as a young bull tonight, and I am certain that I could hit harder than in any of my previous fights… I gave him half a dozen terrific left-arm body punches and I knew he was in great

distress. While I fought aggressively from the start, I did not cut loose at any time, reserving myself for a longer fight.... I knew that it was all up with him when I shot the left in his stomach in the fifth round. If you noticed, I frequently put my head out so that Ruhlin would lead. I knew that he could not hurt me, and it gave me the chance to duck under his guard so that I could uppercut him.

Afterwards, Ruhlin had a black eye. He said that in the 3rd round, everything seemed black to him. He lost his ability to judge distance, and he had little control over his own powers of locomotion. Gus tried right crosses after clinches, but without success. Jeff avoided the right by staying close and rendering the blow ineffective.

Ruhlin admitted that two hard jabs in the 4th round dazed him and that he caught a brutal shot in the stomach in the 5th.

I got that bad punch in the stomach. That hurt me, and I left myself open for a second. Jeffries saw his chance and caught me a hard one on the jaw. Everything was black for a while, and I was never really right afterwards. No man can stand up under Jeffries' body blows if they land fairly. ...

There was no use in keeping on. I could probably have gone one or two rounds more, but what was the use of going to slaughter. It was the walloping I got in the belly in the fourth round that finished me most, but that terrible welt that I got on the jaw was worse than all. I was gone entirely and didn't know what I was doing. Jeff smashed me awfully, and I didn't seem to be able to protect myself. I got in all right in the second round, but after that every time I tried for him my blows glanced off. They wouldn't land square no matter how hard I tried. Jeff was in great condition and is a great fighter.

Gus gave Jeff's defense more credit than most of the reporters did.

Ruhlin's poor showing astonished everyone, particularly those who had seen him looking good in sparring with Denver Ed Martin, or had observed him dismantle Sharkey.

Perhaps trying to justify his poor performance and ending the fight on his stool, Ruhlin also claimed that a foul blow put him on the road to defeat. He was doing well, fighting a careful fight. However, Jeff accidentally fouled him in the 3rd round, and, according to him, that had a great deal to do with his going to pieces.

He hit me in the groin and followed it with two hard jolts, one in the pit of the stomach and the other over the heart, and after that I became so weak that I could scarcely keep my feet. I staggered around the ring and at times I could hardly see him. Everything looked black in front of me and I knew it would only be a question of time when I would be knocked out. I could have fought a few more rounds perhaps after the fifth, but I had no chance to win except to land a lucky punch and at that I don't think I had the strength left to do the trick. Once or twice in the clinches Jeffries elbowed me and in my weakened condition the jolts I got didn't do me any good. He kept boring in on me with all his strength in the clinches. ... His punches were good and stiff, but they did not hurt me until I got the jolts in the body and the punch in the groin. I wanted to go on and fight after the fifth round, but I suppose Madden acted for the best. I was a beaten man. ... When I came to my corner after the fifth round I was weak and my head was dizzy. I got to Jeff's ribs very hard two or three times during the fight, but I did not have the strength to follow up the advantage.

Ruhlin also claimed that Jeff unintentionally fouled him in the 2nd round as well. He said that he received a punch to the stomach in the 5th round that no man could have survived.

Jeffries responded to Ruhlin's claims of foul. "He was scared to death from the jump. I did not foul him at all. He simply quit." Some agreed that Jeff had been rough in clinches and had once used his elbow, but neither the referee nor any of the local sources supported the low blow claim.

It was one of Jeff's easiest victories, and an amazing disappointment to the spectators, who at least expected a rough and tough battle, despite feeling that Jeff would eventually win. They were surprised at how quickly and easily Jeffries had subdued his foe.

In George Siler's opinion, Ruhlin landed without difficulty and easily outpointed Jeff during the first 4 rounds. Gus hit cleaner and landed many lefts, but his most effective and powerful blows were the rights to the body.

However, Ruhlin's blows did not have enough steam or effect. He threw and landed often, but was usually looking to move away or clinch afterwards. Gus seemed nervous, lacking confidence. He was clearly outgunned, and what hard punches he did land did not matter to Jeffries, whose "capacity for punishment is enormous.... [I]t seems that Ruhlin's right-hand blows, hard as they appeared to a spectator, had no effect on the champion."

Jeffries did not mind Ruhlin's blows in the least and often did not try to avoid them, remaining upright. It looked as if he was attempting to make Gus "outfight himself." Not using his crouch made Jeffries speedier on his feet. He had often been criticized for not being aggressive enough, but that criticism could not be lodged in this one. He was after Ruhlin all the time. The champion did not throw all that often, but when he did, the blows were powerful. Jeff was just too strong for him, and his pressure, combined with his hard blows, quickly weakened Ruhlin.

Although Jeffries forced the battle, at first he found Ruhlin a hard man to catch. However, a hard left hook in the 3rd almost ended the bout. Gus was clever enough to last out the round by clinching. Siler concluded,

It is questionable whether Ruhlin could have gone much father at the time he stopped. It is a difficult thing to gauge the shape he was in after receiving several hard punches in the stomach from a hitter like Jeffries. Madden declared he saw no use in having his man butchered, and he is a good judge. If Ruhlin could have fought all night he would have had no chance to ultimately win.

The San Francisco Examiner said Jeffries was cool and relaxed, unconcerned by what the seemingly afraid Ruhlin did. Gus barely put up a fight and was completely outclassed. He was given ammonia in the corner to revive him, but it helped little.

The San Francisco Chronicle said that Jeffries went at Ruhlin slowly but surely and kept him running away all the time. Jeff allowed Ruhlin to land on him often without trying to avoid the blows. Yet, Ruhlin at times seemed hesitant to strike, fearing that he would leave an opening. Jeffries paid no attention to the punches, simply smiling and walking him down.

The San Francisco Call said that in the first two rounds, Gus hit cleaner and scored the most blows, but they lacked the champion's terrible punishing power. It felt that Jeff's hardest blow was a short right to the body. "He times his blow to a nicety, delivering it just an instant before a clinch and with his opponent coming toward him." Ultimately, the Call opined that Jeff outclassed Ruhlin and was his complete master.

The day after the fight, hearing all of the criticism lodged at Gus, Jeff came to Ruhlin's defense a bit. "It was no use letting the fight go on any longer. Those blows which I piled in on his stomach are what defeated Ruhlin, and there was more force to them than most people thought. A body blow is a painful blow, and yet it does not look as cruel as a blow on the jaw, but it is worse."

Ruhlin said that the reason he could not land any good blows was because of Jeff's constant aggressiveness. What blows he did land were glancing. "Gus complained of Jim striking him one foul blow below the belt in the third round, but admitted that it did not especial harm." So, Ruhlin had changed his tune a bit about the low blow. Gus said that he needed to keep moving because if he had stood his ground, Jeffries would have knocked his head off. "Jeff is a very strong fellow and has a hard blow."[657]

Offering his thoughts on the fight, Bob Fitzsimmons said, "It is always the man behind the wallop who carries off the money and all that goes with the winner."

In 1903, Jeff spoke about the fact that Ruhlin had been branded a quitter. "Let me tell you, I gave Gus twice the punching that Fitz and Corbett got. Ruhlin ain't a quitter. He got a couple of wallops that would have stopped almost anything. ... When I gave him that body punch that

---

657 San Francisco Bulletin, November 17, 1901.

took his feet off the floor I knew he was gone. He didn't quit – he was just licked, that's all."[658]

Jeffries echoed these sentiments in his autobiography, saying, "My heavy body punches had nearly broken him in two. If he had gone down after that last punch in the body and had been counted out as Corbett was at Carson nobody would have had any chance to find fault."[659]

Despite the quick annihilation, one begrudging writer was critical of Jeffries, saying that he was not a first-class prizefighter:

> He is a tremendously big man, a tremendously strong man, but he lacks vim, and he is not a good boxer. He has got two tremendously dangerous punches, one a left hand body punch, the other a right hand counter delivered at a very short range; but he does not know how to protect himself properly, and he does not take advantage of obvious openings. He is not quick; on the contrary, he is quite slow – slow in his foot work and slow in his hitting. As for stopping, he seldom uses his arms for that purpose, relying almost entirely on protecting his head with his shoulders or ducking under a blow. He is the biggest and strongest man I ever saw in a prize ring.

The National Police Gazette said that Jeffries was not receiving the credit that he deserved, and that he should be favorably compared to fighters of the past, despite the hesitation of some critics to do so.

> It has been said that Corbett or Jackson would have stopped Jeffries' gallop had he been of their day. Possibly. Jeffries has not the mechanical genius as a ringster that either of these men had. At the same time he has many things that they had not. Neither of the men was as strong as Jeffries, nor had the powers of assimilation, nor the grizzly-like paws that he possesses. Neither of them could have cracked Sharkey's ribs as he did. When a fellow has these qualifications and can box some besides he is a bad man to be left alone with in a ring. ... I think he is more of an all-around fighting machine than ever Jackson, Corbett or any one else knew how to be.[660]

The Gazette opined that Jeff would remain in undisputed possession of his title for some time to come.

One *Examiner* writer was quite high on Jeffries, which was more consistent with the overall increasing admiration for his abilities.

> They have no idea of the formidable fighting machine Jeffries has developed into.... He has improved his knowledge of boxing three-fold... I have seen him myself in a practice clinch with Bob

---

658 *San Francisco Bulletin*, August 24, 1903.
659 *My Life and Battles* at 45.
660 *National Police Gazette*, December 7, 1901.

Armstrong. I watched him give a quick wrench of his shoulders and saw the 200-pound negro stagger to the wall. Think of the force this fellow, with his improved knowledge of ringmanship, is able to put into his blows…. The plain truth of it is that Jeffries today is a wonder both in the line of giving and taking punishment.

The Call also believed that there was no man alive who had a chance to defeat the champion, and that if Jeff maintained his present form, he would be champion for many years to come. Over the years, Jeff had shown vast improvement as a fighter. He went from going 20 rounds to a draw with Ruhlin, to having him at his total mercy in 5 rounds.

It was at this point that Jeffries was finally starting to receive the respect that he deserved. He had defeated Fitzsimmons, Sharkey, Corbett, and Ruhlin, all those considered to have any chance to defeat him. Each had their own unique styles, but Jeffries had managed to figure out a way to defeat them all, demonstrating his versatility and adaptability. Many newsmen were finally realizing or acknowledging that Jeffries was special.

The Twentieth Century Athletic Club said the total receipts were $32,700. *The Evening Post* said over $40,000 was taken in. It said Jeff received about $22,000 and Ruhlin $5,000. Referee Harry Corbett was paid $500. *The Chronicle* said 62 ½% of the receipts went to the fighters. Of that, Jeff's share was 75% (about $13,950) to Ruhlin's 25% (about $4,650). *The Call* and *Bulletin* said that the total gate receipts were $30,487.50. Jeff earned $14,056.52 to Ruhlin's $4,685.54.

Regardless of the exact amounts, it was big money at that time. "It would take a laboring man who receives $2 a day for his work nineteen years, working every day in the year, to earn what the ex-boiler-maker made in twenty minutes." Another said that New York State's governor, the highest salaried governor in the country, made $4,000 a year less than what Jeff had made in one night. However, it was still not as much as Jeffries had been making in his New York fights.

CHAPTER 30

On the Horizon

Although the Jeffries-Ruhlin fight was successfully filmed, it was said that the films would have been more valuable had there been a true knockout. Some said that it was bad for boxing for Ruhlin to have retired, because people did not want to pay a bunch of money for such an ending.

However, some raised an equally strong argument that stopping the bout was better for the sport's long-term legal success, because without the brutality, the anti-boxing lobby would have no ammunition. Billy Madden was disturbed by the desire for a complete knockout, saying that it was inhuman, and would have only fueled the anti-boxing folks.

> Ruhlin was knocked into unconsciousness by Fitzsimmons, and it was 6 o'clock the next morning before Gus knew what his name was. Then and there Madden declared that that would be the last time he would let his protégé be 'cut to ribbons.' If there were more managers like Madden there would be fewer accidents in the ring and fewer sermons delivered from the pulpits on the brutality of the prize ring. "If Gus had been carried out of the ring in a helpless condition and remained unconscious for several hours, what a splendid opening it would have been for the preachers today," remarked Madden. "As I ended the fight there was nothing brutal to it and it will be an easy matter to hold another championship contest."

Word was that Tom Sharkey had accepted the San Francisco Athletic Club's tentative offer to fight Jeffries on December 20. However, as a result of the bad impression left by the Ruhlin bout, the promoters held back any discussion of the prospective fight. They wanted to wait for the bad feeling to fade out of the spectators' memories before discussing another fight.

Despite Madden's logical argument that the Ruhlin fight stoppage was good for boxing, because it was considered to have been a poor fight and ultimately a mismatch, the San Francisco Athletic Club's directors were concerned about promoting a fight between Jeffries and Sharkey. They felt that the public would not pay for it, particularly since both Fitz and Ruhlin had stopped Sharkey, and Jeff had just mowed through Ruhlin as if he was nothing. The talent would consider Sharkey to be easy picking, and therefore, like Ruhlin, might put up a disappointing showing. The anticipated outcome would hurt the gate. Therefore, their first choice for a

Jeffries opponent was Fitzsimmons. Jeffries said that he wanted to meet Fitz next, but if Bob was not willing, Sharkey would do.[661]

However, the *Evening Post* went so far as to unfairly call the promoters of the Ruhlin fight "the pirates of pugilism." It said that although it was announced that Jeff and Sharkey would be matched,

> They will do nothing of the kind. San Francisco has had enough of these freebooters. … There is a point where barefaced robbery must cease. We have been robbed so often that we are tiring of the monotony. … We pay our money for genuine brutality and we are filled with wrath when we learn that we have been buncoed. The Jeffries-Ruhlin farce was the straw that broke the camel's back in this city. … The Jeffries-Sharkey fake will not be 'pulled off' in this city.

Clearly, the fact that Ruhlin had not fought to the bitter end had soured many to the sport. They felt swindled out of their money's worth. Feeling that Sharkey would do the same, the newspapers refused to support the fight.

The Evening Post even went so far as to call the recent fight a fake and swindle designed to make money, claiming that the result was cut and dried from the beginning. If Ruhlin had been knocked cold, it would have served to dispel suspicions that the fight was not on the level. Instead, the retirement generated suspicions that it was all a fake.

The following day, the *Evening Post* reported that the storm of public indignation caused the local promoter to drop the Sharkey fight "on the pretext that Sharkey could not prepare himself by December." It felt that the reality was that San Francisco would refuse to be robbed again within so short a period of time. San Franciscans remembered how Sharkey had faked a fight with Fitzsimmons years ago there, which made things even worse for him as a potential opponent.

Further dampening the prospects of a potential fight, the belief that Jeffries had ruined Sharkey by the punishment that he had administered to him in their championship fight was increasingly taking hold amongst the public and reporters. Jeff had done this with only one good arm. He was currently fighting very well with two good arms. On the other hand, Sharkey was on the wane, having been knocked out in his last two bouts.[662]

Jeffries supported this argument, saying that he fought Sharkey while handicapped by an injury to his left arm. After his arm failed him in the 5th round, when he had Tom staggering, he had to fight practically with his right only, and even with that limitation, "Tom got a beating that he never recovered from. … Sharkey was never again the man that he was before." *The Evening Post* agreed. "There are a few who saw those contests and

661 *San Francisco Bulletin*, November 18, 1901.
662 *San Francisco Evening Post*, November 18-20, 1901.

whatever their personal feeling may be toward Jeffries they will admit the truth of Jeffries' remarks."[663]

The National Police Gazette opined that Sharkey had done nothing since his battle with Jeffries to justify him as a challenger. Further, a San Francisco correspondent informed it that the man who was party to a crooked fight in San Francisco once before would not be allowed to fight there again. Even those who wanted to see Tom fight Jeff again agreed that it would be "far better for the healthy condition of the boxing game in this city to keep Sharkey away." *The Gazette* opined, "Sharkey might be able to stay in the ring with Jeffries longer than Ruhlin did, but it is manifest to me that the result would be the same." Hence, there was no third Sharkey fight.

Jeffries went hunting in Fresno, before returning to Los Angeles to visit for a short while.

The press and public were discussing which fighter had any chance with Jeffries. The one that the public most wanted to see Jeff do battle with was Bob Fitzsimmons. Therefore, Jeffries stood to make the most money by fighting him.

Bob Fitzsimmons was retired, but reportedly said that he was considering returning for a fight with Jeff. He again claimed that he was 'dosed' with poison before their fight. Bob said, "Jeffries is not what might be called a knockerout. He is too slow and deliberate, too, and at the same time does not care to take too many chances. Does anybody believe I was myself when he put me to sleep?"

Fitzsimmons was keeping fit, punching the bag and engaging in outdoor exercises. He did not drink. He was weighing about 180 pounds, and said that he would not have to do much to get back into fighting trim.

Some mentioned Corbett as a potential opponent. One writer said that in condition, Jim Corbett was dangerous for anyone. However, he was not a puncher. "He can make a monkey of the cleverest fighter in the ring today, but if he can not hand out a hard wallop he can't win from men of Jeffries' caliber." It was opined that a rematch would be a duplicate of their first fight. Corbett could outpoint anyone, but Jeff would be able to stand anything that Jim could hand him until he finally got the opportunity to land the knockout blow. In a long fight, it was almost a certainty that Jeff would win.[664]

Others felt that neither Fitzsimmons nor any other established fighter would have a chance with Jeffries, that only a developing crop of boxers could possibly eventually give him a real test. But, it would take them time to mature properly to be ready for a monster like Jeffries. Ironically, the increasing perception of Jeffries as being vastly superior to all others was making it difficult to market future fights.

---

663 *San Francisco Evening Post*, December 2, 1901.
664 *National Police Gazette*, December 14, 1901; *San Francisco Evening Post*, December 19, 1901.

Not in many years has a champion stood in such lonesome glory as the immense person from Los Angeles. ... Red Robert Fitzsimmons, a few days ago, was thought to be the one man that the public would fancy as Jim's foe. The feeling has veered around. It is now admitted that the terrible Jeffries of today would whip the aged Bob far more quickly than when they first did battle. Bob is in the sere and yellow – a wonderful boxer, but certainly no better than a year ago, while Jeffries is now in the very zenith of his sturdy vigor. ... Jeffries, bigger than anybody else and with a strength surpassing even his enormous size, has no competitor. Fitzsimmons is verging toward the edge of Hasbeen hill. ... If the champion is to be whipped, a new heavyweight must be caught young and properly educated. And that will take time, a great deal of time.[665]

One of those up and coming fighters seen as a possible challenger on the horizon was Denver Ed Martin, the black fighter who had been Gus Ruhlin's sparring partner and was coming off a KO7 over Hank Griffin. *The Gazette* said that Martin's experience with Ruhlin was of considerable benefit to him.

He is young, almost if not quite as clever as Ruhlin, can punch harder, is ambitious and thoroughly game. As I said several weeks ago, of all the men now looming up on the pugilistic horizon not one has better qualifications for usurping the title than he. ... The next champion will be a black man, mark the prediction.

Martin said that he would bet all he had that Jeffries was a dub whom he could lick in a punch. Martin observed that Jeff left Ruhlin half a dozen openings, and said that if he had been in the ring, he would have landed on Jeff and won. Of course, Martin and Ruhlin really went at it in their sparring sessions in a competitive fashion, and Gus even dropped Martin, whereas the iron-jawed Jeffries easily blew through Ruhlin. Martin's retort was that Ruhlin left his fight in the gym, and was frozen with fear against Jeffries.[666]

Feeling that his defensive skills were underrated, the following year, Jeffries said,

Some people remarked I was easy to reach because Ruhlin got to me several times. All I have to say is his blows did not hurt me. I am very watchful – or I think I am – and when a man starts a punch for my face or body I always gauge the force of it before doing anything. If I make up my mind it is not a damaging punch I allow it to land for the

665 *San Francisco Evening Post*, December 2, 1901.
666 *San Francisco Evening Post*, November 27, 1901.

sake of getting in a counter. If it is a heavy blow I will get out of the way of it quick enough.[667]

Ruhlin had backed Jeff on this point, noting that his blows were glancing and that he could not land solidly on Jeffries. The champion's argument was further supported by the fact that he had never been decked in a fight.

Regardless of his merits as a potential challenger, because he was black, Jeffries was not going to box Denver Ed Martin in a title fight. Although Jeff had boxed black men in non-title bouts, it was said that Jeffries drew the color line when it came to title fights. This was a different official stance than the champion had at the beginning of his reign in 1899, when he then said that he would defend against all comers: "I do not bar anyone, black or white, old or young."

> When Jeff was asked the other day if he would fight Martin, if he beat Ruhlin, Delaney chimed in by saying, "No, we won't fight a negro for the championship. … Suppose he were to fight Martin and be defeated, which does not seem possible. America would have to bow to a negro champion."[668]

This argument was coupled with the fact that boxing was still struggling to gain widespread legal acceptance. More black challengers and possible champions might be an additional impediment to any legal progress. Legislators would be even more uncomfortable about legalizing a sport which threatened the dominant racial hierarchy and social norm of racial separation. Delaney did not want to allow such a bout to take place, irrespective of whether or not it would be competitive.

Delaney's views were consistent with the time's existing racial segregation. As recently as 1896, the U.S. Supreme Court ruled that it was perfectly legal for states to pass laws mandating racial separation, which they did. Many boxing writers, the *Police Gazette* in particular, still argued for fairness when it came to boxing, a sport which did not always honor the color line. However, the general social rule was racial separation.

As the weeks passed, Jeffries said that he would ignore Martin's challenges. He did not strictly draw the color line, but did so when it came to championship bouts. Delaney insisted that Jeff would not fight Martin. "Jeffries does not draw the color line strictly, yet he refuses to box a negro for the championship." Besides, Bob Armstrong, a man whom Jeff had defeated with a broken hand, had in 1899 knocked out Martin in 2 rounds. Still, Martin had been undefeated since then, and had impressed many observers of his sparring with Ruhlin.

Regardless of the color line, the *Police Gazette* noted that although Denver Ed Martin was the only "comer" who looked to have an eventual

---

667 *National Police Gazette*, July 19, 1902.
668 *National Police Gazette*, December 7, 1901.

chance to succeed to the title, he needed time to develop properly. It opined that Martin needed another year of development in order to be ready for Jeffries. "Martin hardly has class enough yet to go after Jeffries, and will do well to wait until he wears the scalps of a few minor factors in the heavyweight game at his belt before he aspires to the title." He needed more experience. Furthermore, he was just recently being noticed, and required time to be properly marketed, for there was no real public demand for his title challenge.[669]

In December 1901 (possibly December 14) at the Theatrical Business Men's Athletic Club at 139 West Forty-First Street in New York, at a members-only smoker, wearing 8-ounce gloves, Bob Fitzsimmons and Tom Sharkey boxed a friendly 5-round bout for points in a 15-foot ring. They went at each other hotly at the end, the blows coming so quickly that they could not be counted. When it was over, the referee declared it a draw.[670]

When asked whether Fitzsimmons had gone back, Sharkey answered in the negative.

> You can just bet Fitz is the same old fellow. Gone back? Anybody who talks that way of Bob should call at Bellevue Hospital and have his sanity tested. It was the same old Fitz I boxed on Saturday night. He was just as quick as he ever was; he had his old punch and he stepped around like a youngster. … Understand, our bout was only a friendly one, but once in a while Fitz would sneak in a jolt just to show that he still had that punch. He side-stepped in his own old-fashioned way, and altogether it does not seem to me that he has in the least forgotten a thing he knew about the fighting game. …
>
> Honestly, I believe he is as good as he ever was in his life. With the necessary training, I do not believe that Jeffries would have anything of a walkover. In fact, Fitz would have an even break, but just how such a battle would terminate I would rather not say. But Fitz is the same old clever fellow with the punch.[671]

One month after the Ruhlin fight, on December 16, 1901, Jeffries was in Salt Lake City, Utah on an exhibition tour with his brother Jack. At each town that he traveled to, Jeff remarked that he would try to get Fitzsimmons to fight him.[672]

Jeffries was in Denver, Colorado on December 20, 1901 to give friendly sparring exhibitions with brother Jack and world featherweight champion Young Corbett II (William Rothwell). Jeff was scheduled to box 6 rounds with each.

---

669 *San Francisco Examiner,* December 28, 1901; *National Police Gazette,* February 1, 1902.
670 *San Francisco Evening Post,* December 16, 1901.
671 *San Francisco Evening Post,* December 26, 1901.
672 *San Francisco Evening Post,* December 17, 1901.

Before a small crowd, Jeffries played around with Young Corbett and had fun in what was called a burlesque. Jeff did things like allowing Corbett to hit him, missing his punches intentionally, and even acting groggy and going down as if to take the count. Still, regardless of the comedy, Jeffries revealed some of his finer points as well, sufficient to impress the viewers.

> He was as agile as a kitten and when he assumed his crouching attitude in the opening round he was like a giant toying with an infant.... He surprised the talent with the shiftiness he displayed. He danced about the ring almost as fast as his smaller opponent, who seemed to be in the pink of condition.

Against his brother Jack, James landed some stiff jabs.

> It is a mistake to say the champion is not clever. He showed wonderful speed, and his blocking and feinting were marvelous. The talent were all one in the opinion that there is not a heavyweight in the fighting world today who can go against his game with success. He is wonderfully endowed by nature with all the qualifications necessary to hold the championship against all comers.[673]

Jeff and his party were said to be headed to Omaha. The champ offered $1,000 to anyone who could induce Fitzsimmons to fight him.[674]

On December 25, 1901 in Kansas City, Missouri, Jeffries and his brother Jack engaged in a lively 6-round sparring exhibition. The champion gave "a most clever exposition of his ability at the game of hit, stop and get away. He gave an exhibition of his marvelous defense, his wonderful speed for a man of his pounds, and cleverness with both hands." James Jeffries had weight, height, reach, speed, science, hitting power, ring generalship, and a cool head. "It is difficult to figure out how any man now in the game could hope to deprive him of the championship honor." Jeff was heading to New York, where he was set to give more exhibitions.[675]

Jeffries wanted to fight Fitzsimmons next because Bob would be the biggest drawing card. He said that other title aspirants would not generate enough revenue, and therefore, in order to fight them, he would need to be induced with a large side bet or a guaranteed purse.

On December 27, 1901 in Oakland, Jack Johnson fought Hank Griffin to a 15-round draw.

That same day, Jeff was in Chicago, again informing the public that he wanted to fight Fitzsimmons.

Fitzsimmons was expected to come out of retirement and make a match with Jeff. Bob had been training quietly for several weeks and had made remarks that he was the only man in the world with a chance to defeat

---

673 *Rocky Mountain News*, December 20, 21, 1901.
674 *San Francisco Chronicle*, December 21, 1901.
675 *Kansas City Star, Brooklyn Daily Eagle*, December 26, 1901.

Jeffries. Fitz knew that he would be a big draw, and therefore could insist on more money.

In late December, the Edison Company advertised the Jeffries-Ruhlin fight films. Jeff's training took up 380 feet of film, and Ruhlin's training 280 feet. The fight required 1,100 feet. A proprietor could purchase a copy of the films for $275.[676]

In his second autobiography, Jeffries said that he had been almost constantly on the road for nearly a four month time span (Sep. – Dec.), boxing every day. During that time, he met U.S. President Teddy Roosevelt.[677]

The National Police Gazette reported that Jeffries had not made much from his road exhibitions. It happily noted, "Getting the money in exhibition bouts, even for the heavyweight champion of the world, is now a thing of the past. The people have acquired wisdom and reluctantly part with their coin to see anything but a real fight. They don't want fancy bouts, fakes, hippodromes, or exhibitions." It said that men like Corbett would talk fight in order to keep solid with the public, but would not mean it. He preferred to make easy money in exhibitions and on the stage, where he did not "get his hair mussed." "Jeffries, however, will fight."[678]

Owing to the fact that Fitzsimmons still had not put in an appearance at the negotiating table, Bill Delaney on Jeff's behalf signed articles of agreement for Jeffries to meet Sharkey if Tom was victorious in his upcoming January 17 bout with Peter Maher. Still, "A second battle between Fitz and Jeffries would excite more public interest than any other that could be arranged, and it is to be hoped that the former champion can be induced to forgo his determination to quit fighting."

Fitzsimmons said that he would come back and fight again, provided that sufficient money was involved. The confident Jeffries wanted to make the fight winner-take-all. He noted, "When I fought Fitzsimmons I was compelled to give him 75 per cent, win or lose." Fitz once again required a guarantee. He would not enter the ring unless it was made worth his while. He knew that their fight would be the biggest draw in boxing, and wanted a guaranteed taste of those revenues, win or lose. Jeff said he would split the purse 65% winner/35% loser. Fitz said that was fair, but wanted to see Jeff in person to consummate the deal. No one was certain whether Bob was serious or not, because his "mind was as changeable as a chameleon's colors." Negotiations were ongoing.

On January 17, 1902 in Philadelphia, Tom Sharkey and Peter Maher boxed in a scheduled 6-round bout. However, the two only engaged in a gentle tapping affair, not even closely resembling a fight. The angry crowd

---

676 *Kansas City Star, New York Clipper, San Francisco Chronicle, Evening Post,* December 28, 1901.
677 *Two Fisted Jeffries* at 204-206.
678 *National Police Gazette,* January 11, 1902.

howled "Fake!" until referee Billy Rocap stopped it in the middle of the 3rd round and declared it a no contest.

Apparently, in advance of the bout, both men were arrested and each placed under $5,000 bonds to keep the peace. Therefore, they could not really fight, or they would forfeit their money. However, the public was not informed about this, and paid for the real thing. In order to induce a large gate, Sharkey and Maher allowed the public to believe that they would fight on the merits. Therefore, the spectators felt swindled out of their money. The press condemned the whole thing as the worst fiasco ever perpetrated. Once again, Tom Sharkey had been involved in a fight that hurt boxing. As a result of the public's disgust with Sharkey, any potential match with Jeffries was declared off.

Instead, Jeffries and Fitzsimmons would fight. Bob was guaranteed $7,500 and a significant portion of the fighter's share of the gross receipts, even should he suffer defeat, a sufficient inducement for him to fight.[679]

On February 15, 1902, Jeffries and Fitzsimmons signed articles of agreement. They were to box 20 rounds before the club offering the largest purse, to be divided 60%/40% to the winner/loser, with the winner receiving all of the moving picture profits. The contestants would be permitted the use of soft surgical bandages, subject to the referee's inspection. The bout was tentatively set to take place in mid-May. Fitz was already doing some training.[680]

At that time, Denver Ed Martin was scheduled to take on then colored heavyweight champion Frank Childs. Childs was described as a tough fighter who "has defeated nearly every prominent colored boxer in the country, and also a number of white pugilists. He hits a very hard punch, is fairly clever, and some time ago [Jan. 1898] he knocked out Armstrong in two rounds." On March 4, 1899, Childs scored a KO6 over Armstrong to win the "colored heavyweight championship of the world." His last loss was a September 1898 20-round decision to George Byers, but he avenged it with a March 1901 KO17 over Byers to gain undisputed recognition as the colored champion.[681]

On February 24, 1902 in Chicago, Denver Ed Martin won a 6-round decision over Frank Childs. As a result, some began calling Martin the colored champion. However, others said that the bout was too short to determine who the better man was. Martin had great advantages in height (at least five inches) and reach, and that, together with his cleverness,

---

679 *National Police Gazette*, January 18, 25, February 1, 8, 15, 1902.
680 *New York Clipper*, February 22, 1902; *National Police Gazette*, March 8, 1902.
681 Childs' record included: 1895 LKOby3 Choynski; 1898 KO2 Armstrong, L20 Byers; 1899 KO6 Armstrong, W8 Dunkhorst, W6 Mexican Pete Everett, W6 John "Klondike" Haines (who was coming off a KO5 win over Jack Johnson), D6 Kennedy, KO3 Haines; 1900 W10 Everett, W10 Fred Russell; 1901 KO17 Byers (gaining the legitimate claim to the colored championship); and 1902 KO4 Bill Hanrahan (who held a recent KO1 over Marvin Hart). Boxrec.com. *National Police Gazette*, March 11, 25, 1899, September 2, 1899.

enabled him to easily outpoint Childs in a short bout. However, it was said that Childs was never known for his cleverness, but rather his ability to knock his man out, and he landed some hard, staggering blows in the bout. On the other hand, it was said that Martin was not a puncher, at least not to the extent that Childs was, for Frank took all his blows with a smile. Therefore, it was unclear regarding who would ultimately win in a lengthier battle.[682]

Despite their agreement, Bob Fitzsimmons had changed his mind, and wanted 50% of everything from his fight with Jeffries, win or lose. Fitz knew that he was the only opponent that the public really wanted to see in the ring with Jeff, and he wanted to capitalize on that fact. Jeffries would not agree, saying that the public would not stand for such terms.[683]

Still, it was looking like the fight would happen, because in March, Bob was training and sparring hard in New York with Gus Ruhlin, who was preparing for a fight with Peter Maher. Fitz took long daily spins on the road. He and Ruhlin wrestled a bit, and then sparred in lively fashion. "Fitzsimmons several times shook up Ruhlin with a stiff whack on the head and once sent him staggering back with a left thrust to the body." Ruhlin returned with a punch to the nose that brought blood.

It was said that Bob would be in great shape when the fight came off. "Fitzsimmons seems to have lost none of his speed, and he is regarded as the most marvelous 'old man' in the fistic world. Ruhlin declares the lanky Australian can hit as stiff a punch as ever." Jeff and Gus were mixing it daily in rough-house style.[684]

On March 21, 1902 in Philadelphia, Gus Ruhlin scored a KO2 over Peter Maher. Gus was still a top fighter.

When Fitzsimmons attempted to negotiate the location of the Jeffries match, and essentially threatened to pull out of the fight, he began taking heat from the press, which called him a flunker. Apparently, this made Bob become more reasonable. He finally agreed that California was the only state in the nation where they could legally fight a championship-length bout and maximize ticket sales. Nevada would allow a fight to the finish, but its isolation made it less attractive. Of course, all the ongoing discussion about the final details caused the bout's date to become less certain.[685]

Jeffries was in Los Angeles with his family, doing some training there. On May 5, he sparred 3 lively rounds with his brother Jack at the Chutes before a good-sized and enthusiastic audience. One or two of the blows would have floored ordinary men.

At that time, Jack Jeffries was in better shape than his brother. James J. was not as concerned with his own training as he was in helping Jack

682 *Chicago Tribune*, February 25, 1902.
683 *National Police Gazette*, March 1, 1902.
684 *Los Angeles Times*, March 15, 1902; *National Police Gazette*, March 22, 1902.
685 *National Police Gazette*, May 3, 10, 1902.

prepare for his upcoming bout with Jack Johnson, who was coming off a March 1902 KO4 over Joe Kennedy. Still, the following day, the champ did about 15 miles on the road, in addition to some other work.

Jeff spars his brother Jack.

In sparring, James J. was allowing brother Jack to punch away at him to his heart's content. Jack hit him with some hard blows, but they utterly failed "to even disconcert the big fellow, who acts as if he liked playing punching bag for a change. Occasionally Jeffries gets shifty in his work and for a large man he shows amazing speed. The champion is a great deal faster now than when he won the world's title from Fitzsimmons." The brothers were sparring daily.

A small majority favored Johnson over Jack Jeffries, although the local newspaper said the fight was really an even-money proposition. The reality was that Jack Jeffries was not much of a fighter. He had primarily earned his living as his brother's sparring partner, rarely engaging in competitive contests. His only pro results were: 1900 KO4 Jack Beauscholte and L6 and D10 Billy Stift.

On May 16, 1902 in Los Angeles, 170-175-pound Jack Johnson easily scored a KO5 over 180-185-pound Jack Jeffries.[686]

In late April or early May 1902 at Wood's Gymnasium in New York, Bob Fitzsimmons and Jim Corbett sparred 3 lively and fast rounds. In the 1st round, Jim was quick, dancing around, jabbing, side-stepping and swinging. Fitz retaliated and they engaged in pretty exchanges. A Corbett left to the lips left its impression and another blow puffed up Bob's nose, but he took it well. Jim was a little slower in the 2nd. Fitz landed a few stiff punches in the wind and Corbett clinched. On the break, he tapped Bob on the ear with a left and hit him hard in the ribs. Fitz sidestepped twice and puzzled Jim with some feints. Neither lost their heads. In the 3rd round, Jim moved well and landed on the face and mouth. Bob hit the jaw and body with his right. They went at it during the final minute with many quick blows. Corbett was puffing at the finish, while Bob seemed fresh.[687]

Hank Griffin accepted a position as Fitzsimmons' sparring partner.

> Hank thinks he is the right man to train with Fitz, as he stood up twice before the big fellow, once for seventeen and once for four rounds. Hank will find that posing as Fitz's sparring partner is no sinecure. Fitz has an unpleasant habit of putting out about three trainers a day when he is feeling well.

Fitzsimmons claimed to be weighing 168 pounds (unproven), and said that he was better now than at any other time in his career. He had always taken excellent care of himself, which was the secret to his longevity.[688]

In early June, Jeffries and Fitzsimmons finally ironed out the details of their fight. They agreed to box on July 25, 1902 in San Francisco. Each made some concessions. Jeffries withdrew his objection to hand bandages. He had noted that Fitz did not allow either Corbett or Jeffries to wear bandages when they had fought him, so Jeff wanted to give Fitz the same treatment. However, Bob made them a requirement because his hands were becoming fragile. He noted that in the original articles, they had agreed that hand bandages could be worn. Fitz said, "All I want is a little bit of sticking plaster on my hand where it was hurt before." Jeffries responded, "I have no objection to that. It will be subject to the inspection of the referee, of course." "Certainly," responded Fitzsimmons. In return, Jeff was able to name the club where the fight would be held. The purse split would be 60%/40% to the winner/loser. Both agreed that the winner would fight Corbett, who wanted another crack at the title.[689]

686 *Los Angeles Herald*, May 6, 10, 12, 16, 1902.
687 *National Police Gazette*, May 17, 1902.
688 *Los Angeles Herald*, May 7, 11, 1902.
689 *National Police Gazette*, June 14, 21, 1902, August 9, 1902.

CHAPTER 31

Championship Training

After having done some training with his brother in Los Angeles, in June 1902, James Jeffries went to Harbin Springs to begin serious training for the Fitzsimmons fight. He worked with Bill Delaney, brother Jack, Joe Kennedy, and Kid Eagan.

Fitzsimmons had already been training for several months in New York. Since December 1901, he had boxed with the likes of Tom Sharkey, Gus Ruhlin, and Jim Corbett. In June 1902, Bob stationed his training camp at Skagg's Springs, which, like Harbin Springs, was north of San Francisco. Bob boxed with Hank Griffin and Soldier Tom Wilson, as well as Chicago's George Dawson, who had trained him for the Ruhlin and Sharkey fights.

According to the *Police Gazette*, Fitzsimmons rose daily at 6:30 a.m. He would walk 2.5 miles and then run back. In the gymnasium, he tossed the medicine ball with his trainers. He punched the ball for 15 minutes, and also hit the "funny fellow," a bag three-feet in diameter by four-feet in length. Fitz then sparred George Dawson, who was described as a giant. Despite his superior size, Dawson was a boy in Bob's hands. Bob would box another 4 rounds with 23-year-old Soldier Tom Wilson, who stood over 6 feet tall and weighed over 200 pounds. Hank Griffin was also "there to take a punching, and it is safe to say that he gets all that is coming to him." Fitz also hit baseballs for an hour.

After dinner, Fitzsimmons would rough it and wrestle with Dawson and Wilson, pushing their heads back, grabbing their necks, and generally mauling each other for half an hour. Next, Bob hit a bag for 6 rounds. He then exercised his legs, feinting, side-stepping, advancing, retreating, and ducking from little rubber balls thrown at him.

Jeff's training generally consisted of running 8 or 10 miles, hitting the sand bag in a way that was "really astonishing," sparring Joe Kennedy and Jack Jeffries (both listed at 6' and 200 pounds or more), typically rotating each for a round for a total of 8 rounds, jumping rope, working the rowing machine, shadow boxing with weights, tossing the medicine ball, and working the pulley machines. "Imagine a man weighing nearly 220 pounds as light on his feet as a maiden just out of dancing school and combining with this the quickness and litheness of a cat – that is Jeffries."

Jeff's former trainer Tommy Ryan looked for Fitzsimmons to put up a much better showing this time. "If he can only stay away and fight clever, like Corbett did, he can get Jeffries. I suppose, though, he will fight the same old way – carry it to the other fellow until he wins or loses." Ryan said that when Jeff won the title, Tommy had told him to fire the right for the body every time that Bob advanced.[690]

Making Jeff's performance and victory over Gus Ruhlin seem all the more impressive, on June 25, 1902 in London, England, in their rubber match, Ruhlin scored a KO11 over Tom Sharkey. Tom adopted his forcing tactics, holding his own for the first 3-5 rounds, but after that, Ruhlin hit him when and where he pleased, giving Tom an awful beating. Sharkey went down four times in the 11th round. After the bell rang to end the round, Tom's seconds threw up the sponge. Not only did Ruhlin's victory over Sharkey boom Jeffries, but it further put Sharkey out of the championship hunt.[691]

Fitz jogs with Griffin while Dawson follows on horseback.

Fitzsimmons was working hard. On the morning of June 28, he ran, and then boxed 4 rounds each with Wilson, Dawson, and Griffin. "The way he goes at these men is really surprising." His sparring partners fought him hard, but he always gave them better than they sent in. Bob could take punishment without the slightest notice and it looked "as if it would take a battering ram to put him out of business." When his manager Clark Ball

690 *New York Clipper*, June 7, 1902; *National Police Gazette*, June 28, July 5, 19, August 23, 1902. For more detail on Jeff's daily training regimen, see the Appendix.
691 *San Francisco Bulletin*, July 11, 1902; *National Police Gazette*, July 19, 26, 1902.

advised him to let up a little on his work and not take so many hard knocks, Bob said, "Why, this work is not bothering me in the least."

On the 30th, Fitz ran 10 miles up and down the hills at a 9-minute mile pace.[692]

On July 1, Fitz ran 10 miles – the first 5 easy, and then 5 miles hard. Over the course of one of those miles, he sprinted 100 yards, and then walked 100 yards, alternating this way for the entire mile.

At a 4th of July celebration, Fitz sparred with George Dawson and Soldier Wilson. He also punched the bag.

Bob showed better form on the 8th than he had since he started training. Discussing Bob's pace on the run, Hank Griffin said,

> Well, Lord, you should see him go. He didn't know when he was going up the hill. It was all level to him. Why, I guess I must have lost my wind before I had gone two miles.... When I came in I was all done up. While Mr. Fitzsimmons, he looked as if he had just done a cakewalk around the barn.

In the afternoon, Fitz hit the bag, and then sparred Dawson, Wilson, and Griffin 2 rounds each for a total of 6 rounds. A blow that Bob tried to hold back dazed Wilson. Griffin was the snappiest and most earnest worker of the bunch. "It is give and take and he is right after Fitz all the time." Fitzsimmons liked working with Hank the most because he could engage and let himself out more. Griffin had made a good impression. "He is a willing worker and exceedingly shifty."

On the 10th, wearing a costume of a baby pink hue, Bob punched the bag, cutting it a bit short on account of the summer heat. He then sparred alternate rounds with Dawson, then Soldier Wilson, and then Griffin, repeating the circuit.[693]

Unfortunately, the parties were unable to negotiate an agreement regarding the fight films. Fitzsimmons was not happy with the biograph company's offer, and rejected the idea of the fight being filmed. Initially, Jeffries did not worry about it too much, but said that he was sorry because he would like to have everyone see just who the better man was.

However, several days later, it was reported that the Jeffries camp was upset by Fitz's "bullheadedness" and "cussedness," which prevented an arrangement with the biograph folks to film the fight. Delaney said, "The whole thing in a nutshell is that Fitz wanted Jeff to put up all the money that was necessary to carry the thing out. He wouldn't give up a cent."

Responding to the Jeffries camp, Bob said, "Delaney thinks I am overlooking a business proposition. Yes, but it was one for the biograph people, but not for me. ... By that agreement we had all to lose, while they were protected to the fullest extent without guaranteeing anything in the

692 *San Francisco Bulletin*, June 29, 30, 1902.
693 *San Francisco Bulletin*, July 3, 5, 9-11, 1902.

way of results." He noted that under the proposed agreement, the biograph company would not have to pay for expenses, while the club and the principals were expected to put up a great deal of money in financing. So, the fight was not filmed.[694]

Fitzsimmons was training hard, and seemed tireless. Harry Corbett noted,

> If Fitzsimmons can fight as well as he can work, he has a great chance. ... The way that fellow runs on the road and then punches the bag and boxes a half dozen hot rounds with Wilson is really wonderful. ... Age seems to have had absolutely no effect upon him. He's as frisky as a little child.

Hank Griffin said that there was nothing to the fight, for Bob would win.[695]

Jeffries shifted his training quarters from Harbin Springs to Oakland's Reliance Club, beginning work there on July 14. First, he punched the bag and skipped rope. He then sparred 8 rounds, 4 rounds each with brother Jack and Joe Kennedy, the two alternating a round at each bell. They boxed with 8-ounce gloves, with no headgear. At 212-213 pounds, Jeffries had taken off 20 pounds during his training. Bill Delaney said, "I have been with Jeff a long time, but I never saw him in such perfect condition as he is at the present time." Onlookers marveled at Jeff's speed and lightness in his footwork. Owing to his superior size, remarkable quickness for a big man, his youth, condition, and great chin, Jeffries was a 2 ½ to 1 and 10 to 4 betting odds favorite.[696]

That same day, the 14th, Fitzsimmons did his morning run with Griffin. In the afternoon, he hit the bag. Then he boxed Dawson 1 round. Wilson was up next, and a relatively light blow dropped him. The next round, Bob banged Griffin hard and often, but Hank took it and fought back. During the next circuit of 3

---

694 *San Francisco Bulletin,* July 8, 13, 14, 1902.
695 *San Francisco Evening Post, San Francisco Bulletin,* July 14, 1902.
696 *San Francisco Call, San Francisco Evening Post,* July 14, 1902; *San Francisco Bulletin,* July 15, 1902.

alternating rounds, Fitz asked each man to fight in a crouch, like Jeffries, which they did. Bob boxed the 7th round against Wilson again, and then Griffin ended the 8 rounds. Fitzsimmons "hammered the colored boy good and plenty. … Bob sent a short jolt into his jaw that gave him a dizzy spell." After the round was over, Hank said, "Did you see him give me that jolt? … It was a dandy. What would it have been if he had meant it? Oh, Lordy!"[697]

On the 15th, Jeff ran 9 miles. He exercised with dumb-bells and pulley weights for 20 minutes. He sparred 8 rounds total, alternating single rounds with Jack Jeffries and Joe Kennedy. "It seemed next to impossible for any man living to master that mass of muscle and strength and giant frame, and the blows of his sparring partners he laughed at." Jack and Joe threw hard punches, but Jeff eluded them by ducking, side-stepping and countering. Jeff finished up by punching the bag for 20 minutes.

Jeffries did not hit his sparring partners anywhere near as hard as he could. He did not dare to, or else he would lose them. Jeff said, "I don't hurt them. I don't treat them as rough as they treat me." Still, Delaney said that Jeffries had already accidentally knocked out Kennedy during the training at Harbin Springs. Kennedy said that Jeffries had improved wonderfully since he last saw him. "He's quicker, stronger, more shifty and it's twice as hard to hit him. When you try to push him away, it's like moving a house."

Delaney said that not only could Jeffries dish it, but he could take it too. In their first fight, Fitz hit him with some cracking shots, and expected Jeff to fall, but when he was right there grinning at him, it broke Bob's heart. Others said Fitz exhausted himself with his own output in trying to knock Jeff out, that Jeffries was the first man whom he hit but could not knock out.[698]

697 *San Francisco Bulletin*, July 15, 1902.
698 *San Francisco Call, San Francisco Evening Post*, July 16, 1902.

Both fighters continued their hard daily training regimens. On the 16th, Jeff emerged from his sparring sessions with a bruise on his right cheek bone. Another said Jeff sustained a cut lip, although it was unclear whether it was the result of a punch or a butt. Stepping on the scales fully clothed, he weighed 220 pounds. Delaney estimated that he would enter the ring for the fight at about 215 pounds. He felt that Jeffries was in his prime, in possession of immense powers of endurance and resistance.

Jeffries spars Joe Kennedy.

Jeff's camp strenuously denied rumors that there were two sets of articles of agreement, one for the public in which there was a 60/40 split, and a private agreement in which they were to split the purse evenly. Delaney said that he had never been accused of faking in his life, and would pay $1,000 to anyone who could prove otherwise.[699]

At Skaggs Springs on the 16th, Fitzsimmons ran 10 miles. He boxed 8 fast rounds with Wilson and Griffin, dropping Wilson several times. Griffin was also knocked down, the first knockdown that Fitz had given him.

699 *San Francisco Bulletin*, July 16, 17, 1902; *San Francisco Evening Post, San Francisco Call*, July 17, 1902.

On the 17th, Bob banged Wilson and Griffin around for 6 rounds. Fitz said, "I never was better in my life. ... I will go into the ring in perfect condition." Dawson agreed that Bob was never better.[700]

Jeffries claimed that he was weighing 212 pounds. Delaney preferred him to weigh 215. There was not an ounce of superfluous flesh in evidence.

Jeff's ear was sore. A 350-pound bag filled with sand had brushed his ear and irritated it, and it had not healed owing to the continual punching on it during sparring.[701]

Fitzsimmons continued claiming that he was doped in their first fight, that he could not see Jeffries or tell where he was. Most experts believed that it was Jeff's fists that made him groggy.

About a week from the fight, both Jeffries and Fitzsimmons started backing off in their training, tapering and sparring less often. Delaney said that as a result, Jeff would gain some weight and enter the ring as strong as a bull, at about 220 pounds. Bill said that when Jeff was out of training, he weighed close to 300 pounds, but did not look it, because it was well distributed over his body. He said that Bob was an easier man to fight than Corbett was because he was easier to hit, but at the same time, Bob was the more dangerous fighter because he hit so much harder.[702]

Bob's son, Fitz, Tom Wilson, Eddie Graney, and George Dawson

700 *San Francisco Evening Post, San Francisco Bulletin,* July 17, 1902;
701 *San Francisco Call,* July 18, 1902.
702 *San Francisco Evening Post,* July 18, 19, 1902.

Ed Graney had been selected to referee the fight, and he met with the fighters to discuss the rules. Referee Graney said that in case of a knockdown, the other man must go to his corner until the man on the mat had regained his feet. The men could hit in the clinches while the other held on, but once he commanded a break, they were required to step back. He noted that the articles of agreement allowed the men to use soft surgical bandages.

In Fitz's 6 rounds of sparring on the 18th, Wilson was dropped to the mat, while a blow to the jaw dazed Griffin and caused him to stop working for a few seconds. Both men worked hard and at a fast pace, giving Bob some pretty hard raps, but none of them had any effect.[703]

That same day, Jeff rowed for an hour on Lake Merritt. However, other than that, he took a day of rest. He felt that he was drawn too fine at 208 pounds, but would try to take on some weight and get up to 215 or 217. He was so confident of winning that he was already having Delaney start negotiations for another fight with Corbett.

On the 19th, Jeffries did an 8-mile morning run, sprinting 20 times along the way. In the afternoon, with 200-300 men watching, he sparred his usual alternating rounds with Kennedy and brother Jack. The champion was relaxed and whistling to himself as he boxed Kennedy. One blow to brother Jack's chin shook him up considerably. At the end of the workout, Jeff weighed in at 210 pounds, and looked as strong as a lion. George Siler said that Jeffries was faster than he had ever seen him, and his condition was superb. The next day, Jeff sparred 8 rounds.

On the 20th, Fitzsimmons transferred his training quarters from Skaggs Springs to San Francisco, where he would work out at the Olympic Club.[704]

Bob commended Hank Griffin as an excellent sparring partner. He stood 6'2", weighed 180 pounds in top condition, and had a very long reach of 81 ½ inches, even longer than Tom Wilson's 80 inches. Fitz said it was no easy task to subdue Griffin, calling him a wonder.

---

703 *San Francisco Bulletin*, July 19, 1902.
704 *San Francisco Call*, July 19-21, 1902.

Bill Delaney expected Jeffries to enter the ring between 218 and 220 pounds. Delaney said,

> The big fellow has all his forces under control, and does not get rattled, no matter how fast the fight, nor how dangerous the surroundings. He knows his powers of administering and receiving punishment. He is aware that he can punch harder than any man that breathes, and knows that he can digest rougher knocks than any other man. He is so strongly built that he is, compared to Fitzsimmons, like a heavily armored modern battleship.[705]

On the 21st, at the Olympic, Fitz took his morning run, boxed with each of his three trainers, and punched the bag. He mostly played defense against Griffin, for 4 rounds allowing him to slug away, while Bob blocked and eluded blows. In the last round, Fitz showed what he could do if he so desired, slugging Hank and keeping him trying to survive. He then wrestled for 30 minutes with Dawson and Griffin, and seemed fresh afterwards. Soldier Wilson showed reporters his cauliflower ear, which he said had become misshapen as a result of Fitz's pounding.

Fitzsimmons looked to be in excellent condition, and those who saw him were of the opinion that he was dangerous and would give Jeffries a real battle. Another paper said that Bob was a freak. At an age when most were retired, he was at the height of physical perfection, showing no signs of decadence. He was bigger and stronger than at any time in his career. He looked to be weighing 180-185 pounds. Still, he was going up against "the biggest, strongest and most powerful man known in the history of the ring." "Jeffries certainly ought to win, but there is always danger in an opponent of Fitzsimmons' class. He has a deadly punch, which if put in with precision, ought to be destructive enough to rock even a Jeffries."[706]

705 *San Francisco Evening Post, San Francisco Bulletin,* July 21, 1902.
706 *San Francisco Evening Post,* July 21, 1902; *San Francisco Call, San Francisco Evening Post,* July 22, 1902.

The consensus of opinion was that Jeffries ought to win, but that Fitzsimmons had a chance. Jeff had advantages in age, height, weight, strength, and a wonderful chin which could assimilate Fitz's power. He was perhaps the only man who could take Bob's punch. *The Police Gazette* wrote,

> Fitz's admirers may claim that their man is more scientific, but this fact I dispute, for in Jeffries' more recent fights he has demonstrated the possession of a well-developed knowledge of the finer points of the fistic game. He blocks and counters superbly and is faster with a lead than any big man I ever saw except Corbett. He is cool and courageous and has the additional advantage of having beaten Fitzsimmons. ... Fitz has been on the shelf two years while Jeff has had four or five fights in that time. ...

> In my opinion Fitz himself has no idea that he can win. Reverses in theatrical and other speculative ventures have left him in a position where ready money is a necessity, and a big losing end (probably an equal division of the purse if the inside facts were known) has tempted him to try it again.[707]

Still, Bob Fitzsimmons was a fighter with a lot of pride, who had been training diligently for over six months. He clearly wanted to reverse his only legitimate loss.

Approaching the fight, Jeffries said,

> I can truthfully say that I feel bigger and stronger than at any time during my career. I have trained long and faithfully for the event and have reached a state of perfect condition. I do not think that the man lives who can whip me. ... I have made a study of Fitzsimmons and think I know his methods better than he does mine, for I feel that during the past three years I have improved greatly while he has but little.

Jeff also said, "I guarantee that the battle will be fast and furious from start to finish. I think I know Fitzsimmons' style of battle and believe I can easily conquer him if I do not allow him to play in and out with me. I shall therefore hurry matters, feeling confident that in such a style of warfare I can stand the better chance of success."

Delaney said, "I don't think Jeffries will have many more fights. He has now met and whipped the best lot of men the world has ever seen. When you look around, you do not find any rising aspirants for championship honors in view. ... Corbett will be the next and probably the last man Jeffries will meet." Bill said that Jeff was weighing 214 pounds.

Fitzsimmons was also confident. "I will win the fight on Friday night. If I did not think I would be able to reverse the decision awarded to Jeffries

---

707 *National Police Gazette*, August 2, 1902.

on our first meeting I never would have signed for a second. ... I am huskier and stronger than ever."

On the 22nd, Fitz did his morning run. In the afternoon, he boxed 3 rounds with Griffin, 3 rounds with amateur heavyweight Andy Gallagher, and 2 rounds with Al Ahrens, a clever Olympic Club welterweight.

That morning, Jeff ran 10 miles. In the afternoon, he weighed in at 217 pounds. Jeffries worked the pulley weights and wrist machine prior to sparring 8 rounds with Jack and Joe, alternating rounds. He went at Kennedy harder than usual. At one point, a punch on the jaw completely turned Joe around. Kennedy came back and landed a right to the nose, drawing blood.[708]

Although Jeff was the favorite, many felt that Bob had a fighting chance. "That he is trained to the hour is beyond question." On the 23rd, with San Francisco Mayor Eugene Schmitz watching, Fitz boxed 4 fast rounds with Griffin. "He hammered Griffin hard and blocked all the heavy blows Hank sent in." The mayor was impressed.

Afterwards, speaking of Griffin, Bob said, "That fellow is one of the hardest men I have ever tried to hit; he has a way of smothering up that leaves nothing but bones in sight." Griffin complimented Bob as well. "When I first came to the camp Mr. Fitzsimmons had hard work getting at me, as I used the crouching position, but now it does not bother him in the least. ... I have been up against Jeffries, and I know how he can hit, and I tell you I am pinning my money on Bob."

Fitzsimmons said of Jeffries, "When I fought him some years ago I held him too cheaply. I thought he was an overgrown amateur, and I attempted to beat him quickly. He proved strong and caught me with a lucky punch. ... I am in better condition than I was when first we met and I feel confident I can beat him."[709]

The night before the fight, Jeffries said,

> There is in my mind no doubt but that I shall win. ... I am not going into the ring underrating him. I know he is a very dangerous man to crowd, and I am not, I assure you, going to make him fight by taking unnecessary chances. ... [In our first fight], I was then hit as hard or harder than I had ever been struck before. Anyone who saw the New York fight will bear me out in the assertion that I was punished as hard as Fitzsimmons could lay it on. Yet I survived. In the midst of his shower of blows I was unrocked. What I then went through I am ready to take again tomorrow night.[710]

---

708 *San Francisco Evening Post, San Francisco Bulletin, San Francisco Call,* July 23, 1902.
709 *San Francisco Call, San Francisco Bulletin,* July 24, 1902.
710 *San Francisco Evening Post,* July 25, 1902.

CHAPTER 32

The War, the Bandages, and the Speaking Knockdown

Just over eight months after his title defense against Gus Ruhlin, on July 25, 1902 in San Francisco, James Jeffries gave former champion Bob Fitzsimmons a rematch. This was the second time a former gloved world heavyweight champion was granted another crack at the title, and both times it was Jeffries granting the former titlist the opportunity.

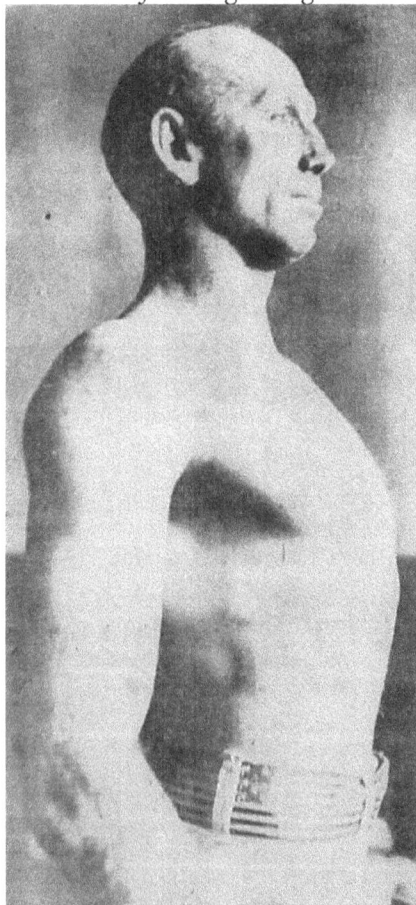

The day of the championship fight, Bob Fitzsimmons said, "I never felt better in my life nor more confident of winning a fight. I feel that I am as good now as when I last fought Jeffries. I was as in good condition then as ever in my life, but I was doped." He also held Jeff too cheaply the first time, underrating his strength and skill. Fitz predicted that he would do better this time, saying that he would fight more carefully. "I know Jeffries' style now and by making a different kind of fight, I am positive that I can turn the tables." "This time I am going to dodge his strength and play to his weakness." Fitz was not bothered by his underdog status. "Odds don't win a fight."[711]

Bob's sparring partner/trainer George Dawson said, "Fitz is in better shape than he ever was, and I think he will win sure. He is a cleverer man than Jeffries and I think he can hit harder, and there is

711 The report of the fight, as well as pre- and post-fight discussion are taken from the *San Francisco Call, San Francisco Bulletin, San Francisco Evening Post, San Francisco Chronicle*, and *San Francisco Examiner*, all July 25-26, 1902; and *National Police Gazette*, August 9, 1902.

no doubt that he is a better general." Hank Griffin said Fitz was a sure winner.

Jeffries said that Fitzsimmons would find a greatly improved man from the one he met in 1899. He was then practically a novice by comparison, and still he knocked out Bob in 11 rounds. Jeff expected to knock him out even more quickly this time. "He has a hard punch; but I have yet to meet a man who can hurt me or knock me down."

Fitz's KO6 over Ruhlin (after Ruhlin knocked out Sharkey in the 15th round) and KO2 over Sharkey (after Sharkey went 25 rounds with Jeffries and had a KO3 over Choynski, but had lost to Ruhlin) clearly made him the most deserving title challenger. However, Bob had not fought in almost two years, not since late August 1900. Still, all of the training reports said that Fitzsimmons was fight sharp and ready, and had remained physically well and active in the intervening two years. He had been steadily training for over six months.

The new outdoor pavilion for the fight had been built on the corner of Fourteenth and Valencia streets. It measured 200' x 215' in the open air. The fighters were to box on an elevated platform which was well lit by strong lights placed by the Independent Electric Light Company. Nearly 200 policemen would be on hand to handle the crowd.

The arrangements of the San Francisco Athletic Club and the police were perfect. There was no trouble or any arrests.

When the arena doors were opened at 6 p.m., there was a line of ticket holders that extended around the block. The arena was practically sold-out a half-hour earlier. "All the $7.50 seats were disposed of early in the afternoon, and then a raid was made on the higher priced ones." Only a few $10, $15, and $20 tickets could be obtained.

The crowd featured folks who had traveled from all over the country to be there. *The Call* said that more than 5,000 people crowded the arena. *The Bulletin* estimated 6,500 people. Some later said 7,000 were in attendance. Scores of ushers were present to assist the ticket holders and direct them to their seats.

High-power electric lights were strung all over the arena so that it was well lit. The ring was bright enough that the men could be seen clearly from the furthest part of the outdoor arena.

The sky was clear, and it was a delightful night to witness a fight outdoors. It was much better than sitting in a stuffy arena breathing in clouds of tobacco smoke and impure air.

Close to the ring were news correspondents from all over the country. During the fight, the clicking of telegraph machines could be heard.

Fitzsimmons arrived a few minutes after 7 p.m. and went to his dressing room. He was rubbed down, and to warm up, he boxed a couple of light rounds with George Dawson.

Jeffries arrived nearly two hours later. He wore a long black overcoat and a Panama hat, which he did not remove until after he entered the ring.

Owing to his great strength and vitality, the odds were 10 to 4 in Jeff's favor. Betting was very light, given the fact that most thought that Jeff would win. After all, he had never been defeated.

Shortly after 10 p.m., accompanied by trainers George Dawson, Hank Griffin, and manager Clark Ball, Fitzsimmons was first to arrive in the ring, wearing a flashy blue bathrobe. The howls and plaudits of the crowd were loud enough to be heard blocks away. The shouts attested to his popularity. Bob bowed in acknowledgement to the deafening applause, and then took his seat in the corner. He was presented with a floral horseshoe, but Fitz was evidently disgusted by it. Most boxers felt it was bad luck to receive a token of esteem in the ring.

Jeffries entered the ring a few minutes later, fully dressed with an overcoat, knee pants, a sweater, and Panama hat. With him were Jack Jeffries, Joe Kennedy, and Bill Delaney. The crowd gave the champion a hearty and cordial greeting as well, but not as great as that given to Fitzsimmons. Jeff bowed in acknowledgement to his fans. Despite the fact that Jeffries was essentially a California native, the underdog Fitz was the decided crowd favorite during the fight. There were plenty of Jeffries admirers, but they were in the minority.

Chewing gum, Jeff nonchalantly walked over and shook hands with Fitz, who rose to his feet. At that point, Jeffries critically and carefully examined the bandages on Bob's hands. He apparently found no fault with them, for he made no objection, and walked over and took his own seat. Jeff wore no hand bandages.

Stakeholder Sam Thall returned the forfeit money that the respective parties had deposited - $2,500 to each of the fighters, and $5,000 to the promoting club, the San Francisco Athletic Club.

Harry Corbett on behalf of his brother James J. announced Jim's challenge to the winner. A challenge from Tom Sharkey was also announced, but it was greeted with groans and jeers from all parts of the house.

Referee Ed Graney appeared in Tuxedo and black satin tie.

When they stripped, Jeff was wearing black trunks, while Fitz wore lavender ones. Both men wore silk American flags for belts. Jeff's gloves were very dark red, while Bob's gloves were a light maroon.

The men were photographed with hands clasped in the center of the ring.

The San Francisco Chronicle said Jeff admitted to weighing in the neighborhood of 218 pounds. Fitzsimmons claimed to weigh only 160 pounds. *The Police Gazette* said Bob weighed 168 to Jeff's 218. Another *Gazette* writer listed Fitz at 180 pounds. *The Examiner's* W.W. Naughton questioned Fitz's reported weight, feeling that he was closer to 190 pounds. As usual, no one knew for sure, because heavyweights were not required to weigh in. In *Two Fisted Jeffries*, Jeff said that Fitz later told him that before their rematch, he weighed 185 pounds. "Weight, however, had little to do with Fitz's great hitting power. He hit as if he weighed three hundred."[712]

Jeffries was 27 years of age, while Fitzsimmons was 39 years old.

Referee Graney said that hitting in the clinches and hugging would be prohibited, which was not in Jeffries' favor, given his style. Apparently, the rules had changed. After the referee gave them instructions about the rules, they both returned to their corners to await the bell. The gong rang at 10:20 p.m.

1st round

Jeffries began the fight in a half-crouching attitude. Fitzsimmons broke ground as Jeff followed, both feinting rapidly. Although Jeff was the aggressor, Bob was the first to lead, sending in some quick rights in more of a jab fashion. Jeff crouched and rushed, but Fitz side-stepped out of the way. Both feinted a lot. "The spectators sat breathless, and watched the two trained boxers fiddle and dance, strike out with the force of piston rods and with the skill of experts."

The aggressive Jeffries anxiously bore in, but Fitzsimmons eluded or neutralized his attacks. As he retreated, Bob shot his left into Jeff's face. Fitz was faster on his feet, his quick leg work getting him out of the way of many rushes. Bob was still willing to exchange though, landing his blows to the head and then moving away. Whenever Jeffries landed to the body, Fitz was back like a flash with one of his hard counters to the head. Jeff landed a hard left to the body, but Bob quickly countered to the head.

One of Fitz's lefts to Jeff's nose started the blood flowing from it in a stream. The quick Fitzsimmons hit him fairly easily, and eluded and countered most of Jeff's blows. Jeffries rushed in, but Bob nimbly hopped out of the way, his hit and move tactics working well. Jeff was repeatedly short with his blows. In a clinch, Jeff sent in a right to body. Bob landed a left to the ear. Jeffries landed a stiff left to the heart. The round concluded with the men sparring, until Jeff landed a right to the breast that momentarily knocked Bob off balance. At the bell, although Jeff's nose was bleeding, he still looked confident.

2nd round

Jeffries kept forcing in determined fashion, going right after Fitzsimmons, but Bob was inclined to retreat. Jeff missed a left and Bob countered with his own jab. Jeff smiled and forced him to a corner, but Bob quickly side-stepped out. Jeff blocked a right. Fitz broke ground from Jeff's lefts, but eventually Bob stopped and landed a stiff left to the face. Jeffries crouched lower, landed a stiff left hook on Fitz's jaw, and then forced Bob back to the ropes with terrific body blows, particularly the left to the body.

---

712 *Two Fisted Jeffries* at 220.

Jeffries kept up such a fast pace that he forced Bob to make a stand and fight back. Fitz landed two left hooks to the face and eluded a left. Jeff went after him and landed a left to the head and Bob clinched. Jeff sent his left to the body and Bob shot his left into the head. The champion landed three lefts to the body before Bob stopped him for a moment with a left jab to the nose, followed by a left to the body and right to the head.

Fitzsimmons landed a stabbing left jab on the nose that brought out the blood again in a stream. The crowd cheered vociferously. Bob's long absence from ring competition had not impaired his judgment of distance, for he seldom missed. He was cool and calm, again fighting intelligently in this round. By the end of the round, Jeff's nose was badly bleeding, the blood flowing down freely. At the bell, Jeff gave Bob a look of mingled surprise and disgust.

The Bulletin, Call, and *Chronicle* all admired Bob's boxing skill. *The Evening Post* said that honors were easy at this point. However, the *Examiner's* W.W. Naughton felt that the round was slightly in favor of Jeffries, "his body blows being telling ones."

3rd round

Jeffries resumed his aggression, forcing matters even as his bloody nose annoyed him a little. He changed tactics just a bit by standing straight up. It left him in less of a defensive stance, but allowed him to move and advance more quickly.

Bob blocked two left leads and countered with a left jab on the sore nose. Jeff tried another left, but Bob stopped him with a left jab to the face. After they clinched, Jeff pushed him back. Fitz landed a stiff left on the nose and Jeff bled freely. Bob also landed a left hook. Jeffries landed the second of two lefts. However, Fitz landed a staggering left counter on the jaw. Jeff fell short with a body blow and received a left and right on the nose.

Fitzsimmons landed a stiff left hook on Jeff's cheek which opened up a cut under his right eye. The blood flowed from the gash, as well as from Jeff's nose. Bob had no marks. Despite Jeff's rushing, Fitz often landed his lefts. Undeterred, Jeffries rushed and swung left and right. Bob blocked those punches, but Jeff landed a hard left to the stomach. Fitz twice jabbed his left to the face, and coolly danced away.

Jeffries twice sent his left to the head. Bob hit the injured nose a couple times. In response, Jeff rushed and landed a hard blow on the neck, then sent both fists to the body. Fitzsimmons countered to the nose, causing the blood to flow in a lavish stream at the bell.

As he returned to his corner, Jeff's face was covered in blood. One said his eye was closing. Another said there was a cut over his right eye as well. Between rounds, Delaney busied himself over Jeffries.

The Examiner said it was Fitz's round. "Jeffries' face was bathed in blood. His nose was swollen and his right eye puffed and cut." *The Evening Post* said, "At this point of the contest honors were easy so far as punishment was concerned. Jeffries, however, appeared to be the greater sufferer, as his face was the recipient, while Fitzsimmons' body did not give evidence of the blows which had landed there."

4th round

Jeff crouched and clenched his lips with a look of angry determination. He went in and set the pace, landing a left to the head, while trying to stay clear of Bob's left jabs. Bob blocked and eluded some blows. They exchanged lefts to the face. Fitz landed a short right to the head and Jeff landed a left on the chest. Bob snapped Jeff's head back with a jab and started the blood flowing again. He also landed a right to the head. Jeffries came in with two left hooks, one for the head and another for the body, but their force was diminished because Fitzsimmons was moving back away from them. Bob landed a stiff left on the body, but Jeff countered with a right on the head. Twice Bob blocked Jeff's lefts.

Jeffries landed a strong right to the body, left to the jaw, and right to the wind. Bob responded with three lefts on Jeff's sore eye. Jeff landed a straight left to the body, a strong left to the jaw, and then shifted back down to the body again. He landed yet another left to the wind. He kept poking at the body with his left. Bob missed some blows as Jeff ducked and they clinched. After breaking, Jeffries landed a hard right to the body, but Fitzsimmons countered him with a half-dozen jabs to the mouth and eye. Fitz boxed carefully, landing clean left jabs. He cleverly ducked and sidestepped Jeff's blows.

Fitzsimmons actually took a turn forcing the fight, landing two hard lefts on the face, causing Jeffries to duck and move away from him. However, Jeff once again forced Fitz across the ring and landed a straight left to the body, which made Bob slightly double up.

Fitz shot out his accurate left again to the nose, and Jeff countered with a right on the jaw. Both landed lefts to the body, but Jeff followed with a left to the body and right to the head that rocked Bob's head back. Fitz landed three lefts to the nose and body. He also landed under the heart. "Jeffries took his medicine as if he liked it, and came back with left on body and right on face." Fitz moved back away out of danger, and then made a stand, shooting his right as Jeff came forward, but the champion ducked.

Between rounds, in the corner, Jeffries looked determined, but a bit worried as he listened to Delaney. It seemed as if he felt that Bob was putting up a much tougher fight than he had expected. Jeff's nose and right eye were still bleeding. *The Examiner* said it was another Fitz round. "He was boxing very neatly, and showed excellent judgment in drawing out of range."

5th round

Jeffries was determined to give Fitzsimmons no rest, so he led for the body. Fitz countered the champion with a left on the face. Jeff's nose was bleeding profusely and the gore was pouring from the cut under the right eye. Despite his face's bad appearance, Jeffries was not at all discouraged, and he kept after Bob and repeatedly punished him hard on the body. They fought rapidly. Fitz pasted Jeff's face with left jabs, and occasionally landed his right to the head. However, Bob's body was sore.

Jeff eagerly rushed, forced Fitz to the ropes, and landed two lefts to the face and a hard left to the stomach. Fitz clinched tightly. *The Bulletin* said this was the turning point in the fight. Jeffries' blows were having an effect. After they broke, Jeff went after him again and swung his left, but Fitz ducked and countered with a right smash to the face and left and right body blows. However, as hard as Fitz hit, Jeffries was undeterred and kept coming, hurrying matters. He seemed to enjoy the rapid pace. He landed a left to the jaw and then shifted it to the body.

With a straight left, Jeff slightly cut Bob's right cheek, just under the eye. Fitz missed a left and clinched. Fitzsimmons could not punch him off, so he resorted to clinching more often. They clinched repeatedly. The problem with holding Jeffries was that he could wear opponents out that way too, because he was so strong and knew how to lay his weight on them so that grabbing him did not get them much rest. However, it was a way to avoid Jeff's punishing blows. The referee warned Bob for holding.

Fitz landed a terrific right on the jaw, and a moment later, a left on the nose. Bob's cutting jabs continued landing. Jeff was bleeding badly. A right to the mouth had Jeff spitting blood. They exchanged blows to the head and body on the inside. Jeff's smashes seemed fierce, but Bob countered well. Jeffries landed a series of hard blows to Bob's body, but received two raps on his bleeding nose. Jeff again smashed Fitz's aching ribs with his left.

Just as the round ended, Fitzsimmons landed a right to the left eyebrow, cutting it open. Jeff's entire face was bleeding freely. He was bleeding from the nose, left eye and right cheek, and mouth. Another said Jeff's left eye was closing. The only mark on Fitz was a slight abrasion on the right cheek from the cutting jab that he received in this round. However, Jeff's body punches were doing their damage internally.

The Bulletin felt that Jeff's pace and body punches were starting to turn the tide of the battle in his favor. *The Evening Post* said this round was the first time that Fitzsimmons showed signs of distress. *The Examiner* opined that the round was slightly in Fitz's favor, but noted that he seemed the more tired of the two.

6th round

Bob's right eye looked slightly swollen as he came up to start the round, and he seemed a bit tired.

Jeff crouched low. He rushed, but Fitz cleverly avoided the blows by blocking and using fast footwork to get out of the way. Bob's defense held up well. Jeffries continued to rush, but Fitzsimmons either smothered, countered, or eluded him with sidesteps. "Fitz's foot work was marvelous." Bob kept landing well and doing the better work. His left to the nose made Jeff's face more swollen. Jeff's eyes were in bad shape. They exchanged lefts on the head; Bob's being the more damaging. Jeff rushed multiple times, but Fitz smothered him and landed three lefts and a right on the face. Jeffries forced Fitzsimmons to the ropes, but received a right and left on the face, which started the blood running again. He could not corner Bob, who seemed a veritable will o' the wisp. Jeff was a fright from the blood which covered him.

Others described a more competitive round. Jeffries twice landed to the body, but Bob blocked the third attempt. Jeff landed a left to the body and Fitz landed a hard right to the head. Jeff landed a left to the jaw, and then smashed his left into the body as Bob backed away.

Bob broke ground, but then gathered himself and attacked in a quick rush, landing rights to the head, body, and nose. Jeff broke ground and moved away for the first time, ducking blows. Fitz again swung both hands with terrific force; hard enough to put out any average man, but Jeffries ignored them and hooked Bob with his left to the eye and followed it up with a body blow, causing Fitzsimmons to clinch.

After they broke, Jeff hit Fitz with the left to the head and body. Fitz then landed his right to the jaw. Jeff answered with a left to the jaw and followed with another smash to the body. Jeffries fought like a mad bull. Bob returned with a left and right to the head. Jeff followed him around the ring.

Fitzsimmons showed remarkable cleverness in eluding Jeff's rushes. He continued landing cutting left jabs, and just as the gong sounded, landed another on the sore mouth and nose. In terms of points, it was Fitz's round.

7th round

This round was full of hard work. Jeffries resumed his rushing tactics, covering up well as he attacked in determined fashion. Jeff landed a couple hard lefts to the body and one on the head, but received a left and right to his head in return. Jeff landed a left and right to the mouth and drove Bob back to the ropes, where he hit Fitz with a left on the body and face, both hard blows.

Jeff's body shots were getting to Fitzsimmons, which stirred up his fighting spirit to retaliate and not allow Jeffries too much momentum. Fitz rallied and landed both fists to Jeff's jaw. He threw a right uppercut and left across. Bob came on again with a right to the body and a right to the nose. The blood poured out from Jeff in a stream. Fitz jabbed him three times on the mouth and forced Jeff back to the ropes, scoring right and left to the jaw. Jeff clinched and Bob's friends cheered.

During the round, Fitz often ducked and retaliated with a right and left on Jeff's bleeding face. He also landed many jabs. Jeff looked terrible, but he was not tired.

Bleeding from all over his face, Jeffries came at him like an enraged bull, forcing Bob to the ropes, landing a left to the body and a right over the heart. Fitz tried to keep him off with left jabs.

Jeff landed a left to the head before they clinched. Jeff hit him in the clinch, which drew some hisses from the spectators. While still clinched, Bob complained about Jeff's hitting in the clinch, and Jeff responded by telling him that it was an accident.

In his autobiography, Jeffries said that during their vicious exchanges, Fitzsimmons grinned and asked, "Well, how do you like it?" Jeff replied, "Suits me all right. You're pretty good for an old fellow." Fitz was smiling, while Jeff was bleeding and looking terrible from the cuts. However, he was still strong on his feet. Jeff's rally at the end of the round showed that he had not lost any of his steam.

It was pretty fighting, and the crowd cheered both at the end. It was, however, another Fitz round. Both men went to their corners looking weary.

8th round

One said, "Jeffries came up strong in the eighth, while Fitzsimmons acted as a man who had had enough of the game." However, they went at it, each landing well. Jeff repeatedly struck the head and body, although his primary focus was the body. Fitz mostly hit the head. Jeffries kept attacking, keeping the pace fast. Bob began to show signs of tiring, as well as discouragement, for he had been punching Jeff squarely on the face and jaw without dazing him. Still, few expected this to be the last round.

Fitzsimmons feinted and broke ground as he drew Jeff in. Jeff forced the fighting, crouching low, carrying his right high and left held far back. Fitz landed a stinging right uppercut. He followed up with a number of quick jabs. Jeffries smiled through his bloody features, ducking a left swing and landing a hard counter left on the ribs. He next swung a left for the jaw and they clinched. After breaking, Jeff went after him. Fitz landed a left jab to the nose, but received a terrific left wallop in the wind. Bob landed a left on the face but took a left on the head and one on the ribs. Bob backed away and landed a right to the body. He missed a right and took a stiff punch on the body. Jeff crouched and landed two left jabs to the face.

Jeffries tore into Fitzsimmons and forced him to the ropes, landing a left on the wind and crashing right to the jaw. Bob fell into a clinch. He tried his uppercut and Jeff landed to the body. Fitz landed a couple blows to Jeff's ribs before they clinched again.

Each local source gave its version of how matters ended. *The Bulletin*, *Evening Post*, and *Chronicle* gave substantially similar accounts.

Jeff forced Bob back into a corner, and, momentarily catching Fitz off his guard from a swing that missed, whipped in a punishing, sledgehammer left just to the right of the navel, one of the terrific body jolts that had made him champion. Bob wobbled, and Jeffries followed up with a right to the jaw which sent Fitzsimmons to the ground, completing the job.

The ex-champion tried to rise, but was unable to beat the count. While the referee was counting, Fitz's face showed clearly that he was suffering excruciating pain. His eyes were bulging from his head like pigeon eggs and there was agony in every feature. As the referee counted to eight, Bob struggled to his hands and knees, but was still down when the ten seconds were counted off. The referee declared Jeffries the winner.

Some other local sources, including the *Call*, *Examiner*, and another *Chronicle* version of the knockout mentioned some talking by Fitzsimmons, either before or after he received the big left to the body. This later became the subject of some controversy.

Call: As Fitz stepped back from the clinch, he smiled and spoke to Jeff, a fatal mistake. Before Bob could get out of the way, Jeffries quickly hooked his left on the body and sent a right to the jaw. Fitz went down, clutching feebly at the lower rope, shaking his head in signal of defeat. The referee counted him out before he could stand erect.

Chronicle (2nd version): "As Fitzsimmons stepped back he smiled and spoke to Jeffries. Before he could get out of reach Jeffries hooked him lightly with his left on the jaw, and as Fitz half turned to slip away he caught him again with a terrific left swing in the solar plexus." Fitz went down on his back, slowly rose, but did not beat the count.

Call (2nd version): Jeff attacked and backed Bob to the ropes. For an instant, Fitz was off his guard, and Jeffries whipped in a short half-arm left hook that caught him in the lower ribs. Bob bent over, shook his head, and as he fell, said to Jeffries, "You've got me." Bob clutched the lower rope. He steadied himself on the rope, partially leaning outside of the ring. Referee Graney counted him out as Bob slowly drew himself up to a standing position. At the end of the count, he was still supporting himself by the top rope. There was no strength left in him.

Examiner: Jeff forced him to the ropes, and,

> [He] swung a left which seemed to catch Fitz above the right hip. Fitz drew away and a second later dropped his hands and spoke to Jeffries. Fitzsimmons' eyes were bright and steady, and he did not seem to be distressed. Suddenly Jeffries let fly the left for the cheek, and Fitzsimmons swung half way round on his feet and went slowly to the floor on his hands and knees…. It was a weird looking thing, for it

seemed inexplicable that Fitz should lower his guard when his manner did not suggest that a damaging blow had been delivered.

Various sources noted that after the count was over and Fitz had struggled to his feet in a doubled-up condition, his eyes were still wobbling in their sockets. Bob walked toward Jeff to shake his hand. Jeffries had started to leave the ring right away, but was called back to shake hands with the beaten man. Fitzsimmons could not stand erect for several minutes.

Answering the cries for a speech, Bob said that the best man in the world had beaten him fairly. "The best man won. I can't whip Jeffries and no one else can. This is my last fight." The crowd cheered. He then removed his gloves and threw them to the audience, which scrambled to secure the souvenirs.

It was said that the battle would go down in the prize-ring annals as one of the greatest ever. The two had thrown powerful blows that would have knocked out any other fighter in the world. Fitz had fought more intelligently and skillfully this time, but he could not beat Jeffries.

Jeffries said that Fitzsimmons gave him the hardest fight of his life. He told the *Chronicle*,

> He seemed faster and stronger than when I met him before, and he reached my head much oftener, but I always had my jaw covered and I knew he could not hit me hard enough on the body to put me out. I am so much bigger and heavier than he is that I knew I would wear him out and win in the end.

> It was a body punch that finished the fight… I simply caught him off his guard after he missed a hook at me, and that was the end.

Jeffries told the *Call*,

> Well, I won, but I'll have to give it to Fitz for being the best old man in the world. He certainly gave me the hardest run for eight rounds that I have had in my career. Gee, but I look pretty well cut up. Say, fellows, does it add to my beauty? This fellow Fitzsimmons has the right material in him. He can go out as old as he is and beat all the other heavyweights in the country. I felt confident that I would win. The blows Fitz landed on me were good and hard, but never made me groggy. He did not knock me down nor did he stagger me. He certainly can wallop some. … The blood flowing from my nose bothered me at first, but I got used to it. The jab I got in the eye did not help me much, but my seconds soon had that patched up. Fitz is game and certainly has cleverness. … When I entered that ring I knew I would win. I took my time and at the right moment ended things. The blow I caught Fitz was a left in the stomach. We were about to clinch and Fitz stepped back into his own corner. He never expected me to follow him up and I must have surprised him. The blow was a

left rip and as soon as I let it go I knew I was the winner. I took no chances, however, but followed it with another in the solar plexus and then walloped him on the head as he was falling. ... Again I say Fitz is the goods and I have to give it to him.

The Evening Post quoted Jeffries as saying,

Well, I won, as I knew I would, but I must admit that the victory brought with it some disagreeable features in the shape of a broken nose, a battered eye and other bruises too numerous to mention.

Fitzsimmons is without doubt the greatest man in the ring outside of myself. ... I had no idea that any man could stand the blows I landed on the body without going down and out before he did. I struck him often with all my force, but he took the gruel and kept coming at me by shooting left and right at my nose and eye. The blood bothered me for a time, but I eventually got used to it and went right in and took his punishment, knowing my ability to withstand his assaults and fully conscious that in time he would have to wilt under my punches.

In his first autobiography, Jeffries mentioned that the new ring platform was built too lightly, which affected him. The lighter Fitz could skip about quickly, but whenever the heavier Jeff moved, the boards bent under him. "It made my footing uncertain and awkward and took away half my speed." He said it was worse when he crouched, so he stood up more. He later said that he walked right into and through Fitz's punches just so he could get close enough to have a chance to land one of his own blows. Jeffries did not mention the ring troubles in his immediate post-fight comments. However, his claim could have been true given that the ring had just recently been built.[713]

Fitzsimmons told the *Call* that he was fairly beaten, and announced his retirement. Bob complained of broken hands, but otherwise had no excuses.

I had to go in. If I'd stayed off he'd have followed me up and beaten my head off. He's always right after you. He'd have killed Corbett if Corbett had fought him as I did. Jeff's a grand fighter. No one can beat him if I can't – and I can't. I thought I had him all the way along. ... It was a left hook that did it – one of my own. The smash on the jaw that followed it did not hurt me. ... I told Jim I was gone as soon as I got that smash.

Speaking about Jeffries with a *Chronicle* reporter, Bob said,

He is a wonder. He had me going in the seventh.... It wasn't that last biff in the eye that did it; it was the smash in the wind. I thought my

713 *My Life and Battles* at 49.

short ribs were broken. When I went down I said with all the wind that was in me, 'Jeff, I'm gone.' On the straight, I might perhaps have pulled out and gone on, but I would have only been chopped to pieces, and I've fought long enough to know when I or any other man has had the finishing punch.

He did me, but if it is the last word that I ever say I will tell you that I wasn't right the first time he put me out…. This time I was as fit as I ever was in my life. Then he was a novice. Now he is a finished fighter….

But ain't I all right for an old man? I don't think that I ever punched anyone harder than I did him in the first four rounds, but he kept coming back. There is no one fighting in the world that has a chance against him. I couldn't do it, and if I can't there is no one that can.

A few years later, Fitz said of the knockout,

He had been bringing his left hand up from a position at his side and I had prepared to block it. But this time he raised his hand high above his head and making somewhat of a circle he brought his hand up into my stomach. It was a terrific blow, for I felt the effects of it for a long time. I lay on the floor trying to get up, but my limbs refused to support me. I said to myself, 'fooled by my own blow.'[714]

Fitzsimmons had seen Corbett try to outbox Jeffries to no avail. Bob had tried a modified version, trying to box and punch him out, but realized that Jeffries was invincible when even his best punches had no effect. No one could keep this Jeffries away, and eventually the champion was going to wear his opponents down and land the big one. Fitz realized this despite all of his effective work and superior points boxing.

In his first autobiography, Jeff backed Fitz's claim that he had hurt hands. "I knew his right hand was gone, for once when he landed a very heavy smash on my forehead I could hear the bones crack, and, although he went right on hitting with it, there wasn't the same weight in the blows." The first two knuckles were broken. Bob later told him that after hurting his hand, he landed his right differently, turning it to land with the knuckles that had not been broken. "And yet he was hitting almost as hard as with a sound hand." Also, "The joints of Bob's left hand were buckled toward the end of the fight, but he didn't hold back his punches."

Fitz trainer and sparring partner George Dawson commented,

I don't see how Bob got beaten. He put up the greatest fight that any man ever fought. … I thought he would win sure as the fight progressed. Bob did wonderful hitting. He hurt one of his hands Thursday while boxing Griffin, and that was against him, but he was

714 *National Police Gazette*, February 5, 1905.

in fine condition otherwise. Jeff is too big for him, that's certain. ... Fitz put up the best fight that could have been made, and the way he mixed it was marvelous. ... Jeff is a giant, and he took smashes that no other man living could have taken and not gone out. That was an unlucky body punch that Bob got, but it happens to the best of them.

Referee Graney said Fitzsimmons was as quick as a cat and displayed intelligent ring generalship. "He danced about the ring so fast sometimes that it was difficult to keep an eye on him, and his blows were aimed with marvelous accuracy." However, his punches did not take the steam away from Jeffries, who was always strong and confident.

It was the greatest fight I ever saw in my life. Fitz was beaten by a left-hand hook in the solar plexus – the very blow that won him the championship from Corbett at Carson. The men fought fairly and squarely. Neither man hit in the clinches. They started to rough it at one stage of the fight and I told them I would take off my coat and give them a good rough house if they did not break when I ordered them. ... Jeffries did not throw his weight on Fitz or resort to hugging. When they clinched each man stepped back and fought nicely. ... It was a clean fight and the best man won. ... When Fitz went down on his knee Jeff moved over to his own corner as provided for in the rules. Fitzsimmons' showing surprised me. I felt satisfied that he would give Jeffries a hard tussle, but I never thought for a moment that he would do so wonderfully well. He certainly is a grand old man.

The experienced George Siler gave his views as well. Jeffries took a "terrible mauling" and his face was "beaten almost to a pulp." Fitz hit him often, especially with the left. Bob would feint Jeff "into a knot," and then stab him with a left jab and dance away. After jabbing him to pieces, in the 5th round, Bob used his right more, and "some of the blows that he landed on Jeffries' jaw with that useful member appeared to be hard enough to fell an ox." However, the blows had no effect on Jeff.

It was only his weight, strength, stamina and capacity of taking punishment that won for him. True, the blow, a left hook which landed directly under the solar plexus, had everything to do with his victory, but, had he not been of cast iron he could never have withstood the blows that Fitz landed on him throughout the fight.

During the bout, Jeffries lunged with many hooks and fell short. After trying unsuccessfully for the head, he switched his focus to the body and found more success. Siler described the end:

Just before the knock-out came Jeffries rushed Bob to the south side of the ropes, and Fitz, as he had done scores of times before, propped him up with the left, and then, as upon previous occasions, attempted to dance out of distance with his back partly turned, then turned suddenly and fetched Jeff coming head on. This time he missed with the left, and as the force of the blow turned him partly around the champion was on top of him like a flash, hooked his left over Fitzsimmons' solar plexus and as the old fellow dropped his hands he crossed him with the right on the jaw, sending him on the lower ropes of the ring.

According to the *Examiner*'s W.W. Naughton, the crowd went home talking about Bob's magnificent showing. "Fitz fought more on the defensive than ever he did in his life, and put up a very effective exhibition." During the fight, the spectators were electrified at the smaller, older, underdog Fitz's performance, and cheered him wildly in each successive round. Fitz was cool, calm, fresh, and never fought better. "He was light on his feet and faultless in his judgment of distance." He outboxed and outpointed Jeffries, who seemed unable to escape his cutting blows. Jeff's nose was bloodied in the 1st, his right eye cut in the 3rd, and both eyes cut in the 6th. He was a sight, bleeding profusely, covered in blood. His crouching attitude did not save him from punishment, and at times, he abandoned it. Fitz landed hard and often. Conversely, Jeff's judgment of distance was off, falling short with most blows, and he was made to look "clumsy and inexpert." Fitzsimmons did not appear distressed by his own exertions. He held the points lead throughout, having the best of the fight up until the knockout.

Jeffries was given his just due credit though. He forced a fast pace, and when he got Fitzsimmons on the ropes, he hit his body hard. Although Bob landed a number of crushing rights and lefts on the jaw, they seemed to have no effect on the Los Angeles giant. He took three punches to one, but could have taken a lot more and still kept going. "His strength and vitality are enough to keep him champion for many a long day." In the 8th, Jeff landed a hard left to the body. Fitz dropped his arm and spoke to Jeff, who then swung for the head and sent him to the floor. Bob arose after the ten-count.

The National Police Gazette said Fitzsimmons for 7 rounds fought "as he had never fought before, cleverly and scientifically, and he surprised even his most faithful adherents. He had the champion cut, bleeding and confused." Jeff's defense seemed off and he had difficulties landing.

The Call said that the fight had been 8 bloody and fiercely contested rounds. Although Jeffries earned the victory, the "honor and glory of the battle rest with the vanquished." For 7 rounds, Fitz had made a "pitiable spectacle" of Jeff, landing at will, cutting his face to ribbons. But then the same blow that Fitzsimmons had knocked out Corbett knocked him out. The fight ended so abruptly that the spectators were surprised.

The battle resembled Corbett-Fitzsimmons in many respects. Fitzsimmons fought both aggressively and defensively, drawing blood from

Jeff's nose in the opening round and making him look like "a Sioux brave in full war-paint." Bob blackened both of Jeff's eyes, cut him deeply on the right cheek, and kept his nose and mouth bleeding continuously. He outboxed and outpointed Jeffries, dancing around, jolting, jabbing, and crossing him as he liked.

However, the champion took it all with bull-dog courage, and landed the harder and more internally damaging blows, particularly to the body. Fitz was the superior boxer, but Jeff applied the determined pressure, looking to land knockout blows, until finally he landed that one fearful punch. His right to the jaw completed the job. Jeffries had landed the one punch that wiped out all of Fitz's good work. His youth, strength, and vitality proved too much for Bob's wonderful science. Fitzsimmons acknowledged that he simply could not beat Jeffries, that the only way to do so was to use a sledgehammer.

This was pretty much how Corbett-Fitzsimmons went, with Jim cutting, bloodying, and outboxing Bob, until Fitz's determination, pressure, and body work finally caught up with Corbett.

Visually, the only mark that Fitzsimmons had was a slight abrasion under his right eye. Dr. Cox said that one of Bob's ribs had been cracked. He had also sprained his left thumb.

The Chronicle said Jeffries received the hardest punishment of his career in a wonderful, furious fight in which Fitzsimmons displayed remarkable cleverness. Bob had the clear points lead from the beginning to the end.

Other papers, such as the *Evening Post* and the *Bulletin*, focused on the fact that Jeffries had worn Fitzsimmons down with effective body blows and his relentless non-stop attack. These newspapers gave Jeff more credit in their round-by-round descriptions and analysis. Jeffries had employed his determined hard-punching strategy and it worked, having stopped Fitzsimmons 3 rounds sooner than he did in their first fight. However, this time, Jeff fought as an attacker, whereas in their first fight, he boxed more cautiously and defensively.

In his first autobiography, Jeff said that during the fight, Delaney had urged him to try to rush matters and stop Fitzsimmons as quickly as possible, due to the fact that Jeff's eyes were closing. "The way the old fellow could hit was a wonder. He was hammering my face in. The blows were as heavy as any I ever felt. ... Fitz looked like a winner, for he was almost unmarked, while I must have been a sight." He later said, "Fitz was boxing a clever, cagy bout, and taking few chances. ... Evidently his plan was to cut me up and lick me piece by piece." However, although Fitzsimmons was punching very hard, Jeff's injuries were all on the surface. "Inside I was as sound and fresh as ever. ... I knew I'd win in time. I was all right still inside, not weak or dazed or even tired. And I knew that Fitzsimmons could not keep up such a terrible pace for twenty rounds."

Regarding the end, Jeffries said that he could feel that Fitzsimmons was growing weaker, for Bob's blows did not hurt and he seemed to be tiring from the pace and the body punishment. Jeff's left landed just to one side of the pit of the stomach, at the edge of the right ribs, driving them in. Bob straightened up and stood perfectly still for a moment, paralyzed. He gasped, "You've got me, Jeff." At the same moment, Jeffries had started the finishing blow for his jaw.

Jeffries had been badly punished by the blows struck with the 5-ounce gloves. His nose was flattened, in line with his cheeks. He required several stitches to sew up the cuts above his left and right eyes, and over his right cheek bone. Given that they wore no mouthpieces back then, "Every tooth in my head was loose. For two days after the fight I couldn't eat. I couldn't move my jaw and I thought it was surely broken. One of my ears was in bad shape." He looked as if he had been run over by a mowing machine. At least that is how Jeff remembered it.[715]

One thing to consider is that back then, fights were never stopped on cuts or swellings. In fact, for most of boxing's history, there was no such thing as a doctor stopping a fight. A cut was just a flesh wound, an impediment that a fighter had to deal with, and Jeffries dealt with the sting of the cuts and the blood in his eyes. The reality is that there rarely is a true medical need for a fight to be stopped on cuts. Rather, it is the politics of the unsightly message that blood brings to the sport that have led to so many premature fight stoppages due to cuts.

The gate receipts were reported to be $31,880. Jeff received a 60% share of 75% of the gross receipts ($14,346), while Fitz received 40% of the same ($9,564). The San Francisco Athletic Club made $7,970. These numbers varied from source to source, but they were all ballpark. *The Bulletin* claimed the fighters only split a 70% share of the gross receipts. It said that Jeff was paid $13,389.60 and Fitz received $8,926.40, or a 60/40 split of 70% of the receipts. The club made $9,564.[716]

One of the topics that boxing fans and historians love to discuss and debate is whether Fitzsimmons wore loaded gloves in this fight. Oddly enough, this topic was given little discussion at the time. Jeffries did tell the *Chronicle*, "It was the bandages that punished me so much. The blows did not daze me, but every time Fitz landed even a glancing blow it seemed to cut me like a knife." The question is whether he meant that Fitz's regular soft bandages allowed him to have a harder or more protected fist which could generate cutting blows, or whether he meant that Fitz's wraps were hardened by plaster of Paris. After all, hand bandages were a new thing, and Jeffries did not wear them, so there was some natural skepticism regarding their effect, even when soft bandages were used.

---

715 *My Life and Battles* at 49-50.
716 *San Francisco Chronicle, San Francisco Call, San Francisco Bulletin,* July 27, 1902.

Jeffries did not mention anything about loaded bandages in his 1910 autobiography. However, in the much later *Two Fisted Jeffries*, he claimed,

> Just as I was going into the ring someone told me that Fitzsimmons had plaster in his bandages, and while still upset about the ring I turned to Delaney and said: 'Make Fitz take those plaster bandages off his hands.' 'Oh let them go,' said Delaney, 'If he can lick you with them on he can lick you with them off.' ... I did not relish those bandages. Rather than have an argument with Delaney at that stage of the proceedings I allowed Fitz to wear the bandages he had on his hands, and, as a result, I received the worst butchering of my life. ... The plaster of Paris in the bandages had hardened and they had the same effect as if he had brass knuckles on each hand.

Jeff also claimed, "After the fight Fitz admitted he had worn plaster of Paris in his bandages, but I held no hard feelings against him and we became the best of friends and chums later. I blamed myself and Delaney for carelessness."[717]

Other later versions claimed that Delaney discovered the plaster of Paris under the bandages before the bout but that Jeff just shrugged and essentially did not care.[718]

It was known before the fight that soft bandages would be allowed. Referee Graney had said so. "By soft bandages is meant the regular linen strips used by surgeons and not heavy bicycle tape. Furthermore the linen must be put on in the ring."

It is clear that both Jeffries and Delaney examined the bandages before the fight and made no objection to them. A local next day report noted, "Jeffries shook hands with Fitz and then examined the bandages on the Cornishman's hands. He turned away as though satisfied." It later said, "The gloves which were to be used by the fighters were examined by the police officials and pronounced satisfactory. ... Delaney scrutinized the bandages on Fitz's hands and took no exception to them. Jeffries wore no bandages." Thus, both Delaney and Jeffries examined the wraps, made no objection, and there was no debate or controversy before the bout. It could be argued that because hand wraps were something of a novelty at that time, there was much speculation as to their impact. Jeffries might have been looking for an excuse for being cut up so much.

However, the overconfident and/or ignorant Jeff and Delaney might have simply decided to let it go, having been previously forewarned that Fitz wanted plaster to protect his weakening hands. In June, Fitzsimmons had insisted on such protection for his hands because of their fragility. He then said, "All I want is a little bit of sticking plaster on my hand where it

---

717 *Two Fisted Jeffries* at 210-213.
718 Rex Lardner, *The Legendary Champions* (N.Y.: American Heritage Press, 1972), 140.

was hurt before." Jeffries responded, "I have no objection to that. It will be subject to the inspection of the referee, of course."[719]

After the fight, Jeffries said, "Fitz should never have cut me up at all. The bandages on his hands did the mischief." Jeffries and Fitzsimmons conversed:

> "Those things on your hands cut me up a lot," said Jeffries, feeling the tape on Fitzsimmons' hands. "You didn't wear them the last time and your blows never cut me up the way they did tonight." "Never mind the bandages, Jim, there were punches behind them. But say, ain't I all right for an old man?" "You are," said Jeffries. "You are the greatest natural fighter that ever was."

It sounded as if Jeffries was not referencing plaster of Paris, but rather the fact that Fitz was wearing wraps at all. Fitz had worn no hand wraps in their first fight, but did so in their second bout, so this, Jeff opined, must explain why he was so cut up. However, Fitz was known for having the hardest punch in boxing, so it should not be that surprising that he did damage.

Still, the following year, when negotiating the terms of a fight with Corbett, Jeffries did not want to allow Corbett to wear hand bandages, saying that they made the hands like plaster of Paris. Jeff said, "When I fought Fitz last time…he wore bandages which were like a plaster cast. Ordinarily my skin is not easy to open, but when Fitz let go those plaster casts they simply cut me open. The bandages were so hard they even hurt Fitz's hands." When Corbett said that Jeff could have a representative observe the wrapping process, Bill Delaney responded, "That's all right, Jim; but you may accidentally 'slip' your hand in a bucket of plaster of paris while meandering from your dressing room to the ring."[720]

Even as early as 1905, the *Police Gazette* wrote, "It is said that Fitz used to put moistened plaster of Paris on his linen bandages and let the mass grow hard. Then he would have a rocky ridge across his hand that could be felt straight through the glove."[721] No definitive answer was given at the time of the fight. All that can be said is that Jeffries blamed the bandages for cutting him up. However, multiple subsequent statements gave the impression that Fitz had indeed dipped his hands into plaster of Paris.

Ironically, if Fitzsimmons had worn loaded wraps, although it might have helped him cut Jeffries and hit harder, the hardened plaster might have also eventually led to Bob's hands being more injured, something which Jeff referenced. Certainly, taking punches from hardened plaster further adds to Jeff's reputation for having an iron chin.

The historically overlooked controversy is that there was an allegation that the fight was fixed, although this appears to have been a product of the

719 *National Police Gazette*, June 14, 21, 1902, August 9, 1902.
720 *Philadelphia Public Ledger, Press, Inquirer*, March 2, 1903; *National Police Gazette*, March 21, 28, 1903.
721 *Police Gazette*, July 15, 1905.

time's yellow journalism, which sought to generate controversy in order to boost newspaper sales. *The San Francisco Examiner's* lead boxing writer, W.W. Naughton, claimed to have received information that Jeff would win in the 8th round, and had given the mayor a sealed letter saying so before the fight. *The Examiner*, under the ownership of William Randolph Hearst, was known to be a bit on the order of the sensational at times.

Naughton said that he received "an intimation" that the fight was to be won by Jeff in the 8th round, and that "one of the party who was with Jeffries at Harbin Springs had told my informants to bet that Jeffries would earn the decision in the round named."

Naughton said the way that Fitz was knocked out seemed very strange.

> He was always on the alert and never to be caught napping in the first part of the fight, but when the crisis came his hands were down by his side and two blows were struck by Jeffries that knocked him out. Fitzsimmons was talking all this time, and seemed wholly off his guard, which, to say the least, is a very strange thing. ... No one could quite understand how Jeffries had won. Fitz seemed to be doing the better work except in the seventh round, and the finish was a puzzle to many. ... Fitzsimmons certainly is a wonderful fighter. I respected his powers last night more than I ever did before, whatever I might think of his honesty.

The suggestion was that Bob allowed Jeff to knock him out.

Mayor Eugene Schmitz confirmed Naughton's allegations. Schmitz said that the *Examiner* gave him a sealed letter that was not to be opened until called for to do so. He opened the letter shortly before midnight on the night of the fight. It said that Jeffries was to win the fight in the 8th round.

The mayor said that it looked to be a fair fight up until the knockout, but that the ending looked odd.

> I am not prepared to say that the fight was a fake, but it certainly looked queer. Both men fought fairly for seven rounds and there was absolutely nothing that happened that might have caused suspicion. Then in the eighth round the unexpected happened. Fitzsimmons had his hands by his side when the blow was struck. Here is the letter left by Mr. Naughton in my possession in which it was stated that the fight would end in the eighth round. It was not to be opened until 11:30 o'clock and I came to my office with witnesses to open it. It is a coincidence that can not be passed with a trivial notice. ... I shall make a careful inquiry and if I find that my suspicions are justified I shall hereafter oppose the granting of permits for prize ring contests in this city.

Naughton and Schmitz questioned why Bob's hands were down. "Perhaps so much stress would not be placed on this fact were it not for the information given to me on the night before the exhibition that the contest would end, and in favor of Jeffries, in the eighth round."

Most of the civil servants and others interviewed from the crowd did not believe the fight was a fake. Quite the contrary, they thought it was the best fight they had ever seen. A police judge said, "If that fight was a fake I want to see nothing but fakes. It was one of the fastest and best fights I ever saw. Fitzsimmons had all the best of it for a time, but he unquestionably got the finishing punch. He was put out and all this talk of fake is the most utter rot. The fight was perfectly honest if I ever saw an honest fight." Another man said, "If it was a fake it was the best fake I have ever seen."

Another police judge said that there was nothing to be gained by Fitzsimmons taking a dive, given that he was the heavy odds underdog and most thought he would lose. Further, Fitz was such an experienced man at the business that if he really wanted to fake a knockout, he would have done it in a way that no one would have suspected. "He would probably have run into a punch that would have really knocked him down and out, for no one ever pretended that Fitz is afraid of a blow."

Chief of Police Wittman said the fight seemed to be on the level. In fact, according to him, when watching the fight live, the mayor said that it was as fine a fight as he ever saw. Wittman said Fitzsimmons put up a good, hard fight, but "he didn't have much chance."

The captain of detectives echoed that Fitz had no chance. He made a grand showing, and had the speed and strength for a few rounds, but his own exertions finished him. "Each punch he gave left him a little weaker. He made a wonderful showing, but he could not beat Jeffries in a thousand years, but fake, oh, no!" The Oakland chief of police said it was the fairest and squarest fight he ever witnessed. "Jeffries is simply a wonder."

One man gave contradictory statements. On one hand, he saw lips move just before the end of the fight and thought Bob said, "Hit me now." However, he also granted that someone at ringside may have said it, as he was very excited. Still, he also said that in his mind, the fight was entirely on the level. "If Fitz did say 'Hit me now,' it was merely that he knew he had received his finish and wanted the fight to end. He was beaten by the terrible body blows he received."

The Alameda county coroner said that anyone who called the fight a fake either did not know what they were talking about or had an ulterior motive.

> The fight was one of the squarest I have ever witnessed, only I think Jeffries was foolish in making certain concessions that explained why his face was so badly cut up. …
>
> The knockout was as pretty a piece of work as I have ever seen. It is all bosh to say Fitz got right up and took the matter smilingly. It was fully five minutes before he recovered from the blow near the solar

plexus, and he had the expression of agony and distress on his face when he stepped up afterward to shake hands with Jeff. I'll bet Fitz's liver will not be right for months to come. Why, sports who lost almost their every cent said they had nothing to complain of.

Bill Delaney said the fake story was ridiculous and absurd.

I think it is a great injustice to Fitz, taking his age and weight into consideration, and after putting up such a great fight, and after being defeated in one of the greatest and gamest battles in the history of heavyweight pugilism, to be denounced as a faker. As to the letter purported to have been received by Mayor Schmitz, I think he has too much intelligence to notice such an absurdity. Jeff's friends, I myself, have been receiving anonymous letters for some time, saying that the fight would be won in a certain number of rounds. Of course one of them had to come right. I never did like Fitz, but his battle last night won me over.

However, it was noted that atypical of a fight winner, Jeffries seemed anxious to leave the ring. *The Post* noted that Jeff did not seem happy, for he "lost little time in getting out of the ring. In fact, he had to be called back to shake hands." One could speculate that he was either upset at his appearance, or was disgusted at the way matters ended, and wanted to get away from it all. Still, Jeff had left the ring quickly after other fights too.

Negotiations to film the fight broke down, mostly as the result of Fitzsimmons, so we cannot independently determine for ourselves the legitimacy of the knockout. Of course, some could use that to argue that the reason Fitz did not want it filmed was so there would be no evidence. However, the real reason appears to have been financial.

Many of the era's fighters had the habit of speaking to their opponents during a fight, including Fitzsimmons. Fitz had had spoken with Jeff in the 7th round as well. It appeared that Jeffries had capitalized on a brief moment of carelessness. That is, if you believe the versions which claimed that Bob spoke to Jeff before the big blows landed. However, other versions said that Fitz spoke with Jeff after he had been hit with the big body shot, letting him know that he had enough.[722]

The Examiner made various claims regarding what Fitzsimmons said prior to the knockout. The referee was quoted as saying that Fitz said, "That was a Peach," after receiving a blow to the stomach. Another claimed that Fitz said, "Hit me now!" Jeff then hit him in the body and down Bob went. Both Jeff and Fitz vehemently denied that claim.

Fitzsimmons insisted that he was hit with a big body blow that either broke or almost broke his ribs. Although he could hardly breathe, he said as Jeff approached, "I'm gone, Jim."

---

722 *National Police Gazette*, August 9, 1902.

Referee Ed Graney felt that the fight was honest. He noted that both men were clearly giving it their best, and argued that if Fitz intended to throw the fight, he would not have hit Jeffries as hard or as often as he did and risk defeating him, nor would he have taken the punishing blows which he did throughout. That punishment explained why he was worn down. He confirmed that a left hook to the body did the trick.

> Fitz was hit in the body two or three times hard enough to knock any man out. There were sixty pounds difference in weight, and the punishing that Fitz took in the body was terrible. He got an awful punching in the round before the last. In the eighth round Fitz turned and said, 'That was a peach.' He referred to the punch he got in the stomach. Then he got a left-hand hook, and then he got a little one on the jaw on top of it, and he went down. During the fight, Fitz hit Jeffries hard enough to knock his head off. In the seventh round he tottered Jeffries with a left-hand punch. He just cut him to pieces. But age was against him. Fitz is a light man. He got hit hard enough to be killed. Fitz was jabbing Jeffries to death. I sat Fitz in his corner myself, and he said, 'I think you broke my rib, Jim.' I thought that Fitz seemed to be as clever as he ever was, and faster than he ever was before..... I think the fight was legitimate.

However, the *Examiner* questioned the referee's version of what was said. It also questioned how a man could speak after getting hit with a supposedly devastating body shot. "Now, those who saw Corbett at Carson after he received that solar plexus punch know that he wasn't saying it was a peach, a plum or a piece of mince pie. He wasn't able to say anything. If Fitzsimmons didn't say, 'Now, hit me,' there is nothing in the reading of lips."

The San Francisco Evening Post, like the *Examiner*, tried to hype and capitalize on the fix claims, also saying that the fight terminated in a fake. Regarding the end, the *Post* said, "Fitz had been talking to Jeff. What he was saying could not be heard, but a moment or so later Fitz was on all fours on the floor, sent there apparently by a light tap on the jaw." Obviously, this writer missed the body shot that everyone else noticed. Many in the crowd were surprised by the suddenness of the ending. They could not understand how Fitz, after having done so well, should so suddenly succumb. "It was the queerest kind of ending to an otherwise exciting fight."

Jeffries laughed at the suggestions that the fight was a fake. "Of course the fight was on the square. It is ridiculous to talk of anything else. Fitz fought a hard fight, the gamest I ever saw."

During the night of the 25th, Fitzsimmons complained about his ribs, some of which he thought were broken. He showed his swollen hands and said that they had been useless since the 2nd round. The day after the fight, Bob had a slight mark under his right eye, and his left wrist, knuckles, and fingers were badly swollen. Bob complained of pains due to the body blows that he had received. He also said that he could not lift his left arm, and had a severe pain under his heart. "I didn't feel that last night. I feel pretty bad today altogether."

The Fitz folks were upset over the fix claims. They asked, "What was there to gain?" A Fitz representative offered $10,000 for any real proof of a fix. Upset and saddened, Fitzsimmons was actually in tears as he denied the story, looking regretfully at his crippled hands.

> It's a damn, malicious lie. ... It's a shame to call it a fake. ... I fought the greatest fight of my life and here I have been branded as a cur. There I was winning all the time, but I couldn't have won anyway. Both hands were gone. I've fought three hundred and twenty-eight battles and have been defeated twice, both times by Jeffries. That shows he is the better man, doesn't it? ... As God is my judge I did my best.

Bob's wife said that the story was a scheme designed to boom the *Examiner*. She said that her Bob had done his best, but had gone down because the other man got in the right punch at the right time. George Dawson, Bob's chief trainer, had sent multiple telegrams to all of his friends advising them to bet on Fitzsimmons. If it was a fake, he would have advised them to bet on Jeffries.

Soldier Tom Wilson, one of Fitz's trainers, stuck up for Bob.

> Fake! Not on your life. If ever a man trained faithfully for a fight it was Bob Fitzsimmons. ... Fitz was determined to win over Jeffries or die in the attempt. No amount of money could have made him lay down or take part in a fake. He was too anxious to win. ... I was with him for weeks at Skagg's Springs and sparred with him daily. ... He left no stone unturned to get in the best possible condition.

Unfortunately, Wilson was unable to see the fight, because the government had ordered him to report to his post of duty and he had to leave two days before the fight. He was back at Fort Meyer, Virginia in the service of Uncle Sam.[723]

Many questioned the source of Naughton's information. Apparently, a mysterious woman had written him a letter telling him that Fitz was to go out in the 8th round. However, various fortune tellers had made these types of predictions before many fights, with varying success. Bob was actually aware of the prediction before the fight.

> I knew some woman had written to Naughton that I was to lay down in the eighth. I was told of it yesterday afternoon. ... When I got in distress in the eighth last night I thought of the letter and tried to stall off the end, but I couldn't do it. I remember that as I went down I

---

723 *National Police Gazette*, August 23, 1902.

said or tried to say, 'I'm gone,' but I guess it wasn't any more than a gasp. He took all the wind out of my body. I did not say, 'That was a peach,' and if I smiled, as they say I did, that must have been a smile of pain. I tried to last, but I couldn't. I got what I gave many a good man. It was the same blow that I gave Corbett, only it was a little to one side, but it did the business.

Sometime during the fight Jeff got in one that caught me under the heart. I didn't feel it much then, but this morning about 2 o'clock it caught me good, and I thought I was going to die. I can't raise my left hand now.

Fitzsimmons said he tried as hard as he could, but just got caught.

It does look funny, but my God! I tried my best. My hands were gone in the second round and I couldn't hurt Jeffries any more. I hit him on the ear with my right and that went. He got me like I got Corbett. ... It only takes a punch to knock a man in a fight, and the punch came.

Why should I go out in this fight? I was offered $750,000 to throw the Corbett fight. ... I was offered $1,000,000 to throw the Sharkey fight, but my honor always stood before me. ... So help me God, I had nothing to do with a fake. ... May God strike me dead if I faked.

If it was a fake, it was a good one, because Bob blasted Jeff with a lot of great punches, and busted him up. Certainly if Fitz was faking, he was risking that he would blow it by knocking Jeffries out first. The punishment to the face nearly closed Jeff's eyes. Fitz was in his best form, and was unaffected by Jeff's crouch. Jeffries appeared fast in his training sessions, but seemed slow when compared to Bob, who stabbed him repeatedly in the face, nose, eyes, and chin. Jeff's face was a sight to remember. "And yet the gladiator from the southland had the hardihood to declare that he was not hurt." Certainly, if one believes that Fitz wore loaded gloves, it would be incongruous to do so while simultaneously intending to take a dive.

Fitzsimmons said it seemed contradictory to say he threw the fight when it was obvious that he was doing his best to knock Jeffries out. "I punished Jeff as I never punished a man before. I split his ear, I broke his nose, I cut his face up – and to say that I was faking!" Bob also said, "If anybody thinks Jeff hasn't got a punch in him, he's badly fooled, I tell you; and if anybody tells you he can't stand punishment, don't you believe him."

Bob said that he would give up his end of the purse if the mayor could prove that he was connected with a fake. That body shot incapacitated him. "I couldn't speak for some time. The blow simply takes away a man's breath, and he can do nothing."

Fitzsimmons intended to sue W.W. Naughton, the *Examiner*, and the Hearst-owned newspapers on the ground of libel, and ask for punitive damages in the sum of $100,000. Bob said that his whole soul was wrapped up in the battle and he badly wanted to win. However, unscrupulous people had tainted his performance. He challenged them to produce evidence other than the letter, which to his mind was simply a lucky guess.

> No man could have fought better than I did; in all my life I never fought better, but after the second round, when my hands began to cave in, I knew that the only chance I had was to keep jabbing. Jeff was too strong and big for me to reach effectively in this way, and when the end came in the eighth that letter, ever in my mind, stirred every bit of gameness in my carcass. I thought, 'If I can only get on my feet.' 'If I can only stall this through to the next round, then that letter will be given the lie.' But nature refused. It was no use. I could not get up. My breath was gone, but my head was clear. The blow that Jeff thought he landed on my jaw went around to my ear, and I knew that Graney was counting me out. I realized it fully, yet, I was helpless to aid myself. I was all in.[724]

Jeffries said that he would give Corbett the next chance to fight him. He acknowledged that Jim was a very nimble and exceedingly clever fighter, tough to beat in a short rounds fight because of his fancy displays. However, he had no doubt that he could stop him in a long fight because he would wear Corbett out. "As you know, such fights as those through which I have passed are not to discover who is the better boxer, but to demonstrate who is the better man. They are to show which of the two opponents can stand the exhausting pace the longer and come out the victor in the end irrespective of the amount of punishment inflicted."

Bill Delaney was concerned that all the fake talk would hinder a possible fight with Corbett. Regarding the allegations, Delaney said, "Why, when Jeffries couldn't see for the blood streaming down his face, he was chasing Fitz around the ring, landing blows on him all the time. Does that look as if he was not trying his utmost to put him out? The idea is ridiculous." Delaney said he picked Jeff to win in 8 rounds, but that was just a prediction based on the fact that Fitz lasted 11 rounds the last time, and he felt that Bob could not last as long this time. He believed that Fitz was on the decline after the 5th round, and instructed Jeffries to press the action. He said it was a right to the stomach under Bob's left that took his wind, and then a follow-up blow to the chin that finished him.

Delaney realized that Jeffries needed time to heal his face, which was puffed up, blackened and bruised. Jeff had four stitches over his left eye. Under his right eye were two stitches drawing together a deep cut. His eyes were visible through narrow slits in his black and blue eyelids, which were swelled up. His nose was puffy and his forehead had a large lump.

---

724 *San Francisco Bulletin,* July 27, 1902.

The surgeon who was treating him said that the cartilage in his nose being separated from the bridge had caused the excessive bleeding. However, he also said that it was not broken. Still, others reported that Jeff had broken cartilage. Clearly though, Jeff's face proved that he had been in with a man who was trying his best to win.[725]

Fitz was practically unmarked but was actually more seriously injured. The knuckles of his left hand were knocked back, allegedly in the 4th round. His hand was swollen to double its size, and he could barely move his left arm. A blow over the heart in the 5th round seemed to paralyze the muscles of the shoulder and arm. Fitz went to one of the bathhouses the day after the fight and fainted while there, not recovering for some minutes.

The Bulletin noted that the gambling results did not support the allegations of a fake. The betting was fairly light, given that most thought that Jeff would win, and at Corbett's saloon, where most of the wagering took place, only one bet was made that Jeff would win in the 8th round, and it was for only $10.

An upset Jeffries said that he had never taken part in a fake and never would.

> If I were a party to a fake, I would never agree to take the beating I did. This is not the first time I have been marked up, but I always bring home the money. I have fought every man who has had championship aspirations and never received credit for my work. ... I was never guilty of a dishonorable act in my life, and I am not going to commence now.

Jeff said that any talk of a fake was ridiculous. "Fitz fought a hard fight, the gamest I ever saw. ... He worked hard all the time and when I got in the double blow on him he was taken off his guard." He angrily said,

> Anyone who says that that fight was a fake is either crazy or a – liar. Look at my face. Does that look like a fake? ... Look at my whole face. Maybe it is painted and is all a fake. Better try and rub some of this color out. Now, let me tell you that I don't have to fight. ... I have money and I can go into many kinds of businesses by which I can make more than I could at my trade. All my life I have tried to be on the square, and I think I have succeeded. ...

> They can all welt me there if they want to, but I'll give it to them in the end. ... [Fitz] walloped me his hardest in the fight we had before in New York. ... He couldn't hurt me there, but I could hurt him where I wanted to, and that was in the wind. ... Not once during the eight rounds was I distressed. With all the blood that was coming from my nose I only had to gargle once, and so that shows how good my wind was and how easily I was going. When a crowd sees blood

725 *San Francisco Examiner*, July 26, 27, 1902.

on a man they think it's all off with him, but I am not one of that kind.

Jeff noted that the money was all wrong for there to be a fake. If anyone was going to take a dive to make a killing in wagers, he should have been the one to do so, because he was the heavy favorite, so betting on Bob would have meant a lot of money if Fitz had won. Instead, because he was such the heavy favorite, his friends were betting thousands on Jeffries in order to win hundreds. Fitz had little to gain by a fix because he was the clear betting underdog. "I think it is a crime to treat Fitz this way, and those who are doing it I don't think much of. He didn't fake."[726]

Local fight promoter J. H. Gibbs brought up the fact that Fitzsimmons years earlier admitted to throwing a fight with Jim Hall early in his career, so he would not put it past him. One writer said Bob's ribs were not cracked.

Jeffries continued to insist it was a legitimate fight, saying, "I only beat him by the same kind of a blow in the body that I have won most of my battles with." He noted that there were some allegations of fake when Ruhlin quit from his body blows as well. It was his belief that critics were not giving him his due credit for his success against a wonderful fighter.[727]

Responding to its competitor's claims, the *San Francisco Chronicle* reported that most denounced the cry of fake as ridiculous. There was no doubt that Fitz was trying to take Jeff out. Jeff's face was badly battered. His cuts required many stitches, and strips of plaster held together the slit in Jeff's upper lip.

The Chronicle said that only one person in a crowd of 7,000 could hear Bob say, 'Hit me now.' "This statement is so much at variance with the facts as to make it ridiculous." It noted that the letter handed to the mayor was "not to be opened unless Jeffries did win in the eighth," demonstrating that Naughton was not all that certain of his knowledge. It observed that usually when a fight is fixed, many pick it up like wildfire and it affects the betting. Yet, there was practically no betting on the fight.

A close ringsider said, "The blow that Jeffries struck Fitzsimmons under the heart in the eighth round was of sufficient force to floor an ox. … It is imbecile to say that he went down on purpose. Up to that moment he had fought the pluckiest fight I ever saw." George Siler insisted that it was a legitimate fight, and ridiculed the idea of a fake. Another referee said, "No mortal man at his age could stand the body punches Jeff gave him."

Joe Gans, the black world lightweight champion, said,

> No way can you look at that affair and call it a fake. It was simply a great fight and one of the best that I have ever seen. Fitz could have licked anyone else in the world last night. His punch was enough to put anyone away barring the man he met. People don't seem to

726 *San Francisco Bulletin*, July 27, 1902.
727 *San Francisco Examiner*, July 27, 1902.

recognize what a marvel of strength that Jeffries is, and how well he knows how to put the steam behind his blows.

A sporting authority who sat ringside said he saw and heard nothing to make him think it was a fix. "I have seen Fitz in his boxing exhibitions do a fake stunt, as though knocked out, and the worst he ever did could be called crude beside the real article last night."[728]

During the afternoon of the 26th, the day after the fight, the two boxers had a chance meeting. Jeff said, "Do I look like I've been in a fake fight?" Bob replied, "I thought maybe I only dreamed I punched you a little last night." Glancing at his own puffed hand, Fitz said, "You have a hard head. I got this when I landed on your forehead and raised that bump." Jeff replied,

> It's lucky for me most of those lefts you landed on the side of my head were high or it would have been all off with me. I thought you had me in the second round when I got that smash in the nose. I didn't feel any too happy in the fourth, either. I told Delaney I would have to get you quickly, as I was afraid my eyes would close on me.

> The ridiculous part of the *Examiner* story is where a writer, who was seated thirty feet from where the fight ended, saw your lips move forming the words 'Now, hit me.' In another place he says: 'Fitz got in a nasty righthander and Jeff ducked from another right which might have settled the fight.' You were certainly careless of consequences if it was fixed for me to win. Those bandages you wore were what cut me up so; they were like knives. I didn't wear bandages, as whenever I do I hurt my hands instead of saving them.

Apparently, Jeff's seconds thought he would win easily, for they only had a small sponge in the corner, and had difficulty in getting rid of the blood on him.[729]

The San Francisco Call's headline on the 27th said, "Sportsmen are Enthusiastic over Fight and Ridicule the Lame Story of a Fake." It said that there was no foundation in fact for such a silly allegation. Experts were satisfied that the fight was not only legitimate, but the greatest battle in history. It called the *Examiner's* attack on the boxers unjust. "If Jeffries and Fitzsimmons did fake – and ninety-nine out of every hundred present at the battle are willing to go broke financially that they did not – then both should enter the vaudeville ranks. They would become famous as the

---

728 *San Francisco Chronicle*, July 27, 1902. In May 1902, American black Joe Gans had won the world lightweight championship with a KO1 over Frank Erne, joining Joe Walcott of Barbados, who won the welterweight title in December 1901, as the only black men to own a world title at that point. Fellow black, Canadian George Dixon, had lost the world featherweight crown in early 1900 with a LKOby9 to Terry McGovern. Gans would hold his lightweight title until mid 1908. Walcott lost his title in 1904 in a fight that was likely fixed by the referee. As a result, Joe continued being considered the champion until losing the title in 1906.
729 *San Francisco Call*, July 27, 1902.

world's great knockout team." *The Call* said that there was only about 15 seconds left in the 8th round, so Bob was certainly cutting it close if he had intended to throw it in that round.

Alex Greggains, on behalf of the San Francisco Athletic Club, offered $1,000 to anyone who could prove the fight was a fake. Fitz said he would give up his share of the purse and his home in Bensonhurst if it could be shown that he was party to any type of improper agreement.

However, both the *Evening Post* and the *Examiner* continued to question the fight's legitimacy. *The Post* held that the strong defense being put up by the fight folks was necessary in order to save pugilism.

> They know that unless some kind of a defense more opaque than the fight is faked up, pugilism is dead in this city. They wish to protect the "sport" and are prepared to do so by originating any kind of a fairy story that will explain why Bob went down and out in the eighth round at a time when he appeared to have Jeffries at his mercy and to be master of the situation.

> Neither Fitzsimmons nor his numerous friends have yet been able to furnish an explanation of the conversation which passed between the two bruisers in Fitzsimmons' corner just before the "knockout" blow was struck. It is very peculiar that men, fighting as they claim, almost for their lives, should hold a chat, at the expiration of which one dropped his arms in a helpless condition and the other administered a blow which sent the faker down and out.[730]

Four days after the fight, despite crediting Jeff's hard blows and the competitive fight Bob put up, Naughton wrote, "The majority of the men who saw that contest think they saw an honest battle. I know I saw a fraudulent knock-out."[731]

When attending a baseball game, Jeff was asked, "What kind of a talk was that you and Fitz had in the ring?" Jeffries replied,

> Talk, talk, all the talk we had was when he started to fight me in the clinch that time. Graney jumped between us and said: 'If you fellows are going to fight that way go ahead.' Fitz replied: 'I don't want to fight that way.' I said, 'Oh, that is all right. That was accidental,' or words to that effect. Now that was every solitary word that passed between us.[732]

Jeff was scheduled to leave on a two-week hunting trip in the Sonoma County mountains. He would then return to Los Angeles, to fish to his heart's content.

---

730 *San Francisco Evening Post*, July 28, 1902.
731 *San Francisco Examiner*, July 29, 1902.
732 *San Francisco Bulletin*, July 31, 1902.

On the 30th, Fitzsimmons met with Mayor Schmitz. Bob vehemently denied that he did anything dishonest. He told the mayor how his hands had failed him and how Jeff struck him in an unguarded, careless moment. Bob impressed the mayor as an honest man with an honest face.

It was revealed that Mrs. Alfred Hall was the one who had claimed that Jeffries would win in the 8th round. Mrs. Hall was a guest at Harbin Springs while Jeff was training there. She was a fortune teller. She used cards to tell Jeffries his fortune one night, and the cards showed that he would win in the 8th round. This statement became generally known amongst the folks at the springs, and when the *Examiner*'s W.W. Naughton visited there, Mrs. Hall told him that Jeff would win in the 8th. "Mrs. Hall now believes that she brought all the trouble upon Fitzsimmons and bravely comes forward to vindicate him." Naughton's inside source had been a fortune teller.[733]

A writer for the *National Police Gazette* said that the prediction and claim of a fix was a trick played by Naughton. He sealed it in an envelope and gave it to the mayor, yet reserved the right to request that the unopened envelope be returned if he was not correct. This trick had been perpetrated many times, but the prediction was only announced afterwards if it happened to be correct. This *Gazette* author said that he had predicted that Jeff would stop Ruhlin in 5 rounds, but did not go around claiming a fix when he was correct. "I didn't shoot off any fireworks and pretend to know that the whole thing was a fraud." A guess was not evidence of a fix, or necessarily of marvelous judgment. He felt that the absence of a motive, together with the splendid battle, disproved the claims. He called Naughton's action a "stunt."

Regarding the fight, Fitzsimmons outclassed Jeffries in science, but Jeff's great strength pulled him through. His face was smashed and cut up, but he was never distressed, and nothing Bob did deterred Jeff's attack. Jeffries landed hard body shots in the 7th round and he kept up a great pace, looking to break his opponent.

> The knockout seemed to come through Fitz's lack of attention for a moment. He made some remark to Jeffries as Jeffries missed with his right. Then came a left hook to the head. Fitz's hands dropped for a moment and he looked as though he would slip under Jeffries' arm again as he had done so often before, but Jeffries brought out his left again and landed a fearful blow just above the solar plexus and Bob fell as though he had been hit by an ax.

This writer did not think it made sense for the men to give and take such punishment if it was a fix. He also believed that given how well Bob was doing, even if it was fixed, he would have double crossed Jeff to win the championship again. Bob could have made big money as champion just

---

733 *San Francisco Call*, July 31, 1902.

as a road attraction. He too noted that given the 3 to 1 odds, the big money would have been made by Jeff taking a dive, not Bob. "No, it was no fake. Fitz lost because he was up against a problem that he, with all his cunning, couldn't solve." It was no surprise to this writer that Jeffries won. Fitzsimmons' wonderful showing made Jeff's victory all the more creditable. He had defeated a very sharp version of Fitz who had been well prepared and fought a great fight, but still could not defeat the great champion.[734]

In late August, the *Police Gazette* reported, "The 'fake' story is gradually being forgotten and the originator of it will hardly again enjoy the public confidence which characterized his career as a sporting writer and critic." It said that the whole thing was an attempt to secure advertising for the newspaper. "Not one man in a hundred believes that the fight was anything but on the level." So, the story was "packed away in moth balls."[735]

---

734 *National Police Gazette*, August 16, 1902.
735 *National Police Gazette*, August 30, 1902.

CHAPTER 33

Media Creation or Legitimate Performance?

Many were excited about the prospect of a Jeffries-Corbett rematch, given how close and competitive their previous bout had been. Jeffries wanted to fight Corbett because he was a big name, likely to generate the most money. Corbett felt that if the bout was 20 rounds instead of 25 that he could win. He was anticipating a bout with Jeffries in November or December 1902, and in August was working out for two hours every morning at Wood's gymnasium in New York.

When Jeffries announced that he would not fight again until the following May, Corbett quit training. Still, Jim said that he would continue taking the best care of himself, anticipating that he would be Jeff's next opponent.[736]

Disconsolate over his second knockout loss to Gus Ruhlin, Tom Sharkey said that he was retiring. He did not enter the ring again for almost two years.

The Police Gazette considered Corbett the "only man now before the public who can claim a legitimate right to meet the champion." It said that if Jeffries could again dispose of Corbett, the champion would likely retire.

> Prize fighting and its attendant notoriety are evidently becoming distasteful to him. … Jeffries has planned to leave the game in two years' time, whether he is defeated in the interim or not, and go into business. … Jeffries has been contemplating retirement from the ring for some time. His parents have urged him to do this, and Jeffries will do so two years from this month. Jeffries is rated as being wealthy. Besides his earnings from boxing, the champion has made money by speculating in stocks and oil.[737]

So, Jeffries had already contemplated retiring no later than late 1904. In the meantime, he went on another one of his lengthy hunting and hiking trips, this time along the Mexican border. An avid outdoorsman, Jeff typically took these excursions between fights.

In November 1902, Corbett was back in training again, expecting to have a fight with Jeffries the following spring. He wanted ample time to get into the best possible condition. "In every city that the former champion

---

736 *National Police Gazette*, August 23, 1902.
737 *National Police Gazette*, November 1, 1902.

visits he selects a gymnasium in which to spend his leisure time when he is not taking road work. He exercises moderately, lives regularly and is keeping pretty well conditioned." Corbett wrote his brother Harry a letter saying that his one desire was to fight Jeffries again. "I know I can whip the big fellow."[738]

In early December, it was reported that Jeff and Corbett were matched to fight in May 1903. Corbett continued training and said that he wanted to be in perfect condition.

Jim Corbett was obviously sincere in his desire to regain the championship, because while he was touring the country with his monologue at vaudeville theaters, every day he was finding time to spend an hour or two at some local gymnasium. He had done the same thing before their first fight. "Corbett asserts that he has been taking a systematic course of training for more than a year, and that he is in better physical condition today than he has been at any time since he won the championship from Sullivan in 1892."

Corbett felt that he had the punch to hurt Jeffries. He noted that despite Jeff's assertion that he was never punched hard enough to be rocked, and had never been knocked down in a fight, Jim again claimed that he had essentially knocked Jeff out while sparring in Carson City.

> He and I used to box every day while in training. One day I accidentally caught him a hard one on the jaw, and it did the business. The big fellow dropped into my arms. If I had not been near him he would have gone to the boards as hard as ever he will in his life. I do not say this to cast any discredit on Jeffries, but then I have seen the incident denied so often that I think out of justice to myself the real truth should be known. When I fought Jim at Coney Island I was not as strong as I am today. I caught him time and again with stiff right-handers that made his massive frame wabble, but he is such a tremendous piece of humanity that it takes an awful blow to put him on his back.[739]

While Jeffries was concerned with scheduling lucrative bouts with top-echelon well-known fighters, other contenders were developing. The same day as the Jeff-Fitz rematch, on July 25 in London, England, avenging an earlier knockout loss, the clever Denver Ed Martin easily won a 15-round decision over Jeff's former sparring partner and opponent, Bob Armstrong, in a battle advertised as being for the colored championship.[740]

In late 1902 and early 1903, Jack Johnson, another black fighter, was also emerging. Johnson's early career had mixed and spotty results, including: 1899 LKOby5 John "Klondike" Haines; 1900 D20 and KO14

---

738 *National Police Gazette*, November 8, 29, 1902.
739 *National Police Gazette*, December 13, 1902.
740 *National Police Gazette*, August 9, 1902; *San Francisco Examiner, San Francisco Call*, July 26, 1902.

Haines; 1901 LKOby3 Joe Choynski, D10 Billy Stift, and L20 and D15 Hank Griffin. 1902 was a much better year for him, and Johnson's results included: KO4 Joe Kennedy, KO5 Jack Jeffries, D20 Hank Griffin, and W20 Mexican Pete Everett. Of course, James Jeffries had fought Choynski to a draw, had knocked out Hank Griffin and Pete Everett, and stopped Kennedy faster.

Still, on October 21, 1902 in Los Angeles, Johnson fought Frank Childs, who some still recognized as the colored champion because Ed Martin had only defeated him in a 6-round decision bout, which they felt was too short to decide a championship. In a terrific fight, Childs dislocated his elbow when striking Jack's head, and after trying to continue, Frank's seconds threw up the sponge to retire him in the 12th round.[741] Just ten days later, on October 31 in San Francisco, Johnson won a 20-round decision over George Gardner, a well-respected fighter who the following year would win the world light heavyweight championship.

On December 10, 1902 in Philadelphia, Ed Martin and Bob Armstrong fought a 6-round no-decision bout which saw both men hit the canvas several times, each narrowly escaping a knockout. Johnson and Martin were headed for a meeting to determine the true colored champion.

In the meantime, after scheduling the Corbett bout, in late 1902, Jeffries and Fitzsimmons negotiated a partnership to tour the country as a sparring combination. Mrs. Fitzsimmons originated the idea, and both Jeff and Bob agreed that they could make good money touring together. The combination made sense, given that they were the two biggest names in boxing, and therefore could attract large crowds. They would spar each other, and sometimes take on local boxers. Their recent fight had increased the respect that Fitz and Jeff felt for one another, and they became friends.[742]

In *Two Fisted Jeffries*, Jeff said Fitz weighed 202 pounds, while he weighed 235. One December report said they went at it pretty hard in a 4-round San Francisco exhibition where 240-pound Jeff tried to stop him early, but Bob came back and cut him up. Another said that in a Seattle exhibition, their

741 *National Police Gazette*, 1902.
742 *National Police Gazette*, November 15, December 6, 1902.

boxing was stopped after 2 rounds when they really mixed it up and Jeff was badly bleeding.[743]

Of course, such reports were likely just hype to stimulate patronage at what were probably generally tame exhibitions. Jeff and Bob likely just worked with each other, although with two greats in the ring, they might have gotten heated up here and there. Two great punchers could not help but land some good ones. One report said, "They do say that when Jeffries and Fitzsimmons get together in their boxing bout, on their present tour, that they put up a smart contest."[744]

Years later, Fitz said of one of their numerous exhibitions,

> While we were giving an exhibition out West one night Jeffries landed a swing on my temple. The effect of the blow glued my feet to the ground. I was stunned, unable to move as I stared at Jeffries. I heard him say, 'the old man is faking again.' He thought I was playing a joke on him, when as a matter of fact I was helpless and he could have come to me with all kinds of wallops and I would have been powerless to resist them.[745]

They exhibited in Spokane, Washington on December 14. Every seat was taken and the aisles were filled in the record house which contained two dozen women and about 1,800 men. Fitz appeared heavier than usual, but was in splendid condition. He showed speed and drove punches into

---

743 *Two Fisted Jeffries* at 220; *Anaconda Standard*, December 19, 20, 1902; *Butte Inter Mountain*, December 20, 1902.
744 *Butte Miner*, December 17, 1902.
745 *National Police Gazette*, February 18, 1905.

Jeff's face and body as if he meant business. Jeff looked fat weighing 230 pounds. However,

> [T]he manner in which [Jeffries] darted around the ring, blocked, feinted, jabbed and swung was a revelation to the uninitiated. The big fellows ducked and clinched, swatted each other on the mouthpiece, landed resounding blows on each other's ribs and were coltish in their actions. They were applauded vigorously.

They were scheduled to appear that week in Coeur d' Alene, Idaho, Missoula, Montana, and at week's end, Butte, Montana.[746] They gave an "intensely realistic" 3-round exhibition in Montana (likely Missoula) on December 18. On December 19, Jeff and Fitz arrived in Butte, Montana.[747]

---

746 *Butte Miner*, December 18, 1902.
747 *Anaconda Standard*, December 20, 1902.

Although Jeffries was intending to give Corbett a rematch in the near future, he thought more of Fitzsimmons, who "gave me the hardest fight of my career, and is still the best of them, next to myself. I would rather take 50 punches from Jim Corbett than to run into one of the pokes that Fitz can hand out. He hits harder than a mule can kick."

Jeffries also said, "I am now entitled to a rest. I am doing pretty well as it is. We are copping off about $10,000 a week, and that is a good deal better than fighting for a purse."

Colored champion "Denver" Ed Martin via his manager Billy Madden (who also managed Ruhlin) had challenged Fitzsimmons, but Bob rebuked his challenge as not being sufficiently financially lucrative. "Yes, I saw that Madden had posted a forfeit…and has given it out that I can make $2,500 by meeting his coon for six rounds…. I dare say that Jeff and I will make that much apiece tonight…. As for that nigger, Martin, he has not claims to fight me." Martin needed to establish himself as a bigger draw.[748]

On December 20, 1902 in Butte, Montana, Jeffries was scheduled to box a 4-round exhibition bout against Jack Munroe, while Fitz was to box Jack Stewart. If either man was to stay the 4 rounds with Jeff or Bob, they would be paid $250, but if they were knocked out, they would receive $100.

It is possible that Munroe had boxed Jack Johnson, although official records do not list this bout. However, one man predicted that the strong 190-pound Munroe would last the 4 rounds against Jeff based on his observation of a Munroe bout with Johnson. "I saw Munro fight Johnson, the heavyweight negro who recently licked George Gardner, and the way Jack cut that big coon up was a caution. He had the negro clean out in the eighth round, but the black one managed to recuperate and stay the limit."[749]

Like Corbett, Munroe had learned to box in San Francisco and had won the Olympic Club's 1900 amateur heavyweight championship. An ex-football player, he was known for having a big punch. As a professional, Munroe used to spar with Tom Sharkey, Joe Kennedy, and Jack O'Brien, but had not fought since losing a 1900 20-round decision to Hank Griffin.[750]

Tom Sharkey said that Munroe was about 6 feet tall, 210 pounds, and was fast, aggressive, and the hardest hitter he ever faced. Munroe was as strong as a bull, and it took all of Tom's power to make Jack break ground. He said that Munroe had knocked out Fred Russell and Yank Kenny. Jack

748 *Butte Inter Mountain*, December 20, 1902; *Butte Miner*, December 21, 1902.

749 *Anaconda Standard, Butte Miner*, December 20, 1902. Jack Johnson was the one who had recently defeated Gardner in a 20-round decision, so perhaps Munroe had fought him. It was not stated when or where this bout took place, or what the scheduled distance or result was. It is possible that the writer confused Johnson with Hank Griffin.

750 *San Francisco Examiner*, December 22, 1902; Boxrec.com. Some secondary source records indicate that in 1901, Munroe possibly fought Griffin to a rematch 20-round draw.

Beauscholte later said that he had boxed Munroe in training, and that Munroe was something of a fighter.[751]

The 26-year-old Munroe said that he had not fought since 1900, having for the past two years worked in the mines. At the time of the Jeffries bout, Munroe was listed as standing 5'11 ½" and weighing 195 pounds.[752]

This was another bout which the result would be questioned, discussed, and debated for years to come. Via telegraph, a sensational story spread around the nation like wildfire. The Hearst-owned *San Francisco Examiner*, which never shied away from an eye-catching story, reported that Jeff had offered $250 to anyone who could last 4 rounds. Earlier in the evening, Fitzsimmons quickly knocked out his opponent, Jack Stewart, in the 1st round. Jeffries and Munroe then fought 4 fast rounds.

> Monroe hit the champion square on the point of the jaw and sent him to his knees, following it up with several ugly jabs that nearly made a knockout possible. Monroe was too shifty for Jeffries and most of the blows of the big champion went wild. Monroe was still aggressive at the end of the fourth.

It further said that Munroe repeatedly landed a number of jabs and "displayed unexpected cleverness, and, although he went down several

751 *Butte Miner*, December 26, 28, 1902.
752 *Anaconda Standard*, December 22, 1902; *National Police Gazette*, January 17, 1903; February 14, 1903.

times, it was more through Jeffries' great weight than the punishment inflicted." However, Munroe took as much of the count as he could each time he went down.

The next day, the *Examiner* followed up with yet another report which said that Jeff was wobbly on his feet in the 4th round and had previously been down by a stiff punch on the jaw. Jeff recovered quickly after the knockdown. Munroe was still aggressive in the 4th and referee Duncan McDonald, a former fighter and James J. Corbett pal (who likely engaged in hippodromes with Corbett), awarded Munroe the decision. Fitz said that Jeff was clearly out of form. Jeff said it was the first decision rendered against him, but that he would have wagered his life that he could have knocked out Munroe in the next round.

This story was echoed throughout the nation. *The Seattle Post-Intelligencer* also reported that Jeff lost a decision after 4 rounds of the fiercest fighting Butte had seen for some years. At one point, Jeff went to his knees, and a knockout looked possible. Munroe, who had been the amateur champion of the Pacific coast, was game to the core, and argued every inch with Jeffries. He repeatedly landed jabs to the face and jarred him considerably. He blocked many vicious uppercuts, and displayed unexpected cleverness. It too noted that although Jack went down several times, it was more as a result of Jeff's great weight than the punishment inflicted. He took the count each time he went down and met all of Jeff's rushes. Jeff was puffing freely at the end, while Munroe had a slightly bloody nose.

Jeffries told the newspapers that the decision was unwarranted, for Munroe was only entitled to the $250 forfeit for lasting 4 exhibition rounds. He said that had the bout gone one more round, he would have knocked Munroe out. The altitude affected him, and he was afraid of overexertion. Still, he also said that Jack could stand a lot of punishment, and he believed that Munroe could whip Tom Sharkey.[753]

Even one semi-local Montana paper, the *Billings Gazette*, said that the miner knew the game, showed cleverness in ducking and blocking, and fought 4 fast rounds. Jeff failed to stop him as agreed to and therefore lost the decision.

> Monroe repeatedly jolted Jeffries in the face and had the big fellow considerably worried…. Jeffries tried his very best to knock the big miner out, but he showed great cleverness in ducking and blocking uppercuts. Jeffries also roughed it in the clinches, but Monroe was with him all the time.
>
> At one time the champion went to his knees and a knockout looked possible.

753 *San Francisco Examiner, Seattle Post-Intelligencer,* December 21, 22, 1902. Various papers spelled Jack's last name "Monroe" or "Munroe," but over time, "Munroe" seems to have won out.

These are the types of reports disseminated around the country. They made Munroe instantly famous and a hot commodity with the public.

However, there is evidence that such reports were embellished. Even after Jeff boxed Munroe, "Jeffries and Fitzsimmons wound up the program with a lively four-round exhibition." If Jeff was fatigued, hurt, and about to be done up, it is not likely that he would continue on with 4 more lively rounds with Bob Fitzsimmons. Furthermore, Fitz afterwards posted an unaccepted forfeit of $500 to knock out Munroe in 4 rounds. If Munroe was so good, why did he not also accept Fitz's proposition for double the money?[754]

Also, the reports appear to do their best to minimize the fact that Munroe went down several times and took as much of the count as possible. Reading between the lines, he was doing what some folks did to survive with John L. Sullivan in his 4-round knockout exhibitions, and what Hank Griffin had done with Jeffries. Munroe was trying to last by killing the clock. His pay depended on survival, not on winning. Was Jeff knocked down? Was he about to be knocked out? The answer is NO!

As usual, this story's veracity must be scrutinized by reviewing the local primary sources, which during the week following the fight provided their own descriptions and discussions of the bout. The national reports appear to be at least partially derived from some local accounts. The local *Butte Miner* next-day report listed Jack Monroe (as this paper spelled it) as 190 pounds, 6 feet tall, and 29 years of age. It said that Monroe showed unexpected cleverness, was game to the core, put up an argument all the way, repeatedly landed jabs to the face, and even jarred Jeff. "[A]lthough he went down several times, it was more through Jeffries' great weight than the punishment inflicted." Jeff roughed it in the clinches when Monroe held.

By the 3rd round, the smile had disappeared from Jeff's face, "and he went in with a determination to do his man up at every punch. Each time Monroe went to his knees he took the count and met all of the big fellow's rushes." A little blood trickled from Monroe's nose, while Jeff was puffing.

In the 4th round, Jeffries did his best to deliver a knockout, but was unable to do so. Referee McDonald gave the decision to Munroe because Jeff had contracted to stop him inside of 4 rounds and had failed to do it. Technically, it was not a decision on the merits, because it was just an exhibition, and there was no contract term allowing for a decision. The referee's decision was on the basis that Jeff had failed to stop his foe as required.

Afterwards, Jeff engaged in a lively 4-round exhibition with Fitzsimmons. The promoter offered Monroe $500 if he could go 4 rounds with Fitz the following Saturday.[755]

---

754 *Billings Gazette*, December 23, 1902.
755 *Butte Miner*, December 21, 1902.

Jeffries laughed at the national fight reports. In an interview with the *Anaconda Standard*, he claimed that he carried Munroe and let him stay the 4 rounds because he wanted the crowd to have some entertainment, given that Fitzsimmons had stopped his man so quickly in the 1st round. The theater's management had asked him to make the go with Munroe look like a good one. He even told Fitz in the corner that he was carrying him. Jeff said that he was afraid that he had unintentionally knocked out Munroe in the 3rd round with a body shot, but the gong saved him. "In the fourth round I was more careful not to hurt Munroe, but even at that time he was scarcely able to stand when the gong ended the affair." Jeffries said that Munroe was no fighter and had no science. Fitzsimmons confirmed that Jeff told him that he was going to let Munroe stay.

Another local paper, the *Butte Intermountain*, confirmed that the management approached Jeffries and asked him to allow Munroe to last the 4 rounds and make a good exhibition because the Fitz-Stewart match had been a farce. As a result, "The champion would swing slowly and let the miner get inside the swing and it was noticeable to all that Jeff never rushed his man." It noted that Jeff was fat, but still could have stopped him if he had tried to do so.

However, the *Butte Miner* disagreed. It said that Jeffries did his best to stop Monroe and failed. "Of course, Monroe was no match for the champion…. But he showed pluck of the highest type, and no matter how viciously Jeffries went at him, he was trying to mix it up with the big fellow at every opportunity." Regardless of whether Jeff was trying to knock him out or not, both local papers agreed that Jeffries was the superior boxer. Neither mentioned anything about Munroe dropping or hurting Jeffries.

Discussing the fight again, the *Butte Miner* said that Jeff let Munroe off easy in the 1st round, thinking that he had an easy task. So it did confirm that he carried him to a certain degree, at least initially. He had evidently intended to carry him for a while to give the fans their money's worth, and then to stop him. However, he found that he had a tougher task ahead of him than he realized.

The surprised Jeffries woke up after Munroe showed some aggressiveness and landed some stiff jabs. Jeff punched freely in the clinches and several times forced Munroe to his knees, but Jack took full advantage of the count to rest. The miner did some nice blocking and eluding of uppercuts. Jeff had him bleeding from the nose in the 3rd round, though Jack also reddened Jeff's nose. Up to the end, Munroe mixed it up. When in danger, he clinched until shaken off. Both were tired at the finish.

> It is conceded that Monroe would not stand as much show with Fitz as he did with Jeffries, for the reason that Fitz is in the better condition. Jeffries has not done any sparring since he last fought Fitz until they started out two weeks ago on this tour.

After the show, Jeff said that he did not cut loose on account of the high altitude. At that time, he admitted that Munroe was tough and much better than he expected him to be. He opined that Jack could make it interesting for many of the aspiring heavyweights. Butte folks were willing to put up $1,000 that no heavyweight could stop Munroe inside of 10 rounds.

Jeffries was upset that the referee had rendered a decision against him. He agreed that Munroe had technically won the money by lasting, but felt that the referee had no right to make a formal decision making it appear that he had lost the bout, for he had not. Still, the local paper said, "This decision goes in the year's record against Jeffries and it will be the first losing mark in his pugilistic career.… No event of the year has attracted so much attention."

The sparring exhibition had generated a $1,500 house. The seats were $3 a piece, which was said to have been too high.[756]

Just two days after the Munroe exhibition bout, on December 22, Jeff and Fitz boxed 3 friendly rounds in Anaconda, Montana.[757]

Jeffries again denied the reports that Munroe had almost knocked him out. In a special dispatch from Helena, Jeff said,

> In the first place, I want to say that the associated press report sent out from Butte that Munroe had me going and that I was down on one knee is absolutely false.… All I can say for Munroe is that he displayed good generalship in going down for the count at least 12 times during the four rounds. That was all that saved him. I would have put him to sleep in the next round as sure as I stand here.

Fitzsimmons confirmed that he had told Jeff to take him out, but Jeffries refused.

Munroe responded to Jeffries, saying,

> When Jeffries says I failed to hit him he is attempting to deny what 1,500 people who witnessed the contest will say is the truth. At least six times I found Jeffries' face, and the fact that it was red and puffy will testify whether or not I hit him. Jeffries did his best to knock me out. Everyone who saw the mill will corroborate what I have said.[758]

The Butte Miner confirmed Munroe's position, saying, "Jeffries' talk now about not desiring to stop Monroe, but that he wanted the people to see an exhibition, will not go down with those who saw the contest."

However, its latest fight description gave Jeffries much more credit than the national reports did. It said that Jeff went at him carelessly in the 1st round, and smiled when Munroe was not afraid and was aggressive. Jack

---

756 *Anaconda Standard, Butte Inter Mountain, Butte Miner,* December 22, 1902.
757 *Anaconda Standard,* December 23, 1902.
758 *Seattle Post-Intelligencer,* December 23, 1902.

landed his left to the nose and sent Jeff's head back with a jar. Before the 2nd round, Fitz urged Jeff to go in and stop Munroe, and the champ tried. The round was lively and Jack went down twice. In the 3rd, Jeff went at him in a determined fashion, but Monroe mixed it up with him. "It is true that in the third round the gong saved Monroe from a knockout. He was down on the floor and taking the count when the gong saved him." Jeff was puffing and less active in the 4th, but tried to deliver a sledgehammer knockout blow. Munroe killed time by hugging, but also struck at the champion.

During the bout, Munroe had repeatedly landed his left, but was more cautious than he might have been, because he wanted to be on guard and prevent a knockout blow. He gave Jeff few opportunities to land a counterpunch. Munroe said, "I was praying to God to stay another round…and that was all I had any hope of doing. I could have landed oftener on Jeff, but I did not want to take chances on a knockout." In conclusion, "It is not contended that Monroe outsparred the champion." However, it insisted that Jeff had tried to put him out and failed.[759]

The Butte Intermountain again confirmed that the nationwide stories had been false.

> It's too bad that an enthusiastic newspaper man allowed himself to be carried away to the extent that he sent an Associated Press report East to the effect that Jack Munroe had knocked Jeffries down. The New York and Chicago papers played the fact up in big type and the papers there sold like hot peanuts. As a matter-of-fact there is not a word of truth in the report. Jeffries has never been knocked down in his life…. As before stated in these columns Munroe put up a great showing and displayed superb grit and generalship, but that "he had Jeff going," is false. He went into the ring to stay four rounds and he succeeded in doing it…. It was in the nature of an exhibition and not a fight. The referee gave Munroe the decision because the miner had entered the ring to stay four rounds and had done it; not because he had the best of the boxing.[760]

During the same week that Jeffries had boxed Munroe, both Jeff and Fitz offered Munroe money to fight either one of them. However, Munroe was holding out for more money, and wanted a greater amount of time to train. Jeff went from offering $500 up to $1,000 for Munroe to stay 4 rounds with him again. Munroe turned it down and said that he was not in any condition to fight successfully against anyone, let alone Jeff or Fitzsimmons. Of course, if he was not in condition to do so, how had he just allegedly done it? His excuse reveals that he had not done as well as some in the media had reported. It also suggests that Munroe might have

759 *Butte Miner*, December 23, 1902.
760 *Butte Inter Mountain*, December 24, 1902.

been aware of the fact that Jeffries held back for at least part of the bout, and perhaps suspected that if Jeff got going sooner, that he might not have lasted the 4 rounds.[761]

However, there was some good business sense to Munroe's refusal to immediately rematch Jeffries. He had become a hot prospect as a result of the nationwide reports of his showing, and intended to milk it for all it was worth. "He has firmly established himself in the public view by standing off the champion for four rounds." Munroe could develop an even bigger payday for himself by waiting.

Jeff and Fitz were set to exhibit in Great Falls, Montana on December 25. In Bozeman, Montana, Jeff did not perform, but Fitz knocked out 180-pound Mike Ranke in the 2nd round. It was said that Jeff wanted to train for a while before undertaking to stop someone again.

Six days after the Munroe bout, the *Butte Miner* noted that some eastern papers were reporting that Munroe had Jeff going. It again said that such was not the case.

> Jeffries has received a good deal of unjust notoriety out of his meeting with Munroe.... At no time did Munroe have the champion going, or anything like it. He stayed with him four rounds and was fighting with him at the close of the fourth, when Jeffries was doing all in his power to stop him. Jeff had him all but out at the close of the third round, and when the time reached the count of three the gong sounded and the seconds of Munroe dragged him to his corner.
>
> Munroe was quickly revived and Jeffries was getting badly winded, as Munroe had caused him to exert himself beyond what he had expected.... He tried repeatedly and missed several lunges...[Munroe] ducked cleverly, and took as much time as he could in hanging on to the big fellow in the clinches....
>
> Munroe could have undoubtedly landed oftener than he did, but he was smart enough not to lay himself open to a knockout punch.

One of the best punches that Jeff landed was in the 3rd round when in a clinch he nailed Jack with a body shot that dropped him.[762]

Although the damage was already done, some newspapers started amending their initial reports. One said, "The sporting world has been given a wrong impression of what actually took place." It quoted the nearby Montana paper, the *Anaconda Standard*, as saying that Munroe exhibited cleverness in the first two rounds, outpointing Jeff. However, Jeffries dropped Munroe in the 2nd round. In the 3rd, Munroe went down three times, and wisely took his counts. "He was there not to whip Jeffries, but to stay four rounds, and he used his head well." Sometimes Munroe clinched

761 *Butte Miner, Anaconda Standard*, December 24, 1902.
762 *Butte Miner*, December 25, 26, 1902.

to save himself, but Jeff hit him on the body. A right to the body at the end of the 3rd dropped Munroe, and the gong saved him. Munroe was punished in the 4th, but he fought back and landed often. Still, his blows lacked steam. He would go down from punches, but always came back gamely after rising. It opined that Jeffries was never a quick knockout artist as Sullivan had been, and therefore should avoid these types of bouts. Fitzsimmons was much better suited to these exhibitions.[763]

Bob Fitzsimmons also spoke of the Munroe exhibition, calling the report that Jeffries was dropped a malicious falsehood.

> Munroe was never in the game during the four rounds. I told Jeff to put him out after the first round. Jeff said no; that he would let him stay and give the people the worth of their money. They have done Jeff a great injustice. I was surprised at the press doing such an injustice to an American champion. To prove that Jeff let him stay four rounds he offered Munroe $1,000 if he would stay four rounds again. Munroe refused, which goes to show that Munroe knows himself that Jeff can put him out in four rounds if he wished to.[764]

However, Fitz admitted that Jeff tried to stop him after the 2nd round. So, Jeffries carried him for 2 rounds, and then went after him in the 3rd and 4th, but had waited too long because Munroe was clever and tough. By not punching very often, Munroe left Jeffries with few openings and counterpunching opportunities. Still, Munroe was saved by the bell in the 3rd round. Jack was also able to clinch, and go down and take his time in rising, in order to kill the clock. Back in Sullivan's day, these were known as Tug Wilson tactics.[765]

How such a skewed view of the Jeffries-Munroe bout got generated and disseminated may be explained by what transpired after the bout. Clark Ball, Fitz's manager, who had been managing the Fitz-Jeffries tour, severed relations with the combination and signed a contract with Munroe. Ball intended to make Munroe the star attraction of an athletic show managed by him.

After Ball separated from them, when Fitzsimmons met Ball in the lobby of an Anaconda hotel late at night, there was some wrangling between the two men. Ball called Fitzsimmons a liar, and Bob floored his former manager with a left hook to the jaw. On the way down, Ball's head struck the corner of the counter, and it was lacerated. The question not overtly raised at the time, but which should be considered, was whether Ball was the one who put forth the tainted reports in order to boost Munroe. This appears to have been the case.[766]

---

763 *Seattle Post-Intelligencer*, December 28, 1902.
764 *Butte Miner*, December 29, 1902.
765 *Butte Miner*, December 29, 1902.
766 *Seattle Post-Intelligencer*, December 30, 1902.

In his first autobiography, Jeff said that the night of the Munroe exhibition, Fitz had a falling out with Ball. Therefore, Ball rushed over and signed Munroe, and began wiring all over the country that Munroe had defeated Jeff and knocked him down.

In *Two Fisted Jeffries,* Jeff said, "The Monroe myth was built on the plot of a press agent who saw a chance to advance himself and get some money for Monroe and himself at my expense." Jeff said that Ball had sent out the story. The only time Jeffries had been down in the bout was when he missed a punch and slipped in trying to get at Munroe. Fitzsimmons was actually angrier than Jeff was, because Ball was his brother-in-law, so he felt responsible. Therefore, when they met in a hotel lobby, Bob knocked Ball out.[767]

The Jeff-Fitz combination was in Pocatello, Idaho on December 30. When Jeff and Fitz sparred, Bob did all of his work with his left, because he had damaged his right in knocking out Ranke.

Responding to the allegations that there was an agreement to allow Munroe to stay the distance, the club manager in Butte agreed that Jeff had carried Munroe for at least 2 rounds. He said,

> Jeff asked me what we had for him and I told him we had a good man. I then asked him to let Munroe stay a couple of rounds as it would be better for the game…. Jeff said to me: 'Billy, I will not let any man make a reputation off of me…. I'll sure hit him and put him out.' … Jeff did his best to put Munroe out after – not before – the second round.

Still, all of the publicity that Munroe received throughout the nation had put him on the map. One writer said, "The heavyweight division was never so well stocked with promising men as it is at present." Rising contenders like Jack Johnson, Sam McVey, and Jack Munroe were good enough to engage Jeff's attention.

The world champions at year end 1902 were: heavyweight – Jeffries, (colored) – Ed Martin, light heavyweight – George Gardner, middleweight – Tommy Ryan, welterweight – Joe Walcott, lightweight – Joe Gans, featherweight – Young Corbett, bantamweight – Harry Forbes.

On January 2, 1903, Jeff and Fitz were in Salt Lake City, Utah. Some said that Jeff would not attempt to put a man out in 4 rounds again unless he was in top condition.[768]

On January 6, Jack Munroe fought Jack Sullivan, and although he did not put him out in 4 rounds, he had Sullivan on the floor 26 times. A fighter named Mose Lafontise stayed 4 rounds with Munroe on January 7, but Munroe was said to be a clever boxer. On January 9, Munroe beat up a black fighter named Ike Hayes over 4 rounds. "Although the negro stayed

767 *My Life and Battles* at 51.; *Two Fisted Jeffries* at 214, 218.
768 *Butte Miner*, December 30, 1902, January 2, 3, 1903; *National Police Gazette*, January 31, 1903.

he was given an awful beating and only his continual clinching enabled him to last the bout out." Ball was building Munroe.[769]

It was reported that Clark Ball intended to place Munroe under Tommy Ryan's tutelage. When they heard about this, both Fitz and Jeff laughed and said that Munroe could earn $1,000 any time he desired to try to stay 4 rounds with either one of them. Fitz said that Munroe could train with Ryan for a year and it would not matter.[770]

Contradictory reports were being sent out regarding Munroe, depending on the source. One edition of the *National Police Gazette* reported that Munroe knocked the champion down, and won a decision with his fistic ability. "Munroe actually outpointed Jeffries in nearly every round and was justly entitled to the decision. He is game and courageous and a good hitter and had Jeffries groggy." All sorts of sensational things were predicted for him.

The Police Gazette also said that the bout's local referee, Duncan McDonald, felt that Jeff did his utmost to stop Munroe, but could not do it. McDonald said,

> No one can ever claim a dishonest decision was rendered when I had the say, and this decision given to Munroe stands absolutely. Munroe deserved it, and if the champion did not want to put him out, as he claims, his actions belied him. Jeff meant business, as every one who witnessed the bout knows. Jeff was out of form all right, but that does not alter the decision or the result. The big champion was outdone that night.[771]

However, McDonald did not say that Jeff was dropped. When Sam Austin later spoke with McDonald, Duncan confirmed that Munroe did not knock the champion down.

Also not mentioned was the fact that McDonald, the ex-champion of Montana, might have had some bias in favor of the local Montana miner.

McDonald also claimed that Jeff and Fitz went to his hotel in Butte after the contest and asked him to change his decision, but that he had refused.[772]

The Gazette opined that it was a good thing that Munroe came to the surface when he did, because there were no legitimate contenders left to challenge Jeffries. Jeff's decisive victory over Fitzsimmons "convinced us that he was the peer of any pugilist now before the public, and the appearance of a new aspirant for championship honors was awaited with eagerness."[773]

---

769 *Butte Miner*, January 3, 7, 8, 10, 1903; *National Police Gazette*, January 31, February 14, 1903. *The Police Gazette* later revealed that Peter Maher had knocked Hayes out in 2 minutes.
770 *National Police Gazette*, January 31, 1903.
771 *National Police Gazette*, January 17, 1903.
772 *Butte Miner*, December 24, 1902.
773 *National Police Gazette*, January 17, 1903.

Despite McDonald's claims, in February 1903, the *Police Gazette* reported that a Western sporting man who had witnessed the bout had vouched for the truthfulness of Jeff's version of events. Jeffries said Munroe clinched and fell to avoid punishment, did not land a single clean punch, and most certainly did not knock him down.

At that point, the *Gazette* opined that it was nonsensical to be booming Munroe as a pugilistic hero simply because he lasted 4 rounds against the champion by dropping and taking counts. It noted that many years ago, Tug Wilson had done the same thing with Sullivan, but the papers did not come out and boost him. "But then, Wilson was not as lucky a man as Munroe and not so fortunate in having a friendly referee to decide the bout in his favor."[774]

Jeff and Fitz continued touring around the country, giving exhibitions with each other and making good money. In late January, they were in St. Joseph and Kansas City, Missouri. In early February, they were scheduled to exhibit in Springfield, St. Louis, Indianapolis, Louisville, and other places on their way east.

Sam Mott, the pair's new representative, said of the Munroe bout, "I was right at the ringside when that affair took place, and I want to say that Monroe won't last thirty seconds if he ever faces Jeffries again. It was entirely due to Jeff's good nature that he remained as long as he did, as the champion did not want to disappoint a big crowd." The other bouts were quick knockouts, and Fitz put his man out in a punch, so Jeff wanted to give the crowd "a run for their money." "When the spectators commenced to yell with delight over the showing Monroe was making, Jeff looked over at them and just laughed. It didn't worry him a bit." Fitz called on Jeffries to knock Munroe out, "but Jeff simply played with the big miner and let him stay."

> The way the latter went to the floor when Jeff made a pass at him was really funny. He lasted the four rounds by hanging on and slipping down whenever Jeff swung, but Jim could have put him away in the first round had he been so disposed. The champion was electrified to hear McDonald giving Monroe a verdict, as no decision should have been rendered at all. The affair was simply a farce so far as Monroe is concerned. I give you my word that he didn't knock down Jeffries at all, or even land hard enough on the champion to bother him.[775]

It was said that Jeffries was holding out for a lengthier fight against Corbett. He wanted a fight to the finish in Carson, whereas Corbett wanted a 20-round bout. The experts felt that although Corbett had a chance to

---

774 *National Police Gazette*, February 14, 1903.
775 *St. Louis Republic*, February 1, 1903.

outpoint Jeff in a limited-rounds contest, he had zero chance to defeat Jeff in a finish fight.[776]

Jeffries was looking big, brawny, and hearty, although with some superfluous rolls of fat. In St. Louis, Jeff told a reporter,

> Drop that Munroe business. I'm sick of it. Before I quit the subject I want to say that the matter has been misrepresented from the start. There were four bouts scheduled that night at Butte and the seats ranged from $2 to $5 in price. The first three were run off so fast that you wouldn't know there was an exhibition on. Bob Fitz put his man out in 15 seconds and one of the other contests ended in two minutes.

> It was up to me to give the house a run for its money. I decided that the proper thing would be to let Munroe stay four rounds, and fought with the idea of sacrificing the $250 forfeit. I thought it would tickle those miners to have their representative stay four rounds.

> Fitz urged me to put Munroe out all the time, but I dallied around and in the last round I hustled about to make it appear that I was trying hard. I had no intention of putting the man out, however.

> Had I known the deal I was to get on the matter later on I would not have dallied with Munroe. There is no doubt about what Munroe is – he is a dub of the first water and the very first time he goes against a man of caliber he will regret it. Sharkey will kill him.

Jeff said that for a fight with Corbett, he would have to drop his lucrative tour, go into training for a couple months, put up with all the sacrifices, and fight 20 hard rounds. To do so, he required sufficient financial incentives. He was making about $2,000 a night with Fitz. Therefore, he could make more by touring and exhibiting for a couple weeks than he likely would earn with one fight, and without all the worry and trouble. Hence, Jeff was not eager to end his tour any time soon. "I don't say I will not fight Corbett later – it is too easy money to throw away, but not now. I'm too busy getting rich and am having a good time."

Jeff assured the press that although his nightly bout with Bob was a mere exhibition, it was far from tame, for occasionally, when they got warmed up, they would really go at it.[777]

Despite his representations and the advertising hyping their exciting exhibitions, their bout on February 5 at the St. Louis West End Club was exceedingly tame. In fact, it was said to be even tamer than typical exhibition bouts. Each of the 3 rounds only lasted about a minute or so,

---

776 *St. Louis Post-Dispatch*, February 3, 1903.
777 *St. Louis Post-Dispatch*, February 5, 1903.

and they took a few minutes of rest between each round. "Despite press agents' tales, no one really expected to see anything like a fight."

However, the fans at least expected something approaching a fair exhibition. The local paper said that the preliminary handshake proved to be the hardest blow struck. It was a farce, as the men clowned around, smiled, and moved about, only using slow and light taps. Some laughed, some hissed, and some left before it was over. "For the most part the crowd accepted, with good-natured acquiescence, that they had been done again." Jeff simply said that they were not being paid enough to fight and show the real thing. The locals felt a bit swindled. "The majority of spectators went away from the club convinced that Jack Munroe stayed four rounds with him on his merits." Jeff looked fat and slow, and was breathing heavily despite little exertion.[778]

Mouthy as ever, from New York, Corbett claimed that Jeff was afraid to fight him, and said that if he did not, that he would claim the title under the old rules that required a champion to accept within 6 months all challenges backed with a forfeit.

It was obvious to the St. Louis newsmen why Jeff was not eager to fight Corbett. "Not only is he too busy making money, but it would take him at least three months to get into anything like shape." Both Jeff and Fitz ate and drank a fair amount while in the city, contradicting the illusion that they were abstemious.[779]

On February 5, 1903 in Los Angeles, Jack Johnson won a 20-round decision over "Denver" Ed Martin to win the undisputed colored heavyweight championship. *The Police Gazette* summarized,

> Johnson showed remarkable cleverness, though he lacked the power to deliver a hard punch. Had he been endowed with that necessary there were times during his bout when he would have knocked out 'Denver Ed.' Martin was the harder hitter, but that did not help him any. Johnson's cleverness was something he could not solve. His left jabs sailed by Johnson's ear nearly every time.[780]

Jeff and Bob continued their money-making exhibition tour. They sparred 3 rounds in Paducah, Kentucky on February 6. Although it is unclear whether this actually happened or was just a press agent's hype, the dispatch reported, "Fitz had his nose slightly skinned and a few drops of blood were brought from Jeffries' cheek." They were also set to travel to places like Evansville, Indianapolis, Cincinnati, and Louisville.[781]

Jack Munroe further spoke about his experience in the ring with Jeffries.

778 *St. Louis Post-Dispatch, St. Louis Daily Globe Democrat, St. Louis Republic*, February 6, 1903.
779 *St. Louis Post-Dispatch, St. Louis Republic*, February 7, 1903.
780 *National Police Gazette*, February 28, 1903.
781 *St. Louis Daily Globe Democrat*, February 8, 1903.

It was the first time I had put the gloves on in two years and I was a bit afraid that I would not acquit myself as well as I hoped to. As soon as I went against Jeffries I saw that the champion was holding me cheaply, expecting to trim me in a few rounds. He was laughing and did a lot of rushing. But I wasn't scared a wee bit and instead of running away, just merged in. Jeffries, who, by the way, was not in the best of shape, was surprised. I remember…the first attempt I made with my right. … It was a hard one, but not as hard as I can hit, because I was only there to stay, not to knock any one out.

Well, when I landed, Jeffries winced and went back a few paces. When the round was over I could see that he was angry, and I expected him to sail in for me in the second. In this respect I was not mistaken for when he came after me he pummeled me often under the heart. The blows hurt and I took them in order to get my right over. We were to have broken clean, but he violated the order and I followed suit. Near the close of the second, as best as I can remember, I nailed him with the right in the solar plexus. He was coming to me and my punch sent him to the ropes, and in coming forward he went to his knees.

I knew then that I would not have any trouble in staying, so we mixed it up in the third, with the result that he put me down with a similar body blow. When the fight was over and the referee gave the decision to me I realized that I had done something unusual, and naturally I felt proud. The next night Jeffries offered me $1,000 to meet him again; but I declined, for I figured that I can get more than that when we fight again.

Angered at the stories that Munroe was circulating, Fitzsimmons said,

I am tired of talking about that dub. I will give him $1,000 if Jeffries or myself cannot stop him in three rounds. I am tired of allowing him to go about this country advertising himself at our expense. I want to go on record as stating that he is a third-rate dub and that if anyone thinks he is not a dub just get him to face me for three rounds and let him earn $1,000 if I fail to knock him out.[782]

Munroe said that he played high school football, and although he was the lightest man at 196 pounds in a rush line that averaged 220 pounds, he held his position for two years and played in 100 games. At San Francisco's Olympic Club, he often boxed for fun, sparring with all the big fighters who came there to train. In particular, he boxed a lot with Jack O'Brien and Jack Moffat. After scoring a few knockouts as an amateur, he turned professional against Hank Griffin, "who had stayed seventeen rounds with

782 *National Police Gazette*, February 7, 1903.

Jeffries." After Munroe lost a 20-round decision to Griffin, he drifted away from boxing and became a miner.

Capitalizing on his new-found fame, Munroe traveled to New York and took on Tommy West in a 3-round tryout. Those who saw Munroe were impressed. "After the bout West acknowledged that the miner had a great blow and that he had felt it more than once during the bout." As a new star, Munroe even acted in a play in New York City in which he sparred four 2-minute rounds with Jack Carey. Munroe was taking full advantage of the advertising which his "defeat" of the champion had brought him.[783]

Jeffries blamed himself for letting up on Munroe and boxing easily to give the fans a show. He was upset at all the publicity that Munroe was receiving and the stories which were circulating about their bout.

> To begin with I made no attempt whatever to land on Munroe for the first two rounds and merely let him stay to make it interesting, as I saw he knew absolutely nothing about the game. In the third I had no trouble to hit him at will, and he began to go to the floor. When what should have been the middle of the round was reached, I sent a left and right to his body, catching him on the solar plexus and he fell to the floor. When the timekeeper counted eight I turned to my corner thinking the bout was over, when to my surprise the gong sounded the end of the round, though we had hardly boxed two full minutes. Doc Flynn and Jerry McCarthy, two of Munroe's seconds, dragged him to his corner and revived him. In the fourth round I could not get at him, as he repeatedly clinched or fell to the floor every time I would make a lead and in this manner he managed to stay the limit. He did not during the four rounds land a single clean punch. The reports sent out that he knocked me down are absolutely untrue, and no one knows this better than Munroe himself.

The Police Gazette said that engaging in 4-round all-comers exhibitions was a dangerous proposition, because it was not that easy to stop everyone in 4 rounds. Jeff had been weighing 240 or 245 pounds and was not at his best. Munroe was in good physical condition and had boxing experience. It remembered when Jeff contracted to put out 195-pound Bob Armstrong but failed to do so in 10 rounds, in part owing to a broken hand and the fact that Bob fought warily. Stopping a man was not always that easy.[784]

---

783 *National Police Gazette*, February 14, 1903. West was more of a middleweight, but had very good experience, including: 1896 LKOby2 Kid McCoy and D19 Joe Walcott; 1897 W20 Walcott; 1898 LKOby14 Tommy Ryan; 1899 KO7 George Byers and KO14 Frank Craig; 1900 KO11 Walcott; 1901 LKOby17 Tommy Ryan; and 1901 LKOby16 Marvin Hart.
784 *National Police Gazette*, February 14, March 28, 1903.

CHAPTER 34

Building the Intrigue

In early 1903, it was said that Jim Corbett was embarrassing Jeffries by posting a $5,000 forfeit and saying that he would claim the title if Jeff would not accept his challenge. When Jeffries said he wanted a fight to the finish, some unfairly criticized him as looking for an excuse to avoid Corbett. Jeffries was willing to fight him, but was making such good money with Fitzsimmons on their exhibition tour that he wanted to put the fight off. He also wanted a sufficient purse inducement.

Corbett was training hard every day, as if a fight was imminent. He spent a few hours a day in the gymnasium. Jim said that he was in the best shape of his life, and was bigger and stronger than ever too, weighing 195 pounds. He was convinced that he could defeat Jeffries. "I am sacrificing speed to be able to punch harder, and when I do fight Jeff I will not hit him as many times as I did in our last fight, but when I do land I will hurt him."

After boxing with Fitzsimmons in Terre Haute, Indiana in late February, Jeffries traveled to New York to negotiate with Corbett on March 1, 1903.

Corbett insisted that he would not box in a fight to the finish. He also insisted on wearing hand bandages because Jeff had a wonderful physique, and to land on him without bandages would do more damage to his hands than to Jeff's jaw. Jim said that he had been developing his muscles for the past year, and felt that he could hit as hard a blow as the champion.[785]

Jeffries did not want to allow Corbett to wear hand bandages. "No one with bandages ever fights me again." Jeff objected to bandages because of the Fitzsimmons fight, fearing that Corbett might make his hands hardened like plaster of Paris, which more easily cut him open, "and I'm not going to have any more of that business." Corbett responded that his hands were too fragile, and could not last 2 rounds without them. He said,

> Do you remember when you were with me, that I always wore them? You know even better than I do that I have worn them in all but my two first fights. What right has Jeffries to kick? Nearly all the men he has met have worn bandages on their hands. I wore them in my fight with him, and why is he kicking now?

Corbett said that Jeffries could have a man in his dressing room to observe him put on the wraps, but Bill Delaney feared that Jim could dip his hands into a bucket of plaster of Paris on the way to the ring.

---

785 *National Police Gazette*, February 28, April 4, 1903.

They finally agreed to a 20-round bout using five-ounce gloves, with either man able to wear soft bandages, but the wraps were to be put on in the ring in full view of the audience and to the satisfaction of the referee. The purse would be divided 75%/25% winner-loser. The rematch was tentatively scheduled to take place in California in June or July. Delaney believed that the California clubs would offer $25,000 or more for the bout. As they were leaving, Fitzsimmons said to Corbett, "I'm going to train Jeffries for this fight, Jim." Fitz would eventually take up a position as a Jeffries trainer and sparring partner.

In training, Corbett was looking good and hitting harder. One reporter said that despite the fact that Jim was 36 and Jeff 27, "the latter must be at his best to land an effective blow before the limit of the bout expires."

In the meantime, Jeffries continued his exhibitions with Fitzsimmons. On March 2, 1903 in Philadelphia, they sparred 3 fast 2-minute rounds in pleasing style. There was much excitement amongst the crowd, although there were a number of empty seats, demonstrating that exhibitions were not the draw that the real thing was. One said, "Both men were in surprisingly good physical condition, although Jeffries was, of course, a trifle corpulent, but the speed they exhibited in their six minutes of give and take work electrified the crowd." Jeff was looking quicker with his hands and feet, and more skillful, but not quite as powerful. Of course, he always held back his power in sparring and exhibitions. Another said, "There is no denying the fact that Jeffries and Fitzsimmons are the greatest fighters of this age."

2,000 people crowded into the armory at Chester, Pennsylvania on March 3 to watch Jeff and Fitz box their 3-round exhibition. Unfortunately, some of the rear seats fell with a crash, carrying many men to the floor. One suffered a broken leg.

Jeff and Fitz again exhibited in Philadelphia on March 4 as part of a larger charity show that included boxers Jack O'Brien, Peter Maher, Tom Sharkey, and Kid McCoy.[786]

---

786 *Philadelphia Public Ledger, Philadelphia Press, Philadelphia Inquirer*, March 2-4, 1903; *National Police Gazette*, March 21, 28, 1903.

On March 6, the Jeffries-Corbett fight was pushed back to August, interestingly enough, at the behest of Corbett. Jim wanted sufficient time to train, and also wanted to finish out his own theatrical contracts, which had probably become more lucrative now that he was matched to fight for the title.

In *Two Fisted Jeffries*, Jeff said that while in Philly, they received a telegram saying that Rose Julian Fitzsimmons had come down with pneumonia and was seriously ill. They closed their show and Bob returned to their Coney Island home. Rose eventually died of pneumonia on April 17, 1903. Since they had canceled their exhibition tour, Jeff was instead booked to appear in vaudeville, and continued with that for 2 months before returning to Los Angeles.[787]

Jack Munroe continued to be "the lion of the hour," and was hoping to be next in line for a lucrative fight with Jeffries. However, he needed to convince the public that he was legitimate. Munroe made his debut at Madison Square Garden in a wrestling contest against Tom Jenkins, and his appearance made a favorable impression.

Nettled by the good press that Munroe was receiving, Jeff said, "My bout with him was a joke. I can whip him in two rounds and am willing to bet on that. He was bustled over the country and advertised as the man who knocked Jeffries down, but he could not knock me down with a hammer. ... So long as he does not fight he will have a reputation, but if he ever fights it will be good-night with him."

Jack Johnson, "the colored heavyweight, who has been trimming them all at Los Angeles," was also out with a challenge to Jeffries. On February 26 in Los Angeles, he had won a 20-round decision over Sam McVey to defend his colored heavyweight title. Afterwards, Johnson said,

> I will challenge Jeffries. I am going to Galveston to spend a month with my people and will return to Los Angeles and put it up to the champion. I am by rights the next man that Jeffries ought to meet, and if the mill comes off I will give the crowd plenty of fun for their money.

In April, Corbett said that although he was 36 years old, he felt ten years younger. He planned to travel to California in May for three months of hard training, but in the meantime, he would continually exercise on the road.[788]

Jim Corbett's last fight was an August 1900 5th round knockout win against Kid McCoy, three years earlier.[789] Although Corbett's victory over McCoy was significant, he had not fought at all subsequently, although he

---

787 *Police Gazette*, June 13, July 4, 1903; *Two Fisted Jeffries* at 221.
788 *Police Gazette*, March 14, 21, April 4, May 2, June 6, 1903.
789 Prior to fighting Corbett, McCoy's results included: 1898 W20 Ruhlin; 1899 LKOby10 Sharkey, W20 Choynski; and 1900 KO5 Maher and KO4 Choynski.

did engage in occasional sparring and exhibitions. His inactivity may have been in part due to the fact that many believed that the McCoy bout was fixed. The other reason was that Corbett refused to fight in anything other than championship-caliber bouts, because he wanted big money to fight.

Corbett claimed to have been keeping active on the road, boxing in various towns with local fighters. It was reported that he had been training for the past year. Amongst those exhibitions, in May 1902, Corbett had sparred Fitzsimmons 3 rounds. In December 1902, he gave a 3-round exhibition with future champion Tommy Burns, then a middleweight.

Corbett said that he would fight Jeffries differently this time. He was going to move a bit less and punch harder. He felt that he did not need to move so much in order to outpoint Jeffries, because he was ten times faster than Jeff, so he could afford to be a bit slower, but punch harder, and still be three times as quick. In their first fight, when using his speed to quickly get in and out, he moved away much further than he needed to, spoiling his chances to hit hard. He was going to fight a bit slower, but in a more powerful fashion. Instead of simply jumping away after landing, he would block counters and land a counter blow of his own. He still felt that he could win on points.

Corbett opined that Jeffries was vulnerable to the body, recalling that he hurt him there when they trained and sparred together. He believed that Jeff's crouch was used to guard against body blows.

> Why did Jeff ever start in with that crouch, which makes him twice as slow as he is naturally? Why, only to make it impossible to reach his body. ... I asked Jack Munroe a while ago if he succeeded in hurting Jeff, and where. Munroe said: "Well, he seemed to wince when I reached his body. I hurt him a good deal with a right-hand punch under the heart. It nearly put him out of business."

The Police Gazette said that the yarns being spun around the country "recounting incidents of dissipation and scandalous proceedings" regarding Jeffries were exaggerated. It speculated that these stories were generated in order to influence the betting, for Jeff was a big favorite. However, unlike Corbett, Jeffries would not train all that long for the fight, only planning on a six-week training camp.

Jeff claimed to be taking care of himself, weighing just over 225 pounds. He was annoyed by the many fake reports of his condition. He weighed 215 pounds in his last fight, and was not far off from that weight. However, in his own autobiography, Jeff admitted to weighing 275 pounds. Regarding how he would fight Corbett, Jeff said, "I have a style of my own, and so far it has been successful."

Reacting to the criticism that he was not training as early as Corbett was; Jeff said that he did not wish to overtrain. Some felt that he was taking chances on his condition, while Corbett was training conscientiously. However, this overlooked the fact that owing to his inactivity, Corbett needed more time to get into top form, whereas Jeff required much less time, given his more recent activity.[790]

It was anticipated that Corbett would try to use his experience, prolong the battle, and win on points, especially given that this contest would only be 20 rounds as opposed to the scheduled 25 rounds that their first fight was. However, Jeffries said that despite the fact that Corbett was a shifty boxer, the fight would not go the limit, for he would do what he needed to in order to catch up with him, regardless of the distance.

> Corbett doesn't give me credit for having improved a bit myself, and that is where I will fool him. I have learned to be a bit clever and while I may not be able to stand up and box with him you know what will happen if I land, and I'll land all right. I propose to go right after him this time. The last time we met I made the serious mistake of trying to fight him at long range. ... This time I will make him fight, not box, and I will win sure, though it may take me a few rounds to get him cornered.[791]

Jeffries had also acquiesced to a 24-foot ring, which was a huge Corbett advantage. It would give Jim a lot of room to move. Jeff had wanted a smaller ring so that Jim could not run away from him. In recent years, nothing larger than a 20- or 22-foot ring had been used in San Francisco. Jeff-Fitz II had been in a 20-foot ring, which helped Jeffries. However, Corbett insisted that the traditional rules required a 24-foot ring for championship bouts.

By allowing bandages, a shorter fight length, and a larger ring, Corbett had the advantage in the conditions. Jeff had also given him additional time to train by scheduling the bout in August. Jeffries wanted Corbett to have no excuses when he was defeated. Fitzsimmons was convinced that Jeffries would win regardless, calling him the greatest fighter ever.

San Francisco's Yosemite Club won the bid for the bout, guaranteeing a $22,500 purse, but the fighters would also have the option to take 70% of the gross receipts instead. The boxers would split their end 75%/25% winner/loser. The fight was set for August 14, 1903 in San Francisco.

Corbett was sparring with Yank Kenny in his theatrical tour. In mid-June, Jim ended his tour to begin serious training at Croll's Gardens in Alameda, California. Observers were satisfied that Corbett had developed a punch, and that Jeff would have to deal with both a clever and hard-hitting opponent.

Jeffries began preliminary training work under Bill Delaney's direction at Harbin Springs. He would continue to do so until Fitzsimmons arrived. However, reports were that Jeff was not doing much, and refused to do

---

790 *Police Gazette*, May 9, 16, 23, 1903; *My Life and Battles* at 51.
791 *Police Gazette*, May 30, 1903.

more until Bob arrived. Fitz was in Chicago, apparently courting a new lady.[792]

Corbett said that he never felt better in his life, and was reportedly fit to make the battle of his life. During the last 12 months, he had spent an hour or two almost every day in gymnasiums across the country. He was training hard. "No fighter ever trained more conscientiously for a contest than Corbett." Jim expected to enter the ring weighing about 190 pounds. He was doing 10-12-mile walks every day, punching the bag, and sparring 3 rounds each with Sam Berger and Yank Kenny. Berger was a tall, experienced amateur heavyweight who would later win a gold medal at the 1904 Olympic Games in St. Louis. Kenny was just a trial horse as a pro, but was the same size as Jeffries. Corbett also worked the rowing machine, engaged in wrestling, did calisthenics designed to build up his muscles, and played baseball. Jim said that if he was beaten, it would not be due to lack of physical preparation.

Corbett even hired Tommy Ryan to be one of his trainers. This could give Jim an edge, because as Jeff's former trainer, Ryan would be better equipped to assist Jim in solving Jeffries and provide him with some inside information.

Corbett spars Yank Kenny.

On the other hand, Jeff's friends were not satisfied with his condition. He was said to be weighing 240 pounds and doing little work. "It is known for a fact that the big fellow has not been living the most abstemious life since his victory over Fitzsimmons." It was also a well-known fact that big

792 *Police Gazette*, June 6, 20, 27, July 4, 1903.

men tire more quickly in battle than smaller ones, and so it was even more important for a big man like Jeff to be in top shape. Going 20 rounds while carrying well over 200 pounds of flesh was not an easy task for the human body to endure. This explains why a lot of trainers tried to get their big heavyweights down in weight.

Jeffries started getting down to real work in July, as promised. Although Fitz was going to be Jeff's chief sparring partner, and would give him tips and suggestions, Bill Delaney was still the chief trainer. Delaney's plan was for Jeff not to overtrain, to be big and strong, but also to work on his speed of hand and foot because Corbett, although not as strong as Fitz, was faster and more elusive.

Fitzsimmons said that Jeffries was much faster with his footwork than he was when seen on the east coast. He said that Corbett would find a much improved man, one who would quickly catch up with him. He predicted that Jeff would win inside of 10 rounds.[793]

The Police Gazette reported that Jeff was supremely confident of winning despite having neglected training to go on hunting trips. Still, the consensus of opinion was that Jeffries would win. Corbett had not fought since 1900, while Jeff had stopped Ruhlin and Fitzsimmons. The two were opposites. Corbett could "hit faster and get away quicker than any boxer that ever lived." However, Jeffries could "hit harder than any man that ever stepped into a ring." He could also take any amount of punishment without weakening. The experts felt that Corbett's only hope was to evade Jeff's "pile-driving blows" for 20 rounds and win on points. Ultimately, the *Gazette* did not rely on the reports that Jeff was not taking care of himself, feeling that such stories were circulated in the interests of betting men. However, it agreed that the champion was likely a bit overconfident because he believed himself the winner even before the first gong clanged.[794]

Adding to the already bad press surrounding his training, in late July, a bear badly bit Jeffries. One of the boys kept a bear named Brownie chained up near the hotel. One day, Jeff boxed with the bear for fun, but he must have hit it a little too hard, because the bear then attacked him, biting his wrist and then left calf. The bear chewed holes in Jeff's leg before the pugilist got away.

Fitz attempted to sew up the wound with needle and thread, but found the skin so tough that the needle failed to puncture it. Therefore, according to one source, he used a hammer to drive it through. Another said Fitz used a knife to cut holes for the needle.[795]

---

793 *Police Gazette*, July 11, 18, 1903.
794 *Police Gazette*, July 25, August 1, 8, 1903.
795 *San Francisco Call*, August 2, 1903.

Unfortunately, soon thereafter, Jeff became feverish and broke out in inflamed sores. His leg swelled and was black up to the knee. A physician said he had a case of blood poisoning and advised him to quit training.[796]

The July 25, 1903 *San Francisco Evening Post* said that Jeffries had been forced to abandon training in order to nurse a case of blood poisoning induced by a bear bite. Some speculated that Jeff's blood was in bad condition owing to the effects of the wild life he led in Chicago before coming to the coast to train. Yosemite Club promoter James Coffroth said that the doctors declared that Jeff would quickly recover.[797]

A couple days after the report about Jeff's leg, Corbett said that Jeffries had better not ask for a continuance, that he would claim the championship if Jeff was not ready to fight on August 14. A disgusted Jeffries responded that he had no intention to ask for additional time. Bill Delaney told Jeff not to worry, that Corbett was using his old tactics to upset him. Jeff's doctor said the leg was healing up nicely, and would not bother him at all.[798]

The Police Gazette noted that at best, Jeffries would have only two weeks of hard training to prepare. "Up to this time there has really been no training worthy of note. What there has been will not compare with Corbett's long, steady pull of more than a year." However, it realized that Jeff was in good shape owing to his long hunting trips in the mountains, and his frequent work with the rowing machine, weights, punching bag, and jump rope. Still, he had been eating and drinking as much as he pleased, and staying up late at night. "The truth probably is that he dreads the work incident to a fight until he sees that it is inevitable; then he plunges in with all the vigor of one who never gives up."

Jeffries was only out of training for a short while. On July 31, to start off, he jumped rope 1,000 times; shadow boxed with dumbbells, and used the wrist and rowing machines. Fitzsimmons teased Jeff about his thinning hairline, saying that he would soon look like he and Delaney did.

Jeff then wrestled with the 203-pound Fitzsimmons, tugging, pushing, pulling, and leaning on him for seven minutes straight, until Bob asked for time to be called. Afterwards, Jeff laughingly said to Bob, "You're pretty strong for a little fellow." Bob told Jeff that if he tried leaning on Corbett that Jim would rub his hand over his face. Jeff replied that he would bet that Jim would never put his hand in his face, fearing the consequences.[799]

Fitzsimmons said that Jeffries would have no trouble in disposing of Corbett because Jeff was the world's greatest fighter, could hit a

---

796 *Police Gazette*, August 8, 1903; *My Life and Battles* at 51-52.

797 *San Francisco Evening Post*, July 25, 1903. Jeff later said that he wanted to postpone the fight. However, promoter Jim Coffroth argued that it would cost a lot of money, and would upset a lot of folks who had traveled across the country to see him fight. Jeff agreed to go forward. After a few days, the leg felt better.

798 *San Francisco Evening Post*, July 28, 1903.

799 *San Francisco Call, San Francisco Bulletin*, August 1, 1903. On July 25 in San Francisco, the recently widowed Bob Fitzsimmons got married again, to Julia Gifford. A week later, Bob was training Jeffries.

tremendous blow, and "there is no doubt that his blows will gradually knock Corbett into a state of helplessness." Jeffries was a 2 to 1 and even 3 to 1 betting favorite.

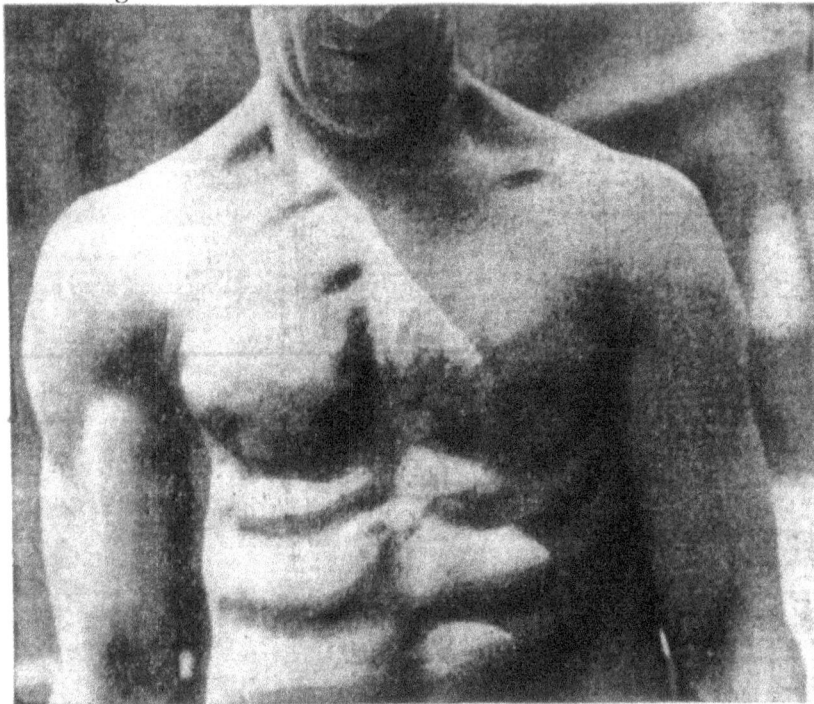

EX-CHAMPION JAMES J. CORBETT HAS BEEN TRAINING FOR TWO YEARS TO DEVELOP THE MUS-CLES OF HIS BODY AS SHOWN IN THE ABOVE PICTURE. CORBETT CLAIMS THAT WITH THIS ARMOUR JEFFRIES' LOW PUNCHES WILL HAVE NO EFFECT, AS THE STOMACH WILL BE FULLY PROTECTED IN THAT CASE JEFFRIES WILL HAVE TO DIRECT ALL HIS BLOWS TO THE HEAD.

Corbett was confident, saying that he did not believe Jeffries could land a knockout blow on him. Still, the question was whether he would be able to avoid Jeff's terrific swings. "Jeffries has become much faster in speed in the last two years. In fact, he has shown considerable aggressiveness in his last two battles, and from all accounts it is his intention to rush Corbett from the start. Jeffries is quoted as saying that Corbett cannot hurt him with a punch."[800]

On August 1, Jeffries went on a short run, and boxed for the first time in camp with Bob Fitzsimmons, as well as Joe Kennedy and brother Jack Jeffries, 2 rounds with each man. Fitz sparred in a lively fashion, attempting to mimic Corbett's tactics, quickly moving away and then stopping suddenly to slip in a left swing or jab. Next, Jeff again went outdoors for half an hour of 100-yard sprints, showing more speed than any of his trainers.

The scale had been removed from the training camp. Delaney did not want Jeff to worry about how much he weighed, as long as he felt strong

---

800 *Police Gazette*, August 15, 1903.

and in condition. Bill said that in the past, it was the fashion to send a horse or boxer into action lean and gaunt, but recently he saw that bigger horses and fleshier fighters were stronger and faster. He saw no problem with Jeff weighing around 230 pounds.[801]

With his leg healed, Jeffries was doing the work of three men. On the 2nd, he went deer hunting again. After exercising for a couple of hours with the pulleys, light dumbbells, punching bag, and skipping rope, he boxed 2 rounds each with Fitz, Joe Kennedy and Jack Jeffries. Fitzsimmons was not a believer in love taps, and he and Jeffries mixed things in a lively fashion. Bob kept Jeff chasing him constantly, emulating Corbett's style.[802]

On August 3, Jeff and Fitz sparred 3 fast rounds.

> He continued to hustle the big Cornishman about without a let up. At the end of the third round Fitzsimmons came reeling from the ring and, exhausted, sank into a chair while flecks of crimson showed on his lips and dropping to the pink tights that he wore, bespattered them for the first time in many a day. Jeffries, though not even breathing to excess, also received a slight cut in his mouth. The go was a very fast one.

---

801 *San Francisco Evening Post*, August 1, 1903; *San Francisco Call*, August 2, 1903.
802 *San Francisco Call*, August 4, 1903.

After that bout, Jeff sparred 6 more rounds, alternating rounds between his brother Jack and Joe Kennedy. Jeffries "is undoubtedly faster at the present time than at any in his career."

Jeff spars brother Jack.

One man who observed their sparring that day said that Jeffries fought like a demon, tearing into Fitzsimmons like a cyclone. They went at it, and Fitz was panting for wind after 3 rounds. Jeff was tireless and strong. This observer predicted that Jeffries was certain to sap Corbett's vitality and reduce his agility to a point where he could get at him and put him out. If hard hitters like Sharkey, Ruhlin, and Fitz could not damage him, then Corbett could not do so either.

Another report said that all three sparring partners were winded, while Jeff was fresh and strong. Fitz was Jeff's most ardent admirer. He slapped him on the back and announced that he was unbeatable. "What surprises me more than anything is that I made so good a fight against you as I put up. Your strength is overpowering and your stamina so great that I do not understand how any man can hope to cope with you."

Contrary to the view of many who believed that Jim would try to run and last, Jeffries predicted that Corbett would tear in and try to knock him out within 6 rounds. Corbett knew it was his only chance to win because he had already once tried to keep away and box, but failed. "He can't keep away from me for twenty rounds and he knows it." Running and moving would only tire out Jim and delay the inevitable. By trying to fight, at least he had a chance, or so Jeff thought.

Corbett was allegedly weighing about 186 ½ pounds. Jim heard that Jeff was weighing 230 pounds, but that did not concern him. "I believe the bigger he is the slower he will be." His trainer, Tommy Ryan, said, "He will not be good with all that beef hanging to him." Tommy heard that Jeffries had been drinking and eating excessively, and opined that right about now Jeff was wishing he had taken better care of himself.

In sparring large heavyweights like 240-pound Yank Kenny and 185-pound Sam Berger, Corbett was looking strong and speedy, like a dancing dervish, and the same clever boxer he ever was. After sparring 3 rounds with

Corbett spars Sam Berger.

each on the 3rd, Jim was fresh and strong, while they were tired.[803]

On August 4, Jeffries took a short walk and run, worked the gymnasium apparatus for an hour, and skipped rope 1,200 times. He then went 3 corking rounds with Fitzsimmons. Jeff's footwork was rapid and improved, such that Fitz found it almost impossible to escape his rushes, even in a 25-foot training ring. They exchanged hard blows. In the 2nd round, Jeff caught a left uppercut which caused him to bite his tongue slightly. At the close, Bob's mouth was bleeding. Jeff then boxed 3 rounds each with Joe Kennedy and Jack Jeffries, going at each man hard, yet still finishing up fresh.

---

803 *San Francisco Evening Post*, August 3-5, 7, 1903; *San Francisco Evening Post*, August 4, 1903; *San Francisco Examiner*, August 4, 5, 1903.

The Jeffries of the future will unquestionably be a different man from the Jeffries of the past. He will no longer take matters quietly, permitting his opponents to wear themselves out vainly endeavoring to cause dents in his anatomy or puncture the skin on his face, but will rush and mix matters as Sullivan of old did. At this game he looks invincible.

After lunch, Jeff went hunting with his rifle. In the evening, he punched the bag for an hour, then took a swim and had a rubdown.[804]

On the 5th, Corbett sparred Sam Berger 19 minutes straight without a rest, and then sparred some more with Yank Kenny. Yank eventually had to stop after Corbett's blows rendered him defenseless.

That same day, Jeff worked 4 rounds with Fitz and 3 each with Jack and Joe. The pace was not mild, but the intensity was less than it had been.[805]

During the morning of August 6, eight days before the fight, Jeff spent a couple of hours in the gymnasium, where a crowd watched him keep up a terrific tattoo on the punching bag. In the afternoon, he played baseball.

In the evening, at the Harbin Springs Music Hall, for a charity benefit performance, Jeff sparred 3 rounds each with Fitz, Kennedy, and brother Jack in a lively fashion before a standing-room-only crowd. First Jeff sparred with Fitz, engaging in fast and fierce exchanges that left Bob well winded at the finish. Jeffries was so fast with both hands and feet that Fitzsimmons found it difficult to either sidestep or duck his rushes.

> Jeff was fast and forced Fitz to break ground continually. Using at times his low crouch and again standing erect, he frequently got home a punch that left its mark. Fitz stabbed back hard, but his piston-like drives that found lodgment had only the effect of stimulating the champion to greater speed. In the second round a ripping left uppercut from Jeff took Fitz in the ribs and his eyes rolled for a moment. The final round was the fastest yet put up here between the two men, and Jeff on his feet and with his arms acquitted himself somewhat after the fashion of a lightweight.[806]

Kennedy, a favorite with the women, also set a merry pace. Jack Jeffries sparred more cautiously. However, the champion emerged from the bouts with a swollen lip and a slight cut on the head, caused by a collision with the top of his brother's head.[807]

Speaking of their sparring, Fitz said that he tried to hustle Jeff, "but it was like punching at a mountain. You can't hurt the concentrated mass of energy and muscle, no matter how you attempt to take him on." Bob said Corbett could not keep away from him.

---

804 *San Francisco Call*, August 5, 1903; *San Francisco Evening Post*, August 4, 1903.
805 *San Francisco Call*, August 6, 7, 1903.
806 *San Francisco Examiner*, August 8, 1903.
807 *San Francisco Call*, August 8, 1903.

He did the dancing master's act at Coney Island, but it did not avail him. Jeffries now knows his style, and will wade into the slaughter conscious of the fact that he will not be hurt. He knows he can beat down Corbett's guard, and will then follow with a punch to the jaw. ... You know I know what I am talking about. Jeffries' wallops hurt.

Bob also said that Jeff was much improved, and was even better than when he met him.

I have found that he has developed speed and is clever. Mark what I tell you, Corbett will have some trouble in getting to Jeff. ... You might as well talk of a rabbit crushing a grizzly. You can't hurt that monster. Corbett may cut him up a bit like a mosquito, but his punches will not go beneath the skin.

Delaney said that at between 225 and 230 pounds, Jeffries was as hard as iron, clever and fast, and his condition perfect.

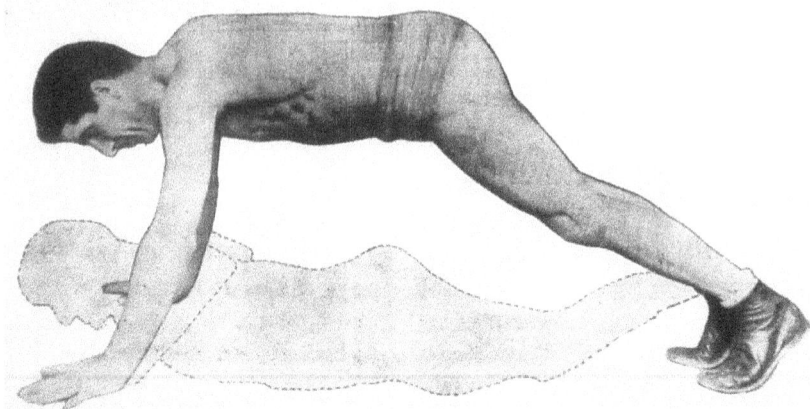

That same day, the 6th, Corbett did his usual sparring with Berger and Kenny at Alameda, tiring them both out. Jim did not see how he could lose. "I am in better condition than when I met Jeffries in New York. … Tommy Ryan has given me some valuable hints on the big fellow, and I will avail myself of his advice and fight accordingly."

Promoter Jim Coffroth believed that Jeffries would win. "He is such a giant in stature and such a glutton for punishment that I hold him to be invulnerable." He felt that although Corbett might outbox him early, Jim would eventually tire and be at Jeff's mercy.[808]

Corbett's friends said that he would win because he was in great shape, and they felt that Jeff would not be at his best. "It is admitted by everyone who recently seen Corbett at his work that he is in much better condition than ever before." The alliance with Tommy Ryan meant a lot to Corbett, "despite the attempt to ridicule it by Jeffries." No love was lost between Ryan and Jeff, and so Tommy was trying to aid Jim in every way he could. Still, Jeff's admirers were offering 2 to 1 odds.[809]

After working with Jeffries for only a week, Fitzsimmons left with his wife on the 7th. Some felt that his leaving was a sign that he was not too happy with Jeff buffeting him about so much in their bout the night before at the benefit. Jeff looked speedy and strong as an ox. "Crafty and cunning as is Bob Fitzsimmons, he was only a boy in the hands of Jeff."

However, the rumors were groundless, for there was no friction. Fitz actually wanted to do more boxing with Jeff, but Jeffries said that he was satisfied with his condition. Fitz said, "Just think! I came 3,000 miles to box ten light rounds with Jeffries. … I thought he ought to have boxed more, and so did Delaney, but Jeffries had a different opinion, and he had his way.

808 *San Francisco Evening Post*, August 7, 1903.
809 *Police Gazette*, August 15, 1903.

Jeffries is very stubborn in his views, and when he gets his mind made up there is no changing it."

Contradicting Fitzsimmons, Delaney said he was happy with Jeff's condition and did not want him to risk injury either to his hands or from one of Bob's powerful blows. Fitz was well compensated for his time. He was paid $55 per round of sparring. Apparently, they boxed six times, 3 rounds each time, for a total of 18 rounds, which cost Jeff $1,000. Bob was still set to be a second for the fight.[810]

Jeffries said that the reports that he was not in condition, that his blood was poisoned, that his training was indifferent, and that the bear bite was serious, were all false. As a result, an upset Jeffries said that no one other than a select few would be admitted to his training quarters from that point on.

For the remainder of his training, Jeff would mostly punch the bag, use the pulley weights and dumbbells, skip rope, wrestle Jack and Joe, and take hunting hikes in the canyons, along with the occasional game of baseball.

It was said that Corbett could not be in any better shape. Still, despite all the talk about his fine condition, it was even money that Jim would not last 12 rounds.[811]

On the 9th, Corbett took a 14-mile run. He punched the bag for a half hour. He was weighing 187 pounds, and expected to enter the ring close to 190. He said,

> I am much better than I was when I last went against him. He may be faster, but I doubt it. He is heavier than before, and my experience teaches me that a man cannot put on ten or fifteen pounds after reaching a limit of 200 without seriously interfering with his locomotion. He then becomes a truck horse. ...

> I am a much stronger puncher now than I have ever been and I firmly believe that I will be able to put force enough into my blows to knock Jeffries down and put him out.[812]

---

810 *San Francisco Call, San Francisco Bulletin,* August 9, 1903.
811 *San Francisco Bulletin,* August 8, 9, 1903.

As of the 10th, Delaney said that Jeffries was stronger and more rugged than ever at close to 230 pounds, but was not high in flesh even at that weight. "He can put up a faster pace and maintain it with greater persistency than ever before. He will go into the ring with Corbett a veritable giant in physique and power and will win though the onslaught he will maintain from start to finish." Jeff would fight Corbett with such strength, speed and agility that he would quickly end the bout and not allow it to drag on needlessly. Even if Jim managed to extend the bout's length, Jeff would win in the stretch.

Most of the experts felt that Jeffries would win, for he was too big and strong. Tom Sharkey said that Corbett was clever and scientific, but Jeff had the punch that counted, and would win in about 10 rounds. Kid McCoy also predicted a 10th round knockout victory for Jeff. Corbett had not fought for some time, while Jeffries had improved. Gus Ruhlin said Jim would make Jeff work for 10-12 rounds, and then youth would be served. Sporting man Jim Wakely said, "Jeff will win if he is in any kind of shape. He is the best man in the world at the game. I have never seen his equal." Joe Kennedy said Jeff would win as he pleased. Jack Root picked Jeff. Marvin Hart said Jeff would win in 12 rounds. "He is a natural born fighter, and I don't believe Corbett could hit him hard enough to hurt him at any stage of the game."

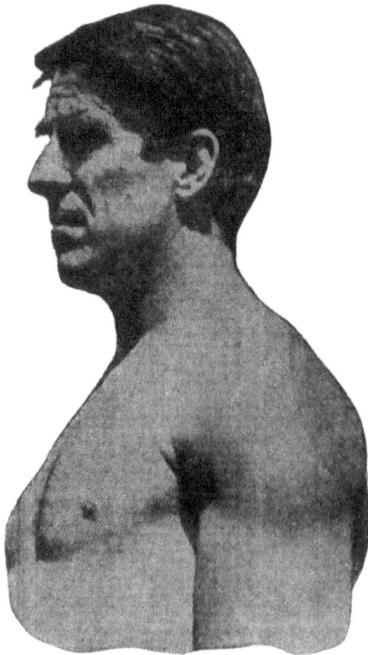

Still, Corbett had his supporters. "That small men often whip big ones is proved by the numerous victories achieved by Tommy Ryan and Joe Walcott over gladiators many sizes heavier." Sam McVey predicted that Corbett would win a 20-round decision. "When you hit at Corbett he has just moved away somewhere." Yank Kenny said Corbett would win a decision. Honest John Kelly said if Jim lasted 10 rounds, he would go on to win a decision. Corbett trainer Professor Dare felt quite sure that Jim would win. Abe Attell picked Corbett. Joe Gans expected the fight to go the limit and said the winner would be

812 *San Francisco Evening Post*, August 10, 1903.

hard to pick. Hank Griffin suspected that Corbett would win on points, or at least earn a draw. Jack Kitchen picked Corbett by decision. "He is a better man today than when he fought John L. Sullivan."[813]

On the 10th, Corbett boxed 12 rounds with Yank Kenny and Sam Berger, taking on each alternately round after round. He also worked the machines.

After working out for an hour in the gym on the 11th, Jeff tipped the scales at 225 pounds.

In his workouts, the 185-pound Corbett showed no signs of fatigue. Jim said that on public form shown in training, he should be the favorite rather than the other way around.[814]

In addition to sparring Berger and Kenny, Corbett had been boxing Tommy Ryan in private as well. Ryan had suggested to Jim that instead of breaking ground and retreating that he should close in, throw his weight on Jeff's arms, and then punch on the breakaway. Jim said, "I shall keep my head, and will punch that big fellow until he will see fists in all directions. I know I am faster and cleverer."[815]

Joe Kennedy said that he had boxed with both Jeffries and Corbett, and did not see how Corbett had a chance. "I was Jeffries' sparring partner when he was training for Fitzsimmons, and the week before that fight I could make a stand-off of it then. I could not keep away from Jeffries at present for four rounds if I had a 20-acre lot to do it." Fitzsimmons called Jeff the greatest fighter in the world and predicted that he would knock Jim out.[816] Clearly, they felt that Jeffries was in his prime.

Delaney said that Jeff was faster and heavier than when he last fought. All of his work in the woods and hills had helped him. The wound on his right leg, just below the knee, where the bear had bitten him, had healed nicely. There was only a small scar showing the spot. He also had a slight scar on his right forearm, a few inches above the wrist, also caused by the bear.

On the 13th, the day before the fight, Corbett sparred 2 rounds with each of his sparring partners (4 rounds total). Jim sprang back and side-stepped as if he were on springs, surprising spectators with his elasticity. Neither Kenny nor Berger could land on him. Jim also worked 2 rounds with the small punching bag and took an 8-mile walk.

Transferring training venues from Harbin Springs to Oakland's Reliance Club, on the 13th, 250 people watched Jeff train. Wearing his black trunks, he shadow-boxed for 23 minutes. "He darted up and down the room with the agility of a panther, and all those present who had not seen him for some time were unanimous in the decision that he had improved

813 *San Francisco Evening Post*, August 10, 11, 1903.
814 *San Francisco Call*, August 11, 12, 1903; *San Francisco Bulletin*, August 11, 1903.
815 *San Francisco Evening Post*, August 12, 1903.
816 *San Francisco Examiner*, August 12, 1903; *Police Gazette*, August 15, 1903.

wonderfully in speed." He then skipped rope for 10 minutes and worked with the apparatus.

After the rubdown, his brother claimed that Jeff would enter the ring weighing 215 pounds, although this was less than what most expected. Jeff did not step on a scale. Another source said that Jeff's weight *after* working out was 218 pounds.

Jeffries said that Corbett could not keep away from him for too long, that whenever the opportunity to land a punch arose, he would seize it, and Corbett and his admirers would know something had happened when he landed. Jeff succinctly and simply said, "I will win." He made no prediction regarding the round.[817]

817 *San Francisco Evening Post*, August 13, 1903.

CHAPTER 35

Leaving No Doubt

Approaching the Corbett-Jeffries championship rematch, some folks were upset that ticket scalpers had already purchased most of the tickets. After the tickets were on sale for only a few hours, it was announced that all of the $5, $10, and $15 seats had already been sold. Fans were concerned that the scalpers would mark up the prices.[818]

On the cusp of the fight, each of the fighters gave their final thoughts. Jeff said,

> I am in perfect condition and expect to win quickly. In my training I have developed my strength but have not sacrificed my speed. ... I will be able to make a more aggressive fight than I have in any of my contests of the past. ... I am certain he cannot hit me hard enough to hurt me, while I am positive that a good, square blow means his certain defeat. ... I feel so much better today than I did on the eve of the mills with Ruhlin, Fitzsimmons and Sharkey. ...

> Corbett will be willing to admit tonight that I have finished my apprenticeship and that I have not forgotten any of the points in the pugilistic game that he and his chief adviser, Tommy Ryan, are alleged to have taught me.

Jeff said that he was never better in his life and was certain that he would win. "On the eve of a championship battle I have never been nervous. It is not my nature and my friends say that I have no nerves."

The day of the fight, Corbett said,

> I shall go into the ring tonight with the greatest confidence in my ability to win. For the past fifteen months I have been employed in preparing myself for this occasion. ... While traveling about the country for over a year past I have shown a great deal of self-denial in regard to indulging in the good things of life. Instead of following in the pleasures that come and go to the showman, I sought the gymnasiums of athletic clubs and there put in my spare time building up my muscles and strengthening my constitution. ... I can truthfully state that I left no stone unturned.

Corbett had studied every one of Jeff's methods and was prepared to meet any possible tactics that he might use. "I have profited, of course, by

818 *San Francisco Bulletin*, August 13, 1903; *San Francisco Call*, August 14, 1903.

597

my former meeting with Jeffries and I in no wise underestimate his capabilities. ... I am in better condition now than I have ever been before in my life."[819]

Tommy Ryan said that although Jeffries was a strong and hard fighter, Corbett had a fine chance to win. "I have given Corbett the benefit of every feature about Jeffries' fighting that is familiar to me. ... Of course, the two men represent entirely different styles of fighting. Jeffries is powerful and tough, but has not the brain or generalship of Corbett."

Even Bill Delaney said that there was no denying that Corbett was as quick as a flash of lightning. However, he was certain that the big fellow would catch him before too many rounds had expired.

> In every fight in which Jeff has participated until the coming engagement his mania was for getting off weight. I have cried out against the system time and time again, for I realize that a man of his massive frame should go into action at nothing short of 220 pounds, but you know Jeff. He had different views and you could not stop him with a battleship. For this engagement things have been different. I outlined a plan of preparatory work that was to his liking and he went to it. ... Jeff could not be better. The title is in no danger.[820]

Corbett's sparring partners had faith in him. Yank Kenny was never more confident in his life about a man winning a fight.

> There are a great many people who think that Corbett has not developed a knockout punch. Well, all I have got to say is that he has. I received the punch myself, and I ought to know. When Jim landed that punch on me I saw a dozen Corbetts. ... I never saw a man so determined. He will rough it, too, with Jeff, and he won't run away like he did at Coney Island. I fully expect to see Corbett knock Jeff out.

Sam Berger said, "Those people who think that Jeffries has everything his own way in this fight are going to be handed a big surprise. ... I feel certain that Corbett will win because he feels so confident himself. I never saw the man in better condition."

However, Jeff's sparring partners were just as confident in him. Fitzsimmons said,

> It will be a repetition of the Jeffries-Jackson affair. Old Peter looked just as good as Corbett does now, he was just as scientific, just as graceful in the ring and could deliver a much harder wallop than Corbett ever could and you remember what a chance he had with the champion. ... You can say that I will be behind Jeff in his corner

---

819 *San Francisco Evening Post*, August 14, 1903.
820 *San Francisco Bulletin*, August 14, 1903.

tonight and if I ever coached in a winning corner, I have scheduled this evening to be that time.

Jack Jeffries said that his brother James was stronger, faster, and harder than ever and would win by knockout. Kid Egan said that youth would be served. Joe Kennedy said that in training, Jeff could give him, Jack Jeffries and Bob Fitzsimmons all they could handle in 3-round doses, and there was no chance for Corbett alone to handle him for 20 rounds.

Referee Eddie Graney spoke about the rules. In the clinches, the man with his arms free could punch, but no holding and hitting would be allowed. He would insist on the men obeying orders to break, but they would be entitled to fight on the breakaways, and therefore had to protect themselves at all times. This was strictly following Queensberry rules. If a man was to fall or be knocked down, the other had to go to his corner and remain there until the other boxer rose.[821]

In *Two-Fisted Jeffries*, Jeff told an interesting story regarding how Graney was chosen to referee the fight.

> Jim was always a smart general, in and out of the ring, and an artist at irritating an opponent. There was a lot of argument as to the referee… As a matter of fact I was determined all the time to force Corbett into naming the man himself, because he had a way of forcing opponents to choose and providing an alibi in case a decision went against him.

So Jeff picked Jim's brother Harry. Naturally, Harry said that would not do because he was Jim's brother. When Jeff started to leave, Corbett asked, 'How about Eddie Graney?' and Jeff agreed. "Then I sat down and laughed, knowing that all the time both of us had wanted Graney, and each wanted the other to choose him."[822]

Just over one year after his last title defense against Bob Fitzsimmons, on August 14, 1903 in San Francisco, the 28-year-old 225-230-pound Jeffries again took on then 36-year-old (almost 37) 186-190-pound former champion James J. Corbett. There was much intrigue regarding the bout because Jim had done so well against Jeff in their May 1900 bout, when Jeffries stopped Corbett in the 23rd round. This was Jeff's third defense against a former heavyweight champion. He was a 2 to 1 betting favorite.[823]

The greatest throng that ever crowded into Mechanics' Pavilion attended the contest. At 3 p.m., there was a line halfway around the pavilion waiting for the doors to open at 6:30 p.m. By 5 p.m., the line of humanity stretched completely around the big building. Small boys who had taken places in line for the purpose of selling their positions reaped a small

821 *San Francisco Bulletin, San Francisco Evening Post*, August 14, 1903.
822 *Two-Fisted Jeffries* at 229-230.
823 The following fight discussion and analysis is taken from the *San Francisco Evening Post, Call, Bulletin, Examiner*, and *Chronicle*, August 15, 1903; *National Police Gazette*, August 22, 1903.

fortune. There were many scraps over the places, and every now and again, the police were called upon to quell disturbances. When the doors were thrown open, there was a seething sea of struggling humanity.

Inside the building, there was comparative order. Uniformed police and Pinkerton men were stationed around the building. Aside from some minor disputes, everything was orderly and the crowd well-behaved.

10,669 people, who generated $62,340 in gate receipts, breaking all attendance and gate records in the state of California, attended the fight. It was said that it would be a long time before a boxing contest would again attract so many people. There were no vacant seats. *The Chronicle* said, "The largest crowd that ever witnessed a prize-fight in San Francisco – some say in the United States – attended the match last night." The $62,340 taken in made it the third highest in box receipts on record for a fight anywhere. The receipts were even greater than Jeff-Fitz II, which allegedly amounted to $40,000. Only Corbett-McCoy and Jeffries-Fitzsimmons in New York had been higher. Actually, a greater number of people saw Jeffries-Corbett II, but the ticket prices were lower. The highest price for a seat was $20, while the prices for Corbett-McCoy had been as high as $35.

At 9:15 p.m., Jeffries was the first to enter the arena and ring. He wore black trunks which extended nearly to his knees. Around his waist was an American flag. Upon seeing him, the immense crowd gave a tremendous cheer. Following him were Bill Delaney, Bob Fitzsimmons, Jack Jeffries, and Joe Kennedy.

Corbett appeared shortly thereafter, clad in a white bathing robe. When they saw him, the crowd went wild. Many rose to their feet, giving him an ovation, hats in hands, cheering "Jim, Jim, our Jim!" The native San Franciscan Corbett had the most admirers and friends. During the fight, they cheered him lustily every time he landed. With him were Tommy Ryan, Professor Dare, Tom Corbett, Yank Kenny, and Sam Berger.

When he entered, Corbett walked across the ring over to Jeff and shook his hand. Both were smiling.

Master of Ceremonies Billy Jordan announced the men. Corbett was given an ovation. The champion received a hearty reception as well. Referee Eddie Graney was introduced to cheers. He wore a Tuxedo.

Challenges were read from Jack Munroe and Jack Johnson. Munroe's challenge was received with jeers, but Johnson's received applause. Jeff turned to Delaney and said he would not fight a colored man, but was ready to meet Munroe. Eddie Cook, Jeff's theatrical manager, sent a telegram wishing him luck.

The bandaging of Corbett's hands took place in the ring, which Delaney and Fitzsimmons carefully watched. Ironically, both Fitzsimmons and Delaney protested Corbett's bandages. Delaney went over and consulted Jeffries. Jeff walked over to inspect, made an examination of the wraps by feeling them, and then nodded his approval and made no objection.

Jeffries wore no hand bandages. He thought they were of no protection and actually led to injury. "In every fight where I have worn bandages I have hurt my hands more than when I left them off."

Sam Berger watched Jeff insert his hands into the gloves. Ryan spoke with Corbett. He helped remove Jim's white dressing robe. Corbett also wore plain black trunks. The photos show he wore a breech clout. He presented the appearance of a perfectly trained athlete. His skin looked healthy and his bulk was greater than in previous contests.

After the men put on and adjusted their gloves, they stood at ring center to be photographed. The boxers then retired to their corners.

Graney called the men to ring center for a final word. Jim's skin looked like marble besides Jeff's swarthy skin. Jordan announced that they would fight straight Queensberry rules and would break on the referee's order. Before the bell, Jeff's American flag was removed.

1st round

Jeffries did not wait on Corbett, but immediately and consistently attacked. Jeff was remarkably light on his feet, standing up straight so that he could quickly move in. Corbett began nervously and resorted to clinching when Jeff drew close. Utilizing little of his usual footwork, Corbett held his ground, punched, and then grabbed. There was a great deal of pulling and hauling on the inside, but Jeff was clearly the stronger fighter. Jim did not land very often, and he could not keep Jeff away. Jeffries forced Corbett to the ropes more than once, and drove in lefts to the body. Either Corbett had consciously decided not to waste his energy moving as much, or Jeffries' fast attack did not allow Corbett to escape as much. Perhaps it was a combination of both.

Jeffries showed remarkable skill as he maintained a fast pace. He feinted, then led and landed on the cleverest man on earth. Jeff ducked Jim's punches and countered in the stomach. Corbett landed his left jab, although without effect, as well as some good rights to the body. He would then close in and clinch for defense, owing to Jeff's relentless pressure. Jim tried to land his right on the break, and often landed his right over the heart on the inside.

Jeffries focused on the body, and landed a crushing blow over the heart which hurt, and Jim again clinched. Corbett would clinch every time Jeff landed to his body. It was clearly Jeff's round.

In between rounds, Corbett's handlers brought out a new wrinkle in caring for a man. Instead of waving fans and towels, Corbett had an immense oxygen tank concealed under the ring platform in his corner. To this was attached a long rubber tube, on the end of which was a spraying machine. After each round, when Jim returned to his corner, a stream of oxygen was sprayed on his face, which had a remarkable reviving effect. Corbett had secretly trained with it and found its effects to be beneficial. No one but Corbett's seconds knew that it would be used on fight night.

2nd round

Corbett landed rights to the body and some lefts to the head, landing more blows than Jeffries did, but they had no effect, while Jeff's counter blows jarred Jim. They mixed it up a bit, with Jeff landing his hook to the body and head, but receiving a hard counter hook to the jaw. There were several clinches, mostly initiated by Corbett, who was ducking Jeff's blows.

After Jeffries missed a left, they clinched. They would not break, Corbett claiming that Jeff was holding on. On the break, Jeff swung his left to the head. He forced Corbett to the ropes, and they clinched. On the break, Corbett hooked a left to the jaw. Jim sent in a left and right to the body, but received a left hook to the head. Jeff came on quickly, but Jim clinched. Thus far, Corbett had shown very little speed, while Jeff showed improvement in speed and cleverness.

During this round, Corbett came within an ace of going out. After separating from a clinch, he attempted to clinch again as Jeff stepped in and landed a terrible stinging left in the pit of the stomach which doubled Jim up. Corbett kept his feet and saved himself by clinching. His face took on a deathly pallor for a moment, and he looked like a beaten man, although it quickly passed away. However, the blow had a long-term effect. It took a heap of fight out of him. Afterwards, many said this was the decisive blow of the fight.

Jeffries also landed a right which caught Corbett in the center of the body and made him wince. The suffering Corbett stalled and used some light blows to the face to keep Jeff off. Actually, according to the *Evening Post*, Corbett did so well with his clever boxing at the end of the round and landed so many punches that he caused some to think that he had the better of the round on points, including the *Examiner.*

However, Jeff's big body blow had the effect of gradually sapping Jim's strength. Jeff was as spry as a kitten and seemed just as clever as Corbett. He could afford to take a chance every time that Corbett did.

3rd round

Corbett saw that he could not elude the relentless Jeffries with footwork, so he took to ducking and holding. When clinching, Corbett would bump his shoulder into Jeff, who then retaliated so roughly that the crowd thought that Jeff was fouling. Jeffries worked his free hand in the clinches, mostly landing his left to the body and head. He was fighting fast and asserting himself, landing hard jabs to the head and body. Corbett landed three lefts in succession to the face, but in the clinch, Jeff worked his right and two lefts to the body. There was some rough fighting, Corbett working in close and directing his blows at the stomach.

The pace and body punishment were beginning to tell on Jim, because he was slow, while Jeff was clever and fast. Corbett did not punch very much, but rather ducked and clinched. Jeff extricated himself from a clinch by pushing Jim away. Corbett blocked a lead with his glove and landed a right to the heart, and then followed with a clinch. Every time they came together, Corbett would clinch to get a respite. When Jeff would miss, Corbett would clinch. Jim landed a right to the body, but Jeff answered with a left swing to the side that hurt. Jim again clinched.

Jeffries hooked his left to the neck but Jim jolted him over the ribs with his right. Corbett ran away to avoid a rush, but then turned quickly and put in a hard right over the heart. There was a lot of clinching. After some light exchanges, Jeff pulled his arms free from a clinch and nailed Jim with some heavy left and rights to the body. Jeff barely missed a right and roughed Jim in the clinch, to some hooting from the galleries. Jeff forced Jim, fighting fiercely. Three times Corbett landed his left hook to the jaw. He landed another hook in the stomach. Jeff only smiled and continued forcing Jim around the ring. Corbett taunted him and then mixed it up, landing a hard right.

The Examiner said it was Jeff's round, and the *Evening Post* agreed that the round was much in his favor. *The Bulletin* also said that Jeff continued to outbox and outpoint Jim, which was a big surprise. However, the *Chronicle* said it was Corbett's round. *The Call* said, "It was a rough round, with honors even as to the matter of blows landed, but Jeffries gave indications of forcing matters at infighting."

4th round

During the round, Jeffries went after Corbett as if he intended to end the fight. Corbett went to the ropes often, but kept up his clinching and clever blocking in order to prevent significant damage. Jeff occasionally slammed Jim on the body and head, but the head blows seemed to do no harm. It was the body blows that counted.

The fight was delayed for a moment, because the seam along the thumb of Jeff's left glove had opened up and the gray padding showed through. The 5-ounce glove had split open due to all the hammering, and because Jeff's hands were so big. After momentarily examining the glove, Referee Graney told them to fight on.

Corbett was clinching more and Jeffries continued hitting him in the body. A left to the head forced Jim to clinch again. He was quite eager to clinch. Jeff fought hard in the clinches, but Corbett got in too close for Jeff to do any real damage. Jeffries swung a hard left on the chest, but Corbett countered with a left on the mouth and right over the heart. Jim jabbed Jeff several times, but the blows were so light that Jeffries laughed and came right back.

Despite his survival tactics, for the first time in the fight, Corbett got dropped, by a mighty left hook which landed either in the pit of the stomach or on the short ribs. Jim sank to the floor on his knees. It looked as if the fight was over. "Corbett's eyes rolled in their sockets and his face took on a look of terrible agony." However, Jim showed that he was a fighter, rising at eight. He blocked another body shot and held on, showing his generalship. Jim survived, and soon thereafter, the gong saved him.

Between rounds, Police Captain Mooney entered the ring, examined Jeff's split glove, and then he and Graney both ordered that a new glove be procured to replace the burst one, whose padding was slipping out. When the minute interval expired, the glove had not yet been replaced. Fitz cut the left glove off and gave Jeff a new one. Replacing the glove caused the rest to be 30-35 seconds longer, which benefited Corbett, who remained in his corner welcoming the extra oxygen and recovery time after the gong had rung to begin the 5th round. Although unclear, this might have shortened the 5th round's duration. Some suggested that part of the 5th expired before they resumed again.

5th round

Jeffries continually fought for the body. Corbett did some fast stepping to keep away as Jeff chased him about the ring. Jim excited the crowd by jabbing Jeff on the face and getting away from returns. However, the enthusiasm was short-lived, for Jeffries followed him up and fought Corbett all over the ring. Jim alternately threw hooks to the head and rights to the heart. He repeatedly tried his right for the heart, his best blow, and frequently landed it, but Jeff only smiled. Jim's left hooks did not seem to have enough power in them to keep Jeff off either. Corbett did throw some hard looking lefts and rights, but they had no effect.

Jeffries stood up straight, walked right in and twice hooked Corbett in the stomach. Jeff sent a right to the ribs again. Jim clinched often, and Jeff worked hard to free himself. Jeffries landed some short jarring lefts to the body and head, forcing Jim to clinch each time. Corbett held his guard low to protect the body, and so Jeff landed his left to the head more often. The champ landed a hard left hook to the jaw, following it up with a left and right to the body. Jim held on.

Corbett possibly landed more blows than Jeff did, but every time Jeffries landed, Corbett's knees would wobble. One observer said the fight was clearly in Jeff's favor at this point. Another said Corbett was tired, and his blows lacked steam. Another said the round was even. *The Evening Post* said the 5th through 7th rounds were similar to the early rounds. Corbett mostly held, or would punch and grab, while Jeff led with hard blows, focused on the body, kept the pace fast, and was much stronger.

6th round

Jeffries feinted and forced Corbett around the ring. Jim momentarily picked it up, landing many jabs. He even tried to attack, thinking that Jeff was fatiguing. However, Jeffries scored another knockdown, each local source giving a different account of how it happened.

Chronicle: Jeff feinted, which caused Jim to drop his guard, and then Jeffries dropped him with a left hook to the jaw. Another version said that during a hot rally, Jeff dropped Jim with a left jolt to the neck
Call: Jeffries crouched for a moment and landed his left jab to the head. He then stood up straight and landed the left hook to the chin.
Bulletin: Corbett ran into a stiff right to the body that doubled him up and dropped him again.
Examiner: Jeff dropped Corbett with a right to the jaw.

Corbett remained down for almost the full count, rising at nine. He stalled by moving away, but then clinched. Jeff hit him with short inside shots, including a double hook to the body and head, followed by a right uppercut to the body.

Although it looked like he would be finished, to the wonderment of all, Corbett recuperated and fought back gamely. He took it and mixed it up, fighting fast at close quarters, crossing Jeff's jaw with a right and also countering with a good right uppercut to the chin, which he then repeated after a clinch. Jeff paid no attention to the uppercuts. When Jim jabbed Jeff on the chin at the gong, the crowd gave him a loud cheer.

The *Bulletin* said Corbett finished the round strong, but the *Call* said the round ended with Corbett weak but smiling. He had shown very little of his once wonderful cleverness, but it had to be conceded that Jeffries had improved in cleverness, making the contrast in generalship less striking than was expected.

7th round

Corbett altered his style and went back to his old stick and move tactics, which worked for a while. Jeff attacked ferociously as Jim used his famous footwork to escape. Corbett evoked tremendous cheering by jabbing Jeff repeatedly, and ducking away from returns. However, one writer said that Jim was unsuccessful at landing his left very solidly. Corbett landed his right to the heart, but Jeff came back with a left to the body.

Whenever Jeffries drew close, Corbett held on. He repeatedly clinched. Each time, the old veteran used his psychological tactics, talking to the audience and to Jeffries. "He can't knock me out. He can't knock me out." "Come on you big duffer." "Why don't you knock me out?" It appeared that Jim was trying to induce Jeff to exert himself more by talking to him. Corbett said, "I'm a pretty hard old guy. You can't knock me out. Just try it if you think you can. What a baby elephant!" Jeff made no reply, but stuck to his work.

As Corbett held and spoke, Jeffries worked his body. Jim was absorbing severe body punishment. Jeff appeared to be trying to knock him out. Corbett landed several short-arm lefts and rights to the head, and even some combinations, but Jeff kept pressing him to the ropes and landing hard shots until Jim clinched.

As soon as they would break from a clinch, Jeffries was on top of him, forcing Jim to clinch again. Corbett took a left to the head, but uppercut Jeff with the right to the chin. Jim was fighting faster on his feet at this stage, using his fancy boxing tactics, but they were of no use.

8th round

In the early part of the round, Jeff was, as usual, forcing matters, landing on the body and head. However, for the first time in the fight, Jeffries slowed up and showed some fatigue. Sensing this, Corbett really picked it up and did well; landing more often, while showing speed and cleverness in eluding blows with head movement. He was not holding as much, and showed more aggression. Corbett's flash of old-time form set his devoted adherents yelling with excitement.

Corbett landed a left to the nose and ducked a left. Jeff hooked his right to the body. Jim landed a hard right to the head. In close, Corbett landed several right uppercuts to the head and body, as well as his left hook. Corbett then sent in half a dozen snappy lefts and rights on Jeff's face, nose, and chin. Some said he was attempting to put Jeffries out.

However, Jeffries did not seem to care, for Jim's blows had little effect upon him, as he kept coming forward all the time. The few blows that Jeff landed had some wondering how Corbett took them. Still, Jeff appeared tired, holding his arms down. At times, he just moved in and clinched, seeming desirous to take a break, perhaps in some distress. Corbett went at him and peppered him with jabs and swings. Jeffries landed a hard left to the body, received two left stabs to the face, but then replied with a left to the head.

Fighting cleverly, Corbett stabbed the eyes and sent in several lefts and rights on the jaw. He seemed to have improved 100%, having changed his style from previous rounds, using more footwork, rapid punches, and his old-time cleverness in ducking and blocking.

At the bell, the crowded house wildly cheered for Corbett, who had won the round. According to Corbett's autobiography, Jim felt that Jeffries was tiring, so he poured it on. However, he was unable to do significant damage because the debilitating body punishment had sapped his power.

9th round

Jeff commenced roughing it from the start, attacking like a bull, throwing his shoulder into Corbett and leaning on him in the clinch. He scored with a left to the head and a right and left to the body.

However, thinking that Jeffries was still tired, and, encouraged by Ryan, Corbett came right back and rushed in dealing out blows, landing a right to the body and then a right and left to the head. Jeff appeared tired. Corbett continued smashing Jeff, landing lefts to the head and rights to the body. He landed quite often, even in the clinches, doing his best work in the fight. There was a long series of clinches. Corbett seemed as strong as ever. Jim landed three rights to the body at close quarters. He also landed three left hooks to the jaw and crossed with the right. He blocked Jeff's efforts and landed three more rights to the body and one on the jaw.

Corbett also jabbed quite a bit, repeatedly stabbing Jeff on the mouth. Each time he landed, the crowd cheered. They were clearly with him. Still, Jim's left cheek showed a lump from one of Jeff's inside blows. Jeff had a similar mark.

Despite all of the blows Corbett landed, Jeffries was able to disregard and shrug them off. At the end of the round, Jeff caught his second wind and showed that he was still strong. He landed a body shot that clearly hurt Corbett. *The Examiner* said it was a right to the body, while the *Chronicle* said it was a strong straight left to the body. *The Call* said Jeff hooked the left to the body and Corbett clinched hard. Corbett weakened and looked beaten. The referee had trouble separating them. Jim stabbed Jeff's mouth with his left three times, but the blows were light. The spectators continued cheering for Corbett.

Apparently, in the corner, Corbett told his seconds that he was "all in," but would do his best until knocked out.

In his autobiography, Jeff said that after hurting Corbett with his big hook to the body, as Corbett returned to his corner, his legs seemed heavy and his feet dragged, so he knew that he had him. Fitzsimmons was begging him to go out and end the fight, sore because Jim had already gone 9 rounds, when Jeff had put Bob out in 8 rounds.

10th round

The battle came to an end in this round. Jeffries stood straight up and went right after Corbett in earnest, without hesitation. Corbett tried to make it a waiting fight. They exchanged some lefts to the face and clinched in between exchanges. Each local source described the end.

Examiner: Corbett landed two lefts on the temple, but Jeffries dropped him with a hard left to the pit of the stomach. Jim rose at nine looking helpless. He shouldered into a clinch, but a right to the body dropped Corbett again. One observer said it was more of a right uppercut to the body.

Chronicle: A Jeffries right on the body made Jim shake his head. A moment later a left in the solar plexus or over the heart dropped Corbett. He rose, but a right to the body dropped him again.

Evening Post: Jeff took a few punches to the head in order to raise Corbett's guard, so that he could counter to the body. When the opportunity arrived, Jeffries landed a right and left to the stomach. Corbett went to the mat and stayed down until the count of nine. He rose, but another punch to the body dropped him again.

Bulletin: Jeff dropped Corbett with a massive sledgehammer left to the body. Corbett staggered to his feet at nine and immediately went into a clinch to recuperate. Jeffries shook him off easily, and shifting, drove his right into the body. Jim sank down in a heap, the suffering and agony clearly pictured on his grimacing face.

Call: Jeffries landed a jolty left to the head and followed it with a vicious, crushing left to the body. Corbett sank down slowly and gazed vacantly out of his eyes. As he groped about on his hands and knees, there was a look of agony on his face. He rose at nine but was defenseless. Jeff feinted and then ripped in his terrible left hook to the body, landing slightly to the right of center. It seemed to paralyze Corbett, who fell to his knees again, clutching his side in terrible pain. His facial features were distorted.

Seeing that his man was beaten and had enough, in order to save him from further punishment, Corbett's cornerman Tommy Ryan retired Jim before the count was over, as Corbett was still struggling to rise. Ryan tossed a big palm leaf fan into the ring, signifying the retirement and acknowledging defeat. He then entered the ring.

Corbett staggered to his feet, doubled over in pain. His seconds helped him onto his chair, which had been brought to ring center, right where Corbett went down. He sat in a doubled over position. It was a number of minutes before Jim could straighten up.

When Corbett's breath returned, Jeffries walked over and they shook hands. Jim said, "I am an old man, Jeff. I thought I could whip you, but I realize now my mistake. The man who can take your measure has not yet been created. I fought the best I knew how, but from the first there was nothing to it." Another quoted Corbett as saying, "I thought I could beat you. I've tried it twice and failed. Now I want to be counted one of your admirers. You are a great fighter."

Bob Fitzsimmons told Harry Corbett, "Take him out of the ring, Harry." Jim, who was speaking with Jeffries, caught he remark, turned and said, "You mind your business or I'll punch you in the nose."

One writer said Corbett had ugly red blotches about his stomach, but otherwise he showed no marks of the ordeal. Another said that Jim showed few marks of the contest, only a few scratches on his shoulders and a slight puffing of the upper lip.

Corbett admitted that he had been frightfully punished. He said that his injuries were not skin deep, but of the kind that would be with him for many a day. In his dressing room, he complimented Jeffries. Various newspapers quoted him as saying the following:

> Jeffries surprised me. He has made wonderful improvement. I never saw him so fast. I am certain that he was not that quick when he fought Fitzsimmons. His footwork has improved and his hitting is cleaner. He did not employ his crouch in the manner that he did in our previous contest. ...

> It's fifteen months gone out of my life, but I don't feel bad.... I was in perfect condition. Science cuts no figure when you are against a man of Jeffries' bulk. ... I tried to give Jeff a hard fight, and I think I did. But he's too big and powerful. No man can put him out. He's abnormal – a giant of strength. It isn't science that counts with him, because no matter how many times you land you can't put him out.... There's not a living man in the ring to-day who can put him out. He's too big and powerful – that's it, that's the whole thing. ...

> No man living today, nor was there ever one, has any business with Jeffries. He is in a class by himself. He is just as strong as he ever was, much cleverer and in the ring tonight his speed was a revelation to me. It was my ill fortune to find him at his best and I have paid the penalty.

Corbett essentially knew the fight was over in the 2nd round when Jeffries landed that heart-breaking left just under his elbow in the short ribs. True, he went right back at Jeff, but it was only a bluff. He thought, cunning pugilist that he is, that his show of aggressiveness would lead Jeff to believe that the best he had was doing no damage, that Corbett was not hurt. However, he told Ryan after the round, "It is all over. That punch took all of the fight out of me." Still, even in the face of a losing battle, Jim fought on gamely.

> I was beaten by the blow to the stomach in the second round. ... That blow caused me to alter my entire plan of battle. ... Many thought that it was my intention to make a runaway fight. It might have been, too, but after that frightful body jolt in the second round there was no runaway in me. ...

I knew that I could not last many rounds longer, so I decided to wade right in and fight Jeffries after his own style. … I was forced to fight close, as every step was wearying, and I thought that if I made the big fellow believe that I was following him up he would extend himself, give me a chance to get at him, and with it, a chance to win the fight. … I kept jollying him and told him he would have to put me out and he tried time and again to do so. …

I saw that I was losing my strength and I tried to give the people a run for their money. He had youth and strength in his favor and I was all in. For a couple of rounds it was nip and tuck, but he was too big and strong. I saw that if I ran away from him I would tire myself. I therefore slugged and tried that way. I had him tired in a couple of rounds. … The blows he landed on my body did the trick. The oxygen used on me after each round refreshed me and my wind was perfect, but I could not assimilate his terrible blows. …

To be candid though, I must admit that Jeffries was my superior in strength and stamina. There is no need of a man 'conning' himself. I am not so good as I once was, while Jeffries is the best man that ever stepped into a ring. In addition to his great hitting powers he can assimilate punishment that would render any other man powerless. To give him his due, I will say that I do not believe the man lives who can whip him.

Corbett felt that he had Jeff in distress for two rounds (the 8th and 9th), but he was too tired and not strong enough to take advantage. He admitted that he taunted Jeff and told him that he could not knock him out, trying to make him angry. Of the knockout, Jim said, "The blow struck me in the upper portion of the stomach and caused me great agony. I was completely out."

In his autobiography, Corbett said that Jeffries was a natural left hander and the fastest for his weight that he ever saw.[824]

Despite his defeat, Corbett still had many admirers. He took his punishment like a man. "The terrible drubbing Jim took about the body will hurt him for several days. Every once in a while last night after the fight Corbett opened his mouth and closed his eyes, wincing with pain. Once he said: 'Well, I'm going to do all my talking tonight. I'll be too sore to talk tomorrow.'" However, Jim told reporters not to feel bad for him.

Corbett erroneously thought he went down in the 2nd round. "I was certainly down in the second, because I remember that I was hurt more then than at any other time." Like Corbett, Referee Graney said Jim went down in the 2nd from a left hook to the body. Either they were wrong as to the round or all of the reporters were. None of the fight reports indicated

824 Corbett at 318-322.

that Jim went down in the 2nd, but rather for the first time in the 4th. Corbett's trainer confirmed that a body shot in the 2nd round took Corbett's strength. However, he remained up.

The official figures said Corbett went down in the 4th, 6th, and twice in the 10th, but not in the 2nd round. The vast majority agreed that Corbett was badly hurt and doubled over in the 2nd, but he did not actually go down. George Siler, Colonel Martin Brady (Corbett's timekeeper), Harry Corbett, and Billy Jordan all said the first knockdown was in the 4th round. The Jeffries brothers both recalled that Corbett went down in the round during which Jeff's glove broke and there was a delay to get a new glove. This was at the end of the 4th. Jack remembered it was the 4th round because he remarked that it was too bad to give Corbett a rest right after a knockdown. Dick Adams said that he distinctly remembered that in the 2nd, Jim made an awful face but stayed up and stalled until the bell. After the first knockdown of the fight in the 4th round, he thought that it was a lucky thing for Jim that Jeff's glove had to be replaced.[825]

Jeffries did not show a great deal of enthusiasm or joy, taking the victory matter-of-factly. He said, "I always knew that I was Corbett's master. When you go into a ring with a man knowing absolutely that you can whip him, I see no reason why you should jump in the air and shout for joy when the referee says the coin is yours."

Jeff said that he was never in better condition in his life, and had added speed and cleverness to his weight and strength. "I was much faster tonight and in better condition than I was at our former meeting. ... I demonstrated what I had repeatedly claimed, that I had improved in science and speed."

The champion had formerly believed that he needed to make a certain weight for a fight, and took off too much flesh. This time, he never stepped on the scale and did not concern himself with losing weight. He did not know what he weighed for the fight.

Jeffries believed that he had proven his superiority over every heavyweight in the world. He said,

> I'm Dutch; that's why I went at him with caution... If I had run in at the first and skipped about I might have got a wallop that would have hurt me. But I never had the slightest doubt that I should put him out. I was not in distress at any time. You can see I have not a scratch, and I was not struck a single blow which I felt. ... Corbett had lots of steam behind his punches, but he never feazed me. ... I gave Corbett my head frequently in the fight, in order that he would hurt his hands. ...There was never a moment in the contest that I was in danger. ...

---

825 *San Francisco Bulletin*, August 17, 1903.

I thought I had him in the second round. The blow I landed was a terrific body punch and would have settled any other man. He surprised me by continuing. ...

He made the kind of a fight I like. I was afraid he would keep away. ... Corbett tried to 'kid' me during the fight, but I laughed at him. I knew he could not beat me and I did not hurry myself. ...

I knew Corbett was tired and my strength was increasing. I knew it was only a matter of time when I would get him. ...

Of course I believe that the end would have come sooner but for the broken glove. That delayed the game for at least thirty-five seconds, and that is a world of time to a leg-weary fighter. When Corbett came up after that long rest it was almost like starting over again, but I had located his weak spot; it was already sore, and I knew that it was only a question of a few minutes when I would find it with right or left and close the evening's engagement.

The Bulletin said that not a blow landed by Corbett affected Jeff at all, and he left the bout without a mark. However, the *Call* said Jeff's nose was puffed and he had a slight swelling of the lips.

Speaking of his future, Jeffries said,

I have always stood ready to defend my title against any man in the world. I bar negroes, however. ... I am now ready to meet all white men for the championship. ... If Jack Monroe wants to fight me I am ready to make some easy money.

Referee Graney was extremely impressed by Jeffries, saying that he was fast, wicked, and clever. He felt that Jeff could easily whip any fighter in the world.

Jeffries showed wonderful improvement. He fought better and faster than he did when he met Fitzsimmons in this city. He even hit harder and his blows had more direction. ... Jeffries showed grand science and great hitting power. He boxed as well as Corbett and was strong as a lion. ...

I was not prepared to see Jeffries outbox Corbett. He lost none of his overpowering strength by taking on the newly acquired cleverness, and every blow told.... His class is so absolute that no boxer in the world can hope to cope with him and a new generation of fighters must come up before the championship will leave his hands. He has ten years to go, with that grand physique of his, and then I doubt if the equal of his present self will ever exist. ... I believe many years will elapse before a new champion arrives.

As good as Jeffries was, Graney still gave Corbett a lot of credit for putting up a skillful and gritty battle.

> It was the best heavyweight contest I have ever seen. Both men fought fairly and with great determination. ... The punches Corbett received in the body hurt him. ... Corbett was extremely clever. He should not be cast down by defeat, as he did splendidly. At one time I thought Jeffries was a little tired, but his natural strength came back to him, and he proved much stronger than his opponent. ... He was virtually beaten in the second round from the blow Jeffries dealt him to the body. ... The blow was a terrible one. He received another hard one near the close of the ninth round, and I knew it was all over. Corbett stalled cleverly, but had to succumb to the terrible blows Jeffries dealt him in the body. The condition of both men was splendid. I allowed first blood to Jeffries. I think Corbett put up the best fight in his whole career.

Graney said Corbett fought differently than before, mixing it up, willing to take a beating. Jim had the advantage in the last few rounds. However, a left to Corbett's body at the end of the 9th did the real damage. He confirmed that the left to the body dropped him in the 10th and that a right uppercut to the body put him out.

Professor Dare, one of Corbett's trainers, said that Corbett's condition was perfect, but he took punishment that would kill an ordinary man. This time, Jim was bigger and stronger, and the oxygen between rounds did him a world of good. However, he simply could not overcome the terrible blows. "I don't think any man could withstand them. Had Corbett not been in such fine fettle he would have succumbed in the second round." It was a testament to this toughness, determination, and condition that he was able to last as long as he did.

Even Tommy Ryan gave Jeffries credit for both power and skill. He agreed that the body blow in the 2nd round took the fight out of Corbett and slowed him down.

> Jeffries is a hard man to beat. He is so big and strong that one must conclude it is impossible to find a man who will be able to take his measure. Before last night's encounter I thought a clever, strong man could beat him, but when he stepped into the ring and showed as much science as Corbett I was forced to take off my hat and acknowledge his superiority.

As usual, the local papers provided their analysis, and they were fairly unanimous in their assessments. The fight was a surprise in that Jeff was quicker than Corbett and actually outboxed him, despite his enormous size. This was doubly impressive because Corbett was deemed without an equal in ring agility. Jeffries had shown a marvelous increase in speed and astonishing cleverness as a scientific boxer. He proved a master at boxing, and his superb condition surprised the spectators. His muscles were hard, yet flexible. He fought as if he knew that he could not lose.

His clumsy leads were absent; his awkward efforts to set himself after missing were a thing of the past. In the year since he beat Bob Fitzsimmons down and out he has added wonderful science to his enormous bulk and unbeatable strength. He could have acquired his knowledge in but one way – from Bob Fitzsimmons, with whom he toured the country and boxed almost nightly.

George Siler said that unlike their first fight, Jeffries "did not rush at him and swing wildly, but moved swiftly toward him, measured his distance carefully, and did not attempt to hit unless Corbett was within distance."

The fight was also surprising in that instead of jabbing and dancing away, Corbett went in and battled with Jeff at close range. Corbett either did not try to stay away or could not do so owing to Jeff's speedy footwork. When Jeff led, Jim would duck and come up with a jolt in close. Corbett's best punch was the right uppercut on the break, particularly to the heart. However, Jeff was better at the inside game.

Corbett surprised many with his grim determination and ability to slug, putting up a plucky and game effort. At times, he showed to advantage in the slugging, and flashes of his old-time speed, but Jeff was systematically beating him down. Corbett's punches would have hurt others, but the mountain of muscle did not even tremble. None of Jim's blows left any impression upon Jeffries, who appeared good-natured, often smiling, conscious of his own strength and fearing no harm. It was the first fight in quite some time that Jeff did not bleed.

Corbett battled gamely in a fast fight, in part because he was in great shape. While he escaped some terrible swings, he was badly punished with short-arm blows. He assimilated a great deal of punishment that only a well-conditioned man could handle. One said that either he had lost some of his vaunted skill or Jeff's improvements were so marked as to eclipse Jim's efforts. His condition enabled him to recover quickly when hurt. Another said it was a great battle because Corbett showed wonderful defensive work when pressed hard, as well as a display of gameness and ability to rally after being hit hard enough to put almost anybody on earth out. However, from the start, it seemed just a matter of time before Corbett would succumb to Jeff's relentless rushes and terrible blows. Corbett's struggle appeared hopeless.

Tom Corbett later said that every time Jim led and Jeff came back with a left swing, Corbett stepped inside of it. That strategy worked well during the 1st round. However, in the 2nd round, "instead of swinging around with it as he had been doing Jeff suddenly brought it in as Jim stepped toward him, and it landed right in his stomach. It was an awful wallop and practically ended the fight." That solar plexus blow completely demoralized Corbett.[826]

---

826 *Police Gazette*, June 11, 1904.

Jeffries rained a storm of blows on Corbett, who fought a desperate fight. Jeff showed speed and cleverness and was as fast with his hands and feet as Corbett. "He never stood, as in other fights, stolidly in his place, doubled into a defensive crouch, but kept on the move with an agility that he never showed before, standing upright most of the time and meeting Corbett with a style of fighting something like his own." Siler said that Jeff was just as accurate if not more so than Corbett. Jim was floored in the 4th and 6th with hooks to the body.

Just when Corbett looked to be done in, he showed the most energy. He changed his tactics in the 7th and moved more. Jeff outpointed him in all but two rounds – the 8th and 9th, when Corbett made his best showing and peppered Jeff with many jolty rights and lefts and followed with uppercuts on the inside, making his last stand. Corbett may have had more points, but despite his wonderful efforts, his blows were not effective. Jeff just grinned and smilingly kept at his work, his confidence evident. "Jeffries walked into them just for the opportunity of landing one himself." Prior to that, Corbett had been "stalling," as he said, thinking Jeff was not in the best condition and that his exertions would tire him. However, his hopes were shattered, as there was no slackening of speed in Jeff's work, and when he came on strong in the 10th, Corbett got stopped. The knockout came from the hook to the body that dropped him, and then a right to the body that finished it.

Jeff was essentially master of the situation from start to finish. At the end, Corbett was helpless and no longer able to defend himself. Age and a great fighter had caught up with him. Despite all his great training, Corbett was outclassed. Lightweight Jimmy Britt said the fight proved the old adage that a good little man cannot lick a good big man.

The San Francisco Bulletin said Jeffries was alone in his glory, that not one of the division's big men was a match for him.

> Like Alexander of old, he has conquered the pugilistic realm and is sighing for new fields to invade, but just now none appear on the horizon. There is absolutely not a fighter in America, Europe or Australia who is worthy of the big boilermaker's attention, and he is right in the prime of his life, too. ... Jeffries stands out alone and in a class by himself.

The San Francisco Call noted that this was Jeff's sixth championship battle in less than four years. It said that Jeffries stood above all of the former ring champions.

The San Francisco Evening Post was also extremely high on Jeffries. It said he fought the best battle of his life and proved that he was the greatest fighter on earth. "James J. Jeffries is invulnerable." Jeff was "perhaps the greatest marvel the pugilistic world has ever beheld." In looking over the pugilistic field, one was led to the conclusion that he would hold the title for a very long time. "In his present form Jeffries is invulnerable."

Jimmy Britt said Jeff added laurels by showing himself to be fast and clever. "It was not the Jeffries that fought Sharkey and Fitzsimmons. ... The improvement in his style, speed and agility was simply marvelous. He is a grand fighter, and I can see nobody looming up on the pugilistic horizon who has even a small chance to bring Jeffries down." Jeff showed the public that there were few things about boxing that he did not know. He was clever, fast, and shifty, showing remarkable swiftness in all of his movements. He also remained calm when Corbett handed out intervals of quick snappy spasms of punishment.

Some said that Corbett was "not there" in pugilistic parlance. "And neither would anybody else be there after taking one or two of Jeff's well directed jolts in the midriff." Corbett said that he was never in his life in better condition. "He was certainly in great shape to stand the punishment he did. In the last three rounds Corbett did some brilliant work. He gave the champion a fight and the people a run for their money." But Jeffries was just too good. "Edison will have to invent a man to lick Jeffries. He has a long lease on his title."

Observers agreed that the champion was without an equal, and unbeatable. One said, "I don't believe the superior of the victor walks the earth. Of one thing I am certain – his peer as to physique and strength does not exist. His massive frame and giant muscles proclaim his invulnerability. ... His last win satisfied me that he is invincible."

The San Francisco Examiner said Jeff dominated, was the fastest big man alive, had improved his footwork and defense, and also opined that no boxer alive could defeat him. Jeff was too strong and clever.[827]

On the east coast, the *Police Gazette* said that by going at Jeff and fighting him, it was the equivalent of handing him the purse. "The Los Angeles man was born to fight that way, and swapping blows is his long suit. He showed it by putting Corbett down four times." However, Jeffries did not wait for Corbett, but rushed rather than playing a waiting game. He had done this with Ruhlin and Fitzsimmons (in their second bouts) as well. Thus, in this fight both men took on tactics directly opposite to the ones they had used in their first fight. Jeff was not as patient, and Jim did not move as much.

The Police Gazette was higher on Jeffries than ever. It called him the greatest champion ever known and indisputably pre-eminent over all other fighters. He had qualified himself in every essential point of fistic skill and ability. The champion was in a class by himself. He could fight with both strength and cleverness. Sam Austin wrote,

> Corbett's excuse that Jeffries was too big for him will reasonably explain his defeat to his own satisfaction, but it is doubtful if the result would have been any different if there was a parity of equality in their respective weights. Jeffries' fighting qualities would have

827 *San Francisco Examiner*, August 15, 16, 1903.

offset any little advantage Corbett might have had in the matter of boxing skill, and it is the fighting ability which tells.

Austin even opined that Jeffries could have defeated John L. Sullivan. The question, then, was who could give him a legitimate fight. Jack Munroe, who was at ringside and saw the slaughter, evidently had no intention of getting into the ring with the champion.

> [Jeffries] stands indisputably supreme as a pugilist. He has qualified in every essential point of artistic endeavor. Coupled with this, great bulk and strength give him advantages which no other pugilist in the world can surmount. He is a champion and the greatest the world has ever seen.[828]

John L. Sullivan said, "Jeffries is a great fighter. He has strength and lots of science, and can make any fighter in the world look like 30 cents." When asked if he thought that Jeff was as good a man as he was in his prime, Sully said, "Well, he's just as good, anyhow. I don't know whether he would be able to go a fight like that which I put up against Ryan or Kilrain. Fighting today is play business compared with what it was when I held the belt."

The day after the fight, Corbett and Jeffries met at Harry Corbett's and discussed the previous night's contest in a friendly manner. Jeff asked, "How do you feel?" Jim responded, "Devilish sore, Jeff. Did not sleep a wink all night. Was so sore in my body where you punched me that I couldn't find a spot in bed where I could rest without getting a pain." There were bruises everywhere that Jeffries had hit him. Corbett acknowledged that the body blow in the 2nd round took the fight out of him. Jeff replied, "You stopped a bunch of hot ones. In fact, you took more punishment than Fitzsimmons." Jeff had no marks on his face, while Corbett only had a slight swelling on the left cheek bone, scarcely noticeable.

Corbett told Jeffries, "You were never stronger or faster in your life. Unless you dissipate and ruin yourself you ought to be champion as long as you have a foot out of the grave." "You can whip any two men in the business."

Jeff replied that he had trained differently. He spent more time hunting, and did not worry about his weight as he had in the past. Jim said, "To give you an idea of how strong you were… When you threw your left shoulder against me you almost knocked me over, and when I tried to stop one of your left leads your glove carried my blocks back and you made me hit myself thereby. I never had this happen to me before."

Corbett also said that Jeffries would have beaten John L. Sullivan on the best day that Sullivan ever saw.[829]

828 *Police Gazette*, August 29, 1903.
829 *San Francisco Bulletin*, August 16, 1903.

Despite all the accolades, Jeffries was growing tired of the fight game. "I am not proud of being the champion fighter of the world. It means nothing to me except that I make my living out of the game." If he could be a championship fisher or hunter, he would be proud of those titles, for those were his true passions. However, boxing made him the big money.[830]

The fighters received about 70% of the $62,340 taken in, with Jeff receiving approximately 75% of that ($32,728.50) and Corbett 25% ($10,909.50). The Yosemite Club realized $18,702.

It was later said that Corbett actually made less. Fearing that the gate would be small, he made a side agreement with promoter Jim Coffroth wherein he would be guaranteed 75% of $25,000 if he won, and 25% of that amount if he lost. Thus, he came away with $6,250, and Coffroth made another $4,659.50.

In the days following the fight, Corbett was complimented for his gameness. He was outclassed in weight and hitting powers, but he did not break ground as he had in the past. Jeffries went at him in utter disregard for his punches, confident that Corbett could not knock him out. Jeff's lack of fear made him appear even cleverer.

Even Bob Fitzsimmons, no friend of Corbett's, gave Jim credit for the game fight that he put up. "I know full well how Jeffries can hit and I think Corbett, as I have said before, made a great showing."

A week or so after the fight, Corbett further said of Jeffries, "The more I think about him and his style - … the more I admire him. He is a great fighter and worthy of every praise for skill and strength, but he was too strong for me in spite of my own training to meet that very condition. It was that awful punch in the second round that done me."

Jeff said that his favorite punch was the left hook to the body, and he had defeated Ruhlin, Fitzsimmons, and Corbett with that punch.[831]

Speaking of the fight a month or so later, Corbett said,

> I never got such a beating as Jeffries gave me. He is the one fellow I want to duck when it comes to fighting. He can lick two men in a ring any time. He'll never be beaten unless he is caught out of condition. … He bent one of my ribs with that punch in the second round and it will take me at least six months to get over it.[832]

Jeff later returned the compliment, saying, "They said this fellow Corbett could not punch. I discovered that he could wallop, as a number of his blows certainly stung me good and hard. Corbett took an awful beating in our fight. He never flinched, however, until he could fight no longer."[833]

830 *San Francisco Call*, August 16, 1903.
831 *San Francisco Call*, *San Francisco Evening Post*, August 17, 1903; *Police Gazette*, September 12, 1903; *San Francisco Bulletin*, August 23, 24, 1903.
832 *Police Gazette*, October 10, 1903.
833 *Police Gazette*, November 7, 1903.

CHAPTER 36

Justifying Challenges

Following the mid-August 1903 Corbett fight, it appeared that James Jeffries had cleaned out the division. He was so good that there was no one that the public or press really demanded that he face. Sure, there were some up and coming contenders, but they had not yet elevated themselves to the level of public esteem of those whom Jeff had already fought.

> Jeffries now fears there is no pugilist on earth capable of giving him a battle. He laughs at Jack Monroe and smiles when Jack Johnson is mentioned. The negro may be a good, clever fellow, but he would be outclassed worse than Corbett was. He has a soft punch, and could not hurt the big gladiator in a month.

> There is one man who might have a faint chance of success, and that is Sam McVey, the Oxnard giant. He weighs in excess of 200 pounds, and has a very hard wallop. He is the only kind of a man of whom the champion would stand in the least bit of danger. Punchers like Gardner, Monroe, Sharkey and Ruhlin are easy game for the champion.[834]

Jack Johnson said,

> They say there's only two men left who have a chance [with Jeffries]; that's Sam McVey and myself. Well, I have beaten this Mr. McVey once and can do it again any time he gets a side bet ready. … My man now is Jeffries. I'm big enough, weigh near 200, and I'll tell you the fight won't be one-sided. He can't touch a man with his right, and I'm sure I could take care of that left and slip him a few on the side.

However, Hank Griffin said that he wanted to fight Johnson. He noted that he had a victory over Johnson, and the best that Jack could do against him was to draw. "According to that, I must be the [colored] champion and not Mr. Johnson." Jeffries had stopped Griffin once, and easily handled and decked him several times in their 4-round exhibition.[835]

Jeffries said that he would fight any white man on earth, but "there is no chance of his ever crawling through the ropes with a coon."

Jack Johnson opined that Jeff was right in drawing the color line against any old colored fighter, but felt that after all of the colored fighters had

---

834 *San Francisco Evening Post*, August 17, 1903.
835 *San Francisco Bulletin*, August 18, 1903.

faced one another and one emerged as the best, that Jeff would withdraw his objections and accept his challenge. Johnson said that he would challenge the winner of the upcoming Ed Martin–Sam McVey fight.[836]

Racial perceptions, prejudices, and analysis in the fight game were alive and well. One writer noted,

> It wasn't but a few generations back that Ireland and England produced all the fighters. The English boxer of those days was rugged, bulldog in his pluck, occasionally well-scienced, but never brainy or intellectual, while the Irish fighter always had the native wit and quick thinking powers of his race. The French or German boxer was unheard of, Australia had developed no scrappers, and the Jews of the ring were all English Hebrews – some of them among the best men of the day.

> When Australia began to turn out stars, they were men of the Irish blood, and the champions who rose up in America were Irish, too…. Since that golden day, the other nations which have migrated to America have learned the art, and the grade of English boxers has deteriorated.

> Italians have fairly swarmed into the ring in recent years. The Italian is imitative, and took to the ring not because he was a fighter, but because the first Italians to try the game made money. It was at first thought that they would quit when hurt, but punishment only seems to make the Italian boxer wrathful, and when an Italian's dark face looms up in a corner the spectator can settle back in his seat, satisfied that he will see some good going.

> Jewish boxers have thinned out in the past three years, and there are not nearly as many Hebrews in the ring as there were a short time ago. The Jewish boxer is always fairly scientific, crafty and an admirable ring general. It is usually supposed that the Jewish boxer, like Choynski, saves his money, but as a plain fact most of them have been of the gay type…and have blown their money as fast as it came in.

> German fighters are now numerous…[T]hey are game, but they do not rise to the heights of topmost fame and championships. The German is generally a slugger…and delights the crowd, win or lose. Bohemian boxers have just begun to shine. Root, of course, is the star…the Bohemian is thoroughly courageous, and the fairest, squarest kind of a fighting man.

> It is amusing to note the way in which the crowd at a ringside receives the different nationalities of fighter. There is always a hearty cheer

---

836 *San Francisco Bulletin*, August 24, 27, 1903.

and earnest backing for the Irishman; grins and good-humored tolerance for the German, and virulent hostility to the Italian and the negro. Put a boy of any other race in with an Italian, and everybody in the house who is not himself of Italian origin at once begins to root frantically against the son of ancient Rome. It is to the credit of the Italians that they have pushed so far forward against such adverse influences.

Racial attitudes continued to influence the heavyweight champion. Jeffries freely admitted that he would not defend the title against a black challenger, announcing, "I will fight any white man in the world, but will not fight a negro."

The Police Gazette's Sam Austin said that Jack Johnson could provide Jeff some trouble in a couple years, if properly developed. Still, even if Johnson was considered a worthy challenger, Jeffries was not going to fight him due to his race. Some criticism was made of Jeff's color line stance.

> Jeff knows him, and has followed his career with no little interest ever since he burst upon the scene as an eligible opponent for titular honors. George Gardiner, the present light heavyweight champion, who believes he can whip Fitzsimmons, proved to be little more than a plaything for this burly black fellow, and the latter did awful things to 'Sandy' Ferguson, a second-rate heavyweight fighter who knocked out Bob Armstrong in one round the other night. Johnson likewise put a terrific crimp in the championship aspirations of Denver Ed Martin, the giant black whom we all thought a year or two ago was the legitimate successor to the title. Just because he happens to be black, Sharkey, Ruhlin, Corbett and Fitzsimmons can't see him when he assumes a fighting attitude, and now Jeffries has found his eyesight so acute that he can differentiate between colors, and draws the line, although he was, perhaps, afflicted with a peculiar sense of blindness when he fought Peter Jackson, Bob Armstrong and Hank Griffin.

> Notwithstanding the prevailing objection to color, just keep your eyes on this black fellow. He has all the qualifications needed to face Jeffries but experience – size, weight, strength and ability. Give him a chance to get ring-wise by facing him against the whole group of second-raters, and I am confident that in two years time he will give Mr. Jeffries a surprisingly good fight.[837]

Still, even the *Gazette*, which was historically a big proponent of racial equality in boxing, felt that Johnson required another couple years of experience before he would be ready for Jeffries. What Austin failed to recognize was the fact that Jeff was willing to fight blacks if it was not a

---

837 *Police Gazette*, August 22, September 5, 1903. On August 20, 1903, Sandy Ferguson scored a KO1 over Bob Armstrong.

championship bout. However, he did not want to give a black man even the opportunity to win the crown, consistent with the general social norm of the day, particularly when it came to the top prize – the heavyweight championship.

Regardless of the color line issue, Jeffries was considered peerless. Most discussions regarding who would be his next opponent focused on Jack Munroe. "Munroe is a big, husky, strong fellow who gave the champion a hard argument. ... Those who were at the ringside maintain that he had the better of the bout." Jeffries denied the truth of those reports and offered to put the miner out in 6 rounds or forfeit all interest in the purse. Since meeting Jeff, Munroe was said to have improved a great deal, so much so that he was now saying that if they met again, he would put Jeffries out. The only way to settle the issue was for them to get into the ring again.[838]

Munroe was touring around giving boxing and wrestling exhibitions, working on his skill, and trying to impress the general public as to his worth. He was also capitalizing on his new-found fame as a result of the reports of the Butte affair.

Ultimately, the public did not believe that anyone had much of a realistic chance with Jeff. He had defeated all different types of fighters. *The Police Gazette* said that Fitzsimmons had tried terrific hitting power and cunning tactics, and failed. Ruhlin futilely tried his bulk and boxing. Sharkey used bullrushing vigor, and it did not work. Corbett used science and speed, and there was nothing doing. "What, then, can be put in the ring with Jeffries?"[839]

The reports of his performance against Munroe had upset Jeff, and he wanted to clear things up. In September 1903, he signed articles to fight Jack Munroe in a 20-round bout, the fight to be held in October. However, Munroe wanted additional time to train, desiring the fight be held in November.

Some said that Munroe was reticent to fight Jeff, preferring to continue capitalizing on his new-found fame in exhibitions and wrestling bouts. Still, he talked a good game. He said that no one could knock him out in 20 rounds, let alone 4, including Jeffries. Munroe held fast to the version that he had knocked Jeff down. "I've been aching for a whack at that man Jeffries ever since I knocked him down in our exhibition bout." Munroe insisted on having adequate time to prepare, so the match was temporarily off because he did not feel ready.

The Gazette criticized that if Munroe was sincere, he would sign to fight some contender in order to prove himself. "As for his beating Jeffries that is the most ludicrous thing I ever heard of. ... Munroe and his manager evidently see an opportunity to get a big loser's end." It felt that they were

838 *San Francisco Evening Post*, August 28, 1903.
839 *Police Gazette*, September 5, 12, 1903.

trying to build up a fight with Jeffries so that they could make more money in the end.

The Gazette continued harping on Jeff's color line stance. The fact that he drew the line actually helped gain Jack Johnson more support and publicity from that paper than he might have otherwise received. Johnson was campaigning for a shot at Jeffries, hoping to perform well enough in his fistic engagements to obtain the public's support in his demands for a title fight.

> While Jeffries continues to reiterate that he will not fight a black man for the title of heavyweight champion of the world, the curtain-colored individual whom he believes to be the only menacing factor to his remaining in undisputed possession of that title, has started on a campaign of fistic engagements which he hopes will in time justify the support of public opinion in his demands upon Jeffries for a fight. That person is Jack Johnson, who is now the recognized colored champion heavyweight. Johnson is matched to fight Sandy Ferguson in the new fistic arena at Colma, Cal., on Oct. 16. Ferguson and Johnson have already fought a couple of draws in Massachusetts, where ten rounds is about as far as the authorities will allow fighters to go, but at Colma these big fellows will be privileged to scrap for twenty-five rounds if they can't settle their argument in less time....

> Though not quite twenty-one years old Sandy weighs 226 pounds in condition and stands 6 feet 3 inches in his stocking feet. This makes him a bigger chunk of humanity than the present champion, who is no Lilliputian. Ferguson is no untried soldier in the arena. Aside from meeting Johnson twice he has a draw with Gus Ruhlin and two wins over Bob Armstrong, whom he defeated in a round each time. Tim McGrath, who is training him, says that Ferguson does not know his own strength. He has seen him play with 500 pound iron dumb-bells as if they were so much wood.[840]

On September 15, 1903 in Los Angeles, Sam McVey scored a KO1 over Denver Ed Martin. *The Detroit Free Press* wrote,

> It really looks as if Jeffries will have to fight a black man or quit the game. McVey's easy victory over Ed Martin has boomed the first named's stock at the coast, and a battle between McVey and Jack Johnson should now be a big drawing card. With this over, there would be nothing further to consider but a match between the winner and Jeffries. The champion is doubtless right in his contention that a black champion would be repugnant to most sport followers. Still, we have a few of them now, with Gans at the top of the lightweight division and Walcott the leader of the welters. Their accessions to

---

840 *Police Gazette*, September 19, 26, 1903.

their respective thrones did not result in civil war. Dixon was the boss of his class for years, and was popular, though never so great an idol as he would have been had his skin been white. It is possibly up to Jeffries to show us that in some of the divisions that white talent is better than black. And defeat of Jeffries would merely result in greater activity in the heavyweight class, in the effort to bring to light a white man capable of recovering the lost laurels.[841]

THOSE DARK CLOUDS.

However, despite the fact that he believed that he could not be defeated, Jeffries was determined not to even take the chance of losing the championship to a negro. He said that when there were no viable white contenders to fight, he would quit the business.

Jeffries had boxed against a number of blacks before his reign. He even sparred black fighters as champion, and had an exhibition with Hank Griffin, but he never did have an official *title defense* against a black fighter.

At that time, racial discrimination was not something boxers felt the need to hide. It was practically stated as a matter of pride. The color-line was an understood barrier that existed to protect the heavyweight championship for whites. Jeff could not even risk the possibility of the championship falling into the hands of a black man.[842]

Quite frankly, as of 1903, not many reporters were clamoring for Jeffries to fight a black fighter. No contender, white or black, particularly stood out as a genuine threat. The general consensus of sportswriters was that Jeffries

---

841 *Detroit Free Press*, September 20, 1903. George Dixon, a Canadian black fighter who won the world featherweight crown in 1898, made seven successful title defenses in 1899 until losing the title in 1900 to Terry McGovern, a white fighter.
842 Randy Roberts, *Papa Jack*, (N.Y.: The Free Press, 1983), 31, citing the *Los Angeles Times*, September 30, 1903, and *Bakersfield Daily Californian*, August 19, 1903; Al-Tony Gilmore, *Bad Nigger!* (N.Y.: Kennikat Press, 1975), 30; Jack Johnson, *Jack Johnson Is A Dandy* (N.Y.: Chelsea House Publishers, 1969), 171. Johnson said of Jeffries, "For a long time he declared that he had drawn the color line."

was in a class by himself and unbeatable. Even the *Police Gazette* said that Jeff was indisputably supreme and the greatest champion ever.[843]

Some historians have felt that Jeffries' color line stance was made in response to Jack Johnson's ascendancy. However, Jeff had drawn the color line against Ed Martin as well. Jeff's trainer/manager Bill Delaney was a staunch believer in the color line and likely influenced him.

Johnson had gained some respect at that point, but still had not yet established himself as a true threat to the perceived as invincible Jeffries, so there was little pressure from the general public for a fight between them. In fact, Jeffries had been more impressive against common opponents:

Hank Griffin

Jeffries – 1893? KO14 or 15 and 1901 EX4 – easily handling and dropping Griffin multiple times.
Johnson - 1901 L20, D15, 1902 D20 (twice?).

Joe Choynski

Jeff - 1897 D20.
Johnson - 1901 LKOby3.

Joe Kennedy

Jeff - 1901 KO2.
Johnson - 1902 KO4.

Pete Everett

Jeff - 1898 KO3.
Johnson - 1902 W20.

Former champion John L. Sullivan gave Jeff his stamp of approval as a fighter, but ironically, disapproved of his drawing the color line.

> Jeffries is one of the greatest heavyweights this world ever saw, and there is no one today that has any show with him. They have got to get a bigger man than him to down him, but I do not see any one at present that is good enough to meet him. I don't see how he can draw the color line, however. He has met colored boxers before now, and I cannot see how he can bar them now. I do not believe in white men meeting colored men, but the boxers never followed my example.[844]

---

843 *Police Gazette*, August 29, 1903.
844 *Detroit Free Press*, September 27, 1903. The legendary Sullivan also gave his opinion on other matters. "There is a great boxer in Bob Fitzsimmons, and people may call him an old man, but, in my opinion, he can defeat any one in the world, bar Jeffries.... There is one thing that amuses me, and that is this talk by some of these boxers who say they have invented new blows. It is ridiculous. The blows nowadays are the same as those used years ago.... This continual cry of fake is tiresome, for I don't believe there have been many fakes pulled off. If they continue to make that howl about crookedness, it will have a tendency to hurt the sport, which is the best in the world."

Jeffries said, "When there are no more white men to fight I shall quit the game." Unfortunately, though, "There are no men for me to fight in America except negroes, and I don't intend to fight colored men."

Again speaking of his bout with Munroe, Jeff said that he allowed him to last 4 rounds out of consideration for the local Butte folks. "Now Munro goes around the country saying, 'I licked Jeffries; I knocked Jeff down.'"[845]

It seemed that there was not a white fighter left who had any chance of defeating Jeffries. He was going to wait to defend his title until there was a marketable white boxer whom the public was willing to pay to see him fight.

> It is probably Jeffries' purpose to lay back for a while and watch the new candidates fight it out among themselves; then if he sees that any one of them impresses the public with the idea that he would give Jeffries an interesting fight, the big fellow will, as usual, not be found backward about making a match.[846]

Although championing Jack Johnson's right to fight Jeffries, even the *Police Gazette* did not think he or any other black fighter had much of a chance to defeat him. "There are a few negroes in the game, who might do for a few rounds, but they will not be given an opportunity by the champion, who within the past year or so has drawn the color line."

In October 1903, Jeff stopped off in Chicago. He said, "I am still in the game, and will fight any white man they can trot out, but I draw the line on colored men. Not that I am afraid of the dark skinned fighters, but if I am booked for a licking I want a white man to do the trick."

Speaking of his other favorite topic, Jack Munroe, Jeff said, "Oh, yes, he is the fellow that has been strutting as a fighter because I failed to knock him out in four rounds. I do not think he could be hauled into a ring with me with a black and tackle."

Since the Corbett fight, Jeff had been mostly hunting. He had taken a trip down the Yuma River into Mexico. Jeff preferred spending months in the mountains hunting to fighting for thousands of dollars. He was growing tired of the fight game, and said that he would willingly give up his boxing title for the honor of being known as the champion hunter.

> I was virtually forced into the fighting game, and will admit I fancied it at first. The honor of being champion was as pleasing to me as was the money I could earn by becoming champion. It is an old story with me now, but I suppose I have got to go through with it now that I am so deeply mixed up in it.[847]

---

845 *Los Angeles Times*, October 21, 22, 1903.
846 *Police Gazette*, October 31, 1903.
847 *Chicago Tribune*, October 17, 18, 1903.

One exchange said that Jeff would eventually be compelled to fight or retire. Folks such as 20-year-old 220-pound Sam McVey wanted a chance at the title. However, Jeff said that he would have nothing to gain by fighting black fighters. Clearly irked by Munroe's boasts, Jeffries wanted to fight Munroe in order to wipe out his claim that he was Jeff's conqueror, which he held was a fabrication.

On October 27, 1903 in Los Angeles, Jack Johnson won a 20-round decision over Sam McVey, again defending his colored heavyweight title. The fight generated $7,500. *The Los Angeles Times* wrote that Johnson was now the logical contender for Jeff's title. He was the master of his race, possessed of undeniable ability, and a man against whom Jeff could show the best there was in him.[848]

Jeffries changed his mind about wanting to fight Jack Munroe. He was concerned that a fight between them would not draw a sufficient attendance, and therefore he would not reap a sufficient financial reward. He wanted Munroe to fight some legitimate bouts in order to prove to the public that he was worthy of a title shot. Jeff said that Munroe was living on his fifteen minutes of fame.[849]

Indeed, on November 7, 1903 in Philadelphia, Munroe took on Peter Maher. Although the 34-year-old Maher had seen his better days, he was still a powerful puncher, vastly more experienced than Munroe, and a "name" fighter.[850]

In the 1st round, Munroe dropped Maher with a left. Later in the round, Maher landed a right to the jaw that dropped Munroe, but the bell saved him. During the 2nd round, a butt in the clinch cut Munroe. Still, Munroe landed a right that dropped Maher, who rose and fought hard as the gong rang. They exchanged heavy blows in the 3rd. In the 4th round, they continued exchanging. Munroe forced the fighting; raining in a rapid succession of blows until Maher sank to the floor exhausted, taking the full count. Jack Munroe had shown that he could fight. He could give and take a punch.

Jack Johnson sent the *Police Gazette* a letter saying, "I feel that notwithstanding the heroic efforts of Mr. Jeffries to erect the color barricade, I will yet get in the square with him, in the event of which I promise a good account of myself." A lot of people felt the same way. Johnson was 25 years old and weighed 190 pounds. His recent record included 1902 KO5 Jack Jeffries, D20 Hank Griffin, KO12 Frank Childs, WDQ8 Fred Russell, W20 George Gardiner, and W10 Sandy Ferguson; and

848 *Los Angeles Times*, October 25, 29, 1903; *Police Gazette*, November 7, 1903.
849 *Police Gazette*, November 14, 1903. Four rounds of three minutes in length plus the three minutes total rest between rounds equals fifteen minutes. Hence the phrase "Fifteen minutes of fame."
850 Peter Maher's results over the past few years included: 1900 KO1 Steve O'Donnell, KO5 John Klondike Haines, KO2 Jim Jeffords, and L6 Gus Ruhlin; 1901 KO2 Jeffords; 1902 NC3 Sharkey, LKOby2 Ruhlin, W6 Fred Russell, KO1 Jeffords, L6 and D6 Jack O'Brien, and LKOby2 Kid Carter; and 1903 LKOby2 Joe Choynski, LKOby1 George Gardner, and WDQ3 Joe Grim.

1903 W20 Ed Martin and W20 Sam McVey. *The Gazette* asked, "Doesn't that make him look to you like a comer? Does to me."

Still, the *Police Gazette* acknowledged that Jeff's color line stance had nothing to do with fear. "Nobody can honestly believe that Jeff has anything to fear in the outcome of a meeting, but a lot of unthinking people will jump to the conclusion that he fears he will be beaten and offer that as a reason for his declining to fight." Jeffries said, "I am ready to meet any fighter in the world, if he is a white man, and as far as a licking is concerned, I don't fear any black man, but if such a thing should happen that I was to be beaten, I would rather give up my title to a white man." However, this writer felt that if there were no white men left to fight, then Jeff's only alternative would be to become color blind.

Speaking of Jeff's refusal to defend the title against blacks, Bill Delaney said, "If ever a colored man should happen to win the championship the white people would have to move out of San Francisco."[851]

Jack Munroe was next matched to fight Al Limerick, the 6'4" 220-pound heavyweight who had recently dropped Philadelphia Jack O'Brien for the ten-count in the 1st round of an impromptu scrap. The 5'11 ½" 195-200-pound Munroe engaged both Bob Armstrong and Jack "Twin" Sullivan to spar with him to prepare. Munroe claimed to be 27 years old, and did not drink or smoke or dissipate. He was working hard all the time.[852]

On December 7 at Boston's Old Howard, spectators watched Munroe spar 3 rounds with Bob

Jack Munroe, on right

851 *Police Gazette*, November 21, 28, 1903.
852 *Police Gazette*, November 28, December 12, 1903; *Boston Post*, December 1, 11, 1903. Jack Twin Sullivan was said to be a 160-pound middleweight who had fought 160 ring battles. In a 1903 6-round no decision bout, Sullivan dropped Jack O'Brien twice, and it was all O'Brien could do to last the distance. However, in a December 1903 rematch, Sullivan lost a 15-round decision to O'Brien. *Police Gazette*, September 10, 1904.

628

Armstrong. Jack was more of a fighter than a boxer, but was quick on his feet and displayed considerable cleverness. He had a superb physique and was very strong, several times landing on Armstrong harder than he had intended. "He undoubtedly has the punch, and would make trouble for any heavyweight in the ring." That week, Munroe gave two appearances per day with Armstrong.

Jeffries was also in Boston to fill a sparring engagement at the Palace Theater with Joe Kennedy. It was his first sparring engagement since he returned east from California. On December 7, Jeffries gave two performances, sparring 3 rounds with Kennedy in both the afternoon and evening. He too was set to give exhibitions twice a day every day that week. He was also doing light gym work with Steve O'Donnell. Jeff was weighing 244.7 pounds. The doctor who weighed him said that back in 1899, Jeff was 228 pounds.[853]

On December 10, 1903 at Steve O'Donnell's gym in Boston, Jeff was scheduled to spar 10 rounds, alternating 1 round each with Kennedy and O'Donnell, back and forth. However, in round 7, Kennedy began to rough it. He landed a right to the body and left to the face. Jeff backed away, and as Joe swung his left for the head, Jeff ducked and landed a straight right to the jaw, and Joe went to the floor, completely knocked out. That was enough for him for one day.[854]

On December 11, 1903 at Colma, California, Jack Johnson won an unimpressive 20-round decision over Sandy Ferguson in a fight that was called uninteresting. Neither really tried to force the fighting, and the crowd was not slow to voice its disapproval by hissing. "Johnson did most of the leading, but his blows lacked steam." The slightly more aggressive Johnson landed his left often. Ferguson occasionally landed his jab, but without effect. Johnson's performance was called disappointing. Neither had any marks afterwards.

Jack Johnson's cautious, slow-paced, mostly defensive style, and lack of a big punch certainly did not help foster any big momentum or public demand for his obtaining a title shot. He was very clever, but not that entertaining. His stock dropped. Even the *Police Gazette*, which had previously supported Johnson, said he had no chance with Jeffries, who could easily defeat him.

> If his fight the other night was the best evidence of his ability that Jack Johnson can give then he had better chloroform his ambition to ever become heavyweight champion of the world and content himself with occupying a less exalted sphere. Incidentally, Jim Jeffries is to be pitied for so hastily drawing the color line, and by so doing cheating

853 *Boston Post, Boston Herald, Boston Globe,* December 7-10, 1903. Jeffries said the hardest fight of his career was with Tom Sharkey at Coney Island, owing to the fact of the injury to his left arm and the terrible heat from the thousands of lights directly above their heads.
854 *Boston Globe,* December 11, 1903.

himself out of a chance to add many thousands of dollars to his already plethoric bank roll by doing up the negro with neatness and celerity. It is plainly evident now that Jack Johnson, the huge Texan Black, has no pugilistic claims to justify his classification with the champion. He is all right in his own division and is probably the best negro fighter in the world today, but that isn't saying very much, for since the days of Peter Jackson there hasn't been a black skinned fighter who merited serious consideration as an aspirant for championship honors. Johnson fought twenty rounds with Sandy Ferguson, [which was] about as uninteresting an affair as heavyweights could furnish. Neither man showed enough form to try conclusions with the champion. Jeffries, without extending himself, could defeat both men in the same ring.

What might be called the only clean knockdown occurred in the seventh round, and it was Ferguson's. Johnson, at the same time, was fooling near the ropes and creating the belief that he was under a pull. Later it was thought by many of the ringsiders that it was Ferguson's awkwardness that bothered the negro. At this point Ferguson saw an opening and whipped his right across on the chin, dropping Johnson to the mat.

Ferguson was on the floor in some of the rounds that followed and was also pushed through the ropes a couple of times, but was never knocked to the mat with a punch. It was his manner of floundering when hard pressed that put him off his balance.

The contest created universal disgust. For a while the impression prevailed that Johnson was under a wrap, so that his friends could get a bet down on him. Ferguson was badly battered and took a lot of punishment, but Johnson's showing was a great disappointment to those who imagined that he might be pitted against Jeffries.[855]

Jeffries later said, "As for Jack Johnson, I will pass him up. There would be no money in it for me to fight him. He failed to put out Ferguson, and there is where the public would draw the line."[856] Of course, even had Johnson looked good, Jeff was not going to fight him. But Johnson's showing gave him another excuse. Jeffries further said,

If the public demands that I should fight Johnson I will surely have to decline. … If I am defeated, the championship will go to a white man, for I will not fight a colored one. Now mind, I am not shirking from this match because I am afraid of Johnson, for I think I could lick him as easily as I have the rest, but I simply will not fight a colored

855 *Police Gazette*, December 26, 1903.
856 *Detroit Free Press*, January 31, 1904.

man for the championship. The only regret I feel is that Sandy Ferguson did not whip Johnson. I would have willingly given Ferguson a match – I was anxious that he should win in order that I might do so.[857]

Speaking of Jack Johnson, Jim Corbett told a reporter that "a fight with him for the championship would be no attraction, and there would be nothing but Jeffries to it. He said he did not blame Jeffries for drawing the color line, and thought that Johnson should meet such men as Ruhlin, Munroe, Hart and one or two others before going after the world's champion."[858]

On December 15, 1903 in Boston, Jack Munroe took on Al Limerick in a scheduled 15-round bout. Despite the fact that Al was taller, had a longer reach, and was as big as Jeffries was, Munroe gave Limerick a severe pummeling, showing aggressiveness and punching power. Limerick's seconds threw up the sponge after 1 minute and 50 seconds of the 4th round. One reporter said, "Munroe was cheered to the echo and he deserved it. He has gone up another rung of the pugilistic ladder, and has stronger claims than ever for a match with Jeffries."

The next day, Jeffries "admitted that Jack has a stronger claim for a match for the title than he had a week ago. Jeff says that if Munroe will fight a couple more of the big fellows and beat them he will give him a match." *The Boston Post*'s Rob Roy said, "Munroe stands today before the sporting world the one and only legitimate rival that Champion Jim Jeffries has. … As a puncher he is one of the most tremendous I ever saw." He felt that no one but Jeffries could defeat Munroe.[859]

Regardless of the talk about various contenders, the *Police Gazette* said that Jeff was in a class by himself. Jim Corbett said, "How to beat Jeffries is something somebody more advanced in the fighting game than I will have to tell." Jim said it would be hard to find someone as big, as strong, and as quick as Jeff. Corbett called him invincible. Jeffries could punch hard, move quickly on his feet, and take a great punch as well. No one could run from him, and no one could outslug him. "How to beat Jeff is a question the next generation of fighters may figure out. I can't." Bob Fitzsimmons agreed. He said that hitting Jeff was like pounding a stone wall. "I don't think Jeff can be knocked out by a punch on the jaw."[860]

In his continued attempt to earn a sufficient reputation to justify a lucrative title challenge, Munroe scheduled a fight with Tom Sharkey, whom the *Gazette* said was the first really good pugilist that Jack would face since Jeffries. Jeff said, "Munroe has done the proper thing by taking on Sharkey, whom I consider a hard proposition. If he whips him he will be in

857 *Boston Globe*, December 14, 1903.
858 *Boston Herald*, December 15, 1903.
859 *Boston Post, Boston Globe, Boston Herald*, December 16, 17, 1903.
860 *Police Gazette*, December 26, 1903.

line for heavyweight honors." Few mentioned the fact that Sharkey had been inactive from serious bouts for nearly two years. Regardless, Tom was a tough and experienced fighter. By defeating him, Munroe could prove himself.[861]

As of February 1904, Jeff said, "I don't think the public wants me to defend my title against any one but a white man. Don't think I am afraid of a negro. I'm not. They can be licked just as easily as anybody else."[862] Still, over the next year, Jack Johnson continued being watched and discussed as a potential contender for Jeff's title.

In February, Jeffries was in New York. On the 15th at the Gotham Theatre, he had a lively 4-round set-to with Kennedy. Jeff continued giving exhibitions with Kennedy, sometimes twice a day.[863]

On February 15, 1904 in Philadelphia, Jack Johnson "won" a 6-round no-decision bout against Black Bill. However, once again, his punching power was questioned. Larry Temple had knocked out Bill in 4 rounds, but Johnson had failed to do so.

Philadelphia won the bid for Sharkey-Munroe. However, since that state only allowed for a 6-round no-decision bout, there could be no official points decision. That said, even if there was no knockout, but there was a consensus winner amongst the crowd and reporters, that fighter would be treated as the winner. Jeff said that he would fight whoever won, if they won decisively. Munroe trained and sparred with Kid McCoy.[864]

On February 27, 1904, Jeffries was in attendance at Philadelphia's Second Regiment Armory to witness Jack Munroe "win" a 6-round no-decision bout against Tom Sharkey. 27-year-old Munroe weighed 196 pounds to 30-

---

861 *Police Gazette*, February 6, 1904. On December 17, 1903 at Kitty Hawk, North Carolina, Wilbur and Orville Wright became the first humans to successfully invent and fly a motorized airplane. 1903 was also the year that Henry Ford began mass-producing automobiles.
862 *Philadelphia Inquirer*, February 6, 1904.
863 *Philadelphia Inquirer*, February 17, 1904.
864 *New York Journal*, February 16, 1904.

year-old Sharkey's 182 pounds. In the 1st round, Munroe dropped Tom with a left to the ribs. However, a Sharkey right dropped Munroe. Jack survived the round by clinching. After the 1st round, the fight was one-sided in Munroe's favor. Acting according to Kid McCoy's instructions, he mostly used his left jab and right to the body. Munroe used effective ring generalship to jab and move away or to step in and avoid Sharkey's swings and counter to the body. Munroe was also strong enough to push Tom off when he tried to clinch. He landed well to both the head and body, and at times had Sharkey wobbly, as well as cut and bloody over both eyes.

Some said that the internal punishment Sharkey had suffered at Jeff's hands had been responsible for his subsequent defeats. However, against Munroe, "Sharkey proved his ability to fight as well as ever, was quite as aggressive and willing and demonstrated a good knowledge of ring tactics and fistic ability, but he lacked the ability to stand the bombardment of blows which Munroe rained upon his body." Munroe hammered at his body throughout, which weakened Tom and had him "almost in a state of collapse" at the end. *The Police Gazette* said that if there were a few more rounds, Munroe would have knocked out Sharkey. Jack Munroe had outboxed and outslugged Tom Sharkey.[865]

This victory made a Jeffries-Munroe bout all the more intriguing. Munroe's wins over hard punchers like Maher, Limerick, and Sharkey served to legitimize him as a threat to Jeffries and demonstrate that he was no fluke. The doubts about Munroe went out the window. He was a fighter.

James Jeffries learns Jiu Jitsu.

865 *Police Gazette*, March 12, 1904; *Boston Post*, February 28, 1904.

CHAPTER 37

Setting the Record Straight

Because Jack Munroe's victory over Tom Sharkey was decisive, San Francisco's Yosemite Athletic Club guaranteed a $25,000 purse for a 20-round Jeffries-Munroe fight. On February 29, the parties signed articles of agreement for a fight originally set to be held at the end of May 1904.

The Police Gazette said that Munroe was a legitimate candidate who had earned a right to a title shot by his recent performances, particularly by defeating Sharkey.

> In this battle Jeff will be granted a sort of revenge. He will be given the chance he so long desired of demonstrating to the world that the meeting between himself and Munroe at Butte was not what the reports would have us believe. He will show that Munroe has not got a chance in the world against him and repudiate all the stories of Munroe knocking him down.[866]

Jeffries said that he was always willing to fight Munroe, but wanted him to prove to the public that he was a worthy opponent to ensure that a fight between them would draw a gate. He agreed that Munroe had proven himself against Sharkey, outpointing Tom two to one. "I watched the bout with considerable interest, and, while I believe that Munroe has improved 100 per cent since I met him at Butte, I don't think there will be anything to it when we come together again. I will defeat him so quickly that he won't know where he is at." Still, Jeff said that he was not underestimating him, and would train with his usual vigor. He said that he would be heavier than ever.

In March, Jeff began light gymnasium training and continued boxing with Joe Kennedy. He was weighing about 235 pounds. "He intends to retire after his encounter with Munroe unless the public should will otherwise and there is some one to meet him."

It was reported that Munroe had difficulty finding sparring partners, for he had already injured three since he had gone on the road.[867]

At the end of March, Jeffries finished his stage engagements in New York and started West towards San Francisco to train for the May 30 bout. He wanted to get in eight weeks of solid work. "The champion has been taking things easy for the past couple of months. In fact, since his bout with

---

866 *Police Gazette*, March 12, 1904.
867 *Police Gazette*, March 19, April 2, 1904.

Corbett he has done very little exercise." En route to San Francisco, Jeff planned to give exhibitions with Kennedy and work out in local gymnasiums at various cities they visited.

However, as often happened with championship bouts, the date of the big fight got pushed back, at first to June 17. Munroe said that he was not ready to begin training. The real reason was that Munroe wanted to capitalize upon the fact that he was matched to fight for the championship. Curious fans wanted to see the man who would be fighting Jeffries. Therefore, Munroe could make good money giving exhibitions on the road, as much as $750 a week. He wanted to keep that up for as long as possible.[868]

Munroe certainly talked a good game though, and was good at promoting himself. He said that he could defeat Jeffries.

> I know Jeffries is a wonderfully strong man, but so is Sam McVey, whom I defeated recently at Los Angeles. McVey is a marvel of strength and he expected to rough me in the clinches. I met him at his own game and fought him all over the ring. I believe I will be able to take just as good care of myself with Jeffries as I did with McVey.[869]

It is unclear whether this was an official bout, an exhibition, or sparring session. McVey was preparing for a bout with Jack Johnson.

On April 22, 1904 in San Francisco, Jack Johnson knocked out Sam McVey in the 20th round. Once again, the *Police Gazette* jumped on Johnson's bandwagon. It said that by defeating McVey, Johnson, "the dusky hero of a score of fights, has placed himself in a position to legitimately claim a fight with Jim Jeffries for the championship of the world." It said that the victory made him the undisputed best black fighter in the world and also the best black fighter since Peter Jackson. It believed that after Jeff fought Munroe, that Johnson should be next.

> There does not appear to be a ringman in all the wide area where pugilism holds sway with sufficient inches and heft to meet the world's champion after Munroe than Johnson, the conqueror of McVey....
>
> Johnson is the cleverest big man now before the public. He simply toys with all his opponents and he wins his fights through their inability to hit him, rather than the punishment he administers.[870]

Still, Johnson was not an easy sell to the general public, despite his recognized boxing abilities. He was mostly a defender, and although he could punch hard, he rarely kept it up consistently, preferring to tap, move, or grab. He often kept a slow pace. His style was seen as effective but dull.

---

868 *Police Gazette*, April 23, May 7, 1904.
869 *Police Gazette*, April 30, 1904.
870 *Police Gazette*, May 14, 1904.

Johnson said,

> I feel that Jeffries will fight me. He has been advised by certain of his friends to draw the color line, and I think he will accept my challenge, just as soon as he convinces himself that the public believes I am the proper man to oppose him. ... He can dictate all the terms. The only thing I will insist upon is that the contest shall be for the championship of the world.[871]

However, because Jeffries was considered so good that no boxer was his peer, and because Johnson, while respected, did not garner an overwhelming amount of public support, Jeffries could avoid him without too much criticism. Sportswriters called Jeffries unbeatable, and the champion of champions. They also said that no fighter who ever lived could have defeated him. He was in a class of his own. He was even called a throwback to the human ancestors who hunted and killed with their bare hands. Thus, it did not really matter who he fought. The press thought that he would easily handle all challengers. It was just that some, like Johnson, might last longer than others, particularly because like Corbett, Johnson was a safety-first boxer.[872]

Bill Delaney said that Jeffries was planning to retire within a year. He was entering his 30th year of age, and if no big fights could be arranged within a year, Jeff would step away from the game.

Growing tired of boxing, Jeffries wanted to embark on a new life. On April 24, 1904, he got married to a lady named Freda Mayer.[873]

A week later, Jeff started training for the Munroe fight at Harbin Springs. He punched the bag, skipped rope, and worked the dumbbells and wrist machines. He ran and walked as he liked.

Munroe trained with Kid McCoy and Tim McGrath. *The Police Gazette* opined that Jeff's opponents always got into great shape because they knew that it was necessary in order to save them from permanent injury as a result of the punishment Jeffries inflicted. Jeffries could outpunch, outbox, and outstay anyone.

Tom Corbett said that Jeff's secret was that he was left-handed, but took the position of a right-handed fighter.

> In fighting he takes the position of a right-handed man, with his left arm extended and the right across the body, but it is that left he used to pound the rivets back in the early days and gave him the punch that would kill a horse. ... Here is a man whose leading arm holds both the science and the punch. ... He can hook, jab and swing with it, and any one of his blows is like the kick of a mule. ...

---

871 *Police Gazette*, April 30, 1904.
872 *New York Journal*, March 2, 1904.
873 *Police Gazette*, May 7, 14, 1904.

I have watched Jeffries fight for years, and I think that every time he goes in a battle he learns something new with that hand. He has learned enough about the fighting game now to make his crouch unnecessary, and he will now stand up and go after these fellows like he did after Jim.[874]

The Gazette said that the Munroe fight would be the first time that Jeff fought a man like himself – strong, huge, rough, and rugged. Still, Jeff had become a clever boxer, who actually "outfooted" and outsped Corbett, fighting with better judgment. Jeffries liked to denigrate Munroe, saying that he was a dub who stayed 4 rounds with him by clinching and holding. "He wouldn't dare to stand up and fight me face to face."[875]

On June 1, 1904, while sparring, Jeffries "disabled both brother Jack and Joe Kennedy." Jack Jeffries thought he had a broken rib. Joe Kennedy was so sore the following day that he could not box. Jeff admitted that he might have been too rough with them.[876]

---

874 *Police Gazette*, June 11, 1904.
875 *Police Gazette*, June 18, 1904.
876 *Chicago Tribune*, June 3, 1904. Heavyweight Sam Berger was in town and "may put on the gloves with Jeff." Berger would go on to win an Olympic gold medal in the heavyweight division at the 1904 Olympics, held in St. Louis from August 29 to September 3. The 1904 Olympics was a six-day event and contained mostly Americans and Canadians.

On June 3, 1904 at Chicago's Empire Athletic Club, Jack Johnson won a boring 6-round decision over Frank Childs. The bout was called "six rounds of the slowest fighting imaginable." Although victorious, Johnson's performance was less than impressive. As it had done after the Ferguson fight, once again the *Police Gazette* said that based on this showing, Jack Johnson would not be conceded a chance even against a second-rater. Observers left sadly disappointed, and "wondering why Jeff is overlooking the chance to make the easiest kind of money."

> It took Johnson nearly a year to convince Chicago matchmakers that he has learned to fight and he was at last given a chance to show his prowess, but after his showing he could never command a $50 purse in the Windy City. The fight, if such it can be called, went the limit of six rounds. During the entire time four light blows were landed, and as Johnson landed them the referee was forced to give him the decision.[877]

It seemed to be a theme for Johnson that sometimes he was lauded for his skill, while at other times denigrated for his style and lackluster performances. The fact that Jeff drew the color line against him actually put the press on his side even more than if he had not drawn the line. However, Johnson did not always fully justify the push that was being made on his behalf, and so a backlash of harsh critiques followed. Johnson was skillful, but very boring. That was not the type of fighter who was going to garner huge public momentum. *The Gazette* said that there was nobody left to fight the champion, and therefore he would retire after beating Munroe.[878]

Bob Armstrong disputed Johnson's claim to the colored title. He noted that Johnson had only won a 20-round decision over Ed Martin in February '03, while Armstrong had scored a KO3 over Martin in June '03. Armstrong said that Johnson was afraid of him and refused to fight him. However, Armstrong had losses to Frank Childs and Sandy Ferguson, both of whom Johnson had defeated. Still, Armstrong remained a top black fighter that Johnson did not fight, and one whom Jeffries had. By not defeating either Hank Griffin or Bob Armstrong, Johnson had not even cleaned out the colored division.[879]

About a week or so prior to the mid-June Jeffries-Munroe bout, James Jeffries developed water on the knee, the left knee joint swelling until it was impossible to walk. At first, he only asked for a two-week delay, so they agreed upon June 30. However, a physician said it would take much longer, and ordered Jeff to bed. This necessitated a postponement until late August.

The postponement ignited speculation that Jeff did not want the fight, that he was not prepared, or was trying to manipulate the odds. Others

---

877 *Police Gazette*, June 18, 1904.
878 *Police Gazette*, August 13, 1904.
879 *San Francisco Evening Post*, July 22, 1904.

theorized that the real cause of the delay was that there was not enough money in the fight. Regardless, Jeff had been looking to be in good shape. Munroe was not overly disappointed, because he returned to making money giving wrestling and boxing exhibitions.

The knee injury appeared to be legitimate. Jeffries was seen hobbling on crutches in Los Angeles. Delaney said that Jeff had been in bed for ten days prior to that. Even after discontinuing the use of crutches, he was still limping badly.

In an interview, Jeff said that the left knee had not been well for some time, since an enthusiastic friend jumped on his back in San Francisco on the night of the second Corbett fight. "I slipped and my knee hit the curbstone, and it hasn't been right since."[880]

Jack Munroe continued his confident talk, promoting himself with bombast. "I am not a lank-armed, bald-headed 'has-been' or a skinny-legged ranger on the timber border of pugilistic fame, but a man just 26 years of age, who has never drunk a drop of liquor in his life, who comes nearer being of Jeffries' weight than any man whom he has ever met. ... I have no fear of him."

On July 18, Jeff and his wife left Los Angeles heading for Harbin Springs to begin training yet again for the Munroe fight. The rest had helped him, for there was no suspicion of a limp in his walk. However, during his idleness as a result of the knee, Jeff had gone up in weight, all the way up to 250 pounds.[881]

Both boxers each posted $5,000 forfeits to guarantee their appearance for their now scheduled August 26 fight.[882]

While training, Jeff went on a two-day hunting trip. He felt that several days in the hills was a great conditioner. When he returned from his trip on August 2, Jeff was wearing a bandage on his knee.

In the meantime, on August 2, Jack Munroe ran, worked the weight machines, and hit the two punching bags. He also boxed 6 rounds, 2 rounds each with Harry Chester, the big Olympic Club heavyweight,

880 *Police Gazette*, July 2, 9, 16, 23, 30, 1904, August 13, 1904.
881 *San Francisco Evening Post*, July 15, 19, 1904; *Police Gazette*, August 13, 1904.
882 *Police Gazette*, August 27, 1904.

middleweight Jack "Twin" Sullivan, who was both shifty and could give and take hard wallops, and Andy Gallagher. Munroe sparred them daily.[883]

His own pet bear bit Munroe on the hand, and it drew a little blood, but he was okay. Jack was already following in Jeff's footsteps.

On the 3rd, Jeff ran 3 miles at a good clip. He spent several hours in the gym in the afternoon, but did not spar. When Jeffries held the huge 350-pound sandbag on his head, everyone grew frightened that he would be injured, but he was fine. Jeff enjoyed demonstrating his superhuman strength.

On the morning of the 4th, Jeff again worked with the 350-pound sandbag, handling it with no effort. In the afternoon, he played baseball. In the evening, Jeff went hunting, and again demonstrated his physical prowess in a way that was said to make Hercules' cleaning of the Augean stables look easy. After killing a steer, Jeff lifted the carcass without any apparent effort and placed it into a wagon. After it was cut up and weighed, the scales showed 510 pounds. Jeff would continue working in the gym for several more days before engaging in sparring.[884]

On the 11th, first Munroe sparred 2 rounds with Harry Chester. While sparring with his next partner, Munroe floored Twin Sullivan with a short right. Sullivan was groggy. Munroe was looking better than ever before.[885]

Jeffries was looking forward to licking Munroe, and wanted to hurt him.

> Munroe has talked so much and made so many mean cracks that I think he deserves just as hard a beating as I can give him. You know in all my fights I have held a great deal in reserve. I have never had to cut loose with a punch with every ounce behind it because I never had to go so hard as that. I never wanted to be brutal...for fear of possible consequences. I have always had a horror of being mixed up with a killing in the ring. With Munroe I will feel no compunction

883 *San Francisco Call*, August 3, 4, 1904.
884 *San Francisco Call*, August 5, 7, 1904.
885 *San Francisco Call*, August 6, 11, 12, 1904; *San Francisco Evening Post*, August 9, 1904.

about slugging him. He has accused me of drunkenness, of being chicken-hearted and of being physically afflicted. He has acted in a low down way for several months and I propose getting good and even when we get together in the ring.[886]

Jeffries' training on the 12th was a bit unconventional. He went for a long day's hunting excursion through the Lake County Mountains, lasting 20 hours, without food. He brought back two deer and twenty doves.

On the 13th, Jeffries ran 10 miles and worked in the gym for an hour. In the afternoon, he went to the gym again and spent another hour with the various apparatus. Some thought that Jeff was weighing around 245 pounds. He spent most of his free time with his wife. And he still had done no sparring.

On August 14, in the morning, Jeff ran 12 miles. He also did 100 yard sprints, something which admirers enjoyed watching. In the afternoon, he worked the wrist machines and spring bag, tugging at it unceasingly. Jeffries also sparred for the first time, boxing 6 rounds total (3 rounds each) with Jack Jeffries and Joe Kennedy.

Once again, Kid McCoy became an added fixture to the Munroe camp. On the 15th, in the morning, Munroe ran 8 miles and punched the bag 6 rounds. In the afternoon, he sparred 2 rounds each with Chester and Gallagher. Munroe then went 3 more rounds with McCoy. The Kid said that Jack had improved wonderfully.

That same day, Jeff worked an hour and a half in the gym. He sparred 4 rounds each with Jack and Joe.

On the 16th, Munroe sparred 3 rounds with Kid McCoy, and 2 rounds each with Twin Sullivan, Andy Gallagher, and Harry Chester, for a total of 9 rounds.

886 *San Francisco Call*, August 12, 1904.

Jeff continued sparring Jack Jeffries and Joe Kennedy, 4 rounds each on the 16th and 17th. He worked in the gym for over 2 hours on the 17th.

Jeffries was doing his gym work in the morning, resting during the day, and doing a little road work in the evening. He increased his gym work to 3 hours on the 18th. That day, he only sparred Joe Kennedy, for Jack was nursing sore hands. Kennedy's cauliflower ear had been giving him troubles, but he sacrificed himself.

Jeff was a 4-10 odds favorite. Munroe was looking good, but the champion was considered invincible. He was pronounced a marvel of agility and strength. He was weighing around 240 pounds, but it was all muscle

On the 19th, Munroe floored all three of his boxing partners – Chester, Sullivan, and Gallagher. Kid McCoy did not spar due to having injured his wrist. The Kid instructed Munroe to keep blocking and countering, leading very seldom, and that strategy worked.

M'COY SHOWS MUNROE A STRAIGHT LEFT.

On the 20th, Jeff left Harbin Springs to wind up his training at Oakland's Reliance Club. Jeffries said that his knee was as good as it ever was, and he was in first-class condition.

That day, Munroe ran 8 miles. He also sparred McCoy, Chester, Sullivan, and Gallagher, 7-12 rounds total, depending on the source.[887]

From l to r: Saginaw Kid, Frank McDonald, Kid McCoy, Andy Gallagher, Jack Munroe, Harry Chester, Tim McGrath, Jack "Twin" Sullivan

On Sunday the 21st, Jeff took a short walk around town. He later alternated between walking and running, varying the slower pace with short hard sprints, for a total of about 6 miles. He also went rowing on Lake Merritt for an hour.

Jeff said that his work leading up to the fight would consist of running in the morning, boxing and wrestling with Jack and Joe, exercising with the rope apparatus, bag punching, skipping rope, and shadow boxing. "After next Friday, I will tell my side of the Butte incident. The sporting world has heard how Munroe beat me to my knees and had me hanging to the ropes, but my version may prove of equal interest."

As of the 22nd, it was even money that Munroe would get knocked out inside of 10 rounds, which was the favorite betting proposition.

It was reported that Jeff was weighing around 222 pounds, but he was keeping his weight a secret. Munroe was weighing about 212 pounds.

Three days before the fight, on August 23, Jeff jumped rope, and then shadow-boxed with light dumbbells for nearly half an hour. He then boxed 8 rounds, 4 rounds each with Joe and Jack, alternating with each round after round. Thus, each sparring partner received four minutes of rest. Even though Jeff was not letting himself out, he still sent his partners reeling back from short-arm jolts delivered at close range. At one point, Jack Jeffries ran

---

887 *San Francisco Call, San Francisco Evening Post, San Francisco Bulletin*, August 14-21, 1904

into an uppercut which sent him to the floor, flat on his back. In the afternoon, Jeff rowed for an hour. He said this would be his last day of sparring and bag punching, for he did not want to risk injury to his hands. He would run, row, shadow box and work with the gym apparatus. Jeff announced that he weighed 225 pounds, having begun training at 250.

That day, Munroe went 4 rounds with McCoy and 3 each with Chester and another man named Foley, for 10 rounds total. He also ran 5 miles.

Referee Eddie Graney said that the men would need to protect themselves in clinches and breakaways, but would have to break upon his command. The fighters agreed. There would be two pairs of gloves at ringside, in view of the fact that one of Jeff's gloves broke during the Corbett fight. The articles called for soft bandages to be put on in the dressing rooms, but the referee would examine them when they entered the ring.

Munroe said he was weighing about 210 pounds *after* heavy training, but would take on some weight over the next two days and enter the ring at around 220 pounds. Jeffries was expected to weigh 240 pounds when he entered the ring. Betting was 3 ½ to 10 with Jeff the favorite.

On the 24th, Jeffries worked with the weights and the wrist machine, skipped rope for 30 minutes, and then shadow boxed with light dumbbells, displaying marvelous footwork. He worked for 2 hours total and appeared to be in great shape.[888]

Tom Sharkey, who had been in the ring with both, said that although he expected Munroe to give a good account of himself, Jeffries would win. There was not a man in the world who could force the fighting with Jeff and get the best of it. If a fighter did not go to Jeff, he would come after him and make him fight. Therefore, there was no escape from his blows. Furthermore, hitting Jeffries was like "running into the side of a house."

Munroe expressed confidence, saying that he was a faster, stronger, and younger man than that which Jeffries had been up against in a long time, and he had improved since their first meeting. However, a reporter said that Jeff's "record is one that justifies his supporters in proclaiming him the greatest heavyweight that ever breathed."

A sports writer who claimed to have seen Jeff on the scales on the 25th said that he weighed just 219 pounds. Munroe was 210. Still, most felt that Jeff would go into the ring weighing 230-240 pounds. Jeffries claimed to be weighing 225 pounds.

It was said that Munroe would be the heaviest and most rugged man that Jeffries had ever faced. Regardless, the champ remained the strong favorite. "Jeffries, despite his bulk, moves about with the speed of a lightweight. He is a tireless worker and goes at his training like a man who enjoys every moment of it."

---

888 *San Francisco Call, San Francisco Examiner, San Francisco Evening Post,* August 22-25, 1904.

Jeff was confident. "I am stronger, faster and heavier than at any time in my ring career. ... I expect to prove my superiority over Munroe in a decisive manner. He will not have me at the disadvantage as regards the high altitudes which affected me in the Butte fight."

Jack Johnson said he would be on hand at the fight to challenge the winner, notwithstanding that Jeff had repeatedly avowed that he would not defend his title against a colored fighter. "I've been taking on a chunk of weight, and I now weigh 200 pounds. That puts me in the champion's class, and I think I'm entitled to a fight with him. I believe he would have given me a chance before this, but Billy Delaney stands in the way." Johnson picked Jeff to defeat Munroe.[889]

On Friday August 26, 1904 in San Francisco, James J. Jeffries made his sixth official title defense (although he had two additional victories over Kennedy and Finnegan), taking on Jack Munroe.[890]

As early as 3 p.m., there was a long line of men and boys camped along the side of Mechanics' Pavilion, the fight site. By 6:30 p.m., the club was assured of a big attendance. At 7:30 p.m., ticket holders were allowed to enter. Many prominent men were there, including doctors and lawyers, curling smoke from cigars. Announcer Billy Jordan refrained from issuing the usual request to stop smoking because he knew it would be of no use. One lone woman was present. Many spectators had traveled thousands of miles to see the fight. *The Evening Post* claimed that it was doubtful if there was ever a bigger crowd inside the Pavilion.

---

889 *San Francisco Bulletin, San Francisco Examiner, San Francisco Call,* August 25, 26, 1904.
890 The following account of the fight and post-fight analysis is taken from the *San Francisco Call, San Francisco Evening Post, San Francisco Bulletin, San Francisco Examiner,* and *San Francisco Chronicle,* all August 27, 1904; and *National Police Gazette,* September 3, 1904.

Jeff was a 3 ½ to 10 betting odds favorite. There was considerable betting at ringside, but mostly on the line regarding whether Jeff would or would not win in less than 10 rounds. His adherents freely offered even money on the proposition that he would win inside of 10 rounds. John Brink, who backed Jeff every time that he fought, bet $1,000 that Jeff would stop him within 10 rounds.

At 9:17 p.m., Munroe was the first to be seen approaching the ring, wearing a long black overcoat, which he kept wearing until after the gloves were put on. Underneath the coat, Munroe wore green tights with a blue elastic band. His belt consisted of a red, white and blue ribbon. His hands were encased in bandages that looked bulky. With him were Kid McCoy, Twin Sullivan, Tim McGrath, Frank McDonald, and Harry Pollok. Entering the ring at 9:20 p.m., the miner looked a bit worried.

Jeffries entered right after him, stripped for action wearing only his usual black trunks that came half-way down to his knees, and American flag belt twisted around his waist, which had been in service for most of his battles. Jeff looked formidable, chewing gum, his dark face wreathed in confident smiles. He entered the ring as if he owned it, his big grin evident as he chewed away. Unlike Munroe, Jeffries wore no hand bandages. With him were attendants Bill Delaney, Jack Jeffries, Joe Kennedy, and Jimmy Britt, the lightweight champion. Jeff looked calm as he smiled at the crowd. He looked at the miner and chuckled.

Billy Jordan did the usual introductions. Unfortunately, his splendid voice could barely be heard amid the tumult and shouting of the immense crowd. He announced Munroe as "the miners' pride, of Butte, Montana." The crowd gave Munroe a mighty cheer. The generous reception accorded Munroe made Jeffries smile. Jordan then announced "the only champion of the world," and the cheers drowned out Jeff's name. Jeff smiled some more. Although the crowd gave him a hearty reception, it was not as loud as that which greeted the challenger. Referee Eddie Graney wore an immaculate Tuxedo.

The weights were unofficially announced as 224½ pounds for Jeffries, and 208 for Munroe. *The Call* said Jeff weighed 225 pounds, while Munroe weighed about 215 pounds. However, Jeff looked much more muscular. The bulk of his weight was above the waist, while Munroe's was below. *The Police Gazette* said Jeff weighed about 225 and Munroe 212. Most estimated that Jeff would weight close to 230 pounds while Munroe would weight close to 220 pounds.

A small fight amongst the spectators for possession of a chair interested the fighters for about 30 seconds.

While waiting, Jeff said to Delaney, "Take a look at his hands." Bill responded, "I did; they're all right." Perhaps not trusting Delaney's inspection, Jeff went over to shake hands and examine the wraps himself. He lodged no objection. The gloves were given to both camps, and each side examined them as well. Jeff inspected his own gloves, for he did not want them to break, as was the case in the Corbett fight.

The fighters submitted to being photographed. Jeff grasped Munroe's hand and posed. Jeffries looked very confident, while Munroe looked a bit nervous.

Jordan announced that they were to fight straight Queensberry rules and protect themselves in the clinches. He gave his final familiar cry, "Let 'er go," and the automatic gong clanged.

1st round

Jeffries only slightly crouched, keeping his left well out, feinting. Munroe led with punches to the body, but he threw them as if he was afraid of getting hurt, landing only lightly. Jeff danced around a bit, chewing gum and smiling. Munroe rushed in with his head down, but Jeff just clinched.

When Munroe tried to reach Jeff with his left and right, like a flash Jeffries hooked a counter left into his body. Quickly clinching, Munroe looked to be hurt from this first landed punch. Jeff easily pushed Jack away from the clinch. Munroe swung over Jeff's head and they clinched again. On the break, Munroe landed a right to the ribs, but Jeffries countered with a piledriver left to his stomach. A death-like pallor overspread the miner's features. Jeff then landed a left to the head, which shook up Munroe. The champ followed it with a hard left uppercut, and then sent in a right to the body. Munroe was hurt. Jeff kept smiling, chewing his gum. After another clinch, Jeff pushed his man away.

At the same time that Munroe attempted a right to the body, Jeffries landed a terrific short left hook on the temple which floored Munroe. The crowd was on its feet, for the end was already in sight. Jeff stood away as Jack quickly rose in 3-4 seconds.

After he got up, Jeff hit Munroe with a short left on the jaw which must have felt like a mule's kick. When Jack attempted to go inside with his head down, Jeff landed a left uppercut and then followed with a left hook. Jeff backed him up to the ropes with a left to the body and right to the head. He also landed a right to the head and left to the body. Munroe was game enough to take a grueling, but he was not in Jeff's class. He tried to grab, but the big fellow beat him up with short-arm jolts, particularly to the body. In quick succession, Jeff landed a left uppercut to the body and left hook to the head. Another right and left staggered Munroe.

Munroe started to drop from a left hook to the jaw, but before he was fully down, Jeff caught him with a cracking right uppercut on the jaw.

Munroe staggered to his feet after eight or nine seconds, only to be dropped for the third time in the round by one of those fearful left hooks, which nearly closed his right eye. His face was bleeding. Munroe got up and clinched until the bell saved him.

The miner's face and eyes were badly puffed and blackened. He had not landed a single effective blow in the round. The fight seemed to be just about over, as Jack appeared out of it as his seconds led him to his corner.

2nd round

Between rounds, Jeffries rubbed his shoes in the resin box and laughed at his foe. Munroe was all in, but he told his seconds not to throw up the sponge under any circumstances. When the bell rang, Jack looked hurt and fatigued as he walked wearily to the ring center. Still chewing his gum, Jeff went right after the still dazed Munroe, hitting him when and where he pleased, continuing the slaughter.

Twice Jeff landed a left to the body and left to the head combination. Munroe spit blood, lowered his head and went in. Jeff pushed him back and hit him with a left to the nose that made it bleed. Munroe came in again, but Jeff timed the advancing Munroe with a left uppercut that sent his head back. He also sent in a right uppercut when Munroe attempted to clinch.

Jeffries smashed him to the body with both hands, and then dropped Munroe with a short-arm left to the jaw. Blood flowed from Jack's face and mouth. He rose and punched aimlessly until another left hook sent him down. The house was in tumult as the timekeeper counted off the ten seconds.

The referee looked appealingly to Munroe's corner, expecting them to toss up a sponge to retire him. However, they did not. Apparently, the timekeeper counted off the ten seconds and said Munroe was out. However, either the referee believed he had beaten the count, or he could not hear the timekeeper amidst the crowd noise. So the fight continued.

Jeffries pounced on him and rained in vicious body shots that made his fists seem to disappear into Munroe's body all the way to the wrists. Jack doubled over. With some lefts to the head and body, Jeff sent him staggering back to the ropes. Jeffries advanced and was about to throw a decisive finishing right, but then the referee out of sheer mercy stepped between them and stopped it in order to save the wobbling and insensible Munroe from further punishment.

Graney saw Munroe's helpless condition, and wanted to prevent a ring tragedy, for Jeffries had punched him terribly. The stoppage was humane, for another blow would certainly have knocked him out.

The crowd booed and called Munroe a fake. One reporter said, "Jeffries hits with so much ease that the spectators never appreciate the terrible force he puts into his blows." The fight had only lasted 45 or 46 seconds into the 2nd round.

Assisted by his seconds, Munroe tottered to his corner, bleeding profusely from a number of cuts about the face. Eventually, Munroe commenced spitting blood, indicating that he had been hurt internally. The crowd cheered Jeffries, but a few minutes later, when Munroe got up from his chair and started out of the ring, the gallery groaned at him. Still, "The public is always an easy mark and loves to be humbugged, and will be quite ready to subscribe from $2 to $20 a seat for the next big mill."

The Call and *Examiner* agreed that it had been an unequal contest. It was all Jeffries from the start, clearly dominating. He was light on his feet and never wasted a punch. He toyed with Munroe, handling him with ridiculous ease. Jack did not land an effective blow during the contest. It appeared that a left uppercut to the body took all the fight out of him. Various reporters quoted Jeff as saying it was a left to the jaw or a left to the body which started Munroe on the downward path.

The Bulletin said, "Jeff was at his best last night. He was the perfect fighting machine and could have whipped half a dozen Munroes." He beat him into helplessness in the 1st round, and finished him off in the 2nd.

The Evening Post said that Munroe was awkward looking in comparison with the finished fighter that Jeffries was. Jeff had become a good boxer and quick as a flash. In the first minute, it was evident that he had the superior punch and science, while Munroe seemed clumsy and frightened. He was not in Jeff's class. It was like an amateur going up against his teacher. It was no fight, and the crowd was thoroughly disappointed and disgusted. They paid big money to see a fight, but witnessed a slaughter.

Jeff was called the wonder of the age. Most agreed that he was the best in the world by far and that no one could defeat him. They said he would remain champion until he was an old man. In fact, many, including the *Police Gazette*, said that Jeffries was the greatest fighter who ever lived, and stood alone. Others believed that he was the greatest fighter who had lived since the days of Sullivan. Jeffries was quick and easy with his movements, like those of a panther. It was as if his feet were set on steel springs.[891]

There were discrepancies regarding the gate receipts. Some said only $21,800 had been taken in. The fighters received 60%, or $13,080, to be split 60%/40% based on winner/loser. Thus, Jeff came away with $7,848, close to $2,000 per minute of the fight, and the miner earned $5,232. The club earned $8,720, of which the promoter's share was $6,540. Graney received $500.

However, other local reports said the gross receipts were $31,800. Under those numbers, Jeff earned about $11,448 and Munroe $7,632. Regardless, the fighters and promoter Jim Coffroth had made good money. Jack's right eye was closed, but he made more money than he could have earned working for many long days in the mines.

Jeffries said that he was in even better shape than when he met Corbett, and could have fought all night. However, it was an easy fight. As soon as he hit Munroe with the first punch, he knew that it would be over soon. He had Jack at his mercy from the start.

> Well, fellows, I didn't even get warmed up. ... I felt just like fighting tonight, but he did not give me a chance. ...
>
> [A]fter I hit him in the stomach with that first left I knew there was nothing to it. I can hit a fearful blow with my left, and it was the first hook to the jaw that started him going. ... I knew he was mine. ... When I fought Corbett and Fitz I stalled for a few rounds, but not tonight. ... I weighed just 220 pounds when I entered the ring, the same weight at which I fought Fitz and Corbett. ...
>
> Now the people can judge for themselves as to what he did at Butte. ... It was just the same as this, except that he laid down as often as he could so I couldn't hit him. Tonight's fight is my answer to all the things that have been said about me and the Butte fight. It was the

891 *Police Gazette*, September 10, 1904.

easiest fight I ever had. ... I have nothing to say against Munroe, but I think his handlers treated me unfairly when they spread all those stories about me.

Referee Graney said, "I stopped the fight to save Munroe from being killed." He had appealed to McCoy to throw up the sponge, but he refused. Graney knew Munroe was helpless, so he stopped it. The stoppage was met with approval.

Graney said that Jeffries did not even have to work up a sweat, for Munroe was a baby in his hands. Jeff had always claimed that his Butte bout was not worth considering, and the fight proved him correct. Graney opined that Jeff could be champion for another ten years.

> Jeffries is bigger, faster and better than ever. He improves in each fight. Nature has been kind to the champion. He is too strong and hits too hard for any man. ... Munroe should not take his defeat to heart, as he was beaten by a champion of champions. ...

> He was always a fairly hard puncher, a clever boxer and a monument of endurance. He has increased in cleverness and punishing force and he is a marvel of speed. Above all things he has learned to economize so far as energy is concerned. He wastes no power and misplaces no blows. A twist of his forearm and a turn of his wrist speeds a punch that causes as much damage as a crack from a bludgeon.

Indeed, the following year, on June 26, 1905 in Philadelphia, Munroe went the full 6-round distance with Jack Johnson, although Johnson pummeled him. Still, Johnson was criticized. "It was a roughhouse battle, devoid of science on one side and almost everything else on the other. Jeff need not have drawn the color line, for he could have met both of these men in the same ring simultaneously, so far as their ability to do him is concerned."[892]

Munroe admitted that Jeff was his master and that he beat him fairly and squarely. "That left in the jaw in the first is what did it. I was dazed and could not defend myself." He did his best, but had underrated Jeffries, who was just too good. "He is a great fighter and can beat any of them." He said that Jeff was the best the world could produce, and would not be defeated for years to come.

Munroe's face was cut up and he had a badly blackened eye. He was spitting blood after he left the ring.

Kid McCoy said it was the first punch in the stomach that started Munroe going.

Bob Fitzsimmons told reporters, "I told you so. ... Munroe 'as been travelin on a bloomin fake reputation for years." Before the bout began,

---

892 *Police Gazette*, July 15, 1905.

Bob told Jeff not to carry him at all, to remember Butte, and to "cop im at the start."

Fitz once again said that the manager at Butte asked Jeffries to carry Munroe. "The manager of that show was kicking because we was puttin' them down like ten pins, and he says ter Jeff, 'Ow the devil am I to get gate money if you go on bowlin' 'em hover like this. Let 'em stay, let 'em stay.'"[893]

Bill Delaney said that Munroe was hopelessly outclassed. "Jeff hit harder tonight than he ever did before in his life and Munroe received some punches that were something terrible."

In the days following the fight, Jeff further discussed his performance. When Tim McGrath asked Jeffries why he was so vicious with Munroe, he responded, "Because he made cracks about me up in Butte." Jeff said that he did not know whether Munroe had said all that he was quoted as saying, but at any rate, he stood for it, "and that was why I pitched in at him the way I did. I don't say bad things about other people, and I don't like to have them roast me, calling me a quitter and a cur. We can go along and fight without indulging in such kind of talk." Jeff had gone after Munroe like a hungry panther pouncing on a young calf. He said that if Munroe and his manager had not said such things, he might have allowed him to stay a while and make a showing. "I let the other fellows stay when I could have put them away. Ruhlin and Corbett were just as easy."[894]

Jeffries agreed that Graney stopped the fight at the right time, for Munroe was helpless, and might have been seriously injured. Jeff said that the timekeeper had previously counted out Munroe, but the referee did not hear it due to the crowd noise. Although Jeff realized that 10 seconds had elapsed, he did not care, because he was quite content to fight a little longer and pound on Munroe some more.

Jeff said that he was in great shape. The champ was so fast that he could run 100 yards in 10.5 seconds. He complimented Billy Delaney as a great trainer. "Nobody ever gave me better advice than Delaney."[895]

Bill Delaney felt that Jeffries should retire. He had no equal, and there were no marketable challengers for him on the horizon. Delaney said, "This may be Jeff's last fight. He has met and beaten them all, and now I do not see whom they can bring to the front. . ... I would like him to retire on his laurels. If he has to wait for a couple of years he may not be in such good form." He also said, "I can't think of a soul who is entitled to a match, but

---

893 *San Francisco Bulletin*, August 28, 1904.

894 *San Francisco Evening Post*, August 29, 1904.

895 *San Francisco Bulletin*, August 28, 1904. Speaking of the past, Jeff said that Sharkey caught him out of condition. He had hurt his left arm in training, and could barely use it. He dropped Tom with it in the 2nd round, but it hurt so badly that he never led with it for the next 10 rounds. He had to fight with his right. The first time he fought Sharkey, his hands were so swollen and sore that it pained him every time that he hit him.

somebody may spring up." Delaney preferred Jeff to retire than to go stale waiting for a challenger to emerge.

The Call agreed that there were no more men for Jeffries to meet, and that he might as well retire. "In the condition he showed last night he could defeat a whole ring full of aspirants for the championship." There was no true top contender in sight, whom the public really wanted to see Jeff fight. Promoters were not interested in digging up a man to put against him, for no one was good enough to draw a big gate.[896]

Indeed, it was announced that starting October 1, Jeffries would be joining a theatrical company and tour the coast and southern states, playing the role of Davy Crockett. Still, Jeff said that if there was a foe who had made a strong argument for himself, whom the press and public really wanted to see him fight, he would accommodate them and defend his title again. However, that person would have to make himself known before Jeff was inactive for so long that it would be impossible to be at his best. Otherwise, he would retire.[897]

The Bulletin said that Jeffries was too good for his own good. The public would not be overly enthusiastic about seeing him in the ring with anyone, because he was simply in another league. Jeff was "the greatest champion the world has ever seen. That is just the trouble with him – he is too confoundedly great for his own good." It felt that the only fighter with the ghost of a chance to make even a respectable fight was Jack Johnson. He was of a fair size and possessed an unusual amount of cleverness, and therefore had at least a remote chance against Jeffries.

The Bulletin noted that Jack Johnson was present at the Munroe fight, and tried to get through the ropes to challenge Jeff, but the management would not allow him to do so. *The Call* told a different story. "Jack Johnson had announced his intention of challenging the winner, but one glance at Jeffries caused him to change his mind. He maintained a discreet silence."

Regardless, the next day, Johnson's manager, Zick Abrams, was out with a challenge on Jack Johnson's behalf, saying that Johnson would make an immeasurably better showing than did Munroe. He gave the *Bulletin* a check for $2,500 as a guarantee of good faith in the challenge. He said that they were willing to bet $10,000, and would make the fight winner-take-all. *The Bulletin* said, "Johnson is the only heavyweight in sight who has the size, cleverness and punching ability to make the champion get busy in order to win."

Jeffries had said that he was not willing to enter the ring with a negro when the title was on the line. However, the *Bulletin* said that he did not seem as determined on this point as he was six months ago. Jeff gave economic reasons, saying, "We wouldn't draw. ... Johnson hasn't any

---

896 *San Francisco Call*, August 31, 1904. A rumor that Jeff might fight Jack O'Brien was quickly dispelled, for "the knowing ones here would not stand for anything of the kind."
897 *San Francisco Call*, August 28, 1904.

reputation. What's he ever done, and besides he has a shady record aside from being shady in color." It opined that if the public demanded the fight, and no white challenger loomed up in the near future, that Jeff would brush aside the color line. The public might demand the fight if Johnson sufficiently proved himself, because the general boxing public had no prejudice about mixed race boxing matches. "It matters little to the average ring-goer whether the fighters be white or black as long as the sport is of a high order and the best man wins. And Jeffries' popularity would not suffer a particle if he fought Johnson, for some of the best liked pugilists the world knows never drew the color line." It was up to Johnson to give strong enough performances to garner public momentum on his behalf.[898]

Still, a couple days after the fight, Jeff gave indications of being firm regarding the color line. When Tim McGrath said that he had a man that Jeff would have to fight - Jack Johnson, Jeff responded, "Well, you might as well forget that, because I'll never fight a nigger. I could put him away in less time than I did Munroe, but I'll never fight a nigger."[899]

Jeff instead toured with the play *Davy Crockett*. After the curtain, he and Joe Kennedy would put on the gloves for a 3-round exhibition. The show was a financial success, and played all the way through April 1905.[900]

898 *San Francisco Bulletin*, August 28, 1904.
899 *San Francisco Evening Post*, August 29, 1904.
900 *Two Fisted Jeff* at 239-240; *Police Gazette*, April 22, 1905.

CHAPTER 38

Leaving the Game

Following his victory over Jack Munroe, James Jeffries was strongly considering retirement. He felt that it would take years before a suitable white challenger was found, and by then he would have been idle for too long. Jeffries said that he would not fight a black man. "I have no desire to see a colored man even get a chance to win the world's championship, and I will never meet one."

The Police Gazette said that no living pugilist could defeat Jeffries. It agreed that he was safe in the possession of the title until he retired. Jeff was great because he was skillful, resourceful, immensely strong, and able to withstand harder blows than anyone could inflict. It too felt that the want of somebody to lick him meant that he would have to retire. "There doesn't appear to be any living pugilist capable of lowering his colors. All the great ones tried, were defeated and tried again with the same result. ... His opponents were cleverer and stiffer punchers and speedier than the champions of former days."[901]

Jeff said that his rivals had to qualify before challenging him, and he saw no logical opponent.

> I do not want to meet another Jack Munroe, nor will I do so. A fight with a man of Munroe's caliber hurts the game. Whenever a dub like the miner is touted as a world beater and then makes a sorry showing pugilism loses hundreds of friends. Another fight like that would put me on the blink as a drawing card. ...
>
> As matters now stand I do not see that there is a man in the fighting business who has a right to meet me. Of course, there are several who would take a licking for the small end of the big purse, but that's not the sort of scrapper I want to cross arms with. However, let any of the men who are crying for fight prove to the satisfaction of the sporting press of the country that they should be given a chance and they are as good as signed.

Speaking of his prospective rivals, Jeff said,

> All that Sandy Ferguson has to base a demand for a fight on is the fact that he has beaten Gus Ruhlin and a few third and fourth raters. He doesn't class, and a fight with him wouldn't draw flies. I do not

---

think he is game, and would be willing to meet six men of his capacity in an evening.

Jack Johnson is a fair fighter, but he is black, and for that reason I will never fight him. If I were not the champion I would as soon meet a negro as any other man, but the title will never go to a black man if I can help it. I do not think this fellow has anything on a lot of heavies that I have licked. He's a good man, but not as good as Fitz and Sharkey. He is an in-and-outer, and has some queer fights in his record.[902]

In Los Angeles, on October 18, 1904, Jack Johnson knocked out Denver Ed Martin in the 2nd round. Martin was coming off an August rematch W10 over Sam McVey. However, prior to that, in 1903, Bob Armstrong had knocked out Martin in 3 rounds and McVey had stopped Martin in 1 round. Denver Ed had chin issues.

Still, Johnson's impressive victory over Martin served to further his cause. "Johnson showed wonderful class when he knocked out Martin, a powerful negro pugilist, who can fight like a demon. … Private advices say that Johnson looked every bit a whirlwind heavy of the kind that would make Jeffries fight for his life. Jeffries has no right to draw the color line."

Johnson said that Jeffries knew that he was the only fighter that could make him extend himself, so he was sidestepping behind the color line.

I will not rest until public opinion forces Jeffries to recognize my claim for a fight with him. His drawing the color line is all bosh. His famous battle with Peter Jackson out here, his fight with Bob Armstrong in New York, and his tussle with Hank Griffin, all negroes, makes his drawing of the color line ridiculous.

The Police Gazette agreed. "Jim Jeffries' lament over not being able to find an opponent worthy of his consideration would be silenced in short order if he would sidestep his prejudices and agree to fight a black man…. Jeffries has no right to draw the color line."[903]

---

902 *Police Gazette*, October 1, 8, 1904. Ferguson had fought Ruhlin to a May 1903 15-round draw.
903 *Police Gazette*, November 5, 1904.

While most felt that the unbeatable Jeffries would defeat Johnson, the *Police Gazette* said that by refusing to fight him, Jeffries opened himself up to a charge of cowardice, even if it was not true.

> Jeff does not seem to care one bit how many people may knock him and even accuse him of cowardice in warding off Johnson with the old-time color line dodge. He won't budge from his position, notwithstanding the public clamor that he fight the negro champion.
>
> Jack Johnson's record entitles him to a match with Jeffries and he is the only man now in sight who would seem to have a chance with the hitherto invincible rivet driver. Jeff will not add any to his popularity by sticking to his lately adopted color line. On his part, this position is most inconsistent, as Jeffries has fought more than one negro in the past. ...
>
> Ordinarily fighters don't make much of a hit when they draw the color line. The fighting game is not a calling that permits of such finely drawn social distinctions. The public does not care whether the champion in a certain class is black or white or green as long as he's a good, game fighter and willing to fight any deserving aspirant for his title without surrounding his championship pedestal with a lot of impossible and unreasonable conditions....
>
> So, taken on the whole, the color line is looked upon as a pretty shallow excuse for a good fighter to use in side-tracking a good match. There are but few who think Jeffries has any fear of Jack Johnson, but he, nevertheless, lays himself open to an accusation of cowardice in refusing to meet the husky negro.
>
> Jeffries has a strong hold on the American people. He is a most popular champion. But a fighter is expected to fight, not to rest on his laurels, where there is a man in sight who has a possible chance for the title. Jeff's most partisan admirer must admit that Johnson has a chance. His record certainly gives him a stronger title to fight for the world's heavyweight championship than Jack Munroe had. ... The fight loving public wants to see Jeffries fight and fight soon. Jack Johnson stands ready. It's up to Jeffries to forget the color line until he has rubbed this big black speck off his title.[904]

By drawing the color line, Jeffries gave the *Gazette* something to write about, and ironically helped garner Johnson even more free press. It was not that the *Gazette* thought Johnson would defeat Jeff, but it simply did not like the fact that he drew the color line.

One writer, Sandy Griswold, although criticizing Jeff's color-line stance, did not think it had anything to do with fear of Johnson. "Not that I think

904 *Police Gazette*, December 3, 1904.

for a moment that Jeff has the slightest apprehension as to the outcome with Johnson, for I believe he would be as easy as Jack Munroe, but his lofty stand is ridiculous to the extreme."

A Black Cloud in Sight.

Jeff said that if the newsmen did not select a capable white challenger within the next few months, he would retire. However, there was no white man ready for Jeffries. Johnson was the only fighter remotely capable of competing. "Rather than swap punches with a negro Jeffries says he will go without an engagement and retire from the ring."

One white fighter who felt that he had a chance against Jeffries was Marvin Hart. He said that he intended to defeat Johnson before fighting Jeff. Of this prospective challenge, the *Police Gazette* wrote that Hart may "put it all over Johnson, but he hardly has a chance to beat Jeffries."

Regardless of the occasional talk about Johnson, Jeffries was still considered invincible. By late 1904, the *Police Gazette* commented, "That Jim Jeffries is the peer of all fighters is a fact admitted; that fact makes it apparent, too, that the fighting game, so far as the heavyweight division is concerned, will languish and remain inactive until he goes into voluntary retirement and leaves the title to be recontested." Another expert said, "The sporting world is now confronted with the serious problem of getting rid of the greatest fighter that ever put on a glove. ... Jeffries is so good he is a bad thing to have around." No one could compete with him.

Jeffries was being called "the greatest fighter that ever put on a glove." His "opponents were cleverer and stiffer punchers and speedier than the champions of former days. Boxing has improved and most of his antagonists have kept apace with the march of time." While Sullivan held the title for a longer period of time, Jeff in a shorter space of time had defeated better opponents. "Jeff held down the honor at a time when three of the greatest men known to ring history were trying to keep him from landing the coveted prize, namely, Bob Fitzsimmons, Jim Corbett, and Tom Sharkey." It was predicted that it would be years to come before the boxing world would see his equal. "Jim Jeffries is the champion of all champions and the greatest wonder known to the world of sport." In early 1905, Bill Delaney announced that like Jeffries, he was retiring.[905]

Interestingly enough, on March 2, 1905 at Grand Rapids, Michigan, perhaps somewhat motivated by all the comparisons with Jeffries, at age 47, weighing 273 pounds, John L. Sullivan boxed in a scheduled 4-round bout with 196-pound Jim McCormick. Sullivan scored a clean knockout at 1 minute and 23 seconds of the 2nd round. John L. used his famous rushing right swing to the jaw to do the trick. McCormick dropped unconscious and was out cold for five minutes.

McCormick had an 1899 KO1 victory over Kid McCoy, although top contenders had had mostly knocked him out, including LKOby8 to McCoy in the rematch. Still, in 1900, McCormick went 7 rounds with Jack Johnson. The comparison showed that Johnson was not the biggest puncher. Just a week or so prior to the Sullivan bout, McCormick went 6 rounds with McCoy in a no-decision bout. After Sullivan stopped him, in August 1905, McCormick lasted into the 8th round with Gus Ruhlin before being taken out. Even at his advanced age, out of shape and inactive for years, Sullivan showed that he had some serious power and talent, in case they had forgotten.[906]

Seeking to prove himself further to the general boxing public, Jack Johnson scheduled a match with Marvin Hart for late March 1905 in San Francisco. Hart was coming off a 12-round draw with Gus Ruhlin in his last fight. Jeff told a reporter, "I'm not going to discuss Johnson's abilities as a boxer. He may be a wonder and all that, but if any one is to take my title I want that man to be of my own color. If Hart wins I will cheerfully give him a fight."

One reason why there had not been a great public demand for Jeffries to fight Johnson was that Jack Johnson had a somewhat dull style. He was cautious and defensive a majority of the time. Therefore, fight fans were not overly enthusiastic about paying to see him fight. A local paper said,

> Johnson's predilection for loafing during an engagement is well-known, but in meeting Hart he goes against a ripping, smashing fighter.... Hart is not clever, except in a way that is peculiarly his own, but he has worlds of steam and willingness. His reputation is that of a short finisher, with a wallop that Jeff himself might well fear, and any hopes Johnson may have of easily getting away with something may be rudely shattered.

There was concern that Johnson might attempt to reproduce his most recent performance against Sam McVey, which was considered a clever but boring bout for 20 rounds until Johnson put him away in the final round. "Nobody is questioning his ability to fight, but the jeers hurled at him

---

905 *Police Gazette*, September 24, December 10, 17, 24, 31, 1904. February 4, 1905.
906 *Police Gazette*, March 18, 1905; Boxrec.com.

through nineteen slow rounds were sufficient indication that no repetition of that sort of milling will be allowed." Despite the popular view of historians and sociologists, the prejudice which existed against Johnson was as much the result of his style as his race, and even more so by those who only wanted to pay for entertaining fights.[907]

Marvin Hart was described as "loving to root in and carry the fight to his opponent. Nothing can daunt him." Johnson's skills were recognized, but his style was not appreciated.

> Johnson likes a different kind of game. The shifty big fellow prefers to hit and run away, winning his contests by the decision route. This sort of milling has made the dusky giant rather unpopular with the sports in this city and if Johnson wants to reinstate himself in popular favor he will have to try for a clean knockout....
>
> Jeffries has, of course, persistently declared his determination to draw the color line. If Johnson, however, would give incontestable proof that he is a knockout fighter as well as a boxer there is no telling what popular clamor might do to disabuse the world's champion of his prejudices.[908]

Still, Bill Delaney said that Jeff would fight Hart if he won, but would not fight Johnson.

> In June 1905 Jeffries will arrive in California, and if by that time there is no white man ready to make a match with him Jeff will forever retire from the ring. I understand Jeff thoroughly, and know that in order to fight well he must fight often. I do not propose to have Jeff make the mistake that all former champions have made – that is, of fighting once too often.[909]

On March 28, 1905, Marvin Hart was awarded a close 20-round decision over Jack Johnson. The local *San Francisco Examiner* titled its article, "Pluck and Awkwardness Better Than Mixture of Cleverness and Cowardice."

> [Hart won the decision by being] persistently aggressive and steadfastly game. Though his face was prodded into a condition of puffiness by Johnson's straight lefts he never faltered for an instant. Except when carried back by the force of blows he was constantly pressing towards his opponent.
>
> Johnson simply fought when he felt like it. He gave an admirable imitation of his Colma affair with Sandy Ferguson. He held himself in reserve until the ninth round was reached and then he cut loose as though bent on finishing his man in double quick time.

907 *San Francisco Chronicle*, March 26, 27, 1905.
908 *San Francisco Examiner*, March 28, 1905.
909 *Washington Post*, March 28, 1905; *Louisville Times*, March 29, 1905.

He kept up his lick for a couple of rounds and then slowed up. With nothing else to guide him but the yells of disgust from Johnson's corner a tyro would have no difficulty in determining that Johnson's confidence had deserted him. The indifference to punishment and great pluck displayed by the white man seemed to discourage the negro. Johnson beyond a doubt showed that he lacks that essential fighting qualification – grit....

It would be ridiculous to say that Hart is a better ringster than Johnson. If Johnson were only as stout-hearted as the man from Louisville the chances are the negro would dispose of his opponent of last night in ten rounds.

Johnson did his best work with a straight left. He also bruised the side of Hart's face with right crosses. Hart, although anything but a neat boxer, had an awkwardly clever way of stopping Johnson's uppercuts.

Hart scored his biggest successes with a heart punch. He reached Johnson's ribs with this blow a number of times in every round. He also clouted Johnson on the temple and jaw with right swings.

There was a sameness between the rounds from the tenth onward. Johnson spurted occasionally and hammered Hart to the ropes. Then Marvin would pull himself together and force the big negro back across the ring. Johnson's seconds seemed to be in despair. They leaned in through the ropes and railed at the weak-hearted colored champion.

Johnson's seconds cried to him, "You can't win unless you hit him." Instead, Johnson clinched a great deal. His manager said, "For goodness sake go after him." However, "All this time the man from Louisville kept up a fast and even gait, hurling himself against the negro and bringing yelps of satisfaction from the watchers every time he planted what appeared to be a telling blow." The 20th round saw Johnson, as usual, "inclined to clinch," and Hart, as always, the aggressor. Some thought the fight was a draw.

Referee Alex Greggains explained his decision for Hart. "I gave the fight to Hart because he was the aggressor throughout.... Johnson, in my opinion, dogged it. He held at all times in the clinches." Greggains was also quoted as saying, "I gave the decision to Hart because he was the aggressor and carried the fighting all the way. The damage to Hart's face was done by a few jabs. Hart blocked the majority of the colored man's blows. I always give the gamest and most aggressive man the decision." One writer said, "Hart was the aggressor all the way and the referee could do nothing but give him all the glory."

Hart said,

Johnson is a big, clever nigger with a long left arm, and that is why I wear this battered face. Outside of his straight left jabs he had no punch. I nearly broke his ribs with the blows I sent in with both hands. ... I did all the leading and wasn't blowing a bit at the finish. He didn't hurt me any, although, of course his jabs bothered me. He has eight inches longer reach and that counted.

Although Johnson criticized the decision and claimed that he was robbed, he admitted, "Hart is a big, tough fellow, very awkward and hard to hit."

The San Francisco Chronicle said that Johnson was strong on points, but at all times Hart was the aggressor and much more active. Johnson was "clever but unwilling."[910]

The Police Gazette, which had generally been a Johnson advocate, noted that Hart was badly puffed and bruised while Johnson was unmarked. In fairness though, it recognized that Johnson held on considerably, was not nearly as active, and did not have as much power, while Hart fought on the aggressive throughout. Although Johnson landed blows which left their mark, "His blows, though, did not have as much steam behind them as did Hart's. The Southerner, when he landed, hurt his man. ... Johnson undoubtedly prejudiced the referee by holding until he was ready to break." Johnson had the edge in points of cleverness and total number of blows landed, but Hart threw and attacked more, landed harder, fought consistently, and did not hold. Marvin "fought doggedly and like a man who would not be beaten." Regardless of any debate about the decision, the loss hurt Johnson's prestige, because he had fought so close with a man who could do no better than obtain a draw with Gus Ruhlin in his last fight. And Jeffries had blown through Ruhlin.

A day after the bout, referee Greggains put forth an additional explanation for his decision. "Hart wanted to fight all the time. Johnson just loosened up in spots. ... He kept holding in the clinches. ... I think that if every referee would let it be known that aggressiveness would weigh the most when there was no knockout, he would have better contests."[911]

Jeffries said that he was willing to meet Hart only if there was public demand for the fight.

> I am glad Marvin Hart won over Johnson last night. Not that it means a prospective candidate for my title, but it places the negro out of the running. If Johnson had won he would never have fought me. My decision never to meet a negro while I am champion would have been faithfully kept.... I will retire from the ring this year, and when I do retire it will be forever.[912]

Hart wanted to fight Jeffries. "I am the only man in the world who would have a chance to beat him. I have beaten Jack Johnson, a man

---

910 *San Francisco Examiner, San Francisco Chronicle*, March 29, 1905.
911 *Police Gazette*, April 15, 1905; *San Francisco Examiner*, March 30, 1905.
912 *Trenton Times*, March 29, 1905.

Jeffries has been side-stepping for months, and I can put it on the boilermaker, too."

> Hart and his friends are so jubilant over the way he polished off the colored man…. They say that to outfight Johnson as he did, giving the negro many pounds and a beating, shows that Hart is the best heavyweight in the world, outside of Jeffries…. Every man who saw the fight gave Hart credit for the battle he put up, and there were many who said the Kentucky man would make Jeff extend himself to the limit to win.[913]

However, there was some dispute as to Hart's relative merits. W.W. Naughton said Hart "would be candy for Jeff." Analyzing such a matchup, he said, "Jeffries has all that Hart has in the matter of strength and ruggedness. He is heavier, more forceful and more durable than Hart. He is as fast as a featherweight and he would have little difficulty in landing on Hart."

The Police Gazette felt that there would not be a demand to see Hart fight Jeffries. "Jim Jeffries says he will fight Marvin Hart if the public demands it. As the critical public was not favorably impressed by the manner in which Hart won from Jack Johnson…there will hardly be any crying demand for such an unequal match."

The following week's issue of the *Police Gazette* said of a match with Jeffries, "Hart has a Chinaman's chance. He will be the softest proposition that ever crossed the path of the Herculean Californian. … Had Jack Johnson fought up to his standard he would have beaten Hart…. When he did mix it up, Hart looked like a handful of nondescript change." The problem for Johnson was that he did not mix it up enough.[914]

Still, another reporter from the same newspaper gave Hart more of a chance against Jeffries.

> It is true that Hart's victory over Johnson was not a decisive one…. But he won, just the same, and a win by a close margin is as good as a win by mile. Hart…scales over 190 pounds, and at this weight he is quick and agile in his movements. In point of physique, strength for strength, blow for blow, Hart cannot be compared to the boilermaker. …. Hart is a fighter who keeps coming all the time, and these tactics enabled him to predispose Referee Greggains in his favor…. As to Hart's gameness there is not the shadow of doubt. He took all that any man of his physique could stand in his mill with Johnson and never faltered. It is true that Johnson is not one-third the hitter that Jeffries is, but it must be admitted that the champion is

---

913 *Trenton Times, Newark Evening News*, March 30, 1905.
914 *Police Gazette*, April 15, 22, 1905.

not as clever as Johnson. The deduction is, it seems at this stage, that Hart has a fair chance of making a good fight.[915]

However, another reporter said, "Marvin Hart is now considered the next best man to Jeffries, but to borrow an expression from another game, there is a broad streak of daylight between Jeffries and Hart." Ultimately, by May, the *Police Gazette* opined that Jeffries "has not a rival in pugilism today." With no great demand for it, a Hart-Jeffries bout would not occur.

For some time, there had been talk of Jeffries retiring, although there was some uncertainty as to whether he really was going to do so. However, just over a month after Marvin Hart defeated Jack Johnson, it was reported on May 2, 1905 that Jeffries announced that he would be retiring. Jeff was quoted as saying, "The principal reason for my retiring from the ring and from the stage is that my wife objects.... I have determined, along with my wife, that it is not worth while to go into the ring any more. The public is fickle."[916]

On May 13, 1905 in Chicago, Jeffries sparred 3 rounds with Joe Kennedy. Afterwards, at age 30, Jeffries announced his retirement as undefeated heavyweight champion of the world. "I have concluded to retire because there is no one in sight capable of giving the public a run for its money, and as I never took any money on false representations, it is too late to begin now." There was not sufficient public clamor and excitement for Jeffries to fight Marvin Hart, and seeing that there would not be a sufficient financial inducement to fight him, Jeff decided to retire. "The younger crop of champion aspirants do not appear formidable."[917]

Jeffries lamented the fact that there were no big paydays on the horizon for the near future. Still, during his career, Jeff had made vast sums of money from his fights. If he had stuck to boilermaking, he would have been working 10 hours or more per day for about $18 or $20 per week. Boxing had made James Jeffries a rich man.[918]

In *Two Fisted Jeffries*, the champion said, "I realized how Alexander felt when he sighed for more worlds to conquer." There were no big fights left for him, and "I found no pleasure in the idea of going around and knocking out a lot of young fellows with more courage than skill or strength." He did not want to wait around for a big fight to develop. "I figured that, by the time any boxer developed in the class of the great heavies who had held the center of the stage when I started upward, I would be far past my prime."

In his first autobiography, Jeff quoted Delaney as telling him, "It will be at least two or three years before they can bring up another man capable of making any kind of a showing against you. Two years of idleness will spoil

---

915 *Police Gazette*, April 29, 1905.
916 *Police Gazette*, April 29, May 20, 1905; *Seattle Post-Intelligencer*, May 3, 1902.
917 *Chicago Tribune*, May 14, 1905; *Philadelphia Inquirer*, May 15, 1905.
918 *Police Gazette*, May 27, 1905.

any fighter and if you have to wait that long I'd rather see you leave the game for good."

Jeff "never cared for fighting just for the sake of fighting." He was content to live a quiet family life with the fortune he had earned. He purchased a 145-acre ranch near Los Angeles and became a farmer again, growing alfalfa. He would also hunt and fish. He did not need to box.

Despite being retired, it was reported mid-year that Jeff boxed 4 rounds with his brother Jack in Los Angeles at a benefit. However, he was done with serious boxing.[919]

James J. Jeffries had defeated the most deserving contenders of his era and had twice defeated two former champions. Thus, his title reign was as impressive if not more so than the reign of any champion before him. Only Sullivan could compare. Sullivan reigned longer and fought more often, but it could be argued that Jeffries defeated a higher caliber of opponents.

The Police Gazette said that the most conservative critics agreed that Jeffries "is a greater pugilist today on the eve of his retirement than Sullivan ever was the best day of his life." It said that Jeff was retiring without "a rival in pugilism today."[920]

Of course, Sullivan later had his own retort to any criticisms.

> I could produce sports who will tell you that I could strike more blows in ten seconds than any man living could strike in a minute, and these blows counted some, as they were delivered solidly while I was square on my feet, so that all the heft of my body was in every one of them. I've ducked plenty of them.[921]

However, as years passed, Sullivan did not necessarily mind the comparison to Jeffries. He just wanted respect for himself as a skillful fighter. In a surprising and eerily self-deprecating 1907 interview (perhaps displaying the then admired trait of modesty), Sullivan said,

> I don't mid saying that I believe the style of fighting of today is far and away ahead of the old style… Jeffries at his best and me at my best, Jeffries could have put it on me. I never was a really scientific fighter…. My game was the old game – standing up and fighting and depending upon sheer power and pure strength and endurance to get by. I won most of my fights by rushing…. But if a big man today were to fight the same way I did and try those rushes on with a man like Jeffries he'd get slaughtered, that's all. He'd get himself killed…. Jeffries, with his quickness and his impenetrable crouch, and his immense power of endurance, and his vast hitting power, and with all of the foot-shiftiness of the new style-there can't be any doubt that, had it been possible for Jeff and I to meet when we were both at our

919 *Two Fisted Jeffries* at 243-244; *My Life and Battles* at 54; *Police Gazette*, August 12, 1905.
920 *Police Gazette*, May 20, 1905.
921 *Police Gazette*, March 31, 1906.

best, he would have sent it over on me. More than that, I never saw the man that I thought could stand a chance to lick Jeffries. If he's wise he'll not fight any more. He's too big to get down to trim.[922]

Bob Fitzsimmons called Jeffries the greatest fighter in the world and the best man he ever fought. He called Corbett the cleverest fighter he ever met, and Sharkey the best slugger, depending entirely on his strength. He said Choynski had hit him the single hardest blow he had ever received. The body shot Jeffries hit him with in their rematch was the next wallop he most remembered.[923]

Like his predecessors, Jeffries refused to defend against any top black challenger while he was champion. This was only relevant at the tail end of his reign, and at the time, the rising Jack Johnson was nowhere near as highly regarded as a legitimate threat to Jeffries the way Peter Jackson was to Sullivan or Corbett. His fights were often lackluster and dull, and when Johnson lost a close bout to Marvin Hart, most who saw that bout felt that neither Hart nor Johnson had much of a chance to defeat Jeffries. With no mega-fights in sight, Jeffries retired.

It is well known that eventually, Jeffries was lured back into the ring to take on then champion Jack Johnson on July 4, 1910. The public had pressured Jeff to return to dethrone Johnson. Furthermore, the offer of a $101,000 purse, to be split 60%/40% based on winner/loser, was astronomical for the time, and perhaps too good to refuse. Jeff later wrote, "I did not want to return to the ring. I had been idle, as far as boxing went, for six years, and for practically a year before that I had not fought one serious match. For almost five years I scarcely had touched a boxing glove except to spar for fun, or for some charity." Furthermore, he weighed more than 260 pounds and had been enjoying food and beer. He remembered how the old and inactive John L. Sullivan could not be gotten back into condition again even after three years. However, "I had no fear of Johnson, whom I regarded, and still regard, as one of the most overrated fighters that ever was a champion." Although he lacked the snap and pep he once had, and knew he was not anywhere near as good as he once was, he still felt that he was good enough to beat Johnson. However, father time had done him in, and Johnson stopped Jeffries in the 15th round. Historians can today debate just how different the fight would have been had Jeffries taken on Johnson in 1905. One thing that is absolutely certain is that given his many years of inactivity, Jeff was a mere shell of himself in 1910. In 1905, when he retired, James J. Jeffries was considered invincible, and the greatest fighter of all time.[924]

---

922 *Los Angeles Times*, May 12, 1907.
923 *National Police Gazette*, February 5, 1905.
924 *Two Fisted Jeffries* at 272-276.

Appendix:
James J. Jeffries' Record

BORN : April 15, 1875; just outside of Carroll, Ohio.
DIED : March 3, 1953; Burbank, California at age 77.

1890?

Jeffries had a scuffle in school with a larger and older boy named Fred Hamilton, but defeated him.

Jeff later also allegedly defeated a black fighter named Bob Luckett in a street fight, as well as five of Luckett's pals.

1892-1893?

At around age 17, Jeff might have done some informal boxing at the East Side Athletic Club in East Los Angeles.

1893-1895?

| ? | Hank Griffin | Los Angeles, CA | KO 13, 14 or 15 |

1894 or 1895?

Jeff trained under Billy Gallagher and later De Witt Van Court.

Jeffries once sparred with the Los Angeles Athletic Club's president and ex-heavyweight champion, John Brink.

1895

Jeff engaged in an impromptu bout with Jim Barber on the Santa Monica beach, mostly wrestling.

There are unconfirmed claims that Jeffries scored a KO1 George Griffin, KO2 Frank Childs, and KO2 Joe Cotton, as well as KO2 Charles Allen and KO1 J. Morrissey, likely in exhibition smoker bouts, if they indeed took place.

| Oct 29 | Hank Lorraine | Los Angeles, CA | EX KO 2 |

1896

| Jan 10 | Isidore Magnin | Los Angeles, CA | EX 3 |

Magnin was a young boy who weighed 80 pounds.

| May | Jeffries sparred with Billy Gallagher. |

| Jun | Jeffries sparred with Australian Billy Smith, and also Billy Gallagher. |

| Jul 2 | Dan Long | San Francisco, CA | KO 2 |

Although next matched to fight Theodore Van Buskirk, Jeffries came down with a severe case of pneumonia. After recovering, an attempt was made to re-schedule the bout, but the promoters refused to pay the fighters' purse demands.

1897

| Feb | Jeffries sparred with James "Soldier" Walker. |

| Feb 22 | Jack Stelzner | Los Angeles, CA | SCH |

Stelzner pulled out of this bout, claiming a back injury.

Feb 24   Jeff arrived at Shaw's Hot Springs, just outside Carson City, Nevada, set to train and spar with Jim Corbett. Jeff claimed to have run with Corbett almost every day for 10-12 miles. "Sometimes we walked and ran alternately, sometimes we ran the whole way at an easy trot, finishing with a two or three hundred yard spurt."

| Feb 25 | Jim Corbett | Shaw's Hot Springs, NV | EX |

They sparred for about 20 minutes total, including rests.

| Feb 26 | Jim Corbett | Shaw's Hot Springs, NV | EX 4 |

| Feb 27 | Jim Corbett | Shaw's Hot Springs, NV | EX |

Although the Hearst-owned *New York Journal* and *San Francisco Examiner* reported that Corbett dropped Jeffries, Jeff later denied the reports, claiming that they were fabrications designed to boost Corbett.

| Mar 1 | Jim Corbett | Shaw's Hot Springs, NV | EX 3 |

Corbett rotated each boxer in and out for 1 round each, until each sparring partner had gone 3 total rounds.

| Mar 3 | Corbett and Jeffries covered 12 miles of walking, jogging, hill-climbing, and sprinting. |

| Mar 5 | Jim and Jeff went on a walk and run lasting one hour and twenty minutes. |

| Mar 5 | Jim Corbett | Shaw's Hot Springs, NV | EX 3 or 4 |

Round-robin sparring of 1 round at a time with the champ, who went from sparring partner to sparring partner in a rotating circuit.

| Mar 6 | Jim Corbett | Shaw's Hot Springs, NV | EX 4 |

Round-robin sparring of 1 round at a time with the champ.

| Mar 7 | Jim Corbett | Shaw's Hot Springs, NV | EX 4 |

Round-robin sparring of 1 round at a time with the champ.

| Mar 8 | Jim Corbett | Shaw's Hot Springs, NV | EX 4 |

The sparring circuit might have been repeated later in the day.

| Mar 9 | Corbett and Jeffries plodded through the slushy snow for about two and a half hours, running at least 10 miles. |

| Mar 9 | Jim Corbett | Shaw's Hot Springs, NV | EX |

| Mar 10 | Corbett and Jeffries ran 9 miles. |

| Mar 10 | Jim Corbett | Shaw's Hot Springs, NV | EX 4 |

| Mar 11 | Jeffries and Corbett jogged 8 miles, sprinting the final ¼ mile. |

| Mar 11 | Jim Corbett | Shaw's Hot Springs, NV | EX 3 |

| Mar 12 | Corbett and Jeffries ran 10 miles. |

| Mar 12 | Jim Corbett | Shaw's Hot Springs, NV | EX 3 |

Corbett sparred in usual round-robin circuit fashion of 1 round with each sparring partner until each went 3 rounds.

| Mar 13 | Corbett ran 10 miles with Jeffries in the morning. |

| Mar 13 | Jim Corbett | Shaw's Hot Springs, NV | EX 4 |

Usual round-robin circuit, with Jeff sparring 1 round at a time.

| Mar 14 | Jim Corbett | Shaw's Hot Springs, NV | EX 2 |

Round-robin circuit.

| Mar 15 | Jim Corbett | Shaw's Hot Springs, NV | EX 1 |

Jeff likely sparred with Billy Woods, and possibly Danny Needham, in preparation for the Van Buskirk fight.

| Apr 8 | Billy Woods | Oakland, CA | EX 4 |

| Apr 9 | Theodore Van Buskirk | San Francisco, CA | KO 2 |

| Apr 27 | Billy Woods | Los Angeles, CA | EX 6 |

They gave a representation of the Corbett-Fitzsimmons fight.

Jeff trained and sparred for the Baker fight with his brother Jack Jeffries and Billy Woods at Oakland's Reliance Club. De Witt Van Court helped with conditioning work.

| May 18 | Henry Baker | San Francisco, CA | KO 9 |

Jeff prepared for the Ruhlin bout with Billy Woods, Billy Gallagher, and Bill Delaney.

| Jul 16 | Gus Ruhlin | San Francisco, CA | D 20 |

Jeffries sparred with Jack Stelzner in preparation for the Choynski fight.
In addition to Coach Bill Delaney, De Witt and Eugene Van Court were also training Jeffries.

Nov 30	Joe Choynski	San Francisco, CA	D 20

1898

Jeffries and Tom Sharkey scheduled a bout for Jan 7, but the San Francisco authorities would not issue a permit.

In preparation for the Goddard fight, Jeffries sparred with Tommy Ryan.

Feb 28	Joe Goddard	Los Angeles, CA	KO 3 or 4

Goddard retired after the 3rd round. Referee John Brink awarded Jeff the decision, but told Goddard that he would not be paid if he did not continue. After two minutes had elapsed, the boxers continued into the 4th round, but seeing that Goddard was just getting beaten up; Brink stopped the contest and again awarded the bout to Jeffries. Jeff later said that Brink threatened to declare it a no-contest, which would mean no pay, which got Goddard to continue.

Jeff prepared for the Jackson fight by sparring Jack Jeffries and De Witt Van Court, under Bill Delaney's direction.

Mar 22	Peter Jackson	San Francisco, CA	KO 3

Following the Jackson fight, Jeffries signed a contract to give nightly sparring exhibitions at a local San Francisco theater on Market Street.

Apr 6	Jim Jeffords	Angels Camp, CA	EX 4

Preparing for the Everett and Sharkey bouts, Jeffries trained at Oakland's Reliance Club, sparring with Jack Jeffries and Jack Stelzner. De Witt and Eugene Van Court and Bill Delaney also coached him.

Apr 22	"Mexican" Pete Everett	San Francisco, CA	KO 3
May 4	Jack Jeffries	Oakland, CA	EX 3
May 6	Tom Sharkey	San Francisco, CA	W 20
Aug 5	Bob Armstrong	New York, NY	W 10
Aug 5	Steve O'Donnell	New York, NY	SCH

These two bouts were scheduled for the same evening; but the O'Donnell bout was cancelled as a result of Jeffries breaking his left thumb on Armstrong's head.

1899

Jan 29   Jeffries arrived in New York. He then traveled to Boston, set to exhibit there with Jack Jeffries.

Feb 20   Jeff opened his exhibitions at New York's Miner's Bowery Theater, sparring that week with his brother Jack Jeffries.

Mar 20	Jim McCormick	New York, NY	EX 3

Jeffries began giving sparring exhibitions with McCormick at New York's Star Theater.

Jeffries went on an exhibition tour, sparring with Jim Daly.

Apr 4	Jim Daly	Dayton, OH	EX
Apr 5	Jim Daly	Kansas City, MO	EX

Apr 6-8   Jeffries gave afternoon and evening exhibitions at the St. Louis Standard Theater, sparring 3 one-minute rounds at each performance with Jim Daly.

Apr 9   Jeff began his week of exhibitions at Chicago's Great Northern Theater, sparring 3 rounds with Jim Daly.

Bill Delaney said that Jeff had been privately sparring and training with Tommy Ryan.

Apr 17-22 Jeffries and Daly exhibited in Philadelphia, performing in the afternoon and evening.

Apr 24   Jeff began hard training at Loch Arbor, near Asbury Park, New Jersey, the site of his training camp for the world title fight.

Jeff's trainers were Bill Delaney, Kid Egan, and sparring partners Tommy Ryan, Jim Daly, and Jack Jeffries. Jeff claimed to have sparred Ryan nearly every day. He sparred all three on most days.

May 30   Jeff cut down his road work to a few miles. When sparring with Ryan, Jeff worked on his footwork. When sparring Daly, Jeff engaged in more rough work, while Daly tried all of Corbett's tricks. Jack Jeffries also spent considerable time wrestling with Jeff.

May 31   In the morning, Jeff ran 7 miles, sprinting the last 500 yards. Jeff then skipped rope for five minutes. In the afternoon, Jeff boxed 6 rounds with Tommy Ryan. He then hit the punching ball for 30 minutes without letup. Following that, Jeff engaged in another sparring bout, this time with Jim Daly. Next Jeff played three games of handball, threw the medicine ball, and worked the wrist machine.

Jun 2   Jeff did a fast 4-mile run. Following the run, without rest, he jumped rope 1,400 times. He did his usual afternoon work.

Jun 4   Jeff went on a 3-mile run up the beach. After a rubdown, he hit the bag for a short while. He also worked the medicine ball for 30 minutes with Jim Daly.

Jun 5   Jeff walked 10 miles and also played handball. He worked with the punching bag, medicine ball, wrist machine, and jump rope. He sparred Ryan, Daly, and brother Jack for 30 minutes.

Jun 6   Jeff ran 5 or 6 miles at an astonishing gait. Back at camp, he punched the bag for 5 minutes and skipped rope for 15 minutes. He then wrestled and roughed it with Jack Jeffries, tugging and pulling for 4 rounds, "Jim slamming the 200 pounds of Jack against the walls until the windows rattled." He did no sparring. Jeff also swam for an hour.

Jun 7   Jeff just walked in the morning. In the afternoon, he threw the medicine ball, wrestled a bit, skipped rope, swam for 20 minutes, and hit the bag.

Jun 7	Jim Daly	Asbury Park, NJ	EX 3

In the evening, they sparred 3 short rounds between acts of a play.

Jun 8   Jeff punched the bag for 20 minutes, skipped rope for a short while, and threw the medicine ball. He ran 2 miles, and then plunged in the ocean.

Jun 9	Bob Fitzsimmons	Coney Island, NY	KO 11

World Heavyweight Championship

Jun 10	Jim Daly	Philadelphia, PA	EX

Jun 11   Jeff umpired a baseball game at Paterson, NJ.

Jun 12	Jim Daly	Coney Island, NY	EX 3

One-minute rounds.

Jeff gave daily exhibitions, often twice a day, at first primarily sparring with Daly. He was scheduled to exhibit in places like Boston, Wilmington, Providence, Meriden, Hartford, Bridgeport, Buffalo, Rochester, Syracuse (boxing Tommy Ryan), and again at Coney Island.

Jun 15	Jim Daly	New London, CT	EX 3

5,000 people watched Jeff spar and umpire a baseball game.

Jeff was in New York on the 17th to spar with Daly at the Casino Roof Garden.

On the 18th, Jeff umpired two baseball games. He first umpired a game at Weehawken, NY. He then went to New Haven, CT, to umpire a ball game there.

Jun 18	Jack Jeffries	New Haven, CT	EX 3

Jeff was scheduled to box Jack Jeffries on his subsequent tour, because Jim Daly needed a rest. His itinerary included: June 19, afternoon, Utica, evening, Syracuse (boxing Tommy Ryan); 20th, afternoon, Rochester, evening, Buffalo; 21, afternoon, Scranton, evening, Wilkes-Barre; 22, Pittsburg; 23, Cincinnati; 24, Louisville; 25, St. Louis; 26, Chicago; 27, Omaha; 28, Kansas City; 30, Denver; July 1, Salt Lake City; 4, Los Angeles. Jeff would return east the second week in July, then set sail for Europe.

Jun 23	Jack Jeffries	Wheeling, WV	EX
Jun 24	Jack Jeffries	Louisville, KY	EX 5
Jun 25	Jack Jeffries	St. Louis, MO	EX 3

In the afternoon, Jeff umpired a semi-pro baseball game at Athletic Park, and boxed a few brief rounds with brother Jack during the 7th inning.

| Jun 25 | Jack Jeffries | St. Louis, MO | EX 4 |

In the evening at the Standard Theater, Jeff gave another exhibition of 4 short and tame rounds of only 15 seconds each. His brother Jack helped him demonstrate how he won the title from Fitzsimmons.

| Jun 26 | Jack Jeffries | Chicago, IL | EX 4 |

The 4th round was a recreation of the Fitz knockout, with Jack playing Bob.

| Jul 3 | Jack Jeffries | Salt Lake City, UT | EX 4 |

On July 4, still in Salt Lake, Jeff and his brother exhibited at each of two baseball games, the attendance being 1,300 and 2,500 respectively. Jeff umpired the games, and exhibited after the 2nd inning, going 3 short rounds. Jeff "surprised many by his quick and clever ducks."

| Jul 6 | Alex Greggains | San Francisco, CA | EX 3 |
| Jul 6 | Jack Jeffries | San Francisco, CA | EX 3 |

Jeff was in Oakland on the 7th.

On the 8th, in San Jose, Jeff was to umpire a ball game and exhibit with Jack.

| Jul 9 | Jack Jeffries | San Francisco, CA | EX 4 |
| Jul 10 | Jack Jeffries | Los Angeles, CA | EX 4 |

One-minute rounds.

| Jul 14 | Jack Jeffries | Oakland, CA | EX 4 |

Jeff may have exhibited in Sacramento on the 15th.

Jul 25	Jack Jeffries	Cincinnati, OH	EX
Jul 27	From New York, Jeffries sailed for England.		
Aug 4	Jack Jeffries	London, ENG	EX 4

They boxed nightly at London's Royal Aquarium.

| Aug 7 | George Chrisp | London, ENG | EX 2 |
| Aug 7 | Jack Jeffries | London, ENG | EX |

In England, Jack Jeffries was boxing under the name of "Ed Dunkhorst" and sometimes "Jack Dunkhorst."

The August 12 advertisement for Jeff's boxing that night at the Royal Aquarium said that he would be boxing Dunkhorst (which was Jack Jeffries) "and Another."

The ad for the August 14 show said that Jeff would box "Bendoff, Champion of Africa, and Dunkhorst, Ex-Champion of America."

| Aug 15 | Jack Scales | London, ENG | EX |

The London advertisement for the August 16 show said that Jeff would box Jack Walsh and Dunkhorst.

| Aug 17 | Arthur Morris | London, ENG | EX |
| Aug 17 | Jack Jeffries | London, ENG | EX |

On the 18th, Jeff was advertised to box Jack Scales and Dunkhorst once again.

On subsequent days, Jeff boxed Jack, and sometimes one of the locals. The 21st said he would box Arthur Morris (again) and Dunkhorst, while the 22nd said Jeff would box Wolf Bendoff (again) and "Jack Dunkhorst." The 23rd was Jack Walsh (again) and Jack Dunkhorst, while on the 24th, only Dunkhorst was mentioned as the opponent. The last advertised Jeffries appearance at London's Royal Aquarium was on August 29.

Jeff next exhibited in Paris, France with Jack Jeffries.

Jeff also said they toured Liverpool, England, Scotland, Wales, and Ireland (Dublin and Queenstown).

Jeff sailed home on September 15, and arrived in Boston on September 22.

Sep 22	Jack Jeffries	Boston, MA	EX
Sep 23	Jack Jeffries	New York, NY	EX

They appeared at Ulmer Park for the benefit of the Boilermaker's Union, of which Jeff was a member.

On the 24th, Jeff left for his training camp at Allenhurst, NJ, to train for the Sharkey fight. He began training the next day.

Oct 4   Jeffries skipped rope for a half hour, punched the bag, and played handball. After lunch, he ran to Long Branch and back, about 11 miles.

Oct 5   Jeff began the day with his 11-mile run to Long Branch, taking him one hour and 15 minutes. After lunch, he jumped rope for 15 minutes, tossed the medicine ball with Jack Jeffries for 15 minutes, and then punched the bag for 20 minutes. He next played three games of handball. His day's work closed by roughing it and wrestling for nearly half an hour for the first time in camp with Ernest Roeber, the wrestling champion. The usual rub down and shower followed.

While training, Jeff badly injured his left forearm and elbow when a medicine ball struck him awkwardly.

Oct 16   Jeff ran and played handball, but "avoided using his injured left arm as much as possible and in one game never used it at all." He also skipped rope and performed some light leg exercise.

Oct 17   Jeff ran 4 miles, and did a little gymnasium work. He had to rest the left arm and do no sparring.

Oct 19   Jeff took his long run to Long Branch and back. In the gymnasium, he punched the bag moderately for 15 minutes. In the afternoon, he took a bike ride and played two games of handball.

Oct 20   Jeff ran 6 miles, 3 of which were run at a fast gait. In the afternoon, he spent two hours in the gym, wrestling with Roeber and Jack Jeffries, jumping rope, punching the bag, and playing handball.

Oct 24   Jeff reduced his morning run by several miles. In the afternoon, he tested his left arm in sparring for the first time, boxing Tommy Ryan 6 rounds.

Oct 25   Jeff went running with Ryan in the morning for several hours. After breakfast and a rest, he played handball. Jeffries next sparred 6 lively rounds with Tommy Ryan. He then did some wrestling with Ernest Roeber.

Oct 26   Jeff ran 5 miles, sparred 6 rounds with Ryan, and wrestled Roeber. He also played handball, skipped rope, and punched the bag. However, another report said that Jeff had a stiff neck, and so he let up on his training, only running, playing two games of handball, bag punching, rope-skipping and engaging in a light tussle with brother Jack. It claimed that he did no sparring owing to the stiff neck.

Oct 27   Jeffries did his customary morning spin along Shore Road. He played handball, boxed with Jack Jeffries and Tommy Ryan, and punched the bag.

Oct 29   Jeffries punched the bag, skipped rope, and went through his other exercises.

Oct 30   After his road work, Jeff sparred Ryan (6 rounds) and Jack, and wrestled with Roeber. Jeff jumped rope a thousand times and punched the bag for 15 minutes. He also played handball. The afternoon was taken up by a short run and a spin on the bicycle.

Oct 31   Jeff walked to Deal Lake, and rowed across the lake, a distance of about 3 miles. His schedule called for a stroll for several hours. Later, Jeff went at the punching bag with vim, and worked the wrist machine. He boxed Ryan 6 rounds in no tame affair. Jeff cut loose at him more than usual, forcing Ryan to hustle to get away. Then Jeff sparred Jack. "It was not very long before his brother measured his length on the floor in temporary slumber. A left jab settled him." He also likely wrestled with Roeber.

Nov 1   Jeff did several long sprints on the road with Ryan, from 3-5 miles. He would sprint 100 yards, then slow down for a like distance and sprint at the end. After a rubdown and a meal, Jeff skipped rope, punched the bag and sparred some fast rounds with Ryan for the edification of Mike Donovan. Jeff later played some croquet, and punched the bag for 15 minutes.

Nov 2   Jeffries biked to a barber shop and got a shave. He later punched the bag and skipped rope, and possibly worked the pulley machines a bit.

Nov 3	Tom Sharkey	Coney Island, NY	W 25

World Heavyweight Championship

Jeff was scheduled to give a Nov. 4 exhibition with Joe Goddard in Philadelphia. He might have boxed either Tommy Ryan or Jack Jeffries.

Starting Nov. 6, Jeffries began performing in a new burlesque show, "Around New York in Eighty Minutes," at New York's Koster and Blals, during which he gave an exhibition with brother Jack. This was scheduled to continue for a month.

Nov 16   Jeff and Tom Sharkey acted out a one-round retake of the 25th round of their fight, owing to the fact that the cameras had failed to capture it.

After a month in New York, Jeff toured around giving theatrical and boxing exhibitions.

1900

Mar   Jeff did some preliminary training for the Corbett fight with Tommy Ryan and Jack Jeffries.

Apr 6   John/Jack Finnegan   Detroit, MI   KO 1
This was a scheduled 10-round bout.

Jeff trained at Allenhurst, NJ for the Corbett fight.

Apr 16   Jeff ran 12 miles, two more than he had been doing over the previous week. That afternoon, Jeff would began working with Ed Dunkhorst (who weighed 260-300 pounds), doing some roughing with him after Jeff had boxed with brother Jack and with Tommy Ryan.

Apr 24   Jeff sparred 10 total rounds – 3 with brother Jack, 3 with big Ed Dunkhorst, and 4 rounds with chief trainer Tommy Ryan.

Apr 29   John L. Sullivan   New York, NY   EX 3
They boxed 3 tame half-minute rounds with two minutes of rest in between.

May 3   Jeffries rowed 4 miles on Deal Lake. He also did his usual 10-mile run. In the afternoon, he punched the bag 17 minutes, boxed 4 rounds each with Jack Jeffries and Tommy Ryan, tossed the medicine ball with Ed Dunkhorst for 15 minutes, jumped rope 1,000 times without a break, and worked the wrist machine and pulley weights.

May 5   Jeff began his morning by rowing 4 miles on Deal Lake. Upon returning, he and Jack went on a 10-mile run, jogging the first 6 miles, but briskly running the last 4 miles. The afternoon began with a 10-minute session punching the bag, after which Jeff boxed Ryan 5 rounds, mixing stiff punches with science. After that, Dunkhorst came on for 3 more rounds of hard sparring. Jeff constantly encouraged Dunk, and called out to him, "Slam in; I'll take all you can give." Jeff closed his day's work with 10 minutes on the wrist machine and 15 minutes at the pulley weights, followed by the rub-down salt-water wash and shower bath.

May 8   Jeff took an 8-mile jaunt on the road and sprinted the last ¼-mile home. He played 2 games of handball and boxed 2 rounds with reporter W.O. Inglis. Jeff then sparred his brother Jack.

May 9   Jeff rowed 4 miles on Deal Lake and then took his usual long run at a pace fast enough that a fellow accompanying him on a bike had to pedal hard to keep up. In the afternoon, he punched the bag, exercised with the medicine ball and pulley weights, and skipped rope 1,000 times.

May 11   Jim Corbett   Coney Island, NY   KO 23
World Heavyweight Championship

Jeff went on a lengthy baseball umpiring tour.

May 12   Jeff was paid $2,000 for umpiring a baseball game in Philadelphia.

May 13   Jeff umpired a baseball game at Weehawken.

Jeffries said that he was going to be a full fledged actor the following season, and star in a play written for him entitled "A Country Sheriff."

May 17   Jack McCormick   Reading, PA   EX 4

Jeff umpired baseball games in such places as Painted Post and Battle Axe, Michigan.

Aug 27   Jack McCormick   Norfolk, VA   EX 3

Aug 29   John L. Sullivan   New York, NY   EX 3
Each round lasted less than a minute.

Jeffries was scheduled to umpire baseball games until Sep. 20. After that, he toured with a play - *The Man from the West*.

1901

Jan 7   Jeffries began training at Allenhurst for the Ruhlin fight, sparring with Bob Armstrong and Jack Jeffries.

Jan 22   Jeff began training in Cincinnati at his Price Hill training quarters. He ran 6 miles in the morning. In the afternoon, he skipped rope 2,000 times, threw the medicine ball with brother Jack, and then exhibited his footwork. "Jeffries is a marvelous big man on his feet."

Jan 24   Jeff played baseball for a little over half an hour. He then played handball against Jack Jeffries and Bob Armstrong, and defeated both. He then worked a rowing machine. Jeff would spend several hours a day with it.

Jan 25   Jeff played a game of indoor baseball, then played handball, then worked the rowing machine, skipped rope, and finally spent an hour or more striking the punching bag.

Jan 26   Bob Armstrong   Cincinnati, OH   EX 4
Jeff also jumped rope, punched the bag, worked with dumbbells and the rowing machine, and ran 4 miles.

The typical Jeffries day was said to include: 2-mile walk, boxing with brother Jack and Bob Armstrong, rowing and bag punching, pulleys and rope skipping, dumbbell and wrist machine, short run, 10-mile run, and more machine exercises. Sometimes Jeff rode his bicycle as well.

Jan 28   Jeffries injured his kneecap when he fell during a handball game trying to make a difficult return. The knee became inflamed and he walked with a perceptible limp.

Jan 29   Jeff skipped the run and just did a short walk. He punched the bag for 20 minutes without rest. He also worked the rowing machine.

Feb 15   Gus Ruhlin   Cincinnati, OH   SCH
Governor Nash of Ohio prevented the bout.

Jeff returned to performing in *The Man From the West*, traveling around the country.

May 15   In Pittsburg, Jeffries closed his theatrical season.

In early June, when his contract with Bill Brady expired, Jeff thereafter elected to be handled by Bill Delaney.

Sep   Jeff went on an exhibition tour of Southern California with Jack Jeffries.

Sep 15   Jack Jeffries   San Francisco, CA   EX 3

Sep 16   Jack Jeffries   Los Angeles, CA   EX 3
The champ "dodged some pretty stiff and vicious punches…. Jeffries was fast on his feet, and as quick as lighting with his hands."

Sep 17   Hank Griffin   Los Angeles, CA   EX 4
Griffin lasted the 4-round distance to earn $100.

Sep 21   Jack Jeffries   Fresno, CA   EX 3
California's Armory Hall.

Jeff was next set to go to Visalia to exhibit.

Sep 24   Joe Kennedy   Oakland, CA   KO 2
This was not an exhibition, but a scheduled 4-round bout fought on the merits.

Sep 25   Jack Jeffries   Stockton, CA   EX

Oct 2   Jack Jeffries   Bakersfield, CA   EX

Jeffries trained for the Ruhlin fight at Harbin Springs with Bob Armstrong and Jack Jeffries.

Oct 31   Jeffries took a 20-mile jaunt over the hills. He later played a game of baseball. In the afternoon, he boxed Bob Armstrong and Jack Jeffries 4 rounds each. After the sparring, Jeff vigorously hit the bag for 10 minutes. He then worked with the rowing machine for a couple of miles.

Nov 1   After he had already taken one of his long 4-hour treks over the hills, a doctor who examined Jeffries said that he weighed 214 pounds. Jeff said that was going to be his last long run. That day, Jeffries skipped the gymnasium and just played a couple games of baseball and did some light work with the chest weights. Jeff said that in subsequent days, he would play handball, skip rope, punch the bag, and row.

Nov 2   In the morning, Jeffries punched the bag, jumped rope, played four games of handball, and worked with the medicine ball and the rowing machine. In the afternoon, he went on a 10-mile run. In the evening, Jeff worked over his sparring partners. He rested on the 3rd, honoring the Sunday Sabbath.

Nov 4   Jeff played three fast games of handball and showed his wonderful speed. He then sparred 4 hot rounds with Armstrong. Without rest, Jeff then took on Jack and mostly played defense. Jeff then tossed the heavy medicine ball with Armstrong, skipped rope, and worked the rowing machine.

Nov 5   Jeff sparred Jack Jeffries and Bob Armstrong 3 rounds each. After one minute of rest, he skipped rope. Then he worked the rowing machine for 10 minutes, followed by bag punching for 10 minutes. He wrapped up that session by tossing the 20-pound medicine ball for 15 minutes. In the afternoon, Jeffries ran 4 miles to Middletown, and then, on the return 4-mile journey, he spurted all the way. Following this, Jeff hit a nearly 200-pound bag of sand for 15 minutes.

Nov 8   For his final days of preparation, Jeffries moved his training camp from Harbin Springs to Oakland's Reliance Club.

Nov 11   In the morning, Jeff punched the bag and then boxed 8 fast rounds with Armstrong and brother Jack, alternating a round with each. He then skipped rope and worked with the rowing and wrist machines. In the afternoon, Jeff shadow boxed with weights, jumped rope, and sparred before the motion picture camera.

Nov 12   Jeffries exercised for 2 hours at the Reliance Club. He skipped rope for a while (1,000 revolutions), and then punched the inflated sphere bag for 20 minutes, breaking the rope. He then pulled and hauled big Bob Armstrong all over the ring, and shadow boxed with dumbbells.

Nov 13   Jeff punched the bag for 20 minutes, showing his power. For another 20 minutes, he danced about the ring with hand weights, showing his agile footwork and feinting. He then worked with the rowing machine and chest weights, and did his other exercises. "For twenty minutes he lifted twenty pounds with either arm, and at the end he was breathing as calmly as a babe." His legs were "like the columns of a Greek temple." In the afternoon, he took a 5-mile walk, and then ran 3 more miles.

Nov 14   Jeff punched the bag and shadow-boxed around the ring with dumbbells in his hands.

| Nov 15 | Gus Ruhlin | San Francisco, CA | KO 5 |
| **World Heavyweight Championship** | | | Ruhlin retired after the 5th round. |

Jeff went on an exhibition tour with his brother Jack Jeffries.

Dec 16	Jack Jeffries	Salt Lake City, UT	EX
Dec 20	Young Corbett II	Denver, CO	EX 6
Dec 20	Jack Jeffries	Denver, CO	EX 6

Jeff and Jack next exhibited in Omaha.

| Dec 25 | Jack Jeffries | Kansas City, MO | EX 6 |
| Dec 27 | Jeff was in Chicago, where he likely exhibited. |

Jeff was heading to New York, where he was set to give more exhibitions.

1902

| May | Jeff helped train Jack Jeffries for Jack's upcoming bout with Jack Johnson. |
| May 5 | Jack Jeffries | Los Angeles, CA | EX 3 |

Jack and Jeff continued sparring almost daily until the fight on the 16th.

Jun   For the Fitzsimmons rematch, Jeff began serious training at Harbin Springs with Joe Kennedy, brother Jack, Kid Eagan, and Bill Delaney.

Jun 28   Jeffries ran 8 miles. He had done considerable work over the past week and was in splendid condition. He had given up handball and was working a lot with the gym apparatuses. The way he hit the sand bag was "really astonishing." He would gradually increase the amount of boxing with Jack Jeffries and Joe Kennedy.

Jul 1   Jeffries went for a 10-mile run, two more than usual. In the afternoon, he sparred a few rounds with Jack Jeffries and Joe Kennedy.

Jul 3   Jeff did his usual routine, punching the bag, jumping rope, and boxing with Kennedy and Jack.

Jul 8   Jeff did some road work, and boxed 4 fast rounds with his brother.

Jul 10   Jeff went through his regular exercise routine, including sparring both Joe Kennedy and Jack Jeffries. In the morning, he ran 4.5 miles at a pace of just under 6 minutes per mile. Jeff's exercises included the rowing machine for 15 minutes, the punching bag for the same amount of time, and then skipping rope for well over 1,000 revolutions.

Jul 11   Jeff cut out his road work on account of the summer heat. He worked in the gymnasium, including sparring 4 rounds each with Kennedy and brother Jack.

Jeff shifted from Harbin Springs to Oakland's Reliance Club, beginning work there on July 14.

Jul 14   First, Jeff punched the bag and skipped rope. He then sparred 8 rounds, 4 rounds each with brother Jack and Joe Kennedy, the two alternating a round at each bell.

Jul 15   Jeff ran 9 miles. He exercised with dumb-bells and pulleys for 20 minutes. He sparred 8 rounds total, alternating single rounds with Jack Jeffries and Joe Kennedy. Jeff finished up by punching the bag for 20 minutes.

Jul 16   Jeff spent an hour with the weights, jumped rope, and used the rowing machine. He sparred 8 rounds with Jack and Joe. Another source said he did two 8-round sparring sessions. Jeff also punched the bag and used the pulleys.

Jul 17   Jeff ran 9 miles. He rowed on Lake Merritt. He used the pulley weights for 10 minutes and punched the bag for 15 minutes.

Jul 18   Jeff rowed for an hour on Lake Merritt.

Jul 19   Jeff did an 8-mile morning run, sprinting 20 times along the way. In the afternoon, with 200-300 men watching, he sparred his usual alternating rounds with Kennedy and brother Jack.

Jul 20   Other than sparring 8 rounds, Jeffries took things easy, just swimming.

Jul 21   Jeff ran for an hour, doing sprints, and went through some light exercises. He sparred 8 rounds total with Jack and Joe.

Jul 22   That morning, Jeff ran 10 miles. In the afternoon, Jeffries worked the pulley weights and wrist machine prior to sparring 8 rounds with Jack and Joe, alternating rounds.

Jul 23   Jeff boxed 12 rounds with Joe Kennedy and Jack Jeffries He also rowed on the lake.

| Jul 25 | Bob Fitzsimmons | San Francisco, CA | KO 8 |

World Heavyweight Championship

Dec   Jeffries and Fitzsimmons went on an exhibition sparring tour, sparring with each other, and sometimes taking on locals. They exhibited in San Francisco.

| Dec 14 | Bob Fitzsimmons | Spokane, WA | EX |

They were scheduled to appear that week in Coeur d' Alene, Idaho, and Missoula, Montana.

| Dec 18 | Bob Fitzsimmons | Missoula?, MT | EX 3 |

| Dec 20 | Jack Munroe | Butte, MT | EX 4 |

Although Referee Duncan McDonald raised Munroe's hand and declared him the winner, he had no right to do so, because it was a mere exhibition bout in which Munroe was entitled to a monetary bonus for lasting the distance.

| Dec 20 | Bob Fitzsimmons | Butte, MT | EX 4 |

| Dec 22 | Bob Fitzsimmons | Anaconda, MT | EX 3 |

Jeff and Fitz were set to exhibit in Great Falls, Montana on December 25.

Dec 30	Bob Fitzsimmons	Pocatello, ID	EX

1903

Jan 2   Jeff and Fitz were in Salt Lake City, Utah.

In late January, they were in St. Joseph and Kansas City, Missouri. In early February, they were scheduled to exhibit in Springfield, St. Louis, Indianapolis, Louisville, and other places on their way east.

Feb 5	Bob Fitzsimmons	St. Louis, MO	EX 3

One-minute rounds.

Feb 6	Bob Fitzsimmons	Paducah, KY	EX 3

They were also set to travel to places like Evansville (Feb. 12?), Indianapolis, Cincinnati, and Louisville. In late February, Jeff boxed Fitz in Terre Haute, Indiana.

Mar 1   Jeff was in New York negotiating a bout with Corbett.

Mar 2	Bob Fitzsimmons	Philadelphia, PA	EX 3

Two-minute rounds.

Mar 3	Bob Fitzsimmons	Chester, PA	EX 3
Mar 4	Bob Fitzsimmons	Philadelphia, PA	EX

They closed their show when Rose Julian Fitzsimmons became seriously ill with pneumonia.

Jeff was instead booked to appear in vaudeville, and continued with that for 2 months before returning to Los Angeles, California.

Jul   Jeffries began training for the Corbett fight at Harbin Springs.

While training, Jeff was bitten by a pet bear.

Jul 31   Jeff jumped rope 1,000 times; shadow boxed with dumbbells, and used the wrist and rowing machines. He then wrestled Fitzsimmons for 7 minutes straight.

Aug 1   Jeffries went on a short run, and boxed for the first time in camp with Bob Fitzsimmons, as well as Joe Kennedy and brother Jack Jeffries, 2 rounds with each man. Next, Jeff again went outdoors for half an hour of 100-yard sprints.

Aug 2   Jeff went deer hunting. After exercising for a couple of hours with the pulleys, light dumbbells, punching bag, and skipping rope, he boxed 2 rounds each with Fitz, Joe and Jack.

Aug 3   Jeff and Fitz sparred 3 fast rounds. Jeff then sparred 6 more rounds, alternating between his brother Jack and Joe Kennedy.

Aug 4   Jeff took a short walk and run, worked the gymnasium apparatus for an hour, and skipped rope 1,200 times. He then went 3 corking rounds each with Fitz, Joe and Jack. After lunch, Jeff went hunting with his rifle. In the evening, he punched the bag for an hour, then took a swim and had a rubdown.

Aug 5   Jeff worked 4 rounds with Fitz and 3 each with Jack and Joe.

Aug 6   During the morning, Jeff spent a couple of hours in the gymnasium, where a crowd watched him keep up a terrific tattoo on the punching bag. In the afternoon, he played baseball. In the evening, at the Harbin Springs Music Hall, for a charity benefit performance, Jeff sparred 3 rounds each with Fitz, Kennedy, and brother Jack in a lively fashion before a standing-room only crowd. This was the last sparring between Jeff and Fitz.

Aug 7   The 232-pound Jeffries walked down the canyon and shot small game. For the remainder of his training, Jeff would mostly punch the bag, use the weights, skip rope, wrestle with Jack and Joe, and take hunting hikes in the canyons, along with the occasional game of baseball.

Aug 10   Jeff worked for an hour in the gym, pounding away at the punching bag and then wrestling with Joe and Jack.

Aug 11   Jeff put in an hour in the gym punching the bag, skipping rope and working the pulley weights. In the afternoon, he played baseball, and in the evening, he indulged in some more gym work.

He worked 11 rounds with the punching bag, and then wrestled 4 rounds with Jack and Joe. He skipped rope 800 times, and ended the day with the pulley weights.

Aug 13   Jeff shadow-boxed for 23 minutes, skipped rope for 10 minutes, and worked with the apparatus.

Aug 14   James J. Corbett   San Francisco, CA   KO 10
World Heavyweight Championship

Jeff went on a hunting trip down the Yuma River into Mexico.

Dec   In early December, Jeffries arrived in Boston to fill a sparring engagement at the Palace Theater with Joe Kennedy. It was his first sparring engagement since he returned east from California. Jeff was set to give exhibitions every afternoon and evening.

Dec 7   Joe Kennedy   Boston, MA   EX 3
Dec 7   Joe Kennedy   Boston, MA   EX 3

Jeff gave afternoon and evening exhibitions with Kennedy every day that week at the Palace Theater. He was also doing light gym work with Steve O'Donnell.

Dec 10   At Steve O'Donnell's gym, first Jeff worked with the gym apparatus for 15 minutes. He was scheduled to spar 10 rounds, alternating 1 round each with Kennedy and O'Donnell, back and forth. However, in round 7, Jeff landed a straight right to the jaw, and Joe went to the floor, completely knocked out.

1904

Jan 13   Joe Kennedy   Springfield, MA   EX 2
The police told them to cut it one round short so as not to violate the local anti-boxing statute.

Feb   Jeff was sparring in New York.

Feb 15   Joe Kennedy   New York, NY   EX 4

Jeff continued giving exhibitions with Kennedy at the Gotham Theatre, sometimes twice a day.

Mar   Jeff began light gymnasium training for the Munroe bout and continued boxing with Joe Kennedy.

At the end of March, Jeff finished his stage engagements in New York and started West towards San Francisco to train for the Munroe bout. En route, Jeff planned to give exhibitions with Kennedy and work out in local gymnasiums at various cities they visited. However, the Munroe bout got delayed. Munroe wanted more time.

Apr 24   Jeffries married Freda Mayer.

Jun 1?   Jeffries began training for the Munroe fight at Harbin Springs. He punched the bag, skipped rope, worked the dumbbells and wrist machines, and sparred Joe Kennedy and Jack Jeffries. He ran and walked as he liked.

About a week prior to the scheduled June 17 Munroe bout, Jeffries developed water on the knee, which necessitated a delay to August.

On July 18, Jeff and his wife left Los Angeles heading for Harbin Springs to begin training yet again for the Munroe fight.

While training, Jeff went on a two-day hunting trip in the hills, returning on August 2.

Aug 3   Jeff ran 3 miles at a good clip. He spent several hours in the gym in the afternoon, but did not spar. Jeff held the 350-pound bag on his head.

Aug 4   In the morning, Jeff again worked with the 350-pound sandbag, handling it with no effort. In the afternoon, he played baseball. In the evening, Jeff went hunting. After killing a steer, Jeff lifted the 510-pound carcass without any apparent effort and placed it into a wagon. Jeff would continue working in the gym for a couple more days before engaging in sparring.

Aug 5   Jeff ran 4 miles and also engaged in his usual gym work.

Jeff still had not sparred as of the 9th, for Kennedy's ear was injured.

Aug 12   Jeffries went for a long day's hunting excursion through the Lake County Mountains, lasting 20 hours, without food.

Aug 13   Jeffries ran 10 miles and worked in the gym for an hour. In the afternoon, he went to the gym again and spent another hour with the various apparatus. He still had done no sparring.

Aug 14   In the morning, Jeff ran 12 miles. He also did 100 yard sprints. In the afternoon, he worked the wrist machines and spring bag, tugging at it unceasingly. Jeffries also sparred for the first time, boxing 6 rounds total (3 rounds each) with Jack Jeffries and Joe Kennedy.

Aug 15   Jeff worked an hour and a half in the gym. He sparred 4 rounds each with Jack and Joe.

Jeffries continued sparring Jack and Joe, 4 rounds each on the 16th and 17th. Jeff worked in the gym for over 2 hours on the 17th.

Aug 18   Jeffries was doing his gym work in the morning, resting during the day, and doing a little road work in the evening. He increased his gym work to 3 hours. He only sparred Joe Kennedy, for Jack was nursing sore hands.

Aug 20   Jeff left Harbin Springs to wind up his training at Oakland's Reliance Club.

Aug 21   Jeff took a short walk around town. He later alternated between walking and running, varying the slower pace with short hard sprints, for a total of about 6 miles. He also went rowing on Lake Merritt for an hour.

Jeff said that his work leading up to the fight would consist of running in the morning, boxing and wrestling with Jack and Joe, exercising with the rope apparatus, bag punching, skipping rope, and shadow boxing.

Aug 22   Jeff punched the bag for several speedy rounds, and he also boxed 4 rounds each with Joe and Jack. Another report said Jeff did no boxing, just doing 2 hours of gym work, as well as running and rowing.

Aug 23   Jeff skipped rope, and then shadow-boxed with light dumbbells for nearly half an hour. He then boxed 8 rounds, 4 rounds each with Joe and Jack, alternating with each round after round. In the afternoon, Jeff rowed for an hour. Jeff said this would be his last day of sparring and bag punching, for he did not want to risk injury to his hands. He would run, row, shadow box and work with the gym apparatus.

Aug 24   Jeff worked with the weights and the wrist machine, skipped rope for 30 minutes, and then shadow boxed with light dumbbells, displaying marvelous footwork. He worked for 2 hours total.

Aug 26   Jack Munroe   San Francisco, CA   KO 2
World Heavyweight Championship

Oct   Jeff was set to tour with a theatrical company in a play called *Davy Crockett*, which played until April 1905.

1905

May 2   Jeff announced that he would be retiring.

May 13   Joe Kennedy   Chicago, IL   EX 3

Jeffries announced his retirement from boxing.

1910

Jul 4   Jack Johnson   Reno, NV   LKOby15
World Heavyweight Championship

For more on Jeff's post-1905-retirement refereeing and exhibitions, as well as miscellaneous exhibitions post-1910, take a look at the record Tracy Callis posted on Jeffries at Cyberboxingzone.com in the encyclopedia section.

Acknowledgments

I want to thank all those who helped in some way with the research, photographs, editing, promotion, or general support of my endeavors:

Randy Essing
Clay Moyle
Tracy Callis
Tom Seemuth
Cheryl Huyck
Christine Klein
Brian Boru
Shirley and Gary Wurst
Steve Compton
Ralph Buoncristiani
Edith Weil
Philip Halprin
Stephen Gordon
Todd Hodgson
Joan Parsons
Cindy Parsons
Zachary Daniels
John Griffin
H.E. Grant
Michael Hunnicut
Ron Marshall
Ashley Koebel
Don Scott
Rob Snell
Pam Barta-Kacena
Kelly Richard Nicholson
Henry Morrison Flagler Museum
Library of Congress, Prints and Photographs Division
Cyberboxingzone.com
Boxrec.com
Pugilibri
Eastsideboxing.com
Ringmemorabilia.com
Boxing Collectors Newsletter
Pugilistica.com
Boxingbiographies.com
University of Iowa Interlibrary Loan Services
University of Iowa Media Services

INDEX

Kelly, John, 162, 167, 170, 171, 228, 242, 359, 414, 419, 422, 594

Kennedy, Joe, 3, 49, 56, 114, 124, 255, 319, 339, 347, 400, 418, 462, 465, 467, 471-475, 479, 480, 509, 511, 513, 516-518, 520, 523, 526, 559, 562, 586, 588-590, 594, 595, 599, 600, 625, 629, 632, 634, 635, 637, 641, 642, 645, 646, 654, 664, 674, 676-679

Kenny, Yank, 60, 146, 189, 193, 199, 201, 205, 208, 209, 216, 221, 234, 243, 350, 400, 562, 582, 583, 589, 590, 592, 594, 595, 598, 600

Knipe, Joe, 420

LaBlanche, George, 185, 433

Lacy, William, 9

Law, 15, 29, 43, 54, 71, 85, 97, 106, 121, 142, 167, 168, 180, 184, 191, 192, 202, 210, 212, 213, 219, 242, 271, 283, 317, 321, 335, 339, 340-342, 353, 399, 410, 411, 442, 453, 456-459, 461, 464, 481, 505, 525, 542, 545, 551, 583, 600, 674, 678

Lenox Athletic Club, 142, 143, 147, 160, 162, 177, 185, 191, 192, 208, 212, 213, 253, 262, 410

Lewis, Assemblyman, 335, 340, 343, 354, 442

Long, Dan, 22, 23, 26, 72, 122, 466, 667

Lorraine, Hank, 19, 20, 22, 667

Los Angeles Athletic Club, 14, 17-21, 26, 92, 122, 256, 667

Luckett, Bob, 9, 667

Lustig, Dr., 54

Madden, Billy, 57, 61, 62, 68, 181, 362, 364, 401, 407, 410, 412, 413, 416, 450, 453, 481, 485, 486, 488, 493-495, 497, 498, 501, 562

Magnin, Isidore, 20, 667

Maher, Peter, 27, 60, 71, 90, 91, 96, 99, 100, 110, 111, 121, 124, 142, 160, 192, 202, 203, 255, 319, 320, 339, 347-350, 400, 406, 432-434, 449, 452, 453, 464, 471, 475, 508-510, 572, 579, 580, 627, 633

Martin, Ed, 208, 453, 462, 464, 465, 466, 475, 477-479, 482, 484, 486, 488, 496, 504, 505, 509, 558, 559, 562, 571, 575, 620, 621, 623, 625, 628, 638, 656

McAuliffe, Joe, 27, 71, 72, 91, 100, 255, 478

McCormick, Jack/Jim, 188, 260, 262, 319, 344, 345, 350, 399, 400, 418, 430, 462, 659, 669, 673

McCoy, Charles, 141, 142, 160, 161, 183, 185, 189, 195, 211, 222, 225, 226, 227, 231, 243, 244, 255, 257, 260, 262, 272, 319, 339, 342, 348, 358, 364, 366-369, 371, 372, 376, 379, 382, 388, 395, 400, 406, 419, 433, 434, 440, 443, 444, 447-449, 475, 577, 579, 580, 594, 632, 633, 636, 641-643, 646, 651, 659

McCue, Marty, 147, 200, 208, 268

McDonald, Duncan, 564, 572, 676

McDonald, Jim, 74, 81, 88, 104, 106

McGrath, Tim, 124, 283, 623, 636, 643, 646, 652, 654

McKinley, William, 116, 465

McVey, Jim, 28, 40, 42-45, 160, 162, 167-183, 410, 443, 619, 620, 623, 635, 656

McVey, Sam, 462, 571, 580, 594, 619, 623, 627, 628, 635, 656, 659

Mechanics' Pavilion, 61, 122, 128, 599, 645

Miller, William, 27

Mitchell, Charles, 162, 170, 177, 186, 189, 252, 258, 260, 354, 357, 438

Morris, Arthur, 259, 260, 671

Other Books By Adam J. Pollack

John L. Sullivan: The Career of the First Gloved Heavyweight Champion

See mcfarlandpub.com or amazon.com

In the Ring With James J. Corbett

See lulu.com (hardcover or paperback) or amazon.com (paperback only)

In the Ring With Bob Fitzsimmons

See winbykopublications.com or amazon.com

Adam J. Pollack is a staff writer for Cyberboxingzone.com, a boxing coach (icorboxing.com), promoter, chair of USA Boxing's Judicial Committee, amateur judge and referee, and an attorney practicing law in Iowa City, Iowa.